ISBN 978-0-259-19555-9
PIBN 10808073

English
Français
Deutsche
Italiano
Español
Português

www.forgottenbooks.com

Mythology Photography **Fiction**
Fishing Christianity **Art** Cooking
Essays Buddhism Freemasonry
Medicine **Biology** Music **Ancient
Egypt** Evolution Carpentry Physics
Dance Geology **Mathematics** Fitness
Shakespeare **Folklore** Yoga Marketing
Confidence Immortality Biographies
Poetry **Psychology** Witchcraft
Electronics Chemistry History **Law**
Accounting **Philosophy** Anthropology
Alchemy Drama Quantum Mechanics
Atheism Sexual Health **Ancient History**
Entrepreneurship Languages Sport
Paleontology Needlework Islam
Metaphysics Investment Archaeology
Parenting Statistics Criminology
Motivational

THE

ROYAL GALLERY.

OF

POETRY AND ART.

AN ILLUSTRATED BOOK

OF THE

Favorite Poetic Gems of the English Language,

THE

CHOICEST PRODUCTIONS OF AUTHORS, LIVING AND DEAD,

FOR

THE UNCROWNED KINGS AND QUEENS OF AMERICAN HOMES.

WITH AN INTRODUCTION BY

REV. W. H. MILBURN, D. D.,

Chaplain National House of Representatives, Washington, D. C.,

Author of " The Pioneer Preachers and People of the Mississippi Valley ;" " The Rifle·
Axe and Saddlebags ;" " Ten Years of Preacher Life," Etc., Etc.

THE HEART OF ENGLISH LITERATURE IN ONE VOLUME, ENRICHED WITH
400 BEAUTIFUL ENGRAVINGS.

NEW YORK AND ST. LOUIS:
N. D. THOMPSON PUBLISHING CO.
1886.

Entered according to Act of Congress in the year 1885,
N. D. THOMPSON PUBLISHING CO.,
In the office of the Librarian of Congress at Washington, D. C.

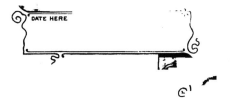
DATE HERE

CONTENTS.

CONTENTS. v

GRIEF AND PATHOS.

THE NOBILITY OF LIFE.

THE BETTER LAND.

Illustrations

INTRODUCTION.

OUR life is mystic, unfathomable—open to manifold subtle influences which help to make or mar us. Who needs be told that we are embosomed in Immensity, when beneath the nightly heavens the eye is greeted by the light of stars, which, notwithstanding the speed of its flight (nearly two hundred thousand miles a second), has been journeying for ages from its source to reach our planet. If sunrise could be witnessed but once a year, who would be abed on the morning of that more than imperial pageant; yet is the splendor less, because almost every day it streams along the sky? In our impatience of the commonplace, in eager search of beauty and inspiration, we cross the sea to Britain, France, or Italy, and come back no richer than we went, because the beauty and inspiration must go with us or we shall not find them anywhere.

The fault of spiritual poverty is in ourselves, not in our surroundings. The heavens by night or day are as beautiful, grand and sacred over the humblest home in America as over the greatest gallery or cathedral in Europe; and he who cannot find the treasures of life here, will discover no treasures there.

Doorways to the infinite knowledge, glory and blessedness of the universe are near the path of every " traveller betwixt life and death"—the humblest as well as the highest; the latchstring is always on the outside, and whoso wills it may enter and find riches, "where moth and rust do not corrupt, nor thieves break through and steal."

At school or college, at the handles of the plow, or with a hoe in the fist, at the carpenter's bench, on the bricklayer's scaffold, in the blacksmith's shop, behind the tradesman's counter, in the merchant's office, in the wife's and mother's round of ceaseless toil and care, wherever our appointed task is to be done—and woe to him who has not found his task, or shrinks from doing it—there must the secrets of the world be learned and the power gained, by use of which we enter into and possess the estate of the soul.

Few in this land are so bereft, so desolate, that visions of ineffable beauty, messages from a world above matter, are denied to them; but the eye must be clarified to see the vision, the ear opened to hear the beatific tidings.

" While this muddy vesture of decay doth grossly close us in," and while custom lies upon us with a weight heavy as frost, and deep almost as life, it is hard for us to behold

> "The light that never was on land or sea,
> The consecration and the poet's dream;"
> To hear the harmony that is in immortal souls."

We are so immersed in the life of the senses, so cheated by the shows of things, occupied by greetings in the market-place, trifles in the street, fashions of dress, the cut of a coat, the mode of a bonnet, the glitter of a brooch, the costume of a dude or belle; we give such time and attention to gossip of newspapers and society, that the eye becomes dull and we see not, the ear heavy and we hear not, and the soul forgets its privilege—is defrauded of its heritage.

We delude ourselves that happiness is to be found, and only found, at the winning-post of life's race; that he alone can have it who gains the wager of the contest, is greeted by the applause of the on-looking throng, crowned with gilt or gold by the judges at the stand:—and so our life is heated, eager, passionate, spectacular. We like the haste and din of crowds, the shuffle of feet and clapping of hands; the ear loses its sense of harmony, and noise becomes music; the eye its discretion, and we mistake paste for diamonds, and fancy that gas-light is better than sunshine.

> " The world is too much with us, late and soon:
> Getting and spending we lay waste our powers."

God deals with us as with sons, and the blows of affliction fall, not to punish, but correct. There is a vacant chair in every home; there are few hearts that have not known the discipline of sorrow; each one hath its own grief with which no stranger intermeddles. Silence and solitude are appointed to us for seasons, that they may do what the bustle and the crowd cannot; and they bid us open our minds and hearts to the ministry of healing, the consolation of higher influences, and persuade us that while on one side we are of the earth earthy, the children of Adam, the man of the red clay, on the other we are His brethren who is the Lord from Heaven. Religion, philosophy, science, the arts and letters, are friendly guides to lead us away from the dissipations and deceptions of the world, from the deceit and allurements of our own hearts to the palace of the Great King in whose courts and gardens we may find health, sanity, strength, and so come back to the working-day world as giants refreshed with new wine.

What power is found in books! A well-chosen library, though small and inexpensive, may introduce us to the best company the world has known, bring us upon terms of intimacy with the kingly spirits of our race, admit us to their confidence so that they tell us the secrets of their hearts, show us the weapons with which they cònquered the world and themselves, breathe upon us the spirit of their courage, enthusiasm, faith, hope and love; teach us the secret of their nobleness, heroism, divinity, until in the wrapt communion we grow into their manners, aims, achievements, and make them our own.

The value of a book depends upon the use we make of it; it is little worth except to the good reader. If its true office be performed for us we must eat, drink, digest, assimilate it so that its nourishment becomes a part of our own being, recruiting our life with its intelligence, wisdom, inspiration.

When books were rare and costly, chained to columns in monasteries, borrowed with pledges that might have been the ransom of princes, men studied, devoured them, and so appropriated their virtue. Now, when books may be bought for a song, when Homer, Dante, Shakespeare, Goethe, Wordsworth, may be had for the asking, we glance at, caress with compliments and pass them by as fish swim among pearls and know not of their value.

When Gen. Jackson, as President of the United States, gave year by year the series of state dinners at the White House, while his distinguished guests banqueted upon the countless dishes and courses, surfeiting their stomachs, addling their brains with the dainties and wines of an English dinner, the sturdy old host stuck to the simple fare, with the dessert of mush and milk, to which he had been used at the "Hermitage," and so kept his head and will, as well as stomach, inviolate; his guests departing with indigestion, often unable to recognize their own homes on reaching them.

Our intéllectual feasts are in many courses, with wines of many vintages—liqueurs, cognac, absinthe, added: what wonder, then, that there is so much literary dyspepsia, apoplexy and paralysis? A wise man once said of an omniverous reader, "He read so much he came at last to know nothing." "A good book," said Milton, " is the precious life-blood of a master spirit, embalmed and treasured up on purpose to a life beyond life:" and he who by devout and constant reading of a few such will realize in his spirit all that is claimed for the transfusion of blood in the veins; recover him from disease, make the shrunken frame dilate, cause the languid eye and pallid cheek to glow and sparkle with the health of immortal youth, lend the voice the music and accents of courage and joy. Through well-chosen books we become heirs of the ages, and when the pencil of the artist and burin of the engraver embody in living form the writer's thought, we have the presence and the glory of a sacrament—"an outward and visible form of an inward and spiritual grace." What pains and expense we are at, what dresses don, and ordeals undergo to gain access to the drawing-rooms of the great, to be presented to princes, to bow and curtsey to kings and queens, and, after all our toil and trouble, often feel in coming away that we have only looked at blocks with wigs on them. We sigh or struggle for invitations to balls and parties, and then learn to our cost that patés, terrapin and champagne apologize to the stomach for the absence of wit and wisdom we hoped to find; and that the proper legend for the entertainment would be, "Panorama of a caravan wandering through the Desert of Sahara." But good books never cheat us thus: they are "a perpetual feast where no crude surfeit reigns;" not harsh and crabbed, as dull fools suppose, but musical as is Apollo's lute." We can apply to them with justice Wordsworth's lines on the Ministry of Nature:

> " Oft, in lonely rooms, and 'mid the din
> Of towns and cities, I have owed to them,
> In hours of weariness, sensations sweet,
> Felt in the blood, and felt along the heart:
> And passing even into my purer mind,
> With tranquil restoration; feelings too
> Of unremembered pleasure; such, perhaps,
> As have no slight or trivial influence
> On that best portion of a good man's life,
> His little, nameless, unremembered acts
> Of kindness and of love: nor less, I trust,
> To them I may have owed another gift,
> Of aspect more sublime: that blessed mood,
> In which the burthen of the mystery,
> In which the heavy and the weary weight
> Of all this unintelligible world
> Is lightened:—that serene and blessed mood,
> In which the affections gently lead us on—
> Until, the breath of this corporeal frame
> And even the motion of our human blood
> Almost suspended, we are laid asleep
> In body, and become a living soul:
> While with an eye made quiet by the power
> Of harmony, and the deep power of joy,
> We see into the life of things."

Homer's Iliad wrought itself into the soul of Alexander, and became the brain and sword with which he conquered the world. A young man walking one day on the river's bank saw something floating in the current, drew it ashore, found it to be a parchment Bible which had been thrown into the flood by command of the apostate Emperor Julian. The youth dried the volume, read it until its contents took possession of him, winning him from the study of Greek Philosophy, and he became the "Golden-mouthed" John of Antioch, afterwards Archbishop of Constantinople, known to the world as St. John Chrysostom, the most powerful preacher the East has known since the days of St. Paul. A young African, who had run a course of intellectual and animal excess, paced to and fro, one pleasant summer afternoon, in a Roman garden, and heard a child in the next garden reading aloud; he paused to listen, heard words which took hold of his conscience and heart, for they were words of the Holy Scriptures. He got the book and studied it, and became the most renowned Doctor and Father of the Christian Church—St. Augustine. But why multiply instances of the power of books.

In presenting you this volume, the publishers have spared neither pains nor expense to make it as nearly perfect as a volume of the kind can be.

The admirable selection from the writers of our tongue, ranges from Chaucer, Spenser and Shakespeare, to our own Hayne, Aldrich and Gilder, and includes pieces well known as household words, and others not easily reached except in these pages.

Of the illustrations a blind man is not competent to speak, but I doubt not they are most excellent, and will help to convey and impress the meaning of the writers.

If the men and women, young or old, into whose hands this book may come, will "read, mark, learn and inwardly digest" its contents until each day "memory have its fraught," they will find it a treasure beyond price, attuning the ear to the melodies of our noble speech, refining the taste, purging the eye to behold the things most real but invisible to mortal sense, informing the mind with "thoughts that wander through eternity," and storing the recollection with truths and images which cannot die; making them to hear

" Oftentimes
The still, sad music of humanity,
Nor harsh nor grating, though of ample power
To chasten and subdue, and they may feel
A presence that disturbs them with the joy
Of elevated thoughts; a sense sublime
Of something far more deeply interfused,
Whose dwelling is the light of setting suns,
And the round ocean and the living air,
And the blue sky, and in the mind of man:
A motion and a spirit, that impels
All thinking things, all objects of all thought,
And rolls through all things."

Sir Richard Steele's famous compliment may have a new application when I say, to have it will be a liberal education.

W. H. MILBURN.

WASHINGTON, April, 1886.

HOME AND FIRESIDE.

"Th' expectant wee-things, toddlin, stacher through,
To meet their dad, wi' flichterin noise and glee."

THE COTTER'S SATURDAY NIGHT.

MY loved, my honoured, much respected
    friend!
  No mercenary bard this homage pays;
With honest pride, I scorn each selfish end:
  My dearest meed, a friend's esteem and
    praise:

To you I sing, in simple Scottish lays,
  The lowly train in life's sequestered scene;
The native feelings strong, the guileless ways;
  What Aiken in a cottage would have been;
Ah! though his worth unknown, far happier there I
  ween.

2

November chill blaws loud wi' angry sugh;
  The shortening winter-day is near a close;
The miry beasts retreating frae the pleugh;
  The blackening trains o' craws to their repose;
The toil-worn Cotter frae his labor goes,
  This night his weekly moil is at an end,
Collects his spades, his mattocks, and his hoes,
  Hoping the morn in ease and rest to spend,
And weary, o'er the moor, his course does hame-
      ward bend.

His wee bit ingle, blinkin bonnily,
  His clean hearth-stane, his thriftie wifie's smile,
The lisping infant prattling on his knee,
  Does a' his weary carking cares beguile,
An' makes him quite forget his labor an' his toil.

Belyve, the elder bairns come drapping in,
  At service out, amang the farmers roun';
Some ca' the pleugh, some herd, some tentie rin
  A cannie errand to a neebor town:

" 'Tis when a youthful, loving, modest pair,
In other's arms breathe out the tender tale."

At length his lonely cot appears in view,
  Beneath the shelter of an aged tree;
The expectant wee-things, toddlin, stacher
      through,
  To meet their dad, wi' flichterin noise and glee,

Their eldest hope, their Jenny, woman grown,
  In youthfu' bloom, love sparkling in her e'e,
Comes hame, perhaps, to show a braw new gown
  Or deposite her sair-won penny-fee,
To help her parents dear, if they in hardship be.

Wi' joy unfeigned brothers and sisters meet,
  An' each for other's welfare kindly spiers:
The social hours, swift-winged, unnoticed fleet;
  Each tells the uncos that he sees or hears;
The parents, partial, eye their hopeful years,
  Anticipation forward points the view.
The mother, wi' her needle an' her shears,
  Gars auld claes look amaist as weel's the new;
The father mixes a' wi' admonition due.

Lest in temptation's path ye gang astray,
  Implore his counsel and assisting might:
They never sought in vain that sought the Lord
  aright! "

But, hark! a rap comes gently to the door;
  Jenny, wha kens the meaning o' the same,
Tells how a neebor lad cam o'er the moor,
  To do some errands, and convoy her hame.

" They round the ingle form a circle wide;
The sire turns o'er wi' patriarchal grace,
The big ha'-Bible, ance his father's pride."

Their master's an' their mistress's command,
  The younkers a' are warnèd to obey;
An' mind their labors wi' an eydent hand,
  An' ne'er, though out o' sight, to jauk or play:
"An', O, be sure to fear the Lord alway,
  An' mind your duty, duly, morn an' night!

The wily mother sees the conscious flame
  Sparkle in Jenny's e'e, and flush her cheek;
Wi' heart-struck anxious care, inquires his name,
  While Jenny hafflins is afraid to speak;
Weel pleased the mother hears, it 's nae wild worth-
  less rake.

Wi' kindly welcome Jenny brings him ben;
 A strappan youth; he takes the mother's eye,
Blythe Jenny sees the visit's no ill ta'en;
 The father cracks of horses, pleughs, and kye.
The youngster's artless heart o'erflows wi' joy,
 But, blate and laithfu', scarce can weel behave,
The mother, wi' a woman's wiles, can spy
 What makes the youth sae bashfu' an' sae grave;
Weel pleased to think her bairn's respectèd like the
  lave.

Is there, in human form, that bears a heart,—
 A wretch! a villain! lost to love and truth!
That can, with studied, sly, ensnaring art,
 Betray sweet Jenny's unsuspecting youth?
Curse on his perjured arts! dissembling smooth!
 Are honor, virtue, conscience, all exiled?
Is there no pity, no relenting ruth,
 Points to the parents fondling o'er their child?
Then paints the ruined maid, and their distraction
  wild!

"The priest-like father reads the sacred page."

O happy love! where love like this is found!
 O heartfelt raptures! bliss beyond compare!
I've pacèd much this weary, mortal round,
 And sage experience bids me this declare:
If Heaven a draught of heavenly pleasure spare,
 One cordial in this melancholy vale,
'T is when a youthful, loving, modest pair,
 In other's arms breathe out the tender tale,
Beneath the milk-white thorn that scents the evening
  gale!

But now the supper crowns the simple board,
 The halesome parritch, chief o' Scotia's food:
The soup their only hawkie does afford,
 That 'yont the hallan snugly chows her cood·
The dame brings forth in complimental mood,
 To grace the lad, her well-hained kebbuck fell,
An' aft he's prest, an' aft he ca's it guid;
 The frugal wifie, garrulous, will tell
How 't was a towmond auld, sin' lint was i' the
  bell.

The cheerfu' supper done, wi' serious face,
  They, round the ingle, form a circle wide;
The sire turns o'er, wi' patriarchal grace,
  The big ha'-Bible, ance his father's pride:
His bonnet reverently is laid aside,
  His lyart haffets wearing thin an' bare;
Those strains that once did sweet in Zion glide,
  He wales a portion with judicious care;
And "Let us worship God!" he says, with solemn
    air.

Or noble "Elgin" beets the heavenward flame,
  The sweetest far of Scotia's holy lays:
Compared with these, Italian trills are tame;
  The tickled ears no heartfelt raptures raise;
Nae unison hae they with our Creator's praise.

The priest-like father reads the sacred page,
  How Abram was the friend of God on high;
Or Moses bade eternal warfare wage
  With Amalek's ungracious progeny;

"The parent pair their secret homage pay."

They chant their artless notes in simple guise;
  They tune their hearts, by far the noblest aim:
Perhaps "Dundee's" wild warbling measures
    rise,
  Or plaintive "Martyrs," worthy of the name;

Or how the royal Bard did groaning lie
  Beneath the stroke of Heaven's avenging ire;
Or Job's pathetic plaint, and wailing cry;
  Or rapt Isaiah's wild, seraphic fire;
Or other holy seers that tune the sacred lyre.

Perhaps the Christian volume is the theme,
  How guiltless blood for guilty man was shed;
How He, who bore in Heaven the second name,
  Had not on earth whereon to lay His head;
How His first followers and servants sped;
  The precepts sage they wrote to many a land:
How He, who lone in Patmos banishéd,
  Saw in the sun a mighty angel stand;
And heard great Babylon's doom pronounced by
    Heaven's command.

There ever bask in uncreated rays,
  No more to sigh, or shed the bitter tear,
Together hymning their Creator's praise,
  In such society, yet still more dear;
While circling time moves round in an eternal sphere.

Compared with this, how poor Religion's pride,
  In all the pomp of method, and of art,
When men display to congregations wide
  Devotion's every grace, except the heart!

"He who stills the raven's clamorous nest."

Then kneeling down, to Heaven's Eternal King,
  The saint, the husband, and the father
    prays:
Hope "springs exulting on triumphant wing,"
  That thus they all shall meet in future days;

The Power, incensed, the pageant will desert,
  The pompous strain, the sacerdotal stole;
But haply, in some cottage far apart,
  May hear, well pleased, the language of the soul;
And in His book of life the inmates poor enroll.

Then homeward all take off their several way;
   The youngling cottagers retire to rest:
The parent-pair their secret homage pay,
   And proffer up to Heaven the warm request,
That He, who stills the raven's clamorous nest,
   And decks the lily fair, in flowery pride,
Would, in the way His wisdom sees the best,
   For them and for their little ones provide;
But chiefly, in their hearts with grace divine
     preside.

From scenes like these old Scotia's grandeur springs.
   That make her loved at home, revered abroad:
Princes and lords are but the breath of kings;
   "An honest man's the noblest work of God:"
And certes, in fair virtue's heavenly road,
   The cottage leaves the palace far behind;
What is a lordling's pomp? a cumbrous load,
   Disguising oft the wretch of human kind,
Studied in arts of hell, in wickedness refined!

O Scotia! my dear, my native soil!
   For whom my warmest wish to Heaven is sent!
Long may thy hardy sons of rustic toil
   Be blest with health, and peace, and sweet content!
And, O, may Heaven their simple lives prevent
   From luxury's contagion, weak and vile!
Then, howe'er crowns and coronets be rent,
   A virtuous populace may rise the while,
And stand a wall of fire around their much-loved
     isle.

O Thou! who poured the patriotic tide
   That streamed through Wallace's undaunted heart;
Who dared to nobly stem tyrannic pride,
   Or nobly die, the second glorious part,
(The patriot's God, peculiarly Thou art,
   His friend, inspirer, guardian, and reward!
O never, never Scotia's realm desert;
   But still the patriot, and the patriot-bard,
In bright succession raise, her ornament and guard!

ROBERT BURNS.

MAKE HOME-LIFE BEAUTIFUL.

LET me say to parents: Make the home-life beautiful, without and within, and they will sow the seeds of gentleness, true kindness, honesty and fidelity, in the hearts of their children, from which the children reap a harvest of happiness and virtue. The memory of the beautiful and happy home of childhood is the richest legacy any man can leave to his children. The heart will never forget its hallowed influences. It will be an evening enjoyment, to which the lapse of years will only add new sweetness. Such a home is a constant inspiration for good, and as constant a restraint from evil.

If by taste and culture we adorn our homes and grounds and add to their charms, our children will find the quiet pleasures of rural homes more attractive than the whirl of city life. Such attractions and enjoyments will invest home-life, school-life, the whole future of life with new interests and with new dignity and joyousness, for life is just what we make it. We may by our blindness live in a world of darkness and gloom, or in a world full of sunlight and beauty and joy; for the world without only reflects the world within. Also, the

A Country Home.

tasteful improvement of grounds and home exerts a good influence not only upon the inmates, but upon the community. An elegant dwelling, surrounded by sylvan attractions, is a contribution to the refinement, the good order, the taste and prosperity of every community, improving the public taste and ministering to every enjoyment.

B. G. NORTHRUP.

SONGS OF SEVEN.

SEVEN TIMES ONE.—EXULTATION.

HERE'S no dew left on the daisies and clover,
    There's no rain left in heaven.
I've said my "seven times" over and over—
    Seven times one are seven.

I am old—so old I can write a letter;
    My birthday lessons are done.
The lambs play always—they know no better;
    They are only one times one.

I hope, if you have, you will soon be forgiven,
    And shine again in your place.

O velvet Bee! you're a dusty fellow—
    You've powdered your legs with gold.
O brave marsh Mary-buds, rich and yellow,
    Give me your money to hold!

O Columbine! open your folded wrapper,
    Where two twin turtle-doves dwell!

"I am seven times one to-day."

O Moon! in the night I have seen you sailing
    And shining so round and low.
You were bright—ah, bright—but your light is falling;
    You are nothing now but a bow.

You Moon! have you done something wrong in heaven,
    That God has hidden your face?

O Cuckoo-pint! toll me the purple clapper
    That hangs in your clear green bell!

And show me your nest, with the young ones in it—
    I will not steal them away;
I am old! you may trust me, linnet, linnet!
    I am seven times one to-day.

SEVEN TIMES TWO.—ROMANCE.

YOU bells in the steeple, ring, ring out your changes
    How many soever they be,
And let the brown meadow-lark's note as he ranges
    Come over, come over to me.

Yet bird's clearest carol by fall or by swelling
    No magical sense conveys,
And bells have forgotten their old art of telling   .
    The fortune of future days.

I wait for the day when dear hearts shall discover,
    While dear hands are laid on my head;
" The child is a woman, the book may close
    over,
    For all the lessons are said."

I wait for my story—the birds cannot sing it,
    Not one, as he sits on the tree;
The bells cannot ring it, but long years, O bring it!
    Such as I wish it to be.

" I leaned out of window, I smelt the white clover,
Dark, dark was the garden, I saw not the gate."

"Turn again, turn again," once they rang cheerily,
    While a boy listened alone;
Made his heart yearn again, musing so wearily
    All by himself on a stone.

Poor bells! I forgive you; your good days are over,
    And mine, they are yet to be;
No listening, no longing shall aught, aught discover:
    You leave the story to me.

The fox-glove shoots out of the green matted heather,
    Preparing her hoods of snow;
She was idle, and slept till the sunshiny weather:
    O children take long to grow.

I wish, and I wish that the spring would go faster,
    Nor long summer bide so late;
And I could grow on like the fox-glove and aster,
    For some things are ill to wait.

SEVEN TIMES THREE.—LOVE.

I LEANED out of window, I smelt the white clover,
    Dark, dark was the garden, I saw not the gate;
" Now, if there be footsteps, he comes, my one
    lover—
    Hush, nightingale, hush! O sweet nightingale,
    wait
        Till I listen and hear
        If a step draweth near,
        For my love he is late!

" The skies in the darkness stoop nearer and nearer,
    A cluster of stars hangs like fruit in the tree,
The fall of the water comes sweeter, comes clearer:
    To what art thou listening, and what dost thou see?
        Let the star-clusters glow,
        Let the sweet waters flow,
        And cross quickly to me.

"You night-moths that hover where honey brims over
    From sycamore blossoms, or settle or sleep;
You glow-worms, shine out, and the pathway discover
    To him that comes darkling along the rough steep.
            Ah, my sailor, make haste,
            For the time runs to waste,
            And my love lieth deep—

"Too deep for swift telling; and yet, my one lover,
    I've conned thee an answer, it waits thee to-night."
By the sycamore passed he, and through the white
            clover;
    Then all the sweet speech I had fashioned took flight;
            But I'll love him more, more
            Than e'er wife loved before,
            Be the days dark or bright.

SEVEN TIMES FOUR.—MATERNITY.

EIGH-HO! daisies and buttercups,
    Fair yellow daffodils, stately and tall!
When the wind wakes how they rock in the
            grasses,
And dance with the cuckoo-buds slender and small!
Here's two bonny boys, and here's mother's own
            lasses,
    Eager to gather them all.

Heigh-ho! daisies and buttercups!
    Mother shall thread them a daisy chain;
Sing them a song of the pretty hedge-sparrow,
    That loved her brown little ones, loved them full
            fain;
Sing, "Heart, thou art wide, though the house be but
            narrow,"—
        Sing once and sing it again.

Heigh-ho! daisies and buttercups,
    Sweet wagging cowslips, they bend and they bow;
A ship sails afar over warm ocean waters,
    And haply one musing doth stand at her prow.
O bonny brown sons, and O sweet little daughters,
        Maybe he thinks on you now!

Heigh-ho! daisies and buttercups,
    Fair yellow daffodils, stately and tall—
A sunshiny world full of laughter and leisure.
And fresh hearts unconscious of sorrow and thrall
Send down on their pleasure-smiles passing its meas-
            ure,
        God that is over us all!

SEVEN TIMES FIVE.—WIDOWHOOD.

SLEEP and rest, my heart makes moan,
    Before I am well awake;
"Let me bleed! Oh, let me alone,
    Since I must not break!"

For children wake, though fathers sleep,
    With a stone at foot and at head;
O sleepless God! forever keep,
    Keep both living and dead!

I lift mine eyes, and what to see,
    But a world happy and fair;
I have not wished it to mourn with me,
    Comfort is not there.

O what anear but golden brooms!
    And a waste of reedy rills;
O what afar but the fine glooms
    On the rare blue hills!

"Let me bleed! Oh, let me alone."

I shall not die, but live forlore—
    How bitter it is to part!
O to meet thee, my love, once more!—
    O my heart, my heart!

No more to hear, no more to see!
    O that an echo might awake
And waft one note of thy psalm to me,
    Ere my heart-strings break!

I should know it how faint so e'er,
    And with angel voices blent;
O once to feel thy spirit anear,
    I could be content!

O once between the gates of gold,
    While an angel entering trod;
But once—thee sitting to behold
    On the hills of God.

SEVEN TIMES SIX.—GIVING IN MARRIAGE.

To bear, to nurse, to rear,
　To watch, and then to lose:
To see my bright ones disappear,
　Drawn up like morning dews;—
To bear, to nurse, to rear,
To watch, and then to lose:
This have I done when God drew near
Among his own to choose.

To hear, to heed, to wed,
　And with thy lord depart
In tears that he, as soon as shed,
Will let no longer smart.—
To hear, to heed, to wed,
　This whilst thou didst I smiled,
For now it was not God who said,
　"Mother, give ME thy child."

O fond, O fool, and blind,
　To God I gave with tears;
But, when a man like grace would find,
My soul put by her fears.
O fond, O fool, and blind,
　God guards in happier spheres;
That man will guard where he did bind
Is hope for unknown years.

To hear, to heed, to wed,
　Fair lot that maidens choose,
Thy mother's tenderest words are said,
Thy face no more she views;
Thy mother's lot, my dear,
　She doth in naught accuse;
Her lot to bear, to nurse, to rear,
　To love—and then to lose.

———————✦———————

SEVEN TIMES SEVEN.—LONGINGS FOR HOME.

A Song of a Boat.

THERE was once a boat on a billow:
　Lightly she rocked to her port remote,
And the foam was white in her wake like
　snow,
And her frail mast bowed when the breeze
　would blow,
　And bent like a wand of willow.

I shaded mine eyes one day when a boat
　Went curtseying over the billow,
I marked her course till a dancing mote,
She faded out on the moonlit foam,

And I stayed behind in the dear loved home;
And my thoughts all day were about the boat,
　And my dreams upon the pillow.

I pray you hear my song of a boat,
　For it is but short:—
My boat, you shall find none fairer afloat,
　In river or port.
Long I looked out for the lad she bore,
　On the open desolate sea;
And I think he sailed to the heavenly shore,
　For he came not back to me—
　　　　　　Ah, me!

A Song of a Nest.

THERE was once a nest in a hollow,
　Down in the mosses and knot-grass pressed,
Soft and warm and full to the brim;
　Vetches leaned over it purple and dim;
　With buttercup buds to follow.

I pray you hear my song of a nest,
　For it is not long:—
You shall never light in a summer quest
　The bushes among—
Shall never light on a prouder sitter,
　A fairer nestful, nor ever know
A softer sound than their tender twitter,
　That wind-like did come and go.

I had a nestful once of my own—
　Ah, happy, happy I!
Right dearly I loved them; but when they were
　grown
They spread out their wings to fly.
Oh, one after one they flew away,
　Far up to the heavenly blue,
To the better country, the upper day;
　And—I wish I was going, too.

I pray you, what is the nest to me,
　My empty nest?
And what is the shore where I stood to see
　My boat sail down to the west?
Can I call that home where I anchor yet,
　Though my good man has sailed?
Can I call that home where my nest was set,
　Now all its hope hath failed?
Nay, but the port where my sailor went,
　And the land where my nestlings be:
There is the home where my thoughts are sent,
　The only home for me—
　　　　　　Ah, me!

　　　　　　　　　JEAN INGELOW.

THE OLD OAKEN BUCKET.

OW dear to my heart are the scenes of my child-
hood,
When fond recollection presents them to view!—
The orchard, the meadow, the deep-tangled wild-
wood,
And every loved spot which my infancy knew!
The wide-spreading pond, and the mill that stood by
it;
The bridge, and the rock where the cataract fell;

How ardent I seized it, with hands that were glowing,
And quick to the white-pebbled bottom it fell!
Then soon, with the emblem of truth overflowing,
And dripping with coolness, it rose from the well—
The old oaken bucket, the iron-bound bucket,
The moss-covered bucket arose from the well.

How sweet from the green, mossy brim to receive it,
As, poised on the curb. it inclined to my lips!

" The cot of my father, the dairy-house nigh it;
And e'en the rude bucket that hung in the well—"

The cot of my father, the dairy-house nigh it;
And e'en the rude bucket that hung in the well—
The old oaken bucket, the iron-bound bucket,
The moss-covered bucket which hung in the well.

That moss-covered vessel I hailed as a treasure;
For often at noon, when returned from the field,
I found it the source of an exquisite pleasure—
The purest and sweetest that nature can yield.

Not a full, blushing goblet could tempt me to leave it,
The brightest that beauty or revelry sips.
And now, far removed from the loved habitation,
The tear of regret will intrusively swell,
As fancy reverts to my father's plantation,
And sighs for the bucket that hangs in the well—
The old oaken bucket, the iron-bound bucket,
The moss-covered bucket that hangs in the well!

SAMUEL WOODWORTH.

GRAVES OF A HOUSEHOLD.

THEY grew in beauty side by side,
  They filled one home with glee;
Their graves are severed far and wide
  By mount, and stream, and sea.
The same fond mother bent at night
  O'er each fair sleeping brow;
She had each folded flower in sight—
  Where are those dreamers now?

One sleeps where southern vines are dressed
  Above the noble slain;
He wrapped his colors round his breast
  On a blood-red field of Spain.
And one—o'er her the myrtle showers
  Its leaves, by soft winds fanned;
She faded 'mid Italian flowers,
  The last of that bright band.

"One 'mid the forest of the West,
  By a dark stream is laid;
The Indian knows his place of rest,
  Far in the cedar shade."

One 'mid the forests of the West,
  By a dark stream is laid;
The Indian knows his place of rest,
  Far in the cedar shade.
The sea, the blue lone sea, hath one—
  He lies where pearls lie deep;
He was the loved of all, yet none
  O'er his low bed may weep.

And, parted thus, they rest who played
  Beneath the same green tree,
Whose voices mingled as they prayed
  Around one parent-knee!
They that with smiles lit up the hall,
  And cheered with song the hearth·
Alas for love, if thou wert all,
  And naught beyond, O Earth!

FELICIA DOROTHEA HEMANS.

MY CHILDHOOD HOME.

HERE'S a little low hut by the river's side,
Within the sound of its rippling tide;
Its walls are grey with the mosses of years,
And its roof all crumbled and old appears;
But fairer to me than castle's pride
Is the little low hut by the river's side!

The little low hut was my natal rest,
When my childhood passed—Life's springtime blest;
Where the hopes of ardent youth were formed,
And the sun of promise my young heart warmed,
Ere I threw myself on life's swift tide,
And left the dear hut by the river's side.

That little low hut, in lowly guise,
Was soft and grand to my youthful eyes,
And fairer trees were ne'er known before,
Than the apple-trees by the humble door—
That my father loved for their thrifty pride—
That shadowed the hut by the river's side.

That little low hut had a glad hearthstone,
That echoed of old with a pleasant tone,
And brothers and sisters, a merry crew,
Filled the hours with pleasure as on they flew;
But one by one the loved ones died,
That dwelt in the hut by the river's side.

The father revered and the children gay
The graves of the world have called away:
But quietly, all alone, here sits
By the pleasant window, in summer, and knits,
An aged woman, long years allied
With the little low hut by the river's side.

That little low hut to the lonely wife
Is the cherished stage of her active life;
Each scene is recalled in memory's beam,
As she sits by the window in pensive dream
And joys and woes roll back like a tide
In that little low hut by the river's side.

My mother—alone by the river's side
She waits for the flood of the heavenly tide,
And the voice that shall thrill her heart with its call
To meet once more with the dear ones all,
And forms in a region beautified,
The band that once met by the river's side.

The dear old hut by the river's side
With the warmest pulse of my heart is allied—
And a glory is over its dark walls thrown,
That statelier fabrics have never known—
And I shall love with a fonder pride
That little low hut by the river's side.

B. P. SHILLABER (MRS. PARTINGTON).

RAIN ON THE ROOF.

HEN the humid shadows hover
Over all the starry spheres,
And the melancholy darkness
Gently weeps in rainy tears,
What a bliss to press the pillow
Of a cottage-chamber bed
And to listen to the patter
Of the soft rain overhead!

Every tinkle on the shingles
Has an echo in the heart;
And a thousand dreamy fancies
Into busy being start,
And a thousand recollections
Weave their air-threads into woof,
As I listen to the patter
Of the rain upon the roof.

Now in memory comes my mother
As she used long years agone,
To regard the darling dreamers
Ere she left then till the dawn;
Oh, I see her leaning o'er me,
As I list to this refrain
Which is played upon the shingles
By the patter of the rain.

Then my little seraph sister,
With her wings and waving hair
And her star-eyed cherub brother
A serene angelic pair!—
Glide around my wakeful pillow,
With their praise or mild reproo
As I listen to the murmur
Of the soft rain on the roof.

And another comes to thrill me
With her eyes' delicious blue;
And I mind not, musing on her,
That her heart was all untrue:
I remember but to love her
With a passion kin to pain,
And my heart's quick pulses vibrate
To the patter of the rain.

Art hath naught of tone or cadence
That can work with such a spell
In the soul's mysterious fountains,
Whence the tears of rapture well
As that melody of nature,
That subdued, subduing strain
Which is played upon the shingles
By the patter of the rain.

COATES KINNEY.

BAIRNIES, CUDDLE DOON.

THE bairnies cuddle doon at nicht,
  Wi' muckle faucht an' din';
"Oh try and sleep, ye waukrif rogues,
  Your feyther's comin' in!"
They dinna hear a word I speak;
  I try an' gie a frown,
But aye I hap them up and cry,
  "O bairnies, cuddle doon!"

Wee Jaimie, wi' the curly heid,
  He aye sleeps next the wa',
Bangs up and cries, "I want a piece'"
  The rascal starts them a'!
I rin an' fetch them pieces—drinks—
  They stop a wee the soun',
Then draw the blankets up and cry
  "O weanies, cuddle doon!"

But scarce five minutes gang. wee Rab
  Cries out frae neath the claes:
"Mither, mak Tam gie ower at ance!
  He's kittlin wi' his taes!"
The mischief's in that Tam for tricks,
  He'd baither half the toun;
But still I hap them up and cry,
  "O bairnies, cuddle doon!"

At length they hear their feyther's step,
  And as he nears the door
They draw their blankets o'er their heids,
  And Tam pretinds to snore.
"Hae a' the weans been guid?" he asks,
  As he pits off his shoon;
"The bairnies, John, are in their beds,
  And lang since cuddled doon."

And just afore we bed oursels
  We look at our wee lambs;
Tam has his airm round wee Rab's neck,
  And Rab his airm round Tam's.
I lift wee Jaimie up the bed,
  And as I straik each crown,
I whisper, till my hairt fills up,
  "O bairnies, cuddle doon!"

The bairnies cuddle doon at nicht,
  Wi' mirth that's dear to me,
For sure the big warl's cark an' care
  Will quaten doon their glee.
But coom what will to ilka ane,
  May he who sits abune
Aye whisper, tho' their pows be bald,
  "O bairnies, cuddle doon!"

ALEXANDER ANDERSON.

OLD FOLKS AT HOME.

WAY down upon de Swanee Ribber,
  Far, far away—
Dare's wha my heart is turning ebber—
  Dare's wha de old folks stay.
All up and down de whole creation,
  Sadly I roam;
Still longing for de old plantation,
  And for de old folks at home.

    All de world am sad and dreary,
      Eb'rywhere I roam;
    Oh, darkeys, how my heart grows weary,
      Far from de old folks at home.

All round de little farm I wandered,
  When I was young;

Den many happy days I squandered,
  Many de songs I sung.
When I was playing wid my brudder,
  Happy was I;
Oh! take me to my kind old mudder!
  Dare let me live and die!

One little hut among de bushes—
  One dat I love—
Still sadly to my memory rushes,
  No matter where I rove.
When will I see de bees a-humming,
  All round de comb?
When will I hear de banjo tumming
  Down in my good old home?

STEPHEN COLLINS FOSTER.

HOME, SWEET HOME.

MID pleasures and palaces though we may roam,
Be it ever so humble there's no place like home!
A charm from the skies seems to hallow us there,
Which, seek through the world, is ne'er met
  with elsewhere.
Home! home! sweet, sweet home!
There's no place like home!

An exile from home, splendor dazzles in vain:
Oh, give me my lowly thatched cottage again!
The birds singing gaily that came at my call—
Give me them—and the peace of mind dearer than all!
Home! home! sweet, sweet home!
There's no place like home!

JOHN HOWARD PAYNE.

BE KIND.

E kind to thy father, for when thou wast young,
  Who loved thee as fondly as he?
He caught the first accents that fell from thy
    tongue,
  And joined in thine innocent glee.
Be kind to thy father, for now he is old,
  His locks intermingled with gray,
His footsteps are feeble, once fearless and bold;
  Thy father is passing away.

Be kind to thy mother, for, lo! on her brow
  May traces of sorrow be seen:
Oh, well may'st you cherish and comfort her now,
  For loving and kind hath she been.
Remember thy mother, for thee will she pray
  As long as God giveth her breath;
With accents of kindness then cheer her lone way,
  E'en to the dark valley of death.

Be kind to thy brother, his heart will have dearth,
  If the smile of thy love be withdrawn;
The flowers of feeling will fade at their birth,
  If the dew of affection be gone.
Be kind to thy brother, wherever you are,
  The love of a brother shall be
An ornament, purer and richer by far,
  Than pearls from the depths of the sea.

Be kind to thy sister, not many may know
  The depth of true sisterly love;
The wealth of the ocean lies fathoms below
  The surface that sparkles above.
Thy kindness shall bring to thee many sweet
    hours,
  And blessings thy pathway to crown,
Affection shall weave thee a garland of flowers,
  More precious than wealth or renown.

MY OLD KENTUCKY HOME.

HE sun shines bright in our old Kentucky home;
  'Tis summer, the darkeys are gay;
The corn-top's ripe and the meadow's in the
    bloom,
  While the birds make music all the day;
The young folks roll on the little cabin floor,
  All merry, all happy, all bright;
By'm by hard times comes a knockin' at the door—
  Then my old Kentucky home, good night!

    Weep no more, my lady; O, weep no more
      to-day!
    We'll sing one song for the old Kentucky home,
    For our old Kentucky home far away.

They hunt no more for the 'possum and the coon,
  On the meadow, the hill and the shore;
They sing no more by the glimmer of the moon,
  On the bench by the old cabin door;
The day goes by, like a shadow o'er the heart,
  With sorrow, where all was delight;
The time has come when the darkeys have to part,
  Then my old Kentucky home, good night!

The head must bow, and the back will have to bend,
  Wherever the darkey may go;
A few more days, and the troubles all will end,
  In the fields where the sugar-cane grow;
A few more days to tote the weary load,
  No matter, it will never be light;
A few more days till we totter on the road,
  Then my old Kentucky home, good night!

                    STEPHEN COLLINS FOSTER.

MOTHERS, SPARE YOURSELVES.

ANY a mother grows old, faded, and feeble long before her time, because her boys
    and girls are not thoughtfully considerate and helpful. When they become old
    enough to be of service in a household, mother has become so used to doing all
herself, to taking upon her shoulders all the care, that she forgets to lay off the burden
little by little, on those who are so well able to bear it. It is partly her own fault, to be
sure, but a fault committed out of love and mistaken kindness for her children.

IN A STRANGE LAND.

OH, to be home again, home again, home again!
Under the apple-boughs, down by the mill;
Mother is calling me, father is calling me,
Calling me, calling me, calling me still.

Oh, how I long to be wandering, wandering
Through the green meadows and over the hill;

Sisters are calling me, brothers are calling me,
Calling me, calling me, calling me still.

Oh, once more to be home again, home again,
Dark grows my sight, and the evening is chill—
Do you not hear how the voices are calling me,
Calling me, calling me, calling me still?

JAMES THOMAS FIELDS.

THE PATTER OF LITTLE FEET.

UP with the sun in the morning,
Away to the garden he hies,
To see if the sleeping blossoms
Have begun to open their eyes.

Running a race with the wind,
With a step as light and fleet,
Under my window I hear
The patter of little feet.

Now to the brook he wanders,
In swift and noiseless flight,
Splashing the sparkling ripples
Like a fairy water-sprite.

No sand under fabled river
Has gleams like his golden hair,
No pearly sea-shell is fairer
Than his slender ankles bare.

Nor the rosiest stem of coral,
That blushes in ocean's bed,
Is sweet as the flash that follows
Our darling's airy tread.

From a broad window my neighbor,
Looks down on our little cot,
And watches the "poor man's blessing"—
I cannot envy his lot.

He has pictures, books, and music,
Bright fountains, and noble trees,
Rare store of blossoming roses,
Birds from beyond the seas.

But never does childish laughter
His homeward footsteps greet;
His stately halls ne'er echo
To the tread of innocent feet.

This child is our "sparkling picture,"
A birdling that chatters and sings,
Sometimes a sleeping cherub,
(Our other one has wings.)

His heart is a charméd casket,
Full of all that's cunning and sweet,
And no harpstring holds such music
As follows his twinkling feet.

When the glory of sunset opens
The highway by angels trod,
And seems to unbar the city
Whose builder and maker is God—

Close to the crystal portal,
I see by the gates of pearl,
The eyes of our other angel—
A twin-born little girl.

And I ask to be taught and directed
To guide his footsteps aright;
So to live that I may be ready
To walk in sandals of light—

And hear, amid songs of welcome,
From messengers trusty and fleet,
On the starry floor of heaven,
The patter of little feet.

3

CATCHING SHADOWS.

WHEN the day and dark are blended,
  And the weary tasks are ended,
Sits the little mother humming,
Waiting sound of his dear coming,
Who, the lord of love's domain,
  Yet to her yields all again.

Then the winsome, wee one, nestling
In her bosom, spies the wrestling,
Dancing shadows rise and fall,
Phantom-like upon the wall,
As the flickering firelight flashes
From among the flames and ashes.

Loud he laughs, in baby glee.
At their elfin revelry;
At the lilting, lithe, elastic,
Airy, fairy forms fantastic,
Now receding, now advancing.
Coy as love from young eyes glancing.

Not eclipse and umbrage dim,
These are sentient things to him;
Wherefore, wistful welcome lending,
Tiny hands are soon extending.
Snatching, catching, quick and eager,
At the shapes that him beleaguer.

Oft he clasps them, grasps them, yet
They but fool him, they coquet;
Vain his striving and endeavor,
They elude and mock him ever,
They delude and still deceive him,
They perplex and vex and grieve him.

Much he wonders, ponders why
When they beckon yet they fly,
And the tear in his blue eye
Shines as rain from sunny sky.
Soon he turns—the cruel seeming
Fades away, and he lies dreaming.

E. HANNAFORD.

A CRADLE HYMN.

HUSH! my dear, lie still, and slumber,
  Holy angels guard thy bed!
Heavenly blessings without number
  Gently falling on thy head.

Sleep, my babe; thy food and raiment,
  House and home thy friends provide;
All without thy care or payment,
  All thy wants are well supplied.

How much better thou 'rt attended
  Than the Son of God could be,
When from heaven he descended,
  And became a child like thee.

Soft and easy is thy cradle:
  Coarse and hard thy Saviour lay:
When his birthplace was a stable,
  And his softest bed was hay.

See the kinder shepherds round him,
  Telling wonders from the sky!

There they sought him, there they found him,
  With his virgin mother by.

See the lovely Babe a-dressing;
  Lovely Infant, how he smiled!
When he wept, the mother's blessing
  Soothed and hushed the holy Child.

Lo! he slumbers in his manger,
  Where the hornéd oxen fed;
Peace, my darling, here 's no danger,
  Here 's no ox anear thy bed.

Mayst thou live to know and fear him,
  Trust and love him all thy days;
Then go dwell forever near him,
  See his face, and sing his praise!

I could give thee thousand kisses,
  Hoping what I most desire;
Not a mother's fondest wishes
  Can to greater joys aspire.

ISAAC WATTS.

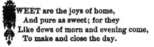

"And yet a happy family
Is but an earlier heaven."

JOYS OF HOME.

SWEET are the joys of home,
  And pure as sweet; for they
Like dews of morn and evening come,
  To make and close the day.

The world hath its delights,
  And its delusions, too;
But home to calmer bliss invites,
  More tranquil and more true.

JOHN ANDERSON, MY JO.

OHN ANDERSON, my jo, John,
  When we were first acquent,
Your locks were like the raven,
  Your bonnie brow was brent;
But now your brow is bald, John,
  Your locks are like the snow;
But blessings on your frosty pow,
  John Anderson, my jo.

John Anderson, my jo, John,
  We clamb the hill thegither;
And monie a canty day, John,
  We've had wi' ane anither.
Now we maun totter down, John,
  But hand in hand we'll go;
And sleep thegither at the foot,
  John Anderson, my jo.

ROBERT BURNS.

CHRISTMAS STOCKINGS.

ERE the stockings were swung in their red,
  white, and blue,
All fashioned to feet that were light as the
  dew.
Ah, the fragrant old faith when we watched the
  cold gray
Reluctantly line the dim border of day,

When we braved the bare floor with our little bare
  feet—
No shrine to a pilgrim was ever so sweet.
When each heart and each stocking was burdened
  with bliss—
On the verge of two worlds there is nothing like this
But a mother's last smile and a lover's first kiss!

BENJAMIN F. TAYLOR.

LOVE AND FRIENDSHIP.

"The little hand outside her muff—
To keep it warm I had to hold it."

ON THE DOORSTEP.

THE conference meeting through at last,
  We boys around the vestry waited
To see the girls come tripping past
  Like snowbirds willing to be mated.

Not braver he that leaps the wall
  By level musket-flashes litten,
Than I, who stepped before them all,
  Who longed to see me get the mitten.

37

But no; she blushed, and took my arm!
  We let the old folks have the highway,
And started toward the Maple Farm
  Along a kind of lover's by-way.

I can't remember what we said,
  'T was nothing worth a song or story;
Yet that rude path by which we sped
  Seemed all transformed and in a glory.

The snow was crisp beneath our feet,
  The moon was full, the fields were gleaming,
By hood and tippet sheltered sweet
  Her face with youth and health was beaming.

The little hand outside her muff—
  O sculptor, if you could but mold it!
So lightly touched my jacket-cuff,
  To keep it warm I had to hold it.

To have her with me there alone—
  'T was love and fear and triumph blended.
At last we reached the foot-worn stone
  Where that delicious journey ended.

The old folks, too, were almost home;
  Her dimpled hand the latches fingered,
We heard the voices nearer come,
  Yet on the doorstep still we lingered.

She shook her ringlets from her hood,
  And with a "Thank you, Ned," dissembled,
But yet I knew she understood
  With what a daring wish I trembled.

A cloud passed kindly overheard,
  The moon was slyly peeping through it,
Yet hid its face, as if it said,
  "Come, now or never! do it! *do it!*"

My lips till then had only known
  The kiss of mother and of sister,
But somehow, full upon her own
  Sweet, rosy, darling mouth—I kissed her!

Perhaps 't was boyish love, yet still,
  O listless woman, weary lover!
To feel once more that fresh, wild thrill
  I'd give— But who can live youth over?
              EDMUND CLARENCE STEDMAN.

THE DEPARTURE.

ND on her lover's arm she leant,
  And round her waist she felt it fold;
And far across the hills they went
  In that new world which is the old.
Across the hills, and far away
  Beyond their utmost purple rim,
And deep into the dying day,
  The happy princess followed him.

"I'd sleep another hundred years,
  O love, for such another kiss;"
"O wake forever, love," she hears,
  "O love, 't was such as this and this;"
And o'er them many a sliding star,
  And many a merry wind was borne,
And streamed through many a golden bar,
  The twilight melted into morn.

"O eyes long laid in happy sleep!"
  "O happy sleep, that lightly fled!"
"O happy kiss, that woke thy sleep!"
  "O love, thy kiss would wake the dead!"
And o'er them many a flowing range
  Of vapor buoyed the crescent bark;
And, rapt through many a rosy change,
  The twilight died into the dark.

A hundred summers! can it be?
  And whither goest thou, tell me where?
"O seek my father's court with me,
  For there are greater wonders there."
And o'er the hills, and far away
  Beyond their utmost purple rim,
Beyond the night, across the day,
  Through all the world she followed him.
              ALFRED TENNYSON.

FIRST LOVE.

IS sweet to hear,
  At midnight on the blue and moonlit deep,
The song and oar of Adria's gondolier;
  By distance mellowed, o'er the waters sweep.
'Tis sweet to see the evening star appear,
  'Tis sweet to listen as the night-winds creep
From leaf to leaf; 'tis sweet to view on high
The rainbow, based on ocean, span the sky.

'Tis sweet to hear the watch-dog's honest bark
  Bay deep-mouthed welcome as we draw near home;
'Tis sweet to know there is an eye will mark
  Our coming, and look brighter when we come.
'Tis sweet to be awakened by the lark,
  Or lulled by falling waters; sweet the hum
Of bees, the voice of girls, the song of birds,
The lisp of children, and their earliest words.

Sweet is the vintage, when the showering grapes
  In Bacchanal profusion reel to earth,
Purple and gushing; sweet are our escapes
  From civic revelry to rural mirth;
Sweet to the miser are his glittering heaps;
  Sweet to the father is his first-born's birth;
Sweet is revenge, especially to women,
Pillage to soldiers, prize-money to seamen.

*   *   *   *   *

'Tis sweet to win, no matter how, one's laurels,
  By blood or ink; 'tis sweet to put an end
To strife; 'tis sometimes sweet to have our quarrels,
  Particularly with a tiresome friend;

Sweet is old wine in bottles, ale in barrels;
  Dear is the helpless creature we defend
Against the world; and dear the school-boy spot
We ne'er forget, though there we are forgot.

But sweeter still than this, than these, than all,
  Is first and passionate love—it stands alone,
Like Adam's recollection of his fall;
  The tree of knowledge has been plucked—all's
    known—
And life yields nothing further to recall
  Worthy of this ambrosial sin, so shown,
No doubt in fable, as the unforgiven
Fire which Prometheus filched for us from heaven.
LORD BYRON.

NO TIME LIKE THE OLD TIME.

HERE is no time like the old time, when you
    and I were young,
  When the buds of April blossomed, and the birds
    of springtime sung!
The garden's brightest glories by summer suns
    are nursed,
  But, oh, the sweet, sweet, sweet violets, the flowers that
    opened first!

There is no place like the old place where you and I
    were born!
Where we lifted first our eyelids on the splendors of
    the morn,
From the milk-white breast that warmed us, from the
    clinging arms that bore,
Where the dear eyes glistened o'er us that will look
    on us no more!

There is no friend like the old friend who has shared
    our morning days,
No greeting like his welcome, no homage like his
    praise;

Fame is the scentless sunflower, with gaudy crown of
    gold,
But friendship is the breathing rose, with sweets in
    every fold.

There is no love like the old love that we courted in
    our pride;
Though our leaves are falling, falling, and we're
    fading side by side,
There are blossoms all around us with the colors of
    our dawn,
And we live in borrowed sunshine when the light of
    day is gone.

There are no times like the old times—they shall never
    be forgot!
There is no place like the old place—keep green the
    dear old spot!
There are no friends like our old friends—may Heaven
    prolong their lives!
There are no loves like our old loves—God bless our
    loving wives!

MARY MORISON.

MARY, at thy window be!
  It is the wished, the trysted hour!
Those smiles and glances let me see
  That make the miser's treasure poor;
How blithely wad I bide the stoure,
  A weary slave frae sun to sun,
Could I the rich reward secure—
  The lovely Mary Morison.

Yestreen when to the trembling string
  The dance gaed through the lighted ha',
To thee my fancy took its wing—
  I sat, but neither heard nor saw;

Though this was fair, and that was braw,
  And yon the toast of a' the town,
I sighed, and said amang them 'a,
  "Ye are na Mary Morison."

O Mary, canst thou wreck his peace
  Wha for thy sake wad gladly dee?
Or canst thou break that heart of his,
  Whase only faut is loving thee?
If love for love thou wilt na gie,
  At least be pity to me shown;
A thought ungentle canna be
  The thought o' Mary Morison.
ROBERT BURNS.

EARLY LOVE.

AH, I remember well (and how can I
But evermore remember well?) when first
Our flame began, when scarce we knew what
    was
The flame we felt; when as we sat and sighed,
And looked upon each other, and conceived
Not what we ailed, yet something we did ail,
And yet were well, and yet we were not well,
And what was our disease we could not tell.

Then would we kiss, then sigh, then look; and thus,
In that first garden of our simpleness,
We spent our childhood. But when years began
To reap the fruit of knowledge—ah, how then
Would she with sterner looks, with graver brow,
Check my presumption, and my forwardness!
Yet still would give me flowers, still would show
What she would have me, yet not have me know.

SAMUEL DANIEL.

CHERRY-RIPE.

THERE is a garden in her face,
    Where roses and white lilies blow;
A heavenly paradise is that place,
    Wherein all pleasant fruits do grow;
    There cherries grow that none may buy,
    Till cherry-ripe themselves do cry.

Those cherries fairly do inclose
    Of orient pearl a double row,
Which when her lovely laughter shows,
    They look like rosebuds fill'd with snow,

Yet them no peer nor prince may buy,
Till cherry-ripe themselves do cry.

Her eyes like angels watch them still;
    Her brows like bended bows do stand,
Threat'ning with piercing frowns to kill
    All that approach with eye or hand
These sacred cherries to come nigh,
Till cherry-ripe themselves do cry.

RICHARD ALISON.

HOW DO I LOVE THEE.

HOW do I love thee? Let me count the ways:
    I love thee to the depth and breadth and
      height
    My soul can reach, when feeling out of sight
    For the ends of Being and ideal Grace.
I love thee to the level of each day's
Most quiet need, by sun and candlelight.
I love thee freely, as men strive for Right;

I love thee purely, as they turn from praise.
I love thee with the passion put to use
In my old griefs, and with my childhood's faith.
I love thee with a love I seem to lose
With my lost saints,—I love thee with the breath,
Smiles, tears, of all my life!—and, if God choose,
I shall but love thee better after death.

ELIZABETH BARRETT BROWNING.

WINIFREDA.

AWAY! let naught to love displeasing,
  My Winifreda, move your care;
Let naught delay the heavenly blessing,
  Nor squeamish pride, nor gloomy fear.

What though no grants of royal donors
  With pompous titles grace our blood,
We 'll shine in more substantial honors,
  And, to be noble, we 'll be good.

Our name, while virtue thus we tender
  Will sweetly sound where 'er 'tis spoke;
And all the great ones, they shall wonder
  How they respect such little folk.

What though, from fortune's lavish bounty,
  No mighty treasures we possess;
We 'll find, within our pittance, plenty,
  And be content without excess.

Still shall each kind returning season
  Sufficient for our wishes give;
For we will live a life of reason,
  And that 's the only life to live.

Through youth and age, in love excelling,
  We 'll hand in hand together tread;
Sweet-smiling peace shall crown our dwelling,
  And babes, sweet-smiling babes, our bed.

How should I love the pretty creatures,
  While round my knees they fondly clung!
To see them look their mother's features,
  To hear them lisp their mother's tongue!

And when with envy time transported
  Shall think to rob us of our joys,
You 'll in your girls again be courted,
  And I 'll go wooing in my boys.

HER LIKENESS.

A GIRL, who has so many wilful ways
  She would have caused Job's patience to forsake him;
  Yet is so rich in all that 's girlhood's praise,
  Did Job himself upon her goodness gaze,
  A little better she would surely make him.

Yet is this girl I sing in naught uncommon,
And very far from angel yet, I trow.

Her faults, her sweetnesses, are purely human;
Yet she 's more lovable as simple woman
  Than any one diviner that I know.

Therefore I wish that she may safely keep
  This womanhede, and change not, only grow;
From maid to matron, youth to age, may creep,
And in perennial blessedness, still reap
  On every hand of that which she doth sow.

DINAH MARIA MULOCK CRAIK.

AE FOND KISS BEFORE WE PART.

AE fond kiss, and then we sever;
  Ae fareweel, alas, forever!
  Deep in heart-wrung tears I'll pledge thee;
  Warring sighs and groans I'll wage thee.
Who shall say that fortune grieves him,
While the star of hope she leaves him?
Me, nae cheerfu' twinkle lights me;
Dark despair around benights me.

I'll ne'er blame my partial fancy—
Naething could resist my Nancy;
But to see her was to love her,
Love but her, and love forever,

Had we never loved sae kindly,
Had we never loved sae blindly,
Never met—or never parted,
We had ne'er been broken-hearted.

Fare thee weel, thou first and fairest!
Fare thee weel, thou best and dearest!
Thine be ilka joy and treasure,
Peace, enjoyment, love, and pleasure!
Ae fond kiss, and then we sever;
Ae fareweel, alas forever!
Deep in heart-wrung tears I'll pledge thee,
Warring sighs and groans I'll wage thee!

ROBERT BURNS.

LET still the woman take
An elder than herself: so wears she to him,
So sways she level in her husband's heart,
For, boy, however we do praise ourselves,
Our fancies are more giddy and unfirm,

More longing, wavering, sooner lost and won,
Than women's are.
*　　*　　*　　*　　*

Then let thy love be younger than thyself,
Or thy affection cannot hold the bent.

MY TRUE-LOVE HATH MY HEART.

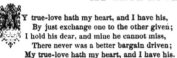

Y true-love hath my heart, and I have his,
 By just exchange one to the other given;
I hold his dear, and mine he cannot miss,
 There never was a better bargain driven;
My true-love hath my heart, and I have his.

His heart in me keeps him and me in one;
 My heart in him his thoughts and senses guides;
He loves my heart, for once it was his own;
 I cherish his because in me it bides;
My true-love hath my heart, and I have his.

SIR PHILIP SIDNEY.

LOVE'S PHILOSOPHY.

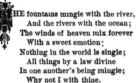

HE fountains mingle with the river,
 And the rivers with the ocean;
The winds of heaven mix forever
 With a sweet emotion;
Nothing in the world is single;
 All things by a law divine
In one another's being mingle;
 Why not I with thine.

See the mountains kiss high heaven,
 And the waves clasp one another;
No sister flower would be forgiven
 If it disdained its brother.
And the sunlight clasps the earth,
 And the moonbeams kiss the sea;
What are all these kissings worth,
 If thou kiss not me?

PERCY BYSSHE SHELLEY.

GOOD BYE.

WEETHEART, good bye! That flut'ring sail
 Is spread to waft me far from thee;
And soon, before the farth'ring gale,
 My ship shall bound upon the sea.
Perchance, all des'late and forlorn,
 These eyes shall miss thee many a year;
But unforgotten every charm—
 Though lost to sight, to memory dear.

Sweetheart, good bye! one last embrace!
 Oh, cruel fate, two souls to sever!
Yet in this heart's most sacred place
 Thou, thou alone, shalt dwell forever;
And still shall recollection trace,
 In fancy's mirror, ever near,
Each smile, each tear, that form, that face—
 Though lost to sight, to memory dear.

THOMAS MOORE.

HOW MANY TIMES.

OW many times do I love thee, dear?
  Tell me how many thoughts there be
  In the atmosphere
  Of a new-fallen year,
Whose white and sable hours appear
  The latest flake of Eternity:
So many times do I love thee, dear.

How many times do I love, again?
  Tell me how many beads there are
  In a silver chain
  Of the evening rain,
Unraveled from the tumbling main,
  And threading the eye of a yellow star:
So many times do I love, again.

THOMAS LOVELL BEDDOES.

ABSENCE.

HEN I think on the happy days
  I spent wi' you, my dearie;
And now what lands between us lie,
  How can I be but eerie!

How slow ye move, ye heavy hours,
  As ye were wae and weary!
It was na sae ye glinted by
  When I was wi' my dearie.

ROBERT BURNS.

COMING THROUGH THE RYE.

OMING through the rye, poor body,
  Coming through the rye,
She draiglet a' her petticoatie,
  Coming through the rye.
Jenny 's a' wat, poor body,
  Jenny's seldom dry;
She draiglet a' her petticoatie,
  Coming through the rye.

Gin a body meet a body
  Coming through the rye;

Gin a body kiss a body—
  Need a body cry?
Gin a body meet a body
  Coming through the glen,
Gin a body kiss a body—
  Need the world ken?
Jenny 's a' wat, poor body;
  Jenny's seldom dry;
She draiglet a' her petticoatie,
  Coming through the rye.

ROBERT BURNS.

COMIN' THROUGH THE RYE.

IN a body meet a body
  Comin' through the rye,
Gin a body kiss a body,
  Need a body cry?
Every lassie has her laddie—
  Ne'er a ane hae I;
Yet a' the lads they smile at me
  When comin' through the rye.

Amang the train there is a swain
  I dearly lo'e mysel';

But whaur his hame, or what his name,
  I dinna care to tell.

Gin a body meet a body
  Comin' frae the town,
Gin a body greet a body,
  Need a body frown?
Every lassie has her laddie—
  Ne'er a ane hae I;
Yet a' the lads they smile at me
  When comin' through the rye.

Adapted from BURNS.

HARK! HARK! THE LARK AT HEAVEN'S GATE SINGS.

ARK! hark! the lark at heaven's gate sings,
  And Phœbus 'gins arise,
His steeds to water at those springs
  On chaliced flowers that lies;

And winking Mary-buds begin
  To ope their golden eyes;
With everything that pretty bin,
  My lady sweet, arise.

WILLIAM SHAKESPEARE.

O FAIREST OF THE RURAL MAIDS.

FAIREST of the rural maids!
Thy birth was in the forest shades;
Green boughs, and glimpses of the sky,
Were all that met thine infant eye.

Thy sports, thy wanderings, when a child,
Were ever in the sylvan wild,
And all the beauty of the place
Is in thy heart and on thy face.

The twilight of the trees and rocks
Is in the light shade of thy locks;

Thy step is as the wind, that weaves
Its playful way among the leaves.

Thine eyes are springs, in whose serene
And silent waters heaven is seen;
Their lashes are the herbs that look
On their young figures in the brook.

The forest depths, by foot unpressed,
Are not more sinless than thy breast;
The holy peace, that fills the air
Of those calm solitudes, is there.

WILLIAM CULLEN BRYANT.

"Take me again to your heart as of yore."

ROCK ME TO SLEEP.

BACKWARD, turn backward, O Time, in your
　　flight,
Make me a child again, just for to-night;
Mother, come back from the echoless shore,
Take me again to your heart as of yore;
Kiss from my forehead the furrows of care,
Smooth the few silver threads out of my hair,
Over my slumbers your loving watch keep —
Rock me to sleep, mother — rock me to sleep.

Backward, flow backward, O tide of the years!
I am so weary of toil and of tears, —
Toil without recompense, tears all in vain, —
Take them and give me my childhood again!
I have grown weary of dust and decay, —
Weary of flinging my soul-wealth away;
Weary of sowing for others to reap; —
Rock me to sleep, mother, — rock me to sleep!

Tired of the hollow, the base, the untrue,
Mother, O mother, my heart calls for you!
Many a summer the grass has grown green,
Blossomed, and faded our faces between,
Yet with strong yearning and passionate pain
Long I to-night for your presence again.
Come from the silence so long and so deep; —
Rock me to sleep, mother, — rock me to sleep!

Over my heart, in the days that are flown,
No love like mother-love ever has shone;
No other worship abides and endures, —
Faithful, unselfish, and patient, like yours:
None like a mother can charm away pain
From the sick soul and the world-weary brain.
Slumber's soft calms o'er my heavy lids creep;—
Rock me to sleep, mother,—rock me to sleep!

Come, let your brown hair, just lighted with gold,
Fall on your shoulders again as of old;
Let it drop over my forehead to-night,
Shading my faint eyes away from the light;
For with its sunny-edged shadows once more
Haply will throng the sweet visions of yore;
Lovingly, softly, its bright billows sweep;—
Rock me to sleep, mother, — rock me to sleep!

Mother, dear mother, the years have been long
Since I last listened your lullaby song:
Sing, then, and unto my soul it shall seem
Womanhood's years have been only a dream.
Clasped to your heart in a loving embrace,
With your light lashes just sweeping your face,
Never hereafter to wake or to weep; —
Rock me to sleep, mother, — rock me to sleep!

ELIZABETH AKERS ALLEN (Florence Percy).

PACK CLOUDS AWAY.

ACK clouds away, and welcome day,
  With night we banish sorrow:
Sweet air, blow soft, mount, lark, aloft,
  To give my love good-morrow.
Wings from the wind to please her mind,
  Notes from the lark I'll borrow;
Bird, prune thy wing! nightingale, sing!
  To give my love good-morrow.
    To give my love good-morrow,
    Notes from them all I'll borrow.

Wake from thy nest, robin-redbreast!
  Sing, birds, in every furrow;
And from each bill let music shrill
  Give my fair love good-morrow!
Blackbird and thrush, in every bush,
  Stare, linnet, and cock-sparrow,
You pretty elves, among yourselves,
  Sing my fair love good-morrow.
    To give my love good-morrow,
    Sing, birds, in every furrow.

THOMAS HEYWOOD.

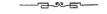

LINGER NOT LONG.

INGER not long! Home is not home without
    thee;
  Its dearest tokens only make me mourn;
Oh! let its memory, like a chain about thee,
  Gently compel and hasten thy return.
        Linger not long!

Linger not long! though crowds should woo thy
    staying,
  Bethink thee, can the mirth of friends, though dear,
Compensate for the grief thy long delaying
  Costs the sad heart that sighs to have thee here?
        Linger not long!

Linger not long! How shall I watch thy coming,
  As evening shadows stretch o'er moor and dell—
When the wild bee hath ceased her busy humming,
  And silence hangs on all things like a spell?
        Linger not long!

How shall I watch for thee when fears grow
    stronger,
  As night draws dark and darker on the hill?
How shall I weep, when I can watch no longer?
  Oh! thou art absent—art thou absent still?
        Linger not long!

Yet though I dream not, though the eye that seem
    thee
  Gazeth through tears that make its splendor dull,
For oh! I sometimes fear, when thou art with me,
  My cup of happiness is all too full!
        Linger not long!

Haste—haste thee home unto thy mountain dwelling;
  Haste as a bird unto its peaceful nest!
Haste as a skiff, when tempests wild are swelling,
  Flies to its haven of securest rest!—
        Linger not long.

SONG.

PLACE in thy memory, dearest,
　　Is all that I claim,
To pause and look back when thou hearest
　　The sound of my name.
Another may woo thee nearer,
　　Another may win and wear;
I care not, though he be dearer,
　　If I am remembered there.

Could I be thy true lover, dearest,
　　Couldst thou smile on me,
I would be the fondest and nearest
　　That ever loved thee.

But a cloud o'er my pathway is glooming,
　　Which never must break upon thine,
And Heaven, which made thee all blooming,
　　Ne'er made thee to wither on mine.

Remember me not as a lover
　　Whose fond hopes are crossed,
Whose bosom can never recover
　　The light it has lost:—
As the young bride remembers the mother
　　She loves, yet never may see,
As a sister remembers a brother,
　　Oh, dearest, remember me.

　　　　　　　　　GERALD GRIFFIN.

LOVE'S YOUNG DREAM.

O, THE days are gone when beauty bright
　　My heart's chain wove!
When my dream of life, from morn till
　　　　night,
　　Was love, still love!
　　New hope may bloom,
　　And days may come,
　Of milder, calmer beam,
But there 's nothing half so sweet in life
　As love's young dream!
O, there 's nothing half so sweet in life
　As love's young dream!

Though the bard to purer fame may soar,
　　When wild youth 's past;
Though he win the wise, who frowned before,
　　To smile at last;
　　He 'll never meet
　　A joy so sweet

　　In all his noon of fame,
As when first he sung to woman's ear
　　His soul-felt flame,
And at every close she blushed to hear
　　The one loved name!

O, that hallowed form is ne'er forgot,
　　Which first love traced;
Still it lingering haunts the greenest spot
　　On memory's waste!
　　'T was odor fled
　　As soon as shed;
　　'T was morning's wingéd dream;
'T was a light that ne'er can shine again
　　On life's dull stream!
O, 't was a light that ne'er can shine again
　　On life's dull stream!

　　　　　　　　　THOMAS MOORE.

LOVE IS ENOUGH.

LOVE is enough. Let us not seek for gold.
　　Wealth breeds false aims, and pride and
　　　　selfishness;
　In those serene, Arcadian days of old,
Men gave no thought to princely homes and dress.
The gods who dwelt in fair Olympia's height,
Lived only for dear love and love's delight;
　　　　Love is enough.

Love is enough. Why should we care for fame?
　Ambition is a most unpleasant guest:
It lures us with the glory of a name
　Far from the happy haunts of peace and rest.
Let us stay here in this secluded place,
Made beautiful by love's endearing grace;
　　　　Love is enough.

Love is enough. Why should we strive for power?
　It brings men only envy and distrust;
The poor world's homage pleases but an hour,
　And earthly honors vanish in the dust.
The grandest lives are ofttimes desolate;
Let me be loved, and let who will be great;
　　　　Love is enough.

Love is enough. Why should we ask for more?
　What greater gift have gods vouchsafed to men?
What better boon of all their precious store
　Than our fond hearts that love and love again?
Old love may die; new love is just as sweet;
And life is fair, and all the world complete;
　　　　Love is enough.

　　　　　　　　　ELLA WHEELER.

IF THOU WERT BY MY SIDE.

IF thou wert by my side, my love!
  How fast would evening fail
In green Bengala's palmy grove,
  Listening the nightingale!

If thou, my love! wert by my side,
  My babies at my knee,
How gayly would our pinnace glide
  O'er Gunga's mimic sea!

But miss thy kind approving eye,
  Thy meek, attentive ear.

But when of morn and eve the star
  Beholds me on my knee,
I feel, though thou art distant far,
  Thy prayers ascend for me.

Then on! then on! where duty leads,
  My course be onward still,

"Thy towers, Bombay, gleam bright, they say,
Across the dark blue sea."

I miss thee at the dawning gray
  When, on our deck reclined,
In careless ease my limbs I lay,
  And woo the cooler wind.

I miss thee when by Gunga's stream
  My twilight steps I guide,
But most beneath the lamp's pale beam,
  I miss thee from my side.

I spread my books, my pencil try,
  The lingering noon to cheer,

O'er broad Hindostan's sultry meads,
  O'er black Almorah's hill.

That course, nor Delhi's kingly gates,
  Nor wild Malwah detain,
For sweet the bliss us both awaits,
  By yonder western main.

Thy towers, Bombay, gleam bright, they say,
  Across the dark blue sea;
But ne'er were hearts so light and gay,
  As then shall meet in thee!

REGINALD HEBER.

PAIN OF LOVE.

TO live in hell, and heaven to behold,
  To welcome life, and die a living death,
  To sweat with heat, and yet be freezing cold,
  To grasp at stars, and lie the earth beneath,
To tread a maze that never shall have end,
To burn in sighs, and starve in daily tears,
To climb a hill, and never to descend,

Giants to kill, and quake at childish fears,
To pine for food, and watch th' Hesperian tree,
To thirst for drink, and nectar still to draw,
To live accurs'd, whom men hold blest to be,
And weep those wrongs which never creature saw;
If this be love, if love in these be founded,
My heart is love, for these in it are grounded.

HENRY CONSTABLE.

BONNIE MARY.

O fetch to me a pint o' wine,
　And fill it in a silver tassie;
That I may drink before I go,
　A service to my bonnie lassie;
The boat rocks at the pier o' Leith;
　Fu' loud the wind blaws frae the ferry;
The ship rides by the Berwick-law,
　And I maun leave my bonnie Mary.

The trumpets sound, the banners fly,
　The glittering spears are rankéd ready;
The shouts o' war are heard afar,
　The battle closes thick and bloody;
It's not the roar o' sea or shore
　Wad make me langer wish to tarry;
Nor shouts o' war that's heard afar—
　It's leaving thee, my bonnie Mary.

ROBERT BURNS.

SWEET HAND.

SWEET hand that, held in mine,
　Seems the one thing I cannot live without,
The soul's one anchorage in this storm and doubt,
　I take thee as a sign

Of sweeter days in store
For life, and more than life, when life is done,
And thy soft pressure leads me gently on
　To Heaven's own evermore.

I have not much to say,
Nor that much in words, at such fond request,

Let my blood speak to thine, and hear the rest
　Some silent heartfelt way.

Thrice blest the faithful hand
Which saves e'en while it blesses; hold me fast;
Let me not go beneath the floods at last,
　So near the better land.

Sweet hand that, thus in mine,
Seems the one thing I cannot live without,
My heart's one anchor in the storm and doubt,
　Take this, and make me thine.

Of all the agonies in life, that which is most poignant and harrowing—that which, for the time, annihilates reason, and leaves our whole organization one lacerated, mangled heart—is the conviction that we have been deceived where we placed all the trust of love.

THREE KISSES.

FIRST time he kissed me, he but only kissed
The fingers of this hand wherewith I write;
And ever since it grew more clean and white—
Slow to world-greetings—quick with its "O,
      list,"
  When the angels speak. A ring of amethyst
I could not wear here, plainer to my sight
Than that first kiss. The second passed in height

The first, and sought the forehead, and half missed,
Half falling on the hair. O beyond meed!
That was the chrism of love, which love's own crown,
With sanctifying sweetness did precede.
The third upon my lips was folded down
In perfect, purple state; since when, indeed,
I have been proud and said, "My love, my own."
                                ELIZABETH BARRETT BROWNING.

TO AN ABSENT WIFE.

'TIS MORN; the sea-breeze seems to bring
    Joy, health, and freshness on its wing;
    Bright flowers, to me all strange and new,
    Are glittering in the early dew;
    And perfumes rise from many a grove
    As incense to the clouds that move
    Like spirits o'er yon welkin clear;
    But I am sad—thou art not here.

'Tis noon; a calm unbroken sleep
Is on the blue waves of the deep;
A soft haze, like a fairy dream,
Is floating over hill and stream;
And many a broad magnolia flower
Within its shadowy woodland bower
Is gleaming like a lovely star;
But I am sad—thou art afar.

'Tis eve; on earth the sunset skies
Are painting their own Eden dyes;
The stars come down, and trembling glow
Like blossoms in the waves below;

And, like some unseen sprite, the breeze
Seems lingering 'mid the orange-trees,
Breathing in music round the spot;
But I am sad—I see thee not.

'Tis midnight; with a soothing spell
The far tones of the ocean swell,
Soft as a mother's cadence mild,
Low bending o'er her sleeping child;
And on each wandering breeze are heard
The rich notes of the mocking-bird
In many a wild and wondrous lay;
But I am sad—thou art away.

I sink in dreams, low, sweet, and clear;
Thy own dear voice is in my ear;
Around my cheek thy tresses twine,
Thy own loved hand is clasped in mine,
Thy own soft lip to mine is pressed,
Thy head is pillowed on my breast.
Oh! I have all my heart holds dear;
And I am happy—thou art here.
                        GEORGE D. PRENTICE.

THE FLOWER O' DUMBLANE.

THE sun has gane down o'er the lofty Ben Lomond,
    And left the red clouds to preside o'er the
      scene,
  While lanely I stray in the calm summer gloamin',
    To muse on sweet Jessie, the Flower o' Dum-
      blane.
How sweet is the brier, wi' its saft fauldin' blossom,
  And sweet is the birk, wi' its mantle o' green;
Yet sweeter and fairer, and dear to this bosom,
  Is lovely young Jessie, the Flower o' Dumblane.

She's modest as ony, and blithe as she's bonnie—
  For guileless simplicity marks her its ain;
And far be the villain, divested of feeling,
  Wha 'd blight in its bloom the sweet Flower o'
    Dumblane.

Sing on, thou sweet mavis, thy hymn to the e'ening!—
  Thou 'rt dear to the echoes of Calderwood glen;
Sae dear to this bosom, sae artless and winning,
  Is charming young Jessie, the Flower o' Dumblane.

How lost were my days till I met wi' my Jessie!
  The sports o' the city seemed foolish and vain;
I ne'er saw a nymph I would ca' my dear lassie
  Till charmed wi' sweet Jessie, the Flower o' Dum-
    blane.

Though mine were the station o' loftiest grandeur,
  Amidst its profusion I 'd languish in pain,
And recken as naething the height o' its splendor,
  If wanting sweet Jessie, the Flower o' Dumblane.
                            ROBERT TANNAHILL.

4

COME INTO THE GARDEN, MAUD.

COME into the garden, Maud,
  For the black bat, night, has flown!
Come into the garden, Maud,
  I am here at the gate alone;
And the woodbine spices are wafted abroad,
  And the musk of the roses blown.

For a breeze of morning moves,
  And the planet of Love is on high,
Beginning to faint in the light that she loves,
  On a bed of daffodil sky,—
To faint in the light of the sun that she loves,
  To faint in its light, and to die.

All night have the roses heard
  The flute, violin, bassoon;
All night has the casement jessamine stirred
  To the dancers dancing in tune,—
Till a silence fell with the waking bird,
  And a hush with the setting moon.

I said to the lily, " There is but one
  With whom she has heart to be gay.
When will the dancers leave her alone?
  She is weary of dance and play."
Now half to the setting moon are gone,
  And half to the rising day;
Low on the sand and loud on the stone
  The last wheel echoes away.

I said to the rose, " The brief night goes
  In babble and revel and wine,
O young lord-lover, what sighs are those
  For one that will never be thine!
But mine, but mine," so I sware to the rose
  " For ever and ever mine!"

And the soul of the rose went into my blood,
  As the music clashed in the hall;
And long by the garden lake I stood,
  For I heard your rivulet fall
From the lake to the meadow, and on to the wood,
  Our wood, that is dearer than all;

From the meadow your walks have left so sweet
  That whenever a March-wind sighs,
He sets the jewel-print of your feet
  In violets blue as your eyes,
To the woody hollows in which we meet
  And the valleys of Paradise.

The slender acacia would not shake
  One long milk-bloom on the tree;
The white lake-blossom fell into the lake,
  As the pimpernel dozed on the lea;
But the rose was awake all night for your sake,
  Knowing your promise to me;
The lilies and roses were all awake,
  They sighed for the dawn and thee.

Queen rose of the rose-bud garden of girls,
  Come hither! the dances are done;
In gloss of satin and glimmer of pearls,
  Queen lily and rose in one;
Shine out, little head, sunning over with curls,
  To the flowers, and be their sun.

There has fallen a splendid tear
  From the passion-flower at the gate.
She is coming, my dove, my dear;
  She is coming, my life, my fate!
The red rose cries, " She is near, she is near; "
  And the white rose weeps, " She is late; "
The larkspur listens, " I hear, I hear; "
  And the lily whispers, " I wait."

She is coming, my own, my sweet!
  Were it ever so airy a tread,
My heart would hear her and beat,
  Were it earth in an earthly bed;
My dust would hear her and beat,
  Had I lain for a century dead;
Would start and tremble under her feet,
  And blossom in purple and red.

ALFRED TENNYSON.

TO ALTHEA, FROM PRISON.

WHEN love with unconfinéd wings
  Hovers within my gates,
And my divine Althea brings
  To whisper at my grates;
When I lie tangled in her hair,
  And fettered with her eye,
The birds that wanton in the air
  Know no such liberty.

When flowing cups run swiftly round,
  With no allaying Thames,
Our careless heads with roses crowned,
  Our hearts with loyal flames;
When thirsty grief in wine we steep,
  When healths and draughts go free,
Fishes that tipple in the deep
  Know no such liberty.

When, linnet-like confinéd, I,
  With shriller note shall sing
The mercy, sweetness, majesty,
  And glories of my king;

Stone walls do not a prison make,
  Nor iron bars a cage;
Minds innocent and quiet take
  That for an hermitage;

"Stone walls do not a prison make,
  Nor iron bars a cage."

When I shall voice aloud how good
  He is, how great should be,
The enlarged winds, that curl the flood.
  Know no such liberty.

If I have freedom in my love,
  And in my soul am free,
Angels alone that soar above
  Enjoy such liberty.

RICHARD LOVELACE.

THERE has nearly always been a good wife behind every great man, and there is a good deal of truth in the saying that a man can be no greater than his wife will let him.

A WOMAN'S QUESTION.

BEFORE I trust my fate to thee,
    Or place my hand in thine,
    Before I let thy future give
    Color and form to mine,
Before I peril all for thee, question thy soul to-night
    for me.

I break all slighter bonds, nor feel
    A shadow of regret:
    Is there one link within the Past
    That holds thy spirit yet?
Or is thy faith as clear and free as that which I can
    pledge to thee?

Does there within my dimmest dreams .
    A possible future shine,
    Wherein thy life could henceforth breathe,
    Untouched, unshared by mine?
If so, at any pain or cost, O, tell me before all is lost.

Look deeper still. If thou canst feel,
    Within thy inmost soul,
    That thou has kept a portion back,
    While I have staked the whole,
Let no false pity spare the blow, but in true mercy
    tell me so.

Is there within thy heart a need
    That mine cannot fulfill?
    One chord that any other hand
    Could better wake or still?
Speak now — lest at some future day my whole life
    wither and decay.

Lives there within thy nature hid
    The demon-spirit change,
    Shedding a passing glory still
    On all things new and strange?
It may not be thy fault alone — but shield my heart
    against thy own.

Couldst thou withdraw thy hand one day
    And answer to my claim,
    That Fate, and that to-day's mistake —
    Not thou — had been to blame?
Some soothe their conscience thus; but thou wilt surely
    warn and save me now.

Nay, answer not — I dare not hear,
    The words would come too late;
    Yet I would spare thee all remorse,
    So, comfort thee, my Fate,—
Whatever on my heart may fall — remember, I would
    risk it all!

             ADELAIDE ANNE PROCTER.

DORIS.

I SAT with Doris, the shepherd maiden:
    Her crook was laden with wreathed flowers;
I sat and wooed her through sunlight wheeling,
    And shadows stealing, for hours and hours.

And she, my Doris, whose lap encloses
    Wild summer roses of rare perfume,
The while I sued her, kept hushed and hearkened
    Till shades had darkened from gloss to gloom.

She touched my shoulder with fearful finger:
    She said, "We linger; we must not stay;
My flock's in danger, my sheep will wander:
    Behold them yonder—how far they stray!"

I answered bolder, "Nay, let me hear you,
    And still be near you, and still adore;
No wolf nor stranger will touch one yearling;
    Ah! stay, my darling, a moment more."

She whispered, sighing: "There will be sorrow
    Beyond to-morrow, if I lose to-day;
My fold unguarded, my flock unfolded,
    I shall be scolded, and sent away."

Said I, replying: "If they do miss you,
    They ought to kiss you, when you get home;
And well rewarded by friend and neighbor
    Should be the labor from which you come."

"They might remember," she answered meekly,
    "That lambs are weakly, and sheep are wild;
But if they love me 'tis none so fervent;
    I am a servant, and not a child."

Then each hot ember glowed quick within me,
    And love did win me to swift reply:
"Ah! do but prove me, and none shall bind you
    Nor fray nor find you, until I die."

She blushed and started, and stood awaiting,
    As if debating in dreams divine;
But I did brave them—I told her plainly
    She doubted vainly; she must be mine.

So we, twin-hearted, from all the valley
    Did rouse and rally the nibbling ewes,
And homeward drove them, we two together,
    Through blooming heather and gleaming dews.

That simple duty fresh grace did lend her—
    My Doris tender, my Doris true:
That I, her warder, did always bless her,
    And often press her, to take her due.

And now in beauty she fills my dwelling
    With love excelling and undefiled;
And love doth guard her, both fast and fervent,
    No more a servant, nor yet a child.

             ARTHUR J. MUNBY.

SAD ARE THEY WHO KNOW NOT LOVE.

SAD are they who know not love,
But, far from passion's tears and smiles,
Drift down a moonless sea, and pass
The silver coasts of fairy isles.

And sadder they whose longing lips
Kiss empty air, and never touch

The dear warm mouth of those they love
Waiting, wasting, suffering much!

But clear as amber, sweet as musk,
Is life to those whose lives unite;
They walk in Allah's smile by day,
And nestle in his heart by night.

THOMAS BAILEY ALDRICH.

O SWALLOW, FLYING SOUTH.

SWALLOW, Swallow, flying, flying South,
Fly to her, and fall upon her gilded eaves,
And tell her, tell her what I tell to thee.

O tell her, Swallow, thou that knowest each,
That bright and fierce and fickle is the South,
And dark and true and tender is the North.

O Swallow, Swallow, if I could follow, and light
Upon her lattice, I would pipe and trill,
And cheep and twitter twenty million loves.

O were I thou, that she might take me in,
And lay me on her bosom, and her heart
Would rock the snowy cradle till I died.

Why lingereth she to clothe her heart with love,
Delaying as the tender ash delays
To clothe herself, when all the woods are green?

O tell her, Swallow, that thy brood is flown;
Say to her, I do but wanton in the South,
But in the North long since my nest is made.

O tell her, brief is life, but love is long,
And brief the sun of summer in the North,
And brief the moon of beauty in the South.

O Swallow, flying from the golden woods,
Fly to her, and pipe and woo her, and make her mine,
And tell her, tell her, that I follow thee.

ALFRED TENNYSON.

SHE WAS A PHANTOM OF DELIGHT.

SHE was a phantom of delight
When first she gleamed upon my sight;
A lovely apparition, sent
To be a moment's ornament;
Her eyes as stars of twilight fair;
Like Twilight's, too, her dusky hair;
But all things else about her drawn
From May-time and the cheerful dawn;
A dancing shape, an image gay,
To haunt, to startle, and waylay.

I saw her upon nearer view,
A spirit, yet a woman too!
Her household motions light and free,
And steps of virgin liberty;
A countenance in which did meet
Sweet records, promises as sweet;

A creature not too bright or good
For human nature's daily food;
For transient sorrows, simple wiles,
Praise, blame, love, kisses, tears, and smiles.

And now I see with eyes serene
The very pulse of the machine;
A being breathing thoughtful breath,
A trav'ler between life and death;
The reason firm, the temperate will,
Endurance, foresight, strength and skill;
A perfect woman, nobly planned,
To warn, to comfort, and command;
And yet a spirit still, and bright
With something of angelic light.

WILLIAM WORDSWORTH.

MARGARET.

MOTHER, I cannot mind my wheel;
My fingers ache, my lips are dry;
Oh, if you felt the pain I feel! —
But oh, who ever felt as I?

No longer could I doubt him true;
All other men may use deceit;
He always said my eyes were blue,
And often swore my lips were sweet.

WALTER SAVAGE LANDOR.

THE MILKING MAID.

HE year stood at its equinox,
  And bluff the north was blowing,
A bleat of lambs came from the flocks,
  Green hardy things were growing;
I met a maid with shining locks
  Where milky kine were lowing.

She wore a kerchief on her neck,
  Her bare arm showed its dimple,

Pathetically rustical,
  Too pointless for the city.

She kept in time without a beat,
  As true as church-bell ringers,
Unless she tapped time with her feet,
  Or squeezed it with her fingers;
Her clear, unstudied notes were sweet
  As many a practiced singer's.

"She wore a kerchief on her neck,
Her bare arm showed its dimple."

Her apron spread without a speck,
  Her air was frank and simple.

She milked into a wooden pail,
  And sang a country ditty—
An innocent fond lover's tale,
  That was not wise nor witty,

I stood a minute out of sight,
  Stood silent for a minute,
To eye the pail, and creamy white
  The frothing milk within it—

To eye the comely milking maid,
  Herself so fresh and creamy.

"Good day to you!" at last I said;
  She turned her head to see me.
"Good day!" she said, with lifted head;
  Her eyes looked soft and dreamy.

And all the while she milked and milked
  The grave cow heavy-laden:
I've seen grand ladies, plumed and silked,
  But not a sweeter maiden.

But not a sweeter, fresher maid
  Than this in homely cotton,
Whose pleasant face and silky braid
  I have not yet forgotten.

Seven springs have passed since then, as I
  Count with a sober sorrow;
Seven springs have come and passed me by,
  And spring sets in to-morrow.

I've half a mind to shake myself
  Free, just for once, from London,
To set my work upon the shelf,
  And leave it done or undone;

To run down by the early train,
  Whirl down with shriek and whistle,
And feel the bluff north blow again,
  And mark the sprouting thistle
Set up on waste patch of the lane
  Its green and tender bristle;

And spy the scarce-blown violet banks,
  Crisp primrose-leaves and others,
And watch the lambs leap at their pranks,
  And butt their patient mothers.

Alas! one point in all my plan
  My serious thoughts demur to:
Seven years have passed for maid and man,
  Seven years have passed for her too.

Perhaps my rose is over-blown,
  Not rosy, or too rosy;
Perhaps in farm-house of her own
  Some husband keeps her cosy,
Where I should show a face unknown,—
  Good-bye, my wayside posy!

CHRISTINA GEORGINA ROSSETTI.

UNDER THE BLUE.

THE skies are low, the winds are slow;
  The woods are bathed in summer glory;
The mists are still, o'er field and hill;
  The brooklet sings its dreamy story.

I careless rove through glen and grove;
  I dream by hill and copse and river;
Or in the shade by aspen made
  I watch the restless shadows quiver.

I lift my eyes to azure skies
  That shed their tinted glory o'er me;
While memories sweet around me fleet,
  As radiant as the scene before me.

And while I muse upon the hues
  Of summer skies in splendor given,
Sweet thoughts arise of rare deep eyes,
  Whose blue is like the blue of heaven.

Bend low, fair skies! Smile sweet, fair eyes!
  From radiant skies rich hues are streaming;
But in the blue of pure eyes true
  The radiance of my life is beaming.

O skies of blue! ye fade from view;
  Faint grow the hues that o'er me quiver;—
But the sure light of dear eyes bright
  Shines on forever and forever!

FRANCIS F. BROWNE.

KISS ME SOFTLY.

KISS me softly and speak to me low,—
  Malice has ever a vigilant ear;
What if Malice were lurking near?
      Kiss me, dear!
Kiss me softly and speak to me low.

Kiss me softly and speak to me low,—
  Envy, too, has a watchful ear;

What if Envy should chance to hear?
      Kiss me, dear!
Kiss me softly and speak to me low.

Kiss me softly and speak to me low;
  Trust me, darling, the time is near
When lovers may love with never a fear;—
      Kiss me, dear!
Kiss me softly and speak to me low.

JOHN GODFREY SAXE.

PEARLS.

NOT what the chemists say they be,
  Are pearls — they never grew;
They come not from the hollow sea,
  They come from heaven in dew!

Down in the Indian sea it slips,
  Through green and briny whirls,

Where great shells catch it in their lips,
  And kiss it into pearls!

If dew can be so beauteous made,
  Oh, why not tears, my girl?
Why not your tears? Be not afraid —
  I do but kiss a pearl!

RICHARD HENRY STODDARD.

A BIRD AT SUNSET.

WILD bird, that wingest wide the glimmering
    moors,
  Whither, by belts of yellowing woods, away?
What pausing sunset thy wild heart allures
  Deep into dying day?

Would that my heart, on wings like thine, could pass
Where stars their light in rosy regions lose —
A happy shadow o'er the warm brown grass,
  Falling with falling dews!

Hast thou, like me, some true-love of thine own,
  In fairy lands beyond the utmost seas;
Who there, unsolaced, yearns for thee alone,
  And sings to silent trees?

Oh, tell that woodbird that the summer grieves
  And the suns darken and the days grow cold;
And, tell her, love will fade with fading leaves,
  And cease in common mould.

Fly from the winter of the world to her!
  Fly, happy bird! I follow in thy flight,
Till thou art lost o'er yonder fringe of fir
  In baths of crimson light.

My love is dying far away from me.
  She sits and saddens in the fading west.
For her I mourn all day, and pine to be
  At night upon her breast.

ROBERT BULWER LYTTON.

SERENADE.

THE western wind is blowing fair
  Across the dark Ægean sea,
And at the secret marble stair
  My Tyrian galley waits for thee.
Come down! the purple sail is spread,
  The watchman sleeps within the town;
O leave thy lily-flowered bed,
  O Lady mine, come down, come down!

She will not come, I know her well,
  Of lover's vows she hath no care,
And little good a man can tell
  Of one so cruel and so fair.
True love is but a woman's toy,
  They never know the lover's pain,
And I who loved as loves a boy
  Must love in vain, must love in vain.

O noble pilot, tell me true,
  Is that the sheen of golden hair?
Or is it but the tangled dew
  That binds the passion-flowers there?

Good sailor, come and tell me now
  Is that my lady's lily hand?
Or is it but the gleaming prow,
  Or is it but the silver sand?

No! no! 'tis not the tangled dew,
  'Tis not the silver-fretted sand,
It is my own dear lady true
  With golden hair and lily hand!
O noble pilot, steer for Troy!
  Good sailor, ply the laboring oar!
This is the Queen of life and joy
  Whom we must bear from Grecian shore!

The waning sky grows faint and blue
  It wants an hour still of day;
Aboard! aboard! my gallant crew
  O Lady mine, away! away!
O noble pilot, steer for Troy!
  Good sailor, ply the laboring oar!
O loved as only loves a boy!
  O loved forever, evermore!

OSCAR WILDE.

BIRD OF PASSAGE.

S the day's last light is dying,
 As the night's first breeze is sighing,
I send you, love, like a messenger-dove, my
 thought through the distance flying;

Let it perch on your sill; or, better,
 Let it feel your soft hand's fetter,
While you search and bring, from under its wing, love,
 hidden away like a letter.

EDGAR FAWCETT.

I FEAR THY KISSES.

FEAR thy kisses, gentle maiden;
 Thou needest not fear mine;
My spirit is too deeply laden
 Ever to burthen thine.

I fear thy mien, thy tones, thy motion;
 Thou needest not fear mine;
Innocent is the heart's devotion
 With which I worship thine.

PERCY BYSSHE SHELLEY.

WHEN THE KYE COMES HAME.

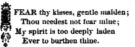

OME, all ye jolly shepherds
 That whistle through the glen,
I 'll tell ye of a secret
 That courtiers dinna ken:
What is the greatest bliss
 That the tongue o' man can name?
'Tis to woo a bonny lassie
 When the kye comes hame!

When the kye comes hame,
 When the kye comes hame,
'Tween the gloaming and the mirk,
 When the kye comes hame!

'Tis not beneath the coronet,
 Nor canopy of state,
'Tis not on couch of velvet,
 Nor arbor of the great,—
'Tis beneath the spreading birk,
 In the glen without the name,
Wi' a bonny, bonny lassie,
 When the kye comes hame!

There the blackbird bigs his nest
 For the mate he loes to see,
And on the topmost bough,
 O, a happy bird is he;
Where he pours his melting ditty,
 And love is a' the theme,
And he 'll woo his bonny lassie
 When the kye comes hame!

When the blewart bears a pearl,
 And the daisy turns a pea,

And the bonny lucken gowan
 Has fauldit up her ee,
Then the laverock frae the blue lift
 Doops down, an' thinks nae shame
To woo his bonny lassie
 When the kye comes hame!

See yonder pawkie shepherd,
 That lingers on the hill,
His ewes are in the fauld,
 An' his lambs are lying still;
Yet he downa gang to bed,
 For his heart is in a flame,
To meet his bonny lassie
 When the kye comes hame!

When the little wee bit heart
 Rises high in the breast,
An' the little wee bit starn
 Rises red in the east,
O there's a joy sae dear,
 That the heart can hardly frame,
Wi' a bonny, bonny lassie,
 When the kye comes hame!

Then since all nature joins
 In this love without alloy,
O, wha wad prove a traitor
 To nature's dearest joy?
O, wha wad choose a crown,
 Wi' its perils and its fame,
And miss his bonny lassie
 When the kye comes hame?

JAMES HOGG.

MAY all go well with you! May life's short day glide on peaceful and bright, with no more clouds than may glisten in the sunshine, no more rain than may form a rainbow; and may the veiled one of heaven bring us to meet again.

THE PATRIOT'S BRIDE.

OH! give me back that royal dream
    My fancy wrought,
When I have seen your sunny eyes
    Grow moist with thought;
And fondly hoped, dear Love, your heart from
    mine
    Its spell had caught;
And laid me down to dream that dream divine,
    But true, methought,
Of how my life's long task would be, to make yours
    blessed as it ought.

To learn to love sweet Nature more
    For your sweet sake,
To watch with you — dear friend, with you! —
    Its wonders break;
The sparkling spring in that bright face to see
    Its mirror make —
On summer morns to hear the sweet birds sing
    By linn and lake;
And know your voice, your magic voice, could still a
    grander music wake!

To wake the old weird world that sleeps
    In Irish lore;
The strains sweet foreign Spenser sung
    By Mulla's shore;
Dear Curran's airy thoughts, like purple birds
    That shine and soar;
Tone's fiery hopes, and all the deathless vows
    That Grattan swore;
The songs that once our own dear Davis sung — ah,
    me! to sing no more.

And all those proud old victor-fields
    We thrill to name,
Whose memories are the stars that light
    Long nights of shame;
The Cairn, the Dan, the Rath, the Power, the Keep,
    That still proclaim
In chronicles of clay and stone, how true, how deep
    Was Eire's fame;
Oh! we shall see them all, with her, that dear, dear
    friend we two have lov'd the same.

Yet ah! how truer, tenderer still
    Methought did seem
That scene of tranquil joy, that happy home
    By Dodder's stream,
The morning smile, that grew a fixéd star
    With love-lit beam,
The ringing laugh, locked hands, and all the far
    And shining stream
Of daily love, that made our daily life diviner than a
    dream.

For still to me, dear Friend, dear Love,
    Or both — dear wife,
Your image comes with serious thoughts,
    But tender, rife;
No idle plaything to caress or chide
    In sport or strife,
But my best chosen friend, companion, guide,
    To walk through life,
Linked hand in hand, two equal, loving friends, true
    husband and true wife.

        SIR CHARLES GAVAN DUFFY.

JANETTE'S HAIR.

OH, loosen the snood that you wear Janette,
    Let me tangle a hand in your hair — my pet;
For the world to me had no daintier sight
    Than your brown hair veiling your shoulder
    white;
    Your beautiful dark brown hair — my pet.

It was brown with a golden gloss, Janette,
It was finer than silk of the floss — my pet;
'Twas a beautiful mist falling down to your wrist,
'Twas a thing to be braided, and jeweled, and kissed —
    'Twas the loveliest hair in the world — my pet.

My arm was the arm of a clown, Janette,
It was sinewy, bristled and brown — my pet;
But warmly and softly it loved to caress
Your round white neck and your wealth of tress,
    Your beautiful plenty of hair — my pet.

Your eyes had a swimming glory, Janette,
Revealing the old, dear story — my pet;

They were gray with that chastened tinge of the sky
When the trout leaps quickest to snap the fly,
    And they matched with your golden hair — my pet.

Your lips — but I have no words, Janette —
They were fresh as the twitter of birds — my pet,
When the spring is young, and roses are wet,
With the dew-drops in each red bosom set,
    And they suited your gold-brown hair — my pet.

Oh, you tangled my life in your hair, Janette,
'Twas a silken and golden snare — my pet;
But, so gentle the bondage, my soul did implore
The right to continue your slave evermore,
    With my fingers enmeshed in your hair — my pet.

Thus ever I dream what you were, Janette,
With your lips and your eyes and your hair — my pet;
In the darkness of desolate years I moan,
And my tears fall bitterly over the stone
    That covers your golden hair — my pet.

        CHARLES GRAHAM HALPINE.

WOOING.

LITTLE bird once met another bird,
 And whistled to her, " Will you be my mate?"
With fluttering wings she twittered, " How
  absurd!
   Oh, what a silly pate! "

And off into a distant tree she flew,
 To find concealment in the shady cover;
And passed the hours in slyly peeping through
  At her rejected lover.

The jilted bard, with drooping heart and wing,
 Poured forth his grief all day in plaintive songs;
Telling in sadness to the ear of Spring
  The story of his wrongs.

But little thought he, while each nook and dell
 With the wild music of his plaint was thrilling,
That scornful breast with sighs began to swell—
  Half-pitying and half-willing.

Next month I walked the same sequestered way,
 When close together on a twig I spied them;
And in a nest half-hid with leaves there lay
  Four little birds beside them.

Coy maid, this moral in your ear I drop:
 When lover's hopes within their hearts you prison,
Fly out of sight and hearing; do not stop
  To look behind and listen.

       JOHN B. L. SOULE.

" Silver sails all out of the west,
Under the silver moon."

SWEET AND LOW.

SWEET and low, sweet and low,
 Wind of the western sea,
Low, low, breathe and blow,
 Wind of the western sea!
  Over the rolling waters go,
Come from the dying moon and blow,
 Blow him again to me;
While my little one, while my pretty one sleeps.

Sleep and rest, sleep and rest,
 Father will come to thee soon:
Rest, rest on mother's breast,
 Father will come to thee soon;
Father will come to his babe in the nest,
 Silver sails all out of the west,
Under the silver moon;
 Sleep, my little one, sleep my pretty one, sleep.

       ALFRED TENNYSON.

THE BROOKSIDE.

WANDERED by the brookside,
  I wandered by the mill;
I could not hear the brook flow —
  The noisy wheel was still;
There was no burr of grasshopper,
  No chirp of any bird,
But the beating of my own heart
  Was all the sound I heard.

I sat beneath the elm-tree;
  I watched the long, long shade,
And as it grew still longer,
  I did not feel afraid;
For I listened for a footfall,
  I listened for a word —
But the beating of my own heart
  Was all the sound I heard.

He came not — no, he came not —
  The night came on alone —
The little stars sat one by one
  Each on his golden throne;
The evening wind passed by my cheek,
  The leaves above were stirred —
But the beating of my own heart
  Was all the sound I heard.

Fast, silent tears were flowing,
  When something stood behind;
A hand was on my shoulder —
  I knew its touch was kind;
It drew me nearer — nearer —
  We did not speak one word,
For the beating of our own hearts
  Was all the sound I heard.

RICHARD MONCKTON MILNES.
(Lord Houghton).

THE OLD STORY.

Y heart is chilled, and my pulse is slow,
  But often and often will memory go,
Like a blind child lost in a waste of snow,
  Back to the days when I loved you so—
    The beautiful long ago.

I sit here dreaming them through and through,
The blissful moments I shared with you—
The sweet, sweet days when our love was new,
When I was trustful and you were true—
    Beautiful days, but few!

Blest or wretched, fettered or free,
Why should I care how your life may be,
Or whether you wander by land or sea?
I only know you are dead to me,
    Ever and hopelessly.

Oh, how often at day's decline
I pushed from my window the curtaining vine,

To see from your lattice the lamp-light shine—
Type of a message that, half divine,
    Flashed from your heart to mine.

Once more the starlight is silvering all;
The roses sleep by the garden wall;
The night bird warbles his madrigal,
And I hear again through the sweet air fall
    The evening bugle call.

But summers will vanish and years will wane,
And bring no light to your window-pane;
No gracious sunshine or patient rain
Can bring dead love back to life again:
    I call up the past in vain.

My heart is heavy, my heart is old,
And that proves dross which I counted gold;
I watch no longer your curtain's fold;
The window is dark and the night is cold,
    And the story forever told.

ELIZABETH AKERS ALLEN.
(Florence Percy).

EVENING SONG.

OOK off, dear Love, across the sallow sands,
  And mark yon meeting of the sun and sea:
How long they kiss in sight of all the lands—
  Ah! longer, longer we.

Now in the sea's red vintage melts the sun,
  As Egypt's pearl dissolved in rosy wine,

And Cleopatra night drinks all. 'Tis done.
  Love, lay thine hand in mine.

Come forth, sweet stars, and comfort heaven's heart;
  Glimmer, ye waves, round else unlighted sands.
O Night! divorce our sun and sky apart —
  Never our lips, our hands.

SIDNEY LANIER.

A PARTING.

SINCE there's no help, come let us kiss and part:
  Nay, I have done; you get no more of me;
  And I am glad, yea, glad with all my heart,
  That thus so clearly I myself can free.
    Shake hands fofever, cancel all our vows,
And, when we meet at any time again,
Be it not seen in either of our brows
That we one jot of former love retain.

Now at the last gasp of Love's latest breath,
  When, his pulse failing, Passion speechless lies;
When Faith is kneeling by his bed of death,
  And Innocence is closing up his eyes,—
Now, if thou wouldst, when all have given him over,
From death to life thou might'st him yet recover.

MICHAEL DRAYTON.

"Watch o'er his slumbers like the brooding dove."

A MOTHER'S LOVE.

HER, by her smile, how soon the stranger knows;
  How soon by his the glad discovery shows,
  As to her lips she lifts the lovely boy,
  What answering looks of sympathy and joy!
  He walks, he speaks. In many a broken word,
  His wants, his wishes, and his griefs are heard;
And ever, ever to her lap he flies,
When rosy sleep comes on with sweet surprise.

Locked in her arms, his arms across her flung,
  (That name most dear forever on his tongue),
As with soft accents round her neck he clings,
And, cheek to cheek, her lulling song she sings:
How blest to feel the beatings of his heart,
Breathe his sweet breath, and bliss for bliss impart:
Watch o'er his slumbers like the brooding dove,
And, if she can, exhaust a mother's love!

SAMUEL ROGERS.

I DO CONFESS THOU 'RT SWEET.

I DO confess thou 'rt sweet, yet find
  Thee such an unthrift of thy sweets.
Thy favors are but like the wind,
  That kisses everything it meets.
And since thou can with more than one,
Thou 'rt worthy to be kissed by none.

The morning rose, that untouched stands,
  Armed with her briers, how sweetly smells!
But plucked and strained through ruder hands,
  Her sweet no longer with her dwells;
But scent and beauty both are gone,
And leaves fall from her, one by one.

SIR ROBERT AYTON.

THE PASSIONATE SHEPHERD TO HIS LOVE.

COME live with me and be my love,
   And we will all the pleasures prove
   That hill and valley, grove and field,
   And all the craggy mountains yield.
   There will we sit upon the rocks,
And see the shepherds feed their flocks
By shallow rivers, to whose falls
Melodious birds sing madrigals.
There will I make thee beds of roses,
With a thousand fragrant posies;
A cap of flowers and a kirtle
Embroider'd all with leaves of myrtle;

A gown made of the finest wool
Which from our pretty lambs we pull;
Slippers lin'd choicely for the cold,
With buckles of the purest gold;
A belt of straw and ivy buds,
With coral clasps and amber studs.
The shepherd swains shall dance and sing
For thy delight each May morning;
And if these pleasures may thee move,
Then live with me and be my love.

CHRISTOPHER MARLOWE.

THE NYMPH'S REPLY TO THE PASSIONATE SHEPHERD.

IF all the world and love were young
   And truth in every shepherd's tongue,
   These pretty pleasures might me move
   To live with thee, and be thy love.

Time drives the flocks from field to fold,
When rivers rage and rocks grow cold;
And Philomel becometh dumb,
The rest complain of cares to come.

The flowers do fade, and wanton fields
To wayward winter reckoning yields;
A honey tongue, a heart of gall,
Is fancy's spring, but sorrow's fall.

Thy gowns, thy shoes, thy beds of roses,
Thy cap, thy kirtle, and thy posies,
Soon break, soon wither, soon forgotten,
In folly ripe, in reason rotten.

Thy belt of straw and ivy buds,
Thy coral clasps and amber studs;
All these in me no means can move
To come to thee and be thy love.

But could youth last, and love still breed,
Had joys no date, nor age no need,
Then these delights my mind might move
To live with thee and be thy love.

SIR WALTER RALEIGH.

LOVE IS A SICKNESS.

LOVE is a sickness full of woes
   All remedies refusing;
   A plant that most with cutting grows,
   Most barren with best using.
     Why so?
More we enjoy it, more it dies;
If not enjoyed, it sighing cries
    Heigh-ho!

Love is a torment of the mind,
   A tempest everlasting;
And Jove hath made it of a kind,
   Not well, nor full, nor fasting.
     Why so?
More we enjoy it, more it dies;
If not enjoyed, it sighing cries
    Heigh-ho!

SAMUEL DANIEL.

FREEDOM IN DRESS.

STILL to be neat, still to be drest,
   As you were going to a feast;
   Still to be powdered, still perfumed —
   Lady, it is to be presumed,
Though art's hid causes are not found,
All is not sweet, all is not sound.

Give me a look, give me a face,
That makes simplicity a grace;
Robes loosely flowing, hair as free —
Such sweet neglect more taketh me
Than all the adulteries of art:
They strike mine eyes, but not my heart.

BEN JONSON.

PHILLIS THE FAIR.

N a hill there grows a flower,
　Fair befall the dainty sweet!
　By the flower there is a bower
　　Where the heavenly muses meet.

In that bower there is a chair,
　Fringéd all about with gold,
Where doth sit the fairest fair
　That ever eye did yet behold.

It is Phillis, fair and bright,
　She that is the shepherd's joy,

She that Venus did despite,
　And did blind her little boy.

Who would not that face admire?
　Who would not this saint adore?
Who would not this sight desire?
　Though he thought to see no more.

Thou that art the shepherd's queen,
　Look upon thy love-sick swain;
By thy comfort have been seen
　Dead men brought to life again.
　　　　　　　　NICHOLAS BRETON.

" We sat in the hush of Summer eves,
Saying but little, yet loving much."

YOU AND I.

HAT if either of us should die?
　Could the hearts that have loved us so tenderly
　Be severed by death? Not so! not so!
　My soul leans out from its house of clay,
When the breeze that has fanned your cheek goes by,
And says: "She's near!" I feel the touch
Of her lip to mine! of her hand, at play

With my hair as it did, when, long ago,
We sat in the hush of summer eves,
Saying but little, yet loving much,
And believing all that Love believes.
And so I know, whate'er I list,
Our souls shall keep thy holy tryst
Through all the years of the life to be.
　　　　　　　　W. H. BURLEIGH.

O, SAW YE THE LASS.

O, SAW ye the lass wi' the bonnie blue een?
Her smile is the sweetest that ever was seen,
Her cheek like the rose is, but fresher, I ween;
She's the loveliest lassie that trips on the green.
The home of my love is below in the valley,
Where wild flowers welcome the wandering bee;
But the sweetest of flowers in that spot that is seen
Is the maid that I love wi' the bonny blue een.

When night overshadows her cot in the glen,
She 'll steal out to meet her loved Donald again;
And when the moon shines on the valley so green,
I'll welcome the lass wi' the bonny blue een.
As the dove that has wandered away from his nest
Returns to the mate his fond heart loves the best,
I'll fly from the world's false and vanishing scene,
To my dear one, the lass wi' the bonny blue een.

RICHARD RYAN.

WE PARTED IN SILENCE.

WE parted in silence, we parted by night,
On the banks of that lonely river;
Where the fragrant limes their boughs unite,
We met — and we parted forever!

The night-bird sung and the stars above
Told many a touching story,
Of friends long passed to the kingdom of love,
Where the soul wears its mantle of glory.

We parted in silence — our cheeks were wet
With the tears that were past controlling;
We vowed we would never, no never, forget,
And those vows at the time were consoling.

But those lips that echoed the sounds of mine
Are as cold as that lonely river;
And that eye, that beautiful spirit's shrine,
Has shrouded its fires forever.

And now on the midnight sky I look,
And my heart grows full of weeping;
Each star is to me a sealéd book,
Some tale of that loved one keeping.

We parted in silence — we parted in tears,
On the banks of that lonely river;
But the odor and bloom of those by-gone years
Shall hang o'er its waters forever.

JULIA CRAWFORD.

COME TO ME, DEAREST.

COME to me, dearest, I'm lonely without thee,
Daytime and night-time, I'm thinking about
thee;
Night-time and daytime, in dreams I behold
thee;
Unwelcome the waking which ceases to fold thee.
Come to me, darling, my sorrows to lighten,
Come in thy beauty to bless and to brighten;
Come in thy womanhood, meekly and lowly,
Come in thy loveliness, queenly and holy.

Swallows will flit round the desolate ruin,
Telling of spring and its joyous renewing;
And thoughts of thy love, and its manifold treasure,
Are circling my heart with a promise of pleasure.
O Spring of my spirit, O May of my bosom,
Shine out on my soul, till it bourgeon and blossom;
The waste of my life has a rose-root within it,
And thy fondness alone to the sunshine can win it.

Figure that moves like a song through the even;
Features lit up by a reflex of heaven;
Eyes like the skies of poor Erin, our mother,
Where shadow and sunshine are chasing each other;

Smiles coming seldom, but childlike and simple,
Planting in each rosy cheek a sweet dimple;—
O, thanks to the Saviour, that even thy seeming
Is left to the exile to brighten his dreaming.

You have been glad when you knew I was glad-
dened;
Dear, are you sad now, to hear I am saddened?
Our hearts ever answer in tune and in time, love,
As octave to octave, and rhyme unto rhyme, love;
I cannot weep but your tears will be flowing,
You cannot smile but my cheek will be glowing;
I would not die without you at my side, love,
You will not linger when I shall have died, love.

Come to me, dear, ere I die of my sorrow,
Rise on my gloom like the sun of to-morrow,
Strong, swift, and fond as the words which I speak,
love,
With a song on your lip and a smile on your cheek,
love.

Come, for my heart in your absence is weary,—
Haste, for my spirit is sickened and dreary,—
Come to the arms which alone should caress thee,
Come to the heart that is throbbing to press thee!

JOSEPH BRENNAN.

ABSENCE.

FROM you have I been absent in the spring,
When proud-pied April, dressed in all his trim,
Hath put a spirit of youth in everything
That heavy Saturn laugh'd; and leaped with him:
Yet nor the lay of birds, nor the sweet smell
Of different flowers in odor and in hue,
Could make me any summer's story tell,
Or from their proud lap pluck them where they grew:

Nor did I wonder at the lily's white,
Nor praise the deep vermilion in the rose;
They were but sweet, but figures of delight,
Drawn after you; you pattern of all those.
Yet seem'd it winter still, and, you away,
As with your shadow I with these did play.

WILLIAM SHAKESPEARE.

WHY SO PALE AND WAN, FOND LOVER.

WHY so pale and wan, fond lover!
Prythee why so pale?
Will, when looking well can't move her,
Looking ill prevail?
Prythee why so pale?

Why so dull and mute, young sinner!
Prythee why so mute?

Will, when speaking well can't win her,
Saying nothing do 't?
Prythee why so mute?

Quit, quit for shame! this will not move,
This cannot take her;
If of herself she will not love,
Nothing can make her:—
The devil take her!

SIR JOHN SUCKLING.

DON'T BE SORROWFUL, DARLING.

DON'T be sorrowful, darling!
And don't be sorrowful, pray;
Taking the year together, my dear,
There isn't more night than day.

'Tis rainy weather, my darling;
Time's waves they heavily run;
But taking the year together, my dear,
There isn't more cloud than sun.

We are old folks now, my darling,
Our heads are growing gray;
But taking the year all round, my dear,
You will always find the May.

We have had our May, my darling,
And our roses long ago;
And the time of the year is coming, my dear,
For the silent night and the snow.

But God is God, my darling,
Of the night as well as the day;
And we feel and know that we can go
Wherever He leads the way.

A God of the night, my darling
Of the night of death so grim;
The gate that leads out of life, good wife,
Is the gate that leads to Him.

REMBRANDT PEALE.

JULIA.

SOME ask'd me where the rubies grew,
And nothing I did say,
But with my finger pointed to
The lips of Julia.

Some ask'd how pearls did grow, and where;
Then spoke I to my girle,

To part her lips, and shewed them there
The quarelets of pearl.

One ask'd me where the roses grew;
I bade him not go seek;
But forthwith bade my Julia show
A bud in either cheek.

ROBERT HERRICK.

"I saw her pace, with quiet grace, the shaded path along."

THE BLOOM WAS ON THE ALDER AND THE TASSEL
ON THE CORN.

HEARD the bob-white whistle in the dewy breath of morn;
The bloom was on the alder and the tassel on the corn.

I stood with beating heart beside the babbling Mac-o-chee,
To see my love come down the glen to keep her tryst with me.

I saw her pace, with quiet grace, the shaded path
along,
And pause to pluck a flower, or hear the thrush's
song.
Denied by her proud father as a suitor to be seen,
She came to me, with loving trust, my gracious little
queen.

Above my station, heaven knows, that gentle maiden
shone,
For she was belle and wide beloved, and I a youth
unknown.
The rich and great about her thronged, and sought on
bended knee
For love this gracious princess gave, with all her
heart, to me.

So like a startled fawn before my longing eyes she
stood,
With all the freshness of a girl in flush of woman-
hood.
I trembled as I put my arm about her form divine,
And stammered, as in awkward speech, I begged her
to be mine.

'Tis sweet to hear the pattering rain, that lulls a dim-
lit dream —
'Tis sweet to hear the song of birds, and sweet the
rippling stream;
'Tis sweet amid the mountain pines to hear the south
winds sigh.
More sweet than these and all beside was the loving,
low reply.

The little hand I held in mine held all I had of life,
To mold its better destiny and soothe to sleep its
strife.
'Tis said that angels watch o'er men, commissioned
from above;
My angel walked with me on earth, and gave to me
her love.

Ah! dearest wife, my heart is stirred, my eyes are dim
with tears —
I think upon the loving faith of all these bygone
years,
For now we stand upon this spot, as in that dewy
morn,
With the bloom upon the alder and the tassel on
the corn.

DON PIATT.

THE GOWAN GLITTERS ON THE SWARD.

THE gowan glitters on the sward,
 The laverock's in the sky,
And Collie on my plaid keeps ward,
 And time is passing by.
 O, no! sad and slow,
  And lengthened on the ground;
 The shadow of our trysting bush
  It wears so slowly round.

My sheep-bells tinkle frae the west,
 My lambs are bleating near;
But still the sound that I love best,
 Alack! I canna hear.
 O, no! sad and slow,
  The shadow lingers still;
 And like a lanely gaist I stand,
  And croon upon the hill.

I hear below the water roar,
 The mill wi' clacking din,
And Lucky scolding frae the door,
 To ca' the bairnies in.
 O, no! sad and slow,
  These are nae sounds for me;
 The shadow of our trysting bush
  It creeps sae drearily.

I coft yestreen, frae Chapman Tam,
 A snood o' bonnie blue,
And promised, when our trysting cam',
 To tie it round her brow.
 O, no! sad and slow,
  The mark it winna' pass;
 The shadow o' that dreary bush
  Is tethered on the grass.

O, now I see her on the way!
 She's past the witch's knowe;
She's climbing up the brownie's brae;
 My heart is in a lowe.
 O, no! 'tis not so,
  'Tis glamrie I hae seen;
 The shadow o' that hawthorn bush
  Will move nae mair till e'en.

My book o' grace I'll try to read,
 Though conned wi' little skill;
When Collie barks I'll raise my head,
 And find her on the hill.
 O, no! sad and slow,
  The time will ne'er be gane;
 The shadow o' our trysting bush
  Is fixed like ony stane.

JOANNA BAILLIE.

SHE WALKS IN BEAUTY.

SHE walks in beauty, like the night
   Of cloudless climes and starry skies,
And all that's best of dark and bright
   Meet in her aspect and her eyes,
Thus mellowed to that tender light
   Which heaven to gaudy day denies.

One shade the more, one ray the less,
   Had half impaired the nameless grace
Which waves in every raven tress
   Or softly lightens o'er her face,

Where thoughts serenely sweet express
   How pure, how dear their dwelling-place.

And on that cheek and o'er that brow
   So soft, so calm, yet eloquent,
The smiles that win, the tints that glow,
   But tell of days in goodness spent—
A mind at peace with all below,
   A heart whose love is innocent.

                  LORD BYRON.

AUX ITALIENS.

AT Paris it was, at the opera there;
   And she looked like a queen in a book that
      night,
   With the wreath of pearls in her raven hair,
   And the brooch on her breast so bright.

Of all the operas that Verdi wrote,
   The best, to my taste, is the Trovatoré;
And Mario can soothe, with a tenor note,
   The souls in purgatory.

The moon on the tower slept soft as snow;
   And who was not thrilled in the strangest way,
As we heard him sing, while the gas burned low,
   " Non ti scordar di me ?"

The Emperor there, in his box of state,
   Looked grave; as if he had just seen
The red flag wave from the city gate,
   Where his eagles in bronze had been.

The Empress, too, had a tear in her eye:
   You'd have said that her fancy had gone back
      again,
For one moment, under the old blue sky
   To the old glad life in Spain.

Well, there in our front-row box we sat
   Together, my bride betrothed and I;
My gaze was fixed on my opera-hat,
   And hers on the stage hard by.

And both were silent, and both were sad—
   Like a queen she leaned on her full white arm,
With that regal, indolent air she had—
   So confident of her charm!

I have not a doubt she was thinking then
   Of her former lord, good soul that he was,
Who died the richest and roundest of men,
   The Marquis of Carabas.

I hope that to get to the kingdom of heaven,
   Through a needle's eye he had not to pass;
I wish him well for the jointure given
   To my lady of Carabas.

Meanwhile, I was thinking of my first love
   As I had not been thinking of aught for years;
Till over my eyes there began to move
   Something that felt like tears.

I thought of the dress that she wore last time,
   When we stood 'neath the cypress-trees together,
In that lost land, in that soft clime,
   In the pleasant evening weather;

Of that muslin dress (for the eve was hot),
   And her warm white neck in its golden chain;
And her full soft hair, just tied in a knot,
   And falling loose again;

Of the jasmine flower that she wore in her breast,
   (O the faint, sweet smell of that jasmine flower!)
And the one bird singing alone in his nest,
   And the one star over the tower.

I thought of our little quarrels and strife,
   And the letter that brought me back my ring;
And it all seemed then, in the waste of life,
   Such a very little thing!

For I thought of her grave below the hill,
   Which the sentinel cypress-tree stands over:
And I thought, "Were she only living still,
   How I could forgive her and love her!"

And I swear, as I thought of her thus, in that hour,
   And of how, after all, old things are best,
That I smelt the smell of that jasmine flower
   Which she used to wear in her breast.

It smelt so faint, and it smelt so sweet,
   It made me creep, and it made me cold!
Like the scent that steals from the crumbling sheet
   Where a mummy is half unrolled.

And I turned and looked: she was sitting there,
   In a dim box over the stage; and drest
In that muslin dress, with that full soft hair,
   And that jasmine in her breast!

I was here, and she was there;
  And the glittering horseshoe curved between!—
From my bride betrothed, with her raven hair
  And her sumptuous scornful mien,

To my early love with her eyes downcast,
  And over her primrose face the shade,
(In short, from the future back to the past.)
  There was but a step to be made.

To my early love from my future bride
  One moment I looked.   Then I stole to the door,
I traversed the passage; and down at her side
  I was sitting, a moment more.

My thinking of her, or the music's strain,
  Or something which never will be exprest,
Had brought her back from the grave again,
  With the jasmine in her breast.

She is not dead, and she is not wed!
  But she loves me now, and she loved me then!
And the very first word that her sweet lips said,
  My heart grew youthful again.

The marchioness there, of Carabas,
  She is wealthy, and young, and handsome still;
And but for her — well, we 'll let that pass;
  She may marry whomever she will.

But I will marry my own first love,
  With her primrose face, for old things are best;
And the flower in her bosom, I prize it above
  The brooch in my lady's breast.

The world is filled with folly and sin,
  And love must cling where it can, I say:
For beauty is easy enough to win;
  But one is n't loved every day.

And I think, in the lives of most women and men,
  There's a moment when all would go smooth and
    even,
If only the dead could find out when
  To come back and be forgiven.

But O, the smell of that jasmine flower!
  And O, the music! and O, the way
That voice rang out from the donjon tower —
  Non ti scordar di me,
  Non ti scordar di me!

ROBERT BULWER LYTTON.

THE WELCOME.

COME in the evening or come in the morning,
  Come when you're looked for, or come without
    warning,
Kisses and welcome you'll find here before you,
  And the oftener you come here the more I'll
    adore you.
Light is my heart since the day we were plighted;
Red is my cheek that they told me was blighted;
The green of the trees looks far greener than ever,
And the linnets are singing, " True lovers, don't
    sever! "

I'll pull you sweet flowers, to wear if you choose them;
Or, after you've kissed them, they'll lie on my bosom.
I'll fetch from the mountain its breeze to inspire you;
I'll fetch from my fancy a tale that won't tire you.
  Oh! your step's like the rain to the summer-vexed
    farmer,
  Or saber and shield to a knight without armor;
  I'll sing you sweet songs till the stars rise above me,
  Then, wandering, I'll wish you, in silence, to love
    me.

We'll look through the trees at the cliff and the eyrie,
We'll tread round the rath on the track of the fairy,
We'll look on the stars, and we'll list to the river,
Till you ask of your darling what gift you can give her.
  Oh! she'll whisper you, "Love, as unchangeably
    beaming,
  And trust, when in secret most tunefully streaming,
  Till the starlight of heaven above us shall quiver,
  As our souls flow in one down eternity's river."

So come in the evening or come in the morning,
Come when you're looked for, or come without warn-
    ing,
Kisses and welcome you'll find here before you,
And the oftener you come here the more I'll adore you!
Light is my heart since the day we were plighted;
Red is my cheek that they told me was blighted;
The green of the trees looks far greener than ever,
And the linnets are singing, "True lovers, don't
    sever."

THOMAS DAVIS.

NEVER burn kindly written letters: it is so pleasant to read them over when the ink
is brown, the paper yellow with age, and the hands that traced the friendly words are
folded over the hearts that prompted them.   Keep all loving letters.   Burn only the harsh
ones, and in burning, forgive and forget them.

A PASTORAL.

Y time, O ye Muses, was happily spent,
When Phœbe went with me wherever I went;
Ten thousand sweet pleasures I felt in my
    breast:
    Sure never fond shepherd like Colin was blest!
    But now she is gone and has left me behind, ·
What a marvellous change on a sudden I find!
When things were as fine as could possibly be,
I thought 't was the Spring; but alas! it was she.

But now I so cross and so peevish am grown,
So strangely uneasy, as never was known.
My fair one is gone, and my joys are all drowned,
And my heart—I am sure it weighs more than a
    pound.

    The fountain that wont to run sweetly along,
And dance to soft murmurs the pebbles among;
Thou know'st, little Cupid, if Phœbe was there,
'T was pleasure to look at, 't was music to hear:

"For ne'er was poor shepherd so sadly forlorn."

With such a companion to tend a few sheep,
To rise up and play, or to lie down and sleep:
I was so good-humored, so cheerful and gay,
My heart was as light as a feather all day;

But now she is absent, I walk by its side,
And still, as it murmurs, do nothing but chide;
Must you be so cheerful, while I go in pain?
Peace there with your bubbling, and hear me
    complain.

My lambkins around me would oftentimes play,
And Phœbe and I were as joyful as they;
How pleasant their sporting, how happy their time,
When Spring, Love, and Beauty were all in their
    prime:
But now, in their frolics when by me they pass,
I fling at their fleeces a handful of grass;
Be still, then, I cry, for it makes me quite mad,
To see you so merry while I am so sad.

My dog I was ever well pleasèd to see
Come wagging his tail to my fair one and me;
And Phœbe was pleased too, and to my dog said,
"Come hither, poor fellow;" and patted his head.
But now, when he's fawning, I with a sour look
Cry "Sirrah!" and give him a blow with my
    crook:
And I'll give him another; for why should not Tray
Be as dull as his master, when Phœbe 's away?

When walking with Phœbe, what sights have I
    seen,
How fair was the flower, how fresh was the green!
What a lovely appearance the trees and the shade,
The cornfields and hedges and everything made!
But now she has left me, though all are still there,
They none of them now so delightful appear:
'T was naught but the magic, I find, of her eyes,
Made so many beautiful prospects arise.

Sweet music went with us both all the wood
    through,
The lark, linnet, throstle, and nightingale, too;
Winds over us whispered, flocks by us did bleat,
And chirp! went the grasshopper under our feet.

But now she is absent, though still they sing on,
The woods are but lonely, the melody's gone:
Her voice in the concert, as now I have found,
Gave everything else its agreeable sound.

Rose, what is become of thy delicate hue?
And where is the violet's beautiful blue?
Does aught of its sweetness the blossoms beguile?
That meadow, those daisies, why do they not smile?
Ah! rivals, I see why it was that you drest,
And made yourselves fine for—a place in her breast;
You put on your colors to pleasure her eye,
To be plucked by her hand, on her bosom to die.

How slowly Time creeps till my Phœbe return!
While amidst the soft zephyr's cool breezes I burn:
Methinks if I knew whereabouts he would tread,
I could breathe on his wings, and 't would melt
    down the lead.
Fly swifter, ye minutes, bring hither my dear,
And rest so much longer for 't when she is here.
Ah, Colin! old Time is full of delay,
Nor will budge one foot faster for all thou canst
    say.

Will no pitying power, that hears me complain,
Or cure my disquiet or soften my pain?
To be cured, thou must, Colin, thy passion remove;
But what swain is so silly to live without love!
No, deity, bid the dear nymph to return,
For ne'er was poor shepherd so sadly forlorn.
Ah! what shall I do? I shall die with despair;
Take heed, all ye swains, how ye part with your
    fair.

JOHN BYROM.

LOVE AT FIRST SIGHT.

THE racing river leaped and sang
    Full blithely in the perfect weather,
All round the mountain echoes rang,
    For blue and green were glad together.

This rains out light from every part,
    And that with songs of joy was thrilling;
But in the hollow of my heart,
    There ached a place that wanted filling.

Before the road and river meet,
    And stepping-stones are wet and glisten,
I heard a sound of laughter sweet,
    And paused to like it, and to listen.

I heard the chanting waters flow,
    The cushat's note, the bee's low humming.
Then turned the hedge, and did not know —
    How could I? that my time was coming.

A girl upon the highest stone,
    Half doubtful of the deed, was standing.

So far the shallow flood had flown,
    Beyond the 'customed leap of landing.

She knew not any need of me,
    Yet me she wanted all unweeting;
She thought not I had crossed the sea,
    And half the sphere, to give her meeting.

I waded out, her eyes I met,
    I wished the moments had been hours;
I took her in my arms and set
    Her dainty feet among the flowers.

Her fellow-maids in copse and lane,
    Ah! still, methinks, I hear them calling;
The wind's soft whisper in the plain,
    That cushat's coo, the water's falling.

But now it is a year ago,
    And now possession crowns endeavor;
I took her in my heart to grow
    And fill the hollow place forever.

JEAN INGELOW.

A SPINNING-WHEEL SONG.

ELLOW the moonlight to shine is beginning;
  Close by the window young Eileen is spinning;
  Bent o'er the fire, her blind grandmother sit-
      ting,
  Is croning, and moaning, and drowsily knit-
      ting.
    "Eileen, achora, I hear some one tapping."
"'Tis the ivy, dear mother, against the glass flap-
    ping."
"Eileen, I surely hear somebody sighing."

And he whispers, with face bent, "I'm waiting for
    you, love.
Get up on the stool, through the lattice step lightly;
We'll rove in the grove while the moon's shining
    brightly."
  Merrily, cheerily, noisily whirring,
  Swings the wheel, spins the reel, while the foot's
      stirring;
  Sprightly, and lightly, and airily ringing,
  Thrills the sweet voice of the young maiden singing.

"Close by the window young Eileen is spinning;
Bent o'er the fire, her blind grandmother, sitting."

"'Tis the sound, mother dear, of the summer wind
    dying."
  Merrily, cheerily, noisily whirring,
  Swings the wheel, spins the reel, while the foot's
      stirring;
  Sprightly, and lightly, and airily ringing,
  Thrills the sweet voice of the young maiden singing.
"What's that noise that I hear at the window, I
    wonder?"
"'Tis the little birds chirping the holly-bush under."
"What makes you be shoving and moving your stool
    on,
And singing all wrong that old song of 'The
    Coolun?'"
There's a form at the casement—the form of her true-
    love;

The maid shakes her head, on her lip lays her fingers,
Steals up from her seat, longs to go — and yet lingers;
A frightened glance turns to her drowsy grandmother,
Puts one foot on the stool, spins the wheel with the
    other.
  Lazily, easily, swings now the wheel round;
  Slowly and lowly is heard now the reel's sound.
  Noiseless and light to the lattice above her
  The maid steps — then leaps to the arms of her lover.
  Slower — and slower — and slower the wheel swings;
  Lower — and lower — and lower the reel rings.
  Ere the reel and the wheel stop their ringing and
      moving,
  Through the grove the young lovers by moonlight
      are roving.

JOHN FRANCIS WALLER.

PHILIP MY KING.

LOOK at me with thy large brown eyes,
    Philip my king,
Round whom the enshadowing purple lies
    Of babyhood's royal dignities:
Lay on my neck thy tiny hand,
With love's invisible scepter laden;
I am thine Esther to command
Till shou shalt find a queen-handmaiden,
    Philip my king.

Up from thy sweet mouth — up to thy brow,
    Philip my king!
The spirit that there lies sleeping now
May rise like a giant and make men bow
As to one Heaven-chosen amongst his peers:
My Saul, than thy brethren taller and fairer
Let me behold thee in future years; —
Yet thy head needeth a circlet rarer,
    Philip my king.

"Lay on my neck thy tiny hand,
With love's invisible sceptre laden."

O the day when thou goest a wooing,
    Philip my king!
When those beautiful lips 'gin suing,
And some gentle heart's bars undoing
Thou dost enter, love-crowned, and there
Sittest love-glorified. Rule kindly,
Tenderly, over thy kingdom fair,
For we that love, ah? we love so blindly,
    Philip my king.

A wreath not of gold, but palm. One day,
    Philip my king,
Thou, too, must tread, as we trod, a way
Thorny and cruel and cold and gray:
Rebels within thee and foes without,
Will snatch at thy crown. But march on, glorious,
Martyr, yet monarch: till angels shout,
As thou sitt'st at the feet of God victorious,
    "Philip the king!"

                  DINAH MARIA MULOCK CRAIK.

FRANK explanations with friends in case of affronts, sometimes save a perishing friendship, and even place it on a firmer basis than at first; but secret discontentment always ends badly.

AFTON WATER.

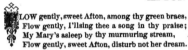

LOW gently, sweet Afton, among thy green braes,
Flow gently, I'll sing thee a song in thy praise;
My Mary's asleep by thy murmuring stream,
Flow gently, sweet Afton, disturb not her dream.

How pleasant thy banks and green valleys below,
Where wild in the woodland the primroses blow;
There oft as mild evening weeps over the lea,
The sweet-scented birk shades my Mary and me.

"How lofty, sweet Afton, thy neighboring hills."

Thou stockdove whose echo resounds through the glen,
Ye wild whistling blackbirds in yon thorny den,
Thou green-crested lapwing, thy screaming forbear,
I charge you disturb not my slumbering fair.

How lofty, sweet Afton, thy neighboring hills,
Far marked with the courses of clear, winding rills;
There daily I wander as noon rises high,
My flocks and my Mary's sweet cot in my eye.

Thy crystal stream, Afton, how lovely it glides,
And winds by the cot where my Mary resides;
How wanton thy waters her snowy feet lave,
As gathering sweet flowerets she stems thy clear wave.

Flow gently, sweet Afton, among thy green braes,
Flow gently, sweet river, the theme of my lays;
My Mary's asleep by thy murmuring stream,
Flow gently, sweet Afton, disturb not her dream.

ROBERT BURNS.

LOVE would put a new face on this dreary old world in which we dwell as pagans and enemies too long; and it would warm the heart to see how fast the vain diplomacy of statesmen, the impotence of armies and navies and lines of defense, would be superseded by this unarmed child.

THE LILY-POND.

OME fairy spirit with his wand,
  I think, has hovered o'er the dell,
And spread this film upon the pond,
  And touched it with this drowsy spell,

For here the musing soul is merged
  In woods no other scene can bring,

And sweeter seems the air when scourged
  With wandering wild-bee's murmuring.

One ripple streaks the little lake,
  Sharp purple-blue; the birches, thin
And silvery, crowd the edge, yet break
  To let a straying sunbeam in.

How came we through the yielding wood,
  That day, to this sweet-rustling shore?
Oh! there together while we stood,
  A butterfly was wafted o'er.

In sleepy light; and even now
  His glimmering beauty doth return
Upon me when the soft winds blow,
  And lilies toward the sunlight yearn.

The yielding wood? And yet 'twas loth
  To yield unto our happy march;
Doubtful it seemed, at times, if both
  Could pass its green, elastic arch.

Yet there, at last, upon the marge
  We found ourselves, and there, behold,
In hosts the lilies, white and large,
  Lay close with hearts of downy gold!

Deep in the weedy waters spread
  The rootlets of the placid bloom:

So sprung my love's flower, that was bred
  In deep still waters of heart's-gloom.

So sprung; and so that morn was nursed
  To live in light, and on the pool
Wherein its roots were deep immersed
  Burst into beauty broad and cool.

Few words were said, as moments passed;
  I know not how it came — that awe
And ardor of a glance that cast
  Our love in universal law.

But all at once a bird sang loud,
  From dead twigs of the gleamy beech;
His notes dropped dewy, as from a cloud,
  A blessing on our married speech.

Ah, Love! how fresh and rare, even now,
  That moment and that mood return
Upon me, when the soft winds blow,
  And lilies toward the sunlight yearn!

              GEORGE PARSONS LATHROP.

CUPID AND CAMPASPE.

CUPID and my Campaspe play'd
  At cards for kisses; Cupid paid.
  He stakes his quiver, bow and arrows,
  His mother's doves and team of sparrows;
  Loses them too, and down he throws
The coral of his lip — the rose
Growing on 's cheek, but none knows how;

With these the crystal on his brow,
And then the dimple of his chin;
All these did my Campaspe win;
At last he set her both his eyes,
She won, and Cupid blind did rise.
O Love, hath she done this to thee?
What shall, alas, become of me!

              JOHN LYLY.

THE DAY RETURNS, MY BOSOM BURNS.

THE day returns, my bosom burns,
  The blissful day we twa did meet;
Though winter wild in tempest toiled,
  Ne'er summer sun was half sae sweet.
Than a' the pride that loads the tide,
  And crosses o'er the sultry line,—
Than kingly robes, and crowns and globes,
  Heaven gave me more; it made thee mine.

While day and night can bring delight,
  Or nature aught of pleasure give,—
While joys above my mind can move,
  For thee and thee alone I live;
When that grim foe of life below
  Comes in between to make us part,
The iron hand that breaks our band,
  It breaks my bliss — it breaks my heart.

              ROBERT BURNS.

CULTIVATE a spirit of love. Love is the diamond amongst the jewels of the believer's breastplate. The other graces shine like the precious stones of nature, with their own peculiar lustre, and various hues: now in white all the colors are united, so in love is centred every other grace and virtue; love is the fulfilling of the law.

GLIMPSES OF NATURE.

"The groves were God's first temples. Ere man learned
To hew the shaft, and lay the architrave."

A FOREST HYMN.

HE groves were God's first temples. Ere man
learned
To hew the shaft, and lay the architrave,
And spread the roof above them—ere he framed
The lofty vault, to gather and roll back
The sound of anthems; in the darkling wood,

Amidst the cool and silence, he knelt down,
And offered to the Mightiest solemn thanks
And supplication. For his simple heart
Might not resist the sacred influences
Which, from the stilly twilight of the place,
And from the gray old trunks that high in heaven

77

Mingled their mossy boughs, and from the sound
Of the invisible breath that swayed at once
All their green tops, stole over him, and bowed
His spirit with the thought of boundless power
And inaccessible majesty. Ah, why
Should we, in the world's riper years, neglect
God's ancient sanctuaries, and adore
Only among the crowd, and under roofs
That our frail hands have raised? Let me, at least,
Here, in the shadow of this aged wood,
Offer one hymn — thrice happy if it find
Acceptance in his ear.

           Father, thy hand
Hath reared these venerable columns; thou
Didst weave this verdant roof. Thou didst look down
Upon the naked earth, and forthwith rose
All these fair ranks of trees. They in thy sun
Budded, and shook their green leaves in thy breeze,
And shot towards heaven. The century-living crow,
Whose birth was in their tops, grew old and died
Among their branches, till at last they stood,
As now they stand, massy and tall and dark,
Fit shrine for humble worshiper to hold
Communion with his Maker. These dim vaults,
These winding aisles, of human pomp or pride
Report not. No fantastic carvings show
The boast of our vain race to change the form
Of thy fair works. But thou art here — thou fill'st
The solitude. Thou art in the soft winds
That run along the summit of these trees
In music; thou art in the cooler breath
That from the inmost darkness of the place
Comes, scarcely felt; the barky trunks, the ground,
The fresh moist ground, are all instinct with thee.
Here is continual worship; — nature, here,
In the tranquillity that thou dost love,
Enjoys thy presence. Noiselessly around,
From perch to perch, the solitary bird
Passes; and yon clear spring, that, midst its herbs,
Wells softly forth and wandering steeps the roots
Of half the mighty forest, tells no tale
Of all the good it does. Thou hast not left
Thyself without a witness, in these shades,
Of thy perfections. Grandeur, strength and grace
Are here to speak of thee. This mighty oak,—
By whose immovable stem I stand and seem
Almost annihilated,— not a prince,
In all that proud old world beyond the deep,
E'er wore his crown as loftily as he
Wears the green coronal of leaves with which
Thy hand has graced him. Nestled at his root
Is beauty, such as blooms not in the glare
Of the broad sun. That delicate forest flower
With scented breath, and look so like a smile.

Seems, as it issues from the shapeless mould,
An emanation of the indwelling Life,
A visible token of the upholding Love,
That are the soul of this wide universe.

     My heart is awed within me when I think
Of the great miracle that still goes on,
In silence, round me, — the perpetual work
Of thy creation, finished, yet renewed
Forever. Written on thy works I read
The lesson of thy own eternity.
Lo! all grow old and die; but see again,
How on the faltering footsteps of decay
Youth presses, — ever gay and beautiful youth
In all its beautiful forms. These lofty trees
Wave not less proudly that their ancestors
Moulder beneath them. O, there is not lost
One of Earth's charms! upon her bosom yet,
After the flight of untold centuries,
The freshness of her far beginning lies,
And yet shall lie. Life mocks the idle hate
Of his arch-enemy Death, — yea, seats himself
Upon the tyrant's throne, the sepulchre,
And of the triumphs of his ghastly foe
Makes his own nourishment. For he came forth
From thine own bosom, and shall have no end.
There have been holy men who hid themselves
Deep in the woody wilderness, and gave
Their lives to thought and prayer, till they outlived
The generation born with them, nor seemed
Less aged than the hoary trees and rocks
Around them; — and there have been holy men
Who deemed it were not well to pass life thus.
But let me often to these solitudes
Retire, and in thy presence reassure
My feeble virtue. Here its enemies,
The passions, at thy plainer footsteps shrink
And tremble, and are still. O God! when thou
Dost scare the world with tempests, set on fire
The heavens with falling thunderbolts, or fill
With all the waters of the firmament,
The swift dark whirlwind that uproots the woods
And drowns the villages; when, at thy call,
Uprises the great deep, and throws himself
Upon the continent, and overwhelms
Its cities,—who forgets not, at the sight
Of these tremendous tokens of thy power,
His pride, and lays his strifes and follies by?
O, from these sterner aspects of thy face
Spare me and mine, nor let us need the wrath
Of the mad unchained elements to teach
Who rules them. Be it ours to meditate,
In these calm shades, thy milder majesty,
And to the beautiful order of thy works
Learn to conform the order of our lives.

              WILLIAM CULLEN BRYANT.

NATURE.

THE bubbling brook doth leap when I come by,
Because my feet find measure with its call;
The birds know when the friend they love is nigh,
For I am known to them, both great and small.
The flower that on the lonely hillside grows
Expects me there when spring its bloom has given;
And many a tree and bush my wanderings knows,

And e'en the clouds and silent stars of heaven;
For he who with his Maker walks aright,
Shall be their lord as Adam was before;
His ear shall catch each sound with new delight,
Each object wear the dress that then it wore;
And he, as when erect in soul he stood,
Hear from his Father's lips that all is good.

JONES VERY.

"A grove
Of large extent, hard by a castle huge."

THE NIGHTINGALE.

AND hark! the Nightingale begins its song,—
"Most musical, most melancholy" bird!
A melancholy bird? oh, idle thought!
In Nature there is nothing melancholy.
. . . . . 'Tis the merry Nightingale,
That crowds, and hurries, and precipitates

With fast thick warble his delicious notes,
As he were fearful that an April night
Would be too short for him to utter forth
His love-chant, and disburden his full soul
Of all its music!

And I know a grove
Of large extent, hard by a castle huge,
Which the great lord inhabits not; and so
This grove is wild with tangling underwood,
And the trim walks are broken up, and grass,
Thin grass and kingcups, grow within the paths
But never elsewhere in one place I knew
So many nightingales; and far and near,
In wood and thicket, over the wide grove,
They answer and provoke each other's song,
With skirmishes and capricious passagings,
And murmurs musical and swift — jug, jug —
And one low piping sound more sweet than all,
Stirring the air with such a harmony,
That, should you close your eyes, you might almost

Forget it was not day! On moonlight bushes,
Whose dewy leaflets are but half disclosed,
You may perchance behold them on the twigs,
Their bright, bright eyes, their eyes both bright and
    full,
Glistening, while many a glow-worm in the shade
Lights up her love-torch.
                    And oft a moment's space,
What time the moon was lost behind a cloud,
Hath heard a pause of silence; till the moon
Emerging, hath awaken'd earth and sky
With one sensation, and these wakeful birds
Have all burst forth in choral minstrelsy,
As if some sudden gale had swept at once
A hundred airy harps!

                    SAMUEL TAYLOR COLERIDGE.

"Wide flush the fields; the softening air is balm."

HYMN ON THE SEASONS.

THESE, as they change, Almighty Father, these
Are but the varied God. The rolling year
Is full of thee. Forth in the pleasing spring
Thy beauty walks, thy tenderness and love,
Wide flush the fields; the softening air is balm;
Echo the mountains round; the forest smiles;
And every sense and every heart is joy.
Then comes thy glory in the summer months,
With light and heat refulgent. Then thy sun
Shoots full perfection through the swelling year,
And oft thy voice in dreadful thunder speaks;
And oft at dawn, deep noon, or falling eve,
By brooks and groves, in hollow-whispering gales,
Thy bounty shines in autumn unconfined,
And spreads a common feast for all that lives.
In winter awful thou! with clouds and storms

Around thee thrown, tempest o'er tempest rolled.
Majestic darkness! on the whirlwind's wing,

Riding sublime, thou bidst the world adore,
And humblest nature with thy northern blast.

Mysterious round! what skill, what force divine,
Deep felt, in these appear! a simple train,
Yet so delightful mixed, with such kind art,
Such beauty and beneficence combined;
Shade, unperceived, so softening into shade;
And all so forming an harmonious whole;

In adoration join; and, ardent, raise
One general song! To him, ye vocal gales,
Breathe soft, whose spirit in your freshness breathes;
O, talk of him in solitary glooms!
Where, o'er the rock, the scarcely waving pine
Fills the brown shade with a religious awe.

"By brooks and groves, in hollow whispering gales."

That, as they still succeed, they ravish still.
But wandering oft, with brute unconscious gaze,
Man marks not thee, marks not the mighty hand,
That, ever busy, wheels the silent spheres;
Works in the secret deep; shoots, steaming, thence
The fair profusion that o'erspreads the spring;

And ye, whose bolder note is heard afar,
Who shake the astonished world, lift high to Heaven
The impetuous song, and say from whom you rage.
His praise, ye brooks, attune, ye trembling rills;
And let me catch it as I muse along.
Ye headlong torrents, rapid and profound;

"Thy bounty shines in Autumn unconfined."

Flings from the sun direct the flaming day;
Feeds every creature; hurls the tempest forth;
And, as on earth this grateful change revolves,
With transport touches all the springs of life,
    Nature, attend! join, every living soul,
Beneath the spacious temple of the sky,
    6

Ye softer floods, that lead the humid maze
Along the vale; and thou, majestic main,
A secret world of wonders in thyself,
Sound his stupendous praise; whose greater voice
Or bids you roar, or bids your roarings fall.
Soft roll your incense, herbs, and fruits, and flowers,

In mingled clouds to him, whose sun exalts,
Whose breath perfumes you, and whose pencil paints.
Ye forests, bend, ye harvests, wave, to him;
Breathe your still song into the reaper's heart,
As home he goes beneath the joyous moon.

While cloud to cloud returns the solemn hymn.
Bleat out afresh, ye hills: ye mossy rocks,
Retain the sound: the broad responsive low,
Ye valleys, raise; for the Great Shepherd reigns;
And his unsuffering kingdom yet will come.

"With clouds and storms,
Around thee thrown, tempest o'er tempest rolled."

Ye that keep watch in heaven, as earth asleep
Unconscious lies, effuse your mildest beams,
Ye constellations, while your angels strike,
Amid the spangled sky, the silver lyre.
Great source of day! best image here below

Ye woodlands all, awake: a boundless song
Burst from the groves! and when the restless day,
Expiring, lays the warbling world asleep,
Sweetest of birds! sweet Philomela, charm
The listening shades, and teach the night his praise.

"Ye headlong torrents, rapid and profound."

Of thy Creator, ever pouring wide,
From world to world, the vital ocean round,
On nature write with every beam his praise.
The thunder rolls: be hushed the prostrate world.

Ye chief, for whom the whole creation smiles,
At once the head, the heart, and tongue of all,
Crown the great hymn; in swarming cities vast,
Assembled men, to the deep organ join

The long resounding voice, oft-breaking, clear,
At solemn pauses, through the swelling bass;
And, as each mingling flame increases each,
In one united ardor rise to Heaven.
Or if you rather choose the rural shade,
And find a fane in every sacred grove,
There let the shepherd's flute, the virgin's lay,
The prompting seraph, and the poet's lyre,

Rivers unknown to song, where first the sun
Gilds Indian mountains, or his setting beam
Flames on the Atlantic isles, 'tis naught to me,
Since God is ever present, ever felt,
In the void waste as in the city full;
And where he vital spreads there must be joy.
When even at last the solemn hour shall come,
And wing my mystic flight to future worlds,

"Since God is ever present, ever felt,
In the void waste as in the city full."

Still sing the God of seasons, as they roll!
For me, when I forget the darling theme,
Whether the blossom blows, the summer ray
Russets the plain, inspiring autumn gleams,
Or winter rises in the blackening east,
Be my tongue mute, may fancy paint no more,
And, dead to joy, forget my heart to beat!
  Should fate command me to the farthest verge
Of the green earth, to distant barbarous climes,

I cheerful will obey; there, with new powers,
Will rising wonders sing: I cannot go
Where universal love not smiles around,
Sustaining all yon orbs, and all their sons;
From seeming evil still educing good,
And better thence again, and better still,
In infinite progression. But I lose
Myself in him, in light ineffable!
Come then, expressive Silence, muse his praise.

JAMES THOMSON.

NIGHT.

ALL heaven and earth are still—though not in
    sleep,
  But breathless, as we grow when feeling most;
    And silent, as we stand in thoughts too deep.
All heaven and earth are still; from the high host
Of stars, to the lulled lake and mountain-coast,
All is concentred in a life intense,
Where not a beam, nor air, nor leaf is lost
  But hath a part of being, and a sense
Of that which is of all Creator and defense.

* * * * * *
And this is in the night—most glorious night!
Thou wert not sent for slumber! let me be
A sharer in thy fierce and far delight, —
A portion of the tempest and of thee!
How the lit lake shines, a phosphoric sea,
And the big rain comes dancing to the earth!
And now again 'tis black — and now, the glee
Of the loud hills shakes with its mountain-mirth,
As if they did rejoice o'er a young earthquake's birth.

LORD BYRON.

THE SEA.

HERE is a pleasure in the pathless woods,
There is a rapture on the lonely shore,
There is society where none intrudes
By the deep sea, and music in its roar:
I love not man the less, but nature more,
From these our interviews, in which I steal
From all I may be, or have been before,
To mingle with the universe, and feel
What I can ne'er express, yet cannot all conceal.

His steps are not upon thy paths — thy fields
Are not a spoil for him — thou dost arise
And shake him from thee; the vile strength he wields
For earth's destruction thou dost all despise,
Spurning him from thy bosom to the skies,
And send'st him, shivering in thy playful spray
And howling, to his gods, where haply lies
His petty hope in some near port or bay,
And dashest him again to earth: — there let him lay.

"Dark-heaving; boundless, endless and sublime."

Roll on, thou deep and dark blue Ocean — roll!
Ten thousand fleets sweep over thee in vain;
Man marks the earth with ruin — his control
Stops with the shore; — upon the watery plain
The wrecks are all thy deed, nor doth remain
A shadow of man's ravage, save his own,
When, for a moment, like a drop of rain
He sinks into thy depths with bubbling groan,
Without a grave, unknelled, uncoffined and unknown.

The armaments which thunderstrike the walls
Of rock-built cities, bidding nations quake
And monarchs tremble in their capitals,
The oak leviathans, whose huge ribs make
Their clay creator the vain title take
Of lord of thee and arbiter of war —
These are thy toys, and, as the snowy flake,
They melt into thy yeast of waves, which mar
Alike the Armada's pride or spoils of Trafalgar.

Thy shores are empires, changed in all save thee;
Assyria, Greece, Rome, Carthage, what are they?
Thy waters wasted them while they were free
And many a tyrant since; their shores obey
The stranger, slave, or savage; their decay
Has dried up realms to deserts: not so thou;
Unchangeable save to thy wild waves' play,
Time writes no wrinkles on thine azure brow;
Such as creation's dawn beheld, thou rollest now.

Thou glorious mirror, where the Almighty's form
Glasses itself in tempests; in all time,
Calm or convulsed, — in breeze, or gale, or storm,
Icing the pole, or in the torrid clime
Dark-heaving; boundless, endless and sublime,

The image of Eternity — the throne
Of the Invisible! even from out thy slime
The monsters of the deep are made; each zone
Obeys thee; thou goes forth, dread, fathomless, alone.

And I have loved thee, Ocean! and my joy
Of youthful sports was on thy breast to be
Borne, like thy bubbles, onward; from a boy
I wantoned with thy breakers — they to me
Were a delight; and if the freshening sea
Made them a terror, 'twas a pleasing fear;
For I was as it were a child of thee,
And trusted to thy billows far and near,
And laid my hand upon thy mane — as I do here.

LORD BYRON.

" Upon the roses it would feed."

THE RAINBOW.

MY heart leaps up when I behold
    A rainbow in the sky:
So was it when my life began;
So is it now I am a man;

So be it when I shall grow old,
    Or let me die!
The child is father of the man;
And I could wish my days to be
Bound each to each by natural piety.

WILLIAM WORDSWORTH.

THE SHEPHERD.

OH, gentle Shepherd! thine the lot to tend,
  Of all that feels distress, the most assail'd,
  Feeble, defenceless; lenient be thy care;
  But spread around thy tenderest diligence
In flowery spring-time, when the new-dropp'd lamb,
Tottering with weakness by his mother's side,
Feels the fresh world about him; and each thorn,
Hillock, or furrow, trips his feeble feet:

Eurus oft flings his hail; the tardy fields,
Pay not their promised food; and oft the dam
O'er her weak twins with empty udder mourns,
Or fails to guard, when the bold bird of prey
Alights, and hops in many turns around,
And tires her also turning: to her aid
Be nimble, and the weakest in thine arms
Gently convey to the warm cote, and oft,

" ——The weakest in thine arms,
Gently convey to the warm cote."

Oh! guard his meek, sweet innocence from all
Th' numerous ills that rush around his life;
Mark the quick kite, with beak and talons prone,
Circling the skies to snatch him from the plain;
Observe the lurking crows: beware the brake —
There the sly fox the careless minute waits:
Nor trust thy neighbor's dog, nor earth, nor sky:
Thy bosom to a thousand cares divide;

Between the lark's note and the nightingale's,
His hungry bleating still with tepid milk; —
In this soft office may thy children join,
And charitable actions learn in sport.
Nor yield him to himself ere vernal airs
Sprinkle the little croft with daisy flowers;
Nor yet forget him; life has rising ills.

JOHN DYER.

THE WORLD IS TOO MUCH WITH US.

HE world is too much with us; late and soon,
Getting and spending, we lay waste our powers;
Little we see in Nature that is ours;
We have given our hearts away, a sordid boon!
This sea that bares her bosom to the moon;
The winds that will be howling at all hours,
And are up-gathered now like sleeping flowers;

For this, for everything, we are out of tune;
It moves us not. Great God! I'd rather be
A pagan suckled in a creed outworn;
So might I, standing on this pleasant lea,
Have glimpses that would make me less forlorn;
Have sight of Proteus rising from the sea,
Or hear old Triton blow his wreathéd horn.

WILLIAM WORDSWORTH.

" Sweet voices in the woods,
And reed-like echoes, that have long been mute."

BREATHINGS OF SPRING.

HAT wak'st thou, Spring?—Sweet voices in the
woods,
And reed-like echoes, that have long been
mute;
Thou bringest back, to fill the solitudes,
The lark's clear pipe, the cuckoo's viewless flute,
Whose tone seems breathing mournfulness or glee,
Even as our hearts may be.

And the leaves greet, Spring!—the joyous leaves,
Whose tremblings gladden many a copse and
glade,
Where each young spray a rosy flush receives,
When thy south wind hath pierced the whispery
shade,
And happy murmurs, running through the grass,
Tell that thy footsteps pass.

And the bright waters—they, too, hear thy call,
  Spring, the awakener! thou has burst their sleep!
Amidst the hollows of the rocks their fall
  Makes melody, and in the forests deep,
Where sudden sparkles and blue gleams betray
    Their windings to the day.

And flowers—the fairy-peopled world of flowers!
  Thou from the dust hast set that glory free,
Coloring the cowslip with the sunny hours,
  And penciling the wood-anemone:
Silent they seem; yet each to thoughtful eye
    Glows with mute poesy.

But what awak'st thou in the heart, O Spring—
  The human heart, with all its dreams and sighs?
Thou that giv'st back so many a buried thing,
  Restorer of forgotten harmonies!
Fresh songs and scents break forth where'er thou art:
    What wak'st thou in the heart?

Too much, O, there too much!—we know not well
  Wherefore it should be thus; yet, roused by thee,
What fond, strange yearnings, from the soul's deep
    cell,
  Gush for the faces we no more may see.
How are we haunted, in thy wind's low tone,
    By voices that are gone!

Looks of familiar love, that never more,
  Never on earth, our aching eyes shall meet,
Past words of welcome to our household door,
  And vanished smiles, and sounds of parted feet—
Spring, 'midst the murmurs of thy flowering trees,
    Why, why reviv'st thou these?

Vain longings for the dead!—why come they back
  With thy young birds, and leaves, and living
    blooms?

"Amidst the hollows of the rocks their fall
  Makes melody."

O, is it not that from thine earthly track
  Hope to thy world may look beyond the tombs?
Yes, gentle Spring; no sorrow dims thine air,
    Breathed by our loved ones there.

           FELICIA DOROTHEA HEMANS.

VARYING IMPRESSIONS FROM NATURE.

CANNOT paint
  What then I was. The sounding cataract
  Haunted me like a passion: the tall rock,
  The mountain, and the deep and gloomy wood,
  Their colors and their forms, were then to me
An appetite, a feeling and a love,
That had no heed of a remoter charm
By thoughts supplied, nor any interest
Unborrowed from the eye.—That time is past,
And all its aching joys are now no more,
And all its dizzy raptures. Not for this
Faint I, nor mourn nor murmur; other gifts
Have followed: for such loss, I would believe,
Abundant recompense. For I have learned
To look on Nature, not as in the hour
Of thoughtless youth; but hearing oftentimes
The still, sad music of humanity,
Not harsh nor grating, though of ample power
To chasten and subdue. And I have felt

A presence that disturbs me with the joy
Of elevated thoughts; a sense sublime
Of something far more deeply interfused,
Whose dwelling is the light of setting suns,
And the round ocean, and the living air,
And the blue sky, and in the mind of man;
A motion and a spirit, that impels
All thinking things, all objects of all thought,
And rolls through all things. Therefore am I still
A lover of the meadows and the woods
And mountains, and of all that we behold
From this green earth; of all the mighty world
Of eye and ear—both what they half create,
And what perceive; well pleased to recognize
In Nature and the language of the sense,
The anchor of my purest thoughts, the nurse,
The guide, the guardian of my heart, and soul
Of all my moral being.

           WILLIAM WORDSWORTH.

EVENING.

T is a beauteous evening, calm and free;
The holy time is quiet as a nun
Breathless with adoration; the broad sun

Is sinking down in its tranquility;
The gentleness of heaven is on the sea.

WILLIAM WORDSWORTH.

HYMN BEFORE SUNRISE IN THE VALE OF CHAMOUNI.

AST thou a charm to stay the morning star
  In his steep course? So long he seems to pause
  On thy bald, awful head, O sovran Blanc!
  The Arve and Arveiron at thy base
Rave ceaselessly; but thou, most awful form!
Risest from forth thy silent sea of pines,
How silently! Around thee and above,
Deep is the air and dark, substantial, black,
An ebon mass: methinks thou piercest it,
As with a wedge! But when I look again,
It is thine own calm home, thy crystal shrine,
Thy habitation from eternity!

Into the mighty vision passing — there,
  As in her natural form, swelled vast to Heaven!
  Awake, my soul! not only passive praise
Thou owest! not alone these swelling tears
Mute thanks and secret ecstacy. Awake,
Voice of sweet song! Awake, my heart, awake!
Green vales and icy cliffs, all join my hymn.

  Thou first and chief, sole sovran of the vale!
O, struggling with the darkness all the night,
And visited all night by troops of stars,
Or when they climb the sky or when they sink:
Companion of the morning star at dawn,

" On thy bald, awful head, O sovran Blanc !"

O dread and silent mount! I gazed upon thee,
Till thou, still present to the bodily sense,
Didst vanish from my thought: entranced in prayer
I worshiped the Invisible alone.

  Yet, like some sweet beguiling melody,
So sweet, we know not we are listening to it,
Thou, the meanwhile, wast blending with my thought,
Yea, with my life and life's own secret joy;
Till the dilating soul, enrapt, transfused,

Thyself earth's rosy star, and of the dawn
Co-herald: wake, O wake and utter praise!
Who sank thy sunless pillars deep in earth?
Who filled thy countenance with rosy light?
Who made thee parent of perpetual streams?

  And you, ye five wild torrents fiercely glad!
Who called you forth from night and utter death,
From dark and icy caverns called you forth,
Down those precipitous, black, jugged rocks,

Forever shattered and the same forever?
Who gave you your invulnerable life,
Your strength, your speed, your fury and your joy,
Unceasing thunder and eternal foam?
And who commanded (and the silence came),
Here let the billows stiffen, and have rest?

Ye ice-falls! ye that from the mountain's brow
Adown enormous ravines slope amain, —
Torrents, methinks, that heard a mighty voice,
And stopped at once amid their maddest plunge, —
Motionless torrents! silent cataracts!
Who made you glorious as the gates of heaven
Beneath the keen, full moon? Who bade the sun
Clothe you with rainbows? Who, with living flowers
Of loveliest blue, spread garlands at your feet —
God! let the torrents, like a shout of nations,
Answer! and let the ice-plains echo, God!
God! Sing, ye meadow streams, with gladsome voice!
Ye pine groves, with your soft and soul-like sounds!
And they, too, have a voice, yon piles of snow,
And in their perilous fall shall thunder, God!
Ye living flowers that skirt the eternal frost!

Ye wild goats sporting round the eagle's nest!
Ye eagles, playmates of the mountain storm!
Ye lightnings, the dread arrows of the clouds!
Ye signs and wonders of the elements!
Utter forth God, and fill the hills with praise!

Thou, too, hoar Mount! with thy sky-pointing peaks,
Oft from whose feet the avalanche, unheard,
Shoots downward, glittering through the pure serene
Into the depth of clouds, that veil thy breast, —
Thou too again, stupendous mountain! thou
That as I raise my head, a while bowed low
In adoration, upward from thy base
Slow traveling with dim eyes suffused with tears,
Solemnly seemest, like a vapory cloud,
To rise before me. — Rise, oh, ever rise,
Rise like a cloud of incense from the earth!
Thou kingly spirit, throned among the hills,
Thou dread ambassador from earth to heaven,
Great hierarch! tell thou the silent sky,
And tell the stars, and tell yon rising sun,
Earth, with her thousand voices, praises God.

SAMUEL TAYLOR COLERIDGE.

TO THE DAISY.

WITH little here to do or see
Of things that in the great world be,
Daisy! again I talk to thee,
For thou art worthy,
Thou unassuming commonplace
Of Nature, with that homely face,
And yet with something of a grace
Which love makes for thee!

Oft on the dappled turf at ease
I sit, and play with similes,
Loose types of things through all degrees,
Thoughts of thy raising:
And many a fond and idle name
I give to thee, for praise or blame,
As is the humor of the game,
While I am gazing.

A nun demure, of lowly port;
Or sprightly maiden, of love's court,
In thy simplicity the sport
Of all temptations;
A queen in crown of rubies drest;
A starveling in a scanty vest;
Are all, as seems to suit thee best,
Thy appellations.

A little cyclops, with one eye
Staring to threaten and defy,
That thought comes next,—and instantly
The freak is over,
The shape will vanish,—and behold
A silver shield with boss of gold,
That spreads itself, some faery bold
In fight to cover!

I see thee glittering from afar,—
And then thou art a pretty star;
Not quite so fair as many are
In heaven above thee!
Yet like a star, with glittering crest,
Self-poised in air thou seem'st to rest;—
May peace come never to his nest,
Who shall reprove thee!

Bright Flower! for by that name at last,
When all my reveries are past,
I call thee, and to that cleave fast,
Sweet, silent creature!
That breath'st with me in sun and air
Do thou, as thou art wont, repair
My heart with gladness, and a share
Of thy meek nature!

WILLIAM WORDSWORTH.

WHAT shall we say of flowers—those flaming banners of the vegetable world, which
march in such various and splendid triumph before the coming of its fruits?

DAWN.

HE night was dark, though sometimes a faint star
  A little while a little space made bright.
  Dark was the night, and like an iron bar
  Lay heavy on the land: till o'er the sea
Slowly, within the East, there grew a light
Which half was starlight, and half seemed to be
The herald of a greater. The pale white
Turned slowly to pale rose, and up the height
Of heaven slowly climbed. The gray sea grew
Rose-colored like the sky. A white gull flew
Straight toward the utmost boundary of the East
Where slowly the rose gathered and increased.
It was as on the opening of a door

By one who in his hand a lamp doth hold,
(Its flame yet hidden by the garment's fold)—
The still air moves, the wide room is less dim.

  More bright the East became, the ocean turned
Dark and more dark against the brightening sky—
Sharper against the sky the long sea line;
The hollows of the breakers on the shore
Were green like leaves whereon no sun doth shine,
Though white the outer branches of the tree.
From rose to red the level heaven burned;
Then sudden, as if a sword fell from on high,
A blade of gold flashed on the ocean's rim.

RICHARD WATSON GILDER.

"The Owl that, watching in the barn,
Sees the mouse creeping in the corn."

THE BARN OWL.

HILE moonlight, silvering all the walls,
  Through every mouldering crevice falls,
  Tipping with white his powdery plume,
  As shades or shifts the changing gloom;
  The Owl that, watching in the barn,

Sees the mouse creeping in the corn,
Sits still, and shuts his round blue eyes
As if he slept,—until he spies
The little beast within his stretch,—
Then starts, and seizes on the wretch!

SAMUEL BUTLER.

"Marshes and swamps and dismal fens."

BEFORE THE RAIN.

WE knew it would rain, for all the morn
  A spirit on slender ropes of mist
Was lowering its golden buckets down
  Into the vapory amethyst

Of marshes and swamps and dismal fens —
  Scooping the dew that lay in the flowers,

Dipping the jewels out of the sea,
  To sprinkle them over the land in showers.

We knew it would rain, for the poplars showed
  The white of their leaves; the amber grain
Shrunk in the wind, and the lightning now
  Is tangled in tremulous skeins of rain.

THOMAS BAILEY ALDRICH.

AFTER THE RAIN.

THE rain has ceased, and in my room
  The sunshine pours an airy flood;
And on the church's dizzy vane
  The ancient Cross is bathed in blood.

From out the dripping ivy-leaves,
  Antiquely carven, gray and high,

A dormer, facing westward, looks
  Upon the village-like an eye:

And now it glimmers in the sun,
  A square of gold, a disk, a speck:
And in the belfry sits a dove
  With purple ripples on her neck.

THOMAS BAILEY ALDRICH.

NIGHT.

MAJESTIC Night!
  Nature's great ancestor! day's elder-born,
And fated to survive the transient sun!
By mortals and immortals seen with awe!
A starry crown thy raven brow adorns,
An azure zone thy waist; clouds, in heaven's
    loom
Wrought through varieties of shape and shade,

In ample folds of drapery divine,
Thy flowing mantle form; and heaven throughout
Voluminously pour thy pompous train.
Thy gloomy grandeurs (Nature's most august,
Inspiring aspect!) claim a grateful verse;
And, like a sable curtain starred with gold,
Drawn o'er my labors past, shall close the scene.

EDWARD YOUNG.

SUMMER.

ROUND this lovely valley rise
The purple hills of Paradise.
  Oh, softly on yon banks of haze
  Her rosy face the summer lays;
Becalmed along the azure sky
The argosies of cloudland lie,
  Whose shores with many a shining rift
  Far-off their pearl-white peaks uplift.

I watch the mowers as they go
Through the tall grass, a white-sleeved row;
  With even stroke their scythes they swing,
  In tune their merry whetstones ring.
Behind, the nimble youngsters run,
And toss the thick swaths in the sun.
  The cattle graze; while warm and still
  Slopes the broad pasture, basks the hill,

" I seek the coolest sheltered seat,
Just where the field and forest meet."

Through all the long midsummer day
The meadow sides are sweet with hay.
  I seek the coolest sheltered seat,
  Just where the field and forest meet,—
Where grow the pine-trees, tall and bland,
The ancient oaks, austere and grand,
  And fringy roots and pebbles fret
  The ripples of the rivulet.

And bright, when summer breezes break,
The green wheat crinkles like a lake.

The butterfly and bumble-bee
Come to the pleasant woods with me;
  Quickly before me runs the quail,
  Her chickens skulk behind the rail;
High up the lone wood-pigeon sits,

"Quickly before me runs the quail.
Her chickens skulk behind the rail."

And the woodpecker pecks and flits.
  Sweet woodland music sinks and swells,
  The brooklet rings its tinkling bells.

The swarming insects drone and hum,
The partridge beats his throbbing drum,
  The squirrel leaps among the boughs,
  And chatters in his leafy house;
The oriole flashes by; and look —
Into the mirror of the brook,

Where the vain bluebird trims his coat,
Two tiny feathers fall and float.

As silently, as tenderly,
The down of peace descends on me.
  Oh, this is peace! I have no need
  Of friend to talk, or book to read;
A dear companion here abides,
Close to my thrilling heart he hides;
  The holy silence is his voice:
  I lie, and listen, and rejoice.

JOHN TOWNSEND TROWBRIDGE.

DAY BREAKING.

SEE, the dapple-grey coursers of the morn
Beat up the light with their bright silver hoofs,
And chase it through the sky.

JOHN MARSTON.

GLIMPSES OF NATURE.

TO THE NIGHTINGALE.

S it fell upon a day
In the merry month of May,
Sitting in a pleasant shade
Which a grove of myrtles made,
Beasts did leap, and birds did sing,
Trees did grow, and plants did spring;
Everything did banish moan,
Save the nightingale alone.
She, poor bird, as all forlorn,
Leaned her breast up-till a thorn;
And there sung the doleful'st ditty
That to hear it was great pity.
Fie, fie, fie! now would she cry;
Teru, teru, by-and-by;
That, to hear her so complain,
Scarce I could from tears refrain;
For her griefs, so lively shown,
Made me think upon mine own.
Ah! (thought I) thou mourn'st in vain;
None takes pity on thy pain;
Senseless trees, they cannot hear thee;
Ruthless bears, they will not cheer thee;
King Pandion, he is dead;
All thy friends are lapped in lead;
All thy fellow-birds do sing,
Careless of thy sorrowing!
Whilst as fickle Fortune smiled,

Thou and I were both beguiled,
Every one that flatters thee
Is no friend in misery.
Words are easy, like the wind;
Faithful friends are hard to find.
Every man will be thy friend
Whilst thou hast wherewith to spend;
But, if stores of crowns be scant,
No man will supply thy want.
If that one be prodigal,
Bountiful they will him call;
And, with such-like flattering,
"Pity but he were a king."
If he be addict to vice,
Quickly him they will entice;
But if Fortune once do frown,
Then farewell his great renown:
They that fawned on him before,
Use his company no more.
He that is thy friend indeed,
He will help thee in thy need;
If thou sorrow, he will weep,
If thou wake, he cannot sleep.
Thus, of every grief in heart,
He with thee doth bear a part.
These are certain signs to know
Faithful friend from flattering foe.

RICHARD BARNFIELD.

THE MOUNT OF THE HOLY CROSS.

HIS wonderful peak of the Rocky Mountain Range is one of the most noted and remarkable mountains in the world. It is among the highest in Colorado, being 14,176 feet high — one of the thirty-three peaks whose summits are 14,000 feet and upward above the sea. A tremendous chasm cleaves it on the eastern side nearly to the top, and right across this, perhaps three-fourths of the way up, is another, and these, filled with snow old as creation, form a perfect and most beautiful cross. It is one of the marked objects visible from Gray's and Pike's Peaks, and from a wide extent of country west of the dividing range of the continent.

THERE is a river in the ocean. In the severest droughts it never fails, and in the mightiest floods it never overflows. Its banks and its bottoms are of cold water, while its current is of warm. The Gulf of Mexico is its fountain, and its mouth is the Arctic Seas. It is the Gulf Stream. There is in the world no other such majestic flow of waters. Its current is more rapid than the Mississippi or the Amazon, and its volume more than a thousand times greater.

THE HEATH-COCK.

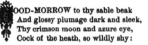

GOOD-MORROW to thy sable beak
And glossy plumage dark and sleek,
Thy crimson moon and azure eye,
Cock of the heath, so wildly shy:

The rarest things, with wayward will,
Beneath the covert hide them still;
The rarest things to break of day
Look shortly forth, and shrink away.

"Cock of the heath, so wildly shy."

I see thee slyly cowering through ·
That wiry web of silvery dew,
That twinkles in the morning air,
Like casements of my lady fair.

A maid there is in yonder tower,
Who, peeping from her early bower,
Half shows, like thee, her simple wile,
Her braided hair and morning smile.

A fleeting moment of delight
I sunn'd me in her cheering sight;
As short, I ween, the time will be
That I shall parley hold with thee.
Through Snowdon's mist red beams the day,
The chirping herd-boy chants his lay;
The gnat-flies dance their sunny ring,—
Thou art already on the wing.

JOANNA BAILLIE.

THERE's rosemary, that's for remembrance; pray you, love, remember:—and there
is pansies, that's for thoughts.

570361

A JUNE DAY.

WHO has not dream'd a world of bliss,
On a bright sunny noon like this,
Couch'd by his native brook's green maze,
With comrade of his boyish days,
While all around them seem'd to be
Just as in joyous infancy?

Through the tall fox-glove's crimson bloom,
And gleaming of the scatter'd broom,
Love you not, then, to list and hear
The crackling of the gorse-flowers near,
Pouring an orange-scented tide
Of fragrance o'er the desert wide?

"Who has not loved, at such an hour,
Upon that heath, in birchen bower."

Who has not loved, at such an hour,
Upon that heath, in birchen bower,
Lull'd in the poet's dreamy mood,
Its wild and sunny solitude?
While o'er the waste of purple ling
You mark a sultry glimmering;
Silence herself there seems to sleep,
Wrapp'd in a slumber long and deep,
Where slowly stray those lonely sheep,

To hear the buzzard whimpering shrill,
Hovering above you high and still?
The twittering of the bird that dwells
Amongst the heath's delicious bells?
While round your bed, o'er fern and blade,
Insects in green and gold array'd,
The sun's gay tribes, have lightly stray'd;
And sweeter sound their humming wings
Than the proud minstrel's echoing strings.

WILLIAM HOWITT.

THE SKY-LARK.

BIRD of the wilderness,
    Blithesome and cumberless,
Sweet be thy matin o'er moorland and lea!
    Emblem of happiness,
    Blest is thy dwelling-place—
Oh, to abide in the desert with thee!

Wild is thy lay and loud,
    Far in the downy cloud
Love gives it energy, love gave it birth.
    Where, on thy dewy wing,
    Where art thou journeying?
Thy lay is in heaven, thy love is on earth.

    O'er fell and fountain sheen,
    O'er moor and mountain green,
O'er the red streamer that heralds the day,
    Over the cloudlet dim,
    Over the rainbow's rim,
Musical cherub, soar, singing, away!

    Then, when the gloaming comes,
    Low in the heather blooms,
Sweet will thy welcome and bed of love be!
    Emblem of happiness,
    Blest is thy dwelling-place—
Oh, to abide in the desert with thee!

JAMES HOGG.

"—— That low plaint oft and oft repeating
To the coy mate that needs so much entreating."

TO THE TURTLE-DOVE.

DEEP in the wood, thy voice I list, and love
Thy soft complaining song, thy tender cooing;
O what a winning way thou hast of wooing!
Gentlest of all thy race — sweet Turtle-dove!
Thine is a note that doth not pass away,
Like the light music of a summer's day:
The merle may trill his richest song in vain —

Scarce do we say, "List! for he pipes again;"
But thou! that low plaint oft and oft repeating
To the coy mate that needs so much entreating,
Fillest the woods with a discursive song
Of love, that sinketh deep, and resteth long;
Hushing the voice of mirth, and staying folly
And waking in the heart a gentle melancholy.

D. CONWAY.

THE RAINBOW.

THUS all day long the full distended clouds
Indulge their genial stores, and well-showered
   earth
Is deep enriched with vegetable life;
Till, in the western sky, the downward sun
Looks out, effulgent, from amid the flush
Of broken clouds, gay-shifting to his beam.
The rapid radiance instantaneous strikes
The illumined mountain through the forest streams,

Bestriding earth, the grand ethereal bow
Shoots up immense; and every hue unfolds,
In fair proportion running from the red
To where the violet fades into the sky.
Here, awful Newton, the dissolving clouds
Form, fronting on the sun, thy showery prism;
And to the sage-instructed eye unfold
The various twine of light, by thee disclosed,
From the white mingling maze.   Not so the boy;

" ———The grand ethereal bow
Shoots up immense."

Shakes on the floods, and in a yellow mist,
Far smoking o'er the interminable plain,
In twinkling myriads lights the dewy gems.
Moist, bright and green, the landscape laughs around.
Full swell the woods; their every music wakes,
Mixed in wild concert with the warbling brooks
Increased, the distant bleatings of the hills,
The hollow lows responsive from the vales,
Whence blending all the sweetened zephyr springs.
Meantime, refracted from yon eastern cloud,

He wondering views the bright enchantment bend,
Delightful, o'er the radiant fields, and runs
To catch the falling glory; but amazed
Beholds the amusive arch before him fly,
Then vanish quite away.   Still night succeeds,
A softened shade, and saturated earth
Awaits the morning beam, to give to light,
Raised through ten thousand different plastic tubes,
The balmy treasures of the former day.

JAMES THOMSON.

AS aromatic plants bestow
No spicy fragrance while they grow;
But, crushed or trodden to the ground,
Diffuse their balmy sweets around.

I KNOW a bank where the wild thyme blows,
Where ox-lips and the nodding violet grows;
Quite over-canopied with luscious woodbine,
With sweet musk-roses, and with eglantine.

TO A WATER-FOWL.

WHITHER, midst falling dew,
  While glow the heavens with the last steps of
    day,
Far, through their rosy depths, dost thou pursue
    Thy solitary way?

Vainly the fowler's eye
Might mark thy distant flight to do thee wrong,
As, darkly painted on the crimson sky,
    Thy figure floats along.

All day thy wings have fanned,
At that far height, the cold, thin atmosphere,
Yet stoop not, weary, to the welcome land,
    Though the dark night is near.

And soon that toil shall end;
Soon shalt thou find a summer home, and rest,
And scream among thy fellows; reeds shall
    bend,
    Soon o'er thy sheltered nest.

" All day thy wings have fanned,
At that far height, the cold, thin atmosphere."

Seek'st thou the plashy brink
Of weedy lake, or marge of river wide,
Or where the rocking billows rise and sink
    On the chafed ocean-side?

There is a Power whose care
Teaches thy way along that pathless coast —
The desert and illimitable air —
    Lone wandering, but not lost.

Thou 'rt gone, the abyss of heaven
Hath swallowed up thy form; yet, on my heart
Deeply hath sunk the lesson thou hast given
    And shall not soon depart:

He who, from zone to zone,
Guides through the boundless sky thy certain flight,
In the long way that I must tread alone,
    Will lead my steps aright.

WILLIAM CULLEN BRYANT.

VIOLETS.

WELCOME, maids of honor!
    You doe bring
    In the spring,
And wait upon her.

She has virgins many
    Fresh and faire;
    Yet you are
More sweet than any.

Y'are the maiden posies,
    And so grac't,
    To be plac't
'Fore damask roses.

Yet though thus respected
    By and by
    Ye doe lie,
Poore girles! neglected.

ROBERT HERRICK.

THE WIND-FLOWER.

THOU lookest up with meek, confiding eye,
 Upon the clouded smile of April's face,
 Unharmed though winter stands uncertain by,
  Eyeing with jealous glance each opening grace.
Thou trustest wisely! in thy faith arrayed,
More glorious thou than Israel's wisest king;
Such fate was his whom men to death betrayed.

As thine who hear'st the timid voice of spring,
While other flowers still hide them from her call,
Along the river's brink and meadows bare,
Thee will I seek beside the stony wall,
And in thy trust with childlike heart would share,
O'erjoyed that in thy early leaves I find,
A lesson taught by him who loved all human kind.

JONES VERY.

" From under the boughs in the snow-clad wood,
The merle and the mavis are peeping."

CHRISTMAS IN THE WOODS.

FROM under the boughs in the snow-clad wood
 The merle and the mavis are peeping.
Alike secure from the wind and the flood,
 Yet a silent Christmas keeping.
  Still happy are they,
  And their looks are gay,
And they frisk it from bough to bough;
  Since berries bright red
  Hang over their head,
A right goodly feast, I trow.

There, under the boughs, in their wintry dress,
 Haps many a tender greeting;
Blithe hearts have met, and the soft caress
 Hath told the delight of meeting.
  Though winter hath come
  To his woodland home,

There is mirth with old Christmas cheer,
  For 'neath the light snow
  Is the fruit-fraught bough,
And each to his love is near.

Yes! under the boughs, scarce seen, nestle they,
 Those children of song together,—
As blissful by night, as joyous by day,
 'Mid the snows and the wintry weather.
  For they dream of spring,
  And the songs they'll sing,
When the flowers bloom again in the mead;
  And mindful are they
  Of those blossoms gay,
  Which have brought them to-day
Such help in their time of need!

HARRISON WEIR.

" The tawny Eagle seats his callow brood
High on the cliff, and feasts his young with blood."

THE EAGLE.

THE tawny Eagle seats his callow brood
   High on the cliff, and feasts his young with
      blood:
  On Snowdon's rocks, or Orkney's wide domain,
    Whose beetling cliffs o'erhang the western
      main,
The royal bird his lonely kingdom forms,
  Amidst the gathering clouds and sullen storms;
Through the wide waste of air he darts his sight,
  And holds his sounding pinions poised for flight;

With cruel eye premeditates the war,
  And marks his destined victim from afar:
Descending in a whirlwind to the ground,
His pinions like the rush of waters sound:
The fairest of the fold he bears away,
And to his nest compels the struggling prey;
He scorns the game by meaner hunters tore,
And dips his talons in no vulgar gore.

                 ANNA LETITIA BARBAULD.

A RAM REFLECTED IN THE WATER.

ORTH we went,
    And down the vale, along the streamlet's edge,
    Pursued our way, a broken company,
    Mute or conversing, singly or in pairs.
    Thus having reach'd a bridge that overarch'd
The hasty rivulet, where it lay becalm'd

On the green turf, with his imperial front.
Shaggy and bold, and wreathéd horns superb,
The breathing creature stood; as beautiful,
Beneath him, show'd his shadowy counterpart.
Each had his glowing mountains, each his sky,
And each seem'd centre of his own fair world;

" A snow-white ram, and in the crystal flood
Another and the same!"

In a deep pool, by happy chance we saw
A twofold image: on a grassy bank
A snow-white ram, and in the crystal flood
Another and the same! Most beautiful,

Antipodes unconscious of each other,
Yet, in partition, with their several spheres,
Blended in perfect stillness, to our sight!
                    WILLIAM WORDSWORTH.

H, there is not lost
    One of earth's charms; upon her bosom yet,
After the flight of untold centuries,
The freshness of her far beginning lies,
And yet shall lie.

SWEET is the breath of morn, her rising sweet,
    With charm of earliest birds; pleasant the sun,
When first on this delightful land he spreads
His orient beams, on herb, tree, fruit, and flower,
Glistering with dew.

THE SQUIRREL-HUNT.

HEN, as a nimble squirrel from the wood,
Ranging the hedges for his filbert-food,
Sits partly on a bough his browne nuts cracking,
And from the shell the sweet white kernell
taking,
TILL (with their crookes and bags) a sort of boyes

The boyes runne dabling through thicke and thin:
One tears his hose, another breakes his shin;
This, torn and tatter'd, hath with much adoe
Got by the bryers; and that hath lost his shoe;
This drops his hat — that headlong falls for haste;
Another cryes behinde for being last:

" He is forced to leave a nut nigh broke,
And for his life leape to a neighbour oake "

(To share with him) come with so great a noyse,
That he is forced to leave a nut nigh broke,
And for his life leape to a neighbour oake;
Thence to a beeche, thence to a row of ashes;
Whilst through the quagmires, and red water plashes,

With stickes and stones, and many a sounding halloo,
The little foole, with no small sport, they follow;
Whilst he from tree to tree, from spray to spray,
Gets to the wood, and hides him in his dray.

WILLIAM BROWNE.

It is computed that the swallow flies upward of sixty, the crow twenty-five, and the hawk forty-two miles an hour. The flight of the English eagle is six thousand feet in a minute.

SUMMER WOODS.

LOVE at eventide to walk alone,
Down narrow lanes, o'erhung with dewy thorn,
Where, from the long grass underneath, the snail,
Jet black, creeps out, and sprouts his timid horn.

While in the juicy corn the hidden quail
Cries, "Wet my foot;" and, hid as thoughts un-
born,
The fairy-like and seldom-seen landrail

"I love at eventide to walk alone."

I love to muse o'er meadows newly mown,
Where withering grass perfumes the sultry air;
Where bees search round, with sad and weary drone,
In vain, for flowers that bloom'd but newly there;

Utters, "Craik!—craik!" like voices under ground,
Right glad to meet the evening dewy veil,
And see the light fade into gloom around.

JOHN CLARE.

NOTHING is better able to gratify the inherent passion of novelty than a garden; for Nature is always renewing her variegated appearance. She is infinite in her productions, and the life of man may come to its close before he has seen half the pictures which she is able to display.

ON A GOLDFINCH.

TIME was when I was free as air,
The thistle's downy seed my fare,
   My drink the morning dew;
I perch'd at will on every spray,
My form genteel, my plumage gay,
   My strains forever new.

For caught and caged, and starved to death,
In dying sighs my little breath
   Soon pass'd the wiry grate.

Thanks, gentle swain, for all my woes,
And thanks for this effectual close
   And cure of every ill!

"The thistle's downy seed my fare."

But gaudy plumage, sprightly strain,
And form genteel, were all in vain,
   And of a transient date;

More cruelty could none express;
And I, if you had shown me less,
   Had been your prisoner still.

WILLIAM COWPER.

CHANGES IN NATURE.

THREE astonishing changes present themselves to our view in the kingdom of Nature. The first is — when a small seed dies in the lap of earth, and rises again in the verdant and flowery splendor of a youthful tree. The next is — when, under a warm and feathery covering, life develops itself in an egg, and a winged bird breaks singing through the shell. The third is — when a creeping caterpillar is transformed into a butterfly, which, with glittering and delicate wing, rocks itself upon the lovely flowers.

MORNING SONG.

UP! quit thy bower! late wears the hour,
Long have the rooks cawed round the tower;
O'er flower and tree loud hums the bee,
And the wild kid sports merrily.
The sun is bright, the sky is clear,
Wake, lady, wake! and hasten here.

Up, maiden fair! and bind thy hair,
And rouse thee in the breezy air!
The lulling stream that soothed thy dream
Is dancing in the sunny beam.

Waste not these hours, so fresh, so gay:
Leave thy soft couch and haste away!

Up! Time will tell the morning bell
Its service-sound has chiméd well;
The aged crone keeps house alone,
The reapers to the fields are gone.
Lose not these hours, so cool, so gay:
Lo! while thou sleep'st they haste away!

JOANNA BAILLIE.

"Ascends the neighboring beech, there whisks his brush."

THE SQUIRREL.

DRAWN from his refuge in some lonely elm,
That age or injury has hollow'd deep,
Where, on his bed of wool and matted leaves,
He has outslept the winter, ventures forth,
To frisk a while and bask in the warm sun,
The Squirrel, flippant, pert, and full of play;

He sees me, and at once, swift as a bird,
Ascends the neighboring beech, there whisks his
brush,
And perks his ears, and stamps and cries aloud,
With all the prettiness of feign'd alarm,
And anger insignificantly fierce.

WILLIAM COWPER.

THE IVY GREEN.

H, a dainty plant is the Ivy Green,
  That creepeth o'er ruins old!
Of right choice food are his meals, I ween,
  In his cell so lone and cold.
The wall must be crumbled, the stone decayed,
  To pleasure his dainty whim;
And the mouldering dust that years have made
  Is a merry meal for him.
      Creeping where no life is seen,
      A rare old plant is the Ivy Green.

Fast he stealeth on, though he wears no wings,
  And a staunch old heart has he;
How closely he twineth, how tight he clings
  To his friend the huge Oak-tree!
And slyly he traileth along the ground,
  And his leaves he gently waves,

As he joyously hugs and crawleth around
  The rich mould of dead men's graves.
  Creeping where grim death has been,
  A rare old plant is the Ivy Green.

Whole ages have fled, and their works decayed,
  And nations have scattered been;
But the stout old Ivy shall never fade
  From its hale and hearty green.
The brave old plant, in its lonely days,
  Shall fatten upon the past;
For the stateliest building man can raise
  Is the Ivy's food at last.
      Creeping on, where time has been,
      A rare old plant is the Ivy Green.

CHARLES DICKENS.

" How true she warp'd the moss to form her nest,
  And model'd it within with wool and clay."

THE THRUSH'S NEST.

ITHIN a thick and spreading hawthorn bush,
  That overhung a mole-hill large and round,
  I heard, from morn to morn, a merry Thrush
  Sing hymns to sunrise, while I drank the
      sound
With joy:—and often, an intruding guest,
  I watch'd her secret toils, from day to day,—
How true she warp'd the moss to form her nest,
  And model'd it within with wool and clay.

And by-and-by, like heath-bells gilt with dew,
  There lay her shining eggs, as bright as
      flowers,
Ink-spotted-over shells of green and blue;
  And there I witness'd, in the summer hours,
A brood of Nature's minstrels chirp and fly,
  Glad as the sunshine and the laughing sky.

JOHN CLARE

"And here he came, pierced by a fatal blow."

THE DYING STAG.

NOW in a grassy dingle he was laid,
  With wild wood primroses befreckled low.
  Over his head the wanton shadows play'd
  Of a young olive, that her boughs so spread,
As with her leaves she seem'd to crown his head.
And here he came, pierced by a fatal blow,

As in a wood he walk'd, securely feeding;
And feeling death swim in his endless bleeding,
His heavy head his fainting strength exceeding,
Bade farewell to the woods that round him wave,
While tears from drooping flowers bedew his turfy
  grave.

GILES FLETCHER.

NIGHT.

NIGHT is the astronomer's accepted time; he goes to his delightful labors when the busy world goes to its rest. A dark pall spreads over the resorts of active life; terrestrial objects, hill and valley, and rock and stream, and the abodes of men disappear; but the curtain is drawn up which concealed the heavenly hosts. There they shine and there they move as they moved and shone to the eyes of Newton and Galileo, of Kepler and Copernicus, of Ptolemy and Hipparchus; yes, as they moved and shone when the morning stars sang together, and all the sons of God shouted for joy. All has changed on earth; but the glorious heavens remain unchanged. The plow passes over the site of mighty cities; the homes of powerful nations are desolate; the languages they spoke are forgotten: but the stars that shone for them are shining for us; the same eclipses run their steady cycle; the same equinoxes call out the flowers of spring, and send the husbandman *to* the harvest; the sun pauses at either tropic as he did when his course began; and sun and moon, and planet and satellite, and star and constellation and galaxy, still bear witness to the power, the wisdom and the love which placed them in the heavens and upholds them there.

EDWARD EVERETT.

TO SENECA LAKE.

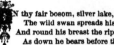

ON thy fair bosom, silver lake,
  The wild swan spreads his snowy sail,
And round his breast the ripples break,
  As down he bears before the gale.

On thy fair bosom, waveless stream,
  The dipping paddle echoes far,
And flashes in the moonlight gleam,
  And bright reflects the polar star.

How sweet, at set of sun, to view
  Thy golden mirror spreading wide,
And see the mist of mantling blue
  Float round the distant mountain's side.

At midnight hour, as shines the moon,
  A sheet of silver spreads below,
And swift she cuts, at highest noon,
  Light clouds, like wreaths of purest snow.

"And round his breast the ripples break,
As down he bears before the gale."

The waves along thy pebbly shore,
  As blows the north wind, heave their foam,
And curl around the dashing oar,
  As late the boatman hies him home.

On thy fair bosom, silver lake!
  Oh, I could ever sweep the oar,
When early birds at morning wake,
  And evening tells us toil is o'er.

JAMES GATES PERCIVAL.

NATURE always springs to the surface, and manages to show what she is. It is vain to stop or try to drive her back. She breaks through every obstacle, pushes forward, and at last makes for herself a way.

8

"And the call of the pheasant
Is frequent and pleasant."

A WOODNOTE.

COME ye, come ye, to the green, green wood;
   Loudly the blackbird is singing,
The squirrel is feasting on blossom and bud,
   And the curling fern is springing:
     Here ye may sleep
     In the moss so deep,
While the noon is so warm and so weary,
     And sweetly awake,
     As the sun through the brake
Bids the fauvette and white-throat sing cheery.

The quicken is tufted with blossom of snow,
   And is throwing its perfume around it;
The wryneck replies to the cuckoo's halloo
   For joy that again she has found it;
     The jay's red breast
     Peeps over her nest,
In the midst of the crab-blossoms blushing;
     And the call of the pheasant
     Is frequent and pleasant,
When all other calls are hushing.

           WILLIAM HOWITT.

"Come ye, come ye, to the green, green wood;
Loudly the blackbird is singing."

NATURE imitates herself. A grain thrown into good ground brings forth fruit; a principle thrown into a good mind brings forth fruit. Everything is created and conducted by the same Master; the root, the branch, the fruits;—the principles, the consequences.

LAMBS AT PLAY.

AY, ye that know, ye who have felt and seen
   Spring's morning smiles and soul-enlivening
     green,
  Say, did you give the thrilling transport way?
    Did your eye brighten when young lambs at play
Leap'd o'er your path with animated pride,
Or grazed in merry clusters by your side?
Ye who can smile, to wisdom no disgrace,
At the arch meaning of a kitten's face;

A thousand wily antics mark their stay,
A startling crowd, impatient of delay.
Like the fond dove, from fearful prison freed,
Each seems to say, "Come, let us try our speed!"
Away they scour, impetuous, ardent, strong,
The green turf trembling as they bound along;
Adown the slope, then up the hillock climb,
Where every molehill is a bank of thyme;
There panting stop: yet scarcely can refrain,

"Did your eye brighten when young lambs at play
Leap'd o'er your path with animated pride?"

If spotless innocence, and infant mirth,
Excite to praise, or give reflection birth,
In shades like these pursue your favorite joy,
'Mid Nature's revels, sports that never cloy.
A few begin a short but vigorous race,
And indolence abash'd soon flies the place;
Then challenged forth. see thither, one by one,
From every side assembling playmates run;

A bird, a leaf, will set them off again:
Or, if a gale with strength unusual blow,
Scattering the wild-briar roses into snow,
Their little limbs increasing efforts try,
Like the torn flower the fair assemblage fly.
Ah, fallen rose! sad emblem of their doom;
Frail as thyself, they perish while they bloom!
            ROBERT BLOOMFIELD.

HE various productions of Nature were not made for us to tread upon, nor only to feed our eyes with their grateful variety, or to bring a sweet odor to us; but there is a more internal beauty in them for our minds to prey upon, did we but penetrate beyond the surface of these things into their hidden properties.

THE HARE.

'TIS instinct that directs the jealous Hare
 To choose her soft abode. With steps reversed
 She forms the doubling maze; then, ere the morn
Peeps through the clouds, leaps to her close recess.

Plot their destruction; or, perchance in hopes
Of plenteous forage, near the ranker mead
Or matted grass, wary and close they sit.
When spring shines forth, season of love and joy,
In the moist marsh, 'mong bed of rushes hid,
They cool their boiling blood. When summer suns

" ——— Ere the morn
Peeps through the clouds, leaps to her close recess."

As wandering shepherds on th' Arabian plains
No settled residence observe, but shift
Their moving camp; now, on some cooler hill,
With cedars crowned, court the refreshing breeze;
And then below, where trickling streams distil
From some precarious source, their thirst allay,
And feed their thirsting flocks: so the wise hares
Oft quit their seats, lest some more curious eye
Should mark their haunts, and by dark treacherous
 wiles

Bake the cleft earth, to thick, wide-spreading fields
Of corn full-grown, they lead their helpless young:
But when autumnal torrents and fierce rains
Deluge the vale, in the dry crumbling bank
Their forms they delve, and cautiously avoid
The dripping covert. Yet, when winter's cold
Their limbs benumbs, thither with speed return'd,
In the long grass they skulk, or shrinking creep
Among the wither'd leaves; thus changing still,
As fancy prompts them, or as food invites.

      WILLIAM SOMERVILLE

TO A SKYLARK.

HAIL to thee, blithe spirit!
 Bird thou never wert,
 That from heaven, or near it,
 Pourest thy full heart
In profuse strains of unpremeditated art.

Higher still and higher,
 From the earth thou springest
Like a cloud of fire;
 The blue deep thou wingest,
And singing still dost soar, and soaring, ever singest.

In the golden lightning
  Of the sunken sun,
O'er which clouds are brightening,
  Thou dost float and run,
Like an unbodied joy whose race is just begun.

The pale, purple even
  Melts around thy flight
Like a star of heaven,
  In the broad daylight
Thou art unseen, but yet I hear thy shrill delight.

Keen as are the arrows
  Of that silver sphere,
Whose intense lamp narrows
  In the white dawn clear,
Until we hardly see, we feel that it is there.

All the earth and air
  With thy voice is loud,
As, when night is bare,
  From one lonely cloud
The moon rains out her beams, and heaven is over-
    flowed.

What thou art we know not:
  What is most like thee?
From rainbow-clouds there flow not
  Drops so bright to see,
As from thy presence showers a rain of melody.

Like a poet hidden
  In the light of thought,
Singing hymns unbidden,
  Till the world is wrought
To sympathy with hopes and fears it heeded not:

Like a high-born maiden
  In a palace tower,
Soothing her love-laden
  Soul in secret hour
With music sweet as love, which overflows her bower:

Like a glow-worm golden,
  In a dell of dew,
Scattering unbeholden
  Its aerial hue
Amongst the flowers and grass which screen it from
  the view.

Like a rose embowered
  In its own green leaves,
By warm winds deflowered,
  Till the scent it gives
Makes faint with too much sweet those heavy-wingéd
  thieves.

Sound of vernal showers
  On the twinkling grass,
Rain-awakened flowers,—
  All that ever was
Joyous and clear and fresh, thy music doth surpass.

Teach us, sprite or bird,
  What sweet thoughts are thine;
I have never heard
  Praise of love or wine
That panted forth a flood of rapture so divine.

Chorus hymeneal,
  Or triumphal chant,
Matched with thine would be all
  But an empty vaunt,—
A thing wherein we feel there is some hidden want.

What objects are the fountains
  Of thy happy strain?
What fields of waves or mountains?
  What shapes of sky or plain?
What love of thine own kind? what ignorance of pain?

With thy clear, keen joyance
  Languor cannot be:
Shadow of annoyance
  Never came near thee:
Thou lovest, but ne'er knew love's sad satiety.

Waking or asleep,
  Thou of death must deem
Things more true and deep
  Than we mortals dream,
Or how could thy notes flow in such a crystal stream?

We look before and after,
  And pine for what is not:
Our sincerest laughter
  With some pain is fraught;
Our sweetest songs are those that tell of saddest
  thought.

Yet if we could scorn
  Hate and pride and fear;
If we were things born
  Not to shed a tear,
I know not how thy joy we ever should come near.

Better than all measures
  Of delightful sound,
Better than all treasures
  That in books are found,
Thy skill to poet were, thou scorner of the ground!

Teach me half the gladness
  That thy brain must know,
Such harmonious madness
  From thy lips would flow,
The world should listen then, as I am listening now.
PERCY BYSSHE SHELLEY.

TO A WILD DEER.

IT couch of repose for a pilgrim like thee!
Magnificent prison inclosing the free!
With rock-wall encircled — with precipice
　　crown'd —
Which, awoke by the sun, thou canst clear at a
　　bound.
Mid the fern and the heather, kind Nature doth keep
One bright spot of green for her favorite's sleep;

Elate on the fern-branch the grasshopper sings,
And away in the midst of his roundelay springs;
'Mid the flowers of the heath, not more bright than
　　himself,
The wild-bee is busy, a musical elf —
Then starts from his labor, unwearied and gay,
And, circling his antlers, booms far, far away.
While high up the mountains, in silence remote,

" With wide-spreading antlers, a guard to his breast,
There lies the wild creature, e'en stately in rest!"

And close to that covert, as clear as the skies
When their blue depths are cloudless, a little lake lies,
Where the creature at rest can his image behold,
Looking up through the radiance, as bright and as
　　bold!
How lonesome! how wild! yet the wildness is rife
With the stir of enjoyment — the spirit of life.
The glad fish leaps up in the heart of the lake,
Whose depths, at the sullen plunge, sullenly quake!

The cuckoo unseen is repeating his note;
The mellowing echo, on watch in the skies,
Like a voice from the loftier climate replies.
With wide-spreading antlers, a guard to his breast,
There lies the wild creature, e'en stately in rest!
'Mid the grandeur of Nature, composed and serene,
And proud in his heart of the mountainous scene,
He lifts his calm eye to the eagle and raven,
At noon sinking down on smooth wings to their haven,

As if in his soul the bold animal smiled
To his friends of the sky, the joint-heirs of the wild.

Yes! fierce looks thy nature, e'en hush'd in repose—
In the depths of thy desert regardless of foes,
Thy bold antlers call on the hunter afar,
With a haughty defiance to come to the war!
No outrage is war to a creature like thee!
The bugle-horn fills thy wild spirit with glee,
As thou barest thy neck on the wings of the wind,
And the laggardly gaze-hound is toiling behind.
In the beams of thy forehead that glitter with death—
In feet that draw power from the touch of the heath—

In the wide-raging torrent that lends thee its roar—
In the cliff that, once trod, must be trodden no more—
Thy trust, 'mid dangers that threaten thy reign!
But what if the stag on the mountain be slain?
On the brink of the rock—lo! he standeth at bay,
Like a victor that falls at the close of the day:
While hunter and hound in their terror retreat
From the death that is spurn'd from his furious feet;
And his last cry of anger comes back from the skies,
As Nature's fierce son in the wilderness dies.

JOHN WILSON (Christopher North).

"——Th' assembled chats
Wave high the tremulous wing, and with shrill notes,
But clear and pleasant, cheer th' extensive heath."

THE HEATH.

ERE the furze,
Enrich'd among its spines with golden flowers,
Scents the keen air; while all its thorny groups,
Wide scatter'd o'er the waste, are full of life;
For, midst its yellow bloom, th' assembled chats
Wave high the tremulous wing, and with shrill notes,
But clear and pleasant, cheer th' extensive heath.
Linnets in numerous flocks frequent it too;
And bashful, hiding in the scenes remote
From his congeners (they who make the woods
And the thick copses echo to their song),

The stonechat makes his domicile; and while
His patient mate with downy bosom warms
Their future nestlings, he his love-lay sings,
Loud to the shaggy wild. The Erica here,
That o'er the Caledonian hills sublime
Spreads its dark mantle (where the bees delight
To seek their purest honey), flourishes,
Sometimes with bells like amethysts, and then
Paler, and shaded like the maiden's cheek
With gradual blushes; other while as white
As rime that hangs upon the frozen spray.

CHARLOTTE SMITH.

HE very soul seems to be refreshed on the bare recollection of the pleasure which the senses receive in contemplating, on a fine vernal morning, the charms of the pink, the violet, the rose, the honey-suckle, the hyacinth, the tulip, and a thousand other flowers, in every variety of figure, scent, and hue; for Nature is no less remarkable for the accuracy and beauty of her works than for variety and profusion.

THE SWALLOW.

THE gorse is yellow on the heath,
  The banks with speedwell flowers are gay,
The oaks are budding; and beneath,
The hawthorn soon will bear the wreath,
  The silver wreath of May.

The welcome guest of settled spring,
  The Swallow too is come at last;
Just at sun-set, when thrushes sing,
I saw her dash with rapid wing,
  And hail'd her as she pass'd.

Come, summer visitant, attach
  To my reed-roof your nest of clay;
And let my ear your music catch,
Low twittering underneath the thatch,
  At the grey dawn of day.

As fables tell, an Indian sage
  The Hindostani woods among,
Could, in his distant hermitage,
As if 'twere marked in written page,
  Translate the wild bird's song.

I wish I did his power possess,
  That I might learn, fleet bird, from thee,
What our vain systems only guess,
  And know from what wild wilderness
You came across the sea.

I would a little while restrain
  Your rapid wing, that I might hear
Whether on clouds that bring the rain
You sail'd above the western main,
  The wind your charioteer.

In Afric, does the sultry gale
  Through spicy bower and palmy grove
Bear the repeated cuckoo's tale?
Dwells there a time the wandering rail,
  Or the itinerant dove?

Were you in Asia? O relate
  If there your fabled sister's woes
She seemed in sorrow to narrate;
Or sings she but to celebrate
  Her nuptials with the rose?

I would inquire how, journeying long
  The vast and pathless ocean o'er,
You ply again those pinions strong,
And come to build anew among
  The scenes you left before?

But if, as colder breezes blow,
  Prophetic of the waning year,
You hide, though none know when or how,
In the cliff's excavated brow,
  And linger torpid here;

Thus lost to life, what favoring dream
  Bids you to happier hours awake,
And tells that, dancing on the beam,
The light gnat hovers o'er the stream,
  The May-fly on the lake?

"The welcome guest of settled spring,
The Swallow too is come at last."

Or if, by instinct taught to know
  Approaching dearth of insect food,
To isles and willowy aits you go,
And, crowding on the pliant bough
  Sink in the dimpling flood;

How learn ye, while the cold waves boom
  Your deep and oozy couch above,
The time when flowers of promise bloom,
And call you from your transient tomb,
  To light, and life, and love?

Alas! how little can be known,
  Her sacred veil where Nature draws;
Let baffled Science humbly own
Her mysteries, understood alone
  By HIM who gives her laws.

                              CHARLOTTE SMITH.

MY heart is awed within me when I think
  Of the great miracle that still goes on
In silence round me—the perpetual work
Of Thy creation, finished, yet renewed
Forever. Written on Thy works I read
The lesson of Thy own eternity.

LO! all grow old and die—but, see again!
  How on the faltering footsteps of decay
Youth presses—ever gay and beautiful youth
In all its beautiful forms. These lofty trees
Wave not less proudly than their ancestors
Moulder beneath them.

THE SIERRAS.

IKE fragments of an uncompleted world,
From bleak Alaska, bound in ice and spray,
To where the peaks of Darien lie curled
In clouds, the broken lands loom bold and gray;
The seamen nearing S· ι Francisco Bay
Forget the compass here; with sturdy hand
They seize the wheel, look up, then bravely lay
The ship to shore by rugged peaks that stand
The stern and proud patrician fathers of the land.

They stand white stairs of heaven—stand a line
Of lifting, endless, and eternal white;
They look upon the far and flashing brine,
Upon the boundless plains, the broken height
Of Kamiakin's battlements. The flight
Of time is underneath their untopped towers;
They seem to push aside the moon at night,
To jostle and to loose the stars. The flowers
Of heaven fall about their brows in shining showers.

They stand a line of lifted snowy isles,
High held above a tossed and tumbled sea, —
A sea of wood in wild unmeasured miles;
White pyramids of Faith where man is free;
White monuments of Hope that yet shall be
The mounts of matchless and immortal song.
I look far down the hollow days; I see
The bearded prophets, simple-soul'd and strong,
That strike the sounding harp and thrill the heeding throng.

Serene and satisfied! supreme! as lone
As God, they loom like God's archangels churl'd:
They look as cold as kings upon a throne;
The mantling wings of night are crush'd and curl'd
As feathers curl. The elements are hurl'd
From off their bosoms, and are bidden go,
Like evil spirits, to an under-world;
They stretch from Cariboo to Mexico,
A line of battle-tents in everlasting snow.

JOAQUIN MILLER.

SNOW-FLAKES.

UT of the bosom of the Air,
Out of the cloud-folds of her garments shaken,
Over the woodlands brown and bare,
Over the harvest-fields forsaken,
Silent and soft and slow
Descends the snow.

Even as our cloudy fancies take
Suddenly shape in some divine expression,
Even as the troubled heart doth make

In the white countenance confession,
The troubled sky reveals
The grief it feels.

This is the poem of the air,
Slowly in silent syllables recorded;
This is the secret of despair,
Long in its cloudy bosom hoarded,
Now whispered and revealed
To wood and field.

HENRY WADSWORTH LONGFELLOW.

THE DOG AND THE WATER-LILY.

HE noon was shady, and soft airs
 Swept Ouse's silent tide,
When, 'scaped from literary cares,
 I wander'd by its side.

My spaniel, prettiest of the race,
 And high in pedigree,
(Two nymphs adorn'd with every grace
 That spaniel found for me).

And puzzling set his puppy brains
 To comprehend the case.

But, with a chirrup clear and strong
 Dispersing all his dream,
I thence withdrew, and follow'd long
 The windings of the stream.

My ramble ended, I return'd;
 Beau, trotting far before,

"I saw him, with that lily cropp'd."

Now wanton'd, lost in flags and reeds,
 Now starting into sight,
Pursued the swallow o'er the meads,
 With scarce a slower flight.

It was the time when Ouse display'd
 Her lilies newly blown;
Their beauties I intent survey'd
 And one I wish'd my own.

With cane extended far, I sought
 To steer it close to land:
But still the prize, though nearly caught,
 Escaped my eager hand.

Beau mark'd my unsuccessful pains
 With fix'd considerate face,

The floating wreath again discern'd,
 And plunging left the shore.

I saw him, with that lily cropp'd,
 Impatient swim to meet
My quick approach, and soon he dropp'd
 The treasure at my feet.

Charm'd with the sight, "The world," I cried,
 "Shall hear of this thy deed:
My dog shall mortify the pride
 Of man's superior breed:

"But chief myself I will enjoin,
 Awake at duty's call,
To show a love as prompt as thine
 To Him who gives me all."

WILLIAM COWPER.

IT is with flowers as with moral qualities — the bright are sometimes poison-
ous, but, I believe, never the sweet.

PLANTING THE APPLE-TREE.

OME, let us plant the apple-tree.
  Cleave the tough greensward with the spade;
  Wide let its hollow bed be made;
  There gently lay the roots, and there
Sift the dark mould with kindly care,
  And press it o'er them tenderly,
As round the sleeping infant's feet
We softly fold the cradle sheet;
  So plant we the apple-tree.

A world of blossoms for the bee,
Flowers for the sick girl's silent room,
For the glad infant sprigs of bloom,
  We plant with the apple-tree.

What plant we in this apple-tree?
Fruits that shall swell in sunny June,
And redden in the August noon,
And drop, when gentle airs come by,

" Boughs where the thrush, with crimson breast,
Shall haunt, and sing, and hide her nest."

What plant we in this apple-tree?
Buds, which the breath of summer days
Shall lengthen into leafy sprays;
Boughs where the thrush with crimson breast
Shall haunt, and sing, and hide her nest;
  We plant, upon the sunny lea,
A shadow for the noontide hour,
A shelter from the summer shower,
  When we plant the apple-tree.

  What plant we in this apple-tree?
Sweets for a hundred flowery springs
To load the May-wind's restless wings,
When, from the orchard row, he pours
Its fragrance through our open doors;

That fan the blue September sky,
  While children come, with cries of glee,
And seek them where the fragrant grass
Betrays their bed to those who pass,
  At the foot of the apple-tree.

  And when, above this apple-tree,
The winter stars are quivering bright,
And winds go howling through the night,
Girls, whose young eyes o'erflow with mirth,
Shall peel its fruit by cottage hearth,
  And guests in prouder homes shall see,
Heaped with the grape of Cintra's vine
  And golden orange of the Line,
  The fruit of the apple-tree.

The fruitage of this apple-tree
Winds and our flag of stripe and star
Shall bear to coasts that lie afar,
Where men shall wonder at the view,
And ask in what fair groves they grew,
And sojourners beyond the sea
Shall think of childhood's careless day
And long, long hours of summer play,
In the shade of the apple-tree.

And time shall waste this apple-tree.
O, when its aged branches throw
Thin shadows on the ground below,
Shall fraud and force and iron will
Oppress the weak and helpless still?
What shall the tasks of mercy be,
Amid the toils, the strifes, the tears
Of those who live when length of years
Is wasting this apple-tree?

"Shall think of childhood's careless day,
And long, long hours of summer play,
In the shade of the apple-tree."

Each year shall give this apple-tree
A broader flush of roseate bloom,
A deeper maze of verdurous gloom,
And loosen, when the frost-clouds lower,
The crisp brown leaves in thicker shower.
The years shall come and pass, but we
Shall hear no longer, where we lie,
The summer's songs, the autumn's sigh,
In the boughs of the apple-tree.

"Who planted this old apple-tree?"
The children of that distant day
Thus to some aged man shall say;
And, gazing on its mossy stem,
The gray-haired man shall answer them:
"A poet of the land was he,
Born in the rude but good old times;
'T is said he made some quaint old rhymes
On planting the apple-tree."

WILLIAM CULLEN BRYANT.

THE DAISY.

HERE is a flower, a little flower
With silver crest and golden eye,
That welcomes every changing hour,
And weathers every sky.

The prouder beauties of the field
In gay but quick succession shine;
Race after race their honors yield,
They flourish and decline.

But this small flower, to Nature dear,
While moons and stars their courses run,
Inwreathes the circle of the year,
Companion of the sun.

It smiles upon the lap of May,
To sultry August spreads its charm,
Lights pale October on his way,
And twines December's arm.

The purple heath and golden broom
  On moory mountains catch the gale;
O'er lawns the lily sheds perfume,
  The violet in the vale.

But this bold floweret climbs the hill,
  Hides in the forest, haunts the glen,
Plays on the margin of the rill,
  Peeps round the fox's den.

The lambkin crops its crimson gem;
  The wild bee murmurs on its breast;
The blue-fly bends its pensile stem
  Light o'er the skylark's nest.

'Tis Flora's page, — in every place,
  In every season, fresh and fair;
It opens with perennial grace,
  And blossoms everywhere.

" 'T is Flora's page—in every place,
In every season, fresh and fair."

Within the garden's cultured round
  It shares the sweet carnation's bed;
And blooms on consecrated ground
  In honor of the dead.

On waste and woodland, rock and plain,
  Its humble buds unheeded rise;
The rose has but a summer reign;
  The daisy never dies!

JAMES MONTGOMERY.

THE sense of beauty in Nature, even among cultured people, is less often met with than other mental endowments.

THE ROBIN.

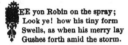EE yon Robin on the spray;
Look ye! how his tiny form
Swells, as when his merry lay
Gushes forth amid the storm.

Yet from out the darkness dreary
Cometh still that cheerful note;
Praiseful aye, and never weary,
Is that little warbling throat.

"Though the snow is falling fast,
Specking o'er his coat with white."

Though the snow is falling fast,
Specking o'er his coat with white —
Though loud roars the chilly blast,
And the evening's lost in night, —

Thank him for his lesson's sake,
Thank God's gentle minstrel there,
Who, when storms make others quake
Sings of days that brighter were.

HARRISON WEIR.

LUTHER always kept a flower in a glass on his writing-table; and when he was waging his great public controversy with Eckins he kept a flower in his hand. Lord Bacon has a beautiful passage about flowers. As to Shakespeare, he is a perfect Alpine valley — he is full of flowers; they spring, and blossom, and wave in every cleft of his mind. Even Milton, cold, serene, and stately as he is, breaks forth into exquisite gushes of tenderness and fancy when he marshals the flowers.

"And birds sit brooding in the snow."

SPRING AND WINTER.

WHEN daisies pied, and violets blue,
    And lady-smocks all silver-white,
And cuckoo-buds of yellow hue,
    Do paint the meadows with delight,
The cuckoo then, on every tree,
Mocks married men, for thus sings he,
        Cuckoo;
Cuckoo, cuckoo,—O word of fear,
Unpleasing to a married ear!

When shepherds pipe on oaten straws,
    And merry larks are ploughmen's clocks,
When turtles tread, and rooks, and daws,
    And maidens bleach their summer smocks,
The cuckoo then, on every tree,
Mocks married men, for thus sings he,
        Cuckoo;
Cuckoo, cuckoo,—O word of fear,
Unpleasing to a married ear!

When icicles hang by the wall,
    And Dick the shepherd blows his nail,
And Tom bears logs into the hall,
    And milk comes frozen home in pail,
When blood is nipped, and ways be foul,
Then nightly sings the staring owl,
        To-who;
Tu-whit, to-who, a merry note,
While greasy Joan doth keel the pot.

When all around the wind doth blow,
    And coughing drowns the parson's saw,
And birds sit brooding in the snow,
    And Marian's nose looks red and raw,
When roasted crabs hiss in the bowl,
Then nightly sings the staring-owl,
        To-who;
Tu-whit, to-who, a merry note,
While greasy Joan doth keel the pot.

WILLIAM SHAKESPEARE.

MARCH.

THE stormy March is come at last,
    With wind, and cloud, and changing skies;
I hear the rushing of the blast,
    That through the snowy valley flies.

Ah, passing few are they who speak,
    Wild, stormy month! in praise of thee;
Yet though thy winds are loud and bleak,
    Thou art a welcome month to me.

For thou, to Northern lands, again
    The glad and glorious sun dost bring,
And thou hast joined the gentle train
    And wear'st the gentle name of Spring.

And in thy reign of blast and storm,
    Smiles many a long, bright sunny day,
When the changed winds are soft and warm,
    And heaven puts on the blue of May.

Then sing aloud the gushing rills
    In joy that they again are free,
And, brightly leaping down the hills,
    Renew their journey to the sea.

The year's departing beauty hides,
    Of wintry storms the sullen threat;
But in thy sternest frown abides
    A look of kindly promise yet.

Thou bring'st the hope of those calm skies,
    And that soft time of sunny showers,
When the wide bloom, on earth that lies,
    Seems of a brighter world than ours.

WILLIAM CULLEN BRYANT.

STATELY Spring! whose robe-folds are valleys, whose breast-bouquet is gardens, and whose blush is a vernal evening.

TO A YOUNG ASS.

POOR little foal of an oppresséd race!
  I love the languid patience of thy face:
  And oft with gentle hand I give thee bread,
  And clap thy ragged coat, and pat thy head.
  But what thy dulled spirits hath dismay'd,
That never thou dost sport along the glade?
And (most unlike the nature of things young)
That earthward still thy moveless head is hung?
Do thy prophetic fears anticipate,
Meek child of misery! thy future fate, —

Poor ass! thy master should have learnt to show
Pity —best taught by fellowship of woe;
For much I fear me that he lives like thee,
Half famish'd in a land of luxury!
How askingly its footsteps hither bend!
It seems to say, " And have I then one friend ? "
Innocent foal! thou poor despised, forlorn!
I hail thee brother, spite of the fool's scorn;
And fain would take thee with me, in the dell
Of peace and mild equality to dwell,

" Is thy sad heart thrilled with filial pain,
To see thy wretched mother's shortened chain?"

The starving meal, and all the thousand aches
" Which patient merit of th' unworthy takes?"
Or is thy sad heart thrill'd with filial pain,
To see thy wretched mother's shorten'd chain?
And truly very piteous is her lot,
Chain'd to a log within a narrow spot,
Where the close-eaten grass is scarcely seen,
While sweet around her waves the tempting green!

Where toil shall call the charmer health his bride,
And laughter tickle plenty's ribless side!
How thou wouldst toss thy heels in gamesome play,
And frisk about as lamb or kitten gay!
Yea, and more musically sweet to me .
Thy dissonant harsh bray of joy would be,
Than warbled melodies, that soothe to rest
The aching of pale fashion's vacant breast!
SAMUEL TAYLOR COLERIDGE.

9

THE FIRST DAY OF SPRING.

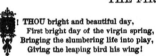

I THOU bright and beautiful day,
  First bright day of the virgin spring,
Bringing the slumbering life into play,
  Giving the leaping bird his wing!

I hear thy voice in the lark's clear note,
  In the cricket's chirp at the evening hour,
In the zephyr's sighs that around me float,
  In the breathing bud and the opening flower.

" In the thousand plants that spring to birth,
On the valley's side in the home of shade."

Thou art round me now in all thy hues,
  Thy robe of green, and thy scented sweets,
In thy bursting buds, in thy blessing dews,
  In every form that my footstep meets.

I see thy forms o'er the parting earth,
  In the tender shoots of the grassy blade,
In the thousand plants that spring to birth,
  On the valley's side in the home of shade.

I feel thy promise in all my veins,
  They bound with a feeling long suppressed,
And, like a captive who breaks his chains,
  Leap the glad hopes in my heaving breast.

There are life and joy in thy coming, Spring!
  Thou hast no tidings of gloom and death:
But buds thou shakest from every wing,
  And sweets thou breathest with every breath.

WILLIAM GILMORE SIMMS.

DAY IS DYING.

DAY is dying! Float, O song,
  Down the westward river,
  Requiem chanting to the Day —
  Day, the mighty Giver.

Pierced by shafts of Time he bleeds,
  Melted rubies sending
Through the river and the sky,
  Earth and heaven blending.

All the long-drawn earthly banks
  Up to cloud-land lifting;

Slow between them drifts the swan,
  'Twixt two heavens drifting.

Wings half open like a flower
  Inly deeply flushing,
Neck and breast as virgin's pure, —
  Virgin proudly blushing.

Day is dying! Float, O swan,
  Down the ruby river;
Follow, song, in requiem
  To the mighty Giver.

MARIAN EVANS LEWES CROSS (George Eliot).

"I steal by lawns and grassy plots;
  I slide by hazel covers;
I move the sweet forget-me-nots
  That grow for happy lovers."

SONG OF THE BROOK.

COME from haunts of coot and hern:
  I make a sudden sally
And sparkle out among the fern,
  To bicker down a valley.

By thirty hills I hurry down,
  Or slip between the ridges,
By twenty thorps, a little town,
  And half a hundred bridges.

Till last by Philip's farm I flow
  To join the brimming river,
For men may come and men may go,
  But I go on forever.

I chatter over stony ways,
  In little sharps and trebles,
I bubble into eddying bays,
  I babble on the pebbles.

With many a curve my banks I fret
  By many a field and fallow,
And many a fairy foreland set
  With willow-weed and mallow.

I chatter, chatter, as I flow
  To join the brimming river;
For men may come and men may go,
  But I go on forever.

I wind about, and in and out,
  With here a blossom sailing,
And here and there a lusty trout,
  And here and there a grayling,

And here and there a foamy flake
  Upon me, as I travel
With many a silvery waterbreak
  Above the golden gravel,

And draw them all along, and flow
  To join the brimming river;
For men may come and men may go,
  But I go on forever.

I steal by lawns and grassy plots;
  I slide by hazel covers;
I move the sweet forget-me-nots
  That grow for happy lovers.

I slip, I slide, I gloom, I glance,
  Among my skimming swallows;
I make the netted sunbeam dance
  Against my sandy shallows;

I murmur under moon and stars
  In brambly wildernesses;
I linger by my shingly bars;
  I loiter round my cresses;

"I chatter over stony ways."

And out again I curve and flow
  To join the brimming river;
For men may come and men may go,
  But I go on forever.

              ALFRED TENNYSON.

HAIL, HOLY LIGHT.

HAIL, holy Light, offspring of Heaven first-born!
Or of the Eternal coeternal beam,
May I express thee unblamed? since God is
    light,
And never but in unapproachéd light
Dwelt from eternity — dwelt then in thee,
Bright effluence of bright essence increate!
Or hear'st thou rather pure ethereal stream,
Whose fountain who shall tell? Before the Sun,
Before the heavens thou wert, and at the voice
Of God, as with a mantle, didst invest
The rising world of waters dark and deep,
Won from the void and formless Infinite!

*   *   *   *   *

For wonderful indeed are all his works.
Pleasant to know, and worthiest to be all
Had in remembrance always with delight!
But what created mind can comprehend
Their number, or the wisdom infinite
That brought them forth, but hid their causes deep?
I saw when, at his word, the formless mass,
This world's material mould, came to a heap:
Confusion heard his voice, and wild uproar
Stood ruled, stood vast Infinitude confined;
Till, at his second bidding, darkness fled,
Light shone, and order from disorder sprung.

              JOHN MILTON.

SPRING.

O! where the rosy-bosomed Hours,
　Fair Venus' train, appear,
　Disclose the long-expecting flowers
　And wake the purple year!
　The Attic warbler pours her throat
Responsive to the cuckoo's note,
The untaught harmony of spring:
While whispering pleasure as they fly,
Cool zephyrs through the clear blue sky
　Their gathered fragrance fling.

And float amid the liquid noon:
Some lightly o'er the current skim,
Some show their gayly gilded trim
　Quick-glancing to the sun.

To Contemplation's sober eye
　Such is the race of man;
And they that creep, and they that fly,
　Shall end where they began.
Alike the busy and the gay
But flutter through life's little day,

" Still is the toiling hand of care;
　The panting herds repose."

Where'er the oak's thick branches stretch
　A broader, browner shade,
Where'er the rude and moss-grown beech
　O'ercanopies the glade,
Beside some water's rushy brink
With me the Muse shall sit, and think
(At ease reclined in rustic state)
How vain the ardor of the crowd,
How low, how little are the proud,
　How indigent the great!

Still is the toiling hand of care;
　The panting herds repose:
Yet hark, how through the peopled air
　The busy murmur glows!
The insect youth are on the wing,
Eager to taste the honeyed spring

In Fortune's varying colors drest:　:
Brushed by the hand of rough mischance
Or chilled by age, their airy dance
　They leave, in dust to rest.

Methinks I hear in accents low
　The sportive kind reply:
Poor moralist! and what art thou?
　A solitary fly!
Thy joys no glittering female meets,
No hive hast thou of hoarded sweets,
No painted plumage to display;
On hasty wings thy youth is flown;
Thy sun is set. thy spring is gone,—
　We frolic while 't is May.

THOMAS GRAY.

A WINTER MORNING.

TIS morning; and the sun, with ruddy orb
  Ascending, fires the horizon; while the clouds
  That crowd away before the driving wind,
  More ardent as the disk emerges more,
  Resemble most some city in a blaze.
Seen through the leafless wood. His slanting ray
Slides ineffectual down the snowy vale,
And, tingeing all with his own rosy hue,
From every herb and every spiry blade
Stretches a length of shadow o'er the field.
Mine, spindling into longitude immense,
In spite of gravity, and sage remark
That I myself am but a fleeting shade,
Provokes me to a smile. With eye askance
I view the muscular proportioned limb
Transformed to a lean shank. The shapeless pair,
As they designed to mock me, at my side
Take step for step; and, as I near approach

The cottage, walk along the plastered wall,
Preposterous sight! the legs without the man.
The verdure of the plain lies buried deep
Beneath the dazzling deluge; and the bents,
And coarser grass upspearing o'er the rest,
Of late unsightly and unseen, now shine
Conspicuous, and in bright apparel clad,
And, fledged with icy feathers, not superb.
The cattle mourn in corners, where the fence
Screens them, and seem half petrified to sleep
In unrecumbent sadness. There they wait
Their wonted fodder; not, like hungering man,
Fretful if unsupplied; but silent, meek,
And patient of the slow-paced swain's delay.
He from the stack carves out the accustomed load,
Deep plunging, and again deep plunging oft,
His broad keen knife into the solid mass;
Smooth as a wall the upright remnant stands,

With such undeviating and even force
He severs it away: no needless care
Lest storms should overset the leaning pile
Deciduous, or its own unbalanced weight.
Forth goes the woodman, leaving unconcerned
The cheerful haunts of men — to wield the axe
And drive the wedge in yonder forest drear,
From morn to eve his solitary task.
Shaggy and lean and shrewd with pointed ears,
And tail cropped short, half lurcher and half cur,
His dog attends him. Close behind his heel
Now creeps he slow; and now, with many a frisk
Wide-scampering, snatches up the drifted snow
With ivory teeth, or ploughs it with his snout;
Then shakes his powdered coat, and barks for joy.

     *   *   *   *

Now from the roost, or from the neighboring pale,
Where, diligent to catch the first faint gleam
Of smiling day, they gossiped side by side,
Come trooping at the housewife's well-known call
The feathered tribes domestic. Half on wing
And half on foot, they brush the fleecy flood,
Conscious and fearful of too deep a plunge.
The sparrows peep, and quit the sheltering eaves
To seize the fair occasion. Well they eye
The scattered grain, and, thievishly resolved
To escape the impending famine, often scared
As oft return, a pert voracious kind.
Clean riddance quickly made, one only care
Remains to each, the search of sunny nook,
Or shed impervious to the blast. Resigned
To sad necessity, the cock foregoes
His wonted strut, and, wading at their head
With well-considered steps, seems to resent

His altered gait and stateliness retrenched.
How find the myriads, that in summer cheer
The hills and valleys with their ceaseless songs,
Due sustenance, or where subsist they now?
Earth yields them naught: the imprisoned worm is safe
Beneath the frozen clod; all seeds of herbs

"The sparrows peep, and quit the sheltering eaves."

Lie covered close; and berry-bearing thorns,
That feed the thrush (whatever some suppose),
Afford the smaller minstrels no supply.
The long protracted rigor of the year
Thins all their numerous flocks. In chinks and holes
Ten thousand seek an unmolested end,
An instinct prompts; self-buried ere they die.

                          WILLIAM COWPER.

WINTRY WEATHER.

INTER, wilt thou never, never go?
  O Summer, but I weary for thy coming,
  Longing once more to hear the Luggie flow,
  And frugal bees, laboriously humming.
Now the east wind diseases the infirm,
  And I must crouch in corners from rough weather;
Sometimes a winter sunset is a charm —
  When the fired clouds, compacted, blaze together,
  And the large sun dips red behind the hills.
I, from my window, can behold this pleasure;
  And the eternal moon, what time she fills
Her orb with argent, treading a soft measure,
  With queenly motions of a bridal mood,
Through the white spaces of infinitude.

                          DAVID GRAY.

    THE key of Nature is laid at man's feet, because he is its divinely-constituted sovereign.

" Then lads and lassies all, be gay,
For this is nature's holiday."

MAY-DAY.

THE daisies peep from every field,
  And violets sweet their odor yield;
The purple blossom paints the thorn,
And streams reflect the blush of morn.
    Then lads and lassies all, be gay,
    For this is nature's holiday.

Let lusty Labor drop his flail,
Nor woodman's hook a tree assail,
The ox shall cease his neck to bow,
And Clodden yield to rest the plough,

Behold the lark in ether float,
While rapture swells the liquid note!
What warbles he, with merry cheer?
" Let love and pleasure rule the year!"

Lo! Sol looks down with radiant eye,
And throws a smile around his sky;
Embracing hill and vale and stream,
And warming nature with his beam.

JOHN WOLCOTT.

THE EARLY PRIMROSE.

MILD offspring of a dark and sullen sire?
  Whose modest form, so delicately fine,
    Was nursed in whirling storms
    And cradled in the winds.

Thee, when young Spring first questioned Winter's
    sway,
And dared the sturdy blusterer to the fight,
    Thee on this bank he threw,
    To mark his victory.

In this low vale the promise of the year,
Serene, thou openest to the nipping gale,
    Unnoticed and alone,
    Thy tender elegance.

So Virtue blooms, brought forth amid the storms
Of chill adversity; in some lone walk
    Of life she rears her head,
    Obscure and unobserved;

While every bleaching breeze that on her blows
Chastens her spotless purity of breast,
    And hardens her to bear
    Serene the ills of life.

HENRY KIRKE WHITE.

IT came o'er my ear like the sweet South,
That breathes upon a bank of violets,
Stealing and giving odors.

LOVES OF THE PLANTS.

OW snow-drops cold and blue-eyed harebells
blend
Their tender tears, as o'er the streams they
bend,
The love-sick violet and the primrose pale
Bow their sweet heads and whisper to the gale;
With secret sighs the virgin lily droops,
And jealous cowslips hang their tawny cups.
How the young rose, in beauty's damask pride,
Drinks the warm blushes of his bashful bride;
With honeyed lips enamored woodbines meet,
Clasp with fond arms, and mix their kisses sweet!

Stay thy soft murmuring waters, gentle rill;
Hush, whispering winds; ye rustling leaves, be still;
Rest, silver butterflies, your quivering wings;
Alight, ye beetles, from your airy rings;
Ye painted moths, your gold-eyed plumage furl,
Bow your wide horns, your spiral trunks uncurl;
Glitter, ye glow-worms, on your mossy beds;
Descend, ye spiders, on your lengthened threads;
Slide here, ye horned snails, with varnished shells;
Ye bee-nymphs, listen in your waxen cells!

ERASMUS DARWIN.

Thou thy Creator's goodness dost declare,
And what dear gifts on thee he did not spare,
A stain to human sense in sin that lowers.
What soul can be so sick which by thy songs
(Attired in sweetness) sweetly is not driven
Quite to forget earth's turmoils, spites, and wrongs,
And lift a reverend eye and thought to heaven?
Sweet artless songster! thou my mind dost raise
To airs of spheres,—yes, and to angels' lays.

WILLIAM DRUMMOND.

TO A NIGHTINGALE.

WEET bird! that sing'st away the early hours
Of winters past, or coming, void of care;
Well pleaséd with delights which present are.
Fair seasons, budding sprays, sweet-smelling
flowers:
To rocks, to springs, to rills, from leafy bowers,

THE ANGLER.

N genial spring, beneath the quivering shade,
Where cooling vapors breathe along the mead,
The patient fisher takes his silent stand,
Intent, his angle trembling in his hand;
With looks unmoved, he hopes the scaly breed,
And eyes the dancing cork, and bending reed.

THE TIGER.

TIGER, tiger, burning bright
 In the forests of the night,
 What immortal hand or eye
 Could frame thy fearful symmetry?

What the hammer, what the chain?
In what furnace was thy brain?
What the anvil? what dread grasp
Dare its deadly terrors clasp?

" Tiger, tiger, burning bright
In the forests of the night."

In what distant deeps or skies
Burnt the fire of thine eyes?
On what wings dare he aspire?
What the hand dare seize thy fire?

And what shoulder, and what art,
Could twist the sinews of thy heart?
And when thy heart began to beat,
What dread hand formed thy dread feet?

When the stars threw down their spears,
And watered heaven with their tears,
Did He smile his work to see?
Did He who made the lamb make thee?

Tiger, tiger, burning bright,
In the forests of the night,
What immortal hand or eye
Dare frame thy fearful symmetry?

WILLIAM BLAKE.

THE thrush derives its name from mistletoe berries, of which it is exceedingly fond. It is famed for its clear, ringing, musical note, and sings loudest, and sweetest, and longest in storms; hence it is no mean teacher to man, whose song of gladness and gratitude should rise to heaven—not only when his sky is clear, but when it is darkened with clouds, and the storm portends fearful disasters.

"He clasps the crag with hookéd hands."

THE EAGLE.

HE clasps the crag with hookéd hands;
Close to the sun in lonely lands,
Ringed with the azure world, he stands.

The wrinkled sea beneath him crawls;
He watches from his mountain walls,
And like a thunderbolt he falls.

ALFRED TENNYSON.

WHAT a desolate place would be this world without a flower! It would be a face without a smile, — a feast without a welcome! Are not flowers the stars of the earth? and are not our stars the flowers of heaven?

A SUMMER MORN.

BUT who the melodies of morn can tell?
The wild brook babbling down the mountain-
   side;
The lowing herd; the sheepfold's simple bell;
The pipe of early shepherd dim descried
In the lone valley; echoing far and wide
The clamorous horn along the cliffs above;

Through rustling corn the hare astonished springs;
Slow tolls the village clock the drowsy hour;
The partridge bursts away on whirring wings;
Deep mourns the turtle in sequestered bower,
And shrill lark carols clear from her aerial tower.

O Nature, how in every charm supreme!
Whose votaries feast on raptures ever new!

"O Nature, how in every charm supreme."

The hollow murmur of the ocean tide;
The hum of bees, the linnet's lay of love,
And the full choir that wakes the universal grove.

The cottage curs at early pilgrim bark;
Crowned with her pail the tripping milkmaid sings;
The whistling ploughman stalks afield, and, hark!
Down the rough slope the ponderous wagon rings;

O, for the voice and fire of seraphim,
To sing thy glories with devotion due.
Blest be the day I 'scaped the wrangling crew
From Pyrrho's maze and Epicurus' sty.
And held high converse with the god-like few
Who to the enraptured heart and ear and eye
Teach beauty, virtue, truth, and love and melody.

JAMES BEATTIE.

SUNSET AT NORHAM CASTLE.

DAY set on Norham's castled steep,
　And Tweed's fair river broad and deep,
　　And Cheviot's mountains lone;
　The battled towers, the donjon keep,
　The loop-hole grates where captives weep,
The flanking walls that round it sweep,
　In yellow lustre shone.

The warriors on the turrets high,
Moving athwart the evening sky,
　Seemed forms of giant height;
Their armor, as it caught the rays,

Above the gloomy portal arch,
Timing his footsteps to a march,
　The warder kept his guard,
Low humming, as he paced along,
Some ancient border-gathering song.

A distant tramping sound he hears;
He looks abroad, and soon appears,
O'er Horncliff hill, a plump of spears
　Beneath a pennon gay:
A horseman, darting from the crowd,
Like lightning from a summer cloud,

" Cheviot's mountains lone."

Flashed back again the western blaze
　In lines of dazzling light.
St. George's banner, broad and gay,
Now faded, as the fading ray
　Less bright, and less, was flung;
The evening gale had scarce the power
To wave it on the donjon tower,
　So heavily it hung.

The scouts had parted on their search,
　The castle gates were barred;

Spurs on his mettled courser proud,
　Before the dark array.

Beneath the sable palisade,
That closed the castle barricade,
　His bugle-horn he blew;
The warder hasted from the wall,
And warned the captain in the hall,
　For well the blast he knew;
And joyfully that knight did call
To sewer, squire, and seneschal.

SIR WALTER SCOTT.

NATURE is like an Æolian harp, a musical instrument whose tones are the re-echo of higher strings within us.

TO THE DANDELION.

EAR common flower, that growest beside the
    way,
  Fringing the dusty road with harmless gold,
  First pledge of blithesome May,
Which children pluck, and, full of pride,
    uphold,
High-hearted buccaneers, o'erjoyed that they
An Eldorado in the grass have found,
  Which not the rich earth's ample round
May match in wealth — thou art more dear to me
Than all the prouder summer-blooms may be.

Gold such as thine ne'er drew the Spanish prow
Through the primeval hush of Indian seas,
  Nor wrinkled the lean brow
Of age, to rob the lover's heart of ease;
  'Tis the spring's largess, which she scatters now
To rich and poor alike, with lavish hand,
  Though most hearts never understand
To take it at God's value, but pass by
The offered wealth with unrewarded eye.

Thou art my tropics and mine Italy;
To look at thee unlocks a warmer clime;
  The eyes thou givest me
Are in the heart, and heed not space or time:
Not in mid June the golden-cuirassed bee
Feels a more summer-like, warm ravishment
  In the white lily's breezy tent,
His conquered Sybaris, than I, when first
From the dark green thy yellow circles burst.

Then think I of deep shadows on the grass, —
Of meadows where in sun the cattle graze,
  Where, as the breezes pass,
The gleaming rushes lean a thousand ways, —
Of leaves that slumber in a cloudy mass,
Or whiten in the wind, — of waters blue
  That from the distance sparkle through
Some woodland gap, — and of a sky above,
Where one white cloud like a stray lamb doth move.

My childhood's earliest thoughts are linked with
    thee;
The sight of thee calls back the robin's song,
  Who, from the dark old tree
Beside the door, sang clearly all day long,
And I, secure in childish piety,
Listened as if I heard an angel sing
  With news from heaven, which he did bring
Fresh every day to my untainted ears,
When birds and flowers and I were happy peers.

How like a prodigal doth nature seem,
When thou, for all thy gold, so common art!
  Thou teachest me to deem
More sacredly of every human heart,
Since each reflects in joy its scanty gleam
Of heaven, and could some wondrous secret show,
  Did we but pay the love we owe,
And with a child's undoubting wisdom look
On all these living pages of God's book.

                   J. R. LOWELL.

HYMN TO THE FLOWERS.

AY-STARS! that ope your eyes with morn to
    twinkle,
  From rainbow galaxies of earth's creation,
  And dew-drops on her lonely altars sprinkle
    As a libation!

Ye matin worshipers! who bending lowly
  Before the uprisen sun — God's lidless eye —
Throw from your chalices a sweet and holy
    Incense on high!

Ye bright mosaics! that with storied beauty
  The floor of Nature's temple tessellate,
What numerous emblems of instructive duty
    Your forms create!

'Neath cloistered boughs, each floral bell that swingeth
  And tolls its perfume on the passing air.
Makes Sabbath in the fields, and ever ringeth
    A call to prayer.

Not to the domes where crumbling arch and column
  Attest the feebleness of mortal hand,

But to that fane, most catholic and solemn,
    Which God hath planned;

To that cathedral, boundless as our wonder,
  Whose quenchless lamps the sun and moon supply—
Its choir the winds and waves, its organ thunder,
    Its dome the sky.

There— as in solitude and shade I wander
  Through the green aisles, or, stretched upon the
    sod,
Awed by the silence, reverently ponder
    The ways of God —

Your voiceless lips, O Flowers, are living preachers,
  Each cup a pulpit, and each leaf a book,
Supplying to my fancy numerous teachers
    From loneliest nook.

Floral Apostles! that in dewy splendor
  " Weep without woe, and blush without a crime,"
Oh, may I deeply learn, and ne'er surrender,
    Your lore sublime!

"Thou wert not, Solomon! in all thy glory,
  Arrayed," the lilies cry, "in robes like ours;
How vain your grandeur! Ah, how transitory
      Are human flowers!"

In the sweet-scented pictures, Heavenly Artist!
  With which thou paintest Nature's wide-spread hall,
What a delightful lesson thou impartest
      Of love to all.

Ephemeral sages! what instructors hoary
  For such a world of thought could furnish scope?
Each fading calyx a *memento mori*,
      Yet fount of hope.

Posthumous glories! angel-like collection!
  Upraised from seed or bulb interred in earth,
Ye are to me a type of resurrection,
      And second birth.

"There — as in solitude and shade I wander
  Through the green aisles, . . . "

Not useless are ye, Flowers! though made for
          pleasure:
  Blooming o'er field and wave, by day and night,
From every source your sanction bids me treasure
      Harmless delight.

Were I, O God, in churchless lands remaining,
  Far from all voice of teachers or divines,
My soul would find, in flowers of thy ordaining,
      Priests, sermons, shrines!

                    HORACE SMITH.

SOLACE IN NATURE.

NATURE never did betray
    The heart that loved her. 'Tis her privilege,
  Through all the years of this our life, to lead
  From joy to joy; for she can so inform
  The mind that is within us, so impress
With quietness and beauty, and so feed
With lofty thoughts, that neither evil tongues,
Rash judgments, nor the sneers of selfish men,
Nor greetings where no kindness is, nor all
The dreary intercourse of daily life,
Shall e'er prevail against us, or disturb
Our cheerful faith, that all which we behold
Is full of blessings.

                    Therefore let the moon
Shine on thee in thy solitary walk;
And let the misty mountain winds be free
To blow against thee; and, in after years,
When these wild ecstasies shall be matured
Into a sober pleasure; when the mind
Shall be a mansion for all lovely forms;
Thy memory be as a dwelling-place
For all sweet sounds and harmonies: oh! then,
If solitude, or fear, or pain, or grief,
Should be thy portion, with what healing thoughts
Of tender joy wilt thou remember me,
And these my exhortations!

                    WILLIAM WORDSWORTH.

JUNE.

EARTH gets its price for what Earth gives us;
    The beggar is taxed for a corner to die in;
    The priest has his fee who comes and shrives us;
      We bargain for the graves we lie in;
At the Devil's booth are all things sold,
Each ounce of dross costs its ounce of gold;
    For a cap and bells our lives we pay,
Bubbles we buy with the whole soul's tasking;
'Tis heaven alone that is given away,
'Tis only God may be had for the asking;
No price is set on the lavish summer,
June may be had by the poorest comer.

Every clod feels a stir of might,
    An instinct within it that reaches and towers,
And, groping blindly above it for light,
    Climbs to a soul in grass and flowers;
The flush of life may well be seen
    Thrilling back over hills and valleys;
The cowslip startles in meadows green,
    The buttercup catches the sun in its chalice,
And there's never a leaf or a blade too mean
    To be some happy creature's palace;
The little bird sits at his door in the sun,
    Atilt like a blossom among the leaves,

" Now is the high-tide of the
    year,
And whatever of life hath
   ebbed away
Comes flooding back, with a
   ripply cheer."

And what is so rare as a day in June?
    Then, if ever, come perfect days;
Then heaven tries the earth if it be in tune,
    And over it softly her warm ear lays.
Whether we look, or whether we listen,
We hear life murmur, or see it glisten;

And lets his illumined being o'errun
    With the deluge of summer it receives;
His mate feels the eggs beneath her wings,
And the heart in her dumb breast flutters and sings,
He sings to the wide world, and she to her nest,—
In the nice ear of Nature, which song is the best?

Now is the high-tide of the year,
 And whatever of life hath ebbed away
Comes flooding back, with a ripply cheer,
 Into every bare inlet and creek and bay;
Now the heart is so full that a drop overfills it,
We are happy now because God wills it;
No matter how barren the past may have been,
'Tis enough for us now that the leaves are green;
We sit in the warm shade and feel right well
How the sap creeps up and the blossoms swell;
We may shut our eyes, but we cannot help knowing
That skies are clear and grass is growing;
The breeze comes whispering in our ear
That dandelions are blossoming near,
 That maize has sprouted, that streams are flowing,
That the river is bluer than the sky,
That the robin is plastering his house hard by;
And if the breeze kept the good news back,
For other couriers we should not lack;

We could guess it all by yon heifer's lowing, —
And hark! how clear bold chanticleer,
Warmed with the new wine of the year,
 Tells all in his lusty crowing!
Joy comes, grief goes, we know not how;
Everything is happy now,
 Everything is upward striving;
'Tis as easy now for the heart to be true
As for grass to be green or skies to be blue,
 'Tis the natural way of living:
Who knows whither the clouds have fled?
In the unscarred heaven they leave no wake,
And the eyes forget the tears they have shed,
 The heart forgets its sorrow and ache;
The soul partakes the season's youth,
 And the sulphurous rifts of passion and woe
Lie deep 'neath a silence pure and smooth,
Like burnt-out craters healed with snow.

JAMES RUSSELL LOWELL.

TO A MOUNTAIN DAISY.

ON TURNING ONE DOWN WITH A PLOUGH.

WEE, modest, crimson-tippéd flower,
 Thou's met me in an evil hour;
For I maun crush amang the stoure
 Thy slender stem:
To spare thee now is past my power,
 Thou bonnie gem.

Alas! it's no thy neebor sweet,
The bonnie lark, companion meet,
Bending thee 'mang the dewy weet,
 Wi' speckled breast,
When upward springing, blithe to greet
 The purpling east!

Cauld blew the bitter-biting north
Upon thy early, humble birth;
Yet cheerfully thou glinted forth
 Amid the storm;
Scarce reared above the parent earth
 Thy tender form!

The flaunting flowers our gardens yield
High sheltering woods and wa's maun shield;
But thou beneath the random bield
 O' clod or stane
Adorns the histie stibble-field,
 Unseen, alane.

There, in thy scanty mantle clad,
Thy snawy bosom sunward spread,
Thou lifts thy unassuming head
 In humble guise;

But now the share uptears thy bed,
 And low thou lies!

Such is the fate of artless maid,
Sweet floweret of the rural shade!
By love's simplicity betrayed,
 And guileless trust,
Till she, like thee, all soiled is laid
 Low i' the dust.

Such is the fate of simple bard,
On life's rough ocean luckless starred!
Unskilful he to note the card
 Of prudent lore,
Till billows rage, and gales blow hard,
 And whelm him o'er!

Such fate to suffering worth is given,
Who long with wants and woes has striven,
By human pride or cunning driven
 To misery's brink,
Till, wrenched of every stay but Heaven,
 He, ruined, sink!

E'en thou who mourn'st the daisy's fate,
That fate is thine — no distant date;
Stern Ruin's ploughshare drives, elate,
 Full on thy bloom,
Till crushed beneath the furrow's weight,
 Shall be thy doom!

ROBERT BURNS.

10

"I in these flowery meads would be,
These crystal streams should solace me."

THE ANGLER'S WISH.

IN these flowery meads would be,
  These crystal streams should solace me;
  To whose harmonious bubbling noise,
I with my Angle would rejoice,
  Sit here, and see the turtle-dove,
  Court his chaste mate to acts of love:

And raise my low-pitch'd thoughts above
Earth, or what poor mortals love:
  Thus free from lawsuits, and the noise
  Of princes' courts, I would rejoice:

Or with my Bryan and a book,
Loiter long days near Shawford Brook;

"Or with my Bryan and a book,
Loiter long days near Shawford Brook."

Or on that bank, feel the west wind
Breathe health and plenty, please my mind
To see sweet dew-drops kiss these flowers,
And then wash off by April showers:
  Here hear my Kenna sing a song,
  There see a blackbird feed her young,

Or a laverock build her nest;
Here give my weary spirits rest,

There sit by him, and eat my meat,
There see the sun both rise and set;
There bid good-morning to next day;
There meditate my time away;
  And angle on, and beg to have
  A quiet passage to a welcome grave.

IZAAK WALTON.

THE BROOM.

H! the broom, the bonny, bonny broom,
On my native hills it grows;
I had rather see the bonny broom,
Than the rarest flower that blows.
Oh! the yellow broom is blossoming,
In my own dear country;
I never thought so small a thing
As a flower my nerveless heart could wring,
Or draw a tear from me.

It minds me of my native hills,
Clad in the heath and fen;
Of the green strath and the flowery brae,
Of the glade and the rockless glen;

It minds me of dearer things than these—
Of love with life entwined,
Of humble faith on bended knees,
Of home joys gone, and memories,
Like sere leaves, left behind!

It minds me of that blessed time,
Of the friends so true to me,
Of my warm-hearted Highland love,
When the broom was the trysting-tree.
I loathe this fair but foreign strand,
With its fadeless summer bloom;
And I swear, by my own dear native land,
Again on the heathy hills to stand,
Where waves the yellow broom.

MARY HOWITT.

" Still on thy banks so gayly green
May numerous flocks and herds be seen."

ODE TO LEVEN WATER.

N Leven's banks, while free to rove
And tune the rural pipe to love,
I envied not the happiest swain
That ever trod th' Arcadian plain.
Pure stream, in whose transparent wave
My youthful limbs I wont to lave,
No torrents stain thy limpid source,
No rocks impede thy dimpling course,
That sweetly warbles o'er its bed,
With white, round, polished pebbles spread;
While, lightly poised, the scaly brood
In myriads cleave thy crystal flood;
The springing trout, in speckled pride;
The salmon, monarch of the tide;

The ruthless pike, intent on war;
The silver eel, and mottled par;
Devolving from thy parent lake,
A charming maze thy waters make,
By bowers of birch and groves of pine,
And edges flowered with eglantine.
Still on thy banks so gayly green
May numerous flocks and herds be seen;
And lasses chanting o'er the pail;
And shepherds piping in the dale;
And ancient faith that knows no guile,
And industry imbrowned by toil,
And hearts resolved, and hands prepared,
The blessings they enjoy to guard.

TOBIAS GEORGE SMOLLET.

A SPRING DAY.

DVANCING spring profusely spreads abroad
  Flowers of all hues, with sweetest fragrance
    stored;
    Where'er she treads Love gladdens over plain,
Delight on tiptoe bears her lucid train;
Sweet Hope with conscious brow before her flies,
Anticipating wealth from Summer skies;

All Nature feels her renovating sway;
The sheep-fed pasture, and the meadows gay;
And trees, and shrubs, no longer budding seen,
Display the new-grown branch of lighter green;
On airy downs the idling shepherd lies,
And sees to-morrow in the marbled skies.

                 ROBERT BLOOMFIELD.

"The sheep-fed pasture, and the meadows gay."

THE LITTLE BEACH-BIRD.

HOU little bird, thou dweller by the sea,
  Why takest thou its melancholy voice?
    Why with that boding cry
    O'er the waves dost thou fly?
O, rather, bird, with me
  Through the fair land rejoice!

Thy flitting form comes ghostly dim and pale,
  As driven by a beating storm at sea;
    Thy cry is weak and scared,
    As if thy mates had shared
The doom of us. Thy wail —
  What does it bring to me?

Thou call'st along the sand, and haunt'st the surge,
  Restless and sad; as if, in strange accord
    With motion and with roar
    Of waves that drive to shore,
One spirit did ye urge —
  The Mystery — the Word.

Of thousands thou both sepulchre and pall,
  Old ocean, art! A requiem o'er the dead,
    From out thy gloomy cells,
    A tale of mourning tells, —
Tells of man's woe and fall,
  His sinless glory fled.

Then turn thee, little bird, and take thy flight
  Where the complaining sea shall sadness bring
    Thy spirit nevermore.
    Come, quit with me the shore,
For gladness and the light,
  Where birds of summer sing.

             RICHARD HENRY DANA.

O daintie flowre or herbe that growes on grownd,
  No arborett with painted blossoms drest
And smelling sweete, but there it might be fownd
To bud out faire, and throwe her sweete smels al
    arownd.

"Hundreds have come to view
My grandeur in decay."

THE AGED OAK AT OAKLEY.

WAS a young fair tree;
Each spring with quivering green
My boughs were clad, and far
Down the deep vale a light
Shone from me on the eyes
Of those who pass'd, — a light
That told of sunny days,
And blossoms, and blue sky;
For I was ever first
Of all the grove to hear
The soft voice underground
Of the warm-working spring,

And ere my brethren stirr'd
Their sheathéd bud, the kine,
And the kine's keeper, came
Slow up the valley path,
And laid them underneath
My cool and rustling leaves,
And I could feel them there
As in the quiet shade
They stood with tender thoughts,
That passed along their life
Like wings on a still lake,
Blessing me; and to God,

The blessed God, who cares
For all my little leaves,
Went up the silent praise;
And I was glad with joy
Which life of laboring things
Ill knows— the joy that sinks
Into a life of rest.
Ages have fled since then,
But deem not my fierce trunk
And scanty leafage serve
No high behest; my name
Is sounded far and wide;
And in the Providence
That guides the steps of men,

Hundreds have come to view
My grandeur in decay;
And there hath pass'd from me
A quiet influence
Into the minds of men:
The silver head of age,
The majesty of laws,
The very name of God,
And holiest things that are,
Have won upon the heart
Of human kind the more,
For that I stand to meet
With vast and bleaching trunk,
The rudeness of the sky.

HENRY ALFORD.

THE PHEASANT.

CLOSE by the borders of the fringèd lake,
    And on the oak's expanded bough, is seen,
    What time the leaves the passing zephyrs shake,
    And gently murmur through the sylvan scene,
    The gaudy Pheasant, rich in varying dyes,
That fade alternate, and alternate glow:
Receiving now his color from the skies,
And now reflecting back the watery bow.
He flaps his wings, erects his spotless crest,
His flaming eyes dart forth a piercing ray;
He swells the lovely plumage of his breast,
And glares a wonder of the Orient day.

THE THRUSH.

SONGSTER of the russet coat,
    Full and liquid is thy note;
    Plain thy dress, but great thy skill,
    Captivating at thy will.

Small musician of the field,
Near my bower thy tribute yield,
Little servant of the ear,
Ply thy task, and never fear.

I will learn from thee to praise
God, the Author of my days;
I will learn from thee to sing,
Christ, my Saviour and my King;
Learn to labor with my voice,
Make the sinking heart rejoice.

AT last the golden oriental gate
    Of greatest heaven 'gan to open fair,
And Phœbus, fresh as bridegroom to his mate,
Came dancing forth, shaking his dewy hair;
And hurls his glistening beams through gloomy air.

SNOW.

THE blessed morn has come again;
        The early gray
Taps at the slumberer's window-pane,
        And seems to say,
Break, break from the enchanter's chain
        Away, away!

'Tis winter, yet there is no sound
        Along the air
Of winds along their battle-ground;
        But gently there
The snow is falling. — all around
        How fair, how fair!

RALPH HOYT.

THE O'LINCOLN FAMILY.

FLOCK of merry singing-birds were sporting
    in the grove:
Some were warbling cheerily, and some were
    making love:
There were Bobolincon, Wadolincon, Winter-
    seeble, Conquedle, —
A livelier set was never led by tabor, pipe, or fiddle.—
Crying, "Phew, shew, Wadolincon, see, see, Bob-
    olincon,
Down among the tickletops, hiding in the buttercups!
I know the saucy chap, I see his shining cap
Bobbing in the clover there, — see, see, see!"

Up flies Bobolincon, perching on an apple-tree,
Startled by his rival's song, quickened by his
    raillery;
Soon he spies the rogue afloat, curvetting in the air,
And merrily he turns about, and warns him to
    beware!
"'Tis you that would a-wooing go, down among the
    rushes O!

But wait a week, till flowers are cheery, — wait a
    week, and, ere you marry,
Be sure of a house wherein to tarry!
Wadolink, Whiskodink, Tom Denny, wait, wait,
    wait!"

Every one's a funny fellow; every one's a little
    mellow;
Follow, follow, follow, follow, o'er the hill and in the
    hollow!
Merrily, merrily, there they hie; now they rise and
    now they fly;
They cross and turn, and in and out, and down in the
    middle, and wheel about, —
With a "Phew, shew, Wadolincon! listen to me, Bob-
    olincon! —
Happy's the wooing that's speedily doing, that's
    speedily doing,
That's merry and over with the bloom of the clover!
Bobolincon, Wadolincon, Winterseeble, follow, follow
    me!"

WILSON FLAGG.

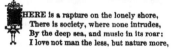

SOLITUDE OF THE SEA.

HERE is a rapture on the lonely shore,
    There is society, where none intrudes,
    By the deep sea, and music in its roar:
    I love not man the less, but nature more,

From these our interviews, in which I steal
From all I may be, or have been before,
To mingle with the universe, and feel
What I can ne'er express, yet cannot all conceal.

LORD BYRON.

SUMMER DROUGHT.

WHEN winter came the land was lean and sere,
   There fell no snow, and oft from wild and
      field
  In famished tameness came the drooping deer,
   And licked the waste about the troughs
     congealed.

And though at spring we plowed and proffered seed,
  It lay ungermed, a pillage for the birds;
And unto one low dam, in urgent need,
  We daily drove the suppliant lowing herds.

But now the fields to barren wastes have run,
  The dam a pool of oozing greenery lies,
Where knots of gnats hang reeling in the sun
  . Till early dusk, when tilt the dragon-flies.

Yet ere the noon, as brass the heaven turns,
  The cruel sun smites with unerring aim,
The sight and touch of all things blinds and burns,
  And bare, hot hills seem shimmering into flame!

On either side the shoe-deep dusted lane
  The meagre wisps of fennel scorch to wire:
Slow lags the team that drags an empty wain,
  And, creaking dry, a wheel runs off its tire.

No flock upon the naked pasture feeds,
  No blithesome "Bob-White" whistles from the
     fence;
A gust runs crackling through the brittle weeds,
  And heat and silence seem the more intense!

" —— A pillage for the birds."

All night the craw-fish deeper digs her wells,
  As shows the clay that freshly curbs them round;
And many a random upheaved tunnel tells
  Where ran the mole across the fallow ground.

But ah, the stone-dumb dullness of the dawn,
  When e'en the cocks too listless are to crow,
And lies the world as from all life withdrawn,
  Unheeding and outworn and swooning low!

There is no dew on any greenness shed,
  The hard-baked earth is split along the walks,
The very burs in stunted clumps are dead,
  And mullein-leaves drop withered from the stalks.

On outspread wings a hawk, far poised on high,
  Quick swooping screams, and then is heard no
     more:
The strident shrilling of a locust nigh
  Breaks forth, and dies in silence as before.

No transient cloud o'erskims with flakes of shade
  The landscape hazed in dizzy gleams of heat;
A dove's wing glances like a parried blade,
  And western walls the beams in torrents beat.

So burning, low and lower still the sun,
  In fierce white fervor, sinks anon from sight,
And so the dread, despairing day is done,
  And dumbly broods again the haggard night!

                  J. P. IRVINE.

"The castled crag of Drachenfels
Frowns o'er the wide and winding Rhine."

THE RHINE.

THE castled crag of Drachenfels
　Frowns o'er the wide and winding Rhine,
Whose breast of waters broadly swells
　Between the banks which bear the vine,
And hill all rich with blossomed trees,
　And fields which promise corn and wine,
And scattered cities crowning these,
　Whose far white walls along them shine,
Have strewed a scene, which I should see
With double joy wert thou with me.

And peasant girls with deep-blue eyes,
　And hands which offer early flowers,
Walk smiling o'er this paradise;
　Above, the frequent feudal towers
Through green leaves lift their walls of gray,
　And many a rock which steeply lowers,
And noble arch in proud decay,
　Look o'er this vale of vintage-bowers;
But one thing want tuese banks of Rhine,—
Thy gentle hand to clasp in mine

I send the lilies given to me:
  Though long before thy hand they touch
I know that they must withered be,
  But yet reject them not as such;
For I have cherished them as dear,
  Because they yet may meet thine eye,
And guide thy soul to mine even here,
  When thou behold'st them drooping nigh,
And know'st them gathered by the Rhine,
And offered from my heart to thine!

The river nobly foams and flows,
  The charm of this enchanted ground,
And all its thousand turns disclose
  Some fresher beauty varying round:
The haughtiest breast its wish might bound
  Through life to dwell delighted here;
Nor could on earth a spot be found
  To nature and to me so dear,
Could thy dear eyes in following mine
Still sweeten more these banks of Rhine.

LORD BYRON.

TO A MOUNTAIN OAK.

PROUD mountain giant, whose majestic face,
  From thy high watch-tower on the steadfast
    rock,
Looks calmly o'er the trees that throng thy base,
How long hast thou withstood the tempest's
  shock?

How long hast thou looked down on yonder vale,
  Sleeping in sun before thee;
Or bent thy ruffled brow to let the gale
  Steer its white, drifting sails just o'er thee?

GEORGE HENRY BOKER.

THERE is a serene and settled majesty in forest scenery that enters into the soul, and dilates and elevates it, and fills it with noble inclinations. The ancient and hereditary groves, too, which everywhere abound, are most of them full of story. They are haunted by the recollections of the great spirits of past ages who have sought relaxation among them from the tumult of arms or the toils of state, or have wooed the muse beneath their shade.

FOREST PICTURES.

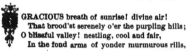 GRACIOUS breath of sunrise! divine air!
   That brood'st serenely o'er the purpling hills;
O blissful valley! nestling, cool and fair,
   In the fond arms of yonder murmurous rills,

The fitful breezes, fraught with forest balm,
   Faint, in rare wafts of perfume, on my brow;
The woven lights and shadows, rife with calm,
   Creep slantwise 'twixt the foliage, bough on bough

" O blissful valley! nestling, cool and fair,
In the fond arms of yonder murmurous rills."

Breathing their grateful measures to the sun;
O dew-besprinkled paths, that circling run
Through sylvan shades and solemn silences,
Once more ye bring my fevered spirit peace!

Uplifted heavenward, like a verdant cloud
Whose rain is music, soft as love, or loud
With jubilant hope, — for there, entranced, apart,
The mock-bird sings, close, close to Nature's heart.

Shy forms about the greenery, out and in,
 Flit 'neath the broadening glories of the morn;
The squirrel — that quaint sylvan harlequin —
 Mounts the tall trunks; while swift as lightning, born

The deer-hound's voice, sweet as the golden bell's,
Prolonged by flying echoes round the dells,
And up the loftiest summits wildly borne,
Blent with the blast of some keen huntsman's horn.

"The squirrel — that quaint sylvan harlequin."

Of summer mists, from tangled vine and tree
Dart the dove's pinions, pulsing vividly
Down the dense glades, till glimmering far and gray
The dusky vision softly melts away!

In transient, pleased bewilderment, I mark
 The last dim shimmer of those lessening wings.
When from lone copse and shadowy covert, hark!
 What mellow tongue through all the woodland
  rings!

And now the checkered vale is left behind;
 I climb the slope, and reach the hill-top bright;
Here, in bold freedom, swells a sovereign wind,
 Whose gusty prowess sweeps the pine-clad height;
While the pines,— dreamy Titans roused from sleep,—
Answer with mighty voices, deep on deep
Of wakened foliage surging like a sea;
And o'er them smiles Heaven's calm infinity!

                    PAUL HAMILTON HAYNE.

FLOWERS.

E valleys low', where the mild whispers rise
  Of shades, and wanton winds, and gushing
    brooks
  On whose fresh lap the swart-star sparely looks:
Throw hither all your quaint enameled eyes,
That on the green turf suck the honeyed showers,
And purple all the ground with vernal flowers.

Bring the rathe primrose that forsaken dies,
The tufted crow-toe, and pale jessamine,
The white pink, and the pansy freaked with jet,
The glowing violet,
The musk-rose, and the well-attired woodbine,
With cowslips wan that hang the pensive head,
And every flower that sad embroidery wears.

                    JOHN MILTON.

"Oft have I walked these woodland paths."

UNDER THE LEAVES.

OFT have I walked these woodland paths,
  Without the blest foreknowing
That underneath the withered leaves
  The fairest buds were growing.

To-day the south wind sweeps away
  The types of autumn's splendor,
And shows the sweet arbutus flowers,
  Spring's children, pure and tender.

O prophet-flowers! — with lips of bloom,
  Out-vying in your beauty
The pearly tints of ocean shells, —
  Ye teach me faith and duty!

"Walk life's dark ways," ye seem to say,
  "With love's divine foreknowing,
That where man sees but withered leaves,
  God sees sweet flowers growing."

ALBERT LAIGHTON.

WINTER.

WINTER, ruler of the inverted year,
  Thy scattered hair with sleet-like ashes filled,
  Thy breath congealed upon thy lips, thy cheeks
  Fringed with a beard made white with other
    snows
Than those of age, thy forehead wrapped in clouds,
A leafless branch thy sceptre, and thy throne
A sliding car, indebted to no wheels,
But urged by storms along its slippery way,
I love thee, all unlovely as thou seem'st,
And dreaded as thou art! Thou hold'st the sun
A prisoner in the yet undawning east,
Shortening his journey between morn and noon,

And hurrying him, impatient of his stay,
Down to the rosy west; but kindly still
Compensating his loss with added hours
Of social converse and instructive ease,
And gathering, at short notice, in one group
The family dispersed, and fixing thought,
Not less dispersed by daylight and its cares.
I crown thee king of intimate delights,
Fireside enjoyments, home-born happiness,
And all the comforts that the lowly roof
Of undisturbed retirement, and the hours
Of long uninterrupted evening know.

WILLIAM COWPER.

THE FLOWER'S NAME.

ERE'S the garden she walked across,
　Arm in my arm, such a short while since:
Hark! now I push its wicket, the moss
　Hinders the hinges, and makes them wince.
She must have reached the shrub ere she turned,
　As back with that murmur the wicket swung;
For she laid the poor snail my chance foot spurned,
　To feed and forget it the leaves among.

Down this side of the gravel-walk
　She went while her robe's edge brushed the box;
And here she paused in her gracious talk
　To point me a moth on the milk-white phlox.
Roses, ranged in valiant row,
　I will never think that she passed you by!
She loves you, noble roses, I know;
　But yonder see where the rock-plants lie!

This flower she stopped at, finger on lip,—
　Stooped over, in doubt, as settling its claim;
Till she gave me, with pride to make no slip,
　Its soft meandering Spanish name.
What a name! was it love or praise?
　Speech half asleep, or song half awake?
I must learn Spanish one of these days,
　Only for that slow sweet name's sake.

Roses, if I live and do well,
　I may bring her one of these days,
To fix you fast with as fine a spell,—
　Fit you each with his Spanish phrase.
But do not detain me now, for she lingers
　There, like a sunshine over the ground;
And ever I see her soft white fingers
　Searching after the bud she found.

Flower, you Spaniard! look that you grow not,—
　Stay as you are, and be loved forever!
Bud, if I kiss you, 'tis that you blow not,—
　Mind! the shut pink mouth opens never!
For while thus it pouts, her fingers wrestle,
　Twinkling the audacious leaves between,
Till round they turn, and down they nestle:
　Is not the dear mark still to be seen?

Where I find her not, beauties vanish;
　Whither I follow her, beauties flee.
Is there no method to tell her in Spanish
　June's twice June since she breathed it with me?
Come, bud! show me the least of her traces;
　Treasure my lady's lightest footfall:
Ah! you may flout and turn up your faces,—
　Roses, you are not so fair, after all!

ROBERT BROWNING.

SPRING IN CAROLINA.

PRING, with that nameless pathos in the air
　Which dwells with all things fair,
　Spring, with her golden suns and silver rain,
　Is with us once again.

Out in the lonely woods the jasmine burns
　Its fragrant lamps, and turns
Into a royal court with green festoons
　The banks of dark lagoons.

In the deep heart of every forest tree
　The blood is all aglee,
And there's a look about the leafless bowers,
　As if they dreamed of flowers.

Yet still on every side we trace the hand
　Of winter in the land,
Save where the maple reddens on the lawn,
　Flushed by the season's dawn;

Or where, like those strange semblances we find
　That age to childhood bind,
The elm puts on, as if in Nature's scorn,
　The brown of autumn corn.

As yet the turf is dark, although you know
　That, not a span below,

A thousand germs are groping through the gloom,
　And soon will burst their tomb.

In gardens you may note amid the dearth
　The crocus breaking earth;
And near the snow-drop's tender white and green,
　The violet in its screen.

But many gleams and shadows needs must pass
　Along the budding grass,
And weeks go by, before the enamored South
　Shall kiss the rose's mouth.

Still there's sense of blossoms yet unborn
　In the sweet airs of morn;
One almost looks to see the very street
　Grow purple at his feet.

At times a fragrant breeze comes floating by,
　And brings, you know not why,
A feeling as when eager crowds await
　Before a palace gate

Some wondrous pageant; and you scarce would start,
　If from a beech's heart
A blue-eyed Dryad, stepping forth, should say,
　"Behold me! I am May!"

　　*　　　*　　　*

HENRY TIMROD.

THE LARK.

O! here the gentle lark, weary of rest,   The sun ariseth in his majesty;
  From his moist cabinet mounts up on high,   Who doth the world so gloriously behold,
  And wakes the morning, from whose silver   That cedar-tops and hills seem burnish'd gold.
    breast   WILLIAM SHAKESPEARE.

GRIZZLY.

COWARD, of heroic size,   O'er the bee's or squirrel's hoard;
  In whose lazy muscles lies   Whiskered chin, and feeble nose,
  Strength we fear, and yet despise;   Claws of steel, on baby toes.—
  Savage,—whose relentless tusks   Here, in solitude and shade,
  Are content with acorn husks;   Shambling, shuffling, plantigrade,
Robber,—whose exploits ne'er soared   Be thy courses undismayed!

Here, where Nature makes thy bed,
Let thy rude, half-human tread
  Point to hidden Indian springs,
Lost in fern and fragrant grasses
Hovered o'er by timid wings.
Where the wood-duck lightly passes,
Where the wild bee holds her sweets—
  Epicurean retreats,
Fit for thee, and better than
Fearful spoils of dangerous man.

In thy fat-jowled deviltry,
Friar Tuck shall live in thee;
Thou may'st levy tithe and dole;
  Thou shalt spread the woodland cheer,
From the pilgrim taking toll;
  Match thy cunning with his fear,
Eat and drink and have thy fill;
Yet remain an outlaw still!

BRET HARTE.

THE VIOLET.

FAINT, delicious spring-time violet!
  Thine odor, like a key,
Turns noiselessly in memory's wards to let
  A thought of sorrow free.

The breath of distant fields upon my brow
  Blows through that open door
The sound of wind-borne bells, more sweet and low
  And sadder than of yore.

It comes afar, from that beloved place,
  And that beloved hour,
When life hung ripening in love's golden grace,
  Like grapes above a bower.

A spring goes singing through its reedy grass;
  The lark sings o'er my head,
Drowned in the sky—O, pass, ye visions, pass!
  I would that I were dead!—

Why hast thou opened that forbidden door,
  From which I ever flee?
O vanished joy! O love, that art no more,
  Let my vexed spirit be!

O violet! thy odor through my brain
  Hath searched and stung to grief
This sunny day, as if a curse did stain
  Thy velvet leaf.

WILLIAM WETMORE STORY.

CALM AND STORM ON LAKE LEMAN.

CLEAR, placid Leman! thy contrasted lake,
  With the wild world I dwelt in, is a thing
  Which warns me, with its stillness, to forsake
Earth's troubled waters for a purer spring.
  This quiet sail is as a noiseless wing
To waft me from distraction; once I loved
Torn ocean's roar, but thy soft murmuring
Sounds sweet as if a sister's voice reproved,
That I with stern delights should e'er have been so
  moved.

It is the hush of night, and all between
Thy margin and the mountains, dusk, yet clear,
Mellowed and mingling, yet distinctly seen,
Save darkened Jura, whose capt heights appear
Precipitously steep; and drawing near,

There breathes a living fragrance from the shore,
Of flowers yet fresh with childhood; on the ear
Drops the light drip of the suspended oar,
Or chirps the grasshopper one good-night carol more:
     *   *   .   *   *

The sky is changed!—and such a change! O night,
And storm, and darkness, ye are wondrous strong,
Yet lovely in your strength, as is the light
Of a dark eye in woman! Far along,
From peak to peak, the rattling crags among
Leaps the live thunder! Not from one lone cloud,
But every mountain now hath found a tongue,
And Jura answers, through her misty shroud,
Back to the joyous Alps, who call to her aloud!

LORD BYRON.

FREEDOM OF NATURE.

CARE not, Fortune, what you me deny:
  You cannot rob me of free Nature's grace;
  You cannot shut the windows of the sky,
Through which Aurora shows her brightening
  face;

You cannot bar my constant feet to trace
The woods and lawns, by living stream, at eve;
Let health my nerves and finer fibres brace,
And I their toys to the great children leave;
Of fancy, reason, virtue, naught can me bereave.

JAMES THOMSON.

11

THREE SUMMER STUDIES.

MORNING.

THE cock hath crowed. I hear the doors un-
  barred;
  Down to the grass-grown porch my way I
  take,
And hear, beside the well within the yard,
  Full many an ancient quacking, splashing
  drake,

The tall, green spears, with all their dewy load,
Which grow beside the well-known pasture-road.

A humid polish is on all the leaves,—
  The birds flit in and out with varied notes,
The noisy swallows twitter 'neath the eaves,
  A partridge whistle through the garden floats,
While yonder gaudy peacock harshly cries,
As red and gold flush all the eastern skies.

"The noisy swallows twitter 'neath the eaves."

And gabbling goose, and noisy brood-hen,—all
Responding to yon strutting gobbler's call.

The dew is thick upon the velvet grass,
  The porch-rails hold it in translucent drops,
And as the cattle from the enclosure pass,
  Each one, alternate, slowly halts and crops

Up comes the sun! Through the dense leaves a spot
  Of splendid light drinks up the dew; the breeze
Which late made leafy music, dies; the day grows hot,
  And slumbrous sounds come from marauding bees:
The burnished river like a sword-blade shines,
Save where 't is shadowed by the solemn pines.

"The passing curls in the river stand,
Telling the coolness which its wave leaves there."

NOON.

Over the farm is brooding silence now,—
  No reaper's song, no raven's clangor harsh,
No bleat of sheep, no distant low of cow,
  No croak of frogs within the spreading marsh,
No bragging cock from littered farmyard crows,—
The scene is steeped in silence and repose.

A trembling haze hangs over all the fields,—
  The panting cattle in the river stand,
Seeking the coolness which its wave scarce yields,
  It seems a Sabbath through the drowsy land;
So hushed is all beneath the Summer's spell,
I pause and listen for some faint church-bell.

The leaves are motionless, the song-birds mute;
  The very air seems somnolent and sick:
The spreading branches with o'er-ripened fruit
  Show in the sunshine all their clusters thick,
While now and then a mellow apple falls
With a dull thud within the orchard's walls.

The sky has but one solitary cloud
  Like a dark island in a sea of ligh.,
The parching furrows 'twixt the corn-rows ploughed
  Seem fairly dancing in my dazzled sight,
While over yonder road a dusty haze
Grows luminous beneath the sun's fierce blaze.

EVENING.

That solitary cloud grows dark and wide,
  While distant thunder rumbles in the air,—

A fitful ripple breaks the river's tide,—
  The lazy cattle are no longer there,
But homeward come, in long procession slow,
  With many a bleat and many a plaintive low.

Darker and wider spreading o'er the west
  Advancing clouds, each in fantastic form,
And mirrored turrets on the river's breast,
  Tell in advance the coming of a storm,—
Closer and brighter glares the lightning's flash,
And louder, nearer sounds the thunder's crash.

The air of evening is intensely hot,
  The breeze feels heated as it fans my brows,—
Now sullen rain-drops patter down like shot,
  Strike in the grass, or rattle mid the boughs.
A sultry lull, and then a gust again,—
And now I see the thick advancing rain!

It fairly hisses as it drives along,
  And where it strikes breaks up in silvery spray
As if 't were dancing to the fitful song
  Made by the trees, which twist themselves and sway
In contest with the wind, that rises fast
Until the breeze becomes a furious blast.

And now, the sudden, fitful storm has fled,
  The clouds lie piled up in the splendid west,
In massive shadow tipped with purplish red,
  Crimson, or gold. The scene is one of rest;
And on the bosom of yon still lagoon
I see the crescent of the pallid moon.

JAMES BARRON HOPE.

" And on the bosom of yon still lagoon
I see the crescent of the pallid moon."

IMAGINATIVE SYMPATHY WITH NATURE.

SKY, mountains, river, winds, lake, lightnings! ye,
  With night, and clouds, and thunder, and a soul
  To make these felt and feeling, well may be
  Things that have made me watchful; the far roll
Of your departing voices is the knoll

Of what in me is sleepless—if I rest.
But where of ye, O tempests! is the goal?
Are ye like those within the human breast?
Or do ye find at length, like eagles, some high nest?

LORD BYRON.

SEPTEMBER.

SWEET is the voice that calls
From babbling waterfalls
In meadows where the downy seeds
    are flying;
    And soft the breezes blow,
    And eddying come and go
In faded gardens where the rose is
    dying.

Among the stubbled corn
The blithe quail pipes at morn,
The merry partridge drums in hidden places,
    And glittering insects gleam
    Above the reedy stream,
Where busy spiders spin their filmy laces.

At eve, cool shadows fall
Across the garden wall,
And on the clustered grapes to purple turning;
    And pearly vapors lie
    Along the eastern sky,
Where the broad harvest-moon is redly burning.

Ah, soon on field and hill
The wind shall whistle chill.
And patriarch swallows call their flocks together,
    To fly from frost and snow,
    And seek for lands where blow
The fairer blossoms of a balmier weather.

The cricket chirps all day,
    "O fairest summer, stay!"
The squirrel eyes askance the chestnuts browning;
    The wild fowl fly afar
    Above the foamy bar,
And hasten southward ere the skies are frowning.

Now comes a fragrant breeze
Through the dark cedar-trees,
And round about my temples fondly lingers,
In gentle playfulness,
Like to the soft caress
Bestowed in happier days by loving fingers.

Yet, though a sense of grief
Comes with the falling leaf,
And memory makes the summer doubly **pleasant**,
In all my autumn dreams
A future summer gleams,
Passing the fairest glories of the present!

GEORGE ARNOLD.

FLOWERS.

WILL not have the mad Clytie,
  Whose head is turned by the sun;
The tulip is a courtly queen,
  Whom, therefore, I will shun:
The cowslip is a country wench,
  The violet is a nun; —
But I will woo the dainty rose,
  The queen of every one.

The pea is but a wanton witch,
  In too much haste to wed,
And clasps her rings on every hand;
  The wolfsbane I should dread;

Nor will I dreary rosemarye,
  That always mourns the dead;
But I will woo the dainty rose,
  With her cheeks of tender red.

The lily is all in white, like a saint,
  And so is no mate for me;
And the daisy's cheek is tipped with a blush,
  She is of such low degree;
Jasmine is sweet, and has many loves;
  And the broom's betrothed to the bee;
But I will plight with the dainty rose,
  For fairest of all is she.

THOMAS HOOD.

STARS.

E stars! which are the poetry of heaven,
  If in your bright leaves we would read the fate
  Of men and empires, — 'tis to be forgiven
  That in our aspirations to be great
  Our destinies o'erleap their mortal state,

And claim a kindred with you; for ye are
A beauty and a mystery, and create
In us such love and reverence from afar,
That fortune, fame, power, life, have named them-
      selves a star.

LORD BYRON.

"The hollow winds begin to blow."

SIGNS OF RAIN.

THE hollow winds begin to blow;
  The clouds look black, the glass is low,
  The soot falls down, the spaniels sleep,
  And spiders from their cobwebs peep.
Last night the sun went pale to bed,
The moon in halos hid her head;
The boding shepherd heaves a sigh,
For see, a rainbow spans the sky!
The walls are damp, the ditches smell,
Closed is the pink-eyed pimpernel.
Hark how the chairs and tables crack!
Old Betty's nerves are on the rack;

Loud quacks the duck, the peacocks cry,
The distant hills are seeming nigh.
How restless are the snorting swine!
The busy flies disturb the kine,
Low o'er the grass the swallow wings,
The cricket, too, how sharp he sings!
Puss on the hearth, with velvet paws,
Sits wiping o'er her whiskered jaws;
Through the clear streams the fishes rise,
And nimbly catch the incautious flies.
The glow-worms, numerous and light,
Illumed the dewy dell last night;

At dusk the squalid toad was seen,
Hopping and crawling o'er the green;
The whirling dust the wind obeys,
And in the rapid eddy plays;
The frog has changed his yellow vest,
And in a russet coat is dressed.
Though June, the air is cold and still,
The mellow blackbird's voice is shrill;

My dog, so altered in his taste,
Quits mutton-bones on grass to feast;
And see yon rooks, how odd their flight!
They imitate the gliding kite,
And seem precipitate to fall,
As if they felt the piercing ball.
'T will surely rain; I see with sorrow,
Our jaunt must be put off to-morrow.

EDWARD JENNER.

"Our jaunt must be put off to-morrow."

DAFFODILS.

I WANDERED lonely as a cloud
    That floats on high o'er vales and hills,
When all at once I saw a crowd,
    A host, of golden daffodils,
Beside the lake, beneath the trees,
Fluttering, dancing in the breeze.

Continuous as the stars that shine
    And twinkle on the Milky Way,
They stretched in never-ending line
    Along the margin of a bay:
Ten thousand saw I at a glance,
Tossing their heads in sprightly dance.

The waves beside them danced, but they
    Outdid the sparkling waves in glee;
A poet could not but be gay
    In such a jocund company;
I gazed, and gazed, but little thought
What wealth the show to me had brought:

For oft, when on my couch I lie,
    In vacant or in pensive mood,
They flash upon that inward eye
    Which is the bliss of solitude;
And then my heart with pleasure fills,
And dances with the daffodils.

WILLIAM WORDSWORTH.

SONNET ON THE RIVER RHINE.

'WAS morn, and beanteous on the mountain's
    brow
  (Hung with the beamy clusters of the vine)
  Streamed the blue light, when on the sparkling
    Rhine
We bounded, and the white waves round the prow
In murmurs parted. Varying as we go,
Lo, the woods open, and the rocks retire,

Some convent's ancient walls or glistening spire
'Mid the bright landscape's track unfolding slow.
Here dark, with furrowed aspect, like despair,
Frowns the bleak cliff; there on the woodland's side
The shadowy sunshine pours its streaming tide;
While Hope, enchanted with the scene so fair,
Would wish to linger many a summer's day,
Nor heeds how fast the prospect winds away.

WILLIAM LISLE BOWLES.

"Here dark, with furrowed aspect, like despair,
Frowns the bleak cliff."

IN itself the ocean panorama is very grand. It would be hard to exaggerate the beauty of both sea and sky, especially in and near the tropics. The sky near the horizon was of pale blue, and often the clouds all round the sea line of a light pink tint, and the sea near the ship like an amethyst or the wing of some tropical bird. In those rare times when the sea was calm, the motion of the ship made it flow in large sheets as of some oily liquid; or, again, like the blue steel of some polished cuirass.

TO THE CUCKOO.

HAIL, beauteous stranger of the grove!
  Thou messenger of spring!
Now Heaven repairs thy rural seat,
  And woods thy welcome sing.

Soon as the daisy decks the green,
  Thy certain voice we hear.
Hast thou a star to guide thy path,
  Or mark the rolling year?

Delightful visitant! with thee
  I hail the time of flowers,
And hear the sound of music sweet
  From birds among the bowers.

The school-boy, wandering through the wood
  To pull the primrose gay,

Starts, thy most curious voice to hear,
  And imitates thy lay.

What time the pea puts on the bloom,
  Thou fliest thy vocal vale,
An annual guest in other lands,
  Another spring to hail.

Sweet bird! thy bower is ever green,
  Thy sky is ever clear;
Thou hast no sorrow in thy song,
  No winter in thy year!

O, could I fly, I'd fly with thee!
  We'd make, with joyful wing,
Our annual visit o'er the globe,
  Attendants on the spring.

                    JOHN LOGAN.

MARCH.

SLAYER of winter, art thou here again?
  O welcome, thou that bring'st the summer nigh!
  The bitter wind makes not thy victory vain,
  Nor will we mock thee for thy faint blue sky.
    Welcome, O March! whose kindly days and dry
Make April ready for the throstle's song,
Thou first redresser of the winter's wrong!

Yea, welcome, March! and though I die ere June,
Yet for the hope of life I give thee praise,
Striving to swell the burden of the tune
That even now I hear thy brown birds raise,

Unmindful of the past or coming days;
Who sing, "O joy! a new year is begun!
What happiness to look upon the sun!"

O, what begetteth all this storm of bliss,
But Death himself, who, crying solemnly,
Even from the heart of sweet Forgetfulness,
Bids us, "Rejoice! lest pleasureless ye die.
Within a little time must ye go by.
Stretch forth your open hands, and, while ye live,
Take all the gifts that Death and Life may give."

                    WILLIAM MORRIS.

THE SHADED WATER.

HEN that my mood is sad, and in the noise
  And bustle of the crowd I feel rebuke,
  I turn my footsteps from its hollow joys
  And sit me down beside this little brook;
  The waters have a music to mine ear
    It glads me much to hear.

It is a quiet glen, as you may see,
  Shut in from all intrusion by the trees,
That spread their giant branches, broad and
    free,
  The silent growth of many centuries;
And make a hallowed time for hapless moods,
  A sabbath of the woods.

A gracious couch — the root of an old oak
  Whose branches yield it moss and canopy —
Is mine, and, so it be from woodman's stroke
  Secure, shall never be resigned by me;
It hangs above the stream that idly flies,
  Heedless of any eyes.

There, with eye sometimes shut, but upward bent,
  Sweetly I muse through many a quiet hour
While every sense on earnest mission sent,
  Returns, thought-laden, back with bloom and
    flower;
Pursuing, though rebuked by those who moil,
  A profitable toil.

"It is a quiet glen, as you may see,
Shut in from all intrusion by the trees."

Few know its quiet shelter, — none, like me,
  Do seek it out with such a fond desire,
Poring in idlesse mood on flower and tree,
  And listening as the voiceless leaves respire, —
When the far-traveling breeze, done wandering,
  Rests here his weary wing.

And all the day, with fancies ever new,
  And sweet companions from their boundless store,
Of merry elves bespangled all with dew,
  Fantastic creatures of the old-time lore,
Watching their wild but unobtrusive play,
  I fling the hours away.

And still the waters, trickling at my feet,
  Wind on their way with gentlest melody,
Yielding sweet music, which the leaves repeat,
  Above them, to the gay breeze gliding by, —
Yet not so rudely as to send one sound
  Through the thick copse around.

Sometimes a brighter cloud than all the rest
  Hangs o'er the archway opening through the trees,
Breaking the spell that, like a slumber, pressed
  On my worn spirit its sweet luxuries, —
And with awakened vision upward bent,
  I watch the firmament.

How like its sure and undisturbed retreat—
  Life's sanctuary at last, secure from storm —
To the pure waters trickling at my feet
  The bending trees that overshade my form!
So far as sweetest things of earth may seem
  Like those of which we dream.

Such, to my mind, is the philosophy
  The young bird teaches, who, with sudden flight,
Sails far into the blue that spreads on high,
  Until I lose him from my straining sight, __
With a most lofty discontent to fly
  Upward, from earth to sky.

WILLIAM GILMORE SIMMS.

"And the gaunt woods, in ragged, scant array,
Wrap their old limbs with sombre ivy-twine."

NOVEMBER.

THE mellow year is hasting to its close;
  The little birds have almost sung their last,
  Their small notes twitter in the dreary blast—
  That shrill-piped harbinger of early snows;—
The patient beauty of the scentless rose,
Oft with the Morn's hoar crystal quaintly glassed,
Hangs, a pale mourner for the summer past,
And makes a little summer where it grows:—

In the chill sunbeam of the faint brief day
The dusky waters shudder as they shine;
The russet leaves obstruct the straggling way
Of oozy brooks, which no deep banks define,
And the gaunt woods, in ragged, scant array,
Wrap their old limbs with sombre ivy-twine.

HARTLEY COLERIDGE.

IT seems as if it were Nature's ain Sabbath, and the verra waters were at rest. Look
  down upon the vale profound, and the stream is without motion! No doubt, if you
were walking along the bank, it would be murmuring with your feet. But here—here up
amang the hills, we can imagine it asleep, even like the well within reach of my staff.

THE SEA IN CALM AND STORM.

VARIOUS and vast, sublime in all its forms,
   When lulled by zephyrs, or when roused by
       storms;
  Its colors changing, when from clouds and sun
   Shades after shades upon the surface run;
Embrowned and horrid now, and now serene
In limpid blue and evanescent green;
And oft the foggy banks on ocean lie,
Lift the fair sail, and cheat the experienced eye!
  Be it the summer noon; a sandy space
The ebbing tide has left upon its place;
Then just the hot and stony beach above,
Light, twinkling streams in bright confusion move;
(For, heated thus, the warmer air ascends,
And with the cooler in its fall contends).
Then the broad bosom of the ocean keeps
An equal motion; swelling as it sleeps,
Then slowly sinking; curling to the strand,
Faint, lazy waves o'ercreep the ridgy sand.

Or tap the tarry boat with gentle blow,
And back return in silence, smooth and slow,

"Ships in the calm seem anchored; for they glide
On the still sea, urged solely by the tide."

"——The petrel, in the troubled way,
Swims with her brood, or flutters in the spray."

Ships in the calm seem anchored; for they glide
On the still sea, urged solely by the tide.

* * * * * *

View now the winter storm! Above, one cloud,
Black and unbroken, all the skies o'ershroud;
The unwieldy porpoise, through the day before,
Had rolled in view of boding men on shore;
And sometimes hid and sometimes showed his form,
Dark as the cloud, and furious as the storm.

Raking the rounded flints, which ages past
Rolled by their rage, and shall to ages last.
Far off, the petrel, in the troubled way,
Swims with her brood, or flutters in the spray;
She rises often, often drops again,
And sports at ease on the tempestuous main.
High o'er the restless deep, above the reach
Of gunner's hope, vast flights of wild-ducks
    stretch;

" ——Their passage tribes of sea-gulls urge."

All where the eye delights, yet dreads, to roam
The breaking billows cast the flying foam
Upon the billows rising—all the deep
Is restless change—the waves, so swelled and steep,
Breaking and sinking and the sunken swells,
Nor one, one moment, in its station dwells;
But nearer land you may the billows trace,
As if contending in their watery chase;
May watch the mightiest till the shoal they reach,
Then break and hurry to their utmost stretch;
Curled as they come, they strike with furious force,
And then, reflowing, take their grating course,

Far as the eye can glance on either side,
In a broad space and level line they glide;
All in their wedge-like figures from the north,
Day after day, flight after flight, go forth.
Inshore their passage tribes of sea-gulls urge,
And drop for prey within the sweeping surge;
Oft in the rough, opposing blast they fly
Far back, then turn, and all their force apply,
While to the storm they give their weak, complain-
    ing cry;
Or clap the sleek white pinion to the breast,
And in the restless ocean dip for rest.

GEORGE CRABBE.

THE MIDGES DANCE ABOON THE BURN.

THE midges dance aboon the burn;
  The dews begin to fa';
The pairtricks down the rushy holm
  Set up their e'ening ca'.
Now loud and clear the blackbirds sang
  Rings through the briery shaw,
While, flitting gay, the swallows play
  Around the castle wa'.

Beneath the golden gloamin' sky
  The mavis mends her lay;
The redbreast pours his sweetest strains
  To charm the lingering day;

While weary yeldrins seem to wail
  Their little nestlings torn,
The merry wren, frae den to den,
  Gaes jinking through the thorn.

The roses fauld their silken leaves,
  The fox-glove shuts its bell;
The honeysuckle and the birk
  Spread fragrance through the dell.
Let others crowd the giddy court
  Of mirth and revelry,
The simple joys that Nature yields
  Are dearer far to me.
                    ROBERT TANNAHILL.

NATURE'S DELIGHTS.

MAKER of sweet poets! dear delight
Of this fair world and all its gentle livers;
Spangler of clouds, halo of crystal rivers,
Mingler with leaves, and dew, and tumbling
    streams;
Closer of lovely eyes to lovely dreams;
Lover of loneliness and wandering,
Of upcast eye and tender pondering!—
Thee must I praise above all other glories
That smile on us to tell delightful stories;
For what has made the sage or poet write,
But the fair paradise of Nature's light?
In the calm grandeur of a sober line
We see the waving of the mountain pine;

And when a tale is beautifully staid,
We feel the safety of a hawthorn glade;
When it is moving on luxurious wings,
The soul is lost in pleasant smotherings;
Fair dewy roses brush against our faces,
And flowering laurels spring from diamond vases;
O'erhead we see the jasmine and sweet-brier,
And bloomy grapes laughing from green attire;
While at our feet the voice of crystal bubbles
Charms us at once away from all our troubles;
So that we feel uplifted from the world,
Walking upon the white clouds wreathed and curled.

                              JOHN KEATS.

HARVEST TIME.

'ER all the land, a vision rare and splendid—
  (What time the summer her last glory yields!)
I saw the reapers, by tall wains attended,
    Wave their keen scythes across the ripened
      fields;
At each broad sweep the glittering grain-stalks parted,
  With all their sunniest lustres earthward bowed,
But still those tireless blade-curves flashed and darted
  Like silvery lightnings from a golden cloud.

Then burst from countless throats in choral thunder
  A strain that rose toward the sapphire dome;—
Hushed in his lay, the mock-bird heard with wonder
  The resonant gladness of their "Harvest Home,"
And Echo to far fells and forest fountains
  Bore the brave burden that was half divine,
While the proud crested eagle of the mountains
  Sent back an answer from his eyried pine.

And still, the tireless steel gleamed in and over
  The bearded cohorts of the rye and wheat,
Till in long swathes, o'ertopped by perfumed
    clover,
  They slept supinely at the laborer's feet;
And still that harvest song rolled on, till even
  Looked wanly forth from night's encircling bars,—
When, like a pearl of music, lost in Heaven
  Its sweetness melted in a sea of stars.

O favored land! thy bursting barns are laden
  With such fair offspring of thine opulent sod,
At length thou art a rich Arcadian Adenne,
  Lapped in the bounteous benison of God.
Pomona vies with Ceres; but less sober,
  Trips down her orchard ways at gleeful ease,
And in the luminous sunsets of October,
  Shakes the flushed fruitage from her rustling trees.

And far as fancy's kindling eyes can follow
  The harvest-landscapes in their hale increase,
O'er radiant hill-top, and through shadowy hollow,
  Gleams the white splendor of the Plant of Peace.
Its bolls, wind-wafted on their airy stations,
  Hold spells of subtlest service, deftly furled —
Soon to unfold through marvellous transformations,
  And weave their warmth and comfort 'round the
     world!

Ah! Christ be praised; where once o'er wold and
     water
Flashed back the fury of war's blood-red glare —
Where once the shrieks of fratricidal slaughter
Died shuddering on the hot, volcanian air —

Only the breeze, in frolic charge, advances,
  To stir the tides, or win the foliaged pass;
The sunbeams only smite with wavering lances
  The frail battalions of the leaves and grass!

Then let our hearts — 'ere grateful fervor falters —
  To HIM, whose love fulfills all pure desire,
Upwaft, as borne from bright, ethereal altars,
  The glow and grace of sacrificial fire.
For Plenty smiles alike on cot and palace,
  And Peace, so long to us an unknown guest,
Pours from the depths of her enchanted chalice
  That heavenly wine which brings the nations rest!

               PAUL HAMILTON HAYNE.

THE EVENING WIND.

PIRIT that breathest through my lattice: thou
  That coolest the twilight of the sultry day!
Gratefully flows thy freshness round my brow;
  Thou hast been out upon the deep at play,
Riding all day the wild blue waves till now,
  Roughening their crests, and scattering high their
     spray,
And swelling the white sail. I welcome thee
To the scorched land, thou wanderer of the sea!

Go, rock the little wood-bird in his nest;
  Curl the still waters, bright with stars; and rouse
The wide old wood from his majestic rest,
  Summoning, from the innumerable boughs,
The strange deep harmonies that haunt his breast.
  Pleasant shall be thy way where meekly bows
The shutting flower, and darkling waters pass,
And where the o'ershadowing branches sweep the
     grass.

"Thou hast been out upon the deep at play,
  Riding all day the wild blue waves till now,
Roughening their crests, ar.d scattering high their spray,
  And swelling the white sail."

Nor I alone,— a thousand bosoms round
  Inhale thee in the fullness of delight;
And languid forms rise up, and pulses bound
  Livelier, at coming of the wind of night;
And languishing to hear thy welcome sound,
  Lies the vast inland, stretched beyond the sight.
Go forth into the gathering shade; go forth, —
God's blessing breathed upon the fainting earth!

Stoop o'er the place of graves, and softly sway
  The sighing herbage by the gleaming stone,
That they who near the churchyard willows stray,
  And listen in the deepening gloom, alone,
May think of gentle souls that passed away,
  Like thy pure breath, into the vast unknown,
Sent forth from heaven among the sons of men,
And gone into the boundless heaven again.

The faint old man shall lean his silver head
  To feel thee: thou shalt kiss the child asleep,
And dry the moistened curls that overspread
  His temples, while his breathing grows more deep;
And they who stand about the sick man's bed
  Shall joy to listen to thy distant sweep,
And softly part his curtains to allow
Thy visit, grateful to his burning brow.

Go,— but the circle of eternal change,
  Which is the life of Nature, shall restore,
With sounds and scents from all thy mighty range,
  Thee to thy birthplace of the deep once more.
Sweet odors in the sea air, sweet and strange,
  Shall tell the homesick mariner of the shore;
And, listening to thy murmur, he shall deem
He hears the rustling leaf and running stream.

WILLIAM CULLEN BRYANT.

"——Where the giraffes browse
With stately head, among the forest boughs."

NATURE'S MAGNIFICENCE.

WHERE the stupendous mountains of the moon
  Cast their broad shadows o'er the realms of
    noon;
    From rude Caffraria, where the giraffes browse
With stately heads among the forest boughs,
To Atlas, where Numidian lions glow
With torrid fire beneath eternal snow;

From Nubian hills that hail the dawn of day,
To Guinea's coast, where evening fades away;
Regions immense, unsearchable, unknown,
Bask in the splendor of the solar zone. —
A world of wonders, where creation seems
No more the works of Nature, but her dreams.

12

Great, wild and beautiful, beyond control,
She reigns in all the freedom of her soul;
Where none can check her bounty when she showers
O'er the gay wilderness her fruits and flowers;
None brave her fury when, with whirlwind breath
And earthquake step, she walks abroad with death.
O'er boundless plains she holds her fiery flight,
In terrible magnificence of light;
At blazing noon pursues the evening breeze,
Through the dim gloom of realm-o'ershadowing trees;

Her thirst at Nile's mysterious fountain quells,
Or bathes in secresy where Niger swells,
An inland ocean, on whose jasper rocks
With shells and sea-flower wreaths she binds her
    locks.
She sleeps on isles of velvet verdure, placed
Midst sandy gulphs and shoals for ever waste;
She guides her countless flocks to cherished rills,
And feeds her cattle on a thousand hills.

                                        JAMES MONTGOMERY.

"Her thirst at Nile's mysterious fountain quells."

SPRING.

DIP down upon the northern shore,
    O sweet new year, delaying long.
    Thou doest expectant Nature wrong;
Delaying long, delay no more.

What stays thee from the clouded noons,
    Thy sweetness from its proper place?
    Can trouble live with April days,
Or sadness in the summer moons?

Bring orchis, bring the fox-glove spire,
    The little speedwell's darling blue,
    Deep tulips dashed with fiery dew,
Laburnums, dropping wells of fire.

O thou, new year, delaying long,
    Delayest the sorrow in my blood,
    That longs to burst a frozen bud,
And flood a fresher throat with song.

                                        ALFRED TENNYSON.

THE SKY—sometimes gentle, sometimes capricious, sometimes awful, never the same for two moments together; almost human in its passions, almost spiritual in its tenderness, almost divine in its infinity—its appeal to what is immortal in us is as distinct as its ministry of chastisement or of blessing to what is mortal, is essential.

IT SNOWS.

"It snows!" cries the School-boy, "Hurrah!" and his shout
   Is ringing through parlor and hall,
   While swift as the wing of a swallow, he's out,
   And his playmates have answered his call;
   It makes the heart leap but to witness their joy;
Proud wealth has no pleasure, I trow,
Like the rapture that throbs in the pulse of the boy,
   As he gathers his treasures of snow;
Then lay not the trappings of gold on thine heirs,
While health, and the riches of nature, are theirs.

And nearer and nearer his soft cushioned chair
   Is wheeled toward the life-giving flame;
He dreads a chill puff of the snow-burdened air,
   Lest it wither his delicate frame;
Oh! small is the pleasure existence can give,
When the fear we shall die only proves that we live!

"It snows!" cries the Traveler, "Ho!" and the word
   Has quickened his steed's lagging pace;
The wind rushes by, but its howl is unheard,
   Unfelt the sharp drift in his face;

" Proud wealth has no pleasure, I trow,
Like the rapture that throbs in the pulse of the boy,
As he gathers his treasures of snow."

"It snows!" sighs the Imbecile, "Ah!" and his breath
Comes heavy, as clogged with a weight:
While, from the pale aspect of nature in death
   He turns to the blaze of his grate;

For bright through the tempest his own home appeared,
   Ay, through leagues intervened he can see;
There's the clear, glowing hearth, and the table prepared,
   And his wife with her babes at her knee;

Blest thought! how it lightens the grief-laden hour,
That those we love dearest are safe from its power!

"It snows!" cries the Belle, "Dear, how lucky!" and
    turns
From her mirror to watch the flakes fall;
Like the first rose of summer, her dimpled cheek
    burns,
While musing on sleigh-ride and ball:
There are visions of conquests, of splendor, and
    mirth,
Floating over each drear winter's day;
But the tintings of Hope, on this storm-beaten earth,
Will melt like the snow-flakes away:

Turn, turn thee to Heaven, fair maiden, for bliss;
That world has a pure fount ne'er opened in this.

"It snows!" cries the Widow, "Oh God!" and her
    sighs
Have stifled the voice of her prayer;
Its burden you'll read, in her tear-swollen eyes,
    On her cheek sunk with fasting and care.
'Tis night, and her fatherless ask her for bread,
    But "He gives the young ravens their food,"
And she trusts, till her dark hearth adds horror to
    dread,
    And she lays on her last chip of wood.
Poor sufferer! that sorrow thy God only knows;
'Tis a most bitter lot to be poor, when it snows!

                                    MRS. S. J. HALE.

"Till the victorious Orb rose unattended,
And every billow was his mirror splendid!"

SUNRISE AT SEA.

WHEN the mild weather came,
    And set the sea on flame,
How often would I rise before the sun,
    And from the mast behold
The gradual splendors of the sky unfold
Ere the first line of disk had yet begun,
Above the horizon's arc,
    To show its flaming gold,
Across the purple dark!

One perfect dawn how well I recollect,
When the whole east was flecked
With flashing streaks and shafts of amethyst,
While a light crimson mist

Went up before the mounting luminary,
And all the strips of cloud began to vary
Their hues, and all the zenith seemed to ope
As if to show a cope beyond the cope!

How reverently calm the ocean lay
    At the bright birth of that celestial day!
How every little vapor, robed in state,
Would melt and dissipate
    Before the augmenting ray,
Till the victorious Orb rose unattended,
And every billow was his mirror splendid!

                                    EPES SARGENT.

INVOCATION TO NATURE.

ARTH, ocean, air, beloved brotherhood!
  If our great mother have imbued my soul
  With aught of natural piety to feel
  Your love, and recompense the boon with
    mine;
If dewy morn, and odorous noon, and even,
With sunset and its gorgeous ministers,
And solemn midnight's tingling silentness;
If Autumn's hollow sighs in the sere wood,

And Winter robing with pure snow and crowns
Of starry ice the gray grass and bare boughs;
If Spring's voluptuous pantings, when she breathes
Her first sweet kisses, have been dear to me;
If no bright bird, insect, or gentle beast
I consciously have injured, but still loved
And cherished these my kindred; — then forgive
This boast, beloved brethren, and withdraw
No portion of your wonted favor now!

PERCY BYSSHE SHELLEY.

TABLE MOUNTAIN, CAPE OF GOOD HOPE.

APE of storms, thy spectre fled,
  See, the angel Hope, instead.
  Lights from heaven upon thine head; —

And where Table-mountain stands;
Barbarous hordes from desert sands,
Bless the sight with lifted hands.

St. Helena's dungeon-keep
Scowls defiance o'er the deep;
There a warrior's relics sleep.

Who he was, and how he fell,
Europe, Asia, Afric, tell;
On that theme all time shall dwell.

JAMES MONTGOMERY.

HAT is there more sublime than the trackless, desert, all-surrounding, unfathomable sea? What is there more peacefully sublime than the calm, gently-heaving, silent sea? What is there more terribly sublime than the angry, dashing, foaming sea? Power —resistless, overwhelming power—is its attribute and its expression, whether in the careless, conscious grandeur of its deep rest, or the wild tumult of its excited wrath.

"To climb the trackless mountain all unseen
With the wild flock that never needs a fold;
Alone o'er steeps and foaming falls to lean."

THE POET'S SOLITUDE.

TO sit on rocks, to muse o'er flood and fell,
  To slowly trace the forest's shady scene,
    Where things that own not man's dominion
        dwell,
  And mortal foot hath ne'er or rarely been;
  To climb the trackless mountain all unseen,
  With the wild flock that never needs a fold;
  Alone o'er steeps and foaming falls to lean,—
This is not solitude; 'tis but to hold
Converse with Nature's charms and view her stores
    unrolled.

But midst the crowd, the hum, the shock of men
  To hear, to see, to feel, and to possess,
  And roam along, the world's tired denizen,
  With none who bless us, none whom we can bless;
  Minions of splendor, shrinking from distress!
  None that, with kindred consciousness endued,
  If we were not, would seem to smile the less
  Of all that flattered, followed, sought and sued;
This is to be alone; this, this is solitude!

                              LORD BYRON.

COUNTRY LIFE.

"When now the cock, the ploughman's horn,
Calls for the lily-wristed morn."

A COUNTRY LIFE.

SWEET country life, to such unknown,
 Whose lives are others', not their own!
 But serving courts and cities, be
 Less happy, less enjoying thee.
  Thou never plough'd the ocean's foam,
To seek and bring rough pepper home;
Nor to the eastern Ind dost rove,
To bring from thence the scorchéd clove;

Nor, with the loss of thy loved rest,
Bring'st home the ingot from the west.
No; thy ambition's masterpiece
Flies no thought higher than a fleece;
Or how to pay thy hinds, and clear
All scores, and so to end the year;
But walk'st about thy own dear grounds,
Not craving others' larger bounds;

For well thou know'st 'tis not th' extent
Of land makes life, but sweet content.
When now the cock, the ploughman's horn,
Calls for the lily-wristed morn,
Then to thy corn-fields thou dost go,
Which, though well soil'd, yet thou dost know
That the best compost for the lands
Is the wise master's feet and hands.·
There, at the plough, thou find'st thy team,
With a hind whistling there to them;
And cheer'st them up by singing how
The kingdom's portion is the plough.
This done, then to th' enamell'd meads
Thou go'st; and, as thy foot there treads,
Thou seest a present god-like power
Imprinted in each herb and flower;

For sports, for pageantry, and plays,
Thou hast thy eves and holy-days,
On which the young men and maids meet
To exercise their dancing feet;
Tripping the comely country round,
With daffodils and daisies crown'd.
Thy wakes, thy quintels, here thou hast,
Thy May-poles, too, with garlands graced;
Thy morris-dance, thy Whitsun ale,
Thy shearing feast, which never fail;
Thy harvest-home, thy wassail-bowl,
That's tost up after fox i' th' hole;
Thy mummeries, thy twelfth-night kings
And queens, and Christmas revellings;
Thy nut-brown mirth, thy russet wit,
And no man pays too dear for it.

"And find'st their bellies there as full
Of short sweet grass, as backs with wool."

And smell'st the breath of great-eyed kine,
Sweet as the blossoms of the vine.
Here thou behold'st thy large, sleek neat,
Unto the dewlaps up in meat;
And, as thou look'st, the wanton steer,
The heifer, cow, and ox, draw near,
To make a pleasing pastime there.

These seen, thou go'st to view thy flocks
Of sheep, safe from the wolf and fox;
And find'st their bellies there as full
Of short sweet grass, as backs with wool;
And leav'st them, as they feed and fill,
A shepherd piping on the hill.

To these thou hast thy time to go,
And trace the hare in the treacherous snow:
Thy witty wiles to draw, and get
The lark into the trammel net;
Thou hast thy cock rood, and thy glade,
To take the precious pheasant made!
Thy lime-twigs, snares, and pitfalls, then,
To catch the pilfering birds, not men.
O happy life, if that their good
The husbandmen but understood!
Who all the day themselves do please,
And younglings, with such sports as these;
And, lying down, have nought t' affright
Sweet sleep, that makes more short the night.

                                  ROBERT HERRICK.

"Around my ivied porch shall spring
Each fragrant flower that drinks the dew."

A WISH.

MINE be a cot beside the hill;
  A beehive's hum shall soothe my ear;
A willowy brook that turns a mill
  With many a fall shall linger near.

The swallow oft beneath my thatch
  Shall twitter from her clay-built nest;
Oft shall the pilgrim lift the latch,
  And share my meal, a welcome guest.

Around my ivied porch shall spring
  Each fragrant flower that drinks the dew;
And Lucy at her wheel shall sing
  In russet gown and apron blue.

The village church, among the trees,
  Where first our marriage vows were given,
With merry peals shall swell the breeze,
  And point with taper spire to heaven.

SAMUEL ROGERS.

CAN anything be so elegant as to have few wants and serve them one's self? Parched corn, and a house with one apartment, that I may be free of all perturbations, that I may be serene and docile to what the mind shall speak, and girt and road-ready for the lowest mission of knowledge or goodness, is frugality for gods and heroes.

TOWN AND COUNTRY.

OD made the country and man made the town.
　What wonder then that health and virtue, gifts
　That can alone make sweet the bitter draught
　That life holds out to all, should most abound
And least be threatened in the fields and groves?
Possess ye, therefore, ye who, borne about
In chariots and sedans, know no fatigue
But that of idleness, and taste no scenes
But such as art contrives, possess ye still
Your element; there only can ye shine;
There only minds like yours can do no harm.
Our groves were planted to console at noon
The pensive wanderer in their shades. At eve

The moonbeam, sliding softly in between
The sleeping leaves, is all the light they wish,
Birds warbling all the music. We can spare
The splendor of your lamps; they but eclipse
Our softer satellite. Your songs confound
Our more harmonious notes: the thrush departs
Scared, and the offended nightingale is mute.
There is a public mischief in your mirth;
It plagues your country. Folly such as yours,
Graced with a sword, and worthier of a fan,
Has made, what enemies could ne'er have done,
Our arch of empire, steadfast but for you,
A mutilated structure, soon to fall.

WILLIAM COWPER.

THE HOMESTEAD.

ROM the old squire's dwelling, gloomy and grand,
　Stretching away on either hand,
　Lie fields of broad and fertile land.

Acres on acres everywhere,
The look of smiling plenty wear,
That tells of the master's thoughtful care.

Sleek cows down the pasture take their ways,
Or lie in the shade through the sultry days,
Idle, and too full-fed to graze.

Ah! you might wander far and wide,
Nor find a spot in the country's side
So fair to see as our valley's pride!

"And here you will find on every hand
Walks and fountains and statues grand,
And trees from many a foreign land."

Here blossoms the clover, white and red,
Here the heavy oats in a tangle spread,
And the millet lifts her golden head;

And, ripening, closely neighbored by
Fields of barley and pale white rye,
The yellow wheat grows strong and high.

And near, untried through the summer days,
Lifting their spears in the sun's fierce blaze,
Stand the bearded ranks of the maize.

Straying over the side of the hill,
The sheep run to and fro at will,
Nibbling of short green grass their fill.

How, just beyond, if it will not tire
Your feet to climb this green knoll higher,
We can see the pretty village spire;

And, mystic haunt of the whippoorwills,
The wood, that all the background fills,
Crowning the tops to the mill-creek hills.

There, miles away, like a faint blue line,
Whenever the day is clear and fine,
You can see the track of a river shine.

Near it a city hides unseen,
Shut close the verdant hills between,
As an acorn set in its cup of green.

And right beneath, at the foot of the hill,
The little creek flows swift and still,
That turns the wheel of Dovecote mill.

Nearer the grand old house one sees
Fair rows of thrifty apple-trees,
And tall straight pears o'ertopping these.

And down at the foot of the garden, low,
On a rustic bench, a pretty show,
White bee-hives, standing in a row.

And here you will find on every hand
Walks and fountains and statues grand,
And trees from many a foreign land.

And flowers, that only the learned can name,
Here glow and burn like a gorgeous flame,
Putting the poor man's blooms to shame.

Far away from their native air
The Norway pines their green dress wear;
And larches swing their long, loose hair.

"Though grave and quiet at any time,
But that now, his head in manhood's prime
Is growing white as the winter's rime."

Here trimmed in sprigs, with blossoms, each
Of the little bees in easy reach,
Hang the boughs of the plum and peach.

At the garden's head are poplars tall,
And peacocks, making their harsh, loud call,
Sun themselves all day on the wall.

Near the porch grows the broad catalpa tree,
And o'er it the grand wistaria
Born to the purple of royalty.

There looking the same for a weary while—
'Twas built in this heavy, gloomy style—
Stands the mansion, a grand old pile.

Always closed, as it is to-day,
And the proud squire. so the neighbors say,
Frowns each unwelcome guest away.

Though some, who knew him long ago,
If you ask, will shake their heads of snow,
And tell you he was not always so,

Though grave and quiet at any time,
But that now, his head in manhood's prime
Is growing white as the winter's rime.

PHŒBE CARY.

"His little boys are with him, seeking flowers,
Or chasing the too venturous gilded fly."

SUNDAY IN THE FIELDS.

HAIL Sabbath! day of mercy, peace, and rest!
   Thou o'er loud cities throw'st a noiseless spell;
   The hammer there, the wheel, the saw, molest
   Pale thought no more. O'er trade's conten-
         tious hell
      Meek Quiet spreads her wings invisible.
But when thou com'st less silent are the fields,
   Through whose sweet paths the toil-freed towns-
         man steals;
To him the very air a banquet yields.
   Envious he watches the poised hawk that wheels
   His flight on chainless winds. Each cloud reveals
A paradise of beauty to his eye.
   His little boys are with him, seeking flowers,
Or chasing the too venturous gilded fly;
   So by the daisy's side he spends the hours,
   Renewing friendship with the budding bowers;
And—while might, beauty, good without alloy,
   Are mirror'd in his children's happy eyes,
In His great temple offering thankful joy
   To Him the infinitely Great and Wise,
   With soul attuned to Nature's harmonies,
Serene and cheerful as a sporting child.

EBENEZER ELLIOT.

THE glory of the country is in its homes, which contain the true elements of national vitality, and are the embodied type of heaven.

BLOSSOM-TIME.

THERE'S a wedding in the orchard, dear,
 I know it by the flowers:
They're wreathed on every bough and branch,
 Or falling down in showers.

The air is in a mist, I think,
 And scarce knows which to be —
Whether all fragrance, clinging close,
 Or bird-song, wild and free.

While whispers ran among the boughs
 Of promises and praise;
And playful, loving messages
 Sped through the leaf-lit ways.

And just beyond the wreathéd aisles
 That end against the blue,
The raiment of the wedding-choir
 And priest came shining through.

" There's a wedding in the orchard, dear,
I know it by the flowers."

And countless wedding-jewels shine,
 And golden gifts of grace:
I never saw such wealth of sun
 In any shady place.

It seemed I heard the flutt'ring robes
 Of maidens clad in white,
The clasping of a thousand hands
 In tenderest delight;

And though I saw no wedding-guest,
 Nor groom, nor gentle bride,
I know that holy things were asked,
 And holy love replied.

And something through the sunlight said:
 "Let all who love be blest!
The earth is wedded to the spring —
 And God, He knoweth best."

MARY E. DODGE.

THE PRAISE OF A SOLITARY LIFE.

THRICE happy he who by some shady grove,
  Far from the clamorous world, doth live his
    own.
  Thou solitary, who is not alone,
    But doth converse with that eternal love,
O how more sweet is bird's harmonious moan,
Or the hoarse sobbings of the widow'd dove,
Than those smooth whisperings near a prince's
    throne,

Which good make doubtful, do the evil approve!
O how more sweet is Zephyr's wholesome breath,
And sighs embalm'd which new-born flowers
    unfold,
Than that applause vain honor doth bequeath!
How sweet are streams to poison drank in gold!
The world is full of horror, troubles, slights:
Woods' harmless shades have only true delights.

WILLIAM DRUMMOND.

" Thrice happy he who by some shady grove,
  Far from the clamorous world, doth live his own."

THE OLD MILL.

BESIDE the stream the grist-mill stands,
  With bending roof and leaning wall;
So old, that when the winds are wild,
  The miller trembles lest it fall:
And yet it baffles wind and rain,
Our brave old Mill, and will again.

Its dam is steep, and hung with weeds:
  The gates are up, the waters pour,
And tread the old wheels slippery round,
  The lowest step forever o'er.
Methinks they fume, and chafe with ire,
Because they cannot climb it higher.

From morn to night in Autumn time,
  When harvests fill the neighboring plains,
Up to the mill the farmers drive,
  And back anon with loaded wains:
And when the children come from school
They stop and watch its foamy pool.

The mill inside is small and dark;
  But peeping in the open door
You see the miller flitting round,
  The dusty bags along the floor.
The whirling shaft, the clattering spout,
And the yellow meal a-pouring out!

All day the meal is floating there,
  Rising and falling in the breeze;
And when the sunlight strikes its mist
  It glitters like a swarm of bees:
Or like the cloud of smoke and light
Above a blacksmith's forge at night.

I love our pleasant, quaint old Mill,
  It still recalls my boyish prime;
'Tis changed since then, and so am I,
  We both have known the touch of time:

The mill is crumbling in decay,
And I—my hair is early gray.

I stand beside the stream of life,
  And watch the current sweep along:
And when the flood-gates of my heart
  Are raised, it turns the wheel of song:
But scant, as yet, the harvest brought
From out the golden fields of Thought.

RICHARD HENRY STODDARD.

FARMING.

WHILE the city is refreshed and renovated by the pure tides poured from the country into its steamy and turbid channels, the cultivation of the soil affords at home that moderate excitement, healthful occupation, and reasonable return, which most conduce to the prosperity and enjoyment of life. It is, in fact, the primitive employment of man,—first in time, first in importance. The newly-created father of mankind was placed by the Supreme Author of his being in the garden which the hand of Omnipotence itself had planted, "to dress and to keep it." Before the heaving bellows had urged the furnace, before a hammer had struck upon an anvil, before the gleaming waters had flashed from an oar, before trade had hung up its scales or gauged its measures, the culture of the soil began. "To dress the garden and to keep it!"—This was the key-note struck by the hand of God himself in that long, joyous, wailing, triumphant, troubled, pensive strain of life-music which sounds through the generations and ages of our race. Banished from the garden of Eden, man's merciful sentence—at once doom, reprieve and livelihood—was "to till the ground from which he was taken," and this, in its primitive simplicity, was the occupation of the gathering societies of men.

To this wholesome discipline the mighty East, in the days of her ascendency, was trained; and so rapid was her progress that in periods anterior to the dawn of history she had tamed the domestic animals, had saddled the horse, and yoked the ox, and milked the cow, and sheared the patient sheep, and possessed herself of most of the cereal grains which feed mankind at the present day. I obtained from the gardens of Chatsworth, and sent to this country, where they germinated, two specimens of wheat raised from grains supposed to have been wrapped up in Egyptian mummy-cloths 3,000 years ago, and not materially differing from our modern varieties; one of them, indeed, being precisely identical—thus affording us the pleasing assurance that the corn which Joseph placed in Benjamin's sack before the great pyramid was built was not inferior to the best of the present day.

EDWARD EVERETT.

I WOULD rather sit on a pumpkin and have it all to myself, than to be crowded on a velvet cushion.

TWO PICTURES.

N old farm-house with meadows wide
And sweet with clover on each side;
A bright-eyed boy, who looks from out
The door with woodbine wreathed about,
And wishes his one thought all day:
" Oh, if I could but fly away
    From this dull spot, the world to see,
How happy, happy, happy,
    How happy I should be! "

Amid the city's constant din,
A man who round the world has been,
Who, mid the tumult and the throng,
Is thinking, thinking, all day long:
" Oh, could I only tread once more
    The field-path to the farm-house door,
The old green meadow could I see,
    How happy, happy, happy,
How happy I should be! "

MARION DOUGLASS.

" Still where he treads the stubborn clods divide,
The smooth, fresh furrow opens deep and wide."

THE PLOUGHMAN.

LEAR the brown path to meet his coulter's gleam!
    Lo! on he comes, behind his smoking team,
    With toil's bright dew-drops on his sunburnt
        brow,
The lord of earth, the hero of the plough!

First in the field before the reddening sun,
Last in the shadows when the day is done,
Line after line, along the bursting sod,
Marks the broad acres where his feet have trod.
Still where he treads the stubborn clods divide,
The smooth, fresh furrow opens deep and wide;
Matted and dense the tangled turf upheaves,
Mellow and dark the ridgy corn-field cleaves;

Up the steep hillside, where the laboring train .
Slants the long track, that scores the level plain,
Through the moist valley, clogged with oozing
        clay,
The patient convoy breaks its destined way;
At every turn the loosening chains resound,
The swinging ploughshare circles glistening round,
Till the wide field one billowy waste appears,
And wearied hands unbind the panting steers.

These are the hands whose sturdy labor brings
The peasant's food, the golden pomp of kings;
This is the page whose letters shall be seen,
Changed by the sun to words of living green;

This is the scholar whose immortal pen
Spells the first lesson hunger taught to men;
These are the lines that heaven-commanded Toil
Shows on his deed,—the charter of the soil!

O gracious Mother, whose benignant breast
Wakes us to life, and lulls us all to rest,
How thy sweet features, kind to every clime,
Mock with their smile the wrinkled front of Time!
We stain thy flowers,—they blossom o'er the dead;
We rend thy bosom, and it gives us bread;
O'er the red field that trampling strife has torn,
Waves the green plumage of thy tasselled corn,
Our maddening conflicts scar thy fairest plain,
Still thy soft answer is the growing grain.
Yet, O our Mother, while uncounted charms
Steal round our hearts in thine embracing arms,
Let not our virtues in thy love decay,
And thy fond sweetness waste our strength away.

No, by these hills whose banners now displayed
In blazing cohorts Autumn has arrayed;
By yon twin summits, on whose splintery crests
The tossing hemlocks hold the eagles' nests;
By these fair plains the mountain circle screens,
And feeds with streamlets from its dark ravines,—
True to their home, these faithful arms shall toil
To crown with peace their own untainted soil;
And, true to God, to freedom, to mankind,
If her chained ban-dogs Faction shall unbind,
These stately forms, that, bending even now,
Bowed their strong manhood to the humble plough,
Shall rise erect, the guardians of the land,
The same stern iron in the same right hand,
Till o'er their hills the shouts of triumph run,—
The sword has rescued what the ploughshare won!

OLIVER WENDELL HOLMES.

"To walk in the air how pleasant and fair."

THE USEFUL PLOUGH.

COUNTRY life is sweet!
In moderate cold and heat,
   To walk in the air how pleasant and fair!
In every field of wheat,
   The fairest flowers adorning the bowers,
And every meadow's brow;
   So that I say, no courtier may
   Compare with them who clothe in gray,
And follow the useful plough.

They rise with the morning lark,
And labor till almost dark,
   Then, folding their sheep, they hasten to sleep
While every pleasant park
   Next morning is ringing with birds that are singing
On each green, tender bough.
   With what content and merriment
   Their days are spent, whose minds are bent
To follow the useful plough.

WEARINESS can snore upon the flint, when restive sloth finds the down pillow hard.

13

"Those fields and hills, this wild brookside,
To me are better beyond measure."

COUNTRY LIFE.

THE merchant tempts me with his gold,
　The gold he worships night and day;
He bids me leave this dreary wold,
　And come into the city gay.
I will not go; I won't be sold;
　I scorn his pleasures and array;
I'll rather bear the country's cold,
　Than from its freedom walk away.

What is to me the city s pride?
　The haunt of luxury and pleasure;
Those fields and hills, this wild brookside,
　To me are better beyond measure.
Mid country scenes I'll still abide;
　With country life and country leisure.
Content, whatever may betide,
　With common good instead of treasure.

THE CITY AND THE COUNTRY.

THE Réverend Robert Collyer made the remark on one occasion that during his twenty years' residence in Chicago he had not known of a single man who had come prominently to the front in any pursuit who was born and bred in a large city. The leading men in every calling—judges, lawyers, clergymen, editors, merchants, and so on—had been reared in the country, away from the follies, the vices and the enervating influences that are known to exist in all large towns. Fashion reduces all young men and women to the same dull and uninteresting level. New York is now an old city. It has produced generations of men. How few of them have ever made their mark, there or elsewhere! It cannot be said that they go into other parts of the country and there develop the higher forms of manhood. They are never heard of except in the aggregated, concrete form of "our fellow-citizens." How much of a man is due to qualities born in him, and how much to his early environment, no philosopher has been able to tell us; but it is impossible to conceive of a sagacious intellect like that of Lincoln, of a glorious mind like Webster's, emerging from the false glitter and noisy commotion of the city. We think of Washington, the patrician sage, pacing among the stately oaks of old Virginia; of Jefferson in his country-seat, and of John Adams tilling his farm in Massachusetts. These men, it is true, flourished at a time when there were no large cities in the United States. But later on we see Lincoln and Garfield reaching the topmost round of fame's ladder from the obscurity of country homes. Not one American President, from first to last, was born in a city.

THE HAYMAKERS.

DOWN on the Merrimac River,
　While the autumn grass is green,
Oh, there the jolly hay-men
　In their gundalows are seen;
Floating down, as ebbs the current,
　And the dawn leads on the day,
With their scythes and rakes all ready,
　To gather in the hay.

The good wife, up the river,
　Has made the oven hot,
And with plenty of pandowdy
　Has filled her earthen pot.
Their long oars sweep them onward,
　As the ripples round them play,
And the jolly hay-men drift along
　To make the meadow hay.

At the bank-side then they moor her,
    Where the sluggish waters run,
By the shallow creek's low edges,
    Beneath the fervid sun—
And all day long the toilers
    Mow their swaths, and day by day,
You can see their scythe-blades flushing
    At the cutting of the hay.

When the meadow-birds are flying,
    Then down go scythe and rake,
And right and left their scattering shots
    The sleeping echoes wake—

For silent spreads the broad expanse,
    To the sand-hills far away,
And thus they change their work for sport,
    At making of the hay.

When the gundalows are loaded—
    Gunwales to the water's brim—
With their little square-sails set atop,
    Up the river how they swim!
At home, beside the fire, by night,
    While the children round them play,
What tales the jolly hay-men tell
    Of getting in the hay!

                        GEORGE LUNT.

"Down on the Merrimac River,
    While the autumn grass is green."

THE SONG OF THE MOWERS.

WE are up and away, ere the sunrise hath kissed
    In the valley below us, that ocean of mist,
    Ere the tops of the hills have grown bright in
        its ray,
        With our scythes on our shoulders, we're up
            and away.

The freshness and beauty of morning are ours,
The music of birds and the fragrance of flowers;
And our trail is the first that is seen in the dew,
As our pathway through orchards and lanes we pursue.

Hurrah! here we are! now together, as one,
Give your scythes to the sward, and press steadily on;
All together, as one, o'er the stubble we pass,
With a swing and a ring of the steel through the
    grass.

Before us the clover stands thickly and tall,
At our left it is piled in a verdurous wall;
And never breathed monarch more fragrant perfumes
Than the sunshine distills from its leaves and its
    blooms.

Invisible censers around us are swung,
And anthems exultant from tree-tops are flung;
And 'mid fragrance and music and beauty we share
The jubilant life of the earth and the air.

Let the priest and the lawyer grow pale in their shades,
And the slender young clerk keep his skin like a
  maid's;

We care not, though dear Mother Nature may bronze
Our cheeks with the kiss that she gives to her sons.

Then cheerly, boys, cheerly! together, as one,
Give your scythes to the sward, and press steadily on;
All together, as one, o'er the stubble we pass,
With a swing and a ring of the steel through the grass.

WILLIAM HENRY BURLEIGH.

THE CORNFIELD.

SOON as the morning trembles o'er the sky,
And, unperceived, unfolds the spreading day,
Before the ripened field the reapers stand.
At once they stoop and swell the lusty sheaves,

While through their cheerful band the rural talk,
The rural scandal, and the rural jest,
Fly harmless, to deceive the tedious time,
And steal unfelt the sultry hours away.

JAMES THOMSON.

SHE bids you on the wanton rushes lay you down,
And rest your gentle head upon her lap,
And she will sing the song that pleaseth you,
And on your eyelids crown the god of sleep,
Charming your blood with pleasing heaviness;

Making such difference betwixt wake and sleep
As is the difference betwixt day and night,
The hour before the heavenly-harnessed team
Begins his golden progress in the east.

THE MOWERS.

HERE mountains round a lonely dale
    Our cottage-roof enclose,
  Come night or morn, the hissing pail
    With yellow cream o'erflows;
And roused at break of day from sleep,
  And cheerly trudging hither—
A scythe-sweep, and a scythe-sweep,
  We mow the grass together.

Gay sunlights o'er the hillocks creep,
  And join for golden weather—
A scythe-sweep, and a scythe-sweep,
  We mow the dale together.

The good-wife stirs at five, we know,
  The master soon comes round,
And many swaths must lie a-row
  Ere breakfast-horn shall sound;

" A scythe-sweep, and a scythe-sweep,
    We mow the grass together."

The fog drawn up the mountain-side
  And scattered flake by flake,
The chasm of blue above grows wide,
  And richer blue the lake;

The clover and the florin deep,
  The grass of silvery feather—
A scythe-sweep and a scythe-sweep,
  We mow the dale together.

The noon-tide brings its welcome rest
  Our toil-wet brows to dry;
Anew with merry stave and jest
  The shrieking hone we ply.
White falls the brook from steep to steep
  Among the purple heather—
A scythe-sweep, and a scythe-sweep,
  We mow the dale together.

For dial, see, our shadows turn;
  Low lies the stately mead;
A scythe, an hour-glass, and an urn—
  All flesh is grass, we read.
To-morrow's sky may laugh or weep,
  To Heaven we leave it, whether—
A scythe-sweep, and a scythe-sweep,
  We've done our task together.

WILLIAM ALLINGHAM.

WHEN THE COWS COME HOME.

LOVE the beautiful evening
  When the sunset clouds are gold;
When the barn-fowls seek a shelter
  And the young lambs seek their fold;
When the four-o'-clocks are open,
  And the swallows homeward come;
When the horses cease their labors,
  And the cows come home.

When the supper's almost ready,
  And Johnny is asleep,
And I beside the cradle
  My pleasant vigil keep:
Sitting beside the window
  Watching for "Pa" to come.
While the soft bells gently tinkle
  As the cows come home.

When the sunset and the twilight
  In mingling hues are blent,
I can sit and watch the shadows
  With my full heart all content:
And I wish for nothing brighter,
  And I long no more to roam
When the twilight's peace comes o'er me,
  And the cows come home.

I see their shadows lengthen
  As they slowly cross the field,
And I know the food is wholesome
  Which their generous udders yield.
More than the tropic's fruitage,
  Than marble hall or dome,
Are the blessings that surround me
  When the cows come home.

MARY E. NEALEY.

COME TO THE SUNSET TREE.

OME to the sunset tree!
  The day is past and gone;
The woodman's ax lies free,
  And the reaper's work is done.

The twilight star to heaven,
  And the summer dew to flowers,
And rest to us is given
  By the cool, soft evening hours.

Come to the sunset tree!
  The day is past and gone;
The woodman's ax lies free,
  And the reaper's work is done.

Yes; tuneful is the sound
  That dwells in whispering boughs;
Welcome the freshness round,
  And the gale that fans our brows.

"Come to the sunset tree,
The day is past and gone."

Sweet is the hour of rest!
  Pleasant the wind's low sigh,
And the gleaming of the west,
  And the turf whereon we lie.

When the burden and the heat
  Of labor's task are o'er,
And kindly voices greet
  The tired one at his door.

But rest more sweet and still
  Than ever nightfall gave,
Our longing hearts shall fill
  In the world beyond the grave.

There shall no tempest blow,
  No scorching noontide heat;
There shall be no more snow,
  No weary wandering feet.

And we lift our trusting eyes,
　From the hills our fathers trod,
To the quiet of the skies,
　To the Sabbath of our God.

Come to the sunset tree!
　The day is past and gone;
The woodman's ax lies free.
　And the reaper's work is done!

FELICIA DOROTHEA HEMANS.

MY LITTLE BROOK.

LITTLE brook half hidden under trees,—
It gives me peace and rest the whole day
　　through,
Having this little brook to wander to,
　So cool, so clear, with grassy banks and these
　Sweet miracles of violets 'neath the trees.

And yet the waves they come I know not whence,
And they flow on from me I know not whither,
Sometimes my fancy pines to follow thither;
　But I can only see the forest dense,—
　Still the brook flows I know not where nor
　　whence.

"I sit here by the stream in full content."

There is a rock where I can sit and see
The crystal ripples dancing down and racing,
Like children round the stones each other chasing,
　Then for a moment pausing seriously,
　In a dark mimic pond that I can see.

The rock is rough and broken on its edge
With jutting corners, but there come alway
The merry ripples with their tiny spray,
　To press it ere they flow on by the sedge,
　They never fail the old rock's broken edge.

I sit here by the stream in full content,
It is so constant, and I lay my hand
Down through its waters on the golden sand.
　And watch the sunshine with its shallows blent,
　Watch it with ever-growing, sweet content.

Who knows from what far hills it threads its way,
What mysteries of cliffs and pines and skies
O'erhang the spot where its first fountains rise.
　What shy wild deer may stoop to taste its spray.
　Through what rare regions my brook threads its way.

I only see the trees above, below,
Who knows through what fair lands the stream may
　　run,
What children play, what homes are built thereon.
　Through what great cities broadening it may go?—
　I only see the trees above, below.

What do I care? I pause with full content,
My little brook beside the rock to see,
What it has been or what it yet may be,
　Naught matters, I but know that it is sent
　Flowing my way, and I am well content.

MARY BOLLES BRANCH.

A HARVEST HYMN.

GREAT GOD! — our heart-felt thanks to Thee!
  We feel thy presence everywhere;
And pray, that we may ever be
  Thus objects of thy guardian care.

We sowed! — by Thee our work was seen,
  And blessed; and instantly went forth
Thy mandate; and in living green
  Soon smiled the fair and fruitful earth.

We toiled! — and Thou didst note our toil;
  And gav'st the sunshine and the rain,
Till ripened on the teeming soil
  The fragrant grass, and golden grain.

And now, we reap! — and oh, our God!
  From this, the earth's unbounded floor,
We send our Song of Thanks abroad,
  And pray Thee, bless our hoarded store!

W. D. GALLAGHER.

THE OLD HOUSE.

I'M standing by the window-sill,
  Where we have stood of yore;
The sycamore is waving still
  Its branches near the door;
And near me creeps the wild-rose vine
  On which our wreaths were hung.—
Still round the porch its tendrils twine,
  As when we both were young.

The little path that used to lead
  Down by the river shore
Is overgrown with brier and weed—
  Not level as before.

But there's no change upon the hill,
  From whence our voices rung —
The violets deck the summit still,
  As when we both were young.

And yonder is the old oak-tree,
  Beneath whose spreading shade,
When our young hearts were light and free,
  In innocence we played;
And over there the meadow gate
  On which our playmates swung,
Still standing in its rustic state,
  As when we both were young.

LOUISA CHANDLER MOULTON.

RURAL NATURE.

WHERE art thou loveliest, O Nature, tell!
　　Oh, where may be thy Paradise? Where grow
　　Thy happiest groves? And down what woody
　　　　dell
Do thy most fancy-winning waters flow?

Eternal summer, while the air may quell
His fury. Is it 'neath his morning car,
Where jeweled palaces, and golden thrones,
Have awed the Eastern nations through all time?
Or o'er the Western seas, or where afar

"And down what woody dell
Do thy most fancy-winning waters flow?"

Tell where thy softest breezes longest blow?
And where thy ever blissful mountains swell
Upon whose sides the cloudless sun may throw

Our winter sun warms up the southern zones
With summer? Where can be the happy climes?
　　　　　　　　　　　　　　　WILLIAM BARNES.

TO walk with the breeze upon one's brow, to trample the level grass exuberant
　　with freshness, to climb upon the mountain, to follow through the meadows
　　some thread of water gliding under rushes and water-plants,—I give you my
　　word for it, there is happiness in this. At this contact with healthy and natural
things, the follies of the world drop off as drop the dead leaves when the spring sap
rises and the young leaves put forth.

THE FARMER'S BOY.

LED now the sullen murmurs of the north,
  The splendid raiment of the Spring peeps forth;
  Her universal green and the clear sky
  Delight still more and more the gazing eye.
  Wide o'er the fields, in rising moisture strong,
Shoots up the simple flower, or creeps along
The mellowed soil, imbibing fairer hues
Or sweets from frequent showers and evening dews
That summon from their sheds the slumbering ploughs,
While health impregnates every breeze that blows.
No wheels support the diving, pointed share;
No groaning ox is doomed to labor there;

Welcome, green headland! firm beneath his feet:
Welcome, the friendly bank's refreshing seat;
There, warm with toil, his panting horses browse
Their sheltering canopy of pendant boughs;
Till rest delicious chase each transient pain,
And new-born vigor swell in every vein.
Hour after hour, and day to day succeeds,
Till every clod and deep-drawn furrow spreads
To crumbling mould,—a level surface clear,
And strewed with corn to crown the rising year;
And o'er the whole, Giles, once transverse again,
In earth's moist bosom buries up the grain.

"For pigs and ducks and turkeys throng the door."

No helpmates teach the docile steed his road
(Alike unknown the ploughboy and the goad):
But unassisted, through each toilsome day,
With smiling brow the plough man cleaves his way,
Draws his fresh parallels, and, widening still,
Treads slow the heavy dale, or climbs the hill.
Strong on the wing his busy followers play,
Where writhing earthworms meet the unwelcome day,
Till all is changed, and hill and level down
Assume a livery of sober brown;
Again disturbed, when Giles with wearying strides
From ridge to ridge the ponderous harrow guides.
His heels deep sinking, every step he goes,
Till dirt adhesive loads his clouted shoes.

The work is done; no more to man is given;
The grateful farmer trusts the rest to Heaven.
  *   *   *   *   *
  His simple errand done, he homeward hies;
Another instantly its place supplies.
The clattering dairy-maid, immersed in steam,
Singing and scrubbing midst her milk and cream,
Bawls out, "Go fetch the cows!"—he hears no
      more;
For pigs and ducks and turkeys throng the door,
And sitting hens for constant war prepared,—
A concert strange to that which late he heard.
Straight to the meadow then he whistling goes;
With well-known halloo calls his lazy cows;

Down the rich pasture heedlessly they graze,
Or hear the summons with an idle gaze.
For well they know the cow-yard yields no
    more
Its tempting fragrance, nor its wintry store.
Reluctance marks their steps, sedate and slow,
The right of conquest all the law they know;
The strong press on, the weak by turns succeed,
And one superior always takes the lead,
Is ever foremost whereso'er they stray,
Allowed precedence, undisputed sway:
With jealous pride her station is maintained,
For many a broil that post of honor gained.
At home, the yard affords a grateful scene,
For spring makes e'en a miry cow-yard clean.
Thence from its chalky bed behold conveyed
The rich manure that drenching winter made,
Which, piled near home, grows green with many
    a weed,
A promised nutriment for autumn's seed.

Forth comes the maid, and like the morning smiles;
The mistress, too, and followed close by Giles.
A friendly tripod forms their humble seat,
With pails bright scoured and delicately sweet.
Where shadowing elms obstruct the morning ray
Begins the work, begins the simple lay;
The full-charged udder yields its willing stream
While Mary sings some lover's amorous dream;
And crouching Giles, beneath a neighboring tree,
Tugs o'er his pail and chants with equal glee;
Whose hat with battered brim, and nap so bare,
From the cow's side purloins a coat of hair,—
A mottled ensign of his harmless trade,
An unambitious, peaceable cockade.
As unambitious, too, that cheerful aid
The mistress yields beside her rosy maid;
With joy she views her plenteous reeking store,
And bears a brimmer to the dairy door;
Her cows dismissed, the luscious mead to roam,
Till eve again recall them loaded home.

ROBERT BLOOMFIELD.

FARM-YARD SONG.

VER the hills the farm-boy goes,
    His shadow lengthened along the land,
    A giant staff in a giant hand;
In the poplar tree, above the spring,
The katydid begins to sing;
        The early dews are falling; —
Into the stone-heap darts the mink;
The swallows skim the river's brink;
And home to the woodland fly the crows,
When over the hill the farm-boy goes,
        Cheerily calling, —
    "Co', boss! co', boss! co'! co'! co'! "
Farther, farther, over the hill,
Faintly calling, calling still, —
    "Co', boss! co', boss! co'! co'! "

Into the yard the farmer goes,
With grateful heart, at the close of day;
Harness and chain are hung away;
In the wagon-shed stand yoke and plough;
The straw's in the stack, the hay in the mow,
        The cooling dews are falling; —
The friendly sheep his welcome bleat,
The pigs come grunting to his feet,
The whinnying mare her master knows,
When into the yard the farmer goes,
        His cattle calling, —
    "Co', boss! co', boss! co'! co'! co'! "
While still the cow-boy, far away,
Goes seeking those that have gone astray, —
    "Co', boss! co', boss! co'! co'! "

Now to her task the milkmaid goes,
The cattle come crowding through the gate,
Lowing, pushing, little and great;
About the trough, by the farm-yard pump,
The frolicsome yearlings frisk and jump,
        While the pleasant dews are falling;
The new-milch heifer is quick and shy,
But the old cow waits with tranquil eye;
And the white stream into the bright pail flows,
When to her task the milkmaid goes,
        Soothingly calling, —
    "So, boss! so, boss! so! so! so! "
The cheerful milkmaid takes her stool,
And sits and milks in the twilight cool,
        Saying, "So! so, boss! so! so! "

To supper at last the farmer goes,
The apples are pared, the paper read,
The stories are told, then all to bed.
Without, the cricket's ceaseless song
Makes shrill the silence all night long;
        The heavy dews are falling.
The housewife's hand has turned the lock;
Drowsily ticks the kitchen clock;
The household sinks to deep repose;
But still in sleep the farm-boy goes
        Singing, calling, —
    "Co', boss! co', boss! co'! co'! co'! "
And oft the milkmaid in her dreams
Drums in the pail with the flashing streams,
        Murmuring, "So, boss! so! "

JOHN TOWNSEND TROWBRIDGE.

HARVEST SONG.

LOVE, I love to see
  Bright steel gleam through the land;
'Tis a goodly sight, but it must be
  In the reaper's tawny hand.

The helmet and the spear
  Are twined with the laurel wreath;
But the trophy is wet with the orphan's tear;
  And blood-spots rust beneath.

I love to see the field
  That is moist with purple stain,
But not where bullet, sword and shield
  Lie strewn with the gory slain.

No, no; 'tis where the sun
  Shoots down his cloudless beams,
Till rich and bursting juice-drops run
  On the vineyard earth in streams.

My glowing heart beats high
  At the sight of shining gold;
But it is not that which the miser's eye
  Delighteth to behold.

A brighter wealth by far
  Than the deep mine's yellow vein,

Is seen around in the fair hills crowned
  With sheaves of burnished grain.

Look forth thou thoughtless one,
  Whose proud knee never bends;
Take thou the bread that's daily spread,
  But think on Him who sends.

Look forth, ye toiling men,
  Though little ye possess, —
Be glad that dearth is not on earth
  To make that little less.

Let the song of praise be poured
  In gratitude and joy,
By the rich man with his garners stored
  And the ragged gleaner-boy.

The feast that Nature gives
  Is not for one alone;
'Tis shared by the meanest slave that lives
  And the tenant of a throne.

Then glory to the steel
  That shines in the reaper's hand,
And thanks to Him who has blest the seed
  And crowned the harvest land.

ELIZA COOK.

THE FARMER'S WIFE.

BIRD-LIKE she's up at day-dawn's blush,
  In summer heats or winter snows—
Her veins with healthful blood aflush,
  Her breath of balm, her cheek a rose,

"Homeward (his daily labors done,
The stalwart farmer slowly plods.''

In eyes—the kindest eyes on earth—
Are sparkles of a homely mirth;

Demure, arch humor's ambush in
The clear curves of her dimpled chin.
Ah! guileless creature, hale and good,
Ah! fount of wholesome womanhood,
Far from the world's unhallowed strife!
God's blessing on the farmer's wife.

I love to mark her matron charms,
  Her fearless steps through household ways,
Her sun-burnt hands and buxom arms,
  Her waist unbound by torturing stays;
Blithe as a bee, with busy care,
She's here, she's there, she's everywhere;
Long ere the clock has struck for noon
Home chords of toil are all in tune;
And from each richly bounteous hour
She drains its use, as bees a flower.
Apart from Passion's pain and strife,
Peace gently girds the Farmer's Wife!

Homeward (his daily labors done)
  The stalwart farmer slowly plods,
From battling, between shade and sun,
  With sullen glebe and stubborn sods.
Her welcome on his spirit bowed
Is sunshine flashing on a cloud!

All vanished is the brief eclipse!
Hark! to the sound of wedded lips,
And words of tender warmth that start
From out the husband's grateful heart!
O! well he knows how vain is life,
Unsweetened by the Farmer's Wife.

But lo! the height of pure delight
  Comes with the evening's stainless joys,
When by the hearthstone spaces bright
  Blend the glad tones of girls and boys;
Their voices rise in gleeful swells,
Their laughter rings like elfin bells,
Till with a look 'twixt smile and frown
The mother lays her infant down,
And at her firm, uplifted hand,
There's silence 'mid the jovial band;

Her signal stills their harmless strife —
Love crowns with law the Farmer's Wife!

Ye dames in proud, palatial halls—
  Of lavish wiles and jeweled dress,
On whom, perchance, no infant calls
  (For barren oft YOUR loveliness) —
Turn hitherward those languid eyes
And for a moment's space be wise;
Your sister 'mid the country dew
Is three times nearer Heaven than you,
And where the palms of Eden stir.
Dream not that ye shall stand by her,
Though in your false, bewildering life,
Your folly scorned the Farmer's Wife!

            PAUL HAMILTON HAYNE.

THE PUMPKIN.

GREENLY and fair in the lands of the sun,
The vines of the gourd and the rich melon run,
And the rock and the tree and the cottage enfold,
With broad leaves all greenness and blossoms all
    gold,
Like that which o'er Nineveh's prophet once grew,
While he waited to know that his warning was true,
And longed for the storm-cloud, and listened in vain
For the rush of the whirlwind and red fire-rain.

On the banks of the Xenil, the dark Spanish maiden
Comes up with the fruit of the tangled vine laden;
And the Creole of Cuba laughs out to behold
Through orange-leaves shining the broad spheres of
    gold;
Yet with dearer delight from his home in the North,
On the fields of his harvest the Yankee looks forth,
Where crook-necks are coiling and yellow fruit shines,
And the sun of September melts down on his vines.

Ah! on Thanksgiving Day, when from East and from
    West,
From North and from South come the pilgrim and
    guest,
When the grey-haired New-Englander sees round his
    board
The old broken links of affection restored,

When the care-wearied man seeks his mother once
    more,
And the worn matron smiles where the girl smiled
    before,
What moistens the lip and what brightens the eye?
What calls back the past, like the rich pumpkin-pie?

O, fruit loved of boyhood! the old days recalling;
When wood-grapes were purpling and brown nuts
    were falling!
When wild, ugly faces we carved in its skin,
Glaring out through the dark with a candle within!
When we laughed round the corn-heap, with hearts
    all in tune,
Our chair a broad pumpkin, our lantern the moon,
Telling tales of the fairy who traveled like steam
In a pumpkin-shell coach, with two rats for her team!

Then thanks for thy present!— none sweeter or better
E'er smoked from an oven or circled a platter!
Fairer hands never wrought at a pastry more fine,
Brighter eyes never watched o'er its baking than thine!
And the prayer, which my mouth is too full to express,
Swells my heart that thy shadow may never be less,
That the days of thy lot may be lengthened below,
And the fame of thy worth like a pumpkin-vine grow,
And thy life be as sweet, and its last sunset sky
Golden-tinted and fair as thy own pumpkin-pie!

            JOHN GREENLEAF WHITTIER.

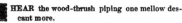

HEAR the wood-thrush piping one mellow des-
    cant more,
And scent the flowers that blow when the heat of
    day is o'er.

ATH not old custom made this life more sweet
    Than that of painted pomp? Are not these
        woods
More free from perils than the envious court?

ROBERT OF LINCOLN.

ERRILY swinging on briar and weed,
  Near to the nest of his little dame,
Over the mountain-side or mead,
  Robert of Lincoln is telling his name:
    Bob-o'-link, bob-o'-link,
    Spink, spank, spink;
Snug and safe is that nest of ours,
Hidden among the summer flowers.
              Chee, chee, chee.

Robert of Lincoln's Quaker wife,
  Pretty and quiet, with plain brown wings,
Passing at home a patient life,
  Broods in the grass while her husband sings:
    Bob-o'-link, bob-o'-link
    Spink, spank, spink;
Brood, kind creature; you need not fear
Thieves and robbers while I am here.
              Chee, chee, chee.

"Robert of Lincoln is telling his name."

Robert of Lincoln is gayly dressed.
  Wearing a bright black wedding coat;
White are his shoulders and white his crest,
  Hear him call in his merry note:
    Bob-o'-link, bob-o'-link,
    Spink, spank, spink;
Look, what a nice new coat is mine,
Sure there was never a bird so fine.
              Chee, chee, chee.

Modest and shy as a nun is she,
  One weak chirp is her only note,
Braggart and prince of braggarts is he,
  Pouring boasts from his little throat:
    Bob-o'-link, bob-o'-link,
    Spink, spank, spink;
Never was I afraid of man;
Catch me, cowardly knaves, if you can.
              Chee, chee, chee.

Six white eggs on a bed of hay,
  Flecked with purple, a pretty sight!
There as the mother sits all day,
  Robert is singing with all his might:
    Bob-o'-link, bob-o'-link,
    Spink, spank, spink;
Nice good wife, that never goes out,
Keeping house while I frolic about.
        Chee, chee, chee.

Soon as the little ones chip the shell
  Six wide mouths are open for food;
Robert of Lincoln bestirs him well,
  Gathering seed for the hungry brood.
    Bob-o'-link, bob-o'-link,
    Spink, spank, spink;
This new life is likely to be
Hard for a gay young fellow like me.
        Chee, chee, chee.

Robert of Lincoln at length is made
  Sober with work, and silent with care;
Off is his holiday garment laid,
  Half forgotten that merry air,
    Bob-o'-link, bob-o'-link,
    Spink, spank, spink;
Nobody knows but my mate and I
Where our nest and our nestlings lie.
        Chee, chee, chee.

Summer wanes; the children are grown;
  Fun and frolic no more he knows;
Robert of Lincoln 's a humdrum crone;
  Off he flies, and we sing as he goes:
    Bob-o'-link, bob-o'-link,
    Spink, spank, spink;
When you can pipe that merry old strain,
Robert of Lincoln, come back again.
        Chee, chee, chee.

                        WILLIAM CULLEN BRYANT.

ON THE BANKS OF THE TENNESSEE.

I SIT by the open window
  And look to the hills away,
Over beautiful undulations
  That glow with the flowers of May —
And as the lights and the shadows
  With the passing moments change,
Comes many a scene of beauty
  Within my vision's range —
But there is not one among them
  That is half so dear to me,
As an old log-cabin I think of
  On the banks of the Tennessee.

Now up from the rolling meadows,
  And down from the hill-tops now,
Fresh breezes steal in at my window,
  And sweetly fan my brow —
And the sounds that they gather and bring
    me,
  From rivulet, and meadow, and hill,
Come in with a touching cadence,
  And my throbbing bosom fill —
But the dearest thoughts thus wakened,
  And in tears brought back to me,
Cluster round that old log-cabin
  On the banks of the Tennessee.

To many a fond remembrance
  My thoughts are backward cast,
As I sit by the open window
  And recall the faded past —
For all along the windings
  Of the ever-moving years,
Lie wrecks of hope and of purpose
  That I now behold through tears—

14

And of all of them, the saddest
  That is thus brought back to me,
Makes holy that old log-cabin
  On the banks of the Tennessee.

  "——An old log-cabin I think of
    On the banks of the Tennessee."

Glad voices now greet me daily,
  Sweet faces I oft behold,
Yet I sit by the open window,
  And dream of the times of old—
Of a voice that on earth is silent,
  Of a face that is seen no more,
Of a spirit that faltered not ever
  In the struggle of days now o'er —
And a beautiful grave comes pictured
  Forever and ever to me,
From a knoll near that old log-cabin
  On the banks of the Tennessee.

                        W. D. GALLAGHER.

SUMMER LONGINGS.

AH! my heart is weary waiting,
　　Waiting for the May,—
Waiting for the pleasant rambles
Where the fragrant hawthorn-brambles,
　　With the woodbine alternating,
　　Scent the dewy way.
　Ah! my heart is weary waiting,
　　Waiting for the May.

Ah! my heart is sick with longing,
　　Longing for the May,—
Longing to escape from study,
To the young face fair and ruddy,
　And the thousand charms belonging
　　To the summer's day.
　Ah! my heart is sick with longing,
　　Longing for the May.

Ah! my heart is sore with sighing,
　　Sighing for the May,—
Sighing for their sure returning,
When the summer beams are burning,

Hopes and flowers that, dead or dying,
　　All the winter lay.
　Ah! my heart is sore with sighing,
　　Sighing for the May.

Ah! my heart is pained with throbbing,
　　Throbbing for the May,—
Throbbing for the seaside billows,
Or the water-wooing willows;
　Where, in laughing and in sobbing,
　　Glide the streams away.
　Ah! my heart, my heart is throbbing,
　　Throbbing for the May.

Waiting sad, dejected, weary,
　　Waiting for the May:
Spring goes by with wasted warnings.—
Moonlit evenings, sunbright mornings,—
　Summer comes, yet dark and dreary
　　Life still ebbs away;
　Man is ever weary, weary,
　　Waiting for the May!

　　　DENIS FLORENCE MAC-CARTHY.

FARM LIFE.

AGRICULTURE is the greatest among the arts, for it is first in supplying our necessities. It is the mother and nurse of all other arts. It favors and strengthens population; it creates and maintains manufactures, gives employment to navigation and materials to commerce. It animates every species of industry, and opens to nations the surest channels of opulence. It is also the strongest bond of well regulated society, the surest basis of internal peace, the natural associate of good morals.

We ought to count among the benefits of agriculture the charm which the practice of it communicates to a country life. That charm which has made the country, in our own view, the retreat of the hero, the asylum of the sage, and the temple of the historic muse. The strong desire, the longing after the country, with which we find the bulk of mankind to be penetrated, points to it as the chosen abode of sublunary bliss. The sweet occupations of culture with her varied products and attendant enjoyments are, at least, a relief from the stifling atmosphere of the city, the monotony of subdivided employments, the anxious uncertainty of commerce, the vexations of ambition so often disappointed, of self-love so often mortified, of factitious pleasures and unsubstantial vanities.

We deplore the disposition of young men to get away from their farm homes to our larger cities, where they are subject to difficulties and temptations, which, but too often, they fail to overcome.

Depend upon it, if you would hold your sons and brothers back from roaming away into the perilous centres, you must steadily make three attempts—to abate the taskwork of farming, to raise maximum crops and profits, and to surround your work with the exhilaration of intellectual progress. You must elevate the whole spirit of your vocation for your vocation's sake, till no other can outstrip it in what most adorns and strengthens a civilized state.

SUMMER WOODS.

HE ceaseless hum of men, the dusty streets,
Crowded with multitudinous life; the din
Of toil and traffic, and the woe and sin,
The dweller in the populous city meets:
These have I left to seek the cool retreats
Of the untrodden forest, where, in bowers
Builded by Nature's hand, inlaid with flowers,
And roofed with ivy, on the mossy seats
Reclining, I can while away the hours
In sweetest converse with old books, or give
My thoughts to God; or fancies fugitive
Indulge, while over me their radiant showers
Of rarest blossoms the old trees shake down,
And thanks to Him my meditations crown!

WILLIAM HENRY BURLEIGH.

THE VILLAGE BOY.

FREE from the cottage corner, see how wild
  The village boy along the pasture hies,
With every smell, and sound, and sight beguiled,
  That round the prospect meets his wondering
    eyes;
Now, stooping, eager for the cowslip peeps,
  As though he'd get them all,—now tired of these,
Across the flaggy brook he eager leaps,
  For some new flower his happy rapture sees;—

Now, leering 'mid the bushes on his knees
  On woodland banks, for blue-bell flowers he
    creeps;—
And now, while looking up among the trees,
  He spies a nest, and down he throws his flowers,
And up he climbs with new-fed ecstasies;
  The happiest object in the summer hours.

                                    CLARKE.

" And up he climbs with new-fed ecstasies."

THE BAREFOOT BOY.

BLESSINGS on thee, little man,
  Barefoot boy, with cheek of tan!
  With thy turned-up pantaloons,
    And thy merry whistled tunes;
With thy red lip, redder still
Kissed by strawberries on the hill;

With the sunshine on thy face,
Through thy torn brim's jaunty grace!
From my heart I give thee joy:
I was once a barefoot boy.
Prince thou art—the grown-up man
Only is republican.

Let the million-dollared ride!
Barefoot, trudging at his side,
Thou hast more than he can buy,
In the reach of ear and eye:
Outward sunshine, inward joy.
Blessings on thee, barefoot boy!

O! for boyhood's painless play,
Sleep that wakes in laughing day,
Health that mocks the doctor's rules,
Knowledge never learned of schools:

Where the ground-nut trails its vine,
Where the wood-grape's clusters shine;
Of the black wasp's cunning way,
Mason of his walls of clay,
And the architectural plans
Of gray hornet artisans!
For, eschewing books and tasks,
Nature answers all he asks;
Hand in hand with her he walks,
Face to face with her he talks,

" With thy turned-up pantaloons,
And thy merry whistled tunes."

Of the wild bee's morning chase,
Of the wild flower's time and place,
Flight of fowl, and habitude
Of the tenants of the wood;
How the tortoise bears his shell,
How the woodchuck digs his cell,
And the ground-mole sinks his well;
How the robin feeds her young,
How the oriole's nest is hung;
Where the whitest lilies blow,
Where the freshest berries grow,

Part and parcel of her joy.
Blessings on the barefoot boy!

O for boyhood's time of June,
Crowding years in one brief moon,
When all things I heard or saw,
Me, their master, waited for!
I was rich in flowers and trees,
Humming-birds and honey-bees;
For my sport the squirrel played,
Plied the snouted mole his spade;

For my taste the blackberry cone
Purpled over hedge and stone;
Laughed the brook for my delight,
Through the day and through the night:
Whispering at the garden wall,
Talked with me from fall to fall;
Mine the sand-rimmed pickerel pond,
Mine the walnut slopes beyond,
Mine, on bending orchard trees,
Apples of Hesperides!
Still, as my horizon grew,
Larger grew my riches too,
All the world I saw or knew
Seemed a complex Chinese toy,
Fashioned for a barefoot boy!

O, for festal dainties spread,
Like my bowl of milk and bread,
Pewter spoon and bowl of wood,
On the door-stone, gray and rude!
O'er me, like a regal tent,
Cloudy-ribbed, the sunset bent:
Purple-curtained, fringed with gold,
Looped in many a wind-swung fold;
While, for music, came the play
Of the pied frogs' orchestra;

And, to light the noisy choir,
Lit the fly his lamp of fire.
I was monarch; pomp and joy
Waited on the barefoot boy!

Cheerily, then, my little man!
Live and laugh as boyhood can;
Though the flinty slopes be hard,
Stubble-speared the new-mown sward,
Every morn shall lead thee through
Fresh baptisms of the dew;
Every evening from thy feet
Shall the cool wind kiss the heat;
All too soon these feet must hide
In the prison-cells of pride,
Lose the freedom of the sod,
Like a colt's for work be shod,
Made to tread the mills of toil,
Up and down in ceaseless moil:
Happy if their track be found
Never on forbidden ground;
Happy if they sink not in
Quick and treacherous sands of sin.
Ah! that thou couldst know thy joy,
Ere it passes, barefoot boy!

JOHN GREENLEAF WHITTIER.

THE COUNTRY LIFE.

NOT what we would, but what we must,
  Makes up the sum of living;
Heaven is both more and less than just
  In taking and in giving.
Swords cleave to hands that sought the plough,
And laurels miss the soldier's brow.

Me, whom the city holds, whose feet
  Have worn its stony highways,
Familiar with its loneliest street—
  Its ways were never my ways.
My cradle was beside the sea,
And there, I hope, my grave will be.

Old homestead! In that old, gray town,
  Thy vane is seaward blowing,
The slip of garden stretches down
  To where the tide is flowing:
Below they lie, their sails all furled,
The ships that go about the world.

Dearer that little country house,
  Inland, with pines beside it;
Some peach-trees, with unfruitful boughs,
  A well, with weeds to hide it:
No flowers, or only such as rise
  Self-sown, poor things, which all despise.

Dear country home! Can I forget
  The least of thy sweet trifles?
The window-vines that clamber yet,
  Whose bloom the bee still rifles?
The roadside blackberries, growing ripe,
And in the woods the Indian Pipe?

Happy the man who tills his field,
  Content with rustic labor;
Earth does to him her fulness yield,
  Hap what may to his neighbor.
Well days, sound nights, oh, can there be
A life more rational and free?

Dear country life of child and man!
  For both the best, the strongest,
That with the earliest race began,
  And hast outlived the longest:
Their cities perished long ago;
Who the first farmers were we know.

Perhaps our Babels too will fall;
  If so, no lamentations,
For Mother Earth will shelter all,
  And feed the unborn nations;
Yes, and the swords that menace now,
  Will then be beaten to the plough.

RICHARD HENRY STODDARD.

HAPPY THE MAN WHOSE WISH AND CARE.

HAPPY the man whose wish and care
  A few paternal acres bound,
Content to breathe his native air
  In his own ground.

Whose herds with milk, whose fields with bread,
  Whose flocks supply him with attire;
Whose trees in summer yield him shade,
  In winter, fire.

Blest, who can unconcern'dly find
  Hours, days, and years slide soft away

In health of body, peace of mind,
  Quiet by day,

Sound sleep by night; study and ease
  Together mixed; sweet recreation,
And innocence, which most does please
  With meditation.

Thus let me live, unseen, unknown;
  Thus unlamented let me die;
Steal from the world, and not a stone
  Tell where I lie.

ALEXANDER POPE.

"The pomp of groves, and garniture of fields."

CONTENTMENT WITH NATURE.

LIBERAL, not lavish, is kind Nature's hand;
  Nor was perfection made for man below:
  Yet all her schemes with nicest art are planned,
  Good counteracting ill, and gladness woe.
With gold and gems if Chilian mountains glow,
If bleak and barren Scotia's hills arise,
There plague and poison, lust and famine, grow;
Here peaceful are the vales and pure the skies,
And freedom fires the soul and sparkles in the eyes.

Then grieve not, thou, to whom the indulgent Muse,
Vouchsafes a portion of celestial fire;
Nor blame the partial Fates, if they refuse
The imperial banquet and the rich attire:
Know thine own worth, and reverence the lyre.

Wilt thou debase the heart which God refined?
No; let thy Heaven-taught soul to Heaven aspire,
To fancy, freedom, harmony, resigned;
Ambition's grovelling crew forever left behind.

O, how canst thou renounce the boundless store
Of charms which Nature to her votary yields!
The warbling woodland, the resounding shore,
The pomp of groves, and garniture of fields;
All that the genial ray of morning gilds,
And all that echoes to the song of even,
All that the mountain's sheltering bosom shields,
And all the dread magnificence of heaven,
O, how canst thou renounce, and hope to be for-
  given!

JAMES BEATTIE.

"While Dobbin through the stable doors
Shows his round shape."

NIGHTFALL: A PICTURE.

NOW burns the summer afternoon;
  A mellow lustre lights the scene;
And from its smiling beauty soon
  The purpling shade will chase the sheen.

The old, quaint homestead's windows blaze;
  The cedars long black pictures show;
And broadly slopes one path of rays
  Within the barn, and makes it glow.

The loft stares out—the cat intent,
  Like carving, on some gnawing rat—
With sun-bathed hay and rafters bent,
  Nooked, cobwebbed homes of wasp and bat.

The harness, bridle, saddle dart
  Gleams from the lower, rough expanse;
At either side the stooping cart,
  Pitchfork, and plow cast looks askance.

White Dobbin through the stable doors
  Shows his round shape; faint color coats
The manger, where the farmer pours,
  With rustling rush, the glancing oats.

A sun haze streaks the dusky shed;
  Makes spears of seams and gems of chinks;
In mottled gloss the straw is spread;
  And the grey grindstone dully blinks.

The sun salutes the lowest west
  With gorgeous tints around it drawn;
A beacon on the mountain's breast,
  A crescent, shred, a star—and gone.

The landscape now prepares for night;
  A gauzy mist slow settles round;
Eve shows her hues in every sight,
  And blends her voice with every sound.

The sheep stream rippling down the dell,
  Their smooth, sharp faces pointed straight;
The pacing kine, with tinkling bell,
  Come grazing through the pasture gate.

The ducks are grouped, and talk in fits;
  One yawns with stretch of leg and wing;
One rears and fans, then, settling, sits;
  One at a moth makes awkward spring.

The geese march grave in Indian file,
  The ragged patriarch at the head;
Then, screaming, flutter off awhile,
  Fold up, and once more stately tread.

Brave chanticleer shows haughtiest air;
  Hurls his shrill vaunt with lofty bend;
Lifts foot, glares round, then follows where
  His scratching, picking partlets wend.

Staid Towser scents the glittering ground;
  Then, yawning, draws a crescent deep,
Wheels his head-drooping frame around
  And sinks with forepaws stretched for sleep.

The oxen, loosened from the plow,
  Rest by the pear-tree's crooked trunk;
Tim, standing with yoke-burdened brow,
  Trim, in a mound beside him sunk.

One of the kine upon the bank,
  Heaves her face-lifting, wheezy roar;
One smooths, with lapping tongue, her flank;
  With ponderous droop one finds the floor.

Freed Dobbin through the soft, clear dark
  Glimmers across the pillared scene,
With the grouped geese—a pallid mark—
  And scattered bushes black between.

The fire-flies freckle every spot
  With fickle light that gleams and dies;
The bat, a wavering, soundless blot,
  The cat, a pair of prowling eyes.

Still the sweet, fragrant dark o'erflows
  The deepening air and darkening ground,
By its rich scent I trace the rose,
  The viewless beetle by its sound.

The cricket scrapes its rib-like bars;
  The tree-toad purrs in whirring tone;
And now the heavens are set with stars,
  And night and quiet reign alone.

ALFRED B. STREET.

BUT now the scene is changed, and all
  Is fancifully new;
The trees, last eve, so straight and tall,
  Are bending on the view,
And streams of living daylight fall
  The silvery arches through.

The boughs are strong with glittering pearls,
  As dewdrops bright and bland,
And there they gleam in silvery curls,
  Like gems of Samarcand,
Seeming in wild fantastic whirls
  The works of fairyland.

THE HOUSE ON THE HILL.

FROM the weather-worn house on the brow of
the hill
  We are dwelling afar, in our manhood, to-day;
But we see the old gables and hollyhocks still,
  As they looked long ago, ere we wandered
away;

We can hear the sharp creak of the farm-gate again,
  And the loud, cackling hens in the gray barn near by,
With its broad sagging floor and its scaffolds of grain,
  And its rafters that once seemed to reach to the sky;
We behold the great beams, and the bottomless bay
Where the farm-boys once joyfully jumped on the hay.

"From the weather-worn house on the brow of the hill
We are dwelling afar, in our manhood, to-day;
But we see the old gables and hollyhocks still,
As they looked long ago, ere we wandered away."

We can see the tall well-sweep that stands by the door,
And the sunshine that gleams on the old oaken floor.

We can hear the low hum of the hard-working bees
  At their toil in our father's old orchard, once more,
In the broad, trembling tops of the bright-blooming
trees,
  As they busily gather their sweet winter store;
And the murmuring brook, the delightful old horn,
And the cawing black crows that are pulling the corn.

We can see the low hog-pen, just over the way,
  And the long-ruined shed by the side of the road,
Where the sleds in the summer were hidden away
  And the wagons and plows in the winter were
stowed;
And the cider-mill, down in the hollow below,
  With a long, creaking sweep, the old horse used to
draw,
Where we learned by the homely old tub long ago,
What a world of sweet rapture there was in a straw;

From the cider-casks there, loosely lying around,
More leaked from the bung-holes than dripped on the
ground.

We behold the bleak hillsides still bristling with rocks,
Where the mountain streams murmured with musical
sound,
Where we hunted and fished, where we chased the
red fox,
With lazy old house-dog or loud-baying hound;

Where we sowed, where we hoed, where we cradled
and mowed,
Where we scattered the swaths that were heavy with
dew,
Where we tumbled, we pitched, and behind the tall
load
The broken old bull-rake reluctantly drew.
How we grasped the old "Sheepskin" with feelings of
scorn
As we straddled the back of the old sorrel mare,

"And the cold, cheerless woods we delighted to tramp."

And the cold, cheerless woods we delighted to tramp
For the shy, whirring partridge, in snow to our
knees,
Where, with neck-yoke and pails, in the old sugar-
camp,
We gathered the sap from the tall maple-trees;
And the fields where our plows danced a furious jig,
While we wearily followed the furrow all day,
Where we stumbled and bounded o'er boulders so
big
That it took twenty oxen to draw them away;

And rode up and down through the green rows of
corn,
Like a pin on a clothes-line that sways in the air,
We can hear our stern fathers reproving us still,
As the careless old creature "comes down on a
hill."

We are far from the home of our boyhood to-day,
In the battle of life we are struggling alone;
The weather-worn farmhouse has gone to decay,
The chimney has fallen, its swallows have flown,

But Fancy yet brings, on her bright golden wings,
  Her beautiful pictures again from the past,
And Memory fondly and tenderly clings
  To pleasures and pastimes too lovely to last.

We wander again by the river to-day;
  We sit in the school-room, o'erflowing with fun,
We whisper, we play, and we scamper away
  When our lessons are learned and the spelling is
    done.

We see the old cellar where apples were kept,
  The garret where all the old rubbish was thrown,
The little back chamber where snugly we slept,
  The homely old kitchen, the broad hearth of stone,
Where apples were roasted in many a row,
Where our grandmothers nodded and knit long ago.

Our grandmothers long have reposed in the tomb;
  With a strong, healthy race they have peopled the
    land;
They worked with the spindle, they toiled at the
    loom,
  Nor lazily brought up their babies by hand.

The old flint-lock musket, whose awful recoil
  Made many a Nimrod with agony cry,
Once hung on the chimney, a part of the spoil
  Our gallant old grandfathers captured at "Ti."

Brave men were our grandfathers, sturdy and strong;
  The kings of the forest they plucked from their
    lands;
They were stern in their virtues, they hated all wrong,
And they fought for the right with their hearts and
    their hands.

Down, down from the hillsides they swept in **their**
    might,
  And up from the valleys they went on their way,
To fight and to fall upon Hubbardton's height,
  To struggle and conquer in Bennington's fray.

Oh! fresh be their memory, cherished the sod
  That long has grown green o'er their sacred
    remains,
And grateful our hearts to a generous God
  For the blood and the spirit that flows in our veins.

Our Allens, our Starks, and our Warners are gone,
  But our mountains remain with their evergreen
    crown.
The souls of our heroes are yet marching on,
  The structure they founded shall never go down.

From the weather-worn house on the brow of the hill
  We are dwelling afar, in our manhood to-day;
But we see the old gables and hollyhocks still,
  As they looked when we left them to wander away.
But the dear ones we loved in the sweet long ago
In the old village churchyard sleep under the snow.

Farewell to the friends of our bright boyhood days,
  To the beautiful vales once delightful to roam,
To the fathers, the mothers, now gone from our
    gaze,
  From the weather-worn house to their heavenly
    home,
Where they wait, where they watch, and will welcome
    us still,
As they waited and watched in the house on the hill.

                              EUGENE J. HALL.

FREEDOM AND PATRIOTISM.

OUR OWN COUNTRY.

HERE is a land, of every land the pride,
Beloved by Heaven o'er all the world beside,
Where brighter suns dispense serener light;
And milder moons imparadise the night;
A land of beauty, virtue, valor, truth,
Time-tutored age, and love-exalted youth:
There is a spot of earth supremely blest,
A dearer, sweeter spot than all the rest,

Where man, creation's tyrant, casts aside
His sword and sceptre, pageantry and pride,
While in his softened looks benignly blend
The sire, the son, the husband, brother, friend.
Where shall that land, that spot of earth be found?
Art thou a man?—a patriot?—look around;
O, thou shalt find, howe'er thy footsteps roam,
That land thy country, and that spot thy home!

JAMES MONTGOMERY.

THE STAR-SPANGLED BANNER.

IN the month of September, 1814, the city of Baltimore was threatened by the approach of a British fleet. The chief defense of the city was Fort McHenry, which on the 13th became the object of a powerful attack. This attack was witnessed, under most remarkable circumstances, by Francis Scott Key, the author of the following song. A friend was held prisoner in the hands of the British. To effect his release, Mr. Key visited the squadron in a cartel, or vessel sent for the exchange of prisoners, and was detained by the Admiral till the termination of the attack. Placed on board a small vessel, he remained for a whole day a spectator of the tremendous cannonading to which the fort was subjected. On its successful resistance depended the fate of his home and friends. All day his eyes watched that low fortification. Night came, and in spite of all the efforts of the enemy the flag of his country was still flying defiantly in the rays of the setting sun. The bombardment continued through the night, and all the while the sleepless watcher paced the deck, straining his eyes to discern, through the smoke and darkness, if the flag was still there. By the fitful and lurid gleams of exploding shells, the Stars and Stripes were from time to time revealed to his eager gaze, and gave cheer to the anxious hours.

Morning came. It found him with eyes still fastened on the fort. The star-spangled banner floated proudly in the morning breeze, and the echoes of defiant cheers were borne from the fort to his ears. At the same moment the outburst of cannon and the thunder of mortars proclaimed that the spirits and courage of its defenders were buoyant as ever. The attack had been foiled; his home, his friends were saved. It was a proud moment; and his emotions found utterance in the picturesque and impassioned ode, which has become forever associated with the national banner:

O, SAY, can you see, by the dawn's early light,
What so proudly we hailed in the twilight's
last gleaming?
Whose broad stripes and bright stars through
the perilous fight,
O'er the ramparts we watched were so gallantly
streaming;
And the rocket's red glare, the bombs bursting in air,
Gave proof through the night that our flag was still
there.
O, say, does that star-spangled banner yet wave
O'er the land of the free and the home of the brave?

On the shore, dimly seen through the mists of the deep,
Where the foe's haughty host in dread silence
reposes,
What is that which the breeze, o'er the towering
steep,
As it fitfully blows, half conceals, half discloses?
Now it catches the gleam of the morning's first beam,
In full glory reflected now shines on the stream.
'Tis the star-spangled banner! O, long may it wave
O'er the land of the free and the home of the brave!

And where is that band who so vauntingly swore
That the havoc of war and the battle's confusion
A home and a country should leave us no more?
Their blood has washed out their foul footsteps'
pollution.
No refuge could save the hireling and slave
From the terror of death and the gloom of the
grave.
And the star-spangled banner in triumph shall wave
O'er the land of the free and the home of the brave!

O, thus be it ever, when freemen shall stand
Between their loved homes and the war's desola-
tion;
Blest with victory and peace, may the heaven-rescued
land
Praise the power that has made and preserved us a
nation.
Then conquer we must, for our cause it is just,
And this be our motto, "In God is our trust."
And the star-spangled banner in triumph shall wave
O'er the land of the free and the home of the brave!

HAIL COLUMBIA.

AIL Columbia, happy land.
Hail, ye heroes! heaven-born band!
  Who fought and bled in Freedom's cause,
  Who fought and bled in Freedom's cause,
And when the storm of war was gone
Enjoyed the peace your valor won.
  Let independence be our boast,
  Ever mindful what it cost;
  Ever grateful for the prize,
  Let its altar reach the skies.
      Firm, united let us be,
      Rallying round our Liberty;
      As a band of brothers joined,
      Peace and safety we shall find.

Immortal patriots! rise once more:
Defend your rights, defend your shore;
  Let no rude foe with impious hand,
  Let no rude foe with impious hand,
Invade the shrine where sacred lies
Of toil and blood the well-earned prize.
  While offering peace sincere and just,
  In Heaven we place a manly trust,

That truth and justice will prevail,
And every scheme of bondage fail.

Sound, sound the trump of Fame!
Let Washington's great name
  Ring through the world with loud applause,
  Ring through the world with loud applause;
Let every clime to Freedom dear
Listen with a joyful ear!
  With equal skill and godlike power,
  He governed in the fearful hour
  Of horrid war; or guides with ease
  The happier times of honest peace.

Behold the chief who now commands,
Once more to serve his country stands—
  The rock on which the storm will beat;
  The rock on which the storm will beat;
But, armed in virtue firm and true,
His hopes are fixed on Heaven and you.
  When hope was sinking in dismay,
  And glooms obscured Columbia's day,
  His steady mind, from changes free,
  Resolved on death or liberty.

JOSEPH HOPKINSON.

THE AMERICAN FLAG.

HEN Freedom, from her mountain height,
  Unfurled her standard to the air,
  She tore the azure robe of night,
    And set the stars of glory there!
She mingled with its gorgeous dyes
The milky baldric of the skies,
And striped its pure celestial white
With streakings of the morning light.
Then, from his mansion in the sun,
She called her eagle bearer down,
And gave into his mighty hand
The symbol of her chosen land!

Majestic monarch of the cloud!
  Who rear'st aloft thy regal form,
To hear the tempest-trumpings loud,
And see the lightning lances driven,
  When strive the warriors of the storm,
And rolls the thunder-drum of Heaven,—
Child of the sun! to thee 'tis given
To guard the banner of the free,
To hover in the sulphur smoke,
To ward away the battle stroke,
  And bid its blendings shine afar,
  Like rainbows on the cloud of war,
    The harbingers of victory!

Flag of the brave! thy folds shall fly,
The sign of hope and triumph high!
When speaks the signal-trumpet tone,
And the long line comes gleaming on,
Ere yet the life-blood, warm and wet,
Has dimmed the glistening bayonet,
Each soldier's eye shall brightly turn
To where thy sky-born glories burn,
And as his springing steps advance,
Catch war and vengeance from the glance.
And when the cannon-mouthings loud
Heave in wild wreaths the battle shroud,
And gory sabres rise and fall
Like shoots of flame on midnight's pall,
Then shall thy meteor glances glow,
  And cowering foes shall shrink beneath
Each gallant arm that strikes below
    That lovely messenger of death.

Flag of the seas! on ocean wave
Thy star shall glitter o'er the brave;
When death, careering on the gale,
Sweeps darkly round the bellied sail,
And frighted waves rushed wildly back
Before the broadsides' reeling rack,

Each dying wanderer of the sea
Shall look at once to heaven and thee,
And smile to see thy splendors fly
In triumph o'er his closing eye.

Flag of the free heart's hope and home,
By angel hands to valor given,

Thy stars have lit the welkin dome,
And all thy hues were born in heaven!
Forever float that standard sheet,
Where breathes the foe but falls before us,
With Freedom's soil beneath our feet,
And Freedom's banner streaming o'er us!

JOSEPH RODMAN DRAKE.

ENGLISH NATIONAL ANTHEM.

OD save our gracious king,
Long live our noble king,
God save the king.
Send him victorious,
Happy and glorious,
Long to reign over us,
God save the king.

O Lord our God, arise,
Scatter his enemies,
And make them fall;

Confound their politics,
Frustrate their knavish tricks;
On him our hopes we fix,
God save us all.

The choicest gifts in store
On him be pleased to pour,
Long may he reign.
May he defend our laws,
And ever give us cause
To sing with heart and voice,
God save the king.

HENRY CAREY.

RULE, BRITANNIA!

HEN Britain first, at Heaven's command,
Arose from out the azure main,
This was the charter of the land,
And guardian angels sung this strain:
"Rule, Britannia, rule the waves;
Britons never will be slaves."

The nations not so blessed as thee
Must in their turns to tyrants fall;
While thou shalt flourish great and free,
The dread and envy of them all.

Still more majestic shalt thou rise,
More dreadful from each foreign stroke;
As the loud blast that tears the skies
Serves but to root thy native oak.

Thee haughty tyrants ne'er shall tame:
All their attempts to bend thee down
Will but arouse thy generous flame,
But work their woe and thy renown.

To thee belongs the rural reign;
Thy cities shall with commerce shine:
All thine shall be the subject main:
And every shore it circles thine.

The Muses, still with freedom found,
Shall to thy happy coast repair;
Blessed isle! with matchless beauty crowned,
And manly hearts to guard the fair.

JAMES THOMPSON.

FRENCH NATIONAL HYMN.

E sons of Freedom. wake to glory:
Hark, hark, what myriads bid you rise;
Your children, wives, and grandsires hoary—
Behold their tears and hear their cries!
Shall hateful tyrants mischief breeding,
With hireling hosts, a ruffian band,

Affright and desolate the land,
While peace and liberty lie bleeding?
To arms, to arms, ye brave!
Th' avenging sword unsheath!
March on! March on!
All hearts resolved on Victory or death!

HALLOWED GROUND.

WHAT'S hallowed ground? Has earth a clod
Its Maker meant not should be trod
By man, the image of his God,
　　Erect and free,
Unscourged by Superstition's rod
　　To bow the knee?

That's hallowed ground where, mourned and
　　missed,
The lips repose our love has kissed;—
But where's their memory's mansion? Is 't
　　Yon churchyard's bowers?
No! in ourselves their souls exist,
　　A part of ours.

A kiss can consecrate the ground
Where mated hearts are mutual bound:
The spot where love's first links were wound,
　　That ne'er are riven,
Is hallowed down to earth's profound,
　　And up to heaven!

For time makes all but true love old;
The burning thoughts that then were told
Run molten still in memory's mould;
　　And will not cool
Until the heart itself be cold
　　In Lethe's pool.

What hallows ground where heroes sleep?
'T is not the sculptured piles you heap!
In dews that heavens far distant weep
　　Their turf may bloom;
Or Genii twine beneath the deep
　　Their coral tomb.

But strew his ashes to the wind
Whose sword or voice has served mankind,—
And is he dead, whose glorious mind
　　Lifts thine on high?—
To live in hearts we leave behind
　　'Is not to die.

Is 't death to fall for Freedom's right?
He's dead alone that lacks her light!
And murder sullies in Heaven's sight
　　The sword he draws:—
What can alone ennoble fight?
　　A noble cause!

Give that,—and welcome War to brace
Her drums, and rend heaven's reeking space!
The colors planted face to face,
　　The charging cheer,
Though Death's pale horse lead on the chase,
　　Shall still be dear.

And place our trophies where men kneel
To Heaven!—but Heaven rebukes my zeal!
The cause of Truth and human weal,
　　O God above!
Transfer it from the sword's appeal
　　To Peace and Love.

Peace, Love! the cherubim, that join
Their spread wings o'er Devotion's shrine,
Prayers sound in vain, and temples shine,
　　Where they are not,—
The heart alone can make divine
　　Religion's spot.

To incantations dost thou trust,
And pompous rites in domes august!
See mouldering stones and metal's rust
　　Belie the vaunt,
That man can bless one pile of dust
　　With chime or chant.

The ticking wood-worm mocks thee, man!
Thy temples,—creeds themselves grow wan!
But there's a dome of nobler span,
　　A temple given
Thy faith, that bigots dare not ban—
　　Its space is heaven!

Its roof, star-pictured Nature's ceiling,
Where, tracing the rapt spirit's feeling,
And God himself to man revealing,
　　The harmonious spheres
Make music, though unheard their pealing
　　By mortal ears.

Fair stars! are not your beings pure?
Can sin, can death, your worlds obscure?
Else why so swell the thoughts at your
　　Aspect above?
Ye must be heavens that make us sure
　　Of heavenly love!

And in your harmony sublime
I read the doom of distant time;
That man's regenerate soul from crime
　　Shall yet be drawn,
And reason on his mortal clime
　　Immortal dawn.

What's hallowed ground? 'T is what gives birth
To sacred thoughts in souls of worth!—
Peace! Independence! Truth! go forth
　　Earth's compass round;
And your high-priesthood shall make earth
　　All hallowed ground.
　　　　　　　　　　THOMAS CAMPBELL.

———————✦—◦◦—✦———————

IN the long vista of the years to roll,
　Let me not see my country's honor fade;

Oh! let me see our land retain its soul!
　Her pride in Freedom, and not Freedom's shade.

HARP OF THE NORTH.

HARP of the North! that mouldering long hast
        hung
    On the witch-elm that shades Saint Fillan's
        spring,
    And down the fitful breeze thy numbers flung,
Till envious ivy did around thee cling,
Muffling with verdant ringlet every string,
    O Minstrel Harp, still must thine accents sleep?
Mid rustling leaves and fountains murmuring,
    Still must thy sweeter sounds their silence keep,
Nor bid a warrior smile, nor teach a maid to weep?

Not thus, in ancient days of Caledon,
    Was thy voice mute amid the festal crowd,
When lay of hopeless love, or glory won,
    Aroused the fearful or subdued the proud.

At each according pause was heard aloud
    Thine ardent symphony sublime and high!
Fair dames and crested chiefs attention bowed;
    For still the burden of thy minstrelsy
Was Knighthood's dauntless deed, and Beauty's
        matchless eye.

O, wake once more! how rude soe'er the hand
    That ventures o'er thy magic maze to stray;
O, wake once more! though scarce my skill command
    Some feeble echoing of thine earlier lay:
Though harsh and faint, and soon to die away,
    And all unworthy of thy nobler strain,
Yet if one heart throb higher at its sway,
    The wizard note has not been touched in vain.
Then silent be no more! Enchantress, wake again!

SIR WALTER SCOTT.

MARCO BOZZARIS.

AT midnight, in his guarded tent,
    The Turk was dreaming of the hour
    When Greece, her knee in suppliance bent,
        Should tremble at his power.
    In dreams, through camp and court, he bore .
The trophies of a conqueror;
    In dreams his song of triumph heard;
Then wore his monarch's signet-ring,
Then pressed that monarch's throne—a king;
As wild his thoughts, and gay of wing,
    As Eden's garden bird.

At midnight, in the forest shades,
    Bozzaris ranged his Suliote band,—
True as the steel of their tried blades,
    Heroes in heart and hand.
There had the Persian's thousands stood,
There had the glad earth drunk their blood,
    On old Platæa's day;
And now there breathed that haunted air
The sons of sires who conquered there,
With arm to strike, and soul to dare,
    As quick, as far, as they.

An hour passed on, the Turk awoke:
    That bright dream was his last;
He woke—to hear his sentries shriek,
    "To arms! they come! the Greek! the Greek!"
He woke—to die midst flame, and smoke,
And shout, and groan, and sabre-stroke,
    And death-shots falling thick and fast
As lightnings from the mountain-cloud;
And heard, with voice as trumpet loud,
    Bozzaris cheer his band:

"Strike—till the last armed foe expires;
Strike—for your altars and your fires;
Strike—for the green graves of your sires,
    God, and your native land!"

They fought, like brave men, long and well;
    They piled the ground with Moslem slain;
They conquered, but Bozzaris fell,
    Bleeding at every vein.
His few surviving comrades saw
His smile, when rang their proud hurrah,
    And the red field was won;
Then saw in death his eyelids close,
Calmly, as to a night's repose,
    Like flowers at set of sun.

Come to the bridal chamber, Death! .
    Come to the mother when she feels
For the first time her first-born's breath;
    Come when the blessed seals
Which close the pestilence are broke,
And crowded cities wail its stroke,
Come in consumption's ghastly form,
The earthquake's shock, the ocean storm;
Come when the heart beats high and warm
    With banquet-song, and dance, and wine,
And thou art terrible: the tear,
The groan, the knell, the pall, the bier,
And all we know, or dream, or fear
    Of agony, are thine.

But to the hero, when his sword
    Has won the battle for the free,
Thy voice sounds like a prophet's word,
And in its hollow tones are heard
    The thanks of millions yet to be.

Come when his task of fame is wrought;
Come with her laurel-leaf, blood-bought;
  Come in her crowning hour—and then
Thy sunken eye's unearthly light
To him is welcome as the sight
  Of sky and stars to prisoned men;
Thy grasp is welcome as the hand
Of brother in a foreign land;
Thy summons welcome as the cry
That told the Indian isles were nigh
  To the world-seeking Genoese,
When the land-wind, from woods of palm,
And orange-groves, and fields of balm,
  Blew o'er the Haytian seas.

Bozzaris! with the storied brave
  Greece nurtured in her glory's time,
Rest thee; there is no prouder grave,
  Even in her own proud clime.
She wore no funeral weeds for thee,
  Nor bade the dark hearse wave its plume,
Like torn branch from death's leafless tree,
In sorrow's pomp and pageantry,
  The heartless luxury of the tomb.

But she remembers thee as one
Long loved, and for a season gone.
For thee her poet's lyre is wreathed,
Her marble wrought, her music breathed;
For thee she rings the birthday bells;
Of thee her babes' first lisping tells;
For thine her evening prayer is said
At palace couch and cottage bed.
Her soldier, closing with the foe,
Gives for thy sake a deadlier blow;
His plighted maiden, when she fears
For him, the joy of her young years,
Thinks of thy fate, and checks her tears.
  And she, the mother of thy boys,
Though in her eye and faded cheek
Is read the grief she will not speak,
  The memory of her buried joys,—
And even she who gave thee birth,—
Will, by her pilgrim-circled hearth,
  Talk of thy doom without a sigh;
For thou art freedom's now, and fame's,—
One of the few, the immortal names
  That were not born to die.

                    FITZ-GREENE HALLECK.

─────────◆─────────

OF OLD SAT FREEDOM ON THE HEIGHTS.

F old sat Freedom on the heights.
    The thunders breaking at her feet;
Above her shook the starry lights,
    She heard the torrents meet.

There in her place she did rejoice,
  Self-gathered in her prophet-mind,
But fragments of her mighty voice
  Came rolling on the wind.

Then stept she down through town and field
  To mingle with the human race,
And part by part to men revealed
  The fullness of her face —

Grave mother of majestic works,
  From her isle-altar gazing down,
Who God-like grasps the triple forks,
  And king-like wears the crown.

Her open eyes desire the truth,
  The wisdom of a thousand years
Is in them. May perpetual youth
  Keep dry their light from tears;

That her fair form may stand and shine,
  Make bright our days and light our dreams,
Turning to scorn with lips divine
  The falsehood of extremes!

                    ALFRED TENNYSON.

─────◆─ක්ෂ─◆─────

FREEDOM.

! FREDOME is a nobill thing!
Fredome mayse man to haiff liking!
Fredome all solace to man giffis:
He levys at ese that frely levys!
A noble hart may haiff nane ese,
Na ellys nocht that may him plese,
Gyff fredome fallythe: for fre liking
Is yearnyt our all othir thing

Na he, that ay hase levyt fre,
May nocht knaw weill the propyrte,
The angyr, na the wrechyt dome,
That is cowplyt to foule thyrldome.
Bot gyff he had assayit it,
Than all perquer he sult it wyt;
And suld think fredome mar to pryse
Than all the gold in warld that is.

                    JOHN BARBOUR.

LOVE OF LIBERTY.

FOR a lodge in some vast wilderness,
Some boundless contiguity of shade,
Where rumor of oppression and deceit,
Of unsuccessful and successful war,
Might never reach me more. My ear is pained,
My soul is sick, with every day's report
Of wrong and outrage with which earth is filled.
There is no flesh in man's obdurate heart,
It does not feel for man, the natural bond
Of brotherhood is severed as the flax
That falls asunder at the touch of fire.
He finds his fellow guilty of a skin
Not colored like his own; and having power
To enforce the wrong, for such a worthy cause
Dooms and devotes him as his lawful prey.
Lands intersected by a narrow frith
Abhor each other. Mountains interposed
Make enemies of nations, who had else

Like kindred drops been mingled into one.
Thus man devotes his brother, and destroys;
And, worse than all, and most to be deplored,
As human nature's broadest, foulest blot,
Chains him, and tasks him, and exacts his sweat
With stripes, that Mercy, with a bleeding heart,
Weeps when she seees inflicted on a beast.
Then what is man? And what man, seeing this,
And having human feelings, does not blush
And hang his head to think himself a man?
I would not have a slave to till my ground,
To carry me, to fan me while I sleep,
And tremble when I wake, for all the wealth
That sinews bought and sold have ever earned.
No: dear as freedom is, and in my heart's
Just estimation prized above all price,
I had much rather be myself the slave,
And wear the bonds, than fasten them on him.

WILLIAM COWPER.

THE SOURCE OF PARTY WISDOM.

HAVE seen the sea lashed into fury and tossed into spray, and its grandeur moves the soul of the dullest man; but I remember that it is not the billows, but the calm level of the sea, from which all heights and depths are measured. When the storm has passed and the hour of calm settles on the ocean, when the sunlight bathes its smooth surface, then the astronomer and surveyor take the level from which to measure all terrestrial heights and depths. Gentlemen of the convention, your present temper may not mark the healthful pulse of our people when our enthusiasm has passed. When the emotions of this hour have subsided we shall find that calm level of public opinion below the storm, from which the thoughts of a mighty people are to be measured, and by which their final action will be determined. Not here in this brilliant circle, where fifteen thousand men and women are assembled, is the destiny of the Republican party to be declared. Not here, where I see the faces of seven hundred and fifty-six delegates waiting to cast their votes in the urn and determine the choice of the republic, but by four million Republican firesides, where the thoughtful voters, with wives and children about them, with the calm thoughts inspired by the love of home and country, with the history of the past, the hopes of the future, and a knowledge of the great men who have adorned and blessed our nation in days gone by—there God prepares the verdict that shall determine the wisdom of our work to-night. Not in Chicago, in the heats of June, but in the sober quiet that comes to them between now and November; in the silence of deliberate judgment will the great question be settled.

JAMES A. GARFIELD.

FREEDOM who loves, must first be wise and good;
But from that mark how far they rove we see,
For all this waste of wealth and loss of blood.

WHO can in reason then or right assume
Monarchy over such as live by right
His equals, if in pow'r or splendor less,
In freedom equal.

A CURSE ON THE TRAITOR.

FOR a tongue to curse the slave,
  Whose treason, like a deadly blight,
Comes o'er the councils of the brave,
  And blasts them in their hour of might!
May life's unblesséd cup for him
Be drugged with treacheries to the brim,—
  With hopes that but allure to fly,
  With joys that vanish while he sips,
Like Dead Sea fruits, that tempt the eye,
  But turn to ashés on the lips.

His country's curse, his children's shame,
Outcast of virtue, peace, and fame;
May he, at last, with lips of flame
On the parched desert, thirsting, die,—
While lakes, that shone in mockery nigh,
Are fading off, untouched, untasted,
Like the once glorious hopes he blasted!
And when from earth his spirit flies,
  Just Prophet, let the damned one dwell
Full in the sight of Paradise,
Beholding heaven, and feeling hell!

                              THOMAS MOORE.

DOWNFALL OF POLAND.

SACRED Truth! thy triumph ceased awhile,
And Hope, thy sister, ceased with thee to
    smile,
When leagued Oppression poured to Northern
    wars
Her whiskered pandoors and her fierce hussars,
Waved her dread standard to the breeze of morn,
Pealed her loud drum, and twanged her trumpet-horn;
Tumultuous horror brooded o'er her van,
Presaging wrath to Poland—and to man!
  Warsaw's last champion from her height surveyed,
Wide o'er the fields, a waste of ruin laid,—
"O Heaven!" he cried, "my bleeding country save,—
Is there no hand on high to shield the brave?
Yet, though destruction sweep those lovely plains,
Rise, fellow-men! our country yet remains!
By that dread name we wave the sword on high!
And swear for her to live!—with her to die!"

He said, and on the rampart-heights arrayed
His trusty warriors, few, but undismayed;
Firm-paced and slow, a horrid front they form,
Still as the breeze, but dreadful as the storm,
Low murmuring sounds along their banners fly,
Revenge, or death!—the watchword and reply;
Then pealed the notes, omnipotent to charm,
And the loud tocsin tolled their last alarm!—
  In vain, alas! in vain, ye gallant few!
From rank to rank your volleyed thunder flew:—
O, bloodiest picture in the book of Time,
Sarmatia fell, unwept, without a crime;
Found not a generous friend, a pitying foe,
Strength in her arms, nor mercy in her woe!
Dropped from her nerveless grasp the shattered spear,
Closed her bright eye, and curbed her high career;—
Hope, for a season, bade the world farewell,
And Freedom shrieked, as Kosciusko fell.

                              THOMAS CAMPBELL.

GREEN FIELDS OF ENGLAND.

GREEN fields of England! whereso'er
  Across this watery waste we fare,
Your image at our hearts we bear,
  Green fields of England, everywhere.

Sweet eyes in England, I must flee
Past where the waves' last confines be,

Ere your loved smile I cease to see,
Sweet eyes in England, dear to me.

Dear home in England, safe and fast,
If but in thee my lot be cast,
The past shall seem a nothing past
To thee, dear home, if won at last;
Dear home in England, won at last.

                              ARTHUR HUGH CLOUGH.

ETERNAL SPIRIT OF THE CHAINLESS MIND.

ETERNAL spirit of the chainless mind!
  Brightest in dungeons, Liberty! thou art;
For there thy habitation is the heart—
  The heart which love of thee alone can bind;

And when thy sons to fetters are consigned—
To fetters, and the damp vault's dayless gloom—
Their country conquers with their martyrdom,
And Freedom's fame finds wings on every wind.

                              LORD BYRON.

BANNOCKBURN.

T Bannockburn the English lay—
The Scots they were na far away,
But waited for the break o' day
    That glinted in the east;

But soon the sun broke through the heath
And lighted up that field o' death,
When Bruce, wi' saul-inspiring breath,
    His heralds thus addressed :—

Scots, who hae wi' Wallace bled,
Scots, wham Bruce has aften led ;
Welcome to your gory bed,
    Or to victorie.

Now's the day, and now's the hour,
See the front o' battle lour;
See approach proud Edward's power—
    Chains and slaverie !

Wha will be a traitor knave?
Wha can fill a coward's grave?
Wha sae base as be a slave?
    Let him turn and flee !

Wha for Scotland's king and law
Freedom's sword will strongly draw,
Freeman stand, or freeman fa'?
    Let him follow me !

By Oppression's woes and pains!
By your sons in servile chains !
We will drain our dearest veins
    But they shall be free !

Lay the proud usurpers low !
Tyrants fall in every foe !
Liberty 's in every blow !
    Let us do, or die !

                        ROBERT BURNS.

OUR COUNTRY'S CALL.

AY down the axe, fling by the spade;
    Leave in its track the toiling plough;
The rifle and the bayonet-blade
    For arms like yours are fitter now;
And let the hands that ply the pen
    Quit the light task, and learn to wield
The horseman's crooked brand, and rein
    The charger on the battle-field.

Our country calls; away! away!
    To where the blood-stream blots the green,
Strike to defend the gentlest sway
    That Time in all his course has seen.
See, from a thousand coverts—see
    Spring the armed foes that haunt her track;
They rush to smite her down, and we
    Must beat the banded traitors back.

Ho! sturdy as the oaks ye cleave,
    And moved as soon to fear and flight;
Men of the glade and forest! leave
    Your woodcraft for the field of fight.
The arms that wield the axe must pour
    An iron tempest on the foe;
His serried ranks shall reel before
    The arm that lays the panther low.

And ye who breast the mountain storm
    By grassy steep or highland lake,
Come, for the land ye love, to form
    A bulwark that no foe can break.

Stand, like your own gray cliffs that mock
    The whirlwind; stand in her defence :
The blast as soon shall move the rock,
    As rushing squadrons bear ye thence.

And ye, whose homes are by her grand
    Swift rivers, rising far away,
Come from the depth of her green land
    As mighty in your march as they;
As terrible as when the rains
    Have swelled them over bank and bourne,
With sudden floods to drown the plains
    And sweep along the woods uptorn'.

And ye who throng beside the deep,
    Her ports and hamlets of the strand,
In number like the waves that leap
    On his long murmuring marge of sand,
Come, like that deep, when, o'er his brim,
    He rises, all his floods to pour,
And flings the proudest barks that swim,
    A helpless wreck against his shore.

Few, few were they whose swords of old,
    Won the fair land in which we dwell;
But we are many, we who hold
    The grim resolve to guard it well.
Strike for that broad and goodly land,
    Blow after blow, till men shall see
That Might and Right move hand in hand,
    And glorious must their triumph be.

              WILLIAM CULLEN BRYANT.

WHAT CONSTITUTES A STATE?

HAT constitutes a state?
  Not high-raised battlement or labored
      mound,
    Thick wall or moated gate;
  Not cities proud with spires and turrets
      crowned;
  Not bays and broad-armed ports,
Where, laughing at the storm, rich navies ride;
  Not starred and spangled courts,
Where low-browed baseness wafts perfume to pride.
  No:—men, high-minded men,
With powers as far above dull brutes endued
    In forest, brake or den,
As beasts excel cold rocks and brambles rude,—
  Men who their duties know,
But know their rights, and knowing, dare maintain;
  Prevent the long-aimed blow.

And crush the tyrant while they rend the chain,—
    These constitute a state;
And sovereign law, that state's collected will,
    O'er thrones and globes elate
Sits empress, crowning good, repressing ill.
    Smit by her sacred frown,
The fiend, Dissension, like a vapor sinks;
    And e'en the all-dazzling crown
Hides his faint rays, and at her bidding shrinks;
    Such was this heaven-loved isle,
Than Lesbos fairer and the Cretan shore!
    No more shall freedom smile?
Shall Britons languish, and be men no more?
    Since all must life resign,
Those sweet rewards which decorate the brave
    'T is folly to decline,
And steal inglorious to the silent grave.

SIR WILLIAM JONES.

THE LOVE OF COUNTRY.

REATHES there the man with soul so dead,
  Who never to himself hath said,
    This is my own, my native land!
  Whose heart hath ne'er within him burned
As home his footsteps he hath turned,
    From wandering on a foreign strand?
  If such there breathe, go, mark him well;
  For him no minstrel raptures swell!

High though his titles, proud his name,
Boundless his wealth as wish can claim:
Despite those titles, power, and pelf,
The wretch, concentred all in self,
Living, shall forfeit fair renown,
And doubly dying, shall go down
To the vile dust, from whence he sprung,
Unwept, unhonored, and unsung.

SIR WALTER SCOTT.

IT'S HAME, AND IT'S HAME.

T'S hame, and it's hame, hame fain wad I be,
  An' it's hame, hame, hame, to my ain countree!
  When the flower is i' the bud, and the leaf is on
      the tree,
  The lark shall sing me hame in my ain countree;
  It's hame, and it's hame, hame fain wad I be,
  An' it's hame, hame, hame, to my ain countree!

The green leaf o' loyaltie 's beginning for to fa',
The bonnie white rose it is withering an' a';
But I'll water 't wi' the blude of usurping tyrannie,
An' green it will grow in my ain countree.
It's hame, and it's hame, hame fain wad I be,
An' it's hame, hame, hame, to my ain countree!

There's naught now frae ruin my country can save
But the keys o' kind heaven to open the grave,
That a' the noble martyrs who died for loyaltie
May rise again and fight for their ain countree.
It's hame, an' it's hame, hame fain wad I be,
An' it's hame, hame, hame, to my ain countree!

The great now are gane, a' who ventured to save,
The new grass is springing on the tap o' their grave;
But the sun through the mirk blinks blythe in my ee,
"I'll shine on ye yet in your ain countree."
It's hame, and it's hame, hame fain wad I be,
An' it's hame, hame, hame, to my ain countree!

ALLAN CUNNINGHAM.

CAMP AND BATTLE.

"Charged with Abercrombie's doom,
Lightning wing'd a cruel ball."

THE BATTLE OF ALEXANDRIA.

HARP of Memnon! sweetly strung
  To the music of the spheres;
While the Hero's dirge is sung,
  Breathe enchantment to our ears.

Let thy numbers, soft and slow,
  O'er the plain with carnage spread
Soothe the dying while they flow
  To the memory of the dead.

Lashed to madness by the wind,
  As the Red Sea surges roar
Leave a gloomy gulf behind,
  And devour the shrinking shore.

Thus, with overwhelming pride,
  Gallia's brightest, boldest boast,
In a deep and dreadful tide,
  Roll'd upon the British host.

233

Now the veteran Chief drew nigh,
  Conquest towering on his crest,
Valor beaming from his eye,
  Pity bleeding on his breast.

On the whirlwind of the war
  High he rode in vengeance dire;
To his friends a leading star,
  To his foes consuming fire.

Charged with Abercrombie's doom,
  Lightning wing'd a cruel ball:
'Twas the Herald of the Tomb,
  And the Hero felt the call—

Felt — and raised his arms on high;
  Victory well the signal knew,
Darted from his awful eye,
  And the force of France o'erthrew.

Harp of Memnon! sweetly strung
  To the music of the spheres;
While the Hero's dirge is sung,
  Breathe enchantment to our ears.

Let thy numbers, soft and slow,
  O'er the plain with carnage spread,
Soothe the dying while they flow
  To the memory of the dead.

Then thy tones triumphant pour,
  Let them pierce the Hero's grave;
Life's tumultuous battle o'er,
  O, how sweetly sleep the brave!

From the dust their laurels bloom,
  High they shoot and flourish free;
Glory's temple is the tomb;
  Death is immortality.

                JAMES MONTGOMERY.

THE BALLAD OF AGINCOURT.

FAIR stood the wind for France,
  When we our sails advance,
Nor now to prove our chance
    Longer will tarry;
But putting to the main,
At Kause, the mouth of Seine,
With all his martial train,
    Landed King Harry.

And taking many a fort,
Furnished in warlike sort,
Marched toward Agincourt
    In happy hour;
Skirmishing day by day
With those that stopped his way,
Where the French general lay
    With all his power.

Which in his height of pride,
King Henry to deride,
His ransom to provide
    To the king sending;
Which he neglects the while,
As from a nation vile,
Yet, with an angry smile,
    Their fall portending.

And turning to his men,
Quoth our brave Henry then:
Though they to one be ten,
    Be not amazed;
Yet have we well begun,
Battles so bravely won
Have ever to the sun
    By fame been raised.

And for myself, quoth he,
This my full rest shall be;
England ne'er mourn for me,
    Nor more esteem me.
Victor I will remain,
Or on this earth lie slain;
Never shall she sustain
    Loss to redeem me.

Poitiers and Cressy tell,
When most their pride did swell,
Under our swords they fell.
    No less our skill is
Than when our grandsire great,
Claiming the regal seat,
By many a warlike feat
    Lopped the French lilies.

The Duke of York so dread
The eager vaward led;
With the main Henry sped
    Amongst his henchmen.
Excester had the rear,
A braver man not there:
O Lord! how hot they were
    On the false Frenchmen.

They now to fight are gone;
Armor on armor shone;
Drum now to drum did groan,
    To hear was wonder;
That with the cries they make
The very earth did shake,
Trumpet to trumpet spake.
    Thunder to thunder.

Well it thine age became,
O noble Erpingham!
Which did the signal aim
   To our hid forces;
When, from a meadow by
Like a storm suddenly,
The English archery
   Struck the French horses.

With Spanish yew so strong,
Arrows a cloth-yard long,
That like to serpents stung,
   Piercing the weather;
None from his fellow starts,
But playing manly parts,
And like true English hearts,
   Stuck close together.

When down their bows they threw,
And forth their bilboes drew,
And on the French they flew,
   Not one was tardy:
Arms were from shoulders sent,
Scalps to the teeth were rent;
Down the French peasants went;
   Our men were hardy.

This while our noble king,
His broadsword brandishing,
Down the French host did ding,
   As to o'erwhelm it;

And many a deep wound rent
His arms with blood besprent.
And many a cruel dent,
   Bruiséd his helmet.

Glo'ster, that duke so good
Next of the royal blood,
For famous England stood,
   With his brave brother
Clarence, in steel so bright,
Though but a maiden knight,
Yet in that furious fight
   Scarce such another.

Warwick in blood did wade;
Oxford the foe invade,
And cruel slaughter made,
   Still as they ran up.
Suffolk his axe did ply;
Beaumont and Willoughby
Bare them right doughtily,
   Ferrers and Fanhope.

Upon Saint Crispin's day
Fought was this noble fray,
Which Fame did not delay
   To England to carry.
O, when shall Englishmen
With such acts fill a pen,
Or England breed again
   Such a King Harry?

              MICHAEL DRAYTON.

YE MARINERS OF ENGLAND.

E mariners of England
That guard our native seas;
Whose flag has braved a thousand years
The battle and the breeze,
Your glorious standard launch again
To match another foe,
And sweep through the deep,
While the stormy winds do blow;
While the battle rages loud and long,
And the stormy winds do blow.

The spirits of your fathers
Shall start from every wave;
For the deck it was their field of fame,
And ocean was their grave:
Where Blake and mighty Nelson fell,
Your manly hearts shall glow,
As ye sweep through the deep,
While the stormy winds do blow;
While the battle rages loud and long,
And the stormy winds do blow.

Britannia needs no bulwarks,
No towers along the steep;
Her march is o'er the mountain-waves,
Her home is on the deep.
With thunders from her native oak,
She quells the floods below,—
As they roar on the shore,
When the stormy winds do blow;
When the battle rages loud and long,
And the stormy winds do blow.

The meteor flag of England
Shall yet terrific burn;
Till danger's troubled night depart,
And the star of peace return.
Then, then, ye ocean-warriors,
Our song and feast shall flow
To the fame of your name,
When the storm has ceased to blow;
When the fiery fight is heard no more,
And the storm has ceased to blow.

              THOMAS CAMPBELL.

THE UNRETURNING BRAVE.

ND Ardennes waves above them her green
    leaves,
  Dewy with nature's tear-drops, as they pass;
  Grieving, if aught inanimate e'er grieves,
Over the unreturning brave;—alas!
Ere evening to be trodden like the grass
Which now beneath them, but above shall grow
In its next verdure, when this fiery mass
Of living valor, rolling on the foe,
And burning with high hope, shall moulder cold and
  low.

Last noon beheld them full of lusty life,
Last eve in beauty's circle proudly gay;
The midnight brought the signal-sound of strife,
The morn the marshaling in arms—the day
Battle's magnificently stern array!
The thunder-clouds close o'er it, which when rent
The earth is covered thick with other clay,
Which her own clay shall cover, heaped and pent,
Rider and horse—friend, foe,—in one red burial blent!

Their praise is hymned by loftier harps than mine;
Yet one I would select from that proud throng,
Partly because they blend me with his line,
And partly that I did his sire some wrong,
And partly that bright names will hallow song:
And his was of the bravest, and when showered
The death-bolts deadliest the thinned files along,
Even where the thickest of war's tempest lowered,
They reached no nobler breast than thine, young,
  gallant Howard!

There have been tears and breaking hearts for thee,
And mine were nothing, had I such to give;
But when I stood beneath the fresh green tree,
Which living waves where thou didst cease to live,
And saw around me the wide field revive
With fruits and fertile promise, and the Spring
Come forth her work of gladness to contrive
With all her reckless birds upon the wing.
I turned from all she brought, to those she could not
  bring.

LORD BYRON.

WATERLOO.

HERE was a sound of revelry by night,
  And Belgium's capital had gathered then
  Her beauty and her chivalry, and bright
  The lamps shone o'er fair women and brave
    men;
  A thousand hearts beat happily; and when
  Music arose with its voluptuous swell,
Soft eyes looked love to eyes which spake again,
And all went merry as a marriage-bell;
But hush! hark! a deep sound strikes like a rising
  knell!

Did ye not hear it? No; 't was but the wind
Or the car rattling o'er the stony street;
On with the dance! let joy be unconfined;
No sleep till morn, when youth and pleasure meet
To chase the glowing hours with flying feet;
But hark!—that heavy sound breaks in once more,
As if the clouds its echo would repeat;
And nearer, clearer, deadlier than before!
Arm! arm! it is—it is—the cannon's opening roar!

Ah! then and there was hurrying to and fro,
And gathering tears, and tremblings of distress,
And cheeks all pale, which but an hour ago
Blushed at the praise of their own loveliness;
And there were sudden partings, such as press

The life from out young hearts, and choking sighs
Which ne'er might be repeated; who could guess
If evermore should meet those mutual eyes,
Since upon night so sweet such awful morn could
  rise!

And there was mounting in hot haste; the steed,
The mustering squadron, and the clattering car,
Went pouring forward with impetuous speed,
And swiftly forming in the ranks of war;
And the deep thunder, peal on peal afar;
And near, the beat of the alarming drum
Roused up the soldier ere the morning star;
While thronged the citizens with terror dumb,
Or whispering, with white lips,—"The foe! They
  come! they come!"

And wild and high the "The Cameron's gather-
  ing" rose!
The war-notes of Lochiel, which Albyn's hills
Have heard, and heard, too, have her Saxon foes;—
How in the noon of night that pibroch thrills,
Savage and shrill! But with the breath which fills
Their mountain-pipe, so fill the mountaineers
With the fierce native daring which instills
The stirring memory of a thousand years,
And Evan's, Donald's fame rings in each clansman's
  ears!

LORD BYRON.

THE CHARGE OF THE LIGHT BRIGADE.

HALF a league, half a league,
　Half a league onward,
　All in the valley of Death
　　Rode the six hundred.
"Forward, the Light Brigade!
Charge for the guns!" he said:
Into the valley of Death
　　Rode the six hundred.

"Forward, the Light Brigade!"
Was there a man dismayed?
Not though the soldiers knew
　Some one had blundered:
Theirs not to make reply,
Theirs not to reason why,
Theirs but to do and die:
Into the valley of Death
　　Rode the six hundred.

Cannon to right of them,
Cannon to left of them,
Cannon in front of them
　Volleyed and thundered;
Stormed at with shot and shell,
While horse and hero fell,
They that had fought so well
Came through the jaws of Death
Back from the mouth of Hell,
All that was left of them,
　Left of six hundred.

Stormed at with shot and shell,
Boldly they rode and well,
Into the jaws of Death,
Into the mouth of Hell
　　Rode the six hundred.

Flashed all their sabres bare,
Flashed as they turned in air,
Sabring the gunners there,
Charging an army, while
　All the world wondered:
Plunged in the battery-smoke,
Right through the line they broke;
Cossack and Russian
Reeled from the sabre-stroke
　Shattered and sundered.
Then they rode back, but not
　Not the six hundred.

Cannon to right of them,
Cannon to left of them,
Cannon behind them
　Volleyed and thundered;
When can their glory fade?
O, the wild charge they made!
　All the world wondered.
Honor the charge they made!
Honor the Light Brigade,
　Noble six hundred!

ALFRED TENNYSON.

SONG OF THE CAMP.

"GIVE us a song!" the soldiers cried,
　The outer trenches guarding,
When the heated guns of the camps allied
　Grew weary of bombarding.

The dark Redan, in silent scoff,
　Lay grim and threatening under;
And the tawny mound of the Malakoff
　No longer belched its thunder.

There was a pause. A guardsman said:
　"We storm the forts to-morrow;
Sing while we may, another day
　Will bring enough of sorrow."

They lay along the battery's side,
　Below the smoking cannon:
Brave hearts from Severn and from Clyde,
　And from the banks of Shannon.

They sang of love, and not of fame;
　Forgot was Britain's glory:
Each heart recalled a different name,
　But all sang "Annie Laurie."

Voice after voice caught up the song,
　Until its tender passion

Rose like an anthem, rich and strong,—
　Their battle-eve confession.

Dear girl, her name he dared not speak,
　But as the song grew louder,
Something upon the soldier's cheek
　Washed off the stains of powder.

Beyond the darkening ocean burned
　The bloody sunset's embers,
While the Crimean valleys learned
　How English love remembers.

And once again a fire of hell
　Rained on the Russian quarters,
With scream of shot, and burst of shell,
　And bellowing of the mortars.

And Irish Norah's eyes are dim
　For a singer dumb and gory;
And English Mary mourns for him
　Who sang of "Annie Laurie."

Sleep, soldiers! still in honored rest
　Your truth and valor wearing;
The bravest are the tenderest—
　The loving are the daring.

BAYARD TAYLOR.

HOHENLINDEN.

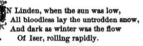

ON Linden, when the sun was low,
All bloodless lay the untrodden snow,
And dark as winter was the flow
    Of Iser, rolling rapidly.

But Linden saw another sight,
When the drum beat, at dead of night,
Commanding fires of death to light
    The darkness of her scenery.

By torch and trumpet fast arrayed,
Each horseman drew his battle-blade,
And furious every charger neighed,
    To join the dreadful revelry.

Then shook the hills with thunder riven,
Then rushed the steed to battle driven,
And louder than the bolts of heaven
    Far flashed the red artillery.

But redder yet that light shall glow
On Linden's hills of stainéd snow,
And bloodier yet the torrent flow
    Of Iser, rolling rapidly.

'Tis morn, but scarce yon level sun
Can pierce the war-clouds rolling dun,
Where furious Frank and fiery Hun
    Shout in their sulphurous canopy.

The combat deepens. On, ye brave,
Who rush to glory or the grave!
Wave, Munich! all thy banners wave,
    And charge with all thy chivalry!

Few, few shall part where many meet!
The snow shall be their winding-sheet
And every turf beneath their feet
    Shall be a soldier's sepulchre.

        THOMAS CAMPBELL.

CARMEN BELLICOSUM.

IN their ragged regimentals,
  Stood the old Continentals,
    Yielding not,
  When the grenadiers were lunging,
  And like hail fell the plunging
    Cannon-shot!
    When the files
    Of the isles,
From the smoky night encampment, bore the banner
  of the rampant
    Unicorn,
And grummer, grummer, grummer, rolled the roll of
  the drummer,
    Through the morn!

Then with eyes to the front all,
  And with guns horizontal,
    Stood our sires;
  And the balls whistled deadly,
  And in streams flashing redly
    Blazed the fires;
    As the roar
    On the shore,
Swept the strong battle-breakers o'er the green-sod-
  ded acres
    Of the plain;
And louder, louder, louder, cracked the black gun-
  powder,
    Cracking amain!

Now like smiths at their forges
  Worked the red St. George's
    Cannoneers;
  And the "villainous saltpetre"
  Rung a fierce, discordant metre
    Round their ears;
    As the swift
    Storm-drift,
With hot sweeping anger, came the horse-guards'
  clangor
    On our flanks:
Then higher, higher, higher, burned the old-fash-
  ioned fire
    Through the ranks!

Then the old-fashioned colonel
  Galloped through the white infernal
    Powder-cloud;
  And his broad-sword was swinging
  And his brazen throat was ringing
    Trumpet loud.
    Then the blue
    Bullets flew,
And the trooper-jackets redden at the touch of the
  leaden
    Rifle-breath;
And rounder, rounder, rounder, roared the iron six-
  pounder,
    Hurling death!

        GUY HUMPHREY McMASTER.

MONTEREY.

[Sept. 19-24, 1846.]

E were not many—we who stood
  Before the iron sleet that day;
Yet many a gallant spirit would
Give half his years if but he could
  Have with us been at Monterey.

Now here, now there, the shot it hailed
  In deadly drifts of fiery spray,
Yet not a single soldier quailed
When wounded comrades round him wailed
  Their dying shout at Monterey.

And on—still on our column kept,
  Through walls of flame, its withering way;
Where fell the dead, the living stept,
Still charging on the guns which swept
  The slippery streets of Monterey.

The foe himself recoiled aghast,
  When, striking where he strongest lay,
We swooped his flanking batteries past,
And, braving full their murderous blast,
  Stormed home the towers of Monterey.

Our banners on those turrets wave,
  And there our evening bugles play;
Where orange-boughs above their grave
Keep green the memory of the brave
  Who fought and fell at Monterey.

We are not many—we who pressed
  Beside the brave who fell that day;
But who of us has not confessed
He'd rather share their warrior rest
  Than not have been at Monterey?

CHARLES FENNO HOFFMAN.

BATTLE-HYMN OF THE REPUBLIC.

INE eyes have seen the glory of the coming of
  the Lord:
He is trampling out the vintage where the
  grapes of wrath are stored;
He hath loosed the fateful lightnings of his terrible,
  swift sword:
His truth is marching on.

I have seen him in the watch-fires of a hundred circling
  camps;
They have builded him an altar in the evening dews
  and damps;
I can read his righteous sentence by the dim and flar-
  ing lamps:
His day is marching on.

I have read a fiery gospel, writ in burnished rows of
  steel:
"As ye deal with my contemners, so with you my
  grace shall deal;

Let the Hero, born of woman, crush the serpent with
  his heel,
Since God is marching on."

He has sounded forth the trumpet that shall never call
  retreat;
He is sifting out the hearts of men before his judgment-
  seat;
O, be swift, my soul, to answer him! be jubilant,
  my feet!
Our God is marching on.

In the beauty of the lilies Christ was born across the
  sea,
With a glory in his bosom that transfigures you and
  me;
As he died to make men holy, let us die to make men
  free,
While God is marching on.

JULIA WARD HOWE.

MY MARYLAND.

HE despot's heel is on thy shore,
  Maryland!
His torch is at thy temple door,
  Maryland!
Avenge the patriotic gore
That flecked the streets of Baltimore,
And be the battle queen of yore,
  Maryland, my Maryland!

Hark to an exiled son's appeal,
  Maryland!
My Mother State, to thee I kneel,
  Maryland!
For life or death, for woe or weal,
Thy peerless chivalry reveal,
And gird thy beauteous limbs with steel,
  Maryland, my Maryland!

Thou wilt not cower in the dust,
   Maryland!
Thy beaming sword shall never rust,
   Maryland!
Remember Carroll's sacred trust,
Remember Howard's warlike thrust,
And all thy slumberers with the just,
   Maryland, my Maryland!

Come! 'tis the red dawn of the day
   Maryland!
Come with thy panoplied array,
   Maryland!
With Ringgold's spirit for the fray,
With Watson's blood at Mouterey,
With fearless Lowe and dashing May,
   Maryland, my Maryland!

Dear Mother, burst the tyrant's chain,
   Maryland!
Virginia should not call in vain,
   Maryland!
She meets her sisters on the plain,
" *Sic semper !* " 'tis the proud refrain
That baffles minions back amain,
   Maryland!
Arise in majesty again,
   Maryland, my Maryland!

Come! for thy shield is bright and strong,
   Maryland!
Come! for thy dalliance does thee wrong,
   Maryland!

Come to thine own heroic throng
Stalking with Liberty along,
And chant thy dauntless slogan-song,
   Maryland, my Maryland!

I see the blush upon thy cheek,
   Maryland!
But thou wast ever bravely meek,
   Maryland!
But lo! there surges forth a shriek,
From hill to hill, from creek to creek,
Potomac calls to Chesapeake,
   Maryland, my Malyland!

Thou wilt not yield the Vandal toll,
   Maryland!
Thou wilt not crook to his control,
   Maryland!
Better the fire upon thee roll,
Better the shot, the blade, the bowl,
Than crucifixion of the soul,
   Maryland, my Maryland!

I hear the distant thunder-hum!
   Maryland!
The " Old Line's bugle, fife and drum,
   Maryland!"
She is not dead, nor deaf, nor dumb;
Huzza! she spurns the Northern scum —
She breathes! She burns! She'll come! She'll come!
   Maryland, my Maryland!

JAMES R. RANDALL.

THE COUNTERSIGN.

ALAS! the weary hours pass slow,
   The night is very dark and still;
   And in the marshes far below
     I hear the bearded whippoorwill;
I scarce can see a yard ahead,
   My ears are strained to catch each sound;
I hear the leaves about me shed,
   And the spring's bubbling through the ground.

Along the beaten path I pace,
   Where white rags mark my sentry's track;
In formless shrubs I seem to trace
   The foeman's form with bending back,
I think I see him crouching low:
   I stop and list—I stoop and peer,
Until the neighboring hillocks grow
   To groups of soldiers far and near.

With ready piece I wait and watch,
   Until my eyes, familiar grown,
Detect each harmless earthern notch,
   And turn guerrillas into stone;

And then, amid the lonely gloom,
   Beneath the tall old chestnut trees,
My silent marches I resume,
   And think of other times than these.

"Halt! Who goes there?" my challenge cry,
   It rings along the watchful line;
"Relief!" I hear a voice reply;
   "Advance, and give the countersign!"
With bayonet at the charge I wait—
   The corporal gives the mystic spell;
With arms aport I charge my mate,
   Then onward pass, and all is well.

But in the tent that night awake,
   I ask, if in the fray I fall,
Can I the mystic answer make
   When the angelic sentries call?
And pray that Heaven may so ordain,
   Where'er I go, what fate be mine,
Whether in pleasure or in pain.
   I still may have the countersign.

THE PICKET GUARD.

"ALL quiet along the Potomac," they say,
  "Except now and then a stray picket
Is shot, as he walks on his beat to and fro,
  By a rifleman hid in the thicket;
'T is nothing—a private or two now and then
  Will not count in the news of the battle;
Not an officer lost—only one of the men,
  Moaning out, all alone, his death-rattle."

All quiet along the Potomac to-night,
  Where the soldiers lie peacefully dreaming;
Their tents in the rays of the clear autumn moon,
  Or the light of the watch-fires, are gleaming.
A tremulous sigh, as the gentle night-wind
  Through the forest-leaves softly is creeping;
While stars up above, with their glittering eyes,
  Keep guard—for the army is sleeping.

There 's only the sound of the lone sentry's tread,
  As he tramps from the rock to the fountain,
And thinks of the two in the low trundle-bed
  Far away in the cot on the mountain.
His musket falls slack—his face, dark and grim,
  Grows gentle with memories tender,

As he mutters a prayer for the children asleep,
  For their mother—may Heaven defend her!

The moon seems to shine just as brightly as then,
  That night, when the love yet unspoken
Leaped up to his lips—when low-murmured vows
  Were pledged to be ever unbroken.
Then drawing his sleeve roughly over his eyes,
  He dashes off tears that are welling,
And gathers his gun closer up to its place,
  As if to keep down the heart-swelling.

He passes the fountain, the blasted pine-tree—
  The footstep is lagging and weary;
Yet onward he goes, through the broad belt of light,
  Toward the shades of the forest so dreary.
Hark! was it the night-wind that rustled the leaves?
  Was it moonlight so suddenly flashing?
It looked like a rifle———"Ah! Mary, good-bye!"
  And the life-blood is ebbing and plashing.

All quiet along the Potomac to-night;
  No sound save the rush of the river;
While soft falls the dew on the face of the dead—
  The picket 's off duty forever!

ETHEL LYNN BEERS.

BETHEL.

WE mustered at midnight, in darkness we formed,
  And the whisper went round of a fort to be
      stormed;
  But no drum-beat had called us, no trumpet
      we heard,
And no voice of command, but our Colonel's low
      word,—
            "Column! Forward!"

And out, through the mist and the murk of the morn,
From the beaches of Hampton our barges were borne;
And we heard not a sound, save the sweep of the
      oar,
Till the word of our Colonel came up from the shore—
            "Column! Forward!"

With hearts bounding bravely, and eyes all alight,
As ye dance to soft music, so trod we that night;
Through the aisles of the greenwood, with vines over-
      arched,
Tossing dew-drops, like gems, from our feet, as we
      marched,—
            "Column! Forward!"

As ye dance with the damsels, to viol and flute,
So we skipped from the shadows, and mocked their
      pursuit;
But the soft zephyrs chased us, with scents of the
      morn,
As we passed by the hay-fields and green waving
      corn,—
            "Column! Forward!"

For the leaves were all laden with fragrance of June,
And the flowers and the foliage with sweets were in
      tune;
And the air was so calm, and the forest so dumb,
That we heard our own heart-beats, like taps of a
      drum,—
            "Column! Forward!"

Till the lull of the lowlands was stirred by a breeze,
And the buskins of Morn brushed the tops of the
      trees,
And the glintings of glory that slid from her track
By the sheen of our rifles were gayly flung back,—
            "Column! Forward!"

16

And the woodlands grew purple with sunshiny mist,
And the blue-crested hill-tops with roselight were
  kissed,
And the earth gave her prayers to the sun in per-
  fumes,
Till we marched as through gardens, and trampled on
  blooms,—
                "Column! Forward!"

Ay! trampled on blossoms, and seared the sweet
  breath
Of the greenwood with low-brooding vapors of death;
O'er the flowers and the corn we were borne like a
  blast,
And away to the fore-front of battle we passed,—
                "Column! Forward!"

For the cannon's hoarse thunder roared out from the
  glades,
And the sun was like lightning on banners and
  blades,

When the long line of chanting Zouaves, like a flood,
From the green of the woodlands rolled, crimson as
  blood,—
                "Column! Forward!"

While the sound of their song, like the surge of the
  seas,
With the "Star-Spangled Banner" swelled over the
  leas;
And the sword of Duryea, like a torch led the way,
Bearing down on the batteries of Bethel that day,—
                "Column! Forward!"

Through green-tasselled corn-fields our columns were
  thrown,
And like corn by the red scythe of fire we were mown;
While the cannon's fierce ploughings new-furrowed
  the plain,
That our blood might be planted for Liberty's grain,—
                "Column! Forward!"

*   *   *   *   *

                AUGUSTINE J. H. DUGANNE.

CIVIL WAR.

"RIFLEMAN, shoot me a fancy shot
    Straight at the heart of yon prowling
        vidette;
  Ring me a ball in the glittering spot
  That shines on his breast like an amulet!"

"Ah, Captain! here goes for a fine-drawn bead
  There 's music around when my barrel 's in tune!"
Crack! went the rifle, the messenger sped,
  And dead from his horse fell the ringing dragoon.

"Now, Rifleman, steal through the bushes, and snatch
  From your victim some trinket to handsel first
      blood—
A button, a loop, or that luminous patch
  That gleams in the moon like a diamond stud."

"O Captain! I staggered, and sunk on my track,
  When I gazed on the face of that fallen vidette;

For he looked so like you as he lay on his back,
  That my heart rose upon me, and masters me yet.

"But I snatched off the trinket—this locket of gold;
  An inch from the centre my lead broke its way,
Scarce grazing the picture, so fair to behold,
  Of a beautiful lady in bridal array."

"Ha! Rifleman, fling me the locket!—'t is she,
  My brother's young bride. and the fallen dragoon
Was her husband—Hush! soldier, 't was Heaven's
      decree;
  We must bury him here, by the light of the moon!

"But, hark! the far bugles their warnings unite;
  War is a virtue—weakness a sin;
There 's lurking and loping around us to-night;
  Load again, Rifleman, keep your hand in!"

                CHARLES DAWSON SHANLY.

"HOW ARE YOU, SANITARY?"

"DOWN the picket-guarded lane
  Rolled the comfort-laden wain,
  Cheered by shouts that shook the plain,
    Soldier-like and merry:
  Phrases such as camps may teach,
  Sabre-cuts of Saxon speech,
  Such as " Bully!" "Them's the peach!"
    "Wade in, Sanitary!"

Right and left the caissons drew
As the car went lumbering through,
Quick succeeding in review
    Squadrons military;
Sunburnt men with beards like frieze,
Smooth-faced boys, and cries like these,—
" U. S. San. Com." " That's the cheese!"
    "Pass in, Sanitary!"

In such cheer it struggled on
Till the battle front was won.
Then the car, its journey done,
    Lo! was stationary;
And where bullets whistling fly,
Came the sadder, fainter cry,
" Help us, brothers, ere we die,—
    Save us, Sanitary! "

Such the work. The phantom files,
Wrapped in battle clouds that rise;
But the brave — whose dying eyes,
    Veiled and visionary,
See the jasper gates swung wide,
See the parted throng outside —
Hears the voice to those who ride :
    " Pass in, Sanitary! "

BRET HARTE.

" How he strode his brown steed ! How we saw his blade brighten
In the one hand still left,—and the reins in his teeth !"

KEARNEY AT SEVEN PINES.

[May 31, 1862.]

O that soldierly legend is still on its journey,—
    That story of Kearney who knew not to
        yield!
'T was a day when with Jameson, fierce Berry,
        and Birney,
    Against twenty thousand he rallied the
        field,

Where the red volleys poured, where the clamor rose
        highest,
Where the dead lay in clumps through the dwarf
        oak and pine,
Where the aim from the thicket was surest and nigh-
        est,—
No charge like Phil Kearney's along the whole line.

When the battle went ill, and the bravest were solemn,
  Near the dark Seven Pines, where we still held our
    ground,
He rode down the length of the withering column,
  And his heart at our war-cry leapt up with a bound;
He snuffed, like his charger, the wind of our powder,—
  His sword waved us on and we answered the sign:
Loud our cheer as we rushed, but his laugh rang the
    louder,
    "There's the devil's own fun, boys, along the whole
    line!"

How he strode his brown steed! How we saw his
  blade brighten
  In the one hand still left,—and the reins in his
  teeth!
He laughed like a boy when the holidays heighten,
  But a soldier's glance shot from his visor beneath.

Up came the reserves to the mellay infernal,
  Asking where to go in,—through the clearing or
    pine?
"O, anywhere! Forward! 'T is all the same, Colonel:
  You'll find lovely fighting along the whole line!'"

O, evil the black shroud of night at Chantilly,
  That hid him from sight of his brave men and tried!
Foul, foul sped the bullet that clipped the white lily,
  The flower of our knighthood, the whole army's .
    pride!
Yet we dream that he still,—in that shadowy region
  Where the dead form their ranks at the wan drum-
    mer's sign,—
Rides on, as of old, down the length of his legion,
  And the word still is Forward! along the whole
    line.

            EDMUND CLARENCE STEDMAN.

THE OLD SERGEANT.

[The "Carrier's New Year Address" of The Louisville Journal, January 1, 1863.]

THE Carrier cannot sing to-day the bal-
    lads
  With which he used to go
Rhyming the glad rounds of the happy New
    Years
  That are now beneath the snow:

For the same awful and portentous Shadow
  That overcast the earth,
And smote the land last year with desolation,
  Still darkens every hearth.

And the Carrier hears Beethoven's mighty
  death-march
  Come up from every mart,
And he hears and feels it breathing in his
  bosom,
  And beating in his heart.

And to-day, a scarred and weather-beaten
  veteran,
  Again he comes along,
To tell the story of the Old Year's struggles
  In another New Year's song.

And the song is his, but not so with the story;
  For the story, you must know,
Was told in prose to Assistant-Surgeon
  Austin,
  By a soldier of Shiloh:

By Robert Burton, who was brought up on
  the Adams,
  With his death-wound in his side;

And who told the story to the Assistant Sur-
  geon
  On the same night that he died.

But the singer feels it will better suit the bal-
  lad,
  If all should deem it right,
To tell the story as if what it speaks of
  Had happened but last night.

        ———

"Come a little nearer, Doctor,—thank you; let me
  take the cup:
Draw your chair up.—draw it closer; just another
  little sup!
May be you may think I'm better; but I'm pretty
  well used up,—
Doctor, you've done all you could do, but I'm just
  a-going up!

"Feel my pulse, sir, if you want to, but it aint much
  use to try"—
"Never say that," said the Surgeon, as he smothered
  down a sigh;
"It will never do, old comrade, for a soldier to say
  die!"
"What you say will make no difference, Doctor,
  when you come to die."

"Doctor, what has been the matter?" "You were
  very faint, they say;
You must try to get to sleep now." "Doctor, have I
  been away?"

"Not that anybody knows of!" "Doctor—Doctor,
please to stay!
There is something I must tell you, and you won't
have long to stay!

"I have got my marching orders, and I'm ready now
to go;
Doctor, did you say I fainted?—but it couldn't ha'
been so,
For as sure as I'm a Sergeant, and was wounded at
Shiloh,
I've this very night been back there, on the old field
of Shiloh!

"This is all that I remember: The last time the
Lighter came,
And the lights had all been lowered, and the noises
much the same,
He had not been gone five minutes before something
called my name:
'ORDERLY SERGEANT — ROBERT BURTON!'—just
that way it called my name.

"And I wondered who could call me so distinctly
and so slow,
Knew it couldn't be the Lighter, he could not have
spoken so,
And I tried to answer, 'Here, sir!' but I couldn't
make it go;
For I couldn't move a muscle, and I couldn't make it
go.

"Then I thought: It's all a nightmare, all a humbug
and a bore;
Just another foolish *grape-vine* * — and it won't come
any more;
But it came, sir, notwithstanding, just the same way
as before:
'ORDERLY SERGEANT — ROBERT BURTON!' — even
louder than before.

"That is all that I remember, till a sudden burst of
light,
And I stood beside the River, where we stood that
Sunday night,
Waiting to be ferried over to the dark bluffs opposite,
When the river was perdition, and all hell was oppo-
site! —

"And the same old palpitation came again in all its
power,
And I heard a Bugle sounding, as from some celestial
Tower;
And the same mysterious voice said: 'IT IS THE
ELEVENTH HOUR!
ORDERLY SERGEANT—ROBERT BURTON—IT IS THE
ELEVENTH HOUR!'

———
*A false story, a hoax.

"Dr. Austin!—what *day* is this?" "It is Wednes-
day night, you know."
"Yes,—to-morrow will be New Year's, and a right
good time below!
What time is it, Dr. Austin?" "Nearly Twelve."
"Then don't you go!
Can it be that all this happened—all this—not an
hour ago!

"There was where the gunboats opened on the dark
rebellious host;
And where Webster semi-circled his last guns upon
the coast;
There were still the two log-houses, just the same, or
else their ghost—
And the same old transport came and took me over —
or its ghost!

"And the old field lay before me, all deserted, far
and wide:
There was where they fell on Prentiss — there Mc-
Clernand met the tide;
There was where stern Sherman rallied, and where
Hurlbut's heroes died, —
Lower down, where Wallace charged them, and kept
charging till he died.

"There was where Lew Wallace showed them he was
of the canny kin,
There was where old Nelson thundered, and where
Rousseau waded in;
There McCook sent 'em to breakfast, and we all began
to win—
There was where the grape-shot took me, just as we
began to win.

"Now, a shroud of snow and silence over everything
was spread;
And but for this old blue mantle and the old hat on
my head,
I should not have even doubted, to this moment, I was
dead,—
For my footsteps were as silent as the snow upon the
dead!

"Death and silence! — Death and silence! all around
me as I sped!
And behold, a mighty Tower, as if builded to the
dead,
To the Heaven of the heavens lifted up its mighty
head,
Till the Stars and Stripes of Heaven all seemed waving
from its head!

"Round and mighty based it towered up into the
infinite —
And I knew no mortal mason could have built a shaft
so bright; .

For it shone like solid sunshine; and a winding stair
  of light
Wound around it and around it till it wound clear out
  of sight!

" And, behold, as I approached it — with a rapt and
  dazzled stare, —
Thinking that I saw old comrades just ascending the
  great stair, —
Suddenly the solemn challenge broke of—'Halt!' and
  'Who goes there?'
'I'm a friend,' I said, 'if you are!' 'Then advance, sir,
  to the Stair!'

"I advanced! That sentry, doctor, was Elijah Bal-
  lantyne!
First of all to fall on Monday, after we had formed
  the line!
'Welcome, my old Sergeant, welcome! Welcome by
  that countersign!'
And he pointed to the scar there, under this old cloak
  of mine.

"As he grasped my hand I shuddered, thinking only
  of the grave;
But he smiled and pointed upward, with a bright and
  bloodless glaive:
'That's the way, sir, to Headquarters.' 'What Head-
  quarters?' 'Of the Brave!'

'But the great Tower?' 'That was builded of the
  great deeds of the Brave!'

"Then a sudden shame came o'er me at his uniform of
  light;
At my own so old and battered, and at his so new and
  bright;
'Ah!' said he, 'you have forgotten the new uniform to-
  night!'
'Hurry back,' — you must be here at just twelve o'clock
  to-night!'

"And the next thing I remember, you were sitting *there*
  and I——
Doctor—did you hear a footstep? Hark!—God bless
  you all! Good bye!
Doctor, please to give my musket and my knapsack,
  when I die,
To my son—my son that's coming—he won't get here
  till I die!

"Tell him his old father blessed him—as he never did
  before,—
And to carry that old musket"——Hark! a knock is
  at the door!——
"Till the Union"——See! it opens!——"Father!
  Father! speak once more!"

"*Bless you*"—gasped the old gray Sergeant. And he
  lay and said no more!

FORCEYTHE WILLSON.

SHERIDAN'S RIDE.

UP from the South at break of day
  Bringing to Winchester fresh dismay,
  The affrighted air with a shudder bore,
  Like a herald in haste, to the chieftain's door,
  The terrible grumble, and rumble, and roar,
  Telling the battle was on once more,
  And Sheridan twenty miles away.

And wider still those billows of war ·
Thundered along the horizon's bar;
And louder yet into Winchester rolled
The roar of that red sea uncontrolled,
Making the blood of the listener cold,
As he thought of the stake in that fiery fray,
And Sheridan twenty miles away.

But there is a road from Winchester town,
A good, broad highway leading down;
And there through the flush of the morning lig' ,
A steed as black as the steeds of night
Was seen to pass, as with eagle flight.
As if he knew the terrible need,
He stretched away with his utmost speed;
Hills rose and fell; but his heart was gay,
With Sheridan fifteen miles away.

Still sprung from those swift hoofs, thundering South
The dust, like smoke from the cannon's mouth,
Or the trail of a comet, sweeping faster and faster,
Foreboding to traitors the doom of disaster.
The heart of the steed and the heart of the master
Were beating like prisoners assaulting their walls,
Impatient to be where the battlefield calls;
Every nerve of the charger was strained to full play,
With Sheridan only ten miles away.

Under his spurning feet, the road
Like an arrowy Alpine river flowed,
And the landscape sped away behind
Like an ocean flying before the wind,
And the steed, like a bark fed with furnace ire,
Swept on, with his wild eye full of fire.
But lo! he is nearing his heart's desire;
He is snuffing the smoke of the roaring fray,
With Sheridan only five miles away.

The first that the General saw were the groups
Of stragglers, and then the retreating troops;
What was done,—what to do,—a glance told him
  both,
And striking his spurs, with a terrible oath,

He dashed down the line, 'mid a storm of huzzas,
And the wave of retreat checked its course there
    because
The sight of the master compelled it to pause.
With foam and with dust the black charger was
    gray;
By the flash of his eye, and his red nostril's play,
He seemed to the whole great army to say,
" I have brought you Sheridan all the way
From Winchester down to save the day."

Hurrah, hurrah for Sheridan!
Hurrah, hurrah for horse and man!
And when their statues are placed on high,
Under the dome of the Union sky,—
The American soldiers' Temple of Fame,—
There with the glorious General's name
Be it said in letters both bold and bright:
" Here is the steed that saved the day
By carrying Sheridan into the fight,
From Winchester, — twenty miles away! "

THOMAS BUCHANAN READ.

"He's in the saddle now!—Fall in!
Steady, the whole brigade!"

STONEWALL JACKSON'S WAY.

OME, cheerily, men, pile on the rails,
    And stir the camp-fires bright;
No matter if the canteen fails,
    We'll have a roaring night!
Here Shenandoah brawls along,
There burly Blue-Ridge echoes strong,
To swell the brigade's rousing song
    Of Stonewall Jackson's way!

We see him now—his old slouched hat
    Cocked o'er his eye askew,
His shrewd, dry smile, his speech so pat,
    So calm, so blunt, so true;
The blue-light Elder knows 'em well,
Says he, "That's Banks—he's fond of shell!
Lord save his soul—we'll give him Hell!"
    That's Stonewall Jackson's way!

Silence! Ground arms! Kneel all! Hats off!
  Old Stonewall's going to pray!
Strangle the fool that dares to scoff!
  Attention! 'Tis his way!
Kneeling upon his native sod
In forma pauperis to God—
"Lay bare thine arm! Stretch forth thy rod!
  Amen!" That's Stonewall's way!

He's in the saddle now—Fall in!
  Steady, the whole brigade!
Hill's at the Ford, cut off! We'll win
  His way out, ball or blade!
No matter if our shoes be worn,
No matter if our feet be torn,—
Quick step! We'll with him before morn,
  In Stonewall Jackson's way!

The sun's bright lances rout the mists
  Of morning, and, by George!—
There's Longstreet struggling in the lists,
  Hemmed by an ugly gorge;
"Pope and his Yankees whipped before!
Bayonets and grape!" hear Stonewall roar;
"Charge, Stuart! Pay off Ashby's score,
  In Stonewall Jackson's way!"

Ah, woman! wait, and watch, and yearn
  For news of Stonewall's band!
Ah, widow! read with eyes that burn
  That ring upon thy hand!
Ah, maiden! weep on, hope on, pray on!
Thy lot is not so all forlorn—
The foe had better ne'er been born
  That gets in Stonewall's way!

J. W. PALMER.

BARBARA FRIETCHIE.

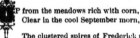

UP from the meadows rich with corn,
  Clear in the cool September morn,

The clustered spires of Frederick stand,
  Green-walled by the hills of Maryland.

Round about them orchards sweep,
  Apple and peach tree fruited deep,

Fair as a garden of the Lord,
To the eyes of the famished rebel horde,

On that pleasant morn of the early Fall.
When Lee marched over the mountain wall,

Over the mountains winding down,
Horse and foot, into Frederick town.

Forty flags with their silver stars,
Forty flags with their crimson bars,

Flapped in the morning wind: the sun
Of noon looked down, and saw not one.

Up rose old Barbara Frietchie then,
Bowed with her fourscore years and ten;

Bravest of all in Frederick town,
She took up the flag the men hauled down.

In her attic-window the staff she set,
To show that one heart was loyal yet.

Up the street came the rebel-tread,
Stonewall Jackson riding ahead.

Under his slouched hat left and right
He glanced: the old flag met his sight.

"Halt!"—the dust-brown ranks stood fast;
"Fire!"—out blazed the rifle-blast.

It shivered the window, pane and sash,
It rent the banner with seam and gash.

Quick, as it fell from the broken staff,
Dame Barbara snatched the silken scarf;

She leaned far out on the window-sill,
And shook it forth with a royal will.

"Shoot, if you must, this old gray head,
But spare your country's flag!" she said.

A shade of sadness, a blush of shame,
Over the face of the leader came;

The nobler nature within him stirred
To life at that woman's deed and word.

"Who touches a hair of yon gray head
Dies like a dog! March on!" he said.

All day long through Frederick street
Sounded the tread of marching feet;

All day long that free flag tossed
Over the heads of the rebel host.

Ever its torn folds rose and fell
On the loyal winds that loved it well;

And through the hill-gaps sunset light
Shone over it with a warm good-night.

Barbara Frietchie's work is o'er,
And the rebel rides on his raids no more.

Honor to her! and let a tear
Fall, for her sake, on Stonewall's bier.

Over Barbara Frietchie's grave.
Flag of Freedom and Union, wave!

Peace and order and beauty draw
Round thy symbol of light and law;

And ever the stars above look down
On thy stars below in Frederick town.

JOHN GREENLEAF WHITTIER.

JOHN BURNS OF GETTYSBURG.

HAVE you heard the story the gossips tell
Of John Burns of Gettysburg? —No? Ah, well,
Brief is the glory that hero earns,
Briefer the story of poor John Burns;
He was the fellow who won renown —
The only man who didn't back down
When the rebels rode through his native town;
But held his own in the fight next day,
When all his townsfolk ran away.
That was in July, sixty-three, —
The very day that General Lee,
The flower of Southern chivalry,
Baffled and beaten, backward reeled
From a stubborn Meade and a barren field.

I might tell how, but the day before,
John Burns stood at his cottage-door,
Looking down the village street,
Where, in the shade of his peaceful vine,
He heard the low of his gathered kine,
And felt their breath with incense sweet;
Or, I might say, when the sunset burned
The old farm gable, he thought it turned
The milk that fell in a babbling flood
Into the milk-pail, red as blood;
Or, how he fancied the hum of bees
Were bullets buzzing among the trees.

But all such fanciful thoughts as these
Were strange to a practical man like Burns,
Who minded only his own concerns,
Troubled no more by his calm-eyed, long-tailed kine,
Than one of his calm-eyed, long-tailed kine,
Quite old-fashioned, and matter-of-fact,
Slow to argue, but quick to act.
That was the reason, as some folks say,
He fought so well on that terrible day.

And it was terrible. On the right
Raged for hours the heavy fight,
Thundered the battery's double bass
Difficult music for men to face;
While on the left — where now the graves
Undulate like the living waves
That all the day unceasing swept
Up to the pits the rebels kept —
Round-shot plowed the upland glades,
Sown with bullets, reaped with blades;

Shattered fences here and there
Tossed their splinters in the air;
The very trees were stripped and bare;
The barns that once held yellow grain
Were heaped with harvests of the slain;
The cattle bellowed on the plain,
The turkeys screamed with might and main,
And brooding barn-fowl left their rest
With strange shells bursting in each nest.

Just where the tide of battle turns,
Erect and lonely, stood old John Burns.

How do you think the man was dressed?
He wore an ancient, long buff vest,
Yellow as saffron — but his best;
And, buttoned over his manly breast
Was a bright blue coat with a rolling collar,
And large gilt buttons — size of a dollar —
With tails that country-folk called " swaller."
He wore a broad-brimmed, bell-crowned hat,
White as the locks on which it sat.
Never had such a sight been seen
For forty years on the village-green,
Since John Burns was a country beau,
And went to the "quilting" long ago.

Close at his elbows, all that day
Veterans of the Peninsula,
Sunburnt and bearded, charged away,
And striplings, downy of lip and chin, —
Clerks that the Home Guard mustered in —
Glanced as they passed at the hat he wore,
Then at the rifle his right hand bore;
And hailed him from out their youthful lore,
With scraps of a slangy *reportoire*:
" How are you, White Hat? " " Put her through? "
" Your head's level! " and, " Bully for you! "
Called him " Daddy " —and begged he'd disclose
The name of the tailor who made his clothes,
And what was the value he set on those;
While Burns, unmindful of jeer and scoff,
Stood there picking the rebels off —
With his long brown rifle and bell-crown hat,
And the swallow-tails they were laughing at.

'Twas but a moment, for that respect
Which clothes all courage their voices checked;

And something the wildest could understand
Spake in the old man's strong right hand,
And his corded throat, and the lurking frown
Of his eyebrows under his old bell-crown;
Until, as they gazed, there crept an awe
Through the ranks in whispers, and some men saw,
In the antique vestments and long white hair
The Past of the Nation in battle there.
And some of the soldiers since declare
That the gleam of his old white hat afar,
Like the crested plume of the brave Navarre,
That day was their oriflamme of war.

Thus raged the battle. You know the rest;
How the rebels, beaten, and backward pressed,
Broke at the final charge and ran.
At which John Burns — a practical man —
Shouldered his rifle. unbent his. brows,
And then went back to his bees and cows.

This is the story of old John Burns;
This is the moral the reader learns:
In fighting the battle, the question's whether
You'll show a hat that's white, or a feather.

BRET HARTE.

THE CHARGE BY THE FORD.

IGHTY and nine with their captain,
   Rode on the enemy's track,
   Rode in the gray of the morning—
   Nine of the ninety came back.

Slow rose the mist from the river,
   Lighter each moment the way;
Careless and tearless and fearless
   Galloped they on to the fray.

Singing in tune, how the scabbards,
   Loud on the stirrup-irons rang,
Clinked as the men rose in saddle,
   Fell as they sank with a clang.

What is it moves by the river,
   Jaded and weary and weak?
Gray-backs—a cross on their banner—
   Yonder the foe whom they seek.

Silence! They see not, they hear not,
   Tarrying there by the marge:
Forward! Draw sabre! Trot! Gallop!
   Charge! like a hurricane, charge.

Ah! 'twas a man-trap infernal—
   Fire like the deep pit of hell!

Volley on volley to meet them,
   Mixed with the gray rebel's yell.

Ninety had ridden to battle,
   Tracing the enemy's track—
Ninety had ridden to battle;
   Nine of the ninety came back.

Honor the name of the ninety;
   Honor the heroes who came
Scatheless from five hundred muskets,
   Safe from the lead-bearing flame.

Eighty and one of the troopers
   Lie on the field on the slain—
Lie on the red field of honor—
   Honor the nine who remain!

Cold are the dead there, and gory,
   There where their life-blood was spilt;
Back come the living. each sabre
   Red from the point to the hilt.

Up with three cheers and a tiger!
   Let the flags wave as they come!
Give them the blare of the trumpet!
   Give them the roll of the drum!

THOMAS DUNN ENGLISH.

THE CAVALRY CHARGE.

ITH bray of the trumpet
   And roll of the drum,
   And keen ring of bugle,
   The cavalry come.
Sharp clank the steel scabbards,
   The bridle-chains ring,
And foam from red nostrils
   The wild chargers fling.

Tramp! tramp! o'er the greensward
   That quivers below,
Scarce held by the curb-bit
   The fierce horses go!
And the grim-visaged colonel,
   With ear-rending shout,
Peals forth to the squadrons
   The order,—"Trot out!"

One hand on the sabre,
 And one on the rein,
The troopers move forward
 In line on the plain.
As rings the word, "Gallop!"
 The steel scabbards clank,
And each rowel is pressed
 To a horse's hot flank:
And swift is their rush
 As the wild torrent's flow,
When it pours from the crag
 On the valley below.

"Charge!" thunders the leader;
 Like shaft from the bow
Each mad horse is hurled
 On the wavering foe.
A thousand bright sabres
 Are gleaming in air;
A thousand dark horses
 Are dashed on the square.

Resistless and reckless
 Of aught may betide,
Like demons, not mortals,
 The wild troopers ride.
Cut right! and cut left!—
 For the parry who needs?
The bayonets shiver
 Like wind-scattered reeds.

Vain—vain the red volley
 That bursts from the square,—
The random-shot bullets
 Are wasted in air.
Triumphant, remorseless,
 Unerring as death,—
No sabre that 's stainless
 Returns to its sheath.

The wounds that are dealt
 By that murderous steel
Will never yield case
 For the surgeon to heal.
Hurrah! they are broken—
 Hurrah! boys, they fly—
None linger save those
 Who but linger to die.

Rein up your hot horses
 And call in your men,—
The trumpet sounds "Rally
 To colors" again.
Some saddles are empty,
 Some comrades are slain,
And some noble horses
 Lie stark on the plain;
But war 's a chance game, boys,
 And weeping is vain.

FRANCIS A. DURIVAGE.

CAVALRY SONG.

OUR good steeds snuff the evening air,
 Our pulses with their purpose tingle;
The foeman's fires are twinkling there;
 He leaps to hear our sabres jingle!
 HALT!
 Each carbine sends its whizzing ball;
 Now, cling! clang! forward all,
 Into the fight!

Dash on beneath the smoking dome:
 Through level lightnings gallop nearer!
One look to Heaven! No thoughts of home:
 The guidons that we bear are dearer. ·

CHARGE!
Cling! clang! forward all!
Heaven help those whose horses fall:
 Cut left and right!

They flee before our fierce attack!
 They fall! they spread in broken surges,
Now, comrades, bear our wounded back,
 And leave the foeman to his dirges
 WHEEL!
The bugles sound the swift recall;
Cling! clang! backward all!
 Home, and good night!

EDMUND CLARENCE STEDMAN.

HE took my arms, and while I forced my way
 Through troops of foes, which did our passage
 stay,
 His buckler o'er my aged father cast,
 Still fighting, still defending, as I past.

EMBATTLED troops with flowing banners pass
 Through flowery meads, delighted, nor distrust
The smiling surface; whilst the caverned ground
Bursts fatal, and involves the hopes of war
In fiery whirls.

THE C. S. ARMY'S COMMISSARY.

963.

"WELL, this is bad!" we sighing said,
    While musing round the bivouac fire,
    And dwelling with a fond desire,
On home and comforts long since fled.

"How gaily came we forth at first!
    Our spirits high, with new emprise,
    Ambitious of each exercise,
And glowing with a martial thirst.

"Our tents—they went a year ago;
    Now kettle, spider, frying-pan
    Are lost to us, and as we can
We live, while marching to and fro.

"Our food has lessened, till at length
    E'en want's gaunt image seems to threat—
    A foe to whom the bravest yet
Must yield at last his knightly strength.

"But while we 've meat and flour enough
The bayonet shall be our spit."

"Equipped as for a holiday,
    With bounteous store of everything
    To use or comfort minist'ring,
All cheerily we marched away.

"But as the struggle fiercer grew,
    Light marching orders came apace,—
    And baggage-wagon soon gave place
To that which sterner uses knew.

"But while we 've meat and flour enough
    The bayonet shall be our spit—
    The ramrod bake our dough on it—
A gum-cloth be our kneading trough.

"We 'll bear privation, danger dare,
    While even these are left to us—
    Be hopeful, faithful, emulous
Of gallant deeds, though hard our fare!"

II—1864.

"Three years and more," we grimly said.
  When order came to "Rest at will"
  Beside the corn-field on the hill,
As on a weary march we sped—

"Three years and more we 've met the foe
  On many a gory, hard-fought field,
  And still we swear we cannot yield
Till Fate shall bring some deeper woe.

" Ill fed, ill clad, and shelterless,
  How little cheer in health we know!
  When wounds and illness lay us low,
How comfortless our sore distress!

" These filmsy rags, that scarcely hide
  Our forms, can naught discourage us;
  But Hunger—ah! it may be thus
That Fortune shall the strife decide.

" But while the corn-fields give supply
We 'll take, content, the roasting-ear."

" Three years and more we 've struggled on,
  Through torrid heat and winter's chill,
  Nor bated aught of steadfast will.
Though even hope seems almost gone.

" But while the corn-fields give supply
  We 'll take, content, the roasting-ear,
  Nor yield us yet to craven fear,
But still press on, to do or die! "

         ED. PORTER THOMPSON.

THE fiery courser, when he hears from far
  The sprightly trumpets and the shouts of war,
Pricks up his ears. and trembling with delight.
Shifts place. and paws, and hopes the promised fight;
On his right shoulder his thick mane reclined,

Ruffles at speed. and dances in the wind:
Eager he stands.—then, starting with a bound,
He turns the turf, and shakes the solid ground;
Fire from his eyes. clouds from his nostrils flow;
He bears his rider headlong on the foe.

SONG OF THE SOLDIERS.

COMRADES known in marches many,
Comrades tried in dangers many,
Comrades bound by memories many,
  Brothers ever let us be.
Wounds or sickness may divide us
Marching orders may divide us,
But whatever fate betide us,
  Brothers of the heart are we.

Comrades known by faith the clearest,
Tried when death was near and nearest,
Bound we are by ties the dearest.
  Brothers evermore to be.
And if spared and growing older,
Shoulder still in line with shoulder,
And with hearts no thrill the colder,
  Brothers ever we shall be.

" But whatever fate betide us,
Brothers of the heart are we."

By communion of the banner,—
Crimson, white, and starry banner,—
By the baptism of the banner,
  Children of one Church are we.

Creed nor faction can divide us,
Race nor language can divide us,
Still, whatever fate betide us,
  Children of the flag are we!

CHARLES G. HALPINE.
(Miles O'Reilly.)

HARK! heard you not those hoofs of dreadful
    note?
Sounds not the clang of conflict on the heath?
Saw ye not whom the reeking sabre smote,
Nor saved your brethren ere they sank beneath
Tyrants and tyrants' slaves?—The fires of death,

The bale-fires flash on high:—from rock to
    rock
Each volley tells that thousands cease to breathe;
Death rides upon the sulphury Siroc.
Red battle stamps his foot, and nations feel the
    shock.

DESCRIPTION AND NARRATION.

"Great garments of rain wrap the desolate night."

"ATLANTIC."

Y, build her long and narrow and deep!
  She shall cut the sea with a scimetar's sweep,
  Whatever betides and whoever may weep!

  Bring out the red wine! Lift the glass to the
    lip!
  With a roar of great guns, and a "Hip! hip!
Hurrah!" for the craft, we will christen the ship!

Dash a draught on the bow! Ah, the spar of white
  wood
Drips into the sea till it colors the flood
With the very own double and symbol of blood!

Now out with the name of the monarch gigantic
That shall queen it so grandly when surges are frantic!
Child of fire and of iron, God save the "Atlantic!"
  *   *   *   *   *   *   *

255

All aboard, my fine fellows! "Up anchor!" the
    word—
Ah, never again shall that order be heard,
For two worlds will be mourning ye gone to a third!

To the trumpet of March wild gallops the sea;
The white-crested troopers are under the lee—
Old World and New World and Soul-World are three.

Great garments of rain wrap the desolate night;
Sweet Heaven disastered is lost to the sight;
"Atlantic," crash on in the pride of thy might!
With thy look-out's dim cry "One o'clock, and all
    right!"

Ho, down with the hatches! The seas come aboard!
All together they come, like a passionate word,
Like pirates that put every soul to the sword!

Their black flag all abroad makes murky the air,
But the ship parts the night as a maiden her hair—
Through and through the thick gloom, from land here
    to land there,
Like the shuttle that weaves for a mourner to wear!

Good night, proud "Atlantic!" One tick of the
    clock,
And a staggering craunch and a shivering shock—
'Tis the flint and the steel! 'Tis the ship and the
    rock!

Deathless sparks are struck out from the bosoms of
    girls,
From the stout heart of manhood, in scintillant whirls,
Like the stars of the Flag when the banner unfurls!

What hundreds went up unto God in their sleep!
What hundreds in agony baffled the deep—
Nobody to pray and nobody to weep!

Alas for the flag of the single "White Star,"
With light pale and cold as the woman's hands are
Who, froze in the shrouds, flashed her jewels afar,
Lost her hold on the world, and then clutched at a
    spar!

God of mercy and grace! How the bubbles come up
With souls from the revel, who stayed not to sup;
Death drank the last toast, and then shattered the
    cup!

                                BENJAMIN F. TAYLOR.

THE WIND IN A FROLIC.

THE Wind one morning sprang up from sleep,
    Saying, "Now for a frolic! now for a leap!
Now for a mad-cap galloping chase!
    I'll make a commotion in every place!"
So it swept with a bustle right through a great
    town,
Creaking the signs, and scattering down
Shutters; and whisking, with merciless squalls,
Old women's bonnets and gingerbread stalls:
There never was heard a much lustier shout.
As the apples and oranges tumbled about;
And the urchins, that stand with their thievish eyes
Forever on watch, ran off each with a prize.
    Then away to the field it went blustering and hum-
        ming,
And the cattle all wondered whatever was coming;
It plucked by the tails the grave matronly cows,
And tossed the colts' manes all over their brows,
'Till, offended at such a familiar salute,
They all turned their backs and stood sulkily mute.
    So on it went, capering and playing its pranks,
Whistling with reeds on the broad river's banks,
Puffing the birds as they sat on the spray,
Or the traveler grave on the king's highway.
    It was not too nice to hustle the bags
Of the beggar, and flutter his dirty rags:
'Twas so bold, that it feared not to play its joke
With the doctor's wig or the gentleman's cloak.

Through the forest it roared, and cried, gayly, "Now,
You sturdy old oaks, I'll make you bow!"
And it made them bow without more ado,
Or cracked their great branches through and through.
    Then it rushed, like a monster, on cottage and farm,
Striking their dwellers with sudden alarm,
So they ran out like bees when threatened with harm.
There were dames with their kerchiefs tied over their
    caps,
To see if their poultry were free from mishaps;
The turkeys they gobbled, the geese screamed aloud,
And the hens crept to roost in a terrified crowd;
There was rearing of ladders, and logs laying on,
Where the thatch from the roof threatened soon to be
    gone.
    But the wind had swept on, and met in a lane
With a school-boy, who panted and struggled in vain;
For it tossed him, and twirled him, then passed, and
    he stood
With his hat in a pool, and his shoe in the mud.
    Then away went the wind in its holiday glee!
And now it was far on the billowy sea;
And the lordly ships felt its staggering blow,
And the little boats darted to and fro:—
But lo! night came, and it sank to rest
On the sea-bird's rock in the gleaming west,
Laughing to think, in its fearful fun,
How little of mischief it had done!

                                WILLIAM HOWITT.

" Through the forest it round, and cried, gayly, { Now,
You sturdy old oaks, I'll make you bow,
And to make them bow, without more ado,
Or cracked their great branches through and through."

IN THE MAINE WOODS.

I.—THE FORESTS.

HAT is most striking in the Maine wilderness is the continuousness of the forest, with fewer open intervals, or glades, than you had imagined. Except the few burnt lands, the narrow intervals on the rivers, the bare tops of the high mountains, and the lakes and streams, the forest is

uninterrupted. It is even more grim and wild than you had anticipated—a damp and intricate wilderness, in the spring everywhere wet and miry. The aspect of the country, indeed, is universally stern and savage, excepting the distant views of the forest from hills, and the lake-prospects, which are mild and civilizing in a degree.

The lakes are something which you are unprepared for; they lie up so high, exposed to the light, and the forest is diminished to a fine fringe on their edges, with here and

there a blue mountain, like amethyst jewels set around some jewel of the first water — so anterior, so superior to all the changes that are to take place on their shores, even now civil and refined, and fair as they can ever be. These

A MOUNTAIN LAKE.

are not the artificial forests of an English king — a royal preserve merely. Here prevail no forest-laws but those of Nature. The aborigines have never been dispossessed, nor Nature disforested. It is a country full of evergreen trees, of mossy silver-birches and watery maples — the ground dotted with insipid, small, red berries, and strewn with damp and moss-grown rocks; a country diversified with innumerable lakes and rapid streams, peopled with trout, with salmon, shad, and pickerel, and other fishes. The forest resounds at rare intervals with the note of the chickadee, the blue-jay, and the woodpecker, the scream of fish-hawk and the eagle, the laugh of the loon, and the whistle of ducks along the solitary streams; at night, with the hooting of owls and the howling of wolves; in summer, swarming with myriads of black flies and mosquitoes, more formidable than wolves to the white man.

Such is the home of the

DENIZENS OF THE FOREST.

moose, the bear, the caribou, the wolf, the beaver, and the Indian. Who shall describe the inexpressible tenderness and immortal life of the grim forest, where Nature, though it be midwinter, is ever in her spring; where the moss-grown and decaying trees are not old, but seem to enjoy a perpetual youth; and blissful, innocent Nature, like a serene infant, is too happy to make a noise, except by a few tinkling, lisping birds, and trickling rills.

II.—SHOOTING RAPIDS.

We reached the dam at noon. The boatmen went through one of the log sluices in the bateau, where the fall was ten feet at the bottom, and took us in below. Here was the longest rapid in our voyage, and perhaps the running this was as dangerous and arduous a task as any. In shooting rapids the boatman has this problem to solve: to choose a circuitous and safe course amid a thousand sunken rocks, scattered over a long distance, at the same time that he is moving steadily on at the rate of fifteen miles an hour. Stop he can not: the only question is, Where will he go? The bow-man chooses the course with all his eyes about him, striking broad off with his paddle, and drawing the boat by main force into her course. The stern-man faithfully follows the bow. Down the rapids we shot at a headlong rate. If we struck a rock, we were split from end to end in an instant. Now like a bait bobbing for some river monster amid the eddies, now darting to this side of the stream, now to that, gliding swift and smooth near to our destruction, or striking broad off with the paddle and drawing the boat to right or left with all our might in order to avoid a rock, we soon ran through the mile, and floated in Quakish Lake.

After such a voyage, the troubled and angry waters, which once had seemed terrible and not be trifled with, appeared tamed and subdued; they had been bearded and worried in their channels, pricked and whipped into submission with the spike-pole and paddle, and all their spirit and their danger taken out of them; and the most swollen and impetuous rivers seemed but playthings henceforth. I began at length to understand the boatmen's familiarity with and contempt for the rapids. "Those Fowler boys," said Mrs. M., "are perfect ducks for the water." They had run down to Lincoln, according to her, thirty or forty miles, in a bateau, in the night, for a doctor, when it was so dark that they could not see a rod before them, and the river was swollen so as to be almost a continuous rapid, so that the doctor cried, when they brought him up by daylight, "Why, Tom, how did you see to steer?" "We didn't steer much—only kept her straight." And yet they met with no accident.

HENRY D. THOREAU.

A LIFE ON THE OCEAN WAVE.

A LIFE on the ocean wave,
  A home on the rolling deep;
Where the scattered waters rave,
  And the winds their revels keep!
Like an eagle caged I pine
  On this dull, unchanging shore:
Oh, give me the flashing brine,
  The spray and the tempest's roar!

Once more on the deck I stand
  Of my own swift-gliding craft:
Set sail! farewell to the land;
  The gale follows fair abaft.

We shoot through the sparkling foam,
  Like an ocean-bird set free,—
Like the ocean-bird, our home
  We'll find far out on the sea.

The land is no longer in view,
  The clouds have begun to frown;
But with a stout vessel and crew,
  We'll say, Let the storm come down!
And the song of our hearts shall be,
  While the wind and the waters rave,
A home on the rolling sea!
  A life on the ocean wave!

EPES SARGENT.

SKIPPER IRESON'S RIDE.

OF all the rides since the birth of Time,
Told in story or sung in rhyme,—
On Apuleius' Golden Ass,
Or one-eyed Calender's horse of brass,
Witch astride of a human back,
Islam's prophet on Al-Borak,—
The strangest ride that ever was sped
Was Ireson's, out from Marblehead!
 Old Floyd Ireson, for his hard heart,
 Tarred and feathered and carried in a cart,
  By the women of Marblehead!

Body of turkey, head of owl,
Wing a-droop like a rained-on fowl,
Feathered and ruffled in every part,
Skipper Ireson stood in the cart.
Scores of women, old and young,
Strong of muscle and glib of tongue,
Pushed and pulled up the rocky lane,
Shouting and singing the shrill refrain:
 "Here's Flud Oirson, fur his horrd horrt,
 Torr'd an' futherr'd an' corr'd in a corrt
  By the women o' Morble'ead!"

Wrinkled scolds with hands on hips,
Girls in bloom of cheek and lips,
Wild-eyed, free-limbed, such as chase
Bacchus round some antique vase;
Brief of skirt, with ankles bare,
Loose of kerchief and loose of hair,
With conch-shells blowing and fish-horns' twang,
Over and over the Mænads sang:
 "Here's Flud Oirson, fur his horrd horrt,
 Torr'd an' futherr'd an' corr'd in a corrt
  By the women o' Morble'ead!"

Small pity for him! He sailed away
From a leaking ship in Chaleur Bay,—
Sailed away from a sinking wreck,
With his own towns-people on her deck!
"Lay by! lay by!" they called to him;
Back he answered, "Sink or swim!
Brag of your catch of fish again!"
And off he sailed through the fog and rain!
 Old Floyd Ireson, for his hard heart,
 Tarred and feathered and carried in a cart,
  By the women of Marblehead!

Fathoms deep in dark Chaleur
That wreck shall lie forevermore.
Mother and sister, wife and maid,
Looked from the rocks of Marblehead
Over the moaning and rainy sea,—
Looked for the coming that might not be!

What did the winds and sea-birds say
Of the cruel captain who sailed away?—
Old Floyd Ireson, for his hard heart,
Tarred and feathered and carried in a cart
 By the women of Marblehead!

Through the street, on either side,
Up flew windows, doors swung wide;
Sharp-tongued spinsters, old wives gray,
Treble lent the fish-horn's bray,
Sea-worn grandsires, cripple-bound,
Hulks of old sailors run aground,
Shook head and fist and hat and cane,
And cracked with curses the hoarse refrain:
 "Here's Flud Oirson, fur his horrd horrt,
 Torr'd an' futherr'd an' corr'd in a corrt
  By the women o' Morble'ead!"

Sweetly along the Salem road
Bloom of orchard and lilac showed.
Little the wicked skipper knew
Of the fields so green and the sky so blue.
Riding there in his sorry trim,
Like an Indian idol, glum and grim,
Scarcely he seemed the sound to hear
Of voices shouting far and near:
 "Here's Flud Oirson, fur his horrd horrt,
 Torr'd an' futherr'd an' corr'd in a corrt
  By the women o' Morble'ead!"

"Hear me, neighbors!" at last he cried,—
"What to me is this noisy ride?
What is the shame that clothes the skin
To the nameless horror that lives within?
Waking or sleeping, I see a wreck,
And hear a cry from a reeling deck!
Hate me and curse me,— I only dread
The hand of God and the face of the dead!"
 Said old Floyd Ireson, for his hard heart
 Tarred and feathered and carried in a cart
  By the women of Marblehead!

Then the wife of the skipper lost at sea
Said, "God has touched him,—why should we?"
Said an old wife, mourning her only son,
"Cut the rogue's tether and let him run!"
So with soft relentings and rude excuse,
Half scorn, half pity, they cut him loose,
And gave him a cloak to hide him in,
And left him alone with his shame and sin.
 Poor Floyd Ireson, for his hard heart,
 Tarred and feathered and carried in a cart
  By the women of Marblehead!

JOHN GREENLEAF WHITTIER.

"——Upon a rustic bridge
We pass a gulf in which the willows dip
Their pendant boughs."

THE RUSTIC BRIDGE.

DESCENDING now (but cautious, lest too fast)
A sudden steep, upon a rustic bridge
We pass a gulf in which the willows dip
Their pendant boughs, stooping as if to drink:
Hence, ankle-deep in moss and flowery thyme,
We mount again, and feel at every step
Our foot half sunk in hillocks green and soft,
Raised by the mole, the miner of the soil.
He, not unlike the great ones of mankind,
Disfigures earth, and plotting in the dark,
Toils much to earn a monumental pile
That may record the mischiefs he has done.

WILLIAM COWPER.

NOON IN MIDSUMMER.

THE summer floats on even wing,
  Nor sails more far, nor draws more near;
Poised calm between the budding spring
  And sweet decadence of the year.

In shadowed fields the cattle stand,
  The dreaming river scarcely flows,
The sky hangs cloudless o'er the land,
  And nothing comes and nothing goes.

A pause of fullness set between
  The sowing and the reaping time;
What is to be and what has been
  Joined each to each in perfect rhyme.

So comes high noon 'twixt morn and eve,
  So comes fu tide 'twixt ebb and flow,
Or midnight 'twixt the day we leave
  And that new day to which we go.

Full, fruitful hours by growing won,
  A restful space 'mid old and new;
When all there was to do is done,
  And nothing yet there is to do.

No days like these so deeply blest,
  That look nor backward nor before;
Their large fulfillment, ample rest,
  Make life flow wider evermore.

                     LOUISA BUSHNELL.

"How silent are the winds! No billow roars;
But all is tranquil as Elysian shores!"

THE SEA IN CALM.

LOOK what immortal floods the sunset pours
Upon us.—Mark! how still (as though in dreams
Bound) the once wild and terrible ocean seems;
How silent are the winds! No billow roars:
But all is tranquil as Elysian shores!
The silver margin which aye runneth round
The moon-enchanted sea hath here no sound;
Even Echo speaks not on these radiant moors!

What! is the giant of the ocean dead,
Whose strength was all unmatched beneath the sun?
No; he reposes! Now his toils are done,
More quiet than the babbling brooks is he.
So mightiest powers by deepest calms are fed,
And sleep, how oft, in things that gentlest be!

                 BRYAN WALLER PROCTOR.
                   (Barry Cornwall.)

BURIAL OF MOSES.

"And he buried him in a valley in the land of Moab, over against Beth-peor; but no man knoweth of his sepulchre unto this day."—DEUT. xxxiv. 6.

BY Nebo's lonely mountain,
  On this side Jordan's wave,
In a vale in the land of Moab,
  There lies a lonely grave;
But no man built that sepulchre,
  And no man saw it e'er;
For the angels of God upturned the sod,
  And laid the dead man there.

That was the grandest funeral
  That ever passed on earth;
Yet no man heard the trampling,
  Or saw the train go forth:

Noiselessly as the daylight
  Comes when the night is done,
And the crimson streak on ocean's cheek
  Grows into the great sun;

Noiselessly as the spring-time
  Her crown of verdure weaves,
And all the trees on all the hills
  Unfold their thousand leaves:
So without sound of music
  Or voice of them that wept,
Silently down from the mountain's crown
  The great procession swept.

Perchance the bald old eagle
On gray Beth-peor's height,
Out of his rocky eyrie
Looked on the wondrous sight;
Perchance the lion stalking
Still shuns that hallowed spot;
For beast and bird have seen and heard
That which man knoweth not.

" Perchance the bald old eagle
On gray Beth-peor's height,
Out of his rocky eyrie
Looked on the wondrous sight."

And give the bard an honored place,
With costly marbles drest,
In the great minster transept
Where lights like glories fall,
And the sweet choir sings, and the organ rings
Along the emblazoned hall.

This was the bravest warrior
That ever buckled sword;
This the most gifted poet
That ever breathed a word;
And never earth's philosopher
Traced with his golden pen
On the deathless page truths half so sage
As he wrote down for men.

But when the warrior dieth
His comrades of the war,
With arms reversed and muffled drums,
Follow the funeral car:
They show the banners taken;
They tell his battles won;
And after him lead his masterless steed,
While peals the minute-gun.

Amid the noblest of the land
Men lay the sage to rest,

And had he not high honor?—
The hillside for a pall!
To lie in state while angels wait,
With stars for tapers tall!
And the dark rock-pines, like tossing plumes,
Over his bier to wave,
And God's own hand, in that lonely land,
To lay him in his grave!—

In that strange grave without a name,
Whence his uncoffined clay
Shall break again—O wondrous thought!—
Before the judgment-day.
And stand, with glory wrapped around,
On the hills he never trod,
And speak of the strife that won our life
With the incarnate Son of God.

O lonely tomb in Moab's land!
O dark Beth-peor's hill!
Speak to these curious hearts of ours,
And teach them to be still;
God hath his mysteries of grace,
Ways that we cannot tell,
He hides them deep, like the secret sleep
Of him he loved so well.

CECIL FRANCES ALEXANDER.

MONEY MUSK.

OH, the buxom girls that helped the boys—
The nobler Helens of humbler Troys—
As they stripped the husks with rustling fold
From eight-rowed corn as yellow as gold.

By the candle-light in pumpkin bowls,
And the gleams that showed fantastic holes
In the quaint old lantern's tattooed tin,
From the hermit glim set up within;

By the rarer light in girlish eyes
As dark as wells, or as blue as skies,
I hear the laugh when the ear is red,
I see the blush with the forfeit paid.

The cedar cakes with the ancient twist,
The cider cup that the girls have kissed.
And I see the fiddler through the dusk
As he twangs the ghost of "Money Musk!"

The boys and girls in a double row
Wait face to face till the magic bow
Shall whip the tune from the violin,
And the merry pulse of the feet begin.

In shirt of check, and tallowed hair,
The fiddler sits in the bulrush chair
Like Moses' basket stranded there
      On the brink of Father Nile.
He feels the fiddle's slender neck,
Picks out the notes with thrum and check,
And times the tune with nod and beck,
      And thinks it a weary while.
All ready! Now he gives the call,
Cries, "Honor to the ladies!" All
The jolly tides of laughter fall
      And ebb in a happy smile.

D-o-w-n comes the bow on every string,
"First couple join right hands and swing!"
As light as any blue-bird's wing
      "Swing once and a half times round."

Whirls Mary Martin all in blue—
Calico gown and stockings new,
And tinted eyes that tell you true,
      Dance all to the dancing sound.

She flits about big Moses Brown,
Who holds her hands to keep her down
And thinks her hair a golden crown
      And his heart turns over once!
His cheek with Mary's breath is wet,
It gives a second somerset!
He means to win the maiden yet,
      Alas for the awkward dunce!

" Your stoga boot has crushed my toe!"
" I'd rather dance with one-legged Joe!"
" You clumsy fellow!" "Pass below!"
      And the first pair dance apart.
Then "Forward six!" advance, retreat,
Like midges gay in sunbeam street;
'Tis Money Musk by merry feet
      And the Money Musk by heart!

" Three-quarters round your partner swing!"
" Across the set!" The rafters ring,
The girls and boys have taken wing
      And have brought their roses out!
'Tis "Forward six!" with rustic grace,
Ah, rarer far than—"Swing to place!"—
Than golden clouds of old point lace
      They bring the dance about.

Then clasping hands all—"Right and left!"
All swiftly weave the measure deft
Across the woof in loving weft
      And the Money Musk is done!
Oh, dancers of the rustling husk,
Good-night, sweethearts, 'tis growing dusk,
Good-night, for aye to Money Musk,
      For the heavy march begun!

BENJAMIN F. TAYLOR.

THE OLD VILLAGE CHOIR.

HAVE fancied, sometimes, the Bethel-bent beam,
That trembled to earth in the patriarch's dream,
Was a ladder of song in that wilderness rest,
From the pillow of stone to the blue of the blest,
And the angels descending to dwell with us
      here,
"Old Hundred," and "Corinth," and "China,"
      and "Mear."

"Let us sing to God's praise," the minister said.
All the psalm-books at once fluttered open at "York;"
Sunned their long dotted wings in the words that he
      read,
While the leader leaped into the tune just ahead,
And politely picked up the key-note with a fork;
And the vicious old viol went growling along
At the heels of the girls, in the rear of the song.

"While the leader leaped into the tune just ahead,
And politely picked up the key-note with a fork."

All the hearts are not dead, not under the sod,
That those breaths can blow open to heaven and
      God!
Ah, "Silver Street" flows by a bright shining road,—
Oh, not to the hymns that in harmony flowed,—
But the sweet human psalms of the old-fashioned
      choir,
To the girl that sang alto—the girl that sang air!

Oh, I need not a wing—bid no genii come
With a wonderful web from Arabian loom,
To bear me again up the river of Time,
When the world was in rhythm, and life was its
      rhyme—
Where the streams of the years flowed so noiseless
      and narrow,
That across it there floated the song of the sparrow—

For a sprig of green caraway carries me there,
To the old village church. and the old village choir,
Where clear of the floor my feet slowly swung,
And timed the sweet pulse of the praise that they
    sung,
Till the glory aslant from the afternoon sun
Seemed the rafters of gold in God's temple begun!

You may smilè at the nasals of old Deacon Brown,
Who followed by scent, till he ran the tune down;

And dear Sister Green, with more goodness than
    grace,
Rose and fell on the tunes as she stood in her place,
And where " Coronation " exultingly flows,
Tried to reach the high notes on the tips of her toes!

To the land of the leal they have gone with their song,
Where the choir and the chorus together belong.
Oh be lifted, ye gates! Let me hear them again—
Blessed song, blessed singers! forever, Amen!

BENJAMIN F. TAYLOR.

THE OLD HOME.

SEE it now, the same unchanging spot,
The swinging gate, the little garden-plot,
The narrow yard, the rock that made its floor,
The flat pale house, the knocker-garnished door.

OLIVER WENDELL HOLMES.

THE POWER OF HABIT.

REMEMBER once riding from Buffalo to the Niagara Falls. I said to a gentleman, " What river is that, sir? " " That," he said, " is Niagara river." " Well, it is a beautiful stream," said I, " bright and fair and glassy; how far off are the rapids? " " Only a mile or two," was the reply. " Is it possible that only a mile from us we shall find the water in the turbuience which it must show near to the Falls? " " You will find it so, sir." And so I found it; and the first sight of Niagara I shall never forget. Now, launch your bark on that Niagara river; it is bright, smooth, beautiful and glassy. There is a ripple at the bow; the silver wake you leave behind adds to the enjoyment.

Down the stream you glide, oars, sails and helm in proper trim, and you set out on your pleasure excursion. Suddenly some one cries out from the bank, "Young men, ahoy!" "What is it?" "The rapids are below you." "Ha! ha! we have heard of the rapids, but we are not such fools as to get there. If we go too fast, then we shall up with the helm and steer for the shore; we will set the mast in the socket, hoist the sail and speed to the land. Then on, boys; don't be alarmed—there is no danger."

"Young men, ahoy there!" "What is it?" "The rapids are below you!" "Ha! ha! we will laugh and quaff; all things delight us. What care we for the future! No man ever saw it. Sufficient for the day is the evil thereof. We will enjoy life while we may; will catch pleasure as it flies. This is enjoyment; time enough to steer out of danger when we are sailing swiftly with the current."

"Young men, ahoy!" "What is it?" "Beware! Beware! The rapids are below you!" Now you see the water foaming all around. See how fast you pass that point! Up with the helm! Now turn! Pull hard! quick! quick! quick! pull for your lives! pull till the blood starts from the nostrils, and the veins stand like whip-cords upon your brows! Set the mast in the socket! hoist the sail!—ah! ah! it is too late! Shrieking, cursing, howling, blaspheming, over they go.

Thousands go over the rapids every year through the power of habit, crying all the while, "When I find out that it is injuring me I will give it up!"

JOHN B. GOUGH.

THE VILLAGE BLACKSMITH.

UNDER a spreading chestnut-tree
  The village smithy stands;
The smith, a mighty man is he,
  With large and sinewy hands;
And the muscles of his brawny arms
  Are strong as iron bands.

His hair is crisp and black and long;
  His face is like the tan;
His brow is wet with honest sweat, —
  He earns whate'er he can,
And looks the whole world in the face,
  For he owes not any man.

Week in, week out, from morn till night,
  You can hear his bellows blow;
You can hear him swing his heavy sledge,
  With measured beat and slow,
Like a sexton ringing the village bell
  When the evening sun is low.

And children coming home from school,
  Look in at the open door;
They love to see the flaming forge,
  And hear the bellows roar,
And catch the burning sparks that fly
  Like chaff from the threshing-floor.

He goes on Sunday to the church,
  And sits among his boys;
He hears the parson pray and preach;
  He hears his daughter's voice
Singing in the village choir,
  And it makes his heart rejoice.

It sounds to him like her mother's voice,
  Singing in Paradise!
He needs must think of her once more,
  How in the grave she lies;
And with his hard, rough hand he wipes
  A tear out of his eyes.

Toiling, rejoicing, sorrowing,
  Onward through life he goes;
Each morning sees some task begin,
  Each evening sees it close;
Something attempted, something done,
  Has earned a night's repose.

Thanks, thanks to thee, my worthy friend,
  For the lesson thou hast taught!
Thus at the flaming forge of life
  Our fortunes must be wrought;
Thus on its sounding anvil shaped
  Each burning deed and thought!

HENRY WADSWORTH LONGFELLOW.

THE DESTRUCTION OF SENNACHERIB.

THE Assyrian came down like the wolf on the fold,
  And his cohorts were gleaming in purple and gold;
And the sheen of their spears was like stars on the sea,
When the blue wave rolls nightly on deep Galilee.

Like the leaves of the forest when Summer is green,
That host with their banners at sunset were seen;
Like the leaves of the forest when Autumn hath flown,
That host on the morrow lay withered and strown.

For the Angel of Death spread his wings on the blast,
And breathed in the face of the foe as he passed;

And the eyes of the sleepers waxed deadly and chill,
And their hearts but once heaved, and forever grew still!

And there lay the steed with his nostril all wide,
But through it there rolled not the breath of his pride;
And the foam of his gasping lay white on the turf,
And cold as the spray of the rock-beating surf.

And there lay the rider distorted and pale,
With the dew on his brow and the rust on his mail;
And the tents were all silent, the banners alone,
The lances unlifted, the trumpet unblown.

And the widows of Ashur are loud in their wail,
And their idols are broke in the temple of Baal;
And the might of the Gentile, unsmote by the sword,
Hath melted like snow in the glance of the Lord!

LORD BYRON.

THE NEW-ENGLAND SCHOOL.

THE morning came, I reached the classic hall;
  A clock-face eyed me, staring from the wall;
  Beneath its hands a printed line I read;
  YOUTH IS LIFE'S SEED-TIME; so the clock-face said.
Some took its counsel, as the sequel showed,—
Sowed — their wild oats, and reaped as they had sowed,
How all comes back! the upward slanting floor—
The masters' thrones that flank the central door—
The long, outstretching alleys that divide
The rows of desks that stand on either side —

The staring boys, a face to every desk,
Bright, dull, pale, blooming, common, picturesque.
Grave is the master's look; his forehead wears
Thick rows of wrinkles, prints of worrying cares;
Uneasy lie the heads of all that rule,
His most of all whose kingdom is a school.
Supreme he sits; before the awful frown
That bends his brows the boldest eye goes down;
Not more submissive Israel heard and saw
At Sinai's foot the Giver of the Law.

OLIVER WENDELL HOLMES.

THE TEMPEST.

E were crowded in the cabin,
　　Not a soul would dare to sleep,—
It was midnight on the waters
　　And a storm was on the deep.

'T is a fearful thing in winter
　　To be shattered by the blast,
And to hear the rattling trumpet
　　Thunder, "Cut away the mast!"

So we shuddered there in silence,—
　　For the stoutest held his breath,
While the hungry sea was roaring,
　　And the breakers talked with Death.

As thus we sat in darkness,
　　Each one busy in his prayers,
"We are lost!" the captain shouted,
　　As he staggered down the stairs.

But his little daughter whispered,
　　As she took his icy hand,
"Is n't God upon the ocean
　　Just the same as on the land?"

Then we kissed the little maiden,
　　And we spoke in better cheer,
And we anchored safe in harbor,
　　When the morn was shining clear.

JAMES THOMAS FIELDS.

THE EVENING CLOUD.

CLOUD lay cradled near the setting sun;
A gleam of crimson tinged its braided snow;
Long had I watched the glory moving on,
O'er the still radiance of the lake below.
Tranquil its spirit seemed, and floated slow —
Even in its very motion there was rest;
While every breath of eve that chanced to blow
Wafted the traveler to the beauteous west:—

Emblem, methought, of the departed soul,
To whose white robe the gleam of bliss is given;
And, by the breath of Mercy, made to roll
Right onward to the golden gates of heaven;
Where, to the eye of faith, it peaceful lies,
And tells to man his glorious destinies.

JOHN WILSON. (Christopher North).

THE STREAM OF LIFE.

IFE bears us on like the current of a mighty river. Our boat at first glides
down the narrow channel, through the playful murmurings of the little brook
and the windings of its grassy borders. The trees shed their blossoms over
our young heads; the flowers on the brink seem to offer themselves to our young
hands; we are happy in hope, and we grasp eagerly at the beauties around
us; — but the stream hurries on, and still our hands are empty. Our course

in youth and manhood is along a wider and deeper flood, amid objects more striking and magnificent. We are animated by the moving pictures of enjoyment and industry passing before us; we are excited by some short-lived success, or depressed and made miserable by some equally short-lived disappointment. But our energy and our depression are both in vain. The stream bears us on, and our joys and griefs are alike left behind us.

We may be shipwrecked — we cannot be delayed; whether rough or smooth, the river hastens to its home, till the roar of the ocean is in our ears, and the tossing of the waves is beneath our feet, and the land lessens from our eyes, and the floods are lifted up around us, and we take our leave of earth and its inhabitants, until of our further voyage there is no witness save the Infinite and Eternal.

REGINALD HEBER.

LUCY GRAY.

FT I had heard of Lucy Gray;
And when I crossed the wild,
I chanced to see, at break of day,
The solitary child.

No mate, no comrade, Lucy knew;
She dwelt on a wide moor,—
The sweetest thing that ever grew
Beside a human door!

You yet may spy the fawn at play,
The hare upon the green;
But the sweet face of Lucy Gray
Will never more be seen.

"To-night will be a stormy night,—
You to the town must go;
And take a lantern, child, to light
Your mother through the snow."

"That, father! will I gladly do;
'T is scarcely afternoon,—
The minster-clock has just struck two,
And yonder is the moon!"

At this the father raised his hook,
And snapped a faggot-band;
He plied his work;—and Lucy took
The lantern in her hand.

Not blither is the mountain roe:
With many a wanton stroke
Her feet disperse the powdery snow,
That rises up like smoke.

The storm came on before its time:
She wandered up and down;
And many a hill did Lucy climb,
But never reached the town.

The wretched parents all that night
Went shouting far and wide;
But there was neither sound nor sight
To serve them for a guide.

At daybreak on the hill they stood
That overlooked the moor;
And thence they saw the bridge of wood,
A furlong from their door.

They wept, and, turning homeward, cried,
"In heaven we all shall meet;"—
When in the snow the mother spied
The print of Lucy's feet.

Then downwards from the steep hill's edge
They tracked the footmarks small;
And through the broken hawthorn hedge,
And by the long stone wall;

And then an open field they crossed;
The marks were still the same;
They tracked them on, nor ever lost;
And to the bridge they came.

They followed from the snowy bank
Those footmarks, one by one,
Into the middle of the plank;
And further there were none!

—Yet some maintain that to this day
She is a living child;
That you may see sweet Lucy Gray
Upon the lonesome wild.

O'er rough and smooth she trips along,
And never looks behind;
And sings a solitary song
That whistles in the wind.

WILLIAM WORDSWORTH.

THE SNOW-STORM.

'TIS a fearful night in the winter-time,
  As cold as it ever can be;
The roar of the blast is heard like the chime
  Of the waves on an angry sea;

"The fence was lost, and the wall of
  stone,
The windows blocked, and the well-
  curbs gone."

The moon is full, but her silver light
The storm dashes out with its wings to-night;
And over the sky, from south to north,
Not a star is seen, as the wind comes forth
  In the strength of a mighty glee.

All day had the snow come down—all day,
  As it never came down before,
And over the hills at sunset lay
  Some two or three feet or more:
The fence was lost, and the wall of stone;
The windows blocked, and the well-curbs gone;
The hay-stack had grown to a mountain-lift;
And the wood-pile looked like a monster drift,
  As it lay by the farmer's door.

The night sets in on a world of snow,
  While the air grows sharp and chill,
And the warning roar of a fearful blow
  Is heard on the distant hill:
And the Norther! See, on the mountain-peak,
In his breath how the old trees writhe and shriek!
He shouts on the plain, Ho-ho! ho-ho!
He drives from his nostrils the blinding snow,
  And growls with a savage will.
  18

Such a night as this to be found abroad
  In the drifts and the freezing air!
Sits a shivering dog in a field by the road,
  With the snow in his shaggy hair;
He shuts his eyes to the wind, and growls;
He lifts his head, and moans and howls;
Then, crouching low from the cutting sleet,
His nose is pressed on his quivering feet;
  Pray, what does the dog do there?

A farmer came from the village plain,
  But he lost the traveled way;
And for hours he trod with might and main
  A path for his horse and sleigh;
But colder still the cold winds blew,
And deeper still the deep drifts grew;
And his mare, a beautiful Morgan brown,
At last in her struggles floundered down,
  Where a log in a hollow lay.

In vain, with a neigh and a frenzied snort,
  She plunged in the drifting snow,
While her master urged, till his breath grew short,
  With a word and a gentle blow;
But the snow was deep, and the tugs were tight;
His hands were numb, and had lost their might;

"The man in his sleigh, and his faithful dog,
  And the beautiful Morgan brown."

So he wallowed back to his half-filled sleigh,
And strove to shelter himself till day,
  With his coat and the buffalo.

He has given the last faint jerk of the rein,
  To rouse up his dying steed;
And the poor dog howls to the blast in vain
  For help in his master's need;
For awhile he strives with a wistful cry,
To catch a glance from his drowsy eye,
And wags his tail if the rude winds flap
The skirt of the buffalo over his lap,
  And whines when he takes no heed.

The wind goes down and the storm is o'er,—
  'Tis the hour of midnight, past;
The old trees writhe and bend no more
  In the whirl of the rushing blast;
The silent moon, with her peaceful light,
Looks down on the hills with snow all white;

And the giant shadow of Camel's Hump,
Of the blasted pine and the ghostly stump,
  Afar on the plain are cast.

But, cold and dead, by the hidden log
  Are they who came from the town,—
The man in his sleigh, and his faithful dog,
  And his beautiful Morgan brown,—
In the wide snow desert, far and grand,
With his cap on his head, and the reins in his hand:
The dog with his nose on his master's feet,
And the mare half seen through the crusted sleet,
  Where she lay when she floundered down.

CHARLES GAMAGE EASTMAN..

CASABIANCA.

[Young Casabianca, a boy about thirteen years old, son of the Admiral of the Orient, remained at his post (in the Battle of the Nile) after the ship had taken fire and all the guns had been abandoned, and perished in the explosion of the vessel, when the flames had reached the powder.]

THE boy stood on the burning deck,
  Whence all but him had fled,
The flame that lit the battle's wreck
  Shone round him o'er the dead.

Yet beautiful and bright he stood,
  As born to rule the storm;
A creature of heroic blood,
  A proud though childlike form.

The flames rolled on; he would not go
  Without his father's word;
The father, faint in death below,
  His voice no longer heard.

He called aloud, " Say, father, say,
  If yet my task be done!"
He knew not that the chieftain lay
  Unconscious of his son.

"Speak, father!" once again he cried,
  "If I may yet be gone!"
And but the booming shots replied,
  And fast the flames rolled on.

Upon his brow he felt their breath,
  And in his waving hair,
And looked from that lone post of death
  In still yet brave despair;

And shouted but once more aloud,
  "My father! must I stay?"
While o'er him fast, through sail and shroud,
  The wreathing fires made way.

They wrapt the ship in splendor wild,
  They caught the flag on high,
And streamed above the gallant child,
  Like banners in the sky.

There came a burst of thunder sound;
  The boy,—Oh! where was he?
Ask of the winds, that far around
  With fragments strewed the sea,—

With shroud and mast and pennon fair,
  That well had borne their part,—
But the noblest thing that perished there
  Was that young, faithful heart.

FELICIA DOROTHEA HEMANS.

THE OLD CANOE.

WHERE the rocks are gray and the shore is steep,
  And the waters below look dark and deep,
  Where the rugged pine, in its lonely pride,
  Leans gloomily over the murky tide,
Where the reeds and rushes are long and rank,
And the weeds grow thick on the winding bank;
Where the shadow is heavy the whole day through,
Lies at its moorings the old canoe.

The useless paddles are idly dropped,
Like a sea-bird's wing that the storm has lopped,
And crossed on the railing, one o'er one.
Like the folded hands when the work is done;
While busily back and forth between
The spider stretches his silvery screen,
And the solemn owl. with his dull "too-hoo,"
Settles down on the side of the old canoe.

The stern, half sunk in the slimy wave,
Rots slowly away in its living grave.
And the green moss creeps o'er its dull decay,
Hiding the mouldering dust away,
Like the hand that plants o'er the tomb a flower,
Or the ivy that mantles the falling tower;
While many a blossom of loveliest hue
Springs up o'er the stern of the old canoe.

The currentless waters are dead and still—
But the light wind plays with the boat at will,
And lazily in and out again
It floats the length of its rusty chain,
Like the weary march of the hands of time,
That meet and part at the noontide chime,
And the shore is kissed at each turn anew
By the dripping bow of the old canoe.

Oh, many a time, with a careless hand,
I have pushed it away from the pebbly strand,

And paddled it down where the stream runs quick,
Where the whirls are wild and the eddies are thick,
And laughed as I leaned o'er the rocking side,
And looked below in the broken tide,
To see that the faces and boats were two
That were mirrored back from the old canoe.

But now, as I lean o'er the crumbling side,
And look below in the sluggish tide,
The face that I see there is graver grown,
And the laugh that I hear has a soberer tone,
And the hands that lent to the light skiff wings
Have grown familiar with sterner things.
But I love to think of the hours that flew
As I rocked where the whirls their white spray threw,
Ere the blossom waved, or the green grass grew,
O'er the mouldering stern of the old canoe.

EMILY R. PAGE.

A GREYPORT LEGEND.

THEY ran through the streets of the seaport town;
They peered from the decks of the ships that lay:
The cold sea-fog that came whitening down
Was never as cold or white as they.
"Ho, Starbuck and Pinckney and Tenterden!
Run for your shallops, gather your men,
Scatter your boats on the lower bay."

Good cause for fear! In the thick midday
The hulk that lay by the rotting pier,
Filled with the children in happy play,
Parted its moorings, and drifted clear,—
Drifted clear beyond reach or call,—
Thirteen children they were in all,—
All adrift in the lower bay!

Said a hard-faced skipper, "God help us all!
She will not float till the turning tide!"
Said his wife, "My darling will hear my call,
Whether in sea or heaven she bide."
　　And she lifted a quavering voice and high,
　　Wild and strange as a sea-bird's cry,
　　　Till they shuddered and wondered at her side.

The fog drove down on each laboring crew,
Veiled each from each and the sky and shore:
There was not a sound but the breath they drew,
And the lap of water and creak of oar;
　　And they felt the breath of the downs, fresh blown
　　O'er leagues of clover and cold gray stone,
　　　But not from the lips that had gone before.

They come no more. But they tell the tale,
That, when fogs are thick on the harbor reef,
The mackerel fishers shorten sail;
For the signal they know will bring relief:
　　For the voices of children, still at play
　　In a phantom hulk that drifts alway
　　　Through channels whose waters never fail.

It is but a foolish shipman's tale,
A theme for a poet's idle page;
But still, when the mists of doubt prevail,
And we lie becalmed by the shores of Age,
　　We hear from the misty troubled shore
　　The voice of the children gone before,
　　　Drawing the soul to its anchorage.

BRET HARTE.

THE GRAPE-VINE SWING.

LITHE and long as the serpent train,
　　Springing and clinging from tree to tree,
Now darting upward, now down again,
　　With a twist and a twirl that are strange to
　　　see;
Never took serpent a deadlier hold,
Never the cougar a wilder spring,
Strangling the oak with the boa's fold,
　　Spanning the beech with the condor's wing.

Yet no foe that we fear to seek,—
　　The boy leaps wild to thy rude embrace;
Thy bulging arms bear as soft a cheek
　　As ever on lover's breast found place;

On thy waving train is a playful hold
　　Thou shalt never to lighter grasp persuade;
While a maiden sits in thy drooping fold,
　　And swings and sings in the noonday shade!

O giant strange of our Southern woods!
　　I dream of thee still in the well-known spot,
Though our vessel strains o'er the ocean floods,
　　And the Northern forest beholds thee not;
I think of thee still with a sweet regret,
　　As the cordage yields to my playful grasp,—
Dost thou spring and cling in our woodlands yet?
　　Does the maiden still swing in thy giant clasp?

WILLIAM GILMORE SIMMS.

MOONLIGHT ON THE PRAIRIE.

BEAUTIFUL was the night. Behind the black
　　wall of the forest,
Tipping its summit with silver, arose the moon.
　　On the river
　　Fell here and there through the branches a
　　　tremulous gleam of the moonlight,
Like the sweet thoughts of love on a darkened and
　　devious spirit.
Nearer and round about her, the manifold flowers of
　　the garden
Poured out their souls in odors, that were their pray-
　　ers and confessions
Unto the night, as it went its way, like a silent Car-
　　thusian.
Fuller of fragrance than they, and as heavy with
　　shadows and night-dews,
Hung the heart of the maiden. The calm and the
　　magical moonlight
Seemed to inundate her soul with indefinable longings,

As, through the garden gate, and beneath the shade of
　　the oak-trees,
Passed she along the path to the edge of the measure-
　　less prairie.
Silent it lay, with a silvery haze upon it, and fire-flies
Gleaming and floating away in mingled and infinite
　　numbers.
Over her head the stars, the thoughts of God in the
　　heavens,
Shone on the eyes of man, who had ceased to marvel
　　and worship,
Save when a blazing comet was seen on the walls of
　　that temple,
As if a hand had appeared and written upon them,
　　"Upharsin."
And the soul of the maiden, between the stars and the
　　fire-flies,
Wandered alone, and she cried, "O Gabriel! O my
　　beloved!

Art thou so near unto me, and yet I cannot behold thee?

Art thou so near unto me, and yet thy voice does not reach me?

Ah! how often thy feet have trod this path to the prairie!

Ah! how often thine eyes have looked on the woodlands around me!

Ah! how often beneath this oak, returning from labor,

Thou hast lain down to rest, and to dream of me in thy slumbers.

When shall these eyes behold, these arms be folded about thee?"

Loud and sudden and near the note of a whippoorwill sounded

Like a flute in the woods; and anon, through the neighboring thickets,

Farther and farther away it floated and dropped into silence.

"Patience!" whispered the oaks from oracular caverns of darkness;

And, from the moonlit meadow, a sigh responded, "To-morrow!"

HENRY WADSWORTH LONGFELLOW.

"O blithely shines the bonny sun
Upon the Isle of May."

WE 'LL GO TO SEA NO MORE.

BLITHELY shines the bonny sun
Upon the Isle of May,
And blithely comes the morning tide
Into St. Andrew's Bay.
Then up, gudeman, the breeze is fair,
And up, my braw bairns three;
There's goud in yonder bonny boat

That sails sae weel the sea!
When haddocks leave the Firth o' Forth,
An' mussels leave the shore.
When oysters climb up Berwick Law,
We 'll go to sea no more,—
No more. .
We 'll go to sea no more.

I 've seen the waves as blue as air,
I 've seen them green as grass;
But I never feared their heaving yet,
   From Grangemouth to the Bass.
I 've seen the sea as black as pitch,
I 've seen it white as snow;
But I never feared its foaming yet,
   Though the winds blew high or low.
     When squalls capsize our wooden walls,
      When the French ride at the Nore,
     When Leith meets Aberdour half way,
      We 'll go to sea no more,—
        No more,
      We 'll go to sea no more.

I never liked the landsman's life,
   The earth is aye the same;
Gie me the ocean for my dower,
   My vessel for my hame.
Gie me the fields that no man plows,
   The farm that pays no fee;
Gie me the bonny fish that glance
   So gladly through the sea.

When sails hang flapping on the masts
   While through the waves we snore,
When in a calm we 're tempest-tossed,
    We 'll go to sea no more,—
      No more,
    We 'll go to sea no more.

The sun is up, and round Inchkeith
   The breezes softly blaw;
The gudeman has the lines on board,—
   Awa, my bairns, awa!
An' ye be back by gloamin' gray,
   An' bright the fire will low,
An' in your tales and sangs we 'll tell
   How weel the boat ye row.
     When life's last sun gaes feebly down,
      An' death comes to our door,
     When a' the world 's a dream to us,
      We 'll go to sea no more,—
        No more,
      We 'll go to sea no more.

               MISS CORBETT.

THE WRECKED SHIP.

AND now, lashed on by destiny severe,
  With horror fraught the dreadful scene drew
      near!
The ship hangs hovering on the verge of death,
Hell yawns, rocks rise, and breakers roar be-
      neath!
   *   *   *   *
In vain the cords and axes are prepared,
For now the audacious seas insult the yard;
High o'er the ship they throw a horrid shade,
And o'er her burst, in terrible cascade.
Uplifted on the surge to heaven she flies,
Her shattered top half buried in the skies,
Then headlong plunging thunders on the ground,
Earth groans! air trembles! and the deeps re-
      sound!

Her giant hulk the dread concussion feels,
And quivering with the wound, in torment reels.
So reels, convulsed with agonizing throes,
The bleeding bull beneath the murderer's blows.
Again she plunges! hark! a second shock
Tears her strong bottom on the marble rock!
Down on the vale of death, with dismal cries,
The fated victims shuddering roll their eyes
In wild despair, while yet another stroke,
With deep convulsion, rends the solid oak:
Till, like the mine, in whose infernal cell
The lurking demons of destruction dwell,
At length, asunder torn, her frame divides,
And crashing spreads in ruin o'er the tides.

              WILLIAM FALCONER.

THE PILOT.

JOHN MAYNARD was well known in the lake district as a God-fearing, honest and intelligent pilot. He was pilot on a steamboat from Detroit to Buffalo. One summer afternoon — at that time those steamers seldom carried boats — smoke was seen ascending from below, and the captain called out, "Simpson, go below and see what the matter is down there." Simpson came up with his face pale as ashes, and said, "Captain, the ship is on fire." Then "Fire! fire! fire!" resounded on shipboard.

All hands were called up. Buckets of water were dashed on the fire, but in vain. There were large quantities of resin and tar on board, and it was found useless to attempt to save the ship. The passengers rushed forward and inquired of the pilot,

"How far are we from Buffalo?" "Seven miles." "How long before we can reach there?" "Three-quarters of an hour at our present rate of steam." "Is there any danger?" "Danger, here — see the smoke bursting out — go forward, if you would save your lives!"

Passengers and crew — men, women and children — crowded the forward part of the ship. John Maynard stood at the helm. The flames burst forth in a sheet of fire; clouds of smoke arose. The captain cried out through his trumpet: "John Maynard!" "Aye, aye, sir!" "Are you at the helm?" "Aye, aye, sir!" "How does she head?" "Southeast by east, sir." "Head her southeast and run her on shore," said the captain.

Nearer, nearer, yet nearer, she approached the shore. Again the captain cried out: "John Maynard!" The response came feebly this time, "Aye, aye, sir!" "Can you hold on five minutes longer, John?" he said. "By God's help, I will."

The old man's hair was scorched from the scalp, one hand disabled, his knee upon the stanchion, and his teeth set; with his other hand upon the wheel, he stood firm as a rock. He beached the ship; every man, woman and child was saved, as John Maynard dropped, and his spirit took its flight to its God.

JOHN B. GOUGH.

THE BURNING OF CHICAGO.

FOUND a Rome of common clay," imperial Cæsar cried;
"I left a Rome of marble!" No other Rome beside!
The ages wrote their autographs along the sculptured stone —
The golden eagles flew abroad — Augustan splendors shone —
They made a Roman of the world! They trailed the classic robe,
And flung the Latin toga around the naked globe!

"I found Chicago wood and clay," a mightier Kaiser said,
Then flung upon the sleeping mart his royal robes of red,
And temple, dome, and colonnade, and monument and spire
Put on the crimson livery of dreadful Kaiser Fire!
The stately piles of polished stone were shattered into sand,
And madly drove the dread simoon, and snowed them on the land!
And rained them till the sea was red, and scorched the wings of prayer!
Like thistle-down ten thousand homes went drifting through the air,

And dumb Dismay walked hand in hand with frozen-eyed Despair!
CHICAGO vanished in a cloud — the towers were storms of sleet,
Lo! ruins of a thousand years along the spectral street!
The night burned out between the days! The ashen hoar-frost fell,
As if some demon set ajar the bolted gates of hell,
And let the molten billows break the adamantine bars,
And roll the smoke of torment up to smother out the stars!
The low, dull growl of powder-blasts just dotted off the din,
As if they tolled for perished clocks the time that might have been!
The thunder of the fiery surf roared human accents dumb;
The trumpet's clangor died away a wild bee's drowsy hum,
And breakers beat the empty world that rumbled like a drum.
O cities of the Silent Land! O Graceland and Rose-hill!
No tombs without their tenantry? The pale host sleeping still?

Your marble thresholds dawning red with holocaustal
    glare,
As if the Waking Angel's foot were set upon the stair!

But ah, the human multitudes that marched before
    the flame —
As 'mid the Red Sea's wavy walls the ancient people
    came!
Behind, the rattling chariots! the Pharaoh of Fire!
The rallying volley of the whips, the jarring of the
    tire!—

And Ruth and Rachel, pale and brave, in silence
    walked beside;
Those Bible girls of Judah's day did make that day
    sublime —
Leave life but them, no other loss can ever bankrupt
    Time!
Men stood and saw their all caught up in chariots of
    flame—
No mantle falling from the sky they ever thought to
    claim,

"Chicago vanished in a cloud."

Looked round, and saw the homeless world as dismal
    as a pyre!—
Looked up, and saw God's blessed Blue a firmament
    so dire!
As in the days of burning Troy, when Virgil's hero
    fled,
So gray and trembling pilgrims found some younger
    feet instead,
That bore them through the wilderness with bold
    elastic stride,

And empty-handed as the dead, they turned away and
    smiled.
And bore a stranger's household gods and saved a
    stranger's child!
What valor brightened into shape, like statues in a
    hall,
When on their dusky panoply the blazing torches fall,
Stood bravely out, and saw the world spread wings of
    fiery flight.
And not a trinket of a star to crown disastered night!

BENJAMIN F. TAYLOR.

A NORTHERN WINTER.

BEHOLD a scene, magnificent and new;
  Nor land nor water meet the excursive view;
  The round horizon girds one frozen plain,
  The mighty tombstone of the buried main,
Where, dark and silent, and unfelt to flow,
A dead sea sleeps with all its tribes below.

Nor shines he here in solitude unknown;
North, south, and west, by dogs or reindeer drawn,
Careering sledges cross the unbroken lawn,
And bring from bays and forelands round the coast,
Youth, beauty, valor, Greenland's proudest boast,
Who thus, in winter's long and social reign,

"North, south, and west, by dogs or reindeer drawn,
Careering sledges cross the unbroken lawn."

But heaven is still itself; the deep blue sky
Comes down with smiles to meet the glancing eye,
Though, if a keener sight its bound would trace,
The arch recedes through everlasting space.
The sun, in morning glory, mounts his throne,

Hold feasts and tournaments upon the main,
When, built of solid floods, his bridge extends
A highway o'er the gulf to meeting friends,
Whom rocks impassable, or winds and tide,
Fickle and false, in summer months divide.

The scene runs round with motion, rings with mirth,
No happier spot upon the peopled earth;
The drifted snow to dust the travelers beat,
The uneven ice is flint beneath their feet.
Here tents, a gay encampment, rise around,
Where music, song, and revelry resound;
There the blue smoke upwreathes a hundred spires,
Where humbler groups have lit their pine-wood fires.

Ere long they quit the tables; knights and dames
Lead the blithe multitude to boisterous games.
Bears, wolves, and lynxes yonder head the chase;
Here start the harnessed reindeer in the race,
Borne without wheels, a flight of rival cars
Track the ice-firmament, like shooting stars,
Right to the goal, — converging as they run,
They dwindle through the distance into one.

JAMES MONTGOMERY.

THE CHILDREN IN THE WOOD.

NOW ponder well, you parents deare,
   These wordes which I shall write;
A doleful story you shall heare,
   In time brought forth to light.
A gentleman of good account,
   In Norfolke dwelt of late,
Who did in honor far surmount
   Most men of his estate.

Sore sicke he was, and like to dye,
   No helpe his life could save;
His wife by him as sicke did lye,
   And both possest one grave.
No love between these two was lost,
   Each was to other kinde;
In love they lived, in love they dyed,
   And left two babes behinde:

The one a fine and pretty boy,
   Not passing three yeares olde;
The other a girl more young than he,
   And framed in beautye's molde.
The father left his little son,
   As plainlye doth appeare,
When he to perfect age should come,
   Three hundred poundes a yeare.

And to his little daughter Jane
   Five hundred poundes in gold,
To be paid downe on marriage-day,
   Which might not be controlled:
But if the children chance to dye,
   Ere they to age should come,
Their uncle should possesse their wealth;
   For so the wille did run.

"Now, brother," said the dying man,
   "Look to my children deare;
Be good unto my boy and girl,
   No friendes else have they here:
To God and you I recommend
   My children deare this daye;
But little while be sure we have
   Within this world to staye.

"You must be father and mother both,
   And uncle all in one;
God knowes what will become of them,
   When I am dead and gone."
With that bespake their mother deare,
   "O brother kinde," quoth shee,
"You are the man must bring our babes
   To wealth or miserie:

"And if you keep them carefully,
   Then God will you reward;
But if you otherwise should deal,
   God will your deedes regard."
With lippes as cold as any stone,
   They kist their children small:
"God bless you both, my children deare; "
   With that the teares did fall.

These speeches then their brother spake
   To this sicke couple there;
"The keeping of your little ones,
   Sweet sister, do not feare.
God never prosper me nor mine,
   Nor aught else that I have,
If I do wrong your children deare,
   When you are layd in grave."

The parents being dead and gone,
   The children home he takes,
And bringes them straite unto his house,
   Where much of them he makes.
He had not kept these pretty babes
   A twelvemonth and a daye,
But, for their wealth, he did devise
   To make them both awaye.

He bargained with two ruffians strong,
   Which were of furious mood,
That they should take these children young,
   And slaye them in a wood.
He told his wife an artful tale:
   He would the children send
To be brought up in faire London,
   With one that was his friend.

Away then went those pretty babes
　Rejoycing at that tide,
Rejoycing with a merry minde,
　They should on cock-horse ride.
They prate and prattle pleasantly,
　As they rode on the waye,
To those that should their butchers be,
　And work their lives' decaye:

So that the pretty speeche they had,
　Made Murder's heart relent:
And they that undertooke the deed,
　Full sore did now repent.
Yet one of them more hard of heart,
　Did vowe to do his charge,
Because the wretch that hired him
　Had paid him very large.

The other won't agree thereto,
　So here they fall to strife;
With one another they did fight,
　About the children's life:
And he that was of mildest mood
　Did slaye the other there,
Within an unfrequented wood,
　The babes did quake for feare!

He took the children by the hand,
　Teares standing in their eye,
And bad them straitwaye follow him,
　And look they did not crye:
And two long miles he ledd them on,
　While they for food complaine:
"Staye here," quoth he, "I'll bring you bread,
　When I come back againe."

These pretty babes, with hand in hand,
　Went wandering up and downe;
But never more could see the man
　Approaching from the towne:
Their prettye lippes with blackberries
　Were all besmeared and dyed,
And when they sawe the darksome night,
　They sat them downe and cryed.

Thus wandered these poor innocents
　Till deathe did end their grief,
In one another's armes they died.
　As wanting due relief:
No burial this pretty pair
　Of any man receives,
Till Robin-redbreast piously
　Did cover them with leaves.

And now the heavy wrathe of God
　Upon their uncle fell;
Yea, fearful fiends did haunt his house,
　His conscience felt an hell;
His barnes were fired, his goodes consumed,
　His landes were barren made,
His cattle dyed within the field,
　And nothing with him stayd.

And in the voyage of Portugal
　Two of his sonnes did dye;
And to conclude, himselfe was brought
　To want and miserye:
He pawned and mortgaged all his land
　Ere seven years came about,
And now at length this wicked act
　Did by this means come out:

The fellowe that did take in hand
　These children for to kill,
Was for a robbery judged to dye,
　Such was God's blessed will:
Who did confess the very truth,
　As here hath been displayed:
Their uncle having dyed in gaol,
　Where he for debt was layd.

You that executors be made,
　And overseers eke
Of children that be fatherless,
　And infants mild and meek;
Take you example by this thing,
　And yield to each his right,
Lest God with such like miserye
　Your wicked minds requite.

THE MASSACRE OF FORT DEARBORN.

[Chicago, 1812.]

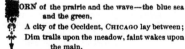

ORN of the prairie and the wave—the blue sea
　and the green,
A city of the Occident, CHICAGO lay between;
Dim trails upon the meadow, faint wakes upon
　the main,
On either sea a schooner and a canvas-covered
　wain.

I saw a dot upon the map, and a house-fly's filmy
　wing—
They said 't was Dearborn's picket-flag when Wilder-
　ness was king;
I heard the reed-bird's morning song—the Indian's
　awkward flail—
The rice tattoo in his rude canoe like a dash of April
　hail—

The beaded grasses' rustling bend —the swash of the lazy tide,
Where ships shake out the salted sails and navies grandly ride!
I heard the Block-house gates unbar, the. column's solemn tread,
I saw the Tree of a single leaf its splendid foliage shed
To wave awhile that August morn above the column's head;
I heard the moan of muffled drum, the woman's wail of fife,

The Dead March played for Dearborn's men just marching out of life.
The swooping of the savage cloud that burst upon the rank
And struck it with its thunderbolt in forehead and in flank,
The spatter of the musket-shot, the rifles' whistling rain—
The sand-hills drift round hope forlorn that never marched again!

BENJAMIN F. TAYLOR.

" Aloft as o'er a buoyant arch they go,
Whose keystone breaks, as deep they plunge below."

THE SHIPWRECKED SAILORS.

THE floods are raging, and the gales blow high,
Low as a dungeon-roof impends the sky;
Prisoners of hope, between the clouds and waves,
Six fearless sailors man yon boat that braves
Peril redoubling upon peril past:
—From childhood nurslings of the wayward blast.
Aloft as o'er a buoyant arch they go,
Whose keystone breaks, —as deep they plunge below;
Unyielding, though the strength of man be vain;
Struggling, though borne like surf along the main;
In front, a battlement of rocks; in rear,
Billow on billow bounding; near, more near,
They verge to ruin;—life and death depend
On the next impulse,—shrieks and prayers ascend.

JAMES MONTGOMERY.

MUSIC IN CAMP.

TWO armies covered hill and plain,
　　Where Rappahannock's waters
Ran deeply crimsoned with the stain
　　Of battle's recent slaughters.

The summer clouds lay pitched like tents
　　In meads of heavenly azure;
And each dread gun of the elements
　　Slept in its high embrasure.

The breeze so softly blew, it made
　　No forest leaf to quiver;
And the smoke of the random cannonade
　　Rolled slowly from the river.

And now where circling hills looked down
　　With cannon grimly planted,
O'er listless camp and silent town
　　The golden sunset slanted.

When on the fervid air there came
　　A strain, now rich, now tender;
The music seemed itself aflame
　　With day's departing splendor.

A Federal band, which eve and morn
　　Played measures brave and nimble,
Had just struck up with flute and horn
　　And lively clash of cymbal.

Down flocked the soldiers to the banks;
　　Till, margined by its pebbles,
One wooded shore was blue with "Yanks,"
　　And one was grey with "Rebels."

Then all was still; and then the band,
　　With movement light and tricksy,
Made stream and forest, hill and strand,
　　Reverberate with "Dixie."

The conscious stream, with burnished glow,
　　Went proudly o'er its pebbles,
But thrilled throughout its deepest flow
　　With yelling of the Rebels.

Again a pause; and then again
　　The trumpet pealed sonorous,

And "Yankee Doodle" was the strain
　　To which the shore gave chorus.

The laughing ripple shoreward flew
　　To kiss the shining pebbles;
Loud shrieked the swarming Boys in Blue
　　Defiance to the Rebels.

And yet once more the bugle sang
　　Above the stormy riot;
No shout upon the evening rang—
　　There reigned a holy quiet.

The sad, slow stream, its noiseless flood
　　Poured o'er the glistening pebbles;
All silent now the Yankees stood,
　　All silent stood the Rebels.

No unresponsive soul had heard
　　That plaintive note's appealing,
So deeply "Home, Sweet Home" had stirred
　　The hidden founts of feeling.

Or Blue, or Grey, the soldier sees,
　　As by the wand of fairy,
The cottage 'neath the live oak trees,
　　The cabin by the prairie.

The cold or warm, his native skies
　　Bend in their beauty o'er him;
Seen through the tear-mist in his eyes,
　　His loved ones stand before him.

As fades the iris after rain,
　　In April's tearful weather,
The vision vanished as the strain
　　And daylight died together.

But Memory, waked by Music's art,
　　Expressed in simple numbers,
Subdued the sternest Yankee's heart,
　　Made light the Rebel's slumbers.

And fair the form of Music shines—
　　That bright celestial creature—
Who still 'mid War's embattled lines
　　Gives this one touch of Nature.

　　　　　　　　　　JOHN R. THOMPSON.

THE DEATH OF NAPOLEON.

WILD was the night, yet a wilder night
　　Hung round the soldier's pillow;
In his bosom there waged a fiercer fight
　　Than the fight on the wrathful billow.

A few fond mourners were kneeling by,
　　The few that his stern heart cherished;
They knew, by his glazed and unearthly eye,
　　That life had nearly perished.

They knew by his awful and kingly look,
　　By the order hastily spoken,
That he dreamed of days when the nations shook,
　　And the nations' hosts were broken.

He dreamed that the Frenchman's sword still slew,
　　And triumphed the Frenchman's eagle,
And the struggling Austrian fled anew,
　　Like the hare before the beagle.

The bearded Russian he scourged again,
　The Prussian's camp was routed,
And again on the hills of haughty Spain
　His mighty armies shouted.

Over Egypt's sands, over Alpine snows,
　At the pyramids, at the mountain,
Where the wave of the lordly Danube flows,
　And by the Italian fountain.

On the snowy cliffs where mountain streams
　Dash by the Switzer's dwelling,

He led again, in his dying dreams,
　His hosts, the broad earth quelling.

Again Marengo's field was won,
　And Jena's bloody battle;
Again the world was overrun,
　Made pale at his cannon's rattle.

He died at the close of that darksome day,
　A day that shall live in story;
In the rocky land they placed his clay,
　"And left him alone with his glory."

　　　　　　　　　ISAAC MCCLELLAN.

THE GRAVE OF BONAPARTE.

IN a lone barren isle, where the wild roaring bil-
　　lows
　Assail the stern rock, and the loud tempests
　　rave,
The hero lies still, while the dew-drooping willows,
Like fond weeping mourners lean over the grave.
The lightnings may flash, and the loud thunders
　　rattle:
He heeds not, he hears not, he 's free from all
　　pain; —
He sleeps his last sleep—he has fought his last bat-
　　tle!
No sound can awake him to glory again!

O shade of the mighty, where now are the legions
　That rushed but to conquer when thou led'st them
　　on?
Alas! they have perished in far hilly regions,
　And all save the fame of their triumph is gone!

The trumpet may sound, and the loud cannon rattle!
　They heed not, they hear not, they're free from all
　　pain:
They sleep their last sleep, they have fought their
　　last battle!
No sound can awake them to glory again!

Yet, spirit immortal, the tomb cannot bind thee,
　For, like thine own eagle that soared to the sun,
Thou springest from bondage and leavest behind
　　thee
A name which before thee no mortal had won.
Though nations may combat, and war's thunders
　　rattle,
　No more on the steed wilt thou sweep o'er the
　　plain;
Thou sleep'st thy last sleep, thou hast fought thy last
　　battle!
No sound can awake thee to glory again!

THE OVERLAND TRAIN.

THE Plains! The shouting drivers at the wheel;
　The crash of leather whips; the crush and roll
　Of wheels; the groan of yokes and grinding
　　steel
And iron chain, and lo! at last the whole
Vast line, that reached as if to touch the goal,
Began to stretch and stream away and wind
Toward the west, as if with one control:
Then hope loomed fair, and home lay far behind;
Before, the boundless plain, and fiercest of their kind.

Some hills at last began to lift and break;
Some streams began to fail of wood and tide.
The sombre plain began betime to take
A hue of weary brown, and wild and wide
It stretched its naked breast on every side.

A babe was heard at last to cry for bread
Amid the deserts; cattle lowed and died
And dying men went by with broken tread,
And left a long black serpent line of wreck and
　　dead.

They rose by night; they struggled on and on
-As thin and still as ghosts; then here and there
Beside the dusty way before the dawn
Men silent laid them down in their despair,
And died. But woman! Woman, frail as fair!
May man have strength to give to you your due;
You faltered not, nor murmured anywhere,
You held your babes, held to your course, and you
Bore on through burning hell your double burthens
　　through.

The dust arose, a long dim line like smoke
From out a riven earth. The wheels went by,
The thousand feet in harness and in yoke,
They tore the ways of ashen alkali,
And desert winds blew sudden, swift and dry.
The dust! It sat upon and filled the train!
It seemed to fret and fill the very sky.
Lo! dust upon the beasts, the tent, the plain,.
And dust, alas! on breasts that rose not up again.

My brave and unremembered heroes, rest;
You fell in silence, silent lie and sleep.
Sleep on unsung, for this, I say, were best;
The world to-day has hardly time to weep;
The world to-day will hardly care to keep
In heart her plain and unpretending brave;
The desert winds, they whistle by and sweep
About you; browned and russet grasses wave
Along a thousand leagues that lie one common grave.

JOAQUIN MILLER.

"The mother—the lads, with their nest, at her knee."

ROBBING THE NEST.

T last we stood at our mother's knee;
    Do you think, sir, if you try,
    You can paint the look of a lie?
    If you can, pray have the grace
    To put it solely in the face
Of the urchin that is likest me:

I think 'twas solely mine, indeed:
    But that's no matter—paint it so;
    The eyes of our mother—take good heed—
    Looking not on the nestful of eggs.
But straight through our faces, down to our lies,
And oh, with such injured, reproachful surprise!

I felt my heart bleed where that glance went, as though
    A sharp blade struck through it.

                          You, sir, know,
That you on the canvas are to repeat
Things that are fairest, things most sweet,—
Woods and cornfields, and mulberry tree,—
The mother,—the lads, with their nest, at her knee;
    But, oh, that look of reproachful woe!
High as the heavens your name I'll shout,
If you paint me the picture and leave that out.

ALICE CARY.

THE FAMINE.

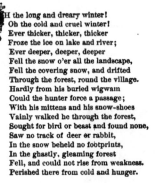

H the long and dreary winter!
Oh the cold and cruel winter!
Ever thicker, thicker, thicker
Froze the ice on lake and river;
Ever deeper, deeper, deeper
Fell the snow o'er all the landscape,
Fell the covering snow, and drifted
Through the forest, round the village.
Hardly from his buried wigwam
Could the hunter force a passage;
With his mittens and his snow-shoes
Vainly walked he through the forest,
Sought for bird or beast and found none,
Saw no track of deer or rabbit,
In the snow beheld no footprints,
In the ghastly, gleaming forest
Fell, and could not rise from weakness,
Perished there from cold and hunger.

Oh the famine and the fever!
Oh the wasting of the famine!
Oh the blasting of the fever!
Oh the wailing of the children!
Oh the anguish of the women!
All the earth was sick and famished;
Hungry was the air around them,
Hungry was the sky above them,
And the hungry stars in heaven
Like the eyes of wolves glared at them!

Into Hiawatha's wigwam
Came two other guests, as silent
As the ghosts were, and as gloomy;
Waited not to be invited,
Did not parley at the doorway,
Sat there without word of welcome
In the seat of Laughing Water;
Looked with haggard eyes and hollow
At the face of Laughing Water.
And the foremost said: "Behold me!
I am Famine, Buckadawin!"
And the other said "Behold me!
I am Fever, Ahkosewin!"
And the lovely Minnehaha
Shuddered as they looked upon her,
Shuddered at the words they uttered,
Lay down on her bed in silence,
Hid her face, but made no answer;
Lay there trembling, freezing, burning
At the looks they cast upon her,
At the fearful words they uttered.

Forth into the empty forest
Rushed the maddened Hiawatha;
In his heart was deadly sorrow,

In his face a stony firmness,
On his brow the sweat of anguish
Started, but it froze and fell not.
Wrapped in furs and armed for hunting
With his mighty bow of ash-tree,
With his quiver full of arrows,
With his mittens, Minjekahwun,
Into the vast and vacant forest
On his snow-shoes strode he forward.

"Gitche Manito, the mighty!"
Cried he with his face uplifted
In that bitter hour of anguish,
"Give your children food, O Father!
Give us food, or we must perish!
Give me food for Minnehaha,
For my dying Minnehaha!"
Through the far-resounding forest,
Through the forest vast and vacant
Rang that cry of desolation,
But there came no other answer
Than the echo of his crying,
Than the echo of the woodlands,
"MINNEHAHA! MINNEHAHA!"

All day long roved Hiawatha
In that melancholy forest,
Through the shadow of whose thickets,
In the pleasant days of summer,
Of that ne'er forgotten summer,
He had brought his young wife homeward
From the land of the Dacotahs;
When the birds sang in the thickets,
And the streamlets laughed and glistened,
And the air was full of fragrance,
And the loving Laughing Water
Said with voice that did not tremble,
"I will follow you, my husband!"

In the wigwam with Nokomis,
With those gloomy guests that watched her,
With the Famine and the Fever,
She was lying, the beloved,
She the dying Minnehaha.
"Hark!" she said, "I hear a rushing,
Hear a roaring and a rushing,
Hear the Falls of Minnehaha
Calling to me from a distance!"
"No, my child!" said old Nokomis,
"'Tis the night-wind in the pine-trees!"
"Look!" she said, "I see my father
Standing lonely at his doorway,
Beckoning to me from his wigwam
In the land of the Dacotahs!"
"No, my child!" said old Nokomis,
"'Tis the smoke that waves and beckons!"

"Ah!" she said, "the eyes of Pauguk
Glare upon me in the darkness,
I can feel his icy fingers
Clasping mine amid the darkness!
Hiawatha! Hiawatha!"

And the desolate Hiawatha,
Far away amid the forest,
Miles away among the mountains,
Heard that sudden cry of anguish,
Heard the voice of Minnehaha
Calling to him in the darkness,
"HIAWATHA! HIAWATHA!"

Over snow-fields waste and pathless,
Under snow-encumbered branches,
Homeward hurried Hiawatha,
Empty-handed, heavy-hearted,
Heard Nokomis moaning, wailing;
"Wahonowin! Wahonowin!
Would that I had perished for you,
Would that I were dead as you are!
Wahonowin! Wahonowin!"
And he rushed into the wigwam,
Saw the old Nokomis slowly
Rocking to and fro and moaning,
Saw his lovely Minnehaha
Lying dead and cold before him,
And his bursting heart within him
Uttered such a cry of anguish,
That the forest moaned and shuddered,
That the very stars in heaven
Shook and trembled with his anguish.

Then he sat down still and speechless,
On the bed of Minnehaha,
At the feet of Laughing Water,
At those willing feet, that never
More would lightly run to meet him,
Never more would lightly follow.

With both hands his face he covered,
Seven long days and nights he sat there,
As if in a swoon he sat there,
Speechless, motionless, unconscious
Of the daylight or the darkness.

Then they buried Minnehaha;
In the snow a grave they made her,
In the forest deep and darksome,
Underneath the moaning hemlocks;
Clothed her in her richest garments,
Wrapped her in her robes of ermine,
Covered her with snow, like ermine;
Thus they buried Minnehaha.
And at night a fire was lighted,
On her grave four times was kindled,
For her soul upon its journey
To the Islands of the Blessed.
From his doorway Hiawatha
Saw it burning in the forest,
Lighting up the gloomy hemlocks;
From his sleepless bed uprising,
From the bed of Minnehaha,
Stood and watched it at the doorway,
That it might not be extinguished,
Might not leave her in the darkness.

"Farewell!" said he, "Minnehaha;
Farewell, O my Laughing Water!
All my heart is buried with you,
All my thoughts go onward with you!
Come not back again to labor,
Come not back again to suffer,
Where the Famine and the Fever
Wear the heart and waste the body,
Soon my task will be completed,
Soon your footsteps I shall follow
To the Islands of the Blessed,
To the Kingdom of Ponemah,
To the Land of the Hereafter!"

HENRY WADSWORTH LONGFELLOW.

THE BRIDE.

HE maid, and thereby hangs a tale,
    For such a maid no Whitsun-ale
        Could ever yet produce:
No grape that's kindly ripe could be
So round, so plump, so soft as she,
    Nor half so full of juice.

Her finger was so small, the ring
Would not stay on which they did bring,—
    It was too wide a peck;
And, to say truth,—for out it must,—
It looked like the great collar—just—
    About our young colt's neck.

10

Her feet beneath her petticoat,
Like little mice, stole in and out,
    As if they feared the light;
But O, she dances such a way!
No sun upon an Easter-day
    Is half so fine a sight.

*   *   *   *

Her cheeks so rare a white was on,
No daisy makes comparison;
    Who sees them is undone;
For streaks of red were mingled there,
Such as are on a Katherine pear,
    The side that's next the sun.

Her lips were red; and one was thin,
Compared to that was next her chin.
　　Some bee had stung it newly;
But, Dick, her eyes so guard her face
I durst no more upon them gaze,
　　Than on the sun in July.

Her mouth so small, when she does speak,
Thou 'dst swear her teeth her words did break,
　　That they might passage get;
But she so handled still the matter,
They came as good as ours, or better,
　　And are not spent a whit.

＊　　　＊　　　＊　　　＊　　　＊

SIR JOHN SUCKLING.

THE OLD MILL.

LONELY by Miami's stream,
　Gray in twilight's fading beam,
　　Spectral, desolate and still;
　Smitten by the storm of years,
Ah! how changed to me appears
　　Yonder old deserted mill.

"Glides the river past the mill,
But the wheels are stark and still."

While my pensive eyes behold
Mossy roof and gable old,
　　Shadowy through obscuring trees,
Memory's vision, quick and true,
Time's long vista looking through,
　　Bygone scenes more plainly sees.

Sees upon the garner floor
Wheat and corn in ample store,—
　　Powdery whiteness everywhere;
Sees a miller, short and stout,
Whistling cheerfully about,
　　Making merry with his care.

Pleased, he listens to the whirr
Of the swift-revolving burr,
　　Deeming brief each busy hour;
Like a stream of finest snow,
Sifting to the bin below,
　　Fall the tiny flakes of flour.

Once, with childhood's vague intent,
Down some furtive way I went,
　　Through a broken floor to peer;
Saw the fearful water drift
In a current, dark and swift,
　　Flying from the angry weir.

Once, with timid steps and soft,
Stealthily I climbed aloft;.
　　Up and up the highest stair;
Iron cogs were rumbling round,—
Every vague and awful sound,
　　Mocked and mumbled at me there.

Wonder if those wheels remain,
And would frighten me again?
　　Wonder if the miller's dead?
Wonder if his ghost at night
Haunts the stairs, a phantom white?
　　Walks the loft with hollow tread?

Glides the river past the mill,
But the wheels are stark and still,
　　Worn and wasting, day by day;
So the stream of years will run
When my busy life is done,
　　So my task-house shall decay.

W. H. VENABLE.

THE beauty of the country surpasses all the grandeur of the city. In the city there
are gardens cultivated with floral skill; but they are not half so lovely even as the
fields, whose swelling grain waves, and nods, and trembles to the whisking wind.

THE FLOOD OF YEARS.

MIGHTY hand from an exhaustless urn
Pours forth the never-ending Flood of Years
Among the Nations. How the rushing waves
Bear all before them! On their foremost edge,
And there alone, is Life; the Present there
Tosses and foams and fills the air with roar
Of mingled noises. There are they who toil,
And they who strive, and they who feast, and they
Who hurry to and fro. The sturdy hind—
Woodman and delver with the spade—are there.
And busy artisan beside his bench,
And pallid student with his written roll.
A moment on the mounting billow seen—
The flood sweeps over them and they are gone.
There groups of revelers, whose brows are twined
With roses, ride the topmost swell awhile,
And as they raise their flowing cups to touch
The clinking brim to brim, are whirled beneath
The waves and disappear. I hear the jar
Of beaten drums, and thunders that break forth
From cannon, where the advancing billow sends
Up to the sight long files of armed men,
That hurry to the charge through flame and smoke.
The torrent bears them under, whelmed and hid,
Slayer and slain, in heaps of bloody foam.
Down go the steed and rider; the plumed chief
Sinks with his followers; the head that wears
The imperial diadem goes down beside
The felon's with cropped ear and branded cheek.
A funeral train the torrent sweeps away,
Bearers and bier and mourners. By the bed
Of one who dies men gather sorrowing,
And women weep aloud; the floods roll on;
The wail is stifled, and the sobbing group
Borne under. Hark to that shrill, sudden shout—
The cry of an applauding multitude
Swayed by some loud-tongued orator who wields
The living mass as if he were its soul!
The waters choke the shout and all is still.
Lo, next, a kneeling crowd, and one who spreads
The hands in prayer! the engulfing wave o'ertakes
And swallows them and him. A sculptor wields
The chisel, and the stricken marble grows
To beauty; at his easel, eager-eyed,
A painter stands, and sunshine at his touch
Gathers upon the canvas, and life glows;
A poet, as he paces to and fro,
Murmurs his sounding lines. Awhile they ride
The advancing billow, till its tossing crest
Strikes them and flings them under while their tasks
Are yet unfinished. See a mother smile
On her young babe that smiles to her again—
The torrent wrests it from her arms; she shrieks,
And weeps, and midst her tears is carried down.

A beam like that of moonlight turns the spray
To glistening pearls; two lovers, hand in hand,
Rise on the billowy swell and fondly look
Into each other's eyes. The rushing flood
Flings them apart; the youth goes down; the maid
With hands outstretched in vain, and streaming eyes,
Waits for the next high wave to follow him.
An agéd man succeeds; his bending form
Sinks slowly; mingling with the sullen stream
Gleam the white locks and then are seen no more.

Lo, wider grows the stream; a sea-like flood
Saps earth's walled cities; massive palaces
Crumble before it; fortresses and towers
Dissolve in the swift waters; populous realms
Swept by the torrent, see their ancient tribes
Engulfed and lost, their very languages
Stifled and never to be uttered more.

I pause and turn my eyes, and, looking back,
Where that tumultuous flood has passed, I see
The silent Ocean of the Past, a waste
Of waters weltering over graves, its shores
Strewn with the wreck of fleets, where mast and hull
Drop away piecemeal; battlemented walls
Frown idly, green with moss, and temples stand
Unroofed, forsaken by the worshipers.
There lie memorial stones, whence time has gnawed
The graven legends, thrones of kings o'erturned,
The broken altars of forgotten gods,
Foundations of old cities and long streets
Where never fall of human feet is heard
Upon the desolate pavement. I behold
Dim glimmerings of lost jewels far within
The sleeping waters, diamonds, sardonyx,
Ruby and topaz, pearl and chrysolite,
Once glittering at the banquet on fair brows
That long ago were dust; and all around,
Strewn on the waters of that silent sea,
Are withering bridal wreaths, and glossy locks
Shorn from fair brows by loving hands, and scrolls
O'erwritten—haply with fond words of love
And vows of friendship—and fair pages flung
Fresh from the printer's engine. There they lie
A moment and then sink away from sight.

I look and the quick tears are in my eyes,
For I behold, in every one of these,
A blighted hope, a separate history
Of human sorrow, telling of dear ties
Suddenly broken, dreams of happiness
Dissolved in air, and happy days, too brief,
That sorrowfully ended; and I think
How painfully the poor heart must have beat
In bosoms without number, as the blow
Was struck that slew their hope or broke their peace.

Sadly I turn, and look before, where yet
The flood must pass, and I behold a mist
Where swarm dissolving forms, the brood of Hope,
Divinely fair, that rest on banks of flowers
Or wander among rainbows, fading soon
And reappearing, haply giving place
To shapes of grisly aspect, such as Fear
Molds from the idle air; where serpents lift
The head to strike, and skeletons stretch forth
The bony arm in menace. Further on
A belt of darkness seems to bar the way,
Long, low, and distant, where the Life that Is
Touches the Life to Come. The Flood of Years
Rolls toward it, near and nearer. It must pass
That dismal barrier. What is there beyond?
Hear what the wise and good have said.
                                        Beyond
That belt of darkness still the years roll on
More gently, but with not less mighty sweep.
They gather up again and softly bear
All the sweet lives that late were overwhelmed
And lost to sight — all that in them was good,
Noble and truly great and worthy of love—

The lives of infants and ingenuous youths,
Sages and saintly women who have made
Their households happy — all are raised and borne
By that great current in its onward sweep,
Wandering and rippling with caressing waves
Around green islands, fragrant with the breath
Of flowers that never wither. So they pass,
From stage to stage, along the shining course
Of that fair river broadening like a sea.
As its smooth eddies curl along their way,
They bring old friends together; hands are clasped
In joy unspeakable; the mother's arms
Again are folded round the child she loved
And lost. Old sorrows are forgotten now,
Or but remembered to make sweet the hour
That overpays them; wounded hearts that bled
Or broke are healed forever. In the room
Of this grief-shadowed Present there shall be
A Present in whose reign no grief shall gnaw
The heart, and never shall a tender tie
Be broken — in whose reign the eternal Change
That waits on growth and action shall proceed
With everlasting Concord hand in hand.

                            WILLIAM CULLEN BRYANT.

THE OLD WATER-WHEEL.

IT lies beside the river, where its marge
Is black with many an old and oarless barge.
And yesty filth and leafage wild and rank
Stagnate and beaten by the crumbling bank.

Once, slow revolving by the industrious mill,
It murmured, — only on the sabbath still;
And evening winds its pulse-like beating bore
Down the soft vale and by the winding shore.

Sparkling around its orbéd motion, flew,
With quick fresh fall, the drops of dashing dew;
Through noontide heat that gentle rain was flung,
And verdant, round, the summer herbage sprung.

Now, dancing light and sounding motion cease,
In these dark hours of cold continual peace;

Through its black bars the unbroken moonlight flows,
And dry winds howl about its long repose!

And mouldering lichens creep, and mosses gray
Cling round its arms, in gradual decay,
Amidst the hum of men, — which doth not suit
That shadowy circle, motionless and mute!

So, by the sleep of many a human heart
The crowd of men may bear their busy part.
Where withered, or forgotten, or subdued,
Its noisy passions have left solitude : —

Ah! little can they trace the hidden truth.
What waves have moved it in the vale of youth!
And little can its broken chords avow
How once they sounded. All is silent, now!

                                    JOHN RUSKIN.

THE DEAD.

I THINK about the dead by day,
   I dream of them at night:
They seem to stand beside my chair,
Clad in the clothes they used to wear,
   And by my bed in white.

The common-places of their lives,
   The lightest words they said,
Revive in me, and give me pain,

And make me wish them back again,
   Or wish that I were dead.

I would be kinder to them now,
   Were they alive once more:
Would kiss their cheeks and kiss their hair,
And love them like the angels there,
   Upon the silent shore.

                        RICHARD HENRY STODDARD.

THE WRECK OF THE SHIP.

UT list! a low and moaning sound
At distance heard, like a spirit's song,
And now it reigns above, around,
As if it called the ship along.
The moon is sunk; and a clouded gray
Declares that her course is run,
And like a god who brings the day,
Up mounts the glorious sun.

But gently now the small waves glide
Like playful lambs o'er a mountain's side.
So stately her bearing, so proud her array,
The main she will traverse forever and aye.
Many ports will exult at the gleam of her mast; —
Hush! hush! thou vain dreamer! this hour is her
    last.

"And like a god who brings the day
Up mounts the glorious sun."

Soon as his light has warmed the seas,
From the parting cloud fresh blows the breeze;
And that is the spirit whose well-known song
Makes the vessel to sail in joy along.
No fears hath she; her giant form
O'er wrathful surge, through blackening storm,
Majestically calm would go
Mid the deep darkness white as snow!

Five hundred souls in one instant of dread
Are hurried o'er the deck;
And fast the miserable ship
Becomes a lifeless wreck.
Her keel hath struck on a hidden rock,
Her planks are torn asunder,
And down come her masts with a reeling shock,
And a hideous crash like thunder.

Her sails are draggled in the brine,
That gladdened late the skies,
And her pennant, that kissed the fair moonshine,
Down many a fathom lies.

"And her pennant, that kissed the fair moonshine,
Down many a fathom lies."

Her beauteous sides, whose rainbow hues
Gleamed softly from below,
And flung a warm and sunny flush
O'er the wreaths of murmuring snow,
To the coral rocks are hurrying down,
To sleep amid colors as bright as their own.

O, many a dream was in the ship
An hour before her death;
And sights of home with sighs disturbed
The sleeper's long-drawn breath.
Instead of the murmur of the sea,
The sailor heard the humming tree
Alive through all its leaves,
The hum of the spreading sycamore
That grows before his cottage-door,
And the swallow's song in the eaves.
His arms enclosed a blooming boy,
Who listened with tears of sorrow and joy
To the dangers his father had passed;
And his wife, — by turns she wept and smiled,
As she looked on the father of her child,
Returned to her heart at last.
He wakes at the vessel's sudden roll,
And the rush of waters is in his soul.
Astounded, the reeling deck he paces,
Mid hurrying forms and ghastly faces;
The whole ship's crew are there!
Wailings around and overhead,
Brave spirits stupefied or dead,
And madness and despair.

JOHN WILSON (Christopher North).

THE GLOVE AND THE LIONS.

KING FRANCIS was a hearty king, and loved a
    royal sport,
And one day as his lions fought, sat looking on
    the court;
The nobles filled the benches, with the ladies in
    their pride,
And 'mongst them sat the Count de Lorge, with
    one for whom he sighed:
And truly 't was a gallant thing to see that crowning
    show,
Valor and love, and a king above, and the royal
    beasts below.

Ramped and roared the lions, with horrid laughing
    jaws;
They bit, they glared, gave blows like beams, a wind
    went with their paws;
With wallowing might and stifled roar they rolled on
    one another;
Till all the pit with sand and mane was in a thunder-
    ous smother;
The bloody foam above the bars came whisking
    through the air;
Said Francis, then, "Faith, gentlemen, we're better
    here than there."

De Lorge's love o'erheard the king, a beauteous, lively
    dame,
With smiling lips and sharp bright eyes, which alway
    seemed the same;
She thought, "The count, my lover, is brave as brave
    can be;
He surely would do wondrous things to show his love
    of me;
King, ladies, lovers, all look on; the occasion is
    divine;
I'll drop my glove, to prove his love; great glory will
    be mine."

She dropped her glove to prove his love, then looked
    at him and smiled;
He bowed, and in a moment leaped among the lions
    wild:
The leap was quick, return was quick, he has regained
    his place,
Then threw the glove, but not with love, right in the
    lady's face.

"By Heaven!" said Francis, "rightly done!" and he
    rose from where he sat:
"No love," quoth he, "but vanity, sets love a task like
    that."

LEIGH HUNT.

THE HERON.

HERE a bright creek into a river's side
Shoots its keen arrow, a green heron sits
Watching the sunfish as it gleaming flits
    From sheen to shade. He sees the turtle
      glide
Through the clear spaces of the rhythmic stream
Like some weird fancy through a poet's dream;
    He turns his golden eyes from side to side,

In very gladness that he is not dead,
While the swift wind-stream ripples overhead
    And the creek's wavelets babble underneath.
O bird! that in a cheerful gloom dost live,
    Thou art, to me a type of happy death;
For when thou flyest away no mate will grieve
    Because a lone, strange spirit vanisheth!

                  JAMES MAURICE THOMPSON.

THE BRIDES OF ENDERBY; OR, THE HIGH TIDE. (1571.)

HE old mayor climbed the belfry tower,
   The ringers rang by two, by three;
"Pull, if ye never pulled before;
   Good ringers, pull your best," quoth he.
"Play uppe, play uppe, O, Boston bells!
   Play all your changes, all your swells,
   Play uppe 'The Brides of Enderby.' "

Men say it was a stolen tyde—
   The Lord that sent it, He knows all;
But in myne ears doth still abide
   The message that the bells let fall:
And there was naught of strange beside
The flight of mews and peewits pied
   By millions crouched on the old sea-wall.

I sat and spun within my doore,
   My thread brake off, I raised myne eyes;
The level sun, like ruddy ore,
   Lay sinking in the barren skies,
And dark against day's golden death
She moved where Lindis wandereth,
   My sonne's faire wife, Elizabeth.

"Cusha! Cusha! Cusha!" calling
   Ere the early dews were falling,
Farre away, I heard her song.
   "Cusha! Cusha!" all along;
Where the reedy Lindis floweth,
   Floweth, floweth,
From the fields where melick groweth
Faintly came her milking song—

"Cusha! Cusha! Cusha!" calling,
   "For the dews will soone be falling;
Leave your meadow grasses mellow,
   Mellow, mellow;
Quit your cowslips yellow;
Come uppe Whitefoot, come uppe Lightfoot,
Quit the stalks of parsley hollow,
   Hollow, hollow;
Come uppe Jetty, rise and follow,
From the clovers lift your head;
Come uppe Whitefoot, come uppe Lightfoot,
Come up Jetty, rise and follow,
   Jetty, to the milking shed."

If it be long, ay, long ago,
   When I begin to think how long,
Againe I hear the Lindis flow,
   Swift as an arrowe, sharp and strong;
And all the aire, it seemeth mee,
Bin full of floating bells (sayth shee),
   That ring the tune of Enderby.

Alle fresh the level pasture lay,
   And not a shadowe mote be seene,
Save where full fyve good miles away
   The steeple towered from out the greene;
And lo! the great bell farre and wide
Was heard in all the country side
   That Saturday at eventide.

The swanherds where there sedges are
   Moved on in sunset's golden breath,
The shepherde lads I heard afarre,
   And my sonne's wife, Elizabeth;
Till floating o'er the grassy sea
Came downe that kindly message free,
   The "Brides of Mavis Enderby."

Then some looked uppe into the sky,
   And all along where Lindis flows
To where the goodly vessels lie,
   And where the lordly steeple shows,
They sayde, "And why should this thing be?
What danger lowers by land or sea?
   They ring the tune of Enderby!

"For evil news from Mablethorpe,
   Of pyrate galleys warping down;
For shippes ashore beyond the scorpe,
   They have not spared to wake the towne;
But while the west bin red to see,
And storms be none, and pyrates flee,
   Why ring 'The brides of Enderby?' "

I looked without, and lo! my sonne
   Came riding down with might and main:
He raised a shout as he drew on,
   Till all the welkin rang again,
"Elizabeth! Elizabeth!"
(A sweeter woman ne'er drew breath
   Than my sonne's wife Elizabeth.)

"The old sea wall (he cried) is downe,
   The rising tide comes on apace,
And boats adrift in yonder towne
   Go sailing uppe the market-place."
He shook as one that looks on death:
"God save you mother!" strait he saith,
   "Where is my wife, Elizabeth?"

"Good sonne, where Lindis winds away,
   With her two bairns, I marked her long;
And ere yon bells beganne to play
   Afar I heard her milking song.
He looked across the grassy lea,
To right, to left, "Ho Enderby!"
   They rang "The Brides of Enderby!"

With that he cried and beat his breast;
For, lo! along the river's bed
A mighty eygre reared his crest,
And uppe the Lindis raging sped.
It swept with thunderous noises loud;
Shaped like a curling snow-white cloud,
Or like a demon in a shroud.

And rearing Lindis backward pressed,
Shook all her trembling bankes amaine,
Then madly at the eygre's breast
Flung uppe her weltering walls again.
Then bankes came downe with ruin and rout—
Then beaten foam flew round about—
Then all the mighty floods were out.

So farre, so fast the eygre drave,
The heart had hardly time to beat,
Before a shallow seething wave
Sobbed in the grasses at oure feet,
The feet had hardly time to flee
Before it brake against the knee,
And all the world was in the sea.

Upon the roofe we sat that night,
The noise of bells went sweeping by;
I marked the lofty beacon light
Stream from the church tower, red and high—
A lurid mark and dread to see;
And awesome bells they were to mee,
That in the dark rang " Enderby."

They rang the sailor lads to guide
From roofe to roofe who fearless rowed;
And I — my sonne was at my side,
And yet the ruddy beacon glowed;
And yet he moaned beneath his breath
"O come in life, or come in death!
O lost! my love, Elizabeth."

And didst thou visit him no more?
Thou did'st, thou did'st, my daughter deare;
The waters laid thee at his doore,
Ere yet the early dawn was clear,

Thy pretty bairns in fast embrace,
The lifted sun shone on thy face,
Downe drifted to thy dwelling place.

That flow strewed wrecks about the grass,
That ebbe swept out the flocks to sea;
A fatal ebbe and flow, alas!
To manye more than myne and me:
But each will mourn his own (she saith),
And sweeter woman ne'er drew breath
Than my sonne's wife, Elizabeth.

I shall never hear her more
By the reedy Lindis shore,
"Cusha! Cusha! Cusha!" calling
Ere the early dews be falling;
I shall never hear her song,
"Cusha! Cusha!" all along
Where the sunny Lindis floweth,
Goeth, floweth,
From the meads where melick groweth,
When the water winding down,
Onward floweth to the town.

I shall never see her more
Where the reeds and rushes quiver,
Shiver, quiver;
Stand beside the sobbing river,
Sobbing, throbbing, in its falling
To the sandy lonesome shore;
I shall never hear her calling,
" Leave your meadow grasses mellow,
Mellow, mellow;
Quit your cowslips, cowslips yellow;
Come uppe Whitefoot, come uppe, Lightfoot;
Quit your pipes of parsley hollow,
Hollow, hollow;
Come uppe Lightfoot, rise and follow;
Lightfoot, Whitefoot.
From your clovers lift the head;
Come uppe Jetty, follow, follow,
Jetty, to the milking-shed."

JEAN INGELOW.

CROQUET.

ATE carved in granite, with griffins at rest,
Arches built grandly to welcome the guest,
Elm-guarded avenue, dim as sea-caves,
Sweep of quaint bridges and rush of clear waves,
Group of acacias, dark cluster of pines,
Mansion half-whelmed in a torrent of vines.
Fountain a shower of fire, lake a soft gloom,
Garden unrolling broad ribbons of bloom,
Lawn smooth as satin and air cool as spray,—
Roland and Christabel deep in croquet!

Christabel—Roland, the flower of our clan,
Noble and bountiful—match them who can.
He fleet and supple, yet strong as young Saul;
She in ten thousand the fairest of all;
He quick to anger, but loving and leal;
She true and tender, though tempered like steel;
Both of all weathers, fine dew and fierce hail,
Ice on the mountain and flowers in the vale:
All their still frostiness melted away,
Just for that nonsense—a game of croquet!

Only croquet? Never trust to the game,
Kindling such raillery, feeding such flame;
Keeping such bird-bolts of laughter in flight,
Tossing such roses of battle in sight!
Roland in triumph and ready to scoff,
Christabel poising her mallet far-off,
Ball speeding on with the wind in its wake,
Smiting its rival and hitting the stake!
Who is the victor! Proud Roland, at bay,
Captures the hand that has won at croquet.

Now is their magic enchainment complete;
Haughty, shy Christabel—far-away sweet.
Caught in that wind from the Aidenn of souls,
Blushes rose-bright as red snow of the poles!
Out of all lovers match these if you can;—
Spotless, great-hearted, the flower of our clan.
If they should quarrel—half-right and half-wrong—
Oaks root them deeper when breezes are strong.
Now may Love lead them away and away,
Through the wide Heavens, from that game of
    croquet!

AMANDA T. JONES.

LORD ULLIN'S DAUGHTER.

CHIEFTAIN, to the Highlands bound,
  Cries, "Boatman, do not tarry!
And I 'll give thee a silver pound,
  To row us o'er the ferry."

" Now who be ye, would cross Lochgyle,
  This dark and stormy water?"
"O I 'm the chief of Ulva's isle,
  And this Lord Ullin's daughter.

"And fast before her father's men
  Three days we 've fled together,
For should he find us in the glen,
  My blood would stain the heather.

"His horsemen hard behind us ride;
  Should they our steps discover,
Then who will cheer my bonny bride
  When they have slain her lover?"

Out spoke the hardy Highland wight,
  "I 'll go, my chief—I'm ready:
It is not for your silver bright,
  But for your winsome lady:

"And by my word! the bonny bird
  In danger shall not tarry;
So, though the waves are raging white,
  I 'll row you o'er the ferry."

By this the storm grew loud apace,
  The water-wraith was shrieking:
And in the scowl of heaven each face
  Grew dark as they were speaking.

But still as wilder blew the wind,
  And as the night grew drearer,
Adown the glen rode armèd men,
  Their trampling sounded nearer.

"O haste thee, haste!" the lady cries,
  "Though tempests round us gather;
I 'll meet the raging of the skies,
  But not an angry father."

The boat has left a stormy land,
  A stormy sea before her,—
When, O! too strong for human hand,
  The tempest gathered o'er her.

And still they rowed amidst the roar
  Of waters fast prevailing:
Lord Ullin reached that fatal shore,
  His wrath was changed to wailing.

For sore dismayed, through storm and shade,
  His child he did discover:
One lovely hand she stretched for aid,
  And one was round her lover.

"Come back! come back!" he cried in grief,
  "Across this stormy water:
And I 'll forgive your Highland chief,
  My daughter!—O my daughter!"

'T was vain; the loud waves lashed the shore,
  Return or aid preventing:
The waters wild went o'er his child,—
  And he was left lamenting.

THOMAS CAMPBELL.

GOODY BLAKE AND HARRY GILL.

H! what's the matter?—what's the matter?
  What is't that ails young Harry Gill,
That evermore his teeth they chatter—
  Chatter, chatter, chatter still?
Of waistcoats Harry has no lack,
  Good duffel gray and flannel fine;
He has a blanket on his back,
  And coats enough to smother nine.

In March, December, and in July,
  'Tis all the same with Harry Gill;
The neighbors tell, and tell you truly,
  His teeth they chatter, chatter still.
At night, at morning, and at noon,
  'Tis all the same with Harry Gill;
Beneath the sun, beneath the moon,
  His teeth they chatter, chatter still!

Young Harry was a lusty drover—
  And who so stout of limb as he?
His cheeks were red as ruddy clover;
  His voice was like the voice of three.
Old Goody Blake was old and poor;
  Ill-fed she was, and thinly clad;
And any man who passed her door
  Might see how poor a hut she had.

All day she spun in her poor dwelling,
  And then her three hours' work at night—
Alas! 'twas hardly worth the telling—
  It would not pay for candle-light.
Remote from sheltering village green,
  On a hill's northern side she dwelt,
Where from sea-blasts the hawthorns lean,
  And hoary dews are slow to melt.

By the same fire to boil their pottage,
  Two poor old dames, as I have known,
Will often live in one small cottage;
  But she—poor woman—housed alone.
'Twas well enough when summer came,
  The long, warm, lightsome summer-day;
Then at her door the canty dame
  Would sit, as any linnet gay.

But when the ice our streams did fetter,
  Oh, then how her old bones would shake!
You would have said, if you had met her,
  'Twas a hard time for Goody Blake.
Her evenings then were dull and dead;
  Sad case it was, as you may think,
For very cold to go to bed,
  And then for cold not sleep a wink!

Oh, joy for her! whene'er in winter
  The winds at night had made a rout,
And scattered many a lusty splinter
  And many a rotten bough about.
Yet never had she, well or sick,
  As every man who knew her says,

A pile beforehand, turf or stick,
  Enough to warm her for three days.

Now, when the frost was past enduring,
  And made her poor old bones to ache,
Could anything be more alluring
  Than an old hedge to Goody Blake?
And now and then, it must be said,
  When her old bones were cold and chill,
She left her fire, or left her bed,
  To seek the hedge of Harry Gill.

Now, Harry he had long suspected
  This trespass of old Goody Blake,
And vowed that she should be detected,
  And he on her would vengeance take.
And oft from his warm fire he'd go,
  And to the fields his road would take;
And there at night, in frost and snow,
  He watched to seize old Goody Blake.

And once, behind a rick of burley,
  Thus looking out did Harry stand;
The moon was full and shining clearly,
  And crisp with frost the stubble-land.
He hears a noise!—he's all awake!—
  Again!—on tiptoe down the hill
He softly creeps. 'Tis Goody Blake!
  She's at the hedge of Harry Gill!

Right glad was he when he beheld her!
  Stick after stick did Goody pull;
He stood behind a bush of elder,
  Till she had filled her apron full.
When with her load she turned about,
  The byway back again to take,
He started forward with a shout,
  And sprang upon poor Goody Blake;

And fiercely by the arm he took her,
  And by the arm he held her fast;
And fiercely by the arm he shook her,
  And cried, " I've caught you, then, at last!"
Then Goody, who had nothing said,
  Her bundle from her lap let fall;
And, kneeling on the sticks, she prayed
  To God, who is the Judge of all.

She prayed, her withered hand uprearing,
  While Harry held her by the arm—
" God, who art never out of hearing,
  Oh, may he never more be warm!"
The cold, cold moon above her head,
  Thus on her knees did Goody pray.
Young Harry heard what she had said,
  And, icy cold, he turned away.

He went complaining all the morrow
  That he was cold and very chill:
His face was gloom, his heart was sorrow—
  Alas! that day for Harry Gill!

That day he wore a riding-coat,
  But not a whit the warmer he;
Another was on Thursday brought,
  And ere the Sabbath he had three.

'Twas all in vain — a useless matter—
  And blankets were about him pinned;
Yet still his jaws and teeth they clatter,
  Like a loose casement in the wind.
And Harry's flesh it fell away;
  And all who see him say, "'Tis plain

That, live as long as live he may,
  He never will be warm again."

No word to any man he utters,
  Abed or up, to young or old;
But ever to himself he mutters,
  "Poor Harry Gill is very cold!"
Abed or up, by night or day,
  His teeth they chatter, chatter still.
Now, think, ye farmers all, I pray,
  Of Goody Blake and Harry Gill!

WILLIAM WORDSWORTH.

"From the fireside with many a shrug he hies,
Glad if the full-orb'd moon salute his eyes."

MOONLIGHT.

IN part these nightly terrors to dispel,
  Giles, ere he sleeps, his little flock must tell.
  From the fireside with many a shrug he hies,
  Glad if the full-orb'd moon salute his eyes,
And through the unbroken stillness of the night
Shed on his path her beams of cheering light.
With sauntering steps he climbs the distant stile,
Whilst all around him wears a placid smile;
There views the white-robed clouds in clusters driven,
And all the glorious pageantry of Heaven;
Low, on the utmost boundary of the sight,
The rising vapors catch the silver light;

Thence Fancy measures, as they parting fly,
Which first will throw its shadow on the eye,
Passing the source of light; and thence away,
Succeeded quick by brighter still than they.
Far yet above these wafted clouds are seen
(In a remoter sky, still more serene)
Others, detached in ranges through the air,
Spotless as snow, and countless as they're fair;
Scattered immensely wide from east to west,
The beauteous semblance of a flock at rest.
These to the raptured eye, aloud proclaim
Their mighty Shepherd's everlasting Name.

ROBERT BLOOMFIELD.

THE RIVER WYE.

FIVE years have passed; five summers with the
    length
    Of five long winters! and again I hear
    These waters rolling from their mountain-
       springs
With a sweet inland murmur. Once again
Do I behold these steep and lofty cliffs,
That on a wild secluded scene impress
Thoughts of more deep seclusion; and connect
The landscape with the quiet of the sky.
The day is come when I again repose
Here, under this dark sycamore, and view
These plots of cottage-ground, these orchard-tufts,

Which at this season, with their unripe fruits,
Are clad in one green hue, and lose themselves
Among the woods and copses, nor disturb
The wild green landscape. Once again I see
These hedge-rows, hardly hedge-rows, little lines
Of sportive wood run wild; these pastoral farms,
Green to the very door; and wreaths of smoke
Sent up in silence, from among the trees
With some uncertain notice, as might seem
Of vagrant dwellers in the houseless woods,
Or of some hermit's cave, where by his fire
The hermit sits alone.

                 WILLIAM WORDSWORTH.

LOCHINVAR'S RIDE.

O YOUNG Lochinvar has come out of the West!
    Through all the wild border his steed was the
      best;
    And save his good broadsword he weapons had
      none!
He rode all unarmed and he rode all alone.
So faithful in love, and so dauntless in war,
There never was knight like the young Lochinvar.

He staid not for brake, and he stopped not for stone;
He swam the Eske river where ford there was none;
But, ere he alighted at Netherby gate,
The bride had consented,—the gallant came late;
For a laggard in love, and a dastard in war,
Was to wed the fair Ellen of brave Lochinvar.

So boldly he entered the Netherby hall,
Among bridesmen, and kinsmen, and brothers, and
    all.

Then spoke the bride's father, his hand on his sword,—
For the poor craven bridegroom said never a word,—
"O come ye in peace here, or come ye in war,
Or to dance at our bridal, young Lord Lochinvar?"

"I long wooed your daughter;—my suit you denied:
Love swells like the Solway, but ebbs like its tide;
And now I am come, with this lost love of mine
To lead but one measure,—drink one cup of wine.
There be maidens in Scotland, more lovely by far,
That would gladly be bride to the young Lochinvar."

The bride kissed the goblet; the knight took it up:
He quaffed off the wine, and he threw down the cup;
She looked down to blush, and she looked up to sigh,
With a smile on her lip, and a tear in her eye;
He took her soft hand ere her mother could bar,—
"Now tread we a measure!" said young Lochinvar.

So stately his form and so lovely her face,
That never a hall such a galliard did grace;
While her mother did fret, and her father did fume,
And the bridegroom stood dangling his bonnet and
plume,
And the bridemaidens whispered, "'twere better by
far,
To have matched our fair cousin with young Loch-
invar."

One touch to her hand, and one word in her ear,
When they reached the hall door, where the charger
stood near;
So light to the croup the fair lady he swung,
So light to the saddle before her he sprung;—

"She is won! we are gone, over bank, bush, and
scaur;
They 'll have fleet steeds that follow!" quoth young
Lochinvar.

There was mounting 'mong Græmes of the Netherby
clan;
Fosters, Fenwicks, and Musgraves, they rode and they
ran;
There was racing and chasing on Cannobie lea,
But the lost bride of Netherby ne'er did they see.
So daring in love, and so dauntless in war;
Have ye e'er heard of gallant like young Lochinvar?

SIR WALTER SCOTT.

THE CLOSING YEAR.

TIS midnight's holy hour—and silence now
Is brooding, like a gentle spirit, o'er
The still and pulseless world. Hark! on the
winds
The bell's deep notes are swelling. 'Tis the
knell
Of the departed year.

No funeral train
Is sweeping past; yet on the stream and wood,
With melancholy light, the moonbeams rest,
Like a pale, spotless shroud; the air is stirred,
As by a mourner's sigh; and on yon cloud,
That floats so still and placidly through heaven,
The spirits of the seasons seem to stand,
Young spring, bright summer, autumn's solemn form,
And winter with his aged locks — and breathe
In mournful cadences, that course abroad
Like the far wind-harp's wild and touching wail,
A melancholy dirge o'er the dead year,
Gone from the earth forever.

'Tis a time
For memory and for tears. Within the deep
Still chambers of the heart, a spectre dim,
Whose tones are like the wizard voice of Time,
Heard from the tomb of ages, points its cold
And solemn finger to the beautiful
And holy visions that have passed away
And left no shadow of their loveliness
On the dead waste of Life. That spectre lifts
The coffin-lid of hope, and joy, and love,
And, bending mournfully above the pale
Sweet forms that slumber there, scatters dead flowers
O'er what has passed to nothingness.

The year
Has gone, and, with it, many a glorious throng
Of happy dreams. Its mark is on each brow,

Its shadow in each heart. In its swift course,
It waved its sceptre o'er the beautiful,
And they are not. It laid its pallid hand
Upon the strong man, and the haughty form
Is fallen, and the flashing eye is dim.
It trod the hall of revelry, where thronged
The bright and joyous, and the tearful wail
Of stricken ones is heard, where erst the song
And reckless shout resounded. It passed o'er
The battle-plain, where sword, and spear, and shield
Flashed in the light of mid-day — and the strength
Of serried hosts is shivered, and the grass,
Green from the soil of carnage, waves above
The crushed and mouldering skeleton. It came
And faded like a wreath of mist at eve;
Yet, ere it melted in the viewless air,
It heralded its millions to their home
In the dim land of dreams.

Remorseless Time:—
Fierce spirit of the glass and scythe! — what power
Can stay him in his silent course, or melt
His iron heart to pity? On, still on
He presses, and forever. The proud bird,
The condor of the Andes, that can soar
Through heaven's unfathomable depths, or brave
The fury of the northern hurricane
And bathe his plumage in the thunder's home,
Furls his broad wings at nightfall, and sinks down
To rest upon his mountain-crag — but Time
Knows not the weight of sleep or weariness,
And night's deep darkness has no chain to bind
His rushing pinion. Revolutions sweep
O'er earth, like troubled visions o'er the breast
Of dreaming sorrow; cities rise and sink,
Like bubbles on the water; fiery isles
Spring, blazing, from the ocean, and go back
To their mysterious caverns; mountains rear
To heaven their bald and blackened cliffs, and bow

Their tall heads to the plain; new empires rise,
Gathering the strength of hoary centuries,
And rush down like the Alpine avalauche,
Startling the nations; and the very stars,
Yon bright and burning blazonry of God,
Glitter awhile in their eternal depths,
And, like the Pleiad, loveliest of their train,

Shoot from their glorious spheres, and pass away,
To darkle in the trackless void : yet Time,
Time the tomb-builder, holds his fierce career,
Dark, stern, all-pitiless, and pauses not
Amid the mighty wrecks that strew his path,
To sit and muse, like other conquerors,
Upon the fearful ruin he has wrought.

GEORGE D. PRENTICE.

THE CLOSING SCENE.

WITHIN the sober realms of leafless trees,
The russet year inhaled the dreamy air;
Like some tanned reaper, in his hour of ease,
When all the fields are lying brown and bare.

The gray barns looking from their hazy hills,
O'er the dun waters widening in the vales,
Sent down the air a greeting to the mills
On the dull thunder of alternate flails.

All sights were mellowed and all sounds subdued;
The hills seemed farther and the stream sang low,
As in a dream the distant woodman hewed
His winter log with many a muffled blow.

The embattled forests, erewhile armed with gold,
Their banners bright with every martial hue,
Now stood like some sad, beaten host of old,
Withdrawn afar in Time's remotest blue.

On slumb'rous wings the vulture held its flight;
The dove scarce heard its sighing mate's complaint;
And, like a star slow drowning in the light,
The village church-vane seemed to pale and faint.

The sentinel-cock upon the hillside crew,—
Crew thrice,— and all was stiller than before;
Silent, till some replying warden blew
His alien horn, and then was heard no more.

Where erst the jay, within the elm's tall crest,
Made garrulous trouble round her unfledged young;
And where the oriole hung her swaying nest,
By every light wind like a censer swung;—

Where sang the noisy martens of the eaves,
The busy swallows circling ever near,—
Foreboding, as the rustic mind believes,
An early harvest and a plenteous year;—

Where every bird which charmed the vernal feast
Shook the sweet slumber from its wings at morn,
To warn the reaper of the rosy east,—
All now was sunless, empty, and forlorn.

Alone from out the stubble piped the quail,
And croaked the crow through all the dreamy
gloom;
Alone the pheasant, drumming in the vale,
Made echo to the distant cottage-loom.

There was no bud, no bloom upon the bowers;
The spiders moved their thin shrouds night by
night,
The thistledown, the only ghost of flowers,
Sailed slowly by — passed noiseless out of sight.

Amid all this — in this most cheerless air,
And where the woodbine shed upon the porch
Its crimson leaves, as if the Year stood there
Firing the floor with his inverted torch,—

Amid all this, the centre of the scene,
The white-haired matron with monotonous tread
Plied the swift wheel, and with her joyless mien
Sat, like a fate, and watched the flying thread.

She had known Sorrow,— he had walked with her,
Oft supped, and broke the bitter ashen crust;
And in the dead leaves still she heard the stir
Of his black mantle trailing in the dust.

While yet her cheek was bright with summer bloom,
Her country summoned, and she gave her all;
And twice War bowed to her his sable plume —
Re-gave the swords to rust upon the wall:

Re-gave the swords, but not the hand that drew
And struck for Liberty the dying blow;
Nor him who, to his sire and country true,
Fell mid the ranks of the invading foe.

Long, but not loud, the droning wheel went on,
Like the low murmur of a hive at noon;
Long, but not loud, the memory of the gone
Breathed through her lips a sad and tremulous tune.

At last the thread was snapped; her head was bowed;
Life dropped the distaff through his hands serene;
And loving neighbors smoothed her careful shroud,
While Death and Winter closed the autumn scene.

THOMAS BUCHANAN READ.

ABRAHAM LINCOLN.

[This tribute appeared in the London "Punch," which, up to the time of the assassination of Mr. Lincoln, had ridiculed and maligned him with all its well-known powers of pen and pencil.]

YOU lay a wreath on murdered Lincoln's bier,
  You, who with mocking pencil wont to trace,
  Broad for the self-complacent British sneer,
    His length of shambling limb, his furrowed
      face,

His gaunt, gnarled hands, his unkempt, bristling hair,
  His garb uncouth, his bearing ill at ease,
His lack of all we prize as debonair,
  Of power or will to shine, of art to please;

You, whose smart pen backed up the pencil's laugh,
  Judging each step as though the way were plain,
Reckless, so it could point its paragraph
  Of chief's perplexity, or people's pain:

Beside this corpse, that bears for winding-sheet
  The Stars and Stripes he lived to rear anew,
Between the mourners at his head and feet,
  Say, scurrile jester, is there room for *you?*

Yes: he had lived to shame me from my sneer,
  To lame my pencil, and confute my pen;
To make me own this hind of princes peer,
  This rail-splitter a true-born king of men.

My shallow judgment I had learned to rue,
  Noting how to occasion's height he rose;
How his quaint wit made home-truth seem more true;
  How, iron-like, his temper grew by blows.

How humble, yet how hopeful, he could be;
  How, in good fortune and in ill, the same;
Nor bitter in success, nor boastful he,
  Thirsty for gold, nor feverish for fame.

He went about his work,—such work as few
  Ever had laid on head and heart and hand,
As one who knows, where there 's a task to do,
  Man's honest will must heaven's good grace com-
    mand;

Who trusts the strength will with the burden grow,
  That God makes instruments to work his will,
If but that will we can arrive to know,
  Nor tamper with the weights of good and ill.

So he went forth to battle, on the side
  That he felt clear was Liberty's and Right's,
As in his peasant boyhood he had plied
  His warfare with rude Nature's thwarting mights;

The uncleared forest, the unbroken soil,
  The iron-bark, that turns the lumberer's ax,
The rapid, that o'erbears the boatman's toil,
  The prairie, hiding the mazed wanderer's tracks,

The ambushed Indian, and the prowling bear,—
  Such were the deeds that helped his youth to train:
Rough culture, but such trees large fruit may bear,
  If but their stocks be of right girth and grain.

So he grew up, a destined work to do,
  And lived to do it; four long-suffering years'
Ill fate, ill feeling, ill report, lived through,
  And then he heard the hisses change to cheers,

The taunts to tribute, the abuse to praise,
  And took both with the same unwavering mood;
Till, as he came on light, from darkling days,
  And seemed to touch the goal from where he stood,

A felon hand, between the goal and him,
  Reached from behind his back, a trigger prest,
And those perplexed and patient eyes were dim,
  Those gaunt, long-laboring limbs were laid to rest!

The words of mercy were upon his lips,
  Forgiveness in his heart and on his pen,
When this vile murderer brought swift eclipse
  To thoughts of peace on earth, good-will to men.

The Old World and the New, from sea to sea,
  Utter one voice of sympathy and shame:
Sore heart, so stopped when it at last beat high;
  Sad life, cut short just as its triumph came!

A deed accurst! Strokes have been struck before
  By the assassin's hand, whereof men doubt
If more of horror or disgrace they bore;
  But thy foul crime, like Cain's, stands darkly out,

Vile hand, that brandest murder on a strife,
  Whate'er its grounds, stoutly and nobly striven;
And with the martyr's crown crownest a life
  With much to praise, little to be forgiven.

                                    TOM TAYLOR.

------◦>◦◆◦<◦------

A GOOD name is properly that reputation of virtue that every man may challenge as his right and due in the opinions of others, till he has made forfeit of it by the viciousness of his actions.

PLACES AND PERSONS.

"The swan on still Saint Mary's Lake
Float double, swan and shadow."

YARROW UNVISITED.

FROM Stirling Castle we had seen
The mazy Forth unraveled;
Had trod the banks of Clyde and Tay,
And with the Tweed had traveled;
And when we came to Clovenford,
Then said my " winsome marrow,"
" Whate'er betide, we'll turn aside,
And see the braes of Yarrow."

" Let Yarrow folk, frae Selkirk town,
Who have been buying, selling,
Go back to Yarrow, 'tis their own;
Each maiden to her dwelling!
On Yarrow's banks let herons feed,
Hares couch, and rabbits burrow!
But we will downward with the Tweed,
Nor turn aside to Yarrow.

"There's Galla Water, Leader Haughs,
Both lying right before us;
And Dryborough, where with chiming Tweed
The lintwhites sing in chorus;
There's pleasant Teviotdale, a land
Made blithe with plough and harrow:
Why throw away a needful day
To go in search of Yarrow?

"What's Yarrow but a river bare,
That glides the dark hills under?
There are a thousand such elsewhere
As worthy of your wonder."
Strange words they seemed of slight and scorn;
My true-love sighed for sorrow,
And looked me in the face, to think
I thus could speak of Yarrow!

"O, green," said I, "are Yarrow's holms,
And sweet is Yarrow flowing!
Fair hangs the apple frae the rock,
But we will leave it growing.
O'er hilly path, and open strath,
We'll wander Scotland thorough;
But, though so near, we will not turn
Into the dale of Yarrow.

"Let beeves and homebred kine partake
The sweets of Burn-mill meadow;
The swan on still Saint Mary's Lake
Float double, swan and shadow!
We will not see them; will not go
To-day, nor yet to-morrow;
Enough, if in our hearts we know
There's such a place as Yarrow.

"Be Yarrow stream unseen, unknown!
It must, or we shall rue it:
We have a vision of our own;
Ah! why should we undo it?
The treasured dreams of times long past,
We'll keep then, winsome marrow!
For when we're there, although 'tis fair,
'Twill be another Yarrow!

"If care with freezing years should come,
And wandering seem but folly, —
Should we be loath to stir from home,
And yet be melancholy, —
Should life be dull, and spirits low,
'Twill soothe us in our sorrow,
That earth has something yet to show,
The bonny holms of Yarrow!"

WILLIAM WORDSWORTH.

YARROW VISITED.

AND is this Yarrow!—this the stream
Of which my fancy cherished
So faithfully, a waking dream?
An image that hath perished!
O that some minstrel's harp were near,
To utter notes of gladness,
And chase this silence from the air,
That fills my heart with sadness.

Yet why?—a silvery current flows
With uncontrolled meanderings;
Nor have these eyes by greener hills
Been soothed, in all my wanderings.
And, through her depths, Saint Mary's Lake
Is visibly delighted;
For not a feature of those hills
Is in the mirror slighted.

A blue sky bends o'er Yarrow Vale,
Save where that pearly whiteness
Is round the rising sun diffused,
A tender hazy brightness; .
Mild dawn of promise! that excludes
All profitless dejection;
Though not unwilling here to admit
A pensive recollection.

Where was it that the famous flower
Of Yarrow Vale lay bleeding?
His bed perchance was yon smooth mound
On which the herd is feeding:
And haply from this crystal pool,
Now peaceful as the morning,
The water-wraith ascended thrice,
And gave his doleful warning.

Delicious is the lay that sings
The haunts of happy lovers,
The path that leads them to the grove,
The leafy grove that covers:
And pity sanctifies the verse
That paints, by strength of sorrow,
The unconquerable strength of love;
Bear witness, rueful Yarrow!

But thou, that didst appear so fair
To fond imagination,
Dost rival in the light of day
Her delicate creation:
Meek loveliness is round thee spread,
A softness still and holy;
The grace of forest charms decayed,
And pastoral melancholy.

That region left, the vale unfolds
Rich groves of lofty stature,
With Yarrow winding through the pomp
Of cultivated nature;
And, rising from those lofty groves,
Behold a ruin hoary!
The shattered front of Newark's towers,
Renowned in border story.

Fair scenes for childhood's opening bloom,
For sportive youth to stray in;
For manhood to enjoy his strength;
And age to wear away in!
Yon cottage seems a bower of bliss,
It promises protection
To studious ease, and generous cares,
And every chaste affection!

How sweet on this autumnal day,
The wild wood's fruits to gather,
And on my true-love's forehead plant
A crest of blooming heather!

And what if I enwreathed my own!
'Twere no offence to reason;
The sober hills thus deck their brows
To meet the wintry season.

I see—but not by sight alone,
Loved Yarrow, have I won thee;
A ray of fancy still survives—
Her sunshine plays upon thee!
Thy ever youthful waters keep
A course of lively pleasure;
And gladsome notes my lips can breathe,
Accordant to the measure.

The vapors linger round the heights,
They melt—and soon must vanish;
One hour is theirs, no more is mine—
Sad thought! which I would banish.
But that I know, where'er I go,
Thy genuine image, Yarrow!
Will dwell with me—to heighten joy,
And cheer my mind in sorrow.

WILLIAM WORDSWORTH.

YARROW STREAM.

THY banks were bonnie, Yarrow stream,
When first on thee I met my lover;
Thy banks how dreary, Yarrow stream,
When now thy waves his body cover!

For ever now, O Yarrow stream,
Thou art to me a stream of sorrow;
For never on thy banks shall I
Behold my love—the flower of Yarrow!

He promised me a milk-white horse,
To bear me to his father's bowers;
He promised me a little page,
To squire me to his father's towers.

He promised me a wedding-ring,
The wedding-day was fixed to-morrow:
Now he is wedded to his grave,
Alas! a watery grave in Yarrow!

Sweet were his words when last we met,
My passion I as freely told him;
Clasped in his arms, I little thought
That I should never more behold him.

Scarce was he gone, I saw his ghost—
It vanished with a shriek of sorrow;
Thrice did the water-wraith ascend,
And give a doleful groan through Yarrow!

His mother from the window looked,
With all the longing of a mother;
His little sister, weeping, walked
The greenwood path to meet her brother.

They sought him east, they sought him west,
They sought him all the forest thorough;
They only saw the clouds of night—
They only heard the roar of Yarrow!

No longer from thy window look—
Thou hast no son, thou tender mother!
No longer walk, thou lovely maid—
Alas! thou hast no more a brother!

No longer seek him east or west,
No longer search the forest thorough,
For, murdered in the night so dark,
He lies a lifeless corpse in Yarrow!

The tears shall never leave my cheek,
No other youth shall be my marrow;
I'll seek thy body in the stream,
And there with thee I'll sleep in Yarrow!

The tear did never leave her cheek,
No other youth became her marrow;
She found his body in the stream,
And with him now she sleeps in Yarrow.

JOHN LOGAN.

MELROSE ABBEY.

F thou wouldst view fair Melrose aright,
Go visit it by the pale moonlight;
For the gay beams of lightsome day
Gild, but to flout, the ruins gray.
When the broken arches are black in night,
And each shafted oriel glimmers white:
When the cold light's uncertain shower
Streams on the ruined central tower;
When buttress and buttress, alternately,
Seem framed of ebon and ivory;
When silver edges the imagery,
And the scrolls that teach thee to live and die;
When distant Tweed is heard to rave,
And the owlet to hoot o'er the dead man's grave,
Then go — but go alone the while —
Then view St. David's ruined pile;
And, home returning, soothly swear,
Was never scene so sad and fair!

SIR WALTER SCOTT.

FAIR GREECE! SAD RELIC OF DEPARTED WORTH.

AIR GREECE! sad relic of departed worth!
Immortal though no more; though fallen, great!
Who now shall lead thy fallen children forth,
And long accustomed bondage uncreate?
Not such thy sons who whilome did await,
The hopeless warriors of a willing doom,
In bleak Thermopylæ's sepulchral strait,—
O, who that gallant spirit shall resume,
Leap from Eurota's banks, and call thee from the
tomb?

LORD BYRON.

THE INCHCAPE ROCK.

O stir in the air, no stir in the sea,—
The ship was as still as she could be;
Her sails from heaven received no motion;
Her keel was steady in the ocean.

Without either sign or sound of their shock,
The waves flowed over the Inchcape rock;
So little they rose, so little they fell,
They did not move the Inchcape bell.

The Holy Abbot of Aberbrothok
Had placed that bell on the Inchcape rock;
On a buoy in the storm it floated and swung,
And over the waves its warning rung.

When the rock was hid by the surges' swell,
The mariners heard the warning bell;
And then they knew the perilous rock,
And blessed the Abbot of Aberbrothok.

The sun in heaven was shining gay,—
All things were joyful on that day;
The sea-birds screamed as they wheeled around,
And there was joyance in their sound.

The buoy of the Inchcape bell was seen,
A darker speck on the ocean green;
Sir Ralph, the rover, walked his deck,
And he fixed his eye on the darker speck.

He felt the cheering power of spring, —
It made him whistle, it made him sing;
His heart was mirthful to excess;
But the rover's mirth was wickedness.

His eye was on the bell and float:
Quoth he, "My men, put out the boat;
And row me to the Inchcape rock,
And I'll plague the priest of Aberbrothok."

The boat is lowered, the boatmen row,
And to the Inchcape rock they go;
Sir Ralph bent over from the boat,
And cut the warning bell from the float.

Down sank the bell with a gurgling sound;
The bubbles rose, and burst around.
Quoth Sir Ralph, " The next who comes to the rock
Will not bless the Abbot of Aberbrothok."

Sir Ralph, the rover, sailed away, —
He scoured the seas for many a day;
And now, grown rich with plundered store,
He steers his course to Scotland's shore.

Quoth Sir Ralph, "It will be lighter soon,
For there is the dawn of the rising moon."

" Canst hear," said one, " the breakers roar?
For yonder, methinks, should be the shore.
Now where we are I cannot tell,
But I wish we could hear the Inchcape bell."

They hear no sound; the swell is strong;
Though the wind hath fallen, they drift along;
Till the vessel strikes with a shivering shock, —
O Christ! it is the Inchcape rock!

Sir Ralph, the rover, tore his hair;
He cursed himself in his despair.

" Without either sign or sound of their shock,
The waves flowed over the Inchcape rock."

So thick a haze o'erspreads the sky
They cannot see the sun on high;
The wind hath blown a gale all day;
At evening it hath died away.

On the deck the rover takes his stand;
So dark it is they see no land.

The waves rush in on every side;
The ship is sinking beneath the tide.

But ever in his dying fear
One dreadful sound he seemed to hear, —
A sound as if with the Inchcape bell
The Devil below was ringing his knell.

ROBERT SOUTHEY.

CAPE HATTERAS.

THE Wind King from the North came down,
Nor stopped by river, mount or town;
But, like a boisterous god at play,
Resistless, bounding on his way,   ·
He shook the lake and tore the wood,

And flapped his wings in merry mood,
Nor furled them, till he spied afar
The white caps flash on Hatteras bar,
Where fierce Atlantic landward bowls
O'er treacherous sands and hidden shoals.

He paused, then wreathed his horn of cloud,
And blew defiance long and loud:
"Come up! come up, thou torrid god,
' That rul'st the Southern sea!
Ho! lightning-eyed and thunder-shod,
  Come wrestle here with me!
As tossest thou the tangled cane,
I 'll hurl thee o'er the boiling main!
  *   *   *   *   *

He drew his lurid legions forth,
And sprang to meet the white-plumed North.

Can mortal tongue in song convey
The fury of that fearful fray?
How ships were splintered at a blow,
Sails shivered into shreds of snow,
And seamen hurled to death below!

"—— That lone hulk stands
Embedded in thy yellow sands."

"Come up! come up, thou torrid god,
Thou lightning-eyed and thunder-shod,
  And wrestle here with me!"
'T was heard and answered: "Lo! I come
  From azure Carribee,
To drive thee cowering to thy home,
And melt its walls of frozen foam."
From every isle and mountain dell,
From plains of pathless chaparral,
From tide-built bars, where sea-birds dwell,

Two gods commingling, bolt and blast,
The huge waves on each other cast,
And bellowed o'er the raging waste;
Then sped, like harnessed steeds, afar,
That drag a shattered battle-car
Amid the midnight din of war!

False Hatteras! when the cyclone came,
Thy waves leapt up with hoarse acclaim
And ran and wrecked yon argosy!

Fore'er nine sank! that lone hulk stands
Embedded in thy yellow sands,—
An hundred hearts in death there stilled,
And yet its ribs, with corpses filled,
  Are now caressed by thee!

    *   *   *   *   *

You lipless skull shall speak for me,
"This is the Golgotha of the sea!
And its keen hunger is the same
In winter's frost or summer's flame!
When life was young, adventure sweet,
I came with Walter Raleigh's fleet,
But here my scattered bones have lain
And bleached for ages by the main!

Though lonely once, strange folk have come,
Till peopled is my barren home.
Enough are here. Oh, heed the cry,
Ye white-winged strangers sailing by!
The bark that lingers on this wave
Will find its smiling but a grave!
Then, tardy mariner, turn and flee,
A myriad wrecks are on thy lee!
With swelling sail and sloping mast,
Accept kind Heaven's propitious blast!
O ship, sail on! O ship, sail fast,
Till, Golgotha's quicksands being past,
Thou gain'st the open sea at last!"

JOSIAH W. HOLDEN.

THE BURIAL OF SIR JOHN MOORE.

NOT a drum was heard, not a funeral note,
  As his corse to the rampart we hurried:
Not a soldier discharged his farewell shot
  O'er the grave where our hero we buried.

We buried him darkly at dead of night,
  The sods with our bayonets turning;
By the struggling moonbeam's misty light,
  And the lantern dimly burning.

No useless coffin enclosed his breast,
  Nor in sheet or in shroud we wound him;
But he lay like a warrior taking his rest,
  With his martial cloak around him.

Few and short were the prayers we said,
  And we spoke not a word of sorrow,
But we steadfastly gazed on the face of the dead,
  And we bitterly thought of the morrow.

We thought, as we hollowed his narrow bed,
  And smoothed down his lonely pillow,
That the foe and the stranger would tread o'er his head,
  And we far away on the billow.

Lightly they 'll talk of the spirit that 's gone,
  And o'er his cold ashes upbraid him;
But little he 'll reck if they let him sleep on
  In the grave where a Briton has laid him.

But half of our heavy task was done,
  When the clock struck the hour for retiring;
And we heard the distant and random gun
  That the foe was sullenly firing.

Slowly and sadly we laid him down
  From the field of his fame fresh and gory;
We carved not a line, we raised not a stone,
  But we left him alone with his glory!

CHARLES WOLFE.

CHARLES XII OF SWEDEN.

IN what foundation stands the warrior's pride,
How just his hopes, let Swedish Charles decide;
A frame of adamant, a soul of fire,
No dangers fright him, and no labors tire;
O'er love, o'er fear, extends his wide domain,
Unconquered lord of pleasure and of pain;
No joys to him pacific sceptres yield,
War sounds the trump, he rushes to the field;
Behold surrounding kings their powers combine,
And one capitulate, and one resign;
Peace courts his hand, but spreads her charms in vain;
"Think nothing gained," he cries, "till naught remain,
On Moscow's walls till Gothic standards fly,
And all be mine beneath the polar sky."
The march begins in military state,
And nations on his eye suspended wait;

Stern Famine guards the solitary coast,
And Winter barricades the realms of Frost;
He comes, nor want nor cold his course delay;—
Hide, blushing Glory, hide Pultowa's day!
The vanquished hero leaves his broken bands,
And shows his miseries in distant lands;
Condemned a needy supplicant to wait,
While ladies interpose and slaves debate,
But did not Chance at length her error mend?
Did no subverted empire mark his end?
Did rival monarchs give the fatal wound,
Or hostile millions press him to the ground?
His fall was destined to a barren strand,
A petty fortress, and a dubious hand;
He left the name at which the world grew pale,
To point a moral, or adorn a tale.

SAMUEL JOHNSON.

ON LEAVING THE WEST.

AREWELL, ye soft and sumptuous solitudes!
Ye fairy distances, ye lordly woods,
Haunted by paths like those that Poussin
      knew,
When after his all gazers' eyes he drew:
I go—and if I never more may steep
An eager heart in your enchantments deep,

A tender blessing lingers o'er the scene,
Like some young mother's thought, fond, yet serene,
And through its life new-born our lives have been.
Once more, farewell—a sad, a sweet farewell;
And if I never must behold you more,
In other worlds I will not cease to tell
The rosary I here have numbered o'er;

Yet ever to itself that heart may say,
Be not exacting—thou hast lived one day—
Hast looked on that which matches with thy mood,
Impassioned sweetness of full being's flood,
Where nothing checked the bold yet gentle wave,
Where naught repelled the lavish love that gave.

And bright-haired Hope will lend a gladdened ear,
And Love will free him from the grasp of Fear,
And Gorgon critics, while the tale they hear,
Shall dew their stony glances with a tear,
If I but catch one echo from your spell:
And so farewell—a grateful, sad farewell!

MARGARET FULLER.

THE KNIGHT'S TOMB.

HERE is the grave of Sir Arthur O'Kellyn?
Where may the grave of that good man be? —
By the side of a spring, on the breast of Hel-
    vellyn,
Under the twigs of a young birch-tree!
The oak that in summer was sweet to hear,

And rustled its leaves in the fall of the year,
And whistled and roared in the winter alone,
Is gone,—and the birch in its stead is grown.
The knight's bones are dust,
And his good sword rust; —
His soul is with the saints, I trust.

SAMUEL TAYLOR COLERIDGE.

COLUMBUS.

E was a man whom danger could not daunt,
Nor sophistry perplex, nor pain subdue,
A stoic, reckless of the world's vain taunt,
And steeled the path of honor to pursue;
So, when by all deserted, still he knew
How best to soothe the heart-sick, or confront
Sedition, schooled with equal eye to view
The frowns of grief, and the base pangs of want.

But when he saw that promised land arise
In all its rare and bright varieties,
Lovelier than fondest fancy ever trod;
Then softening nature melted in his eyes;
He knew his fame was full, and blessed his God;
And fell upon his face, and kissed the virgin sod!

SIR AUBREY DE VERE.

TO THOMAS MOORE.

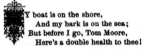

Y boat is on the shore,
    And my bark is on the sea;
But before I go, Tom Moore,
    Here's a double health to thee!

Here's a sigh to those who love me,
    And a smile to those who hate;
And, whatever sky's above me,
    Here's a heart for any fate.

Though the ocean roar around me,
    Yet it still shall bear me on;

Though a desert should surround me,
    It hath springs that may be won.

Were 't the last drop in the well,
    As I gasped upon the brink,
Ere my fainting spirit fell,
    'T is to thee that I would drink.

With that water, as this wine,
    The libation I would pour
Should be—peace to thine and mine,
    And a health to thee, Tom Moore.
                                    LORD BYRON.

TO VICTOR HUGO.

ICTOR in poesy! Victor in romance!
Cloud-weaver of phantasmal hopes and fears!
French of the French, and lord of human tears!
Child-lover, bard, whose fame-lit laurels glance,
Darkening the wreaths of all that would ad-
    vance
Beyond our strait their claim to be thy peers!
Weird Titan, by thy wintry weight of years

As yet unbroken! Stormy voice of France,
Who does not love our England, so they say;
I know not! England, France, all men to be,
Will make one people, ere man's race be run;
And I, desiring that diviner day,
Yield thee full thanks for thy full courtesy
To younger England, in the boy, my son.
                                    ALFRED TENNYSON.

MAZZINI.

LIGHT is out in Italy,
    A golden tongue of purest flame;
We watched it burning, long and lone,
    And every watcher knew its name,
And knew from whence its fervor came:
    That one rare light of Italy,
Which put self-seeking souls to shame!

This light which burnt for Italy,
    Through all the blackness of her night,
She doubted once upon a time,
    Because it took away her sight;
She looked and said, "There is no light!"
    It was thine eyes, poor Italy?
That knew not dark apart from bright.

This flame which burnt for Italy,
    It would not let her haters sleep;
They blew at it with angry breath,
    And only fed its upward leap,
And only made it hot and deep;
    Its burning showed us Italy,
And all the hopes she had to keep.

This light is out in Italy,
    Her eyes shall seek for it in vain!
For her sweet sake it spent itself,
    Too early flickering to its wane—
Too long blown over by her pain.
Bow down and weep, O Italy,
Thou canst not kindle it again!
                    LAURA C. REDDEN (Howard Glyndon).

BYRON.

E touched his harp, and nations heard, entranced.
As some vast river of unfailing source,
Rapid, exhaustless, deep, his numbers flowed,
And oped new fountains in the human heart.
Where Fancy halted, weary in her flight,
In other men, his, fresh as morning, rose,
    And soared untrodden heights, and seemed at
        home
Where angels bashful looked. Others, though great,
Beneath their argument seemed struggling whiles;

He from above descending stooped to touch
The loftiest thought; and proudly stooped, as though
It scarce deserved his verse. With Nature's self
He seemed an old acquaintance, free to jest
At will with all her glorious majesty.
He laid his hand upon " the ocean's mane,"
And played familiar with his hoary locks;
Stood on the Alps, stood on the Apennines,
And with the thunder talked, as friend to friend;
And wove his garland of the lightning's wing,

In sportive twist, the lightning's fiery wing,
Which, as the footsteps of the dreadful God,
Marching upon the storm in vengeance, seemed;
Then turned, and with the grasshopper, who sung
His evening song beneath his feet, conversed.
Suns, moons, and stars and clouds, his sisters were;
Rocks, mountains, meteors, seas and winds and storms
His brothers, younger brothers, whom he scarce
As equals deemed. All passions of all men,
The wild and tame, the gentle and severe;
All thoughts, all maxims, sacred and profane;

All creeds, all seasons, time, eternity;
All that was hated, and all that was dear;
All that was hoped, all that was feared, by man;
He tossed about, as tempest-withered leaves,
Then, smiling, looked upon the wreck he made.
With terror now he froze the cowering blood,
And now dissolved the heart in tenderness;
Yet would not tremble, would not weep himself;
·But back into his soul retired, alone,
Dark, sullen, proud, gazing contemptuously
On hearts and passions prostrate at his feet.

ROBERT POLLOK.

AT THE TOMB OF BYRON.

MASTER! here I bow before a shrine;
Before the lordliest dust that ever yet
Moved animate in human form divine.
Lo! dust indeed to dust. The mould is set
Above thee, and the ancient walls are wet,
And drip all day in dank and silent gloom,
As if the cold gray stones could not forget
Thy great estate shrunk to this sombre room,
But learn to weep perpetual tears above thy tomb.

Through broken panes I hear the schoolboy's shout,
I see the black-winged engines sweep and pass,
And from the peopled narrow plot without,
Well grown with brier, moss, and heaving grass,
I see the Abbey loom an ivied mass,
Made eloquent of faiths, of fates to be,
Of creeds, and perished kings; and still, alas,
O soldier-childe! most eloquent of thee,
Of thy sad life, and all the unsealed mystery.

I look into the dread, forbidding tomb;
Lo! darkness—death. The soul on shifting sand
That belts eternity gropes in the gloom——
The black-winged bird goes forth in search of land,
But turns no more to reach my reaching hand——
O, land beyond the land! I lean me o'er
Thy dust in prayer devout——I rise, I stand
Erect; the stormy seas are thine no more;
A weary white-winged dove has touched the olive
shore.

A bay-wreath woven by the sun-down west
Hangs damp and stained upon the dank gray wall,
Above thy time-soiled tomb and tattered crest;
A bay-wreath gathered by the seas that call
To orient Cathay, that break and fall
On shell-lined shores, before Tahiti's breeze——
A slab, a crest, a wreath, and these are all
Neglected, tattered, torn; yet only these
The world bestows for song that rivaled singing seas.

A bay-wreath wound by one more truly brave
Than Shastan; fair as thy eternal fame,
She sat and wove above the sunset wave,
And wound and sang thy measures and thy name.
'T was wound by one, yet sent with one acclaim
By many, fair and warm as flowing wine,
And purely true, and tall as glowing flame,
That list and lean in moonlight's yellow shine
To tropic tales of love in other tongues than thine.

I bring this idle reflex of thy task,
And my few loves, to thy forgotten tomb:
I leave them here; and here all pardon ask
Of thee, and patience ask of singers whom
Thy majesty has silenced. I resume
My staff, and now my face is to the West;
My feet are worn; the sun is gone, a gloom
Has mantled Hucknall, and the minstrel's zest
For fame is broken here, and here he pleads for rest.

JOAQUIN MILLER.

ON THE PORTRAIT OF SHAKESPEARE.

THIS figure that thou here seest put,
It was for gentle Shakespeare cut,
Wherein the graver had a strife
With nature, to outdo the life:
O could he but have drawn his wit,

As well in brass, as he hath hit
His face; the print would then surpass
All that was ever writ in brass:
But since he cannot, reader, look,
Not on his picture, but his book.

BEN JONSON.

THE LOST OCCASION.

[In memory of Daniel Webster.]

SOME die too late, and some too soon,
  At early morning, heat of noon,
  Or the chill evening twilight. Thou,
  Whom the rich heavens did so endow
With eyes of power and Jove's own brow,
With all the massive strength that fills
Thy home-horizon's granite hills,
With rarest gifts of heart and head
From manliest stock inherited
New England's stateliest type of man.
In port and speech Olympian;
Whom no one met, at first, but took
A second awed and wondering look
(As turned, perchance, the eyes of Greece,
On Phidias' unveiled masterpiece);
Whose words in simplest home-spun clad,
The Saxon strength of Cædmon's had,
With power reserved at need to reach
The Roman forum's loftiest speech,
Sweet with persuasion. eloquent
In passion, cool in argument,
Or, ponderous, falling on thy foes
As fell the Norse god's hammer blows,
Crushing as if with Talus' flail
Through error's logic-woven mail,
And falling only when they tried
The adamant of the righteous side,—
Thou, foiled in aim and hope, bereaved
Of old friends, by the new deceived,
Too soon for us, too soon for thee,
Beside thy lonely Northern sea,
Where long and low the marsh-lands spread,
Laid wearily down thy august head.

Thou shouldst have lived to feel below
Thy feet Disunion's fierce upthrow,—
The late-sprung mine that underlaid
Thy sad concessions vainly made.
Thou shouldst have seen from Sumter's wall
The star-flag of the Union fall,
And armed Rebellion pressing on
The broken lines of Washington!
No stronger voice than thine had then
Called out the utmost might of men,

To make the Union's charter free
And strengthen law by liberty.
How had that stern arbitrament
To thy gray age youth's vigor lent,
Shaming ambition's paltry prize
Before thy disillusioned eyes;
Breaking the spell about thee wound
Like the green withes that Samson bound;
Redeeming, in one effort grand,
Thyself and thy imperilled land!
Ah, cruel fate, that closed to thee,
O sleeper by the Northern sea,
The gates of opportunity!
God fills the gaps of human need,
Each crisis brings its word and deed.

Wise men and strong we did not lack;
But still, with memory turning back,
In the dark hours we thought of thee,
And thy lone grave beside the sea.

Above that grave the east winds blow,
And from the marsh-lands drifting slow
The sea-fog comes, with evermore
The wave-wash of a lonely shore,
And sea-birds melancholy cry,
As Nature fain would typify
The sadness of a closing scene,
The loss of that which should have been.
But, where thy native mountains bare
Their foreheads to diviner air,
Fit emblem of diviner fame,
One lofty summit keeps thy name.
For thee the cosmic forces did
The rearing of that pyramid;
The prescient ages shaping with
Fire, flood, and frost, thy monolith.
Sunrise and sunset lay thereon
With hands of light their benison;
The stars of midnight pause to set
Their jewels in its coronet.
And evermore that mountain mass
Seems climbing from the shadowy pass
To light, as if to manifest
Thy nobler self, thy life at best!

JOHN GREENLEAF WHITTIER.

NATHANIEL HAWTHORNE.

HERE in seclusion and remote from men
  The wizard hand lies cold,
Which at its topmost speed let fall the pen,
  And left the tale half told.

Ah! who shall lift that wand of magic power,
  And the lost clew regain?
The unfinished window in Aladdin's tower
  Unfinished must remain!

HENRY WADSWORTH LONGFELLOW.

HENRY WADSWORTH LONGFELLOW.

(DIED MARCH 24, 1882.)

O ye dead Poets, who are living still
Immortal in your verse.—LONGFELLOW.

E mourn for those whose laurels fade,
Whose greatness in the grave is laid;
Whose memory few will care to keep,
Whose names, forgotten, soon shall sleep;
We mourn Life's vainness, as we bow
O'er folded hands and icy brow.

Wan is the grief of those whose faith
Is bounded by the shores of Death;
From out whose mists of doubt and gloom
No rainbow arches o'er the tomb
Where Love's last tribute of a tear
Lies with dead flowers upon the bier.

O thou revered, beloved!—not yet,
With sob of bells, with eyes tear-wet,
With faltering pulses, do we lay
Thy greatness in the grave away;
Not Auburn's consecrated ground
Can hold the life that wraps thee round.

Still shall thy gentle presence prove
Its ministry of hope and love;
Thy tender tones be heard within
The story of Evangeline;

And by the Fireside, midst the rest,
Thou oft shalt be a welcome guest.

Again the Mystery will be clear;
The august Tuscan's shades appear;
Moved by thy impulse. we shall feel
New longings for thy high ideal;
And under all thy forms of art
Feel beatings of a human heart.

As in our dreams we follow thee
With longing eyes Beyond the Sea,
We see thee on some loftier height
Across whose trembling bridge of light
Our Voices of the Night are borne,
Clasp with white hand the stars of Morn.

O happy Poet! Thine is not
A portion in the common lot;
Thy works shall follow thee; thy verse
Shall still thy living thoughts rehearse;
The Ages shall to thee belong—
An immortality of Song.

FRANCIS F. BROWNE.

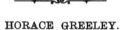

HORACE GREELEY.

ARTH, let thy softest mantle rest
On this worn child to thee returning,
Whose youth was nurtured at thy breast,
Who loved thee with such tender yearning.
He knew thy fields and woodland ways,
And deemed thy humblest son his brother; —
Asleep, beyond our blame or praise,
We yield him back, O gentle Mother!

Of praise, of blame, he drank his fill;
Who has not read the life-long story?
And dear we hold his fame, but still
The man was dearer than his glory.
And now to us are left alone
The closet where his shadow lingers,
The vacant chair — that was a throne, —
The pen just fallen from his fingers.

Wrath changed to kindness on that pen,
Though dipped in gall. it flowed with honey;
One flash from out the cloud, and then
The skies with smile and jest were sunny.

Of hate he surely lacked the art,
Who made his enemy his lover:
O reverend head, and Christian heart!
Where now their like the round world over?

He saw the goodness, not the taint,
In many a poor, do-nothing creature,
And gave to sinner and to saint,
But kept his faith in human nature;
Perchance he was not worldly-wise,
Yet we who noted, standing nearer,
The shrewd, kind twinkle in his eyes,
For every weakness held him dearer

Alas, that unto him who gave
So much so little should be given!
Himself alone he might not save,
Of all for whom his hands had striven.
Place, freedom, fame, his work bestowed;
Men took, and passed, and left him lonely;
What marvel if, beneath his load,
At times he craved — for justice only.

Yet thanklessness, the serpent's tooth,
  His lofty purpose could not alter;
Toil had no power to bend his youth,
  Or make his lusty manhood falter;
From envy's sling, from slander's dart,
  That armored soul the body shielded,
Till one dark sorrow chilled his heart,
  And then he bowed his head and yielded.

Now, now, we measure at its worth
  The gracious presence gone forever!
The wrinkled East, that gave him birth,
  Laments with every laboring river;
Wild moan the free winds of the West
  For him who gathered to her prairies
The sons of men, and made each crest
  The haunt of happy household fairies;

And anguish sits upon the mouth
  Of her who came to know him latest:
His heart was ever thine, O South!
  He was thy truest friend, and greatest!

He shunned thee in thy splendid shame,
  He stayed thee in thy voiceless sorrow;
The day thou shalt forget his name,
  Fair South, can have no sadder morrow.

The tears that fall from eyes unused,
  The hands above his grave united,
The words of men whose lips he loosed,
  Whose cross he bore, whose wrongs he righted, —
Could he but know, and rest with this!
  Yet stay, through Death's low-lying hollow,
His one last foe's insatiate hiss
  On that benignant shade would follow!

Peace! while we shroud this man of men,
  Let no unhallowed word be spoken!
He will not answer thee again,
  His mouth is sealed, his wand is broken.
Some holier cause, some vaster trust
  Beyond the veil, he doth inherit:
O gently, Earth, receive his dust,
  And Heaven soothe his troubled spirit!

EDMUND CLARENCE STEDMAN.

JOSEPH RODMAN DRAKE.

GREEN be the turf above thee,
  Friend of my better days!
None knew thee but to love thee,
  Nor named thee but to praise.

Tears fell, when thou wert dying,
  From eyes unused to weep,
And long, where thou art lying,
  Will tears the cold turf steep.

When hearts whose truth was proven,
  Like thine, are laid in earth,
There should a wreath be woven
  To tell the world their worth;

And I, who woke each morrow
  To clasp thy hand in mine,
Who shared thy joy and sorrow,
  Whose weal and woe were thine, —

It should be mine to braid it
  Around thy faded brow;
But I've in vain essayed it,
  And feel I cannot now.

While memory bids me weep thee,
  Nor thoughts nor words are free;
The grief is fixed too deeply
  That mourns a man like thee.

FITZ-GREENE HALLECK.

DIRGE FOR A SOLDIER.

MAJOR-GENERAL PHILIP KEARNEY.

CLOSE his eyes; his work is done!
  What to him is friend or foeman,
Rise of moon or set of sun,
  Hand of man or kiss of woman?
Lay him low, lay him low,
  In the clover or the snow!
What cares he? he cannot know;
  Lay him low!

As man may, he fought his fight,
  Proved his truth by his endeavor;
Let him sleep in solemn night,
  Sleep forever and forever.

Lay him low, lay him low,
  In the clover or the snow!
What cares he? he cannot know;
  Lay him low!

Fold him in his country's stars,
  Roll the drum and fire the volley!
What to him are all our wars? —
  What but death bemocking folly?
Lay him low, lay him low,
  In the clover or the snow!
What cares he? he cannot know;
  Lay him low!

Leave him to God's watching eye:
Trust him to the hand that made him.
Mortal love weeps idly by;
God alone has power to aid him.

Lay him low, lay him low,
In the clover or the snow!
What cares he? he cannot know;
Lay him low!

GEORGE HENRY BOKER.

VALE.*

"*E mortuis nil nisi bonum.*" When
For me the end has come, and I am dead,
And little voluble chattering daws of men
Peck at me curiously, let it then be said
By some one brave enough to speak the truth:
Here lies a great soul killed by cruel wrong.
Down all the balmy days of his fresh youth,
To his bleak, desolate noon, with sword and song,
And speech that rushed up hotly from the heart,
He wrought for Liberty, till his own wound
(He had been stabbed), concealed with painful art
Through wasting years, mastered him, and he
swooned,
And sank there where you see him lying now,
With that word "Failure" written on his brow.

But say that he succeeded. If he missed
World's honors, and world's plaudits and the
wage
Of the world's deft lacqueys, still his lips were kissed
Daily by those high angels who assuage
The thirstings of the poets—for he was
Born unto singing, and a burthen lay

Mightily on him, and he moaned because
He could not rightly utter in the day
What God taught in the night. Sometimes, nathless,
Power fell upon him, and bright tongues of flame,
And blessings reached him from poor souls in stress,
And benedictions from black pits of shame,
And little children's love, and old men's prayers,
And a Great Hand that led him unawares.

So he died rich. And if his eyes were blurred
With thick films—silence! he is in his grave.
Greatly he suffered; greatly, too, he erred;
Yet broke his heart in trying to be brave.
Nor did he wait till Freedom had become
The popular shibboleth of the courtier's lips,
But smote for her when God Himself seemed dumb
And all his arching skies were in eclipse.
He was a-weary, but he fought his fight,
And stood for simple manhood; and was joyed
To see the august broadening of the light,
And new earths heaving heavenward from the void
He loved his fellows, and their love was sweet—
Plant daisies at his head and at his feet.

RICHARD REALF.

A FRIEND'S GREETING.

TO J. G. WHITTIER ON HIS SEVENTIETH BIRTHDAY.

NOW-BOUND for earth, but summer-souled for
thee,
Thy natal morning shines:
Hail, friend and poet. Give thy hand to me,
And let me read its lines!

For skilled in fancy's palmistry am I,
When years have set their crown;
When life gives light to read its secrets by,
And deed explains renown.

So, looking backward from thy seventieth year
On service grand and free,
The pictures of thy spirit's past are clear,
And each interprets thee.

I see thee, first, on hills our Aryan sires
In time's lost morning knew.
Kindling as priest the lonely altar-fires
That from earth's darkness grew.

Then wise with secrets of Chaldæan lore,
In high Akkadian fane;
Or pacing slow by Egypt's river shore,
In Thothmes' glorious reign.

I hear thee, wroth with all iniquities
That Judah's kings betrayed,
Preach from Ain-Jidi's rock thy God's decrees,
Or Mamre's terebinth shade.

And, ah! most piteous vision of the past,
Drawn by thy being's law,
I see thee. martyr, in the arena cast,
Beneath the lion's paw.

Yet, afterwards, how rang thy sword upon
The paynim helm and shield!
How shone with Godfrey, and at Askalon,
Thy white plume o'er the field.

*Written immediately before his suicide.

Strange contradiction! where the sand waves spread
　The boundless desert sea,
The Bedouin spearmen found their destined head,
　Their dark-eyed chief — in thee!

And thou wert friar in Cluny's saintly cell,
　And Skald by Norway's foam,
Ere fate of poet fixed thy soul to dwell
　In this New England home.

Here art thou poet,— more than warrior, priest;
　And here thy quiet years
Yield more to us than sacrifice or feast,
　Or clash of swords or spears.

The faith that lifts, the courage that sustains,
　These thou wert sent to teach:
Hot blood of battle, beating in thy veins,
　Is turned to gentle speech.

Not less, but more, than others hast thou striven;
　Thy victories remain:
The scars of ancient hate, long since forgiven,
　Have lost their power to pain.

Apostle pure of freedom and of right,
　Thou hadst thy one reward;
Thy prayers were heard, and flashed upon thy sight
　The coming of the Lord!

Now, sheathed in myrtle of thy tender songs,
　Slumbers the blade of truth;
But age's wisdom, crowning thee, prolongs
　The eager hope of youth.

Another line upon thy hand I trace,
　All destinies above:
Men know thee most as one that loves his race,
　And bless thee with their love!

BAYARD TAYLOR.

MY PSALM.

MOURN no more my vanished years:
　Beneath a tender rain,
An April rain of smiles and tears,
　My heart is young again.

The west-winds blow, and, singing low,
　I hear the glad streams run;
The windows of my soul I throw
　Wide open to the sun.

No longer forward nor behind
　I look in hope or fear;
But, grateful, take the good I find,
　The best of now and here.

I plough no more a desert land,
　To harvest weed and tare;
The manna dropping from God's hand
　Rebukes my painful care.

I break my pilgrim staff, — I lay
　Aside the toiling oar;
The angel sought so far away
　I welcome at my door.

The airs of spring may never play
　Among the ripening corn,
Nor freshness of the flowers of May
　Blow through the autumn morn;

Yet shall the blue-eyed gentian look
　Through fringéd lids to heaven,
And the pale aster in the brook
　Shall see its image given; —

The woods shall wear their robes of praise,
　The south-wind softly sigh,
And sweet, calm days in golden haze
　Melt down the amber sky.

Not less shall manly deed and word
　Rebuke an age of wrong;

The graven flowers that wreathe the sword
　Make not the blade less strong.

But smiting hands shall learn to heal,—
　To build as to destroy;
Nor less my heart for others feel
　That I the more enjoy.

All as God wills who wisely heeds
　To give or to withhold,
And knoweth more of all my needs
　Than all my prayers have told!

Enough that blessings undeserved
　Have marked my erring track;—
That wheresoe'er my feet have swerved,
　His chastening turned me back; —

That more and more a Providence
　Of love is understood,
Making the springs of time and sense
　Sweet with eternal good;—

That death seems but a covered way
　Which opens into light,
Wherein no blinded child can stray
　Beyond the Father's sight;—

That care and trial seem at last,
　Through Memory's sunset air,
Like mountain-ranges overpast,
　In purple distance fair; —

That all the jarring notes of life
　Seem blending in a psalm,
And all the angels of its strife
　Slow rounding into calm.

And so the shadows fall apart,
　And so the west-winds play;
And all the windows of my heart
　I open to the day.

JOHN GREENLEAF WHITTIER.

SENTIMENT AND REFLECTION.

ELEGY WRITTEN IN A COUNTRY CHURCHYARD.

THE curfew tolls the knell of parting day,
  The lowing herd winds slowly o'er the lea,
The ploughman homeward plods his weary way,
  And leaves the world to darkness and to me.

Now fades the glimmering landscape on the sight,
  And all the air a solemn stillness holds,
Save where the beetle wheels his droning flight,
  And drowsy tinklings lull the distant folds:

21

Save that from yonder ivy-mantled tower,
  The moping owl does to the moon complain
Of such as, wandering near her secret bower,
  Molest her ancient solitary reign.

For them no more the blazing hearth shall burn,
  Or busy housewife ply her evening care;
No children run to lisp their sire's return,
  Or climb his knees the envied kiss to share.

"The lowing herd winds slowly o'er the lea."

Beneath those rugged elms, that yew-tree's shade,
  Where heaves the turf in many a mouldering heap,
Each in his narrow cell forever laid,
  The rude forefathers of the hamlet sleep.

Oft did the harvest to their sickle yield,
  Their furrow oft the stubborn glebe has broke;
How jocund did they drive their team afield!
  How bowed the woods beneath their sturdy stroke!

"Drowsy tinklings lull the distant folds."

The breezy call of incense-breathing morn,
  The swallow twittering from the straw-built shed,
The cock's shrill clarion, or the echoing horn,
  No more shall rouse them from their lowly bed.

Let not ambition mock their useful toil,
  Their homely joys, and destiny obscure;
Nor grandeur hear with a disdainful smile
  The short and simple annals of the poor.

The boast of heraldry, the pomp of power,
  And all that beauty, all that wealth e'er gave,

Can storied urn, or animated bust,
  Back to its mansion call the fleeting breath?

"Children run to lisp their sire's return."

Await alike the inevitable hour;
  The paths of glory lead but to the grave.

Can honor's voice provoke the silent dust,
  Or flattery soothe the dull cold ear of death?

"Oft did the harvest to their sickle yield."

Nor you, ye proud, impute to these the fault,
  If memory o'er their tomb no trophies raise,
Where through the long-drawn aisle and fretted vault
  The pealing anthem swells the note of praise.

Perhaps in this neglected spot is laid
  Some heart once pregnant with celestial fire;
Hands that the rod of empire might have swayed,
  Or waked to ecstacy the living lyre;

But Knowledge to their eyes her ample page
  Rich with the spoils of time did ne'er unroll;

Full many a flower is born to blush unseen,
  And waste its sweetness on the desert air.

"How jocund did they drive their team afield."

Chill penury repressed their noble rage,
  And froze the genial current of the soul.

Some village Hampden, that, with dauntless breast,
  The little tyrant of his fields withstood,

"Some village Hampden, that with dauntless breast,
The little tyrant of his field withstood."

Full many a gem of purest ray serene
  The dark unfathomed caves of ocean bear;

Some mute inglorious Milton here may rest,
  Some Cromwell guiltless of his country's blood.

The applause of listening senates to command,
  The threats of pain and ruin to despise,
To scatter plenty o'er a smiling land,
  And read their history in a nation's eyes,

Their lot forbade: nor circumscribed alone
  Their growing virtues, but their crimes confined;
Forbade to wade through slaughter to a throne,
  And shut the gates of mercy on mankind:

Their name, their years, spelt by the unlettered Muse,
  The place of fame and elegy supply:
And many a holy text around she strews,
  That teach the rustic moralist to die.

For who, to dumb forgetfulness a prey,
  This pleasing anxious being e'er resigned,
Left the warm precincts of the cheerful day,
  Nor cast one longing, lingering look behind?

"——Wade through slaughter to a throne,
  And shut the gates of mercy on mankind."

The struggling pangs of conscious truth to hide,
  To quench the blushes of ingenuous shame,
Or heap the shrine of luxury and pride
  With incense kindled at the Muse's flame.

Far from the madding crowd's ignoble strife,
  Their sober wishes never learned to stray;
Along the cool sequestered vale of life
  They kept the noiseless tenor of their way.

Yet even these bones from insult to protect,
  Some frail memorial still erected nigh,
With uncouth rhymes and shapeless sculpture decked,
  Implores the passing tribute of a sigh.

On some fond breast the parting soul relies,
  Some pious drops the closing eye requires;
E'en from the tomb the voice of nature cries,
  E'en in our ashes live their wonted fires.

For thee, who mindful of the unhonored dead,
  Dost in these lines their artless tale relate:
If chance, by lonely contemplation led,
  Some kindred spirit shall inquire thy fate,—

Haply some hoary-headed swain may say:
  Oft have we seen him at the peep of dawn
Brushing with hasty steps the dews away,
  To meet the sun upon the upland lawn:

There at the foot of yonder nodding beech,   Now drooping, woful-wan, like one forlorn,
  That wreathes its old fantastic roots so high.   Or crazed with care, or crossed in hopeless love.

"Hard by yon wood, now smiling as in scorn,
Muttering his wayward fancies, he would rove."

His listless length at noontide would he stretch,   One morn I missed him on the customed hill,
  And pore upon the brook that babbles by.   Along the heath, and near his favorite tree;

"Approach and read—for thou canst read—the lay
Graved on the stone beneath yon aged thorn."

Hard by yon wood, now smiling as in scorn,   Another came; nor yet beside the rill,
  Muttering his wayward fancies he would rove;   Nor up the lawn, nor at the wood was he:

The next, with dirges due in sad array,
  Slow through the church-way path we saw him
      borne:—
Approach and read (for thou canst read) the lay
  Graved on the stone beneath yon aged thorn.

THE EPITAPH.

Here rests his head upon the lap of earth,
  A youth, to fortune and to fame unknown:
Fair Science frowned not on his humble birth,
  And Melancholy marked him for her own.

Large was his bounty, and his soul sincere;
  Heaven did a recompense as largely send;
He gave to misery (all he had) a tear,
  He gained from Heaven ('t was all he wished) a
      friend.

No farther seek his merits to disclose,
  Or draw his frailties from their dread abode,
(There they alike in trembling hope repose),
  The bosom of his Father and his God.

THOMAS GRAY.

THANATOPSIS.

To him who in the love of Nature holds
  Communion with her visible forms, she speaks
  A various language; for his gayer hours
  She has a voice of gladness and a smile
And eloquence of beauty; and she glides
Into his darker musings with a mild
And healing sympathy, that steals away
Their sharpness ere he is aware. When thoughts
Of the last bitter hour come like a blight
Over thy spirit, and sad images
Of the stern agony, and shroud, and pall,
And breathless darkness, and the narrow house,
Make thee to shudder, and grow sick at heart—
Go forth under the open sky, and list
To Nature's teachings, while from all around—
Earth and her waters, and the depths of air—
Comes a still voice: Yet a few days and thee
The all-beholding sun shall see no more
In all his course; nor yet in the cold ground,
Where thy pale form was laid, with many tears,
Nor in the embrace of ocean, shall exist
Thy image. Earth, that nourished thee, shall claim
Thy growth, to be resolved to earth again;
And, lost each human trace, surrendering up
Thine individual being shalt thou go
To mix forever with the elements—
To be a brother to the insensible rock,
And to the sluggish clod, which the rude swain
Turns with his share, and treads upon. The oak
Shall send his roots abroad, and pierce thy mould.
  Yet not to thine eternal resting-place
Shalt thou retire alone; nor could'st thou wish
Couch more magnificent. Thou shalt lie down
With patriarchs of the infant world,—with kings,
The powerful of the earth, the wise, the good,
Fair forms, and hoary seers of ages past,
All in one mighty sepulchre. The hills,
Rock-ribbed, and ancient as the sun; the vales
Stretching in pensive quietness between;
The venerable woods; rivers that move
In majesty, and the complaining brooks,

That make the meadows green; and, poured round all,
Old ocean's gray and melancholy waste,—
Are but the solemn decorations all
Of the great tomb of man. The golden sun,
The planets, all the infinite host of heaven,
Are shining on the sad abodes of death,
Through the still lapse of ages. All that tread
The globe are but a handful to the tribes
That slumber in its bosom. Take the wings
Of morning, traverse Barca's desert sands,
Or lose thyself in the continuous woods
Where rolls the Oregon, and hears no sound
Save his own dashings—yet the dead are there;
And millions in those solitudes, since first
The flight of years began, have laid them down
In their last sleep—the dead reign there alone.
So shalt thou rest; and what if thou withdraw
In silence from the living, and no friend
Take note of thy departure? All that breathe
Will share thy destiny. The gay will laugh
When thou art gone, the solemn brood of care
Plod on, and each one as before will chase
His favorite phantom; yet all these shall leave
Their mirth and their employments, and shall come
And make their bed with thee. As the long train
Of ages glide away, the sons of men—
The youth in life's green spring, and he who goes
In the full strength of years, matron and maid,
And the sweet babe, and the gray-headed man—
Shall one by one be gathered to thy side
By those who in their turn shall follow them.

  So live, that when thy summons comes to join
The innumerable caravan that moves
To that mysterious realm where each shall take
His chamber in the silent halls of death,
Thou go not like the quarry-slave at night,
Scourged to his dungeon; but, sustained and soothed
By an unfaltering trust, approach thy grave
Like one who wraps the drapery of his couch
About him, and lies down to pleasant dreams.

WILLIAM CULLEN BRYANT.

I REMEMBER, I REMEMBER.

REMEMBER, I remember
  The house where I was born,
The little window where the sun
  Came peeping in at morn;
He never came a wink too soon,
  Nor brought too long a day,
But now I often wish the night
  Had borne my breath away!

I remember, I remember
  Where I was used to swing,
And thought the air must rush as fresh
  To swallows on the wing;
My spirit flew in feathers then,
  That is so heavy now,
And summer pools could hardly cool
  The fever on my brow.

"I remember, I remember
The house where I was born."

I remember, I remember
  The roses, red and white,
The violets, and the lily-cups,
  Those flowers made of light!
The lilacs, where the robin built,
  And where my brother set
The laburnum on his birthday,—
  The tree is living yet!

I remember, I remember
  The fir-trees dark and high;
I used to think their slender tops
  Were close against the sky.
It was a childish ignorance,
  But now 'tis little joy
To know I 'm farther off from heaven
  Than when I was a boy.

THOMAS HOOD.

THERE appears to exist a greater desire to live long than to live well. Measure by man's desires, he cannot live long enough; measure by his good deeds, and he has not lived long enough; measure by his evil deeds, and he has lived too long.

TWO SONNETS.

I.—SOLITUDE.

O, child of sorrow, to the lonely wood,
And company with trees, and rocks and hills,
With creeping vines, with flow'rs, and gentle
    rills,
  That seem themselves to feel the musing mood,
And feed with thought the charming solitude.
There is a spirit in the groves that fills
The heart with such an influence as steals
The outward sense, and leaves the soul imbued
With pow'r to hold communion with the dead;
And ministering angels here may tell
Some happy story of the spirit home:
Some lov'd one gone, for whom the heart has bled,
May whisper thoughts the sad unrest to quell,
And point to realms of joy and bid thee come.

II.—DESPAIR.

O Death in Life! O grave where grim Despair
  Hath buried hope, and ev'ry pleasing dream
  Of what the years may bring! The fitful gleam
  Of light that lingers yet, but points me where
    A glory might have been; and shapes of fear
Look through the gloom, till my surroundings seem
The work of some malignant thing, supreme
O'er all my pow'rs to plan, to strive, to bear.
Ere yet high noon of days, bereft of strength
To toil for those committed to my hand,
And doomed to see no more a smiling sun,
I find that all is bitterness at length.
Yet, God hath care of us; here let me stand,
And say, with steadfast heart, "His will be done."

ED. PORTER THOMPSON.

"Too late I stayed,—forgive the crime."

TOO LATE I STAYED.

TOO late I stayed,—forgive the crime!
  Unheeded flew the hours:
How noiseless falls the foot of Time
  That only treads on flowers!

And who, with clear account, remarks
  The ebbings of its glass,
When all its sands are diamond sparks,
  That dazzle as they pass?

Oh, who to sober measurement
  Time's happy swiftness brings,
When birds of paradise have lent
  Their plumage to his wings?

WILLIAM ROBERT SPENCER.

MY LIFE IS LIKE THE SUMMER ROSE.

Y life is like the summer rose
  That opens to the morning sky,
But, ere the shades of evening close,
  Is scattered on the ground—to die!
Yet on the rose's humble bed
The sweetest dews of night are shed,
As if she wept the waste to see,—
But none shall weep a tear for me!

My life is like the autumn leaf
  That trembles in the moon's pale ray;
Its hold is frail—its date is brief,
  Restless—and soon to pass away!

Yet, ere that leaf shall fall and fade,
The parent tree will mourn its shade,
The winds bewail the leafless tree,—
But none shall breathe a sigh for me!

My life is like the prints which feet
  Have left on Tampa's desert strand;
Soon as the rising tide shall beat,
  All trace will vanish from the sand;
Yet, as if grieving to efface
All vestige of the human race,
On that lone shore loud moans the sea,—
But none, alas! shall mourn for me!

RICHARD HENRY WILDE.

"Night is the time for toil,
To plough the classic field."

NIGHT.

IGHT is the time for rest;
  How sweet when labors close,
To gather round an aching breast
  The curtain of repose;
Stretch the tired limbs and lay the head
Upon our own delightful bed!

Night is the time for dreams;
  The gay romance of life,
When truth that is, and truth that seems,
  Blend in fantastic strife;
Ah! visions less beguiling far
Than waking dreams by daylight are.

Night is the time for toil;
  To plough the classic field,
Intent to find the buried spoil
  Its wealthy furrows yield;
Till all is ours that sages taught,
That poets sang, or heroes wrought.

Night is the time to weep;
  To wet with unseen tears
Those graves of memory, where sleep
  The joys of other years;
Hopes that were angels in their birth,
But perished young, like things of earth!

Night is the time to watch;
　O'er ocean's dark expanse,
To hail the Pleaides, or catch
　The full moon's earliest glance,
That brings unto the homesick mind
All we have loved and left behind.

Night is the time for care;
　Brooding on hours misspent,
To see the spectre of despair

Beyond the starry pole,
Descries athwart the abyss of night
The dawn of uncreated light.

Night is the time to pray;
　Out Saviour oft withdrew
To desert mountains far away,—
　So will his followers do;
Steal from the throng to haunts untrod,
And hold communion with their God.

"Night is the time to watch,
O'er ocean's dark expanse."

Come to our lonely tent:
Like Brutus, midst his slumbering host,
Startled by Cæsar's stalwart ghost.

Night is the time to muse;
　Then from the eye the soul
Takes flight, and with expanding views

Night is the time for death;
　When all around is peace,
Calmly to yield the weary breath,—
　From sin and suffering cease:—
Think of heaven's bliss, and give the sign
To parting friends:—such death be mine,
　　　　　　　JAMES MONTGOMERY.

MAJESTIC Night!
Nature's great ancestor! day's elder born!
And fated to survive the transient sun!
By mortals and immortals seen with awe:
A starry crown thy raven brow adorns,
An azure zone thy waist; clouds, in heaven's
　　loom
Wrought through varieties of shape and shade,

In ample folds of drapery divine,
Thy flowing mantle form and, heaven throughout,
Voluminously pour thy pompous train:
Thy gloomy grandeurs—Nature's most august,
Inspiring aspect!—claim a grateful verse;
And, like a sable curtain starred with gold.
Drawn o'er my labors past, shall close the scene.

BREAK, BREAK, BREAK.

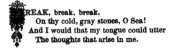

BREAK, break, break,
  On thy cold, gray stones, O Sea!
And I would that my tongue could utter
  The thoughts that arise in me.

And the stately ships go on
  To their haven under the hill;
But O for the touch of a vanished hand,
  And the sound of a voice that is still!

"Break, break, break,
On thy cold, gray stones, O Sea!"

O well for the fisherman's boy,
  That he shouts with his sister at play!
O well for the sailor lad,
  That he sings in his boat on the bay.

Break, break, break,
  At the foot of thy crags, O Sea!
But the tender grace of a day that is dead
  Will never come back to me.

ALFRED TENNYSON.

REFLECTIONS IN WESTMINSTER ABBEY.

WHEN I look upon the tombs of the great, every emotion of envy dies in me; when I read the epitaphs of the beautiful, every inordinate desire goes out; when I meet with the grief of parents upon a tombstone, my heart melts with compassion; when I see the tomb of the parents themselves, I consider the vanity of grieving for those whom we must quickly follow. When I see kings lying by those who deposed them, when I consider rival wits placed side by side, or the holy men that divided the world with their contests and disputes, I reflect with sorrow and astonishment on the little competitions, factions, and debates of mankind. When I read the several dates of the tombs, of some that died yesterday, and some six hundred years ago, I consider that great day when we shall all of us be contemporaries, and make our appearance together.

JOSEPH ADDISON.

BUGLE-SONG.

THE splendor falls on castle walls
  And snowy summits old in story;
  The long light shakes across the lakes,
  And the wild cataract leaps in glory.
Blow, bugle, blow, set the wild echoes flying,
Blow, bugle; answer, echoes, dying, dying,
    dying.

The horns of Elfland faintly blowing!
Blow, let us hear the purple glens replying;
Blow, bugle; answer, echoes, dying, dying, dying.

O love, they die in yon rich sky,
  They faint on hill, or field, or river;
Our echoes roll from soul to soul,

" The splendor falls on castle walls,
And snowy summits old in story."

O, hark! O, hear how thin and clear,
  And thinner, clearer, farther going!
O, sweet and far from cliff and scar

And grow forever and forever.
Blow, bugle, blow, set the wild echoes flying,
And answer, echoes, answer, dying, dying, dying.
             ALFRED TENNYSON.

WHERE the owner of the house is bountiful, it is not for the steward to be niggardly.

THOSE EVENING BELLS.

THOSE evening bells! those evening bells!
How many a tale their music tells
Of youth and home, and that sweet time
When last I heard their soothing chime!

Those joyous hours are passed away;
And many a heart that then was gay

Within the tomb now darkly dwells,
And hears no more those evening bells.

And so 't will be when I am gone.—
That tuneful peal will still ring on;
While other bards shall walk these dells,
And sing your praise, sweet evening bells.

THOMAS MOORE.

"— Its gnarled oaks olden,
Dark with the mistletoe."

PICTURES OF MEMORY.

AMONG the beautiful pictures
That hang on Memory's wall,
Is one of a dim old forest,
That seemeth best of all;

Not for its gnarled oaks olden,
Dark with the mistletoe;
Not for the violets golden
That sprinkle the vale below;

Not for the milk-white lilies
  That lean from the fragrant ledge,
Coquetting all day with the sunbeams,
  And stealing their golden edge;
Not for the vines on the upland,
  Where the bright red berries rest,
Nor the pinks, nor the pale sweet cowslip,
  It seemeth to me the best.

I once had a little brother,
  With eyes that were dark and deep;
In the lap of that old dim forest
  He lieth in peace asleep:
Light as the down of the thistle,
  Free as the winds that blow,
We roved there the beautiful summers,
  The summers of long ago;
But his feet on the hills grew weary,
  And one of the autumn eves,
I made for my little brother
  A bed of the yellow leaves.
Sweetly his pale arms folded
  My neck in a meek embrace,

As the light of immortal beauty
  Silently covered his face;
And when the arrows of sunset
  Lodged in the tree-tops bright.
He fell, in his saint-like beauty,
  Asleep by the gates of light.

"Light as the down of the thistle,
Free as the winds that blow."

Therefore of all the pictures
That hang on Memory's wall,
The one of the dim old forest
Seemeth the best of all.

          ALICE CARY.

THE DIVINITY OF POETRY.

POETRY is the record of the best and happiest moments of the happiest and best minds. We are aware of evanescent visitations of thought and feeling, sometimes associated with place or person, sometimes regarding our own mind alone, and always arising unforeseen and departing unbidden, but elevating and delightful beyond all expression; so that, even in the desire and the regret they leave, there cannot but be pleasure, participating as it does in the nature of its object. It is, as it were, the interpenetration of a diviner nature through our own; but its footsteps are like those of a wind over the sea, which the morning calm erases, and whose traces remain only, as on the wrinkled sand which paves it. These and corresponding conditions of being are experienced principally by those of the most delicate sensibility and the most enlarged imagination; and the state of mind produced by them is at war with every base desire. The enthusiasm of virtue, love, patriotism, and friendship, is essentially linked with such emotions; and whilst they last, self appears as what it is, an atom to a universe. Poets are not only subject to these experiences as spirits of the most refined organization, but they can color all that they combine with the evanescent hues of this ethereal world; a word, a trait in the representation of a scene or passion, will touch the enchanted chord, and reanimate, in those who have ever experienced those emotions, the sleeping, the cold, the buried image of the past. Poetry thus makes immortal all that is best and most beautiful in the world; it arrests the vanishing apparitions which haunt the interlunations of life, and veiling them, or in language or in form, sends them forth among mankind, bearing sweet news of kindred joy to those with whom their sisters abide—abide, because there is no portal of expressions from the caverns of the spirit which they inhabit into the universe of things. Poetry redeems from decay the visitations of the divinity in man.

          PERCY BYSSHE SHELLEY.

THE LESSON OF THE WATER-MILL.

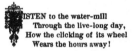

ISTEN to the water-mill
Through the live-long day,
How the clicking of its wheel
Wears the hours away!

And a proverb haunts my mind
As a spell is cast:
" The mill cannot grind
With the water that is past."

" From the field the reapers sing,
Binding up the sheaves."

Languidly the autumn wind
Stirs the forest leaves,
From the fields the reapers sing,
Binding up the sheaves;

Autumn winds revive no more
Leaves that once are shed,
And the sickle cannot reap
Corn once gathered;

Flows the ruffled streamlet on,
　Tranquil, deep and still;
Never gliding back again
　To the water-mill;
Truly speaks that proverb old
　With a meaning vast —
" The mill cannot grind
　With the water that is past."

Take the lesson to thyself,
　True and loving heart;
Golden youth is fleeting by,
　Summer hours depart;
Learn to make the most of life,
　Lose no happy day,
Time will never bring thee back,
　Chances swept away!
Leave no tender word unsaid,
　Love, while love shall last;
" The mill cannot grind
　With the water that is past."

Work while yet the daylight shines,
　Man of strength and will!
Never does the streamlet glide
　Useless by the mill;
Wait not till to-morrow's sun
　Beams upon thy way,
All that thou canst call thine own
　Lies in thy "to-day;"
Power and intellect and health
　May not always last;
"The mill cannot grind
　With the water that is past."

Oh, the wasted hours of life
　That have drifted by!
Oh, the good that might have been,
　Lost without a sigh!

Love that we might once have saved
　By a single word.
Thoughts conceived but never penned,
　Perishing unheard ·

" Listen to the watermill,
Through the livelong day."

Take the proverb to thine heart,
　Take and hold it fast,
" The mill cannot grind
　With the water that is past."

　　　　　　　SARAH DOUDNEY.

A HUNDRED YEARS TO COME.

H, where will be the birds that sing,
　A hundred years to come? ,
The flowers that now in beauty spring,
　A hundred years to come?
The rosy lip, the lofty brow,
The heart that beats so gaily now,
Oh, where will be love's beaming eye,
Joys pleasant smile, and sorrow's sigh,
　A hundred years to come?

Who 'll press for gold this crowded street,
　A hundred years to come?
Who 'll tread yon church with willing feet,
　A hundred years to come?

Pale, trembling age, and fiery youth,
And childhood with its brow of truth;
The rich and poor, on land and sea,
Where will the mighty millions be
　A hundred years to come?

We all within our graves shall sleep
　A hundred years to come!
No living soul for us will weep
　A hundred years to come!
But other men our lands shall till,
And others then our streets will fill,
While other birds will sing as gay,
As bright the sunshine as to-day
　A hundred years to come!

　　　　　　　WILLIAM GOLDSMITH

22

THE TWO WEAVERS.

S at their work two weavers sat,
　Beguiling time with friendly chat,
　They touched upon the price of meat,
　So high a weaver scarce could eat.

"In spite of all the Scripture teaches,
In spite of all the pulpit preaches,
The world, indeed I 've thought so long,
Is ruled, methinks, extremely wrong.

"Quoth John, 'Our ignorance is the cause
Why thus we blame our Maker's laws.'"

"What with my babes and sickly wife,"
Quoth James. "I 'm almost tired of life.
So hard we work, so poor we fare,
'T is more than mortal man can bear.

"How glorious is the rich man's state,
His house so fine, his wealth so great;
Heaven is unjust, you must agree:
Why all to him, and none to me?

"Where'er I look, howe'er I range.
'T is all confused, and hard, and strange:
The good are troubled and opprest,
And all the wicked are the blest."

Quoth John, "Our ignorance is the cause
Why thus we blame our Maker's laws;
Parts of His ways alone we know,
'Tis all that man can see below.

"See'st thou that carpet, not half done,
Which thou, dear James, hast well begun?
Behold the wild confusion there!
So rude the mass, it makes one stare.

"A stranger, ignorant of the trade,
Would say no meaning's there conveyed;
For where's the middle, where's the border?
The carpet now is all disorder."

Quoth James, "My work is yet in bits,
But still in every part it fits;
Besides, you reason like a lout,
Why, man, that carpet's inside out!"

Says John "Thou say'st the thing I mean,
And now I hope to cure thy spleen:
The world, which clouds thy soul with
        doubt,
Is but a carpet inside out.

"As when we view these shreds and ends,
We know not what the whole intends;

So when on earth things look but odd,
They're working still some scheme of God.

"No plan, no pattern can we trace;
All wants proportion, truth, and grace;
The motley mixture we deride,
Nor see the beauteous upper side.

"But when we reach the world of light,
And view these works of God aright,
Then shall we see the whole design,
And own the Workman is divine.

"What now seem random strokes, will there
All order and design appear;
Then shall we praise what here we spurned,
For there the carpet will be turned."

"Thou'rt right," quoth James, "no more I'll
        grumble,
That this world is so strange a jumble;
My impious doubts are put to flight,
For my own carpet sets me right.
                        HANNAH MORE.

APPLE BLOSSOMS.

PLUCKED pink blossoms from my Apple-tree,
    And wore them all that evening in my hair;
Then in due season when I went to see,
    I found no apples there.

With dangling basket all along the grass,
    As I had come, I went the self-same track,
My neighbors mocked me when they saw me pass
    So empty-handed back.

Lilian and Lilias smiled in trudging by,
    Their heaped-up baskets teased me like a jeer;
Sweet-voiced they sang beneath the summer sky—
    Their mother's home was near.

Plump Gertrude passed me with her basket full;
    A stronger hand than hers helped it along;

A voice talked with her through the shadows cool,
    More sweet to me than song.

Ah, Willie, Willie! was my love less worth
    Than apples with their green leaves piled above?
I counted rosiest apples on the earth
    Of far less worth than love.

So once it was with me you stopped to talk,
    Laughing and listening in this very lane:—
To think that by these ways we used to walk
    We shall not walk again!

I let my neighbors pass me, ones and twos
    And groups; the latest said the night grew chill,
And hastened; but I lingered; while the dews
    Fell fast; I lingered still.

JUNE.

GAZED upon the glorious sky,
    And the green mountains round,
And thought that when I came to lie
    At rest within the ground,
'Twere pleasant that in flowery June,
When brooks send up a cheerful tune,
    And groves a joyous sound,
The sexton's hand, my grave to make,
The rich, green mountain turf should break.

A cell within the frozen mould,
    A coffin borne through sleet,
And icy clods above it rolled,
    While fierce the tempests beat —
Away! I will not think of these;
Blue be the sky and soft the breeze,
    Earth green beneath the feet,
And be the damp mould gently pressed
Into my narrow place of rest.

There, through the long, long summer hours
  The golden light should lie,
And thick young herbs and groups of flowers
  Stand in their beauty by.
The oriole should build and tell
His love-tale close beside my cell;
  The idle butterfly
Should rest him there, and there be heard
The housewife bee and humming-bird.

I know that I no more should see
  The season's glorious show,
Nor would its brightness shine for me,
  Nor its wild music flow;
But if, around my place of sleep
The friends I love should come to weep,
  They might not haste to go;
Soft airs, and song, and light and bloom
Should keep them lingering by my tomb.

" And what if, in the evening light,
Betrothéd lovers walk in sight,
    Of my low monument?"

And what if cheerful shouts at noon
  Come, from the village sent,
Or song of maids beneath the moon
  With fairy laughter blent?
And what if, in the evening light,
Betrothéd lovers walk in sight
  Of my low monument?
I would the lovely scene around
Might know no sadder sight nor sound.

These to their softened hearts should bear
  The thought of what has been,
And speak of one who cannot share
  The gladness of the scene;
Whose part in all the pomp that fills
The circuit of the summer hills
  Is that his grave is green;
And deeply would their hearts rejoice
To hear again his living voice.

WILLIAM CULLEN BRYANT.

AS every instinct, or sense, has an end or design, and every emotion in man has its object and direction, we must conclude that the desire of communing with God is but a test of his being destined for a future existence, and the longing after immortality the promise of it.

EVENING PRAYER AT A GIRLS' SCHOOL.

USH! 'tis a holy hour—the quiet room
  Seems like a temple, while yon soft lamp sheds
  A faint and starry radiance, through the gloom,
    And the sweet stillness, down on fair young
       heads,
With all their clust'ring locks, untouched by care,
And bowed, as flowers are bowed with night, in
    prayer.

Gaze on—'tis lovely! Childhood's lip and cheek,
  Mantling beneath its earnest brow of thought—
Gaze—yet what seest thou in those fair, and meek
  And fragile things, as but for sunshine wrought?
Thou seest what grief must nurture for the sky.
What death must fashion for Eternity.

Yet in those flute-like voices, mingling low,
Is woman's tenderness,—how soon her woe!

Her lot is on you—silent tears to weep,
  And patient smiles to wear through suffering's
    hour,
And sumless riches, from affection's deep,
  To pour on broken reeds—a wasted shower!
And to make idols, and to find t   clay,
And to bewail that worship,—therefore pray!

Her lot is on you—to be found untired,
  Watching the stars out by the bed of pain,
With a pale cheek, and yet a brow inspired,
  And a true heart of hope, though hope be vain;

"———Fair young heads,
With all their clust'ring locks, untouched by care,
And bowed, as flowers are bowed with night, in prayer."

O joyous creatures! that will sink to rest
  Lightly, when those pure orisons are done.
As birds with slumber's honey-dew opprest,
  'Midst the dim-folded leaves at set of sun—
Lift up your hearts! though yet no sorrow lies
Dark in the summer-heaven of those clear eyes.

Though fresh within your breasts th' untroubled
    springs
  Of hope make melody where'er ye tread.
And o'er your sleep bright shadows, from the wings
  Of spirits visiting but youth, be spread;

Meekly to bear with wrong. to cheer decay,
And oh! to love through all things—therefore pray!

And take the thought of this calm vesper-time,
  With its low murmuring sounds and silvery
    light,
On through the dark days fading from their prime,
  As a sweet dew to keep your souls from blight:
Earth will forsake—O! happy to have given
Th' unbroken heart's first fragrance unto Heaven!

FELICIA DOROTHEA HEMANS.

WHAT IS LIFE?

AND what 's a life? — a weary pilgrimage,
  Whose glory in one day doth fill the stage
  With childhood, manhood, and decrepit age.

And what 's a life? — the flourishing array
  Of the proud summer meadow, which to-day
  Wears her green plush, and is to-morrow hay.

Read on this dial, how the shades devour
My short-lived winter's day! hour eats up hour;
Alas! the total 's but from eight to four.

Behold these lilies, which thy hands have made,
Fair copies of my life, and open laid
To view, how soon they droop, how soon they fade!

Shade not that dial, night will blind too soon;
My non-aged day already points to noon;
How simple is my suit! — how small my boon!

Nor do I beg this slender inch to wile
The time away or falsely to beguile
My thoughts with joy: here 's nothing worth a smile.

FRANCIS QUARLES.

"Yonder a man at the heavens is staring,
Wringing his hands as in sorrowful case."

CALM IS THE NIGHT.

CALM is the night, and the city is sleeping.
  Once in this house dwelt a lady fair;
Long, long ago, she left it, weeping —
  But still the old house is standing there.

Yonder a man at the heavens is staring.
  Wringing his hands as in sorrowful case;

He turns to the moonlight, his countenance baring—
  O Heaven! he shows me my own sad face!

Shadowy form, with my own agreeing!
  Why mockest thou thus, in the moonlight cold,
The sorrows which here once vexed my being,
  Many a night in the days of old?

CHARLES GODFREY LELAND.
[From the German of Heine.]

SONG.

WE sail toward evening's lonely star.
　That trembles in the tender blue;
One single cloud, a dusky bar,
　Burnt with dull carmine through and through,
Slow smouldering in the summer sky,
　Lies low along the fading west;
How sweet to watch its splendors die,
　Wave-cradled thus, and wind caressed!

The soft breeze freshens; leaps the spray
　To kiss our cheeks with sudden cheer;
Upon the dark edge of the bay
　Light-houses kindle far and near,

And through the warm deeps of the sky
　Steal faint star-clusters, while we rest
In deep refreshment, thou and I,
　Wave-cradled thus, and wind-caressed.

How like a dream are earth and heaven,
　Star-beam and darkness, sky and sea;
Thy face, pale in the shadowy even,
　Thy quiet eyes that gaze on me!
Oh, realize the moment's charm,
　Thou dearest! We are at life's best,
Folded in God's encircling arm,
　Wave-cradled thus. and wind-caressed!

CELIA THAXTER.

"Over the flowery lawn,
Maids are at play."

MAY.

HAS the old glory passed
　From tender May—
That never the echoing blast
Of bugle-horns merry, and fast
Dying away like the past,
　Welcomes the day?

Has the old Beauty gone
　From golden May—
That not any more at dawn

Over the flowery lawn,
Or knolls of the forest withdrawn,
　Maids are at play?

Is the old freshness dead
　Of the fairy May?—
Ah! the sad tear-drops unshed!
Ah! the young maidens unwed!
Golden locks—cheeks rosy red!
　Ah! where are they?

JOHN ESTEN COOKE.

PLEASURES OF MEMORY.

TWILIGHT'S soft dews steal o'er the village green,
With magic tints to harmonize the scene.
Stilled is the hum that through the hamlet broke,
When round the ruins of their ancient oak
The peasants flocked to hear the minstrel play,
And games and carols closed the busy day.
Her wheel at rest, the matron thrills no more
With treasured tales and legendary lore.
All, all are fled; nor mirth nor music flows
To chase the dreams of innocent repose.
All, all are fled; yet still I linger here!
What secret charms this silent spot endear?

As o'er my palm the silver piece she drew,
And traced the line of life with searching view,
How throbbed my fluttering pulse with hopes and
    fears,
To learn the color of my future years!

    *   *   *   *   *   *

Lulled in the countless chambers of the brain,
Our thoughts are linked by many a hidden chain.
Awake but one, and, lo! what myriads rise!
Each stamps its image as the other flies.
Each, as the various avenues of sense
Delight or sorrow to the soul dispense,

"With treasured tales and legendary lore."

Mark yon old mansion frowning through the trees,
Whose hollow turret wooes the whistling breeze.
That casement, arched with ivy 's brownest shade,
First to these eyes the light of heaven conveyed.
The mouldering gateway strews the grass-grown
    court,
Once the calm scene of many a simple sport;
When all things pleased. for life itself was new,
And the heart promised what the fancy drew.

    *   *   *   *   *   *

Down by yon hazel copse, at evening, blazed
The gypsy 's fagot,— there we sat and gazed;
Gazed on her sunburnt face with silent awe,
Her tattered mantle, and her hood of straw.

Brightens or fades; yet all, with magic art,
Control the latent fibres of the heart.
As studious Prospero's mysterious spell
Drew every subject-spirit to his cell;
Each, at thy call advances or retires,
As judgment dictates or the scene inspires.
Each thrills the seat of sense, that sacred source
Whence the fine nerves direct their mazy course,
And through the frame invisibly convey
The subtle, quick vibrations as they play;
Man's little universe at once o'ercast.
At once illumined when the cloud is past.

    *   *   *   *   *   *   *

Hark! the bee winds her small but mellow horn,
Blithe to salute the sunny smile of morn.
O'er thymy downs she bends her busy course,
And many a stream allures her to its source.
'Tis noon, 'tis night. That eye so finely wrought,
Beyond the search of sense, the soar of thought,
Now vainly asks the scenes she left behind;
Its orb so full, its vision so confined!
Who guides the patient pilgrim to her cell?
Who bids her soul with conscious triumph swell?
With conscious truth retrace the mazy clew
Of summer-scents, that charmed her as she flew?
Hail, Memory, hail! thy universal reign
Guards the least link of Being's glorious chain.

*   *   *   *   *   *   *

To meet the changes time and chance present
With modest dignity and calm content.
When thy last breath, ere nature sunk to rest,
Thy meek submission to thy God expressed;
When thy last look, ere thought and feeling fled,
A mingled gleam of hope and triumph shed;
What to thy soul its glad assurance gave,
Its hope in death, its triumph o'er the grave?
The sweet remembrance of unblemished youth, ·
The still inspiring voice of Innocence and Truth!
Hail, Memory, hail! In thy exhaustless mine
From age to age unnumbered treasures shine!
Thought and her shadowy brood thy call obey,
And place and time are subject to thy sway!

" The mouldering gateway strews the grass-grown court."

O thou! with whom my heart was wont to share
From reason's dawn each pleasure and each care;
With whom, alas! I fondly hoped to know
The humble walks of happiness below;
If thy blest nature now unites above
An angel's pity with a brother's love,
Still o'er my life preserve thy mild control,
Correct my views, and elevate my soul;
Grant me thy peace and purity of mind,
Devout yet cheerful, active yet resigned;
Grant me, like thee, whose heart knew no disguise,
Whose blameless wishes never aimed to rise,

Thy pleasures most we feel when most alone;
The only pleasures we can call our own.
Lighter than air. hope's summer-visions die,
If but a fleeting cloud obscure the sky;
If but a beam of sober reason play,
Lo! fancy's fairy frost-work melts away!
But can the wiles of art, the grasp of power,
Snatch the rich relics of a well-spent hour?
These, when the trembling spirit wings her flight,
Pour round her path a stream of living light;
And gild those pure and perfect realms of rest,
Where Virtue triumphs, and her sons are blest!

SAMUEL ROGERS.

A JOY FOREVER.

THING of beauty is a joy forever:
Its loveliness increases; it will never
Pass into nothingness; but still will keep
A bower quiet for us, and a sleep
Full of sweet dreams, and health, and quiet
    breathing.
  Therefore, on every morrow are we wreathing
A flowery band to bind us to the earth,
Spite of despondence, of the inhuman dearth
Of noble natures, of the gloomy days,
Of all the unhealthy and o'er-darkened ways
Made for our searching; yes, in spite of all,
Some shape of beauty moves away the pall

From our dark spirits. Such the sun, the moon,
Trees old and young, sprouting a shady boon
For simple sheep; and such are daffodils
With the green world they live in; and clear rills
That for themselves a cooling covert make
'Gainst the hot season; the mid-forest brake,
Rich with a sprinkling of fair musk-rose blooms:
And such too is the grandeur of the dooms
We have imagined for the mighty dead;
All lovely tales that we have heard or read:
An endless fountain of immortal drink,
Pouring unto us from the Heaven's brink.

                                 JOHN KEATS.

'TIS THE LAST ROSE OF SUMMER.

IS the last rose of summer
  Left blooming alone;
All her lovely companions
  Are faded and gone;
No flower of her kindred,
  No rosebud is nigh,
To reflect back her blushes,
  To give sigh for sigh.

I 'll not leave thee, thou lone one,
  To pine on the stem;
Since the lovely are sleeping,
  Go sleep thou with them.

Thus kindly I scatter
  Thy leaves o'er the bed,
Where thy mates of the garden
  Lie scentless and dead.

So soon may I follow,
  When friendships decay,
And from Love's shining circle
  The gems drop away!
When true hearts lie withered
  And fond ones are flown,
Oh! who would inhabit
  This bleak world alone?

                                 THOMAS MOORE.

THE ISLE OF THE LONG AGO.

H, a wonderful stream is the River Time,
  As it flows through the realm of Tears,
With a faultless rhythm and a musical rhyme,
And a broader sweep and a surge sublime
  As it blends with the ocean of Years.

How the winters are drifting like flakes of snow
  And the summers like buds between;
And the year in the sheaf—so they come and they go
On the River's breast with its ebb and flow,
  As they glide in the shadow and sheen.

There 's a magical Isle up the River Time
  Where the softest of airs are playing;
There 's a cloudless sky and a tropical clime,
And a voice as sweet as a vesper chime,
  And the Junes with the roses are staying

And the name of this Isle is the Long Ago,
  And we bury our treasures there;

There are brows of beauty and bosoms of snow—
  They are heaps of dust, but we loved them so!
  There are trinkets and tresses of hair.

There are fragments of song that nobody sings,
  And a part of an infant's prayer,
There 's a harp unswept and a lute without strings,
There are broken vows and pieces of rings,
  And the garments that she used to wear.

There are hands that are waved when the fairy shore
  By the mirage is lifted in air;
And we sometimes hear through the turbulent roar
Sweet voices we heard in the days gone before,
  When the wind down the River is fair.

Oh, remembered for aye be the blessed Isle
  All the day of our life till night.
And when evening comes with its beautiful smile,
And our eyes are closing in slumber awhile,
  May that "GREENWOOD" of soul be in sight.

                            BENJAMIN F. TAYLOR.

HOPE.

AT summer eve, when Heaven's ethereal bow
Spans with bright arch the glittering hills below,
Why to yon mountain turns the musing eye,
Whose sun-bright summit mingles with the sky?
Why do those cliffs of shadowy tint appear
More sweet than all the landscape smiling near?
'Tis distance lends enchantment to the view,
And robes the mountain in its azure hue.
Thus, with delight, we linger to survey
The promised joys of life's unmeasured way;
Thus, from afar, each dim-discovered scene
More pleasing seems than all the past hath been,

And every form, that Fancy can repair
From dark oblivion, glows divinely there.

* * * * * *

Eternal Hope! when yonder spheres sublime
Pealed their first notes to sound the march of Time,
Thy joyous youth began, — but not to fade.
When all the sister planets have decayed;
When wrapt in fire the realms of ether glow,
And Heaven's last thunder shakes the world below;
Thou, undismayed, shalt o'er the ruins smile,
And light thy torch at Nature's funeral pile.

THOMAS CAMPBELL.

TO A CHILD.

OH, while from me, this tender morn depart
Dreams, vague and vain and wild,
Sing, happy child, and dance into my heart,
Where I was once a child.

Your eyes they send the butterflies before.
Your lips they kiss the rose;
O gentle child, joy opes your morning door —
Joy blesses your repose!

The fairy Echo-Children love you, try
To steal your loving voice;
Flying you laugh — they, laughing while you fly,
Gay with your glee rejoice.

Oh, while from me, this tender morn depart
Dreams vague and vain and wild,
Play, happy child — sing, dance, within my heart,
Where I will be a child!

JOHN JAMES PIATT.

SONNET.

AY follows day; years perish; still mine eyes
Are opened on the self-same round of space;
Yon fadeless forests in their Titan grace,
And the large splendors of those opulent skies.
I watch, unwearied, the miraculous dyes
Of dawn or sunset; the soft boughs which lace
Round some coy Dryad in a lonely place,
Thrilled with low whispering and strange sylvan sighs:

His clear child's soul finds something sweet and new
Even in a weed's heart, the carved leaves of corn
The spear-like grass, the silvery rime of morn,
A cloud rose-edged, and fleeting stars at night!

PAUL HAMILTON HAYNE

"Yon fadeless forests in their Titan grace."

Weary! The poet's mind is fresh as dew,
And oft refilled as fountains of the light.

LIFE'S INCONGRUITIES.

REEN grows the laurel on the bank,
Dark waves the pine upon the hill,
Green hangs the lichen, cold and dank,
Dark springs the hearts-ease by the rill,
Age-mosses clamber ever bright,
Pale is the water-lily's bloom:
Thus life still courts the shades of night,
And beauty hovers o'er the tomb.

So, all through life, incongruous hue
Each object wears from childhood down;
The evanescent — heaven's blue,
The all-enduring — sober brown;
Our brightest dreams too quickly die,
And griefs are green that should be old,
And joys that sparkle to the eye
Are like a tale that's quickly told.

And yet 'tis but the golden mean
That checks our lives' unsteady flow;
God's counterbalance thrown between,
To poise the scale 'twixt joy and woe:
And better so; for were the bowl
Too freely to the parched lip given,
Too much of grief would crush the soul,
Too much of joy would wean from heaven.

EGBERT PHELPS.

EQUINOCTIAL.

HE sun of life has crossed the line;
The summer-shine of lengthened light
Faded and failed—till, where I stand,
'Tis equal day and equal night.

One after one as dwindling hours,
Youth's glowing hopes have dropped away,
And soon may barely leave the gleam
That coldly scores a winter's day.

I am not young—I am not old;
The flush of morn, the sunset calm,
Paling and deepening, each to each,
Meet midway with a solemn charm.

One side I see the summer fields,
Not yet disrobed of all their green;
While westerly, along the hills,
Flame the first tints of frosty sheen.

Ah, middle-point, where cloud and storm
Make battle-ground of this my life!
Where, even matched, the night and day
Wage round me their September strife.

I bow me to the threatening gale:
I know when that is overpast,
Among the peaceful harvest days
An Indian Summer comes at last.

MRS. A. D. T. WHITNEY.

CIRCUMSTANCE.

TWO children in two neighbor villages
Playing mad pranks along the healthy leas;
Two strangers meeting at a festival;
Two lovers whispering by an orchard wall;
Two lives bound fast in one with golden ease;

Two graves grass-green beside a gray church-tower,
Washed with still rains and daisy-blossomed;
Two children in one hamlet born and bred;
So runs the round of life from hour to hour.

ALFRED TENNYSON.

"The nightingale, whose melody is through the green-wood ringing."

THE ROSE UPON MY BALCONY.

THE rose upon my balcony, the morning air perfuming,
Was leafless all the winter-time and pining for the spring;
You ask me why her breath is sweet, and why her cheek is blooming:
It is because the sun is out and birds begin to sing.

The nightingale, whose melody is through the greenwood ringing,
Was silent when the boughs were bare and winds were blowing keen.

And if, Mamma, you ask of me the reason of his singing,
It is because the sun is out and all the leaves are green.

Thus each performs his part, Mamma: the birds have found their voices,
The blowing rose a flush, Mamma, her bonny cheek to dye;
And there's sunshine in my heart, Mamma, which wakens and rejoices.
And so I sing and blush, Mamma, and that 's the reason why.

WILLIAM MAKEPEACE THACKERAY.

THE DEATH OF THE OLD YEAR.

FULL knee-deep lies the winter snow,
And the winter winds are wearily sighing:
Toll ye the church-bell sad and slow.
And tread softly and speak low,
For the old year lies a-dying.

He was full of joke and jest,
But all his merry quips are o'er.
To see him die, across the waste
His son and heir doth ride post-haste,
But he 'll be dead before.

Old year, you must not die;
You came to us so readily,
You lived with us so steadily,
Old year, you shall not die.

He lieth still: he doth not move:
He will not see the dawn of day.
He hath no other life above.
He gave me a friend, and a true true-love,
And the New-year will take 'em away.
Old year, you must not go;
So long as you have been with us,
Such joy as you have seen with us,
Old year, you shall not go.

He frothed his bumpers to the brim;
A jollier year we shall not see.
But, though his eyes are waxing dim,
And though his foes speak ill of him,
He was a friend to me.
Old year, you shall not die;
We did so laugh and cry with you,
I 've half a mind to die with you,
Old year, if you must die.

"Full knee-deep lies the winter snow."

Every one for his own.
The night is starry and cold, my friend,
And the New-year, blithe and bold, my friend,
Comes up to take his own.

How hard he breathes! over the snow
I heard just now the crowing cock.
The shadows flicker to and fro:
The cricket chirps: the light burns low:
'Tis nearly twelve o clock.
  Shake hands before you die.
Old year, we 'll dearly rue for you:
What is it we can do for you?
  Speak out before you die.

His face is growing sharp and thin.
  Alack! our friend is gone.
Close up his eyes: tie up his chin:
Step from the corpse, and let him in
That standeth there alone,
  And waiteth at the door.
There 's a new foot on the floor, my friend,
And a new face at the door, my friend,
  A new face at the door.

           ALFRED TENNYSON.

HOPE.

WHAT song is well sung, not of sorrow?
  What triumph well won without pain?
What virtue shall be, and not borrow
  Bright lustre from many a stain?

What birth has there been without travail?
  What battle well won without blood?
What good shall earth see. without evil
  Ingarnered as chaff with the good?

Lo! the Cross set in rocks by the Roman,
  And nourished by blood of the Lamb,
And watered by tears of the woman,
  Has flourished, has spread like a palm;

Has spread in the frosts, and far regions
  Of snows in the North, and South sands,
Where never the tramp of his legions
  Was heard, nor has reached forth his red hands.

Be thankful; the price and the payment,
  The birth, the privations and scorn,
The cross, and the parting of raiment,
  Are finished. The star brought us morn.

Look starward; stand far and unearthy,
  Free-souled as a banner unfurled;
Be worthy, O brother, be worthy!
  For a God was the price of the world.

           JOAQUIN MILLER.

ALAS! HOW LIGHT A CAUSE MAY MOVE.

ALAS! how light a cause may move
Dissension between hearts that love!
Hearts that the world in vain has tried,
And sorrow but more closely tied;
That stood the storm when waves were rough,
Yet in a sunny hour fall off,
Like ships that have gone down at sea,
When heaven was all tranquillity!

A something light as air, — a look,
  A word unkind or wrongly taken, —
O, love that tempests never shook,
  A breath. a touch like this has shaken!
And ruder words will soon rush in
To spread the breach that words begin;
And eyes forget the gentle ray
They wore in courtship's smiling day;
And voices lose the tone that shed
A tenderness round all they said;
Till fast declining, one by one,
The sweetnesses of love are gone,

And hearts, so lately mingled. seem
Like broken clouds, — or like the stream,
That smiling left the mountain's brow,
  As though its waters ne'er could sever,
Yet, ere it reach the plain below,
  Breaks into floods that part forever.

O you, that have the charge of Love,
  Keep him in rosy bondage bound,
As in the Fields of Bliss above
  He sits, with flowerets fettered round; —
Loose not a tie that round him clings,
Nor ever let him use his wings;
For even an hour, a minute's flight
Will rob the plumes of half their light.
Like that celestial bird, — whose nest
Is found beneath far Eastern skies, —
Whose wings, though radiant when at rest, —
Lose all their glory when he flies!

           THOMAS MOORE.

REASON as the princess, dwells in the highest and inwardest room; the senses are the guards and attendants on the court, without whose aid nothing is admitted into the presence; the supreme faculties are the Peers; the outward parts and inward affections are the Commons.

THE LIBRARY.

MY days among the dead are pass'd;
   Around me I behold,
Where'er these casual eyes are cast,
   The mighty minds of old;
My never-failing friends are they
With whom I converse night and day.

My thoughts are with the dead, with them
   I live in long-past years,
Their virtues love, their faults condemn,
   Partake their griefs and fears;
And from their sober lessons find
Instruction with a humble mind.

"With them I take delight in weal,
And seek relief in woe."

With them I take delight in weal,
   And seek relief in woe;
And while I understand and feel
   How much to them I owe,
My cheeks have often been bedewed
With tears of thoughtful gratitude.

My hopes are with the dead: anon
   With them my place will be;
And I with them shall travel on
   Through all futurity;
Yet leaving here a name, I trust,
Which will not perish in the dust.

ROBERT SOUTHEY.

WOODMAN, SPARE THAT TREE.

WOODMAN, spare that tree!
  Touch not a single bough!
In youth it sheltered me,
  And I 'll protect it now.
'T was my forefather's hand
  That placed it near his cot;
There, woodman, let it stand,
  Thy axe shall harm it not!

When but an idle boy
  I sought its grateful shade;
In all their gushing joy
  Here too my sisters played.
My mother kissed me here;
  My father pressed my hand—
Forgive this foolish tear,
  But let that old oak stand!

" When but an idle boy
  I sought its grateful shade;
In all their gushing joy
  Here too my sisters played."

That old familiar tree,
  Whose glory and renown
Are spread o'er land and sea:
  And would'st thou hew it down?
Woodman, forbear thy stroke!
  Cut not its earth-bound ties;
Oh, spare that aged oak,
  Now towering to the skies!

My heart-strings round thee cling,
  Close as thy bark, old friend!
Here shall the wild-bird sing,
  And still thy branches bend.
Old tree! the storm still brave!
  And, woodman. leave the spot;
While I 've a hand to save,
  Thy ax shall harm it not.

GEORGE P. MORRIS.

SMALL BEGINNINGS.

TRAVELER through a dusty road strewed
    acorns on the lea,
And one took root and sprouted up, and grew
    into a tree.
  Love sought its shade, at evening time, to
    breathe its early vows:
And age was pleased, in heats of noon, to bask be-
    neath its boughs;

He walled it in, and hung with care a ladle at the
    brink,
He thought not of the deed he did, but judged that
    toil might drink.
He passed again, and lo! the well, by summers never
    dried,
Had cooled ten thousand parching tongues, and saved
    a life beside.

"It stood a glory in its place,
A blessing evermore."

The dormouse loved its dangling twigs, the birds
    sweet music bore;
It stood a glory in its place, a blessing evermore.

A little spring had lost its way amid the grass and
    fern,
A passing stranger scooped a well, where weary men
    might turn;

A dreamer dropped a random thought; 't was old,
    and yet 't was new;
A simple fancy of the brain. but strong in being
    true.
It shone upon a genial mind, and lo! its light
    became
A lamp of life, a beacon ray, a monitory flame.

The thought was small; its issue great; a watch-fire
    on the hill,
It sheds its radiance far adown, and cheers the valley
    still!

A nameless man, amid a crowd that thronged the
    daily mart,
Let fall a word of Hope and Love, unstudied, from
    the heart;

A whisper on the tumult thrown, — a transitory
    breath,—
It raised a brother from the dust; it saved a soul from
    death.
O germ! O fount! O word of love! O thought at ran-
    dom cast!
Ye were but little at the first, but mighty at the last.

CHARLES MACKAY.

SONG.

SPIRIT of the Summer-time!
  Bring back the roses to the dells;
The swallow from her distant clime,
  The honey-bee from drowsy cells.

Bring back the friendship of the sun;
  The gilded evenings, calm and late,

When merry children homeward run,
  And peeping stars bid lovers wait.

Bring back the singing; and the scent
  Of meadow-lands at dewy prime;—
Oh bring again my heart's content,
  Thou Spirit of the Summer-time!

WILLIAM ALLINGHAM.

THE RIVER.

GRANDLY flowing River!
O silver-gliding River!
Thy springing willows shiver
  In the sunset as of old;
They shiver in the silence
Of the willow-whitened islands,
While the sun-bars and the sand-bars
  Fill air and wave with gold.

O gray, oblivious River!
O sunset-kindled River!
Do you remember ever
  The eyes and skies so blue

On a summer day that shone here,
When we were all alone here,
And the blue eyes were too wise
  To speak the love they knew?

O stern. impassive River!
O still unanswering River!
The shivering willows quiver
  As the night-winds moan and rave.
From the past a voice is calling,
From heaven a star is falling,
And dew swells in the bluebells
  Above the hillside grave.

JOHN HAY.

HOPE.

IN hope a king doth go to war,
  In hope a lover lives full long;
In hope a merchant sails full far,
  In hope just men do suffer wrong;

In hope the ploughman sows his seed:
Thus hope helps thousands at their need.
Then faint not, heart, among the rest;
Whatever chance, hope thou the best.

RICHARD ALISON.

FIDELITY.

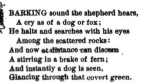

BARKING sound the shepherd hears,
  A cry as of a dog or fox;
He halts and searches with his eyes
  Among the scattered rocks:
And now at distance can discern
A stirring in a brake of fern;
And instantly a dog is seen,
Glancing through that covert green.

It was a cove, a huge recess,
  That keeps till June December's snow;
A lofty precipice in front,
  A silent tarn below!
Far in the bosom of Helvellyn,
Remote from public road or dwelling,
Pathway, or cultivated land,
From trace of human foot or hand.

" The dog had watched about the spot,
    Or by his master's side."

The dog is not of mountain breed;
  Its motions, too, are wild and shy,
With something, as the shepherd thinks,
  Unusual in its cry.
Nor is there any one in sight
All round, in hollow, or on height;
Nor shout, nor whistle, strikes the ear:
What is the creature doing here?

There, sometimes, doth the leaping fish
  Send through the tarn a lonely cheer;
The crag repeats the raven's croak,
  In symphony austere;
Thither the rainbow comes, — the cloud, —
And mists that spread the flying shroud;
And sunbeams, and the sounding blast,
That, if it could, would hurry past;
But that enormous barrier binds it fast.

Not free from boding thoughts, a while
  The shepherd stood; then makes his
    way
Towards the dog, o'er rocks and stones,
  As quickly as he may;
Not far had gone before he found
A human skeleton on the ground!
Th' appalled discoverer, with a sigh,
Looks round to learn the history.

From those abrupt and perilous rocks
  The man had fallen, — that place of fear!
At length, upon the shepherd's mind
  It breaks, and all is clear;
He instantly recalled the name,
And who he was, and whence he came;
Remembered, too, the very day
On which the traveler passed this way.

But hear a wonder, for whose sake
  This lamentable tale I tell!
A lasting monument of words
  This wonder merits well.
The dog. which still was hovering nigh,
Repeating the same timid cry, —
This dog had been, through three months'
    space,
A dweller in that savage place.

Yes, proof was plain, that since that day,
  When this ill-fated traveler died,
The dog had watched about the spot,
  Or by his master's side:
How nourished here, through such long time,
He knows, who gave that love sublime;
And gave that strength of feeling, great
Above all human estimate.

WILLIAM WORDSWORTH.

TOWARD HOME.

BRIGHT flag at yonder tapering mast,
  Fling out your field of azure blue;
Let star and stripe be westward cast,
  And point as freedom's eagle flew!
Strain home! O lithe and quivering spars!
Point home, my country's flag of stars!
My mother, in thy prayer to-night
  There come new words and warmer tears;
On long, long darkness breaks the light,
  Comes home the loved, the lost for years.

Sleep safe, O wave-worn mariner!
  Fear not to-night, or storm or sea:
The ear of heaven bends low to *her!*
  He sails to shore who sails with me.
The wind-tossed spider needs no token
How stands the tree when lightnings blaze;
And, by a thread from heaven unbroken,
  I know my mother lives and prays.

NATHANIEL PARKER WILLIS.

LINES.

WHEN last year the maple bud was swelling,
  When last the crocus bloomed below.
Thy heart to mine its love was telling;
  Thy soul with mine kept ebb and flow;
Again the maple bud is swelling,
  Again the crocus blooms below : —
In heaven thy heart its love is telling,
  But still our souls keep ebb and flow.

When last the April bloom was flinging
  Sweet odors on the air of spring,
In forest aisles thy voice was ringing,
  Where thou didst with the red-bird sing.
Again the April bloom is flinging
  Sweet odors on the air of spring,
But now in heaven thy voice is ringing,
  Where thou dost with the angels sing.

WILLIAM D. GALLAGHER.

A LITTLE WORD IN KINDNESS SPOKEN.

LITTLE word in kindness spoken,
  A motion or a tear,
Has often healed the heart that's broken,
  And made a friend sincere.

A word, a look, has crushed to earth
  Full many a budding flower,

Which, had a smile but owned its birth,
  Would bless life's darkest hour.

Then deem it not an idle thing
  A pleasant word to speak;
The face you wear, the thoughts you bring,
  A heart may heal or break.

COLESWORTHY.

THE WAY TO SING.

THE birds must know. Who wisely sings
          Will sing as they.
The common air has generous wings:
          Songs make their way.

No messenger to run before,
          Devising plan;
No mention of the place, or hour,
          To any man;
No waiting till some sound betrays
          A listening ear;
No different voice, no new delays,
          If steps draw near.

"What bird is that? The song is
          good."
                   And eager eyes
Go peering through the dusky wood
          In glad surprise.

Then, late at night, when by
          his fire,
               The traveler sits,
     Watching the flame grow
          brighter, higher,
          The sweet song flits,
By snatches, through his weary brain,
          To help him rest;
When next he goes that road again,
          An empty nest
On leafless bough will make him sigh:
          "Ah me! last spring,
Just here I heard, in passing by,
          That rare bird sing."

But while he sighs, remembering
          How sweet the song,
The little bird, on tireless wing,
          Is borne along
In other air; and other men,
          With weary feet,
On other roads, the simple strain
          Are finding sweet.

The birds must know. Who wisely sings
          Will sing as they.
The common air has generous wings:
          Songs make their way.

                   HELEN HUNT JACKSON (H. H.).

THE FIRST TRYST.

HE pulls a rose from her rose-tree.
　Kissing its soul to him,—
Far over years, far over dreams
　And tides of chances dim.

He plucks from his heart a poem,
　A flower-sweet messenger,—

Far over years, far over dreams,
　Flutters its soul to her.

These are the world-old lovers,
　Clasped in one twilight's gleam; .
Yet he is but a dream to her,
　And she a poet's dream.

JOHN JAMES PIATT.

" Ye distant spires, ye antique towers,
That crown the watery glade."

ODE ON A DISTANT PROSPECT OF ETON COLLEGE.

E distant spires, ye antique towers,
　That crown the watery glade,
Where grateful Science still adores
　Her Henry's holy shade;
And ye that from the stately brow
Of Windsor's heights the expanse below
　Of grove, of lawn, of mead survey,
Whose turf, whose shade, whose flowers among
Wanders the hoary Thames along
　His silver-winding way :

Ah, happy hills! ah pleasing shade!
　Ah, fields beloved in vain !
Where once my careless childhood strayed,
　A stranger yet to pain !
I feel the gales that from ye blow
A momentary bliss bestow,
　As waving fresh their gladsome wing,
My weary soul they seem to soothe,
And, redolent of joy and youth,
　To breathe a second spring.

Say, Father Thames, for thou hast seen
Full many a sprightly race
Disporting on thy margent green,
The paths of pleasure trace;
Who foremost now delight to cleave,
With pliant arm, thy glassy wave?
The captive linnet which enthrall?
What idle progeny succeed
To chase the rolling circle's speed,
Or urge the flying ball?

While some on earnest business bent
Their murmuring labors ply
'Gainst graver hours that bring constraint
To sweeten liberty:
Some bold adventurers disdain
The limits of their little reign,
And unknown regions dare descry:
Still as they run they look behind,
They hear a voice in every wind,
And snatch a fearful joy.

Gay hope is theirs by fancy fed,
Less pleasing when possest;
The tear forgot as soon as shed,
The sunshine of the breast:
Theirs buxom health of rosy hue,
Wild wit, invention ever new,
And lively cheer of vigor born;
The thoughtless day, the easy night,
The spirits pure, the slumbers light,
That fly the approach of morn.

Alas! regardless of their doom,
The little victims play;
No sense have they of ills to come,
Nor care beyond to-day:
Yet see how all around them wait
The ministers of human fate.
And black Misfortune's baleful train!
Ah, show them where in ambush stand,
To seize their prey, the murderous band!
Ah, tell them they are men!

These shall the fury Passions tear,
The vultures of the mind,
Disdainful Anger, pallid Fear,
And Shame that skulks behind;
Or pining Love shall waste their youth,
Or Jealousy, with rankling tooth,
That inly gnaws the secret heart;
And Envy wan, and faded Care,
Grim-visaged comfortless Despair,
And Sorrow's piercing dart.

Ambition this shall tempt to rise,
Then whirl the wretch from high,
To bitter Scorn a sacrifice,
And grinning Infamy.
The stings of Falsehood those shall try,
And hard Unkindness' altered eye,
That mocks the tear it forced to flow;
And keen Remorse with blood defiled,
And moody Madness laughing wild
Amid severest woe.

Lo! in the vale of years beneath
A grisly troop are seen,
The painful family of Death,
More hideous than their queen:
This racks the joints, this fires the veins,
That every laboring sinew strains.
Those in the deeper vitals rage:
Lo! Poverty, to fill the band,
That numbs the soul with icy hand,
And slow-consuming Age.

To each his sufferings: all are men,
Condemned alike to groan;
The tender for another's pain,
The unfeeling for his own.
Yet, ah! why should they know their fate,
Since sorrow never comes too late,
And happiness too swiftly flies?
Thought would destroy their paradise.
No more: where ignorance is bliss,
'Tis folly to be wise.

THOMAS GRAY.

UPON THE BEACH.

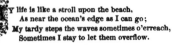

Y life is like a stroll upon the beach,
As near the ocean's edge as I can go;
My tardy steps the waves sometimes o'erreach,
Sometimes I stay to let them overflow.

My sole employment 'tis, and scrupulous care,
To set my gains beyond the reach of tides —
Each smoother pebble, and each shell more rare,
Which ocean kindly to my hand confides.

I have but few companions on the shore,—
They scorn the strand who sail upon the sea;
Yet oft I think the ocean they 've sailed o'er
Is deeper known upon the strand to me.

The middle sea contains no crimson dulse,
Its deeper waves cast up no pearls to view;
Along the shore my hand is on its pulse,
And I converse with many a shipwrecked crew.

HENRY DAVID THOREAU.

SATISFIED.

LIFE is unutterably dear,
   God makes to-day so fair;
Though Heaven is better,—being here
   I long not to be there.

The weights of life are pressing still,
   Not one of them may fall:

Yet such strong joys my spirit fill,
   That I can bear them all.

Though Care and Grief are at my side,
   There would I let them stay,
And still be ever satisfied
   With beautiful To-day!

CHARLOTTE FISKE BATES.

THINK OF ME.

GO where the water glideth gently ever,
   Glideth through meadows that the greenest be;
Go, listen our own beloved river,
      And think of me.

And when the sky is silver-pale at even.
   And the wind grieveth in the lonely tree,
Walk out beneath the solitary heaven,
      And think of me.

"Go where the water glideth gently ever,
Glideth through meadows that the greenest be."

Wander in forests, where the small flower layeth
Its fairy gem beneath the giant tree;
List to the dim brook pining as it playeth,
      And think of me.

And when the moon riseth as she were dreaming,
   And treadeth with white feet the lulléd sea,
Go silent as a star beneath her beaming,
      And think of me.

JOHN HAMILTON REYNOLDS.

ASHES OF ROSES.

SOFT on the sunset sky
   Bright daylight closes.
Leaving when light doth die,
Pale hues that mingling lie—
   Ashes of roses.

When love's warm sun is set,
   Love's brightness closes;
Eyes with hot tears are wet,
In hearts there linger yet
   Ashes of roses.

ELAINE GOODALE.

FOREVER.

THOSE we love truly never die,
  Though year by year the sad memorial wreath,
A ring and flowers, types of life and death,
  Are laid upon their graves.

For death the pure life saves,
And life all pure is love; and love can reach
From heaven to earth, and nobler lessons teach
  Than those by mortals read.

Well blest is he who has a dear one dead:
A friend he has whose face will never change—

A dear communion that will not grow strange;
  The anchor of a love is death.

The blessed sweetness of a loving breath
Will reach our cheek all fresh through weary years.
For her who died long since, ah! waste not tears,
  She 's thine unto the end.

Thank God for one dear friend,
With face still radiant with the light of truth,
Whose love comes laden with the scent of youth,
  Through twenty years of death.
                              JOHN BOYLE O'REILLY.

THE BELLS OF SHANDON.

WITH deep affection
  And recollection
I often think of
    Those Shandon bells,
Whose sounds so wild would,
  In the days of childhood,
Fling round my cradle
    Their magic spells.

On this I ponder
Where'er I wander,
And thus grow fonder,
    Sweet Cork, of thee, —
With thy bells of Shandon,
That sound so grand on
The pleasant waters
    Of the river Lee.

I've heard bells chiming
Full many a clime in,
Tolling sublime in
    Cathedral shrine.
While at a glib rate
Brass tongues would vibrate;
But all their music
    Spoke naught like thine.

For memory, dwelling
On each proud swelling
Of the belfry, knelling
    Its bold notes free,
Made the bells of Shandon
Sound far more grand on
The pleasant waters
    Of the river Lee.

I've heard bells tolling
" Old Adrian's Mole " in,
Their thunder rolling
    From the Vatican,
And cymbals glorious,
Swinging uproarious
In the gorgeous turrets
    Of Nôtre Dame;

But the sounds were sweeter
Than the dome of Peter
Flings o'er the Tiber,
    Pealing solemnly; —
O, the bells of Shandon
Sound far more grand on
The pleasant waters
    Of the river Lee.

There 's a bell in Moscow,
While on tower and kiosk O
In St. Sophia
    The Turkman gets,
And loud in air
Calls men to prayer,
From the tapering summit
    Of tall minarets.

Such empty phantom
I freely grant them;
But there is an anthem
    More dear to me —
'Tis the bells of Shandon,
That sound so grand on
The pleasant waters
    Of the river Lee.
                    FRANCIS MAHONY (Father Prout).

HEARTS THAT HUNGER.

COME hearts go hungering through the world,
  And never find the love they seek;
Some lips with pride or scorn are curled,
  To hide the pain they may not speak;
The eye may flash, the mouth may smile,
  The voice in gladdest music thrill,
And yet beneath them all the while,
  The hungry heart be pining still.

O eager eyes which gaze afar!
  O arms which clasp the empty air.
Not all unmarked your sorrows are,
  Not all unpitied your despair.
Smile, patient lips, so proudly dumb;
  When life's frail tent at last is furled,
Your glorious recompense shall come,
  O hearts that hunger through the world!

"I saw two clouds at morning
Tinged with the rising sun."

I SAW TWO CLOUDS AT MORNING.

I SAW two clouds at morning,
  Tinged with the rising sun,
And in the dawn they floated on,
  And mingled into one;
I thought that morning cloud was blest,
It moved so sweetly to the west.

I saw two summer currents
  Flow smoothly to their meeting,
And join their course, with silent force,
  In peace each other greeting;

Calm was their course through banks of green,
While dimpling eddies played between.

Such be your gentle motion,
  Till life's last pulse shall beat;
Like summer's beam and summer's stream,
  Float on in joy to meet
A calmer sea where storms shall cease,
A purer sky where all is peace.

JOHN G. C. BRAINARD.

SELF-DEPENDENCE.

EARY of myself, and sick of asking
What I am and what I ought to be,
At this vessel's prow I stand, which bears me
Forward, forward, o'er the star-lit sea.

And a look of passionate desire
O'er the sea and to the stars I send .
"Ye who from my childhood have calmed me,
Calm me, ah, compose me to the end!

"Ah, once more," I cried, "ye stars, ye waters,
On my heart your mighty charm renew,
Still, still let me, as I gaze upon you,
Feel my soul becoming vast like you! "

From the intense, clear, star-sown vault of heaven,
Over the lit sea's unquiet way,
In the rustling night-air came the answer:
"Would'st thou be as these are? Live as they.

"Unaffrighted by the silence round them,
Undisturbed by the sights they see,
These demand not that the things without them
Yield them love, amusement, sympathy.

"And with joy the stars perform their shining,
And the sea its long moon-silvered roll,
For self-poised they live, nor pine with noting
All the fever of some differing soul.

"Bounded by themselves, and unregardful
In what state God's other works may be,
On their own tasks all their powers pouring,
These attain the mighty life you see."

O air-born voice! long since, severely clear,
A cry like thine in my own heart I hear:
"Resolve to be thyself; and know that he
Who finds himself, loses his misery! '

MATTHEW ARNOLD.

DAYS OF MY YOUTH.

AYS of my youth, ye have glided away .
Hairs of my youth, ye are frosted and gray:
Eyes of my youth, your keen sight is no more:
Cheeks of my youth, ye are furrowed all o'er:
Strength of my youth, all your vigor is gone:
Thoughts of my youth, your gay visions are
flown.

Day of my youth, I wish not your recall:
Hairs of my youth, I'm content ye should fall:
Eyes of my youth, ye much evil have seen:

Cheeks of my youth, bathed in tears you have been:
Thoughts of my youth, you have led me astray:
Strength of my youth, why lament your decay?

Days of my age, ye will shortly be past:
Pains of my age, yet awhile you can last:
Joys of my age, in true wisdom delight:
Eyes of my age, be religion your light:
Thoughts of my age, dread ye not the cold sod:
Hopes of my age, be ye fixed on your God.

ST. GEORGE TUCKER.

AULD LANG SYNE.

HOULD auld acquaintance be forgot,
And never brought to min'?
Should auld acquaintance be forgot.
And days o' lang syne.
For auld lang syne, my dear,
For auld lang syne,
We 'll take a cup o' kindness yet,
For auld lang syne.

We twa hae rin about the braes,
And pu'd the gowans fine;
But we 've wandered mony a weary foot
Sin' auld lang syne.
For auld lang syne. etc.

We twa hae paidl't i' the burn,
Frae mornin' sun till dine;

But seas between us braid hae roared
Sin' auld lang syne.
For auld lang syne, etc.

And here's a hand, my trusty fier,
And gie 's a hand o' thine;
And we 'll take a right guid willie-waught
For auld lang syne.
For auld lang syne, etc.

And surely ye 'll be your pint-stowp,
And surely I'll be mine;
And we 'll take a cup o' kindness yet
For auld lang syne.
For auld lang syne etc.

ROBERT BURNS.

LAZY.

HARMLESS fellow, wasting useless days,
Am I; I love my comfort and my leisure;
Let those who wish them toil for gold and
praise;
To me the summer day brings more of pleasure.

So, here upon the grass, I lie at ease,
While solemn voices from the past are calling,
Mingled with rustling whispers in the trees,
And pleasant sounds of water idly falling.

There was a time, perhaps, when I had thought
To make a name, a home, a bright existence,
But time has shown me that my dreams are
naught,
Save a mirage that vanished with the distance.

Well, it is gone: I care no longer now
For fame, for fortune, or for empty praises;
Rather than wear a crown upon my brow,
I 'll lie forever here among the daisies.

"So, here upon the grass, I lie at ease."

There was a time when I had higher aims
Than thus to lie among the flowers and listen
To listening birds, or watch the sunset's flames
On the broad river's surface glow and glisten.

So you, who wish for fame, good friend, pass by,
With you I surely cannot think to quarrel;
Give me peace, rest, this bank whereon I lie,
And spare me both the labor and the laurel!

GEORGE ARNOLD.

WE HAVE BEEN FRIENDS TOGETHER.

WE have been friends together,
In sunshine and in shade,
Since first beneath the chestnut-trees
In infancy we played.
But coldness dwells within thy heart,
A cloud is on thy brow;
We have been friends together.
Shall a light word part us now?

We have been gay together,
We have laughed at little jests;
For the fount of hope was gushing
Warm and joyous in our breasts.

But laughter now hath fled thy lip,
And sullen glooms thy brow;
We have been gay together,—
Shall a light word part us now?

We have been sad together,—
We have wept with bitter tears
O'er the grass-grown graves where slumbered
The hopes of early years.
The voices which were silent there
Would bid thee clear thy brow;
We have been sad together,—
O, what shall part us now?

CAROLINE ELIZABETH SARAH NORTON.

A NAME IN THE SAND

ALONE I walked the ocean strand,
A pearly shell was in my hand:
I stooped and wrote upon the sand
    My name, the year and day:—
As onward from the spot I passed,
One lingering look behind I cast,—
A wave came rolling high and fast,
    And washed my line away.

And so, methought, 't will quickly be
With every mark on earth with me:
A wave of dark oblivion's sea
    Will sweep across the place

Where I have trod the sandy shore
Of time, and been to be no more —
Of me, my day, the name I bore,
    To leave no track or trace.

And yet, with Him who counts the sands,
And holds the water in his hands,
I know a lasting record stands,
    Inscribed against my name,
Of all this mortal part has wrought,
Of all this thinking soul has thought,
And from these fleeting moments caught,
    For glory or for shame.

GEORGE D. PRENTICE.

"And I thought of the trees under which we had strayed."

ON VISITING A SCENE OF CHILDHOOD.

LONG years have elapsed since I gazed on the
        scene.
    Which my fancy still robed in its freshness of
        green,—
    The spot where, a school-boy, all thoughtless I
        strayed
By the side of the stream, in the gloom of the shade.

I thought of the friends who had roamed with me there,
When the sky was so blue and the flowers were so
        fair,—
All scattered—all sundered by mountain and wave,
And some in the silent embrace of the grave!

I thought of the green banks, that circled around,
With wild-flowers, and sweet-brier, and eglantine
        crowned,
I thought of the river, all quiet and bright
As the face of the sky on a blue summer night:

And I thought of the trees, under which we had
        strayed,
Of the broad leafy boughs, with their coolness of
        shade;
And I hoped, though disfigured, some token to find
Of the names and the carvings, impressed on the
        rind.

All eager, I hastened the scene to behold,
Rendered sacred and dear by the feelings of old;
And I deemed that, unaltered, my eye should ex-
    plore
This refuge, this haunt, this Elysium of yore.

'T was a dream!—not a token or trace could I view
Of the names that I loved, of the trees that I knew:
Like the shadows of night at the dawning of day,
"Like a tale that is told"—they had vanished away.

Since the birds, that had nestled and warbled above,
Had all fled from its banks, at the fall of the grove.

I paused:—and the moral came home to my heart:—
Behold, how of earth all the glories depart!
Our visions are baseless,—our hopes but a gleam,—
Our staff but a reed,—and our life but a dream.

Then, O, let us look—let our prospects allure—
To scenes that can fade not, to realms that endure,

"I thought of the river all quiet and bright."

And methought the lone river, that murmured along,
Was more dull in its motion, more sad in its song,

To glories, to blessings, that triumph sublime
O'er the blightings of Change, and the ruins of Time.

MOTHER, HOME, HEAVEN.

THREE words fall sweetly on my soul
    As music from an angel lyre,
That bid my spirit spurn control
    And upward to its source aspire;
The sweetest sounds to mortals given
Are heard in Mother, Home, and Heaven.

Dear Mother! ne'er shall I forget
    Thy brow, thine eye, thy pleasant smile!
Though in the sea of death hath set
    Thy star of life, my guide awhile,
Oh, never shall thy form depart
From the bright pictures in my heart.

And like a bird that from the flowers,
    Wing-weary seeks her wonted nest,
My spirit, e'en in manhood's hours,
    Turns back in childhood's Home to rest;
The cottage, garden, hill and stream,
Still linger like a pleasant dream.

And while to one engulfing grave,
    By time's swift tide we 're driven,
How sweet the thought that every wave
    But bears us nearer Heaven!
There we shall meet when life is o'er,
    In that blest Home, to part no more.

WILLIAM GOLDSMITH BROWN.

GIVE ME BACK MY YOUTH AGAIN.

THEN give me back that time of pleasures,
    While yet in joyous growth I sang,—
When, like a fount, the crowding measures
    Uninterrupted gushed and sprang!
Then bright mist veiled the world before me,
    In opening buds a marvel woke,
As I the thousand blossoms broke
Which every valley richly bore me!

I nothing had, and yet enough for youth—
Joy in Illusion, ardent thirst for Truth.

Give unrestrained the old emotion,
The bliss that touched the verge of pain,
The strength of Hate, Love's deep devot'on,—
O, give me back my youth again!

BAYARD TAYLOR.
(*From the German of Goethe.*)

AT LAST.

STOOD beside my window one stormy winter day,
  And watched the light white snow-flakes flutter
    past;
And I saw, though each one wandered its silent,
    separate way.

"'So men must lie down, too,' I said,
      'When life is past.'"

They all sank down upon the ground at last.
  "So men must lie down, too," I said,
    "When life is past."

From out the self-same window, when soft spring
    days were come,
I watched the fair white clouds that sailed the blue;
Could those bright pearly wonders far up in heaven's
    high dome
Be the old wintry snow-banks that I knew?
    "So men shall one day rise again,"
      I whispered, "too."
                              CAROLINE LESLIE.

WAITING.

WALK in sadness and alone
    Beside Time's flowing river;
  Their steps I trace upon the sand
Who wandered with me hand in hand,
    But now are gone forever.

Upon that river, dark and deep
    My boat will soon be tossing;
By earth-sounds growing faint and low,
By mists that blind my eyes, I know
    I must be near the crossing.

And so I walk with silent tread
    Beside Time's flowing river,
And wait the plashing of the oar
That bears me to the Summer Shore,
    To be with friends forever.
                    WILLIAM GOLDSMITH BROWN.

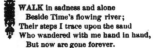

THE BOOK OF JOB.

CALL that, the Book of Job, aside from all theories about it, one of the grandest
things ever written with pen. One feels, indeed, as if it were not Hebrew; such a
noble universality, different from noble patriotism or sectarianism, reigns in it. A
noble book! all men's book! It is our first, oldest statement of the never-ending
problem—man's destiny—and God's way with him here in this earth. And all in such free,
flowing outlines; grand in its sincerity, in its simplicity; in its epic melody, and repose of
reconcilement. There is the seeing eye, the mildly understanding heart. So true every
way; true eyesight and vision for all things; material things no less than spiritual; the
horse—"hast thou clothed his neck with thunder?—he "*laughs* at the shaking of the
spear!" Such living likenesses were never since drawn. Sublime sorrow, sublime recon-
ciliation; oldest choral melody as of the heart of mankind; so soft and great; as the sum-
mer midnight, as the world with its seas and stars! There is nothing written, I think, in
the Bible or out of it, of equal literary merit.
                                    THOMAS CARLYLE.

MORTALITY.

H, why should the spirit of mortal be proud?
Like a fast-flitting meteor, a fast-flying cloud,
A flash of the lightning, a break of the wave,
He passes from life to his rest in the grave.

The leaves of the oak and the willow shall fade,
Be scattered around and together be laid;
And the young and the old, and the low and the high,
Shall moulder to dust and together shall lie.

The child that a mother attended and loved,
The mother that infant's affection that proved,
The husband that mother and infant that blessed,
Each, all, are away to their dwelling of rest.

The maid on whose cheek, on whose brow, in whose eye,
Shone beauty and pleasure, — her triumphs are by;
And the memory of those that beloved her and praised,
Are alike from the minds of the living erased.

The hand of the king that the sceptre hath borne,
The brow of the priest that the mitre hath worn,
The eye of the sage, and the heart of the brave,
Are hidden and lost in the depths of the grave.

The peasant whose lot was to sow and to reap,
The herdsman who climbed with his goats to the steep,
The beggar that wandered in search of his bread,
Have faded away like the grass that we tread.

The saint that enjoyed the communion of heaven,
The sinner that dared to remain unforgiven,
The wise and the foolish, the guilty and just,
Have quietly mingled their bones in the dust.

So the multitude goes, like the flower and the weed,
That wither away to let others succeed;
So the multitude comes, even those we behold,
To repeat every tale that hath often been told.

For we are the same that our fathers have been;
We see the same sights that our fathers have seen, —
We drink the same stream, and we feel the same sun,
And we run the same course that our fathers have run.

The thoughts we are thinking our fathers would think;
From the death we are shrinking from, they too would shrink;
To the life we are clinging to, they too would cling;
But it speeds from the earth like a bird on the wing.

They loved, but their story we cannot unfold;
They scorned, but the heart of the haughty is cold;
They grieved, but no wail from their slumbers may come;
They joyed, but the voice of their gladness is dumb.

They died, — ay! they died: and we things that are now,
Who walk on the turf that lies over their brow,
Who make in their dwellings a transient abode,
Meet the changes they met on their pilgrimage road.

Yea! hope and despondency, pleasure and pain,
Are mingled together like sunshine and rain;
And the smile and the tear and the song and the dirge
Still follow each other, like surge upon surge.

'Tis the wink of an eye, 'tis the draught of a breath,
From the blossom of health to the paleness of death,
From the gilded saloon to the bier and the shroud, —
Oh, why should the spirit of mortal be proud?

WILLIAM KNOX.

OFT IN THE STILLY NIGHT.

FT in the stilly night,
Ere slumber's chain has bound me,
Fond Memory brings the light
Of other days around me:
The smiles, the tears,
Of boyhood's years,
The words of love then spoken;
The eyes that shone,
Now dimmed and gone,
The cheerful hearts now broken.
Thus in the stilly night,
Ere slumber's chain has bound me,
Sad Memory brings the light
Of other days around me.

When I remember all
The friends so linked together
I 've seen around me fall,
Like leaves in wintry weather,
I feel like one
Who treads alone
Some banquet-hall deserted,
Whose lights are fled,
Whose garlands dead,
And all but he departed.
Thus in the stilly night,
Ere slumber's chain has bound me,
Sad Memory brings the light
Of other days around me.

THOMAS MOORE.

24

THE LIGHT-HOUSE.

'ER waves that murmur ever nigh
  My window, opening toward the deep,
The light-house, with its wakeful eye,
  Looks into mine, that shuts to sleep.

Forever there, and still the same;
  While many more besides me mark
On various course, with various aim,
  ·That light that shineth in the dark.

"The light-house, with its wakeful eye,
Looks into mine, that shuts to sleep."

I lose myself in idle dreams.
  And wake in smiles or sighs or fright,
According to my vision's themes,
  And see it shining in the night.

It draws my heart towards those who roam
  Unknown, nor to be known by me;
I see it, and am glad at home,
  They see it, and are safe at sea.

SARAH HAMMOND PALFREY.

AT BEST.

HE faithful helm commands the keel,
  From port to port fair breezes blow;
But the ship must sail the convex sea,
  Nor may she straighter go.

So, man to man; in fair accord.
  On thought and will the winds may wait;

But the world will bend the passing word,
  Though its shortest course be straight.

From soul to soul the shortest line
  At best will bended be;
The ship that holds the straightest course
  Still sails the convex sea.

JOHN BOYLE O'REILLY.

BY THE AUTUMN SEA.

FAIR as the dawn of the fairest day,
Sad as the evening's tender gray,
By the latest lustre of sunset kissed,
That wavers and wanes through an amber
    mist —
There cometh a dream of the past to me,
On the desert sands, by the autumn sea.

That shine with an angel's ruth on me,—
A hopeless waif, by the autumn sea.

The wings of the ghostly beach-birds gleam
Through the shimmering surf, and the curlew's scream
Falls faintly shrill from the darkening height,
The first weird sigh on the lips of Night

"All heaven is wrapped in a mystic veil
And the face of the ocean is dim and pale."

All heaven is wrapped in a mystic veil,
And the face of the ocean is dim and pale,
And there rises a wind from the chill northwest,
That seemeth the wail of a soul's unrest,
As the twilight falls, and the vapors flee
Far over the wastes of the autumn sea.

A single ship through the gloaming glides,
Upborne on the swell of the seaward tides;
And above the gleam of her topmost spar
Are the virgin eyes of the vesper star

Breathes low through the sedge and the blasted tree,
With a murmur of doom, by the autumn sea.

Oh, sky-enshadowed and yearning main,
Your gloom but deepens this human pain;
Those waves seem big with a nameless care,
That sky is a type of the heart's despair,
As I linger and muse by the sombre lea,
And the night-shades close on the autumn sea.

PAUL HAMILTON HAYNE.

TAKE HEART.

ALL day the stormy wind has blown
    From off the dark and rainy sea;
No bird has past the window flown,
The only song has been the moan
    The wind made in the willow-tree.

This is the summer's burial-time:
    She died when dropped the earliest leaves;
And, cold upon her rosy prime,
Fell down the autumn's frosty rime;
    Yet I am not as one that grieves,—

For well I know o'er sunny seas
    The bluebird waits for April skies;
And at the roots of forest trees
The May-flowers sleep in fragrant ease,
    And violets hide their azure eyes.

O thou, by winds of grief o'erblown
    Beside some golden summer's bier,—
Take heart! Thy birds are only flown,
Thy blossoms sleeping, tearful sown,
    To greet thee in the immortal year!

EDNA DEAN PROCTOR.

TIME ROLLS HIS CEASELESS COURSE.

TIME rolls his ceaseless course. The race of yore
Who danced our infancy upon their knee,
And told our marveling boyhood legends store
Of their strange ventures happ'd by land or
    sea,
How are they blotted from the things that be!

How few, all weak and withered of their force,
Wait, on the verge of dark eternity,
Like stranded wrecks, the tide returning hoarse,
To sweep them from our sight! Time rolls his cease-
    less course.

SIR WALTER SCOTT.

"When stars are in the quiet skies,
Then most I pine for thee."

WHEN STARS ARE IN THE QUIET SKIES.

WHEN stars are in the quiet skies,
    Then most I pine for thee;
Bend on me then thy tender eyes,
    As stars look on the sea.
For thoughts, like waves that glide by night,
    Are stillest when they shine;
Mine earthly love lies hushed in light
    Beneath the heaven of thine.

There is an hour when angels keep
    Familiar watch o'er men,
When coarser souls are wrapped in sleep
    Sweet spirit, meet me then;

There is an hour when holy dreams
    Through slumber fairest glide,
And in that mystic hour it seems
    Thou should'st be by my side.

My thoughts of thee too sacred are
    For daylight's common beam;
I can but know thee as my star,
    My angel and my dream!
When stars are in the quiet skies,
    Then most I pine for thee;
Bend on me then thy tender eyes,
    As stars look on the sea.

EDWARD BULWER LYTTON.

DREAMERS.

OH, there be souls none understand,
Like clouds, they cannot touch the land,
Drive as they may by field or town.
Then we look wise at this, and frown,
And we cry "Fool!" and cry "Take hold
Of earth, and fashion gods of gold!"

Unanchored ships, that blow and blow,
Sail to and fro, and then go down
In unknown seas that none shall know,

Without one ripple of renown;
Poor drifting dreamers, sailing by,
That seem to only live to die.

Call these not fools; the test of worth
Is not the bold you have of earth;
Lo, there be gentlest souls, sea blown,
That know not any harbor known;
And it may be the reason is
They touch on fairer shores than this.

JOAQUIN MILLER.

ANSWER TO A CHILD'S QUESTION.

DO you ask what the birds say? The sparrow, the
dove,
The linnet, and thrush say " I love, and I love!"
In the winter they 're silent, the wind is so
strong;
What it says I don't know, but it sings a loud song.
But green leaves, and blossoms, and sunny warm.
weather,
And singing and loving — all come back together.
But the lark is so brimful of gladness and love,
The green fields below him, the blue sky above,
That he sings, and he sings, and forever sings he,
" I love my Love, and my Love loves me."

SAMUEL TAYLOR COLERIDGE.

" Do you ask what the birds say?"

INDIRECTION.

FAIR are the flowers and the children, but their
subtle suggestion is fairer;
Rare is the roseburst of dawn, but the secret that
clasps it is rarer;
Sweet is the exultance of song, but the strain that
precedes it is sweeter;
And never was poem yet writ, but the meaning
out-mastered the metre.

Never a daisy that grows, but a mystery guideth the
growing;
Never a river that flows, but a majesty sceptres the
flowing;
Never a Shakespeare that soared, but a stronger than
he did enfold him;
Nor never a prophet foretells, but a mightier seer
hath foretold him.

Back of the canvas that throbs the painter is hinted
and hidden;
Into the statue that breathes the soul of the sculptor
is bidden;

Under the joy that is felt lie the infinite issues of feel-
ing;
Crowning the glory revealed is the glory that crowns
the revealing.

Great are the symbols of being, but that which is sym-
boled is greater;
Vast the create and beheld, but vaster the inward cre-
ator;
Back of the sound broods the silence, back of the gift
stands the giving;
Back of the hand that receives thrill the sensitive
nerves of receiving.

Space is as nothing to spirit, the deed is outdone by
the doing;
The heart of the wooer is warm, but warmer the heart
of the wooing;
And up from the pits where these shiver, and up from
the heights where those shine.
Twin voices and shadows swim starward, and the es-
sence of life is divine.

RICHARD REALF.

ALONE BY THE HEARTH.

HERE, in my snug fire-lit chamber,
    Sit I alone;
And, as I gaze in the coals, I remember
    Days long agone.

Saddening it is when the night has descended,
    Thus to sit here,
Pensively musing on episodes ended
    Many a year.

'Tis but a wraith of love; yet I linger,
    (Thus passion errs,)
Foolishly kissing the ring on my finger—
    Once it was hers.

Nothing has changed since her spirit departed,
    Here, in this room,
Save I, who, weary, and half broken-hearted,
    Sit in the gloom.

"Saddening it is when the night has descended,
    Thus to sit here,
Pensively musing on episodes ended
    Many a year."

Still in my visions a golden-haired glory
    Flits to and fro;
She whom I loved—but 'tis just the old story:
    Dead, long ago.

Loud 'gainst the window the winter wind dashes,
    Dreary and cold;
Over the floor the red fire-light flashes,
    Just as of old.

Just as of old—but the embers are scattered,
   Whose ruddy blaze
Flashed o'er the floor where the fairy feet pattered
   In other days!

Then, her dear voice, like a silver chime ringing,
   Melted away;
Often these walls have re-echoed her singing,
   Now hushed for aye!

Why should love bring naught but sorrow, I
   wonder?
     Everything dies!

Time and death, sooner or later, must sunder
   Holiest ties.

Years have rolled by; I am wiser and older—
   Wiser, but yet
Not till my heart and my feelings grow colder,
   Can I forget.

So, in my snug little fire-lit chamber,
   Sit I alone;
And, as I gaze in the coals, I remember
   Days long agone!

               GEORGE ARNOLD.

WAITING BY THE GATE.

BESIDE a massive gateway built up in years gone
   by,
   Upon whose top the clouds in eternal shadow
     lie,
While streams the evening sunshine on quiet wood
   and lea,
I stand and calmly wait till the hinges turn for me.

The tree-tops faintly rustle beneath the breeze's
   flight,
A soft and soothing sound, yet it whispers of the
   night;
I hear the wood-thrush piping one mellow descant
   more,
And scent the flowers that blow when the heat of day
   is o'er.

Behold the portals open, and o'er the threshold, now,
There steps a weary one with pale and furrowed
   brow;
His count of years is full, his allotted task is wrought;
He passes to his rest from a place that needs him
   not.

In sadness then I ponder how quickly fleets the hour
Of human strength and action, man's courage and his
   power;
I muse while still the wood-thrush sings down the
   golden day;
And as I look and listen the sadness wears away,

Again the hinges turn, and a youth departing throws
A look of longing backward and sorrowfully goes;
A blooming maid, unbinding the roses from her hair,
Moves mournfully away from amidst the young and
   fair.

Oh glory of our race that so suddenly decays!
Oh crimson flush of morning that darkens as we gaze!

Oh breath of summer blossoms that on the restless
   air
Scatters a moment's sweetness and flies we know not
   where!

I grieve for life's bright promise, just shown and then
   withdrawn;
But still the sun shines round me: the evening bird
   sings on,
And I again am soothed, and, beside the ancient gate,
In the soft evening sunlight, I calmly stand and wait.

Once more the gates are opened; an infant group go
   out,
The sweet smile quenched forever, and stilled the
   sprightly shout.
Oh frail, frail tree of life, that upon the greensward
   strows
Its fair young buds unopened, with every wind that
   blows!

So come from every region, so enter, side by side,
The strong and faint of spirit, the meek, and men of
   pride.
Steps of earth's great and mighty, between those pil-
   lars gray,
And prints of little feet mark the dust along the way.

And some approach the threshold whose looks are
   blank with fear,
And some whose temples brighten with joy in draw-
   ing near,
As if they saw dear faces, and caught the gracious eye
Of Him, the sinless teacher, who came for us to die.

I mark the joy, the terror; yet these within my heart,
Can neither make the dread nor the longing to depart;
And, in the sunshine streaming on quiet wood and
   lea,
I stand and calmly wait till the hinges turn for me.

          WILLIAM CULLEN BRYANT.

THE DUKE OF GLOSTER ON HIS OWN DEFORMITY.

OW are our brows bound with victorious wreaths;
  Our bruised arms hung up for monuments;
  Our stern alarums changed to merry meetings,
  Our dreadful marches to delightful measures.
  Grim-visaged war hath smoothed his wrinkled
      front;
  And now, instead of mounting barbed steeds,
To fright the souls of fearful adversaries,
He capers nimbly in a lady's chamber
To the lascivious pleasing of a lute.
But I, that am not shaped for sportive tricks,
Nor made to court an amorous looking-glass:
I, that am rudely stamped, and want love's majesty,
To strut before a wanton ambling nymph;

I, that am curtailed of this fair proportion,
Cheated of feature by dissembling nature,
Deformed, unfinished, sent before my time
Into this breathing world, scarce half made up,
And that so lamely and unfashionable,
That dogs bark at me, as I halt by them;
Why I, in this weak piping time of peace,
Have no delight to pass away the time,
Unless to spy my shadow in the sun,
And descant on mine own deformity;
And therefore, since I cannot prove a lover,
To entertain these fair well-spoken days,
I am determinèd to prove a villain,
And hate the idle pleasures of these days.

WILLIAM SHAKESPEARE.

SUNBEAMS.

BABY sat on his mother's knee,
  On the golden morn of a summer's day,
Clapping his tiny hands in glee,
  As he watched the shifting sunbeams play.

A sunbeam glanced through the open door,
  With its shimmering web of atoms fine,
And crept along on the sanded floor
  In a glittering, glimmering, golden line.

The baby laughed in his wild delight,
  And clutched at the quivering golden band;
But the sunbeam fled from his eager sight.
  And nought remained in the dimpled hand.

For a cloud had swept o'er the summer sky,
  And gathered the beam to its bosom gray,
And wrapped in a mantle of sombre dye
  The glory and pride of the summer's day.

Thus cheated sore in his eager quest,
  With a puzzled look that was sad to see,

He laid his head on his mother's breast
  And gazed in the dear face wistfully.

The cloud swept by, and the beam returned,
  But the weary child was slumbering now,
And heeded it not, though it glowed and burned
  Like a crown of flame on his baby brow.

And I thought, ah, babe, thou art not alone
  In thy bootless quest for a fleeting toy,
For we all are babes, little wiser grown,
  In our chase for some idle and transient joy.

We are grasping at sunbeams day by day,
  And get but our toil for our weary pains;
For ever some cloudlet obscures the ray,
  And naught in the sordid grasp remains.

But when the lures of our youth depart,
  And our empty strivings are all forgot,
Then down in some nook of the peaceful heart
  The sunbeam glows when we seek it not.

EGBERT PHELPS.

THE VICISSITUDES OF LIFE.

O farewell to the little good you bear me,
  Farewell, a long farewell, to all my greatness!
This is the state of man: to-day he puts forth
  The tender leaves of hope; to-morrow blossoms,
  And bears his blushing honors thick upon him;
The third day comes a frost, a killing frost,
And, when he thinks, good easy man, full surely
His greatness is a-ripening, nips his root,
And then he falls, as I do. I have ventured,
Like little wanton boys that swim on bladders,
This many summers in a sea of glory.
But far beyond my depth: my high-blown pride

At length broke under me, and now has left me,
Weary, and old with service, to the mercy
Of a rude stream, that must for ever hide me.
Vain pomp and glory of this world, I hate ye;
I feel my heart new opened. O, how wretched
Is that poor man that hangs on princes' favors!
There is, betwixt that smile we would aspire to,
That sweet aspect of princes, and their ruin,
More pangs and fears than wars or women have;
And when he falls, he falls like Lucifer,
Never to hope again.

WILLIAM SHAKESPEARE.

ESTRANGEMENT.

LAS! they had been friends in youth;
But whispering tongues can poison truth;
And constancy lives in realms above;
And life is thorny; and youth is vain;
And to be wroth with one we love
Doth work like madness in the brain.

* * * * * * *

A dreary sea now flows between;
But neither heat. nor frost, nor thunder,
Shall wholly do away, I ween,
The marks of that which once hath been.

SAMUEL TAYLOR COLERIDGE.

" Like cliffs which had been rent asunder;
A dreary sea now flows between."

But never either found another
To free the hollow heart from paining, —
They stood aloof, the scars remaining,
Like cliffs which had been rent asunder;

HAMLET'S SOLILOQUY.

O be, or not to be,—that is the question:
Whether 'tis nobler in the mind to suffer
The slings and arrows of outrageous fortune;
Or to take arms against a sea of troubles,
And by opposing, end them?—To die,—to
sleep,—
No more;—and, by a sleep, to say we end
The heart-ache, and the thousand natural shocks
That flesh is heir to,—'t is a consummation
Devoutly to be wish'd. To die;—to sleep;—
To sleep! perchance to dream;—ay, there 's the rub,
For in that sleep of death what dreams may come,
When we have shuffled off this mortal coil,
Must give us pause; there 's the respect
That makes calamity of so long life:
For who would bear the whips and scorns of time,
The oppressor's wrong. the proud man's contumely,
The pangs of despised love, the law's delay,
The insolence of office and the spurns
That patient merit of the unworthy takes,
When he himself might his quietus make
With a bare bodkin? who would fardels bear,
To grunt and sweat under a weary life;
But that the dread of something after death,—
The undiscovered country, from whose bourne
No traveler returns,—puzzles the will;
And makes us rather bear those ills we have,
Than fly to others that we know not of!
Thus conscience does make cowards of us all;
And thus the native hue of resolution
Is sicklied o'er with the pale cast of thought;
And enterprises of great pith and moment,
With this regard, their currents turn a-wry,
And lose the name of action.

WILLIAM SHAKESPEARE.

TO-DAY.

O here hath been dawning
Another blue day;
Think wilt thou let it
Slip useless away.

Out of Eternity
This new Day is born;
Into Eternity
At night will return.

Behold it aforetime
No eye ever did;
So soon it forever
From all eyes is hid.

Here hath been dawning
Another blue day;
Think wilt thou let it
Slip useless away.

THOMAS CARLYLE.

THE STREAM.

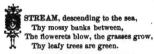

STREAM, descending to the sea,
　　Thy mossy banks between,
The flowerets blow, the grasses grow,
　　Thy leafy trees are green.

In garden plots the children play,
　　The fields the laborers till,
And houses stand on either hand,
　　And thou descendest still.

Strong purposes our minds possess,
　　Our hearts affections fill;
We toil and earn, we seek and learn
　　And thou descendest still.

O end to which our currents tend,
　　Inevitable sea
To which we flow! what do we know,
　　What shall we guess of thee?

" O stream, descending to the sea,
　Thy mossy banks between,
The flowerets blow, the grasses grow,
　Thy leafy trees are green."

O life, descending into death,
　　Our waking eyes behold;
Parent and friend thy lapse attend,
　　Companions young and old.

A roar we hear upon thy shore,
　　As we our course fulfill;
Scarce we divine a sun will shine
　　And be above us still.

ARTHUR HUGH CLOUGH.

GRIEF AND PATHOS.

" Over the river on the hill
Lieth a village white and still."

THE TWO VILLAGES.

OVER the river on the hill
Lieth a village white and still;
All around it the forest trees
Shiver and whisper in the breeze;
Over it sailing shadows go
Of soaring hawk and screaming crow;
And mountain grasses, low and sweet,
Grow in the middle of every street.

Over the river under the hill
Another village lieth still;
There I see in the cooling night
Twinkling stars of household light,
Fires that gleam from smithy's door,
Mists that curl on the river's shore;
And in the road no grasses grow,
For the wheels that hasten to and fro.

In that village on the hill
Never is sound of smithy or mill;
The houses are thatched with grass and flowers,
Never a clock to tell the hours;
The marble doors are always shut;
You may not enter at hall or hut.

In that village under the hill,
When the night is starry and still,
Many a weary soul in prayer
Looks to the other village there,
And weeping and sighing, longs to go
Up to that home from this below;
Longs to sleep by the forest wild,
Whither have vanished wife and child,
And heareth, praying, the answer fall, —
" Patience : That village shall hold ye all! "

ROSE TERRY COOKE.

" Over the river under the hill
Another village lieth still."

All the village lie asleep,
Never a grain to sow or reap;
Never in dreams to moan or sigh —
Silent, and idle, and low, they lie.

THE BLIND BOY.

SAY, what is that thing called light,
    Which I must ne'er enjoy?
What are the blessings of the sight?
    O tell your poor blind boy!

You talk of wondrous things you see,
    You say the sun shines bright;
I feel him warm, but how can he
    Or make it day or night?

My day or night myself I make,
    Whene'er I sleep or play;
And could I ever keep awake,
    With me 't were always day.

With heavy sighs I often hear
    You mourn my hapless woe;
But sure with patience I can bear
    A loss I ne'er can know.

Then let not what I cannot have
    My cheer of mind destroy;
Whilst thus I sing, I am a king,
    Although a poor blind boy.

COLLEY CIBBER.

THE OLD FAMILIAR FACES.

HAVE had playmates, I have had companions,
In my days of childhood, in my joyful school-
    days;
    All, all are gone, the old familiar faces.

I have been laughing, I have been carousing,
Drinking late, sitting late, with my bosom cronies;
All, all are gone, the old familiar faces.

I loved a love once, fairest among women;
Closed are her doors on me. I must not see her;
All, all are gone, the old familiar faces.

I have a friend, a kinder friend has no man;
Like an ingrate I left my friend abruptly;
Left him, to muse on the old familiar faces.

Ghost-like I paced round the haunts of my child-
    hood:
Earth seemed a desert I was bound to traverse,
Seeking to find the old familiar faces.

Friend of my bosom, thou more than a brother,
Why wert not thou born in my father's dwelling?
So might we talk of the old familiar faces,—

How some they have died, and some they have left
    me,
And some are taken from me: all are departed;
All, all are gone, the old familiar faces.

CHARLES LAMB.

THE CHURCHYARD OF THE VILLAGE.

OW sweet and solemn all alone,
 With reverent steps, from stone to stone,
In a small village churchyard lying,
 O'er intervening flowers to move!
And as we read the names unknown,
 Of young and old to judgment go'
 And hear in the calm air above,
Time onward, softly flying,
 To meditate, in Christian love,
Upon the dead and dying!

The friends we loved, long, long ago!
Gliding across the sad retreat,
How beautiful their phantom feet!
What tenderness is in their eyes,
Turned where the poor survivor lies
'Mid monitory sanctities!
What years of vanished joys are fanned
From one uplifting of that hand
In its white stillness! when the shade
Doth glimmeringly in sunshine fade

"And as we read the names unknown,
Of young and old, to judgment gone."

Across the silence seems to go
With dream-like motion wavering slow,
And shrouded in their folds of SLOW,

From our embrace, how dim appears
This world's life through a mist of tears!
Vain hopes! blind sorrows! needless fears!

JOHN WILSON (Christopher North).

MY HEART AND I.

NOUGH! we 're tired, my heart and I;
 We sit beside the headstone thus.
 And wish the name were carved for us;
The moss reprints more tenderly
 The hard types of the mason's knife,
 As Heaven's sweet life renews earth's life,
With which we 're tired, my heart and I.

You see we 're tired, my heart and I;
 We dealt with books, we trusted men,
 And in our own blood drenched the pen,
As if such colors could not fly.
 We walked too straight for fortune's end,
 We loved too true to keep a friend;
At last we 're tired, my heart and I.

How tired we feel, my heart and I;
  We seem of no use in the world;
  Our fancies hang gray and uncurled
About men's eyes indifferently;
  Our voice, which thrilled you so, will let
  You sleep; our tears are only wet;
What do we here, my heart and I?

So tired, so tired, my heart and I;
  It was not thus in that old time
  When Ralph sat with me 'neath the lime
To watch the sun set from the sky:
" Dear Love, you 're looking tired," he said;
  I, smiling at him, shook my head;
'Tis now we 're tired, my heart and I.

So tired, so tired, my heart and I!
  Though now none takes me on his arm
  To fold me close and kiss me warm,

Till each quick breath ends in a sigh
  Of happy languor. Now, alone
  We lean upon his graveyard stone,
Uncheered, unkissed, my heart and I.

Tired out we are, my heart and I.
  Suppose the world brought diadems
  To tempt us, crusted with loose gems
Of powers and pleasures? Let it try.
  We scarcely care to look at even
  A pretty child, or God's blue heaven,
We feel so tired, my heart and I.

Yet, who complains? My heart and I?
  In this abundant earth no doubt
  Is little room for things worn out;
Disdain them. break them, throw them by;
  And if before the days grew rough,
  We once were loved, then — well enough
I think we 've fared, my heart and I.

ELIZABETH BARRETT BROWNING.

WITH THE DEAD.

E hasten to the dead: What seek ye there,
  Ye restless thoughts and busy purposes
  Of the idle brain, which the world's livery wear?
O thou quick heart which pantest to possess
  All that anticipation feigneth fair!—
Thou vainly curious mind which wouldest guess
Whence thou didst come, and whither thou mayst go,

And that which never yet was known wouldst know—
Oh, whither hasten ye, that thus ye press
With such swift feet life's green and pleasant path,
Seeking alike from happiness and woe
A refuge in the cavern of gray death?
O heart, and mind. and thoughts! What thing do you
Hope to inherit in the grave below?

PERCY BYSSHE SHELLEY.

A DEATH-BED.

ER suffering ended with the day;
　Yet lived she at its close,
And breathed the long, long night away
　In statue-like repose.

But when the sun, in all his state,
　Illumed the eastern skies,
She passed through glory's morning-gate,
　And walked in Paradise!

JAMES ALDRICH.

THE DEATH OF THE FLOWERS.

HE melancholy days are come, the saddest of the
　year,
　　Of wailing winds, and naked woods, and mead-
　　ows brown and sear.
　　Heaped in the hollows of the grove, the autumn
　　leaves lie dead;
They rustle to the eddying gust, and to the rabbit's
　tread.
The robin and the wren are flown, and from the shrubs
　the jay,
And from the wood-top calls the crow through all the
　gloomy day.

Where are the flowers, the fair young flowers, that
　lately sprang and stood
In brighter light and softer airs, a beauteous sister-
　hood?
Alas! they all are in their graves; the gentle race of
　flowers
Are lying in their lowly beds with the fair and good
　of ours.
The rain is falling where they lie; but the cold Novem-
　ber rain
Calls not from out the gloomy earth the lovely ones
　again.

The wind-flower and the violet, they perished long
　ago,
And the brier-rose and the orchis died amid the sum-
　mer glow;
But on the hill the golden-rod, and the aster in the
　wood,

And the yellow sunflower by the brook in autumn
　beauty stood,
Till fell the frost from the clear cold heaven, as falls
　the plague on men,
And the brightness of their smile was gone from up-
　land, glade, and glen.

And now, when comes the calm, mild day, as still such
　days will come,
To call the squirrel and the bee from out their winter
　home;
When the sound of dropping nuts is heard, though all
　the trees are still,
And twinkle in the smoky light the waters of the rill;
The south-wind searches for the flowers whose fra-
　grance late he bore,
And sighs to find them in the wood and by the stream
　no more.

And then I think of one who in her youthful beauty
　died,
The fair meek blossom that grew up and faded by my
　side;
In the cold moist earth we laid her, when the forests
　cast the leaf,
And we wept that one so lovely should have a life so
　brief:
Yet not unmeet it was that one, like that young friend
　of ours,
So gentle and so beautiful, should perish with the
　flowers.

WILLIAM CULLEN BRYANT.

SANDS OF DEE.

"MARY, go and call the cattle home,
  And call the cattle home,
  And call the cattle home.

Above the nets at sea?
Was never salmon yet that shone so fair,
  Among the stakes of Dee?"

"And call the cattle home,
Across the sands of Dee."

Across the sands of Dee!"
The western wind was wild and dank with foam,
  And all alone went she.

The creeping tide came up along the sand,
  And o'er and o'er the sand,
  And round and round the sand,
  As far as eye could see;
The blinding mist came down and hid the land:
  And never home came she.

They rowed her in across the rolling foam,—
  The cruel, crawling foam,
  The cruel, hungry foam,—

"To her grave beside the sea."

To her grave beside the sea;
But still the boatmen hear her call the cattle home,
  Across the sands of Dee.

"They rowed her in across the rolling foam."

"O, is it weed, or fish, or floating hair,—
  A tress of golden hair,
  Of drownéd maiden's hair,—

CHARLES KINGSLEY.

———————✳✳———————

E that lacks time to mourn, lacks time to mend.
  Eternity mourns that. 'Tis an ill cure
For life's worst ills, to have no time to feel them.

Where sorrow 's held intrusive and turned out,
There wisdom will not enter, nor true power,
Nor aught that dignifies humanity.

ON THE RECEIPT OF MY MOTHER'S PICTURE.

Y mother! when I learned that thou wast
  dead,
Say, wast thou conscious of the tears I shed?
Hovered thy spirit o'er thy sorrowing son,
Wretch even then, life's journey just begun?
Perhaps thou gavest me, though unfelt, a kiss ·
Perhaps a tear, if souls can weep in bliss—
Ah, that maternal smile! it answers — Yes.
I heard the bell tolled on thy burial day,
I saw the hearse that bore thee slow away,
And, turning from my nursery window, drew
A long, long sigh, and wept a last adieu!
But was it such? It was. Where thou art gone

Adieus and farewells are a sound unknown.
May I but meet thee on that peaceful shore,
The parting words shall pass my lips no more!
Thy maidens, grieved themselves at my concern,
Oft gave me promise of thy quick return.
What ardently I wished, I long believed,
And, disappointed still, was still deceived.
By expectation every day beguiled,
Dupe of to-morrow, even from a child.
Thus many a sad to-morrow came and went,
Till, all my stock of infant sorrows spent,
I learned at last submission to my lot,
But, though I less deplored thee, ne'er forgot.

WILLIAM COWPER.

THE BRIDGE OF SIGHS.

NE more unfortunate,
  Weary of breath,
  Rashly importunate,
  Gone to her death!

Take her up tenderly,
Lift her with care:
Fashioned so slenderly,
Young and so fair!

Look at her garments
Clinging like cerements;
Whilst the wave constantly
Drips from her clothing;
Take her up instantly,
Loving, not loathing.

Touch her not scornfully;
Think of her mournfully,
Gently and humanly;
Not of the stains of her,
All that remains of her
Now is pure womanly.

Make no deep scrutiny
Into her mutiny
Rash and undutiful;
Past all dishonor,
Death has left on her
Only the beautiful.

Still for all slips of hers,
One of Eve's family—
Wipe those poor lips of hers
Oozing so clammily.

Loop up her tresses
Escaped from the comb,
Her fair auburn tresses;
Whilst wonderment guesses
Where was her home?

Who was her father?
Who was her mother?
Had she a sister?
Had she a brother?
Or was there a dearer one
Still, and a nearer one
Yet, than all other?

Alas! for the rarity
Of Christian charity
Under the sun!
O, it was pitiful!
Near a whole city full,
Home she had none.

Sisterly, brotherly,
Fatherly, motherly
Feelings had changed:
Love, by harsh evidence,
Thrown from its eminence;
Even God's providence
Seeming estranged.

Where the lamps quiver
So far in the river,
With many a light
From window and casement,
From garret to basement,
She stood, with amazement,
Houseless by night.

The bleak wind of March
Made her tremble and shiver;
But not the dark arch,
Or the black flowing river:
Mad from life's history,
Glad to death's mystery
Swift to be hurled,—
Anywhere, anywhere
Out of the world!

26

In she plunged boldly,
No matter how coldly
The rough river ran,—
Over the brink of it,
Picture it,—think of it,
Dissolute man!
Leve in it, drink of it,
Then, if you can!

Take her up tenderly,
Lift her with care;
Fashioned so slenderly,
Young, and so fair!

Ere her limbs frigidly
Stiffen too rigidly,
Decently,— kindly —
Smooth and compose them;
And her eyes, close them,
Staring so blindly!

Dreadfully staring
Through muddy impurity.
As when with the daring
Last look of despairing
Fixed on futurity.

Perishing gloomily,
Spurred by contumely,
Cold inhumanity,
Burning insanity,
Into her rest,
Cross her hands humbly
As if praying dumbly,
Over her breast!

Owning her weakness,
Her evil behavior,
And leaving, with meekness,
Her sins to her Saviour!

THOMAS HOOD.

LITTLE SHOES AND STOCKINGS.

LITTLE shoes and stockings!
  What a tale ye speak.
Of the swollen eyelid,
  And the tear-wet cheek;
Of the nightly vigil,
  And the daily prayer;
Of the buried darling,
  Present everywhere!

Brightly plaided stockings
  Of the finest wool;
Rounded feet, and dainty,
  Each a stocking full;
Tiny shoes of crimson,
  Shoes that nevermore
Will awaken echoes
  From the toy-strewn floor.

Not the wealth of Indies
  Could your worth eclipse.
Priceless little treasures,
  Pressed to whitened lips;

As the mother nurses,
  From the world apart,
Leaning on the arrow
  That has pierced her heart.

Head of flaxen ringlets;
  Eyes of heaven's blue;
Parted mouth—a rosebud—
  Pearls just peeping through;
Soft arms, softly twining
  Round her neck at eve;—
Little shoes and stockings,
  These the dreams ye weave.

Weave her yet another,
  Of the world of bliss;—
Let the stricken mother
  Turn away from this;
Bid her dream believing
  Little feet await,
Watching for her passing
  Through the pearly gate.

WHEN WE TWO PARTED.

WHEN we two parted
  In silence and tears,
Half broken-hearted
  To sever for years,
Pale grew thy cheek and cold,
  Colder thy kiss;
Truly that hour foretold
  Sorrow to this.

The dew of the morning
  Sunk chill on my brow,—
It felt like the warning
  Of what I feel now.
Thy vows are all broken,
  And light is thy fame;
I hear thy name spoken,
  And share in its shame.

They name thee before me,
A kuell to mine ear;
A shudder comes o'er me, —
Why wert thou so dear?
They know not I knew thee.
Who knew thee too well : —
Long, long shall I rue thee.
Too deeply to tell.

In secret we met, —
In silence I grieve,
That thy heart could forget,
Thy spirit deceive.
If I should meet thee
After long years,
How should I greet thee? —
With silence and tears.

LORD BYRON.

LITTLE JIM.

THE cottage was a thatched one, the outside old
and mean,
But all within that little cot was wondrous neat
and clean;
The night was dark and stormy, the wind was howling
wild,
As a patient mother sat beside the death-bed of her
child :
A little worn-out creature, his once bright eyes grown
dim :
It was a collier's wife and child — they called him
little Jim.

I have no pain, dear mother, now, but O! I am so dry,
Just moisten poor Jim's lips again, and, mother, don't
you cry."
With gentle, trembling haste she held the liquid to his
lip;
He smiled to thank her as he took each little, tiny sip.
" Tell father, when he comes from work, I said good-
night to him,
And, mother, now I'll go to sleep." Alas! poor little
Jim!
She knew that he was dying; that the child she loved
so dear.

" The cottage was a thatched one, the outside old and mean."

And oh! to see the briny tears fast hurrying down her
cheek,
As she offered up the prayer, in thought, she was
afraid to speak,
Lest she might waken one she loved far better than her
life;
For she had all a mother's heart — had that poor col-
lier's wife.
With hands uplifted, see, she kneels beside the suffer-
er's bed,
And prays that He would spare her boy, and take her-
self instead.

She gets her answer from the child: soft fall the
words from him,
"Mother, the angels do so smile, and beckon little Jim,

Had uttered the last words she might ever hope to hear :
The cottage door is opened, the collier's step is heard
The father and the mother meet, yet neither speak a
word.

He felt that all was over, he knew his child was dead,
He took the candle in his hand and walked towards
the bed;
His quivering lips gave token of the grief he 'd fain
conceal,
And see, his wife has joined him — the stricken couple
kneel :
With hearts bowed down by sadness, they humbly ask
of Him,
In heaven, once more, to meet again their own poor
little Jim.

LAMENT OF THE IRISH EMIGRANT.

'M sittin' on the stile, Mary,
  Where we sat side by side
On a bright May mornin' long ago,
  When first you were my bride;
The corn was springin' fresh and green,
  And the lark sang loud and high;
And the red was on your lip, Mary,
  And the love-light in your eye.

'Tis but a step down yonder lane,
  And the little church stands near—
The church where we were wed, Mary,
  I see the spire from here.
But the graveyard lies between, Mary,
  And my step might break your rest—
For I 've laid you, darling. down to sleep,
  With your baby on your breast.

"Where we sat side by side."

The place is little changed, Mary—
  The day is bright as then;
The lark's loud song is in my ear,
  And the corn is green again;
But I miss the soft clasp of your hand,
  And your breath, warm on my cheek;
And I still keep list'nin' for the words
  You nevermore will speak.

I 'm very lonely now, Mary,
  For the poor make no new friends;
But, O, they love the better still
  The few our Father sends!
And you were all I had. Mary,
  My blessin' and my pride;
There 's nothing left to care for now,
  Since my poor Mary died.

Yours was the good, brave heart, Mary,
  That still kept hoping on.
When the trust in God had left my soul,
  And my arm's young strength was gone;
There was comfort ever on your lip,
  And the kind look on your brow—
I bless you, Mary, for that same,
  Though you cannot hear me now.

I 'm biddin' you a long farewell,
  My Mary, kind and true!
But I 'll not forget you, darling,
  In the land I' m goin' to;
They say there 's bread and work for all,
  And the sun shines always there—
But I 'll not forget old Ireland,
  Were it fifty times as fair!

'T is but a step down yonder lane,
And the little church stands near.''

I thank you for the patient smile,
  When your heart was fit to break—
When the hunger-pain was gnawin' there,
  And you hid it for my sake;
I bless you for the pleasant word,
  When your heart was sad and sore—
O, I'm thankful you are gone, Mary,
  Where grief can't reach you more!

And often in those grand old woods
  I 'll sit and shut my eyes,
And my heart will travel back again
  To the place where Mary lies;
And I 'll think I see the little stile
  Where we sat side by side,
And the springin' corn, and the bright May morn
  When first you were my bride.

LADY DUFFERIN.

THE loves and animosities of youth, where are they? Swept away like the camps that had been pitched in the sandy bed of the river.

THE OLD SEXTON.

IGH to a grave that was newly made.
Leaned a sexton old on his earth-worn spade;
His work was done, and he paused to wait
The funeral train at the open gate.
A relic of bygone days was he,
And his locks were as white as the foamy sea;
And these words came from his lips so thin:
"I gather them in—I gather them in—
Gather—gather—I gather them in.

"I gather them in; for man and boy,
Year after year of grief and joy,
I 've builded the houses that lie around
In every nook of this burial-ground.
Mother and daughter, father and son,
Come to my solitude one by one;
But come they stranger or come they kin,
I gather them in—I gather them in.

"Many are with me, yet I 'm alone;
I 'm King of the Dead, and I make my throne
On a monument slab of marble cold—
My sceptre of rule is the spade I hold.
Come they from cottage, or come they from hall,
Mankind are my subjects, all, all, all!
May they loiter in pleasure, or toilfully spin,
I gather them in—I gather them in.

"I gather them in, and their final rest
Is here, down here, in the earth's dark breast! "
And the sexton ceased as the funeral train
Wound mutely over that solemn plain;
And I said to myself: When time is told,
A mightier voice than that sexton's old
Will be heard o'er the last trump's dreadful din:
"I gather them in—I gather them in—
Gather—gather—gather them in! "

PARK BENJAMIN.

THE OLD ARM-CHAIR.

LOVE it—I love it, and who shall dare
To chide me for loving that old arm-chair!
I've treasured it long as a sainted prize—
I've bedewed it with tears, and embalmed it with
sighs,
'Tis bound by a thousand bands to my heart,
Not a tie will break, not a link will start.
Would you learn the spell? a mother sat there;
And a sacred thing is that old arm-chair.

In childhood's hour I lingered near
The hallowed seat with listening ear;
And gentle words that mother would give,
To fit me to die, and teach me to live.
She told me shame would never betide,
With truth for my creed, and God for my guide;
She taught me to lisp my earliest prayer,
As I knelt beside that old arm-chair.

I sat and watched her many a day,
When her eyes grew dim and her locks were gray,
And I almost worshiped her when she smiled
And turned from her Bible to bless her child.
Years rolled on, but the last one sped—
My idol was shattered—my earth-star fled:
I learnt how much the heart can bear,
When I saw her die in that old arm-chair.

'Tis past! 'tis past! but I gaze on it now
With quivering breath and throbbing brow:
'Twas there she nursed me—'twas there she died,
And memory flowed with lava tide—
Say it is folly, and deem me weak,
While the scalding tears run down my cheek.
But I love it—I love it, and cannot tear
My soul from my mother's old arm-chair.

ELIZA COOK.

MAN WAS MADE TO MOURN

HEN chill November's surly blast
Made fields and forests bare,
One evening, as I wandered forth
Along the banks of Ayr,
I spied a man whose aged step
Seemed weary, worn with care;
His face was furrowed o'er with years,
And hoary was his hair.

"Young stranger, whither wanderest thou? "
Began the reverend sage;
"Does thirst of wealth thy step constrain,
Or youthful pleasures rage?
Or haply, prest with cares and woes,
Too soon thou hast began
To wander forth, with me, to mourn
The miseries of man!

"The sun that overhangs yon moors,
  Outspreading far and wide,
Where hundreds labor to support
  A haughty lordling's pride, —
I 've seen yon weary winter sun
  Twice forty times return;
And every time has added proofs
  That man was made to mourn.

"O man, while in thy early years,
  How prodigal of time!
Misspending all thy precious hours,
  Thy glorious youthful prime!
Alternate follies take the sway;
  Licentious passions burn;
Which tenfold force gives Nature's law,
  That man was made to mourn.

"Look not alone on youthful prime,
  Or manhood's active might;
Man then is useful to his kind,
  Supported in his right;
But see him on the edge of life,
  With cares and sorrows worn,
Then age and want, O ill-matched pair!
  Show man was made to mourn.

"A few seem favorites of fate,
  In pleasure's lap carest;
Yet think not all the rich and great
  Are likewise truly blest.
But, O, what crowds in every land
  Are wretched and forlorn!
Through weary life this lesson learn, —
  That man was made to mourn.

"Many and sharp the numerous ills,
  Inwoven with our frame!
More pointed still we make ourselves,
  Regret, remorse, and shame!

And man, whose heaven-erected face
  The smiles of love adorn,
Man's inhumanity to man
  Makes countless thousands mourn!

"See yonder poor, o'erlabored wight,
  So abject, mean, and vile,
Who begs a brother of the earth
  To give him leave to toil;
And see his lordly fellow-worm
  The poor petition spurn,
Unmindful, though a weeping wife
  And helpless offspring mourn.

"If I 'm designed yon lordling's slave,
  By Nature's law designed, —
Why was an independent wish
  E'er planted in my mind?
If not, why am I subject to
  His cruelty or scorn?
Or why has man the will and power
  To make his fellow mourn?

"Yet let not this too much, my son,
  Disturb thy youthful breast:
This partial view of humankind
  Is surely not the last!
The poor, oppressed, honest man
  Had never, sure, been born,
Had there not been some recompense
  To comfort those that mourn!

"O Death! the poor man's dearest friend,
  The kindest and the best!
Welcome the hour my aged limbs
  Are laid with thee at rest!
The great, the wealthy, fear thy blows,
  From pomp and pleasure torn;
But O, a blest relief to those
  That weary-laden mourn!"

ROBERT BURNS.

THE THREE FISHERS.

HREE fishers went sailing out into the west,
  Out into the west as the sun went down;
  Each thought on the woman who loved him the
    best.
And the children stood watching them out of
    the town;
For men must work, and women must weep,
And there 's little to earn, and many to keep,
  Though the harbor bar be moaning.

Three wives sat up in the lighthouse tower,
  And they trimmed the lamps as the sun went down;
They looked at the squall, and they looked at the
    shower,

And the night-rack came rolling up ragged and
    brown.
But men must work, and women must weep,
Though storms be sudden, and waters deep,
  And the harbor bar be moaning.

Three corpses lay out on the shining sands
  In the morning gleam as the tide went down,
And the women are weeping and wringing their hands
For those who will never come home to the town;
For men must work, and women must weep,
And the sooner it 's over, the sooner to sleep;
  And good-by to the bar and its moaning.

CHARLES KINGSLEY.

THE BEGGAR.

PITY the sorrows of a poor old man!
　　Whose trembling limbs have borne him to
　　　　your door,
　　Whose days are dwindled to the shortest span,
　　　O, give relief, and Heaven will bless your
　　　　store.

These tattered clothes my poverty bespeak,
　These hoary locks proclaim my lengthened years;
And many a furrow in my grief-worn cheek
　Has been the channel to a stream of tears.

"Pity the sorrows of a poor old man."

Yon house, erected on the rising ground,
　With tempting aspect drew me from my road
For plenty there a residence has found,
　And grandeur a magnificent abode.

(Hard is the fate of the infirm and poor!)
　Here craving for a morsel of their bread,
A pampered menial forced me from the door,
　To seek a shelter in a humbler shed.

O, take me to your hospitable home,
　Keen blows the wind, and piercing is the cold!
Short is my passage to the friendly tomb,
　For I am poor and miserably old.

Should I reveal the source of every grief,
　If soft humanity e'er touched your breast,
Your hands would not withhold the kind relief,
　And tears of pity could not be repressed.

Heaven sends misfortunes—why should we repine?
　'Tis Heaven has brought me to the state you see:
And your condition may be soon like mine,
　The child of sorrow and of misery.

A little farm was my paternal lot,
　Then, like the lark, I sprightly hailed the morn;
But ah! oppression forced me from my cot;
　My cattle died, and blighted was my corn.

My daughter,—once the comfort of my age!
　Lured by a villain from her native home,
Is cast, abandoned, on the world's wild stage,
　And doomed in scanty poverty to roam.

My tender wife,—sweet soother of my care!—
　Struck with sad anguish at the stern decree,
Fell,—lingering fell, a victim to despair,
　And left the world to wretchedness and me.

Pity the sorrows of a poor old man!
　Whose trembling limbs have borne him to your
　　　door,
Whose days are dwindled to the shortest span,
　O, give relief, and heaven will bless your store.

THOMAS MOSS.

THE VOICE OF THE POOR.

[In the Irish Famine of '47.]

WAS ever sorrow like to our sorrow,
　　O God above?
　Will our night never change into a morrow
　　Of joy and love?
A deadly gloom is on us, waking. sleeping,
　Like the darkness at noontide
That fell upon the pallid mother, weeping
　By the Crucified.

Before us die our brothers of starvation;
　Around us cries of famine and despair;
Where is hope for us, or comfort, or salvation—
　Where, O where?

If the angels ever hearken, downward bending,
　They are weeping we are sure.
At the litanies of human groans ascending
　From the crushed hearts of the poor.

When the human rest in love upon the human
　All grief is light;
But who bends one kind glance to illumine
　Our life-long night?
The air around is ringing with their laughter—
　God has only made the rich to smile;
But we in rags and want and woe—we follow after,
　Weeping the while.

We never knew a childhood's mirth and gladness,
    Nor the proud heart of youth, free and
        brave;
A deathlike dream of wretchedness and sadness
    Is our life's journey to the grave;
Day by day we lower sink and lower,
    Till the God-like soul within
Falls crushed beneath the fearful demon power
    Of poverty and sin.

We must toil though the light of life is burning,
    Oh, how dim!
We must toil on our sick-bed, feebly turning
    Our eyes to Him
Who alone can hear the pale lip faintly saying,
    With scarce-moved breath,
While the paler hands uplifted are, and praying,
    "Lord, grant us death!"

                LADY WILDE (Speranza).

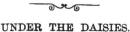

UNDER THE DAISIES.

HAVE just been learning the lesson of life,
    The sad, sad lesson of loving,
And all of its power for pleasure and pain
    Been slowly, sadly proving;
And all that is left of the bright, bright dream,
    With its thousand brilliant phases,
Is a handful of dust in a coffin hid —
    A coffin under the daisies;
      The beautiful, beautiful daisies,
      The snowy, snowy daisies.

And thus forever throughout the world
    Is love a sorrow proving;
There 's many a sad, sad thing in life,
    But the saddest of all is loving.
Life often divides far wider than death;
    Stern fortune the high wall raises;

But better far than two hearts estranged
    Is a low grave starred with daisies;
      The beautiful, beautiful daisies,
      The snowy, snowy daisies.

And so I am glad that we lived as we did,
    Through the summer of love together,
And that one of us, wearied, lay down to rest,
    Ere the coming of winter weather;
For the sadness of love is love grown cold,
    And 'tis one of its surest phases;
So I bless my God, with a breaking heart,
    For that grave enstarred with daisies;
      The beautiful, beautiful daisies,
      The snowy, snowy daisies.

                HATTIE TYNG GRISWOLD.

EXILE OF ERIN.

HERE came to the beach a poor Exile of Erin,
    The dew on his thin robe was heavy and chill;
    For his country he sighed, when at twilight re-
        pairing
      To wander alone by the wind-beaten hill:
But the day-star attracted his eye's sad devotion,
For it rose o'er his own native isle of the ocean,
Where once, in the fire of his youthful emotion,
    He sang the bold anthem of Erin go bragh.

"Sad is my fate!" said the heart-broken stranger;
    "The wild deer and wolf to a covert can flee,
But I have no refuge from famine and danger,
    A home and a country remain not to me,
Never again, in the green sunny bowers,
Where my forefathers lived, shall I spend the sweet
      hours,
Or cover my harp with the wild woven flowers,
    And strike to the numbers of Erin go bragh!

"Erin, my country! though sad and forsaken,
    In dreams I revisit thy sea-beaten shore;
But, alas! in a far foreign land I awaken,
    And sigh for the friends who can meet me no more!

O cruel fate! wilt thou never replace me
    In a mansion of peace,—where no perils can chase me?
Never again shall my brothers embrace me?
    They died to defend me or live to deplore!

"Where is my cabin-door, fast by the wildwood?
    Sisters and sire! did ye weep for its fall?
Where is the mother that looked on my childhood;
    And where is the bosom friend dearer than all?
O, my sad heart! long abandoned by pleasure,
Why did it dote on a fast-fading treasure?
Tears, like the rain-drop, may fall without measure,
    But rapture and beauty they cannot recall.

"Yet, all its sad recollections suppressing,
    One dying wish my lone bosom can draw;
Erin! an exile bequeaths thee his blessing!
    Land of my forefathers! Erin go bragh!
Buried and cold, when my heart stills her motion,
Green be thy fields.— sweetest isle of the ocean!
And thy harp-striking bards sing aloud with devo-
      tion.—
    Erin mavournin,— Erin go bragh!"

                THOMAS CAMPBELL.

WHEN THE GRASS SHALL COVER ME.

WHEN the grass shall cover me,
Head to foot where I am lying;
When not any wind that blows,
Summer blooms nor winter snows,
Shall awake me to your sighing;
Close above me as you pass,
You will say, "How kind she was,"
You will say, "How true she was,"
When the grass grows over me.

When the grass shall cover me,
Holden close to Earth's warm bosom;
While I laugh, or weep or sing
Nevermore for anything;
You will find in blade and blossom,

Sweet, small voices, odorous,
Tender pleaders in my cause,
That shall speak me as I was—
When the grass grows over me.

When the grass shall cover me!
Ah, belovéd, in my sorrow
Very patient, I can wait—
Knowing that or soon or late,
There will dawn a clearer morrow;
When your heart will moan, "Alas!
Now I know how true she was;
Now I know how dear she was."
When the grass grows over me.

INA D. COOLBRITH.

SLEEP.

"He giveth his belovéd sleep."—*Psalm* cxxvi. 2.

OF all the thoughts of God that are
Borne inward unto souls afar,
Among the Psalmist's music deep,
Now tell me if that any is,
For gift or grace, surpassing this,—
"He giveth his belovéd sleep?"

What would we give to our beloved?
The hero's heart, to be unmoved,—
The poet's star-tuned harp, to sweep,—
The patriot's voice, to teach and rouse,—
The monarch's crown, to light the brows?
"He giveth his belovéd sleep."

What do we give to our beloved?
A little faith, all undisproved,—
A little dust to overweep,
And bitter memories, to make
The whole earth blasted for our sake,
"He giveth his belovéd sleep."

"Sleep soft, beloved!" we sometimes say,
But have no tune to charm away
Sad dreams that through the eyelids creep;

But never doleful dream again.
Shall break the happy slumber when
"He giveth his belovéd sleep."

O earth, so full of dreary noise!
O men, with wailing in your voice!
O delvéd gold the wailers heap!
O strife, O curse, that o'er it fall!
God strikes a silence through you all,
And "giveth his belovéd sleep."

His dews drop mutely on the hill.
His cloud above it saileth still.
Though on its slope men sow and reap;
More softly than the dew is shed,
Or cloud is floated overhead,
"He giveth his belovéd sleep."

For me, my heart, that erst did go
Most like a tired child at a show,
That sees through tears the mummers leap,
Would now its wearied vision close,
Would childlike on his love repose
Who "giveth his belovéd sleep."

ELIZABETH BARRETT BROWNING.

THE SONG OF THE SHIRT.

WITH fingers weary and worn,
With eyelids heavy and red,
A woman sat, in unwomanly rags,
Plying her needle and thread—
Stitch! stitch! stitch!
In poverty, hunger, and dirt,
And still, with a voice of dolorous pitch,
She sang the "Song of the Shirt!"

"Work! work! work!
While the cock is crowing aloof!
And work—work—work!
Till the stars shine through the roof!
It's oh! to be a slave
Along with the barbarous Turk,
Where woman has never a soul to save,
If THIS is Christian work!

"Work—work—work!
  Till the brain begins to swim!
Work—work—work!
  Till the eyes are heavy and dim!
Seam, and gusset, and band,
  Band, and gusset, and seam,
Till over the buttons I fall asleep,
  And sew them on in my dream!

Oh! men with sisters dear!
  Oh! men with mothers and wives!
It is not linen you 're wearing out,
  But human creatures' lives!
Stitch—stitch—stitch!
  In poverty, hunger, and dirt,
Sewing at once with a double thread,
  A SHROUD as well as a shirt!

"But why do I talk of death,
  That phantom of grisly bone?
I hardly fear his terrible shape,
  It seems so like my own—
It seems so like my own,
  Because of the fast I keep:
O God! that bread should be so dear,
  And flesh and blood so cheap!

"Work—work—work!
  My labor never flags;
And what are its wages? A bed of straw,
  A crust of bread—and rags:
A shattered roof—and this naked floor—
  A table—a broken chair—
And a wall so blank, my shadow I thank
  For sometimes falling there!

"Work—work—work!
  From weary chime to chime;
"Work—work—work!
  As prisoners work for crime!
Band and gusset, and seam,
  Seam, and gusset, and band,
Till the heart is sick, and the brain benumbed,
  As well as the weary hand!

"Work—work—work!
  In the dull December light;
And work—work—work!
  When the weather is clear and bright:
While underneath the eaves
  The brooding swallows cling,
As if to show me their sunny backs,
  And twit me with the Spring.

"Oh! but to breathe the breath
  Of the cowslip and primrose sweet;
With the sky above my head,
  And the grass beneath my feet:

For only one short hour
  To feel as I used to feel,
Before I knew the woes of want,
  And the walk that costs a meal.

"Oh! but for one short hour!
  A respite, however brief!
No blessed leisure for love or hope,
  But only time for grief!
A little weeping would ease my heart—
  But in their briny bed
My tears must stop, for every drop
  Hinders needle and thread!"

"A wall so blank, my shadow I thank
For sometimes falling there."

With fingers weary and worn,
  With eyelids heavy and red,
A woman sat, in unwomanly rags,
  Plying her needle and thread;
Stitch—stitch—stitch!
  In poverty, hunger, and dirt;
And still with a voice of dolorous pitch!—
  Would that its tone could reach the rich!—
  She sung this "Song of the Shirt!"

THOMAS HOOD.

THE CONQUERED BANNER.

URL that banner, for 'tis weary;
Round its staff 'tis drooping dreary;
  Furl it, fold it, it is best;
For there 's not a man to wave it,
And there 's not a sword to save it,
And there 's not one left to lave it
  In the blood which heroes gave it;
And its foes now scorn and brave it:
  Furl it, hide it — let it rest.

Take that banner down, 'tis tattered!
Broken is its shaft and shattered,
And the valiant host are scattered,
  Over whom it floated high.
Oh, 'tis hard for us to fold it!
Hard to think there's none to hold it;
Hard that those that once unrolled it
  Now must furl it with a sigh.

Furl that banner — furl it sadly —
Once ten thousands hailed it gladly
And ten thousands wildly, madly,
  Swore it should forever wave —
Swore that foeman's sword should never
Hearts like theirs entwined dissever.
'Till that flag should float forever
  O er their freedom or their grave!

Furl it! for the hands that grasped it,
And the hearts that clasped it,
  Cold and dead are lying low;
And that banner — it is trailing!
While around it sounds the wailing
  Of its people in their woe.

For though conquered, they adore it!
Love the cold dead hands that bore it!
Weep for those who fell before it!
Pardon those who trailed and tore it!
But, oh! wildly they deplore it,
  Now, who furl and fold it so.

Furl that banner! True, 'tis gory,
Yet 'tis wreathed around with glory,
And 'twill live in song and story
  Though its folds are in the dust:
For its fame on brightest pages,
Penned by poets and by sages,
Shall go sounding down the ages —
  Furl its folds though now we must.

Furl that banner, softly, slowly;
Treat it gently — it is holy.
  For it droops above the dead.
Touch it not — unfold it never —
Let it droop there furled forever,
  For its people's hopes are dead!

                              ABRAM T. RYAN.

IF.

F. sitting with this little worn-out shoe
  And scarlet stocking lying on my knee,
I knew the little feet had pattered through
  The pearl-set gates that lie 'twixt Heaven and
    me,
I could be reconciled and happy too,
  And look with glad eyes toward the jasper sea.

If in the morning, when the song of birds
  Reminds me of a music far more sweet,
I listen for his pretty, broken words,
  And for the music of his dimpled feet,
I could be almost happy, though I heard
  No answer, and but saw his vacant seat.

I could be glad if, when the day is done,
  And all its cares and heartaches laid away,
I could look westward to the hidden sun,
  And, with a heart full of sweet yearnings, say—
"To-night I 'm nearer to my little one
  By just the travel of a single day."

If I could know those little feet were shod
  In sandals wrought of light in better lands,
And that the foot-prints of a tender God
  Ran side by side with him, in golden sands,
I could bow cheerfully and kiss the rod,
  Since Benny was in wiser, safer hands.

If he were dead, I would not sit to-day
  And stain with tears the wee sock on my knee;
I would not kiss the tiny shoe and say —
  "Bring back again my little boy to me!"
I would be patient, knowing 't was God's way,
  And wait to meet him o'er death's silent sea.

But oh! to know the feet, once pure and white,
  The haunts of vice had boldly ventured in!
The hands that should have battled for the right
  Had been wrung crimson in the clasp of sin!
And should he knock at Heaven's gate to-night,
  To fear my boy could hardly enter in!

                              MAY RILEY SMITH.

S the tree is fertilized by its own broken branches and fallen leaves, and grows out of
  its own decay, so is the soul of man ripened out of broken hopes and blighted
affections.

Some have their dead, where, sweet and calm,
  The summers bloom and go;—
The sea withholds my dead; I walk
  The bar when tides are low,
And wonder how the grave-grass
  Can have the heart to grow.

Flow oh, O unconsenting sea,
  And keep my dead below;
The night-watch set for me is long,
  But, through it all, I know,
Or life comes, or death comes,
  God leads the eternal flow.

HIRAM RICH.

JAMES MELVILLE'S CHILD.

ONE time my soul was pierced as with a sword,
  Contending still with men untaught and wild,
When He who to the prophet lent his gourd
  Gave me the solace of a pleasant child.

A summer gift, my precious flower was given,
  A very summer fragrance was its life;
Its clear eyes soothed me as the blue of heaven,
  When home I turned, a weary man of strife.

With unformed laughter, musically sweet,
  How soon the wakening babe would meet my kiss:
With outstretched arms, its care-wrought father greet!
  O, in the desert, what a spring was this!

A few short months it blossomed near my heart:
  A few short months, else toilsome all, and sad;
But that home-solace nerved me for my part,
  And of the babe I was exceeding glad.

Alas! my pretty bud, scarce formed, was dying,
  (The prophet's gourd, it withered in a night!)
And he who gave me all, my heart's pulse trying,
  Took gently home the child of my delight.

Not rudely culled, not suddenly it perished,
  But gradual faded from our love away:
As if, still, secret dews, its life that cherished,
  Were drop by drop withheld, and day by day.

My blessed Master saved me from repining,
  So tenderly He sued me for His own;
So beautiful He made my babe's declining,
  Its dying blessed me as its birth had done.

And daily to my board at noon and even
  Our fading flower I bade his mother bring,
That we might commune of our rest in Heaven,
  Gazing the while on death, without its sting.

And of the ransom for that baby paid
  So very sweet at times our converse seemed,
That the sure truth of grief a gladness made:
  Our little lamb by God's own Lamb redeemed!

There were two milk-white doves my wife had nour
    ished:
And I, too, loved, erewhile, at times to stand
Marking how each the other fondly cherished,
  And fed them from my baby's dimpled hand!

So tame they grew, that to his cradle flying,
  Full oft they cooed him to his noontide rest;

And to the murmurs of his sleep replying,
  Crept gently in, and nestled in his breast.

'T was a fair sight: the snow-pale infant sleeping,
  So fondly guardianed by those creatures mild,
Watch o'er his closed eyes their bright eyes keeping;
  Wondrous the love betwixt the birds and child!

Still as he sickened seemed the doves too dwining,
  Forsook their food, and loathed their pretty play;
And on the day he died, with sad note pining,
  One gentle bird would not be frayed away.

"And fed them from my baby's dimpled hand."

His mother found it, when she rose, sad hearted,
  At early dawn, with sense of nearing ill;
And when at last, the little spirit parted,
  The dove died too, as if of its heart-chill.

The other flew to meet my sad home-riding,
  As with a human sorrow in its coo;
To my dead child and its dead mate then guiding,
  Most pitifully plained—and parted too.

'T was my first hansel and propine to Heaven;
  And as I laid my darling 'neath the sod,
Precious His comforts—once an infant given,
  And offered with two turtle-doves to God!

MRS. A. STUART MENTEATH.

TO MARY IN HEAVEN.

THOU lingering star, with lessening ray,
    That lov'st to greet the early morn,
Again thou usher'st in the day
    My Mary from my soul was torn.
O Mary! dear departed shade!
    Where is thy place of blissful rest?
See'st thou thy lover lowly laid?
    Hear'st thou the groans that rend his breast?

That sacred hour can I forget, —
    Can I forget the hallowed grove,
Where by the winding Ayr we met
    To live one day of parting love?
Eternity will not efface
    Those records dear of transports past;
Thy image at our last embrace;
    Ah! little thought we 'twas our last!

Ayr, gurgling, kissed his pebbled shore,
    O'erhung with wild woods, thickening **green**;
The fragrant birch, and hawthorn hoar,
    Twined amorous round the raptured scene;
The flowers sprang wanton to be prest,
    The birds sang love on every spray, —
Till soon, too soon, the glowing west
    Proclaimed the speed of wingéd day.

Still o'er these scenes my memory wakes,
    And fondly broods with miser care!
Time but the impression stronger makes,
    As streams their channels deeper wear.
My Mary! dear departed shade!
    Where is thy place of blissful rest?
See'st thou thy lover lowly laid?
    Hear'st thou the groans that rend his breast?

                            ROBERT BURNS.

ANNABEL LEE.

IT was many and many a year ago,
    In a kingdom by the sea,
That a maiden lived whom you may know
    By the name of Annabel Lee;
And this maiden she lived with no other
        thought
    Than to love, and be loved by me.

I was a child and she was a child,
    In this kingdom by the sea;
But we loved with a love that was more than love,
    I and my Annabel Lee,—
With a love that the wingéd seraphs of heaven
    Coveted her and me.

And this was the reason that long ago,
    In this kingdom by the sea,
A wind blew out of cloud-land, chilling
    My beautiful Annabel Lee;
So that her high-born kinsman came
    And bore her away from me,
To shut her up in a sepulchre,
    In this kingdom by the sea.

The angels, not so happy in heaven,
    Went envying her and me.
Yes! that was the reason (as all men know)
    In this kingdom by the sea,
That the wind came out of the cloud by night,
    Chilling and killing my Annabel Lee.

But our love it was stronger by far than the love
    Of those who were older than we,
    Of many far wiser than we;
And neither the angels in heaven above,
    Nor the demons down under the sea,
Can ever dissever my soul from the soul
    Of the beautiful Annabel Lee.

For the moon never beams without bringing me
        dreams
    Of the beautiful Annabel Lee,
And the stars never rise but I feel the bright eyes
    Of the beautiful Annabel Lee.
And so, all the night-tide I lie down by the side
Of my darling, my darling, my life, and my bride,
    In her sepulchre there by the sea,
    In her tomb by the sounding sea.

                            EDGAR ALLAN POE.

WE ARE SEVEN.

A SIMPLE child,
    That lightly draws its breath,
And feels its life in every limb,
    What should she know of death?

I met a little cottage girl:
    She was eight years old she said;
Her hair was thick with many a curl
    That clustered round her head.

She had a rustic woodland air,
And she was wildly clad:
Her eyes were fair, and very fair;—
Her beauty made me glad.

"Sisters and brothers, little maid,
How many may you be?"
"How many? Seven in all," she said,
And wondering looked at me.

"And where are they? I pray you tell."
She answered, "Seven are we;
And two of us at Conway dwell,
And two are gone to sea.

"Two of us in the churchyard lie,
My sister and my brother;
And in the churchyard cottage, I
Dwell near them with my mother."

"You say that two at Conway dwell,
And two are gone to sea,
Yet ye are seven! I pray you tell,
Sweet maid how this may be."

Then did the little maid reply,
"Seven boys and girls are we;
Two of us in the churchyard lie,
Beneath the churchyard tree."

"You run about my little maid,
Your limbs they are alive;
If two are in the churchyard laid,
Then ye are only five."

"Their graves are green, they may be seen,"
The little maid replied,
"Twelve steps or more from my mother's door
And they are side by side.

"My stockings there I often knit,
My kerchief there I hem;
And there upon the ground I sit,
I sit and sing to them.

"And often after sunset, sir,
When it is light and fair,
I take my little porringer,
And eat my supper there.

"The first that died was little Jane;
In bed she moaning lay,
Till God released her of her pain;
And then she went away.

"So in the churchyard she was laid;
And, when the grass was dry.
Together round her grave we played,
My brother John and I.

"And when the ground was white with snow,
And I could run and slide
My brother John was forced to go,
And he lies by her side."

"How many are you, then," said I,
"If they two are in heaven?"
The little maiden did reply,
"O master! we are seven."

"But they are dead; those two are dead?
Their spirits are in heaven!"
'T was throwing words away; for still
The little maid would have her will,
And said, "Nay, we are seven!"

WILLIAM WORDSWORTH.

DIRGE.

SOFTLY!
    She is lying
With her lips apart.
    Softly!
    She is dying
Of a broken heart.

    Whisper!
    She is going
To her final rest.

    Whisper!
    Life is growing
Dim within her breast.

    Gently!
    She is sleeping;
She has breathed her last.
    Gently!
    While you are weeping,
She to heaven has passed.

CHARLES GAMAGE EASTMAN.

WE are what the past has made us. The results of the past are ourselves. The perishable emotions, and the momentary acts of bygone years, are the scaffolding on which we built up the being that we are.

THREE KISSES.

HAVE three kisses in my life,
  So sweet and sacred unto me,
That now, till death-dews on them rest,
  My lips shall ever kissless be.

One kiss was given in childhood's hour,
  By one who never gave another;
Through life and death I still shall feel
  That last kiss of my mother.

The next kiss burned my lips for years;
  For years my wild heart reeled in bliss,

At every memory of that hour
  When my lips felt young love's first kiss.

The last kiss of the sacred three,
  Had all the woe which e'er can move
The heart of woman; it was pressed
  Upon the dead lips of my love.

When lips have felt the dying kiss,
  And felt the kiss of burning love,
And kissed the dead, then nevermore
  In kissing should they think to move.

                        HATTIE TYNG GRISWOLD.

THE BRAVE AT HOME.

HE maid who binds her warrior's sash,
  With smile that well her pain dissembles,
The while beneath her drooping lash
  One starry tear-drop hangs and trembles,

Doomed nightly in her dreams to hear
  The bolts of death around him rattle,
Hath shed as sacred blood as e'er
  Was poured upon the field of battle!

" The wife who girds her husband's sword,
'Mid little ones who weep or wonder."

Though Heaven alone records the tear,
  And fame shall never know her story,
Her heart has shed a drop as dear
  As e'er bedewed the field of glory!

The wife who girds her husband's sword,
  'Mid little ones who weep or wonder,
And bravely speaks the cheering word,
  What though her heart be rent asunder,

The mother who conceals her grief,
  While to her breast her son she presses,
Then breathes a few brave words and brief,
  Kissing the patriot brow she blesses,
With no one but her secret God
  To know the pain that weighs upon her,
Sheds holy blood, as e'er the sod
  Received on Freedom's field of honor!

                        THOMAS BUCHANAN READ.

AULD ROBIN GRAY.

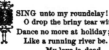

WHEN the sheep are in the fauld, and the kye's
    come hame,
  And a' the weary warld to rest are gane,
  The waes o' my heart fall in showers frae
    my ee,
  Unkempt by my gudeman, wha sleeps sound
    by me.

Young Jamie lo'ed me weel, and sought me for his
    bride,
But saving a crown he had naithing else beside:
To mak' the crown a pound, my Jamie gaed to sea,
And the crown and the pound they were baith for me.

He had nae been gane a twalmonth and a day,
When my faither brak his arm, and the cow was
    stown away;
My mither she fell sick, and my Jamie was at sea,
And auld Robin Gray cam' a courting me.

My faither could na work, my mither could na spin,
I toiled day and night, but their bread I could na win;
Auld Rob maintained them baith, an wi' tears in
    his ee,
Said, "Jeanie, for their sakes, will ye nae marry me?"

My heart it said nay, and I looked for Jamie back,
But the wind it blew hard, and the ship was a wrack—
The ship was a wrack, why did na Jamie dee?
Or why was I spared to cry, Wae's me!

My faither urged me sair, my mither did na speak,
But she looked in my face till my heart was like to
    break:
They gi'ed him my hand, though my heart was in the
    sea,
And so Robin Gray he was gudeman to me!

I had na been a wife a week but only four,
When mournful as I sat on the stane at my door,
I saw my Jamie's wraith, for I could na think it be,
Till he said, "I'm come hame, love, to marry thee."

Sair, sair did we greet, and mickle did we say,—
We took but ae kiss, and tare oursels away:
I wish I were dead, but I am na lik' to dee,
Oh, why was I born to say, Wae's me!

I gang like a gaist, but I care na much to spin;
I dare na think on Jamie, for that wad be a sin;
So I will do my best a gude wife to be,
For auld Robin Gray he is kind to me.

LADY ANNE BARNARD.

MY LOVE IS DEAD.

SING unto my roundelay!
  O drop the briny tear with me!
Dance no more at holiday;
  Like a running river be.
    My love is dead,
    Gone to his death-bed,
    All under the willow tree.

Black his hair as the summer night,
  White his neck as the winter snow,
Ruddy his face as the morning light;
  Cold he lies in the grave below.
    My love is dead, etc.

Sweet his tongue as the throstle's note;
  Quick in dance as thought can be;
Deft his tabor, cudgel stout;
  O, he lies by the willow tree.
    My love is dead, etc.

Hark! the raven flaps his wing
  In the briered dell below;
Hark the death-owl loud doth sing
  To the nightmares as they go.
    My love is dead, etc.

See! the white moon shines on high;
  Whiter is my true-love's shroud,

Whiter than the morning sky,
  Whiter than the evening cloud.
    My love is dead, etc.

Here upon my true-love's grave
  Shall the barren flowers be laid
Nor one holy saint to save
  All the coldness of a maid.
    My love is dead, etc.

With my hands I'll bind the briers
  Round his holy corse to gre;
Ouphant fairy, light your fires;
  Here my body still shall be.
    My love is dead, etc.

Come, with acorn-cup and thorn,
  Drain my heart's blood away;
Life and all its good I scorn,
  Dance by night, or feast by day.
    My love is dead, etc.

Water-witches, crowned with reytes,
  Bear me to your lethal tide.
I die! I come! my true-love waits.
  Thus the damsel spake, and died.

THOMAS CHATTERTON.

OLD TIMES.

"'TWAS thirty years ago, and now
    We meet once more," I sighed and said,
"To talk of Eton and old times;
    But every second word is 'Dead!'"

We fill the glass, and watch the wine
    Rise, as thermometers will do,
Then rouse the fire into a blaze,
    And once more. boys, we share the glow.

"Do you remember Hawtrey's time?
    Pod Major, and the way he read?

And Powis and Old Stokes? Alas!
    Our every second word is 'Dead!'"

Well, springs must have their autumns too,
    And suns must set as they must shine;
And, waiter, here, a bottle more,
    And let it be your oldest wine.

And gather closer to the fire,
    And let the gas flare overhead;
Some day our children will meet thus,
    And they will praise or blame the Dead.

OLD.

BY the wayside, on a mossy stone,
    Sat a hoary pilgrim, sadly musing;
Oft I marked him sitting there alone,
    All the landscape, like a page, perusing;
        Poor, unknown,
By the wayside, on a mossy stone.

"When the stranger seemed to mark our play,
Some of us were joyous, some sad-hearted"

Buckled knee and shoe, and broad-brimmed hat;
    Coat as ancient as the form 't was folding;
Silver buttons, queue, and crimped cravat;
    Oaken staff his feeble hand upholding:
        There he sat!
Buckled knee and shoe, and broad-brimmed hat.

Seemed it pitiful he should sit there,
    No one sympathizing, no one heeding,
None to love him for his thin gray hair,
    And the furrows all so mutely pleading
        Age and care:
Seemed it pitiful he should sit there.

It was summer, and we went to school,
    Dapper country lads and little maidens;
Taught the motto of the "Dunce's stool,"—
    Its grave import still my fancy ladens,—
        "Here 's a fool!"
It was summer, and we went to school.

When the stranger seemed to mark our play,
    Some of us were joyous, some sad-hearted,
I remember well, too well, that day!
    Oftentimes the tears unbidden started
        Would not stay
When the stranger seemed to mark our play.

One sweet spirit broke the silent spell,
    Oh, to me her name was always Heaven!
She besought him all his grief to tell,
    (I was then thirteen, and she eleven,)
        Isabel!
One sweet spirit broke the silent spell.

"Angel," said he sadly, "I am old;
    Earthly hope no longer hath a morrow;
Yet, why I sit here thou shalt be told."
    Then his eye betrayed a pearl of sorrow,
        Down it rolled!
"Angel," said he sadly, "I am old."

"I have tottered here to look once more
    On the pleasant scene where I delighted
In the careless, happy days of yore,
    Ere the garden of my heart was blighted
        To the core:
I have tottered here to look once more.

"All the picture now to me how dear!
  E'en this gray old rock where I am seated
Is a jewel worth my journey here;
  Ah, that such a scene must be completed
      With a tear!
All the picture now to me how dear!

"Old stone school-house!—it is still the same;
  There 's the very step I so oft mounted;
There 's the window creaking in its frame,
  And the notches that I cut and counted
      For the game.
Old stone school-house, it is still the same.

"There the rude, three-cornered chestnut-rails,
  Round the pasture where the flocks were grazing,
Where, so sly, I used to watch for quails
  In the crops of buckwheat we were raising;
      Traps and trails!
There the rude, three-cornered chestnut-rails.

"There 's the mill that ground our yellow grain:
  Pond and river still serenely flowing :
Cot there nestling in the shaded lane,
  Where the lily of my heart was blowing.
      Mary Jane!
There 's the mill that ground our yellow grain.

" There 's the mill that ground our yellow grain."

"In the cottage yonder I was born;
  Long my happy home, that humble dwelling;
There the fields of clover, wheat and corn;
  There the spring with limpid nectar swelling;
      Ah, forlorn!
In the cottage yonder I was born.

"Those two gateway sycamores you see
  Then were planted just so far asunder
That long well-pole from the path to free,
  And the wagon to pass safely under;
      Ninety-three!
Those two gateway sycamores you see.

"There 's the orchard where we used to climb
  When my mates and I were boys together,
Thinking nothing of the flight of time,
  Fearing naught but work and rainy weather:
      Past its prime!
There 's the orchard where we used to climb.

" There 's the gate on which I used to swing,
  Brook, and bridge, and barn, and old red stable;
But alas! no more the morn shall bring
  That dear group around my father's table;
      Taken wing!
There 's the gate on which I used to swing.

I am fleeing; — all I loved have fled.
  Yon green meadow was our place for playing;
That old tree can tell of sweet things said
  When around it Jane and I were straying;
      She is dead!
I am fleeing, — all I loved have fled.

" Yon white spire, a pencil on the sky,
  Tracing silently life's changeful story,
So familiar to my dim old eye,
  Points me to seven that are now in glory
      There on high!
Yon white spire, a pencil on the sky.

Oft the aisle of that old church we trod,
Guided thither by an angel mother;
Now she sleeps beneath its sacred sod;
Sire and sisters, and my little brother,
    Gone to God!
Oft the aisle of that old church we trod.

"There I heard of Wisdom's pleasant ways;
Bless the holy lesson! — but, ah, never
Shall I hear again those songs of praise,
Those sweet voices silent now forever!
    Peaceful days!
There I heard of Wisdom's pleasant ways.

" There my Mary blest me with her hand
When our souls drank in the nuptial-blessing,
Ere she hastened to the spirit-land,
Yonder turf her gentle bosom pressing;
    Broken band!
There my Mary blest me with her hand.

" I have come to see that grave once more,
And the sacred place where we delighted,
Where we worshiped, in the days of yore,
Ere the garden of my heart was blighted
    To the core!
I have come to see that grave once more.

" Angel," said he sadly, " I am old;
Earthly hope no longer hath a morrow,
Now, why I sit here thou hast been told."
In his eye another pearl of sorrow,
    Down it rolled!
" Angel," said he sadly, " I am old."

By the wayside on a mossy stone,
Sat the hoary pilgrim, sadly musing;

" Brook, and bridge, and barn, and old red stable."

Still I marked him sitting there alone,
All the landscape. like a page, perusing;
    Poor, unknown!
By the wayside, on a mossy stone.

RALPH HOYT.

MY MOTHER'S BIBLE.

THIS book is all that 's left me now, —
    Tears will unbidden start. —
With faltering lip and throbbing brow
    I press it to my heart.
For many generations past
    Here is our family tree;
My mother's hands this Bible clasped,
    She, dying, gave it me.

Ah! well do I remember those
    Whose names these records bear;
Who round the hearthstone used to close,
    After the evening prayer,
And speak of what these pages said
    In tones my heart would thrill!
Though they are with the silent dead,
    Here are they living still!

My father read this holy book
    To brothers, sisters, dear;
How calm was my poor mother's look,
    Who loved God's word to hear!
Her angel face, — I see it yet!
    What thronging memories come!
Again that little group is met
    Within the halls of home!

Thou truest friend man ever knew,
    Thy constancy I 've tried;
When all were false, I found thee true,
    My counselor and guide.
The mines of earth no treasures give
    That could this volume buy;
In teaching me the way to live,
    It taught me how to die!

GEORGE P. MORRIS.

BINGEN ON THE RHINE.

A SOLDIER of the Legion lay dying in Algiers,
There was lack of woman's nursing, there was
  dearth of woman's tears;
But a comrade stood beside him, while his life-
  blood ebbed away,
And bent, with pitying glances, to hear what
  he might say.
The dying soldier faltered, as he took that comrade's
  hand,
And he said, "I nevermore shall see my own, my na-
  tive land;
Take a message, and a token, to some distant friends
  of mine,
For I was born at Bingen,—at Bingen on the Rhine.

"Tell my brothers and companions, when they meet
  and crowd around,
To hear my mournful story, in the pleasant vineyard
  ground,
That we fought the battle bravely, and when the day
  was done,
Full many a corse lay ghastly pale beneath the setting
  sun;
And, mid the dead and dying, were some grown old
  in wars,—
The death-wound on their gallant breasts, the last of
  many scars;
And some were young, and suddenly beheld life's
  morn decline,—
And one had come from Bingen,—fair Bingen on the
  Rhine.

"Tell my mother that her other son shall comfort her
  old age,
For I was still a truant bird, that thought his home a
  cage.
For my father was a soldier, and even as a child
My heart leaped forth to hear him tell of struggles
  fierce and wild;
And when he died, and left us to divide his scanty
  hoard,
I let them take whate'er they would,—but kept my
  father's sword;
And with boyish love I hung it where the bright light
  used to shine,
On the cottage wall at Bingen,—calm Bingen on the
  Rhine.

"Tell my sister not to weep for me, and sob with
  drooping head,
When the troops come marching home again with glad
  and gallant tread
But to look upon them proudly, with a calm and stead-
  fast eye,
For her brother was a soldier, too, and not afraid to
  die;

And if a comrade seek her love, I ask her in my name
To listen to him kindly, without regret or shame,
And to hang the old sword in its place (my father's
  sword and mine)
For the honor of old Bingen,—dear Bingen on the
  Rhine.

"There 's another,—not a sister; in the happy days
  gone by
You 'd have known her by the merriment that
  sparkled in her eye;
Too innocent for coquetry,—too fond for idle scorn-
  ing,—
O friend! I fear the lightest heart makes sometimes
  heaviest mourning!
Tell her the last night of my life (for, ere the moon
  be risen,
My body will be out of pain, my soul be out of pris-
  on),—
I dreamed I stood with her, and saw the yellow sun-
  light shine
On the vine-clad hills of Bingen,—fair Bingen on the
  Rhine.

"I saw the blue Rhine sweep along,—I heard, or
  seemed to hear,
The German songs we used to sing, in chorus sweet
  and clear;
And down the pleasant river, and up the slanting hill,
The echoing chorus sounded, through the evening
  calm and still;
And her glad blue eyes were on me, as we passed,
  with friendly talk,
Down many a path beloved of yore, and well-remem-
  bered walk!
And her little hand lay lightly, confidingly in mine,—
But we 'll meet no more at Bingen,—loved Bingen on
  the Rhine."

His trembling voice grew faint and hoarse,—his grasp
  was childish weak —
His eyes put on a dying look,—he sighed and ceased
  to speak;
His comrade bent to lift him, but the spark of life had
  fled,—
The soldier of the Legion in a foreign land is dead!
And the soft moon rose up slowly, and calmly she
  looked down
On the red sand of the battle-field, with bloody corses
  strewn;
Yes, calmly on that dreadful scene her pale light
  seemed to shine,
As it shone on distant Bingen,—fair Bingen on the
  Rhine.

CAROLINE ELIZABETH SARAH NORTON.

THE LAST OF SEVEN.

NAY, be not angry, chide her not,
    Although the child hast erred,
Nor bring the tears into her eyes
    By one ungentle word.

"But now in grief she walks alone
By every garden bed."

When that sweet linnet sang, before
    Our summer roses died,
A sister's arm was round her neck,
    A brother at her side.

But now in grief she walks alone,
    By every garden bed,
That sister's clasping arm is cold,
    That brother's voice is tied.

And when she sits beside my chair,
    With face so pale and meek,
And eyes bent o'er her book, I see
    The tear upon her cheek.

Then chide her not; but whisper now,
    "Thy trespass is forgiven,"—
How canst thou frown on that pale face?
    She is the last of seven.

                 AVIS WILLMOTT.

THE VOICELESS.

WE count the broken lyres that rest
    Where the sweet wailing singers slumber,
But o'er their silent sister's breast
    The wild flowers who will stoop to number?
A few can touch the magic string,
    And noisy fame is proud to win them;
Alas for those that never sing,
    But die with all their music in them!

Nay, grieve not for the dead alone,
    Whose song has told their hearts' sad story:
Weep for the voiceless, who have known
    The cross without the crown of glory!
Not where Leucadian breezes sweep
    O'er Sappho's memory-haunted billow,
But where the glistening night-dews weep
    On nameless sorrow's churchyard pillow.

O hearts that break, and give no sign,
    Save whitening lip and fading tresses,
Till Death pours out his cordial wine,
    Slow-dropped from misery's crushing presses!
If singing breath or echoing chord
    To every hidden pang were given,
What endless melodies were poured,
    As sad as earth, as sweet as heaven!

            OLIVER WENDELL HOLMES.

RESIGNATION.

THERE is no flock, however watched and tended,
    But one dead lamb is there!
There is no fireside, howsoe'er defended,
    But has one vacant chair!

The air is full of farewells to the dying;
    And mournings for the dead;
The heart of Rachel, for her children crying,
    Will not be comforted!

Let us be patient! These severe afflictions
    Not from the ground arise.
But oftentimes celestial benedictions
    Assume this dark disguise.

We see but dimly through the mists and vapors;
    Amid these earthly damps
What seem to us but sad, funereal tapers
    May be heaven's distant lamps.

There is no Death! What seems so is transition;
This life of mortal breath
Is but a suburb of the life elysian,
Whose portal we call Death.

She is not dead, — the child of our affection, —
But gone unto that school
Where she no longer needs our poor protection,
And Christ himself doth rule.

In that great cloister's stillness and seclusion,
By guardian angels led,
Safe from temptation, safe from sin's pollution,
She lives, whom we call dead.

Day after day we think what she is doing
In those bright realms of air;
Year after year, her tender steps pursuing,
Behold her grown more fair.

Thus do we walk with her, and keep unbroken
The bond which nature gives,
Thinking that our remembrance, though unspoken,
May reach her where she lives.

Not as a child shall we again behold her;
For when with raptures wild
In our embraces we again enfold her,
She will not be a child;

But a fair maiden, in her Father's mansion,
Clothed with celestial grace;
And beautiful with all the soul's expansion
Shall we behold her face.

And though at times impetuous with emotion
And anguish long suppressed,
The swelling heart heaves moaning like the ocean,
That cannot be at rest, —

We will be patient, and assuage the feeling
We may not wholly stay;
By silence sanctifying, not concealing,
The grief that must have way.

HENRY WADSWORTH LONGFELLOW.

THE BIVOUAC OF THE DEAD.

THE muffled drum's sad roll has beat
    The soldier's last tattoo;
No more on Life's parade shall meet
    That brave and fallen few.
On Fame's eternal camping ground
    Their silent tents are spread,
And Glory guards, with solemn round,
    The bivouac of the dead.

No rumor of the foe's advance
    Now swells upon the wind;
No troubled thought at midnight haunts
    Of loved ones left behind;
No vision of the morrow's strife
    The warrior's dream alarms;
No braying horn or screaming fife
    At dawn shall call to arms.

Their shivered swords are red with rust,
    Their pluméd heads are bowed;
Their haughty banner, trailed in dust,
    Is now their martial shroud.
And plenteous funeral tears have washed
    The red stains from each brow,
And the proud forms, by battle gashed,
    Are free from anguish now.

The neighing troop, the flashing blade,
    The bugle's stirring blast,
The charge, the dreadful cannonade,
    The din and shout, are past;
Nor war's wild note nor glory's peal
    Shall thrill with fierce delight
Those breasts that never more may feel
    The rapture of the fight.

Like the fierce northern hurricane
    That sweeps his great plateau,
Flushed with the triumph yet to gain,
    Came down the serried foe.
Who heard the thunder of the fray
    Break o'er the field beneath,
Knew well the watchword of that day
    Was "Victory or death."

Long has the doubtful conflict raged
    O'er all that stricken plain,
For never fiercer fight had waged
    The vengeful blood of Spain;
And still the storm of battle blew,
    Still swelled the gory tide;
Not long, our stout old chieftain knew,
    Such odds his strength could bide.

'T was in that hour his stern command
    Called to a martyr's grave
The flower of his belovéd land,
    The nation's flag to save.
By rivers of their fathers' gore
    His first-born laurels grew,
And well he deemed the sons would pour
    Their lives for glory too.

Full many a norther's breath had swept
    O'er Angostura's plain—
And long the pitying sky has wept
    Above the mouldering slain.
The raven's scream, or eagle's flight,
    Or shepherd's pensive lay,
Alone awakes each sullen height
    That frowned o'er that dread fray.

Sons of the Dark and Bloody Ground,
  Ye must not slumber there,
Where stranger steps and tongues resound
  Along the heedless air;
Your own proud land's heroic soil
  Shall be your fitter grave;
She claims from war his richest spoil—
  The ashes of her brave.

So 'neath their parent turf they rest,
  Far from the gory field,
Borne to a Spartan mother's breast,
  On many a bloody shield;
The sunshine of their native sky
  Smiles sadly on them here,
And kindred eyes and hearts watch by
  The heroes' sepulchre.

Rest on, embalmed and sainted dead,
  Dear as the blood ye gave;
No impious footstep here shall tread
  The herbage of your grave;
Nor shall your glory be forgot
  While Fame her record keeps,
Or Honor points the hallowed spot
  Where Valor proudly sleeps.

Yon marble minstrel's voiceless stone,
  In deathless song shall tell,
When many a vanished age hath flown,
  The story how ye fell;
Nor wreck, nor change, nor winter's blight,
  Nor Time's remorseless doom,
Shall dim one ray of glory's light
  That gilds your deathless tomb.

THEODORE O'HARA.

"Bring flowers of early spring
To deck each soldier's grave."

OUR SOLDIERS' GRAVES.

STREW all their graves with flowers,
  They for their country died;
And freely gave their lives for ours,
  Their country's hope and pride.

Bring flowers to deck each sod,
  Where rests their sacred dust;
Though gone from earth, they live to God,
  Their everlasting trust!

Fearless in Freedom's cause
  They suffered, toiled, and bled;

And died obedient to her laws,
  By truth and conscience led.

Oft as the year returns,
  She o'er their graves shall weep;
And wreathe with flowers their funeral urns,
  Their memory dear to keep.

Bring flowers of early spring
  To deck each soldier's grave,
And summer's fragrant roses bring,—
  They died our land to save.

JONES VERY.

BEREAVEMENT.

MARKED when vernal meads were bright,
   And many a primrose smiled,
I marked her, blithe as morning light
   A dimpled three years' child.

A basket on one tender arm
   Contained her precious store
Of spring-flowers in their freshest charm,
   Told proudly o'er and o'er.

The summer months swept by: again
   That loving pair I met.
On russet heath, and bowery lane,
   Th' autumnal sun had set!

And chill and damp that Sunday eve
   Breathed on the mourners' road,
That bright-eyed little one to leave
   Safe in the Saints' abode.

"A basket on one tender arm
Contained her precious store."

The other wound with earnest hold
   About her blooming guide,
A maid who scarce twelve years had told.
   So walked they side by side.

One a bright bud, and one might seem
   A sister flower half blown.
Full joyous on their loving dream
   The sky of April shone.

Behind, the guardian sister came,
   Her bright brow dim and pale—
O cheer thee, maiden! in His Name,
   Who stilled Jairus' wail!

Thou mourn'st to miss the fingers soft,
   That held by thine so fast,
The fond appealing eye, full oft
   Tow'rd thee for refuge cast.

27

Sweet toils, sweet cares, forever gone!
  No more from stranger's face,
Or startling sound, the timid one
  Shall hide in thine embrace.

The first glad earthly task is o'er,
  And dreary seems thy way.
But what if nearer than before
  She watch thee even to-day?

What if henceforth by Heaven's decree
  She leave thee not alone,

But in her turn prove guide to thee
  In ways to Angels known?

O yield thee to her whisperings sweet:
  Away with thoughts of gloom!
In love the loving spirits greet
  Who wait to bless her tomb.

In loving hope with her unseen,
  Walk as in hallowed air.
When foes are strong and trials keen,
  Think, "What if she be there?"

JOHN KEBLE.

THREE ROSES.

HREE roses, wan as moonlight, and weighed
    down,
  Each with its loveliness as with a crown,
  Drooped in a florist's window in a town.

The third, a widow, with new grief made wild,
Shut in the icy palm of her dead child.

THOMAS BAILEY ALDRICH.

"The third, a widow, with new grief made wild,
Shut in the icy palm of her dead child."

The first a lover bought. It lay at rest,
Like flower on flower that night on beauty's breast.

The second rose, as virginal and fair.
Shrank in the tangles of a harlot's hair.

HIGHLAND MARY.

E banks, and braes, and streams around
    The castle o' Montgomery,
Green be your woods, and fair your flowers,
  Your waters never drumlie!
There simmer first unfauld her robes,
  And there the langest tarry;
For there I took the last fareweel
  O' my sweet Highland Mary.

How sweetly bloomed the gay green birk,
  How rich the hawthorn's blossom,
As underneath their fragrant shade
  I clasped her to my bosom!
The golden hours, on angel wings,
  Flew o'er me and my dearie;
For dear to me as light and life
  Was my sweet Highland Mary.

Wi' mony a vow, and locked embrace,
  Our parting was fu' tender;
And, pledging aft to meet again,
  We tore oursels asunder;
But oh! fell death's untimely frost,
  That nipt my flower sae early!
Now green 's the sod, and cauld 's the clay
  That wraps my Highland Mary!

O pale, pale now, those rosy lips
  I aft hae kissed sae fondly!
And closed for aye the sparkling glance
  That dwelt on me sae kindly!
And mouldering now in silent dust
  The heart that lo'ed me dearly!
But still within my bosom's core
  Shall live my Highland Mary.

ROBERT BURNS.

REQUIESCAT.

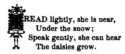READ lightly, she is near,
Under the snow;
Speak gently, she can hear
The daisies grow.

All her bright golden hair
Tarnished with rust,
She that was young and fair
Fallen to dust.

Lily-like, white as snow,
She hardly knew

She was a woman, so
Sweetly she grew.

Coffin-board, heavy stone,
Lie on her breast;
I vex my heart alone,
She is at rest.

Peace, peace; she cannot hear
Lyre or sonnet;
All my life 's buried here —
Heap earth upon it.

OSCAR WILDE.

" Children would run to meet him on his way."

THE BLIND MAN.

BUT list that moan! 'tis the poor blind man's dog,
His guide for many a day, now come to mourn
The master and the friend — conjunction rare :
A man, indeed, he was of gentle soul,
Though bred to brave the deep; the lightning's flash
Had dimmed, not closed, his mild but sightless eyes.
He was a welcome guest through all his range
(it was not wide) ; no dog would bay at him;
Children would run to meet him on his way,
And lead him to a sunny seat, and climb
His knee, and wonder at his oft-told tales:
Then would he teach the elfins how to plait
The rushy cap and crown, or sedgy ship;
And I have seen him lay his tremulous hand
Upon their heads, while silent moved his lips.
Peace to thy spirit! that now looks on me,
Perhaps with greater pity than I felt
To see thee wandering darkling on thy way.

JAMES GRAHAME.

OUT OF THE PLAGUE-STRICKEN CITY.

"E will go, my love, together to the golden
    autumn field;
Ah! mellow falls the sunshine where the
    roses blow;
This day in wood and meadow we 'll forget
    the pale lips sealed;
This day to love and gladness, whate'er the morrows
    yield."
Sweet, sweet the peaceful forest where the cool
    streams flow.

Through the dread plague-stricken city passed the
    lovers on their way,
Far floats the yellow banner in the morning's glow;
Through the ranks of dead and dying, where the fever-
    smitten lay,
Through the wailing and the horror of the fateful
    autumn day.
Ah! God's wrath lieth heavy where the south-winds
    blow.

"Nay, love, why gaze you backward at the dead-cart
    in its round?
Tolls the solemn death-bell, tolling long and slow;
Death holds the pallid city, but we 'll cross its farthest
    bound,
And forget for one brief hour every ghastly sight and
    sound."
List! that voice that crieth, "Woe, ye people,
    woe!"

Like children through the meadows they wandered,
    hand in hand;
Soft the mossy hillocks where the violets grow;
They gathered leaf and flower; but she wrote upon
    the sand,
"Ay, strong is love, but stronger is Death's unsparing
    hand."
Sad the under voices in the river's flow.

"Why speak of death, beloved? to-day is surely ours;
Each hour holds a secret which the angels know;
You gracious sky above us, our feet upon the flowers;

Why vex with thoughts of dolor the peace of happy
    hours?"
Swift the lights and shadows where the aspens
    grow.

The air is thrilled with bird-notes, in the rapture of
    their singing;
Minor chords are sounding in the dove's plaint, soft
    and low;
I am drunken with the gladness that Nature's grace is
    bringing,
Be merry, then, O sweetheart; list the woodland cho-
    rus ringing."
Far-off bells are tolling a requiem, sad and slow.

She closed her heavy eyelids, laid her head upon his
    shoulder;
Nevermore the dreaming of the happy long ago.
"Alas! love, 'neath the flowers I see the dead leaves
    moulder.
I am chill, so chill and weary; has the sunny day
    grown colder?"
Autumn leaves are falling, as the west-winds come
    and go.

Plague-stricken? Yes, O lover, for the Yellow King
    has seized her,
Vast the realm of shadows, where no earth winds
    blow;
Midst the bird songs and the clover and the fresh free
    air he claims her.
Vainly, vainly from his power would thy frantic love
    withhold her,
Weep o'er sweetest flowers, killed by winter's snow.

He laid her 'neath the aspens, but e'er the first gray
    dawning,
Blessed the peaceful garden where God's lilies blow,
Her lovely eyes half opened, and without sigh or
    warning.
Her soul beyond the shadows had sprung to meet the
    morning.
Oh, the blissful morning which His people know!

MARIE B. WILLIAMS.

FOOTSTEPS OF ANGELS.

HEN the hours of day are numbered,
    And the voices of the night
Wake the better soul that slumbered
    To a holy, calm delight;

Ere the evening lamps are lighted,
    And, like phantoms grim and tall,
Shadows from the fitful firelight
    Dance upon the parlor wall;

Then the forms of the departed
    Enter at the open door.—
The beloved ones, the true-hearted,
    Come to visit me once more:

He, the young and strong, who cherished
    Noble longings for the strife,
By the roadside fell and perished,
    Weary with the march of life!

They, the holy ones and weakly,
  Who the cross of suffering bore,
Folded their pale hands so meekly,
  Spake with us on earth no more!

And with them the being beauteous
  Who unto my youth was given,
More than all things else to love me,
  And is now a saint in heaven.

With a slow and noiseless footstep,
  Comes that messenger divine,
Takes the vacant chair beside me,
  Lays her gentle hand in mine;

And she sits and gazes at me
  With those deep and tender eyes,
Like the stars, so still and saint-like,
  Looking downward from the skies.

Uttered not, yet comprehended,
  Is the spirit's voiceless prayer,
Soft rebukes in blessings ended,
  Breathing from her lips of air.

O, though oft depressed and lonely,
  All my fears are laid aside
If I but remember only
  Such as these have lived and died!

HENRY WADSWORTH LONGFELLOW.

THE FATE OF POETS.

THOUGHT of Chatterton, the marvellous boy,
  The sleepless soul that perished in his pride,
Of him who walked in glory and in joy
  Behind his plough along the mountain-side:
By our own spirits are we deified;

"I thought of Chatterton, the marvellous boy,
The sleepless soul, that perished in his pride."

We poets in our youth begin in gladness,
But thereof come in the end despondency and
  madness.

WILLIAM WORDSWORTH.

THE CRADLE.

OW steadfastly she'd worked at it!
  How lovingly had drest
With all her would-be mother's wit
  That little rosy nest!

How longingly she'd hung on it!—
  It sometimes seemed, she said,
There lay beneath its coverlet,
  A little sleeping head.

He came at last, the tiny guest,
  Ere bleak December fled;
That rosy nest he never prest—
  Her coffin was his bed.

AUSTIN DOBSON.

INTO THE WORLD AND OUT.

NTO the world he looked with sweet surprise;
  The children laughed so when they saw his eyes.

Into the world a rosy hand in doubt
He reached—a pale hand took one rose-bud out.

"And that was all—quite all!" No, surely! But
The children cried so when his eyes were shut.

SALLIE M. B. PIATT.

THE REAPER AND THE FLOWERS.

HERE is a Reaper whose name is Death,
  And, with his sickle keen,
He reaps the bearded grain at a breath,
  And the flowers that grow between.

"Shall I have nought that is fair?" saith he;
  "Have nought but the bearded grain?
Though the breath of these flowers is sweet to me,
  I will give them all back again."

He gazed at the flowers with tearful eyes,
  He kissed their drooping leaves;
It was for the Lord of Paradise
  He bound them in his sheaves.

"My Lord has need of these flowerets gay,"
  The Reaper said, and smiled;
"Dear tokens of the earth are they,
  Where He was once a child."

"They shall all bloom in fields of light,
  Transplanted by my care,
And saints, upon their garments white,
  These sacred blossoms wear."

And the mother gave, in tears and pain,
  The flowers she most did love;

She knew she should find them all again
  In the fields of light above.

O, not in cruelty, not in wrath,
  The Reaper came that day;
'T was an angel visited the green earth,
  And took the flowers away.

HENRY WADSWORTH LONGFELLOW.

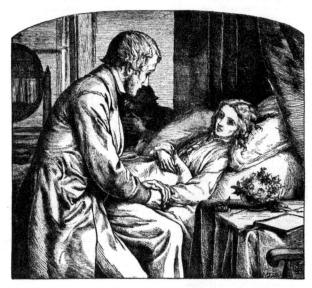

" Touch me once more , my father."

LAST WORDS.

REFRESH me with the bright-blue violet,
  And put the pale faint-scented primrose near,
    For I am breathing yet;
      Shed not one silly tear;
    But when mine eyes are set,
Scatter the fresh flowers thick upon my bier,
And let my early grave with morning dew be wet.

I have passed swiftly o'er the pleasant earth;
  My life hath been the shadow of a dream;
    The joyousness of birth
    Did ever with me seem:

My spirit had no dearth,
But dwelt forever by a full, swift stream,
Lapt in a golden trance of never-failing mirth.

Touch me once more, my father, ere my hand
  Have not answer for thee; — kiss my cheek
      Ere the blood fix and stand
      Where flits the hectic streak;
  Give me thy last command,
Before I lie all undisturbed and meek,
Wrapt in the snowy folds of funeral swathing-band.

HENRY ALFORD.

TEARS, IDLE TEARS.

TEARS, idle tears, I know not what they mean,
Tears from the depths of some divine despair
Rise in the heart, and gather to the eyes,
In looking on the happy Autumn-fields,
And thinking of the days that are no more.

Ah, sad and strange as in dark summer dawns
The earliest pipe of half-awakened birds
To dying ears, when unto dying eyes
The casement slowly grows a glimmering square;
So sad, so strange, the days that are no more.

"In looking on the happy Autumn-fields,
And thinking of the days that are no more."

Fresh as the first beam glittering on a sail
That brings our friends up from the under world,
Sad as the last which reddens over one
That sinks with all we love below the verge;
So sad, so fresh, the days that are no more.

Dear as remembered kisses after death,
And sweet as those by hopeless fancy feigned
On lips that are for others; deep as love,
Deep as first love, and wild with all regret,
O Death in Life, the days that are no more.

ALFRED TENNYSON.

WHO ne'er his bread in sorrow ate —
Who ne'er the mournful midnight hours

Weeping upon his bed hath sate —
He knows you not, ye Heavenly Powers.

DEAD IN NOVEMBER.

HOW can it shine so bright,
　　The garish sun
That shines upon our dead!
Veiled though the pitying stars of night,
No lingering ruth this morn—not one
　　　　Poor cloud to spread,
With softened touch, its brief eclipse
Upon the cold and silent lips,
The weighted eyes, the solemn rest,
The little hands upon the breast,
　　Where he lies—dead!

These roistering winds that toss,
　　In fierce-blown swirl,
The frost-plucked autumn leaves,
Rudely they sport with death and loss,
Or, sinking, mock with sobbing purl
　　　　The heart that grieves:
As joyous and as free as they,
As full of life and glee as they,
Was he, one little week ago,
Who lies in yonder room so low,
　　My boy! and dead!

The peevish crows o'erhead
　　Caw on and on;
The winter-birds chirp clear,
Mid pause in feast of berries red,
Cheery and pert, though song-mates gone,
　　And woods are sere;

Sun-kissed and glad the stream flows on—
Oh God! and all the world goes on
Light-hearted still, the same as when
He breathed it all—the same as then,
　　And yet he's dead!

To-morrow—and the end!
　　The coffin-lid
Will close, and o'er it we
With tears and bursting hearts will bend,
And think of all forever hid,
　　My boy, with thee!
Thy sunny ways, thy kindling joy,
Thy mind's quick reach, my bright-eyed boy!
Thy gracious promise unfulfilled,
The high-set hopes we could but build,
　　All with the dead!

Oh anguish vain! There is
　　No plea to move
The tyrant heart of Death;
No respite, won with agonies
E'en such as Love and Grief approve,
　　With sobbing breath:
Not all Earth's tears the hands could stay
That dig his little grave to-day!
—— Pity, O Christ! our eyes unseal
To see, beyond our sad anele,
　　He lives, though dead!

　　　　　　　　　　E. HANNAFORD

THE CHILD'S FIRST GRIEF.

OH! call my brother back to me!
　　I cannot play alone;
The summer comes with flower and bee—
　　Where is my brother gone?

"The butterfly is glancing bright
　　Across the sunbeam's track;
I care not now to chase its flight—
　　Oh! call my brother back!

"The flowers run wild—the flowers we sow'd
　　Around our garden tree;
Our vine is drooping with its load—
　　Oh! call him back to me!"

"He could not hear thy voice, fair child,
　　He may not come to thee;

The face that once like spring-time smiled,
　　On earth no more thou'lt see.

"A rose's brief bright life of joy,
　　Such unto him was given;
Go—thou must play alone, my boy!
　　Thy brother is in heaven!"

"And has he left his birds and flowers,
　　And must I call in vain;
And, through the long, long summer hours,
　　Will he not come again?

"And by the brook, and in the glade,
　　Are all our wanderings o'er?
Oh, while my brother with me played,
　　Would I had loved him more!"

　　　　　　　　　FELICIA DOROTHEA HEMANS.

A BOSOM empty of a heart of pain makes a lustreless life; but a bosom in which a heart bleeds reveals hidden virtues.

HANNAH BINDING SHOES.

POOR lone Hannah,
　Sitting at the window binding shoes.
　Faded, wrinkled,
　Sitting, stitching in a mournful muse.
　Bright-eyed beauty once was she,
　When the bloom was on the tree;
　Spring and winter
Hannah 's at the window binding shoes.

Not a neighbor
Passing nod or answer will refuse
　To her whisper,
"Is there from the fishers any news?"
　Oh her heart's adrift with one
　On an endless voyage gone!
　Night and morning
Hannah 's at the window binding shoes.

　　Fair young Hannah
Ben, the sunburnt fisher, gaily wooes;
　Hale and clever,
For a willing heart and hand he sues.
　May-day skies are all aglow,
　And the waves are laughing so!
　For her wedding
Hannah leaves her window and her shoes.

May is passing;
Mid the apple-boughs a pigeon cooes.
　Hannah shudders,
For the mild southwester mischief brews.
　Round the rocks of Marblehead,
　Outward bound a schooner sped;
　Silent, lonesome,
Hannah's at the window binding shoes.

'Tis November:
Now no tear her wasted cheek bedews;
　From Newfoundland,
Not a sail returning will she lose,
　Whispering hoarsely, "Fishermen,
　Have you, have you heard of Ben?"

Old with watching,
Hannah's at the window binding shoes.

Twenty winters
Bleach and tear the ragged shore she views;
　Twenty seasons —
Never one has brought her any news.

"Still her dim eyes silently
Chase the white sails o'er the sea."

Still her dim eyes silently
Chase the white sails o'er the sea;
　Hopeless, faithful,
Hannah's at the window binding shoes.

LUCY LARCOM.

THE CROSS.

THE strongest light casts deepest shade,
　The dearest love makes dreariest loss,
　And she his birth so blest had made
　Stood by him dying on the cross.

Yet since not grief but joy shall last,
　The day and not the night abide,
　And all time's shadows, earthward cast,
　Are lights upon the " other side; "

Through what long bliss that shall not fail
　The darkest hour shall brighten on!

Better than any angel's " Hail! "
　The memory of " Behold thy Son! "

Blest in thy lowly heart to store
　The homage paid at Bethlehem;
But far more blessed evermore,
　Thus to have shared the taunts and shame

Thus with thy pierced heart to have stood
　Mid mocking crowds and owned him thine,
True through a world's ingratitude,
　And owned in death by lips divine.

ELIZABETH (RUNDLE) CHARLES.

THE LITTLE MOURNER.

"CHILD, whither goest thou
  Over the snowy hill?
The frost-air nips so keen,
  That the very clouds are still.

Thither go I: — keen the morning
  Bites, and deep the snow;
But, in spite of them,
  Up the frosted hill I go."

"They must be cleared this morning
From the thick-laid snow."

From the golden folding curtains
  The sun hath not looked forth.
And brown the snow-mist hangs
  Round the mountains to the north."

"Kind stranger, dost thou see
  Yonder church-tower rise,
Thrusting its crown of pinnacles
  Into the looming skies?

"Child, and what dost thou?
  When thou shalt be there?
The chancel door is shut —
  There is no bell for prayer;
Yestermorn and yestereven
  Met we there and prayed;
But now none is there
  Save the dead lowly laid."

"Stranger, underneath that tower
　On the western side,
A happy, happy company
　In holy peace abide;
My father, and my mother,
　And my sisters four—
Their beds are made in swelling turf,
　Fronting the western door."

"Child, if thou speak to them
　They will not answer thee;
They are deep down in earth—
　Thy face they cannot see.

Then, wherefore art thou going
　Over the snow hill?
Why seek thy low-laid family,
　Where they lie cold and still?"

"Stranger, when the summer heats
　Would dry their turfy bed,
Duly from this loving hand
　With water it is fed;
They must be cleared this morning
　From the thick-laid snow:—
So now along the frosted field,
　Stranger, let me go."

HENRY ALFORD.

BABY BELL.

HAVE you not heard the poets tell
　How came the dainty Baby Bell
　　Into this world of ours?
The gates of heaven were left ajar:
With folded hands and dreamy eyes,
Wandering out of Paradise,
　She saw this planet, like a star,
　　Hung in the glistening depths of even,—
Its bridges, running to and fro,
O'er which the white-winged angels go,
　Bearing the holy dead to heaven.
She touched a bridge of flowers,—those feet,
So light they did not bend the bells
Of the celestial asphodels,
　They fell like dew upon the flowers,
　Then all the air grew strangely sweet!
And thus came dainty Baby Bell
　　Into this world of ours.

She came, and brought delicious May.
　The swallows built beneath the eaves;
　Like sunlight, in and out the leaves
The robins went the livelong day;
The lily swung its noiseless bell;
　And o'er the porch the trembling vine
　Seemed bursting with its veins of wine,
How sweetly, softly, twilight fell!
O. earth was full of singing-birds
And opening spring-tide flowers,
　When the dainty Baby Bell
　　Came to this world of ours!
O, Baby. dainty Baby Bell,
How fair she grew from day to day!
What woman-nature filled her eyes,
What poetry within them lay!
Those deep and tender twilight eyes,
　So full of meaning, pure and bright
　As if she yet stood in the light
Of those oped gates of Paradise.
And so we loved her more and more:

Ah. never in our hearts before
　Was love so lovely born:
We felt we had a link between
This real world and that unseen—
　The land beyond the morn;
And for the love of those dear eyes,
For love of her whom God led forth
(The mother's being ceased on earth
When Baby came from Paradise.)—
For love of Him who smote our lives.
　And woke the chords of joy and pain,
We said. "Dear Christ!"—our hearts bent down
　Like violets after rain.

And now the orchards, which were white
And red with blossoms when she came,
　Were rich in autumn's mellow prime;
The clustered apples burnt like flame,
The soft-cheeked peaches blushed and fell,
The ivory chestnut burst its shell.
The grapes hung purpling in the grange;
And time wrought just as rich a change
　In little Baby Bell.
Her lissome form more perfect grew,
　And in her features we could trace,
　In softened curves, her mother's face.
Her angel-nature ripened too:
We thought her lovely when she came,
But she was holy, saintly now:—
　Around her pale. angelic brow
We saw a slender ring of flame!

God's hand had taken away the seal
　That held the portals of her speech;
And oft she said a few strange words
　Whose meaning lay beyond our reach.
She never was a child to us,
We never held her being's key;
We could not teach her holy things.
　She was Christ's self in purity.

It came upon us by degrees,
We saw its shadow ere it fell,—
The knowledge that our God had sent
His messenger for Baby Bell.
We shuddered with unlanguaged pain,
And all our hopes were changed to fears,
And all our thoughts ran into tears
  Like sunshine into rain.
We cried aloud in our belief,
"O, smite us gently, gently, God!
Teach us to bend and kiss the rod,
And perfect grow through grief."
Ah, how we loved her, God can tell;

Her heart was folded deep in ours,
  Our hearts are broken, Baby Bell!

At last he came, the messenger,
  The messenger from unseen lands:
And what did dainty Baby Bell?
She only crossed her little hands,
She only looked more meek and fair!
We parted back her silken hair,
We wove the roses round her brow,—
White buds, the summer's drifted snow,—
Wrapt her from head to foot in flowers!
And thus went dainty Baby Bell
  Out of this world of ours!

THOMAS BAILEY ALDRICH.

BEN BOLT.

DON'T you remember sweet Alice, Ben Bolt?
  Sweet Alice, whose hair was so brown,
Who wept with delight when you gave her a
    smile,
  And trembled with fear at your frown?
In the old churchyard in the valley, Ben Bolt,
  In a corner obscure and alone,
They have fitted a slab of the granite so gray,
  And Alice lies under the stone.

Under the hickory-tree, Ben Bolt,
  Which stood at the foot of the hill,
Together we've lain in the noonday shade,
  And listened to Appleton's mill:
The mill-wheel has fallen to pieces, Ben Bolt,
  The rafters have tumbled in,
And a quiet which crawls round the walls as you
    gaze
  Has followed the olden din.

Do you mind the cabin of logs, Ben Bolt,
  At the edge of the pathless woods,
And the button-ball tree with its motley limbs,
  Which nigh by the doorstep stood?

The cabin to ruin has gone, Ben Bolt,
  The tree you would seek in vain;
And where once the lords of the forest waved,
  Grows grass and the golden grain.

And don't you remember the school, Ben Bolt,
  With the master so cruel and grim,
And the shaded nook in the running brook,
  Where the children went to swim?
Grass grows on the master's grave, Ben Bolt,
  The spring of the brook is dry,
And of all the boys who were schoolmates then,
  There are only you and I.

There is change in the things I loved, Ben Bolt,
  They have changed from the old to the new;
But I feel in the deeps of my spirit the truth,
  There never was change in you.
Twelve-months twenty have passed, Ben Bolt,
  Since first we were friends—yet I hail
Thy presence a blessing, thy friendship a truth,
  Ben Bolt, of the salt-sea gale.

THOMAS DUNN ENGLISH.

DECORATION DAY AT CHARLESTON.

SLEEP sweetly in your humble graves,—
  Sleep, martyrs of a fallen cause!
Though yet no marble column craves
  The pilgrim here to pause.

In seeds of laurel in the earth
  The blossom of your fame is blown,
And somewhere, waiting for its birth,
  The shaft is in the stone!

Meanwhile, behalf the tardy years
  Which keep in trust your storied tombs,

Behold! your sisters bring their tears,
  And these memorial blooms.

Small tributes! but your shades will smile
  More proudly on these wreaths to-day,
Than when some cannon-moulded pile
  Shall overlook this bay.

Stoop, angels, hither from the skies!
  There is no holier spot of ground
Than where defeated valor lies,
  By mourning beauty crowned!

HENRY TIMROD.

THE OUTCAST.

BUT who are those who make the streets their couch, and find a short repose from wretchedness at the doors of the opulent? There are strangers, wanderers, and orphans, whose circumstances are too humble to expect redress, and whose distresses are too great even for pity.

Their wretchedness excites rather horror than pity. Some are without the covering even of a few rags, and others emaciated with disease. The world has disclaimed them; society turns its back upon their distress, and has given them up to nakedness and hunger.

Why, why was I born a man, and yet see the sufferings of wretches I cannot relieve? Poor houseless creatures! the world will give you reproaches, but will not give you relief. The slightest misfortunes of the great, the most imaginary uneasiness of the rich, are aggravated with all the power of eloquence, and held up to engage our attention and sympathetic sorrow The poor weep unheeded, persecuted by every subordinate species of tyranny; and every law which gives others security becomes an ememy to them.

OLIVER GOLDSMITH.

THE years back of us are full of voices—voices eloquent and pathetic. You who have lived long, have stood over the grave of many an early dream. Success, when it came, was not what you thought it would be, and even success has often been denied you. You have watched by the couch of many a hope, and seen it fail and die. You have buried many a bright expectation, and laid the memorial wreath over many a joy. Withered garlands are there, and broken rings, and vases once fragrant with flowers, and the white faces of those that sleep.

THE BLUE AND THE GRAY.

BY the flow of the inland river,
　Whence the fleets of iron have fled,
Where the blades of the grave-grass quiver,
　Asleep are the ranks of the dead;—
　　Under the sod and the dew,
　　　Waiting the judgment-day;—
　　Under the one, the Blue;
　　　Under the other, the Gray.

These in the robings of glory,
　Those in the gloom of defeat,
All with the battle-blood gory,
　In the dusk of eternity meet;—
　　Under the sod and the dew,
　　　Waiting the judgment-day;—
　　Under the laurel, the Blue;
　　　Under the willow, the Gray.

From the silence of sorrowful hours
　The desolate mourners go,
Lovingly laden with flowers
　Alike for the friend and the foe;—
　　Under the sod and the dew,
　　　Waiting the judgment-day;—
　　Under the roses, the Blue;
　　　Under the lilies, the Gray.

So with an equal splendor
　The morning sun-rays fall,
With a touch impartially tender,
　On the blossoms blooming for all;—

Under the sod and the dew,
　Waiting the judgment-day;—
'Broidered with gold, the Blue;
　Mellowed with gold, the Gray.

So, when the summer calleth,
　On forest and field of grain
With an equal murmur falleth
　The cooling drip of the rain;—
　　Under the sod and the dew,
　　　Waiting the judgment-day;—
　　Wet with the rain, the Blue;
　　　Wet with the rain, the Gray.

Sadly, but not with upbraiding,
　The generous deed was done;
In the storm of the years that are fading,
　No braver battle was won;—
　　Under the sod and the dew,
　　　Waiting the judgment-day;—
　　Under the blossoms, the Blue;
　　　Under the garlands, the Gray.

No more shall the war-cry sever,
　Or the winding rivers be red;
They banish our anger forever
　When they laurel the graves of our dead!
　　Under the sod and the dew,
　　　Waiting the judgment-day;—
　　Love and tears for the Blue;
　　　Tears and love for the Gray.

FRANCIS MILES FINCH.

THE NOBILITY OF LIFE.

"Once the welcome light has broken, who shall say
What the unimagined glories of the day?"

CLEAR THE WAY.

MEN of thought, be up and stirring, night and
day,
Sow the seed—withdraw the curtain—*clear the
way;*
Men of action, aid and cheer them, as ye may!
There 's a fount about to stream,
There 's a light about to beam,
There 's a warmth about to glow,
There 's a flower about to blow;
There 's a midnight blackness changing into gray.
Men of thought and men of action, CLEAR THE WAY!

Once the welcome light has broken, who shall
say
What the unimagined glories of the day?
What the evil that shall perish in its ray?
Aid the dawning, tongue and pen;
Aid it, hopes of honest men;
Aid it, paper; aid it, type;
Aid it, for the hour is ripe,
And our earnest must not slacken into play.
Men of thought 'and men of action, CLEAR THE
WAY!

431

Lo! a cloud 's about to vanish from the day;
And a brazen wrong to crumble into clay.
Lo! the right 's about to conquer: *clear the way!*
   With the right shall many more
   Enter smiling at the door;

   With the giant wrong shall fall
   Many others, great and small,
That for ages long have held us for their prey.
Men of thought and men of action, CLEAR THE WAY!
                CHARLES MACKAY.

WHAT IS NOBLE?

WHAT is noble?—to inherit
   Wealth, estate, and proud degree?—
There must be some other merit
   Higher yet than these for me!—
Something greater far must enter
   Into life's majestic span,
Fitted to create and centre
   True nobility in man.

What is noble?—'tis the finer
   Portion of our mind and heart,
Linked to something still diviner
   Than mere language can impart:
Ever prompting—ever seeing
   Some improvement yet to plan;
To uplift our fellow-being,
   And, like man, to feel for Man!

What is noble?—is the sabre
   Nobler than the humble spade
here 's a dignity in labor
• Truer than e'er pomp arrayed!
He who seeks the mind's improvement
   Aids the world, in aiding mind!
Every great commanding movement
   Serves not one, but all mankind.

O'er the forge's heat and ashes,—
   O'er the engine's iron head,—
Where the rapid shuttle flashes,
   And the spindle whirls its thread:
There is labor, lowly tending
   Each requirement of the hour,—
There is genius, still extending
   Science, and its world of power!

'Mid the dust, and speed, and clamor,
   Of the loom-shed and the mill;
'Midst the clink of wheel and hammer,
   Great results are growing still!
Though too oft, by fashion's creatures,
   Work and workers may be blamed,
Commerce need not hide its features,—
   Industry is not ashamed!

What is noble?— that which places
   Truth in its enfranchised will,
Leaving steps, like angel-traces,
   That mankind may follow still!
E'en though scorn's malignant glances
   Prove him poorest of his clan,
He 's the Noble—who advances
   Freedom, and the Cause of Man!
                CHARLES SWAIN.

THE LABORER.

STAND up — erect! Thou hast the form
   And likeness of thy God! — Who more?
A soul as dauntless 'mid the storm
   Of daily life, a heart as warm
   And pure, as breast e'er wore.

What then? — Thou art as true a man
   As moves the human mass among;
As much a part of the great plan
That with creation's dawn began,
   As any of the throng.

Who is thine enemy? The high
   In station, or in wealth the chief?
The great, who coldly pass thee by,
With proud step and averted eye?
   Nay! nurse not such belief.

If true unto thyself thou wast,
   What were the proud one's scorn to thee?
A feather which thou mightest cast
Aside, as idly as the blast
   The light leaf from the tree.

No: uncurbed passions, low desires,
   Absence of noble self-respect,
Death, in the breast's consuming fires,
To that high nature which aspires
   Forever, till thus checked; —

These are thine enemies — thy worst:
   They chain thee to thy lowly lot;
Thy labor and thy life accursed.
O. stand erect, and from them burst,
   And longer suffer not.

Thou art thyself thine enemy:
  The great!—what better they than thou?
As theirs is not thy will as free?
Has God with equal favors thee
  Neglected to endow?

True, wealth thou hast not—'tis but dust;
  Nor place—uncertain as the wind;
But that thou hast, which, with thy crust

And water, may despise the lust
  Of both—a noble mind.

With this, and passions under ban,
  True faith, and holy trust in God,
Thou art the peer of any man.
Look up then; that thy little span
  Of life may be well trod.

WILLIAM D. GALLAGHER.

TACT AND TALENT.

ALENT is something, but tact is everything. Talent is serious, sober, grave and respectable: tact is all that, and more too. It is not a sixth sense, but it is the life of all the five. It is the open eye, the quick ear, the judging taste, the keen smell, and the lively touch; it is the interpreter of all riddles, the surmounter of all difficulties, the remover of all obstacles. It is useful in all places, and at all times; it is useful in solitude, for it shows a man his way into the world; it is useful in society, for it shows him his way through the world. Talent is power, tact is skill; talent is weight, tact is momentum; talent knows what to do, tact knows how to do it; talent makes a man respectable, tact will make him respected; talent is wealth, tact is ready money. For all the practical purposes of life, tact carries it against talent ten to one. Take them to the theatre, and put them against each other on the stage, and talent shall produce you a tragedy that will scarcely live long enough to be condemned, while tact keeps the house in a roar, night after night, with its successful farces. There is no want of dramatic talent, there is no want of dramatic tact; but they are seldom together: so we have successful pieces which are not respectable, and respectable pieces which are not successful.

Take them to the bar, and let them shake their learned curls at each other in legal rivalry; talent sees its way clearly, but tact is first at its journey's end. Talent has many a compliment from the bench, but tact touches fees from attorneys and clients. Talent speaks learnedly and logically, tact triumphantly. Talent makes the world wonder that it gets on no faster, tact excites astonishment that it gets on so fast. And the secret is, that it has no weight to carry; it makes no false steps; it hits the right nail on the head; it loses no time; it takes all hints and by keeping its eye on the weathercock, is ready to take advantage of every wind that blows. Take them into the church. Talent has always something worth hearing, tact is sure of abundance of hearers; talent may obtain a living, tact will make one; talent gets a good name, tact a great one; talent convinces, tact converts; talent is an honor to the profession, tact gains honor from the profession.

Take them to court. Talent feels its weight, tact finds its way; talent commands, tact is obeyed; talent is honored with approbation, and tact is blessed by preferment. Place them in the senate. Talent has the ear of the house, but tact wins its heart, and has its votes; talent is fit for employment, but tact is fitted for it. It has a knack of slipping into place with a sweet silence and glibness of movement, as a billiard-ball insinuates itself into the pocket. It seems to know everything, without learning anything. It has served an invisible and extemporary apprenticeship; it wants no drilling; it never ranks in the awkward squad; it has no left hand, no deaf ear, no blind side. It puts on no looks of wondrous wisdom, it has no air of profundity, but plays with the details of place as dexterously as a well-taught hand flourishes over the keys of the piano-forte. It has all the air of commonplace, and all the force and power of genius.

NEVER GIVE UP.

NEVER give up!— it is wiser and better
  Always to hope, than once to despair;
  Fling off the load of doubt's cankering fetters,
  And break the dark spell of tyrannical care.
Never give up, or the burden may sink you,—
  Providence kindly has mingled the cup;
And in all trials and troubles bethink you,
  The watchword of life must be, "Never give up!"

Never give up; there are chances and changes,
  Helping the hopeful, a hundred to one,
And through the chaos, High Wisdom arranges
  Ever success, if you 'll only hold on.

Never give up; for the wisest is boldest,
  Knowing that Providence mingles the cup,
And of all maxims, the best, as the oldest,
  Is the stern watchword of " Never give up! '

Never give up, though the grape-shot may rattle,
  Or the full thunder-cloud over you burst;
Stand like a rock, and the storm or the battle
  Little shall harm you, though doing their worst.
Never give up; if adversity presses,
  Providence wisely has mingled the cup;
And the best counsel in all your distresses
  Is the brave watchword of " Never give up! "

THE GENTLEMAN.

WHEN you have found a *man*, you have not far to go to find a gentleman. You can not make a gold ring out of brass. You can not change a Cape May crystal to a diamond. You can not make a gentleman till you have first a man. To be a gentleman, it will not be sufficient to have had a grandfather. To be a gentleman does not depend upon the tailor, or the toilet. Blood will degenerate. Good clothes are not good habits. A gentleman is just a *gentle*-man; no more, no less; a diamond polished, that was first a diamond in the rough. A gentleman is gentle. A gentleman is modest. A gentleman is courteous. A gentleman is generous. A gentleman is slow to take offense, as being one that never gives it. A gentleman is slow to surmise evil, as being one that never thinks it. A gentleman goes armed only in consciousness of right. A gentleman subjects his appetites. A gentleman refines his taste. A gentleman subdues his feelings. A gentleman deems every other better than himself. Sir Philip Sidney was never so much a gentleman,— mirror though he was of England's knighthood,—as when, upon the field of Zutphen, as he lay in his own blood, he waived the draught of cold spring water, that was brought to quench his mortal thirst, in favor of a dying soldier. St. Paul described a gentleman when he exhorted the Philippian Christians: — "Whatsoever things are just, whatsoever things are pure, whatsoever things are lovely, whatsoever things are of good report, if there be any virtue, and if there be any praise, think on these things."

GEORGE W. DOANE.

WANT OF DECISION.

GREAT deal of labor is lost to the world for the want of a little courage. Every day sends to their graves a number of obscure men, who have only remained in obscurity because their timidity has prevented them from making a first effort, and who, if they had only been induced to begin, would have in all probability gone great lengths in the career of fame. The fact is, that in doing anything in the world worth doing, we must not stand shivering on the bank, thinking of the cold and danger, but jump in, and scramble through as well as we can. It will not do to be perpetually calculating risks and adjusting nice chances; it did all very well before the flood, when a man could consult his friends upon an intended publication for a hundred and fifty years, and live to see its success for six or seven centuries afterward; but at present a man waits and doubts, and consults his brother, and uncles, and his particular friends, till one day he finds that he is sixty-five years of age, and that he has lost so much time in consulting first cousins and particular friends, that he has no more time to follow their advice. There is so little time for over-squeamishness at present, that the opportunity slips away. The very period of life at which a man chooses to venture, if ever, is so confined that it is no bad rule to preach up the necessity, in such instances, of a little violence done to the feelings, and efforts made in defiance of strict and sober calculations.

SIDNEY SMITH.

FOR A' THAT AND A' THAT.

IS there, for honest poverty,
　That hangs his head, and a' that?
The coward-slave, we pass him by,
　We dare be poor for a' that!
　　For a' that, and a' that,
　　Our toils obscure, and a' that,
　　The rank is but the guinea stamp;
　　The man 's the gowd for a' that.

What though on hamely fare we dine,
　Wear hodden-gray, and a' that.
Gie fools their silks, and knaves their wine,
　A man's a man, for a' that;
　　For a' that and a' that:
　　Their tinsel show and a' that:
　　The honest man, though e'er sae poor,
　　Is king o' men for a' that.

Ye see yon birkie, ca'd a lord,
　Wha struts, and stares, and a' that;
Though hundreds worship at his word,
　He 's but a coof for a' that,

For a' that and a' that,
　His riband, star, and a' that,
The man of independent mind,
　He looks and laughs at a' that.

A prince can mak a belted knight,
　A marquis, duke, and a' that;
But an honest man 's aboon his might,
　Guid faith, he mauna fa' that!
　　For a' that, and a' that,
　　Their dignities, and a' that,
　　The pith o' sense, and pride o' worth,
　　Are higher ranks than a' that.

Then let us pray that come it may,
　As come it will for a' that,
That sense and worth, o'er a' the earth,
　May bear the gree, and a' that,
　　For a' that, and a' that,
　　It 's coming yet, for a' that;
　　That man to man, the warld o'er,
　　Shall brothers be for a' that.

ROBERT BURNS.

ODE TO DUTY.

TERN daughter of the voice of God!
O Duty! if that name thou love
Who art a light to guide, a rod
To check the erring, and reprove;
Thou who art victory and law
When empty terrors overawe;
From vain temptations dost set free;
And calm'st the weary strife of frail humanity!

There are who ask not if thine eye
Be on them; who, in love and truth,
Where no misgiving is, rely
Upon the genial sense of youth;
Glad hearts! without reproach or blot;
Who do thy work, and know it not:
May joy be theirs while life shall last!
And thou, if they should totter, teach them to
stand fast!

Serene will be our days and bright,
And happy will our nature be,
When love is an unerring light,
And joy its own security.
And blest are they who in the main
This faith, even now, do entertain:
Live in the spirit of this creed;
Yet find that other strength, according to their
need.

I, loving freedom, and untried:
No sport of every random gust,
Yet being to myself a guide,
Too blindly have reposed my trust;

Full oft, when in my heart was heard
Thy timely mandate, I deferred
The task imposed, from day to day;
But thee I now would serve more strictly, if I may.

Through no disturbance of my soul,
Or strong compunctions in me wrought,
I supplicate for thy control;
But in the quietness of thought;
Me this unchartered freedom tires;
I feel the weight of chance desires:
My hopes no more must change their name,
I long for a repose which ever is the same.

Stern lawgiver! yet thou dost wear
The Godhead's most benignant grace;
Nor know we anything so fair
As is the smile upon thy face;
Flowers laugh before thee on their beds;
And fragrance in thy footing treads;
Thou dost preserve the stars from wrong:
And the most ancient heavens, through thee, are
fresh and strong.

To humbler functions, awful power!
I call thee; I myself commend
Unto thy guidance from this hour;
Oh! let my weakness have an end!
Give unto me, made lowly wise,
The spirit of self-sacrifice;
The confidence of reason give;
And, in the light of truth, thy bondman let me live!

WILLIAM WORDSWORTH.

A GREAT LAWYER.

TRULY Great Lawyer is one of the highest products of civilization. He is a master of the science of human experience. He sells his clients the results of that experience, and is thus the merchant of wisdom. The labors of many generations of legislators and judges enrich his stores. His learning is sufficient to enable him to realize the comparative littleness of all human achievements. He has outlived the ambition of display before courts and juries. He loves justice, law, and peace. He has learned to bear criticism without irritation; censure without anger; and calumny without retaliation. He has learned how surely all schemes of evil bring disaster to those who support them; and that the granite shaft of a noble reputation cannot be destroyed by the poisoned breath of slander.

A Great Lawyer will not do a mean thing for money. He hates vice, and delights to stand forth a conquering champion of virtue. The good opinions of the just are precious in his esteem; but neither love of friends, nor fear of foes, can swerve him from the path of duty. He esteems his office of counselor as higher than political place or scholastic distinction. He detests unnecessary litigation, and delights in averting danger, and restoring peace by wise counsel and skilful plans. The good works of the counsel-room are sweeter to him than the glories of the forum. He proves that honesty is the best policy, and that peace pays both lawyer and client, better than controversy. In a legal contest, he will give his client the benefit of the best presentation of whatever points of fact or of law may be in his power; but he will neither pervert the law, nor falsify the facts to defeat an adversary. The motto of his battle-flag is: Fidelity to the law and the facts, — *semper fidelis.*

C. C. BONNEY.

LABOR.

PAUSE not to dream of the future before us;
Pause not to weep the wild cares that come
o'er us;
Hark! how Creation's deep, musical chorus,
Unintermitting, goes up into Heaven!
Never the ocean-wave falters in flowing;
Never the little seed stops in its growing;
More and more richly the rose-heart keeps glowing,
Till from its nourishing stem it is riven.

"Labor is worship!"—the robin is singing;
"Labor is worship!"—the wild-bee is ringing;
Listen! that eloquent whisper upspringing
Speaks to thy soul from out Nature's great heart.
From the dark cloud flows the life-giving shower;
From the rough sod blows the soft-breathing flower;
From the small insect, the rich coral bower;
Only man, in the plan, shrinks from his part.

Labor is life! 'Tis the still water falleth;
Idleness ever despaireth, bewaileth;
Keep the watch wound, for the dark rust assaileth;
Flowers droop and die in the stillness of noon.
Labor is glory!—the flying cloud lightens;
Only the waving wing changes and brightens;
Idle hearts only the dark future frightens:
Play the sweet keys, wouldst thou keep them in
tune!

Labor is rest from the sorrows that greet us,
Rest from all petty vexations that meet us,
Rest from sin-promptings that ever entreat us,
Rest from world-sirens that lure us to ill,
Work—and pure slumbers shall wait on thy pillow;
Work—thou shalt ride over Care's coming billow;
Lie not down wearied 'neath Woe's weeping-willow;
Work with a stout heart and resolute will!

Labor is health! Lo! the husbandman reaping,
How through his veins goes the life-current leaping!
How his strong arm in its stalwart pride sweeping,
True as a sunbeam the swift sickle guides!
Labor is wealth — in the sea the pearl groweth;
Rich the queen's robe from the frail cocoon floweth;
From the fine acorn the strong forest bloweth:
Temple and statue the marble block hides.

Droop not, though shame, sin, and anguish are round
thee!
Bravely fling off the cold chain that hath bound thee!
Look to yon pure Heaven smiling beyond thee;
Rest not content in thy darkness—a clod!
Work—for some good, be it ever so slowly;
Cherish some flower, be it ever so lowly;
Labor!—all labor is noble and holy!
Let thy great deeds be thy prayer to thy God!

FRANCES SARGENT OSGOOD.

ADVICE TO YOUNG MEN.

YOUNG men, you are the architects of your own fortunes. Rely upon your own strength of body and soul. Take for your star self-reliance, faith, honesty, and industry. Inscribe on your banner, "Luck is a fool, pluck is a hero." Don't take too much advice—keep at your helm and steer your own ship, and remember that the great art of commanding is to take a fair share of the work. Don't practice too much humility. Think well of yourself. Strike out. Assume your own position. Put potatoes in your cart, over a rough road, and small ones go to the bottom. Rise above the envious and the jealous. Fire above the mark you intend to hit. Energy, invincible determination, with a right motive, are the levers that move the world. Don't drink. Don't chew. Don't smoke. Don't swear. Don't deceive. Don't read trashy novels. Don't marry until you can support a wife. Be in earnest. Be self-reliant. Be generous. Be civil. Read the papers. Advertise your business. Make money and do good with it. Love your God and fellow-men. Love truth and virtue. Love your country, and obey its laws. If this advice be implicitly followed by the young men of the country, the millennium is near at hand.

NOAH PORTER.

A PSALM OF LIFE.

WHAT THE HEART OF THE YOUNG MAN SAID TO THE PSALMIST.

TELL me not, in mournful numbers,
    "Life is but an empty dream!"
For the soul is dead that slumbers,
    And things are not what they seem.

Life is real! Life is earnest!
    And the grave is not its goal;
"Dust thou art, to dust returnest,"
    Was not spoken of the soul.

Not enjoyment, and not sorrow,
    Is our destined end or way;
But to act, that each to-morrow
    Find us farther than to-day.

Art is long, and Time is fleeting,
    And our hearts, though stout and brave,
Still, like muffled drums are beating
    Funeral marches to the grave.

In the world's broad field of battle,
    In the bivouac of Life,

Be not like dumb, driven cattle!
    Be a hero in the strife!

Trust no Future, howe'er pleasant!
    Let the dead Past bury its dead!
Act, — act in the living Present!
    Heart within, and God o'erhead!

Lives of great men all remind us
    We can make our lives sublime,
And, departing, leave behind us
    Footprints on the sands of time;

Footprints, that perhaps another,
    Sailing o'er life's solemn main,
A forlorn and shipwrecked brother,
    Seeing, shall take heart again.

Let us, then, be up and doing,
    With a heart for any fate;
Still achieving, still pursuing,
    Learn to labor and to wait.

HENRY WADSWORTH LONGFELLOW.

TRIALS A TEST OF CHARACTER.

VAIN are all the efforts of slander, permanently to injure the fame of a good man! There is a cascade in a lovely Swiss valley which the fierce winds catch and scatter so soon as it pours over the summit of the rock, and for a season the continuity of the fall is broken, and you see nothing but a feathery wreath of apparently helpless spray; but if you look further down the consistency is recovered, and the Staubbach pours its rejoicing waters as if no breeze had blown at all. Nay, the blast which interrupts it only fans it into more marvelous loveliness, and makes it a shrine of beauty where all pilgrim footsteps travel. And so the blasts of calumny, howl they ever so fiercely over the good man's head, contribute to his juster appreciation and to his wider fame. What are circumstances, — I wonder, that they should hinder a true man when his heart is set within him to do a right thing! Let a man be firmly principled in his religion, he may travel from the tropics to the poles, it will never catch cold on the journey. Set him down in the desert, and just as the palm-tree thrusts its roots beneath the envious sand in search of sustenance, he will manage somehow to find living water there. Banish him to the dreariest Patmos you can find, he will get a grand Apocalypse among its barren crags. Thrust him into an inner prison, and make his feet fast in the stocks, the doxology will reverberate through the dungeon, making such melody within its walls of stone that the jailer shall relapse into a man, and the prisoners hearing it shall dream of freedom and of home.

WILLIAM MORLEY PUNSHON.

GRADATIM.

HEAVEN is not reached at a single bound;
 But we build the ladder by which we rise
 From the lowly earth to the vaulted skies,
 And we mount to its summit round by round.

I count this thing to be grandly true,
 That a noble deed is a step toward God,
 Lifting the soul from the common sod
To a purer air and a broader view.

We rise by the things that are under our feet;
 By what we have mastered of good and gain,
 By the pride deposed and passion slain,
And the vanquished ills that we hourly meet.

We hope, we aspire, we resolve, we trust,
 When the morning calls us to life and light;
 But our hearts grow weary, and ere the night
Our lives are trailing in sordid dust.

We hope, we resolve, we aspire, we pray,
 And we think that we mount the air on wings
 Beyond the recall of sensual things,
While our feet still cling to the heavy clay.

Wings for the angels, but feet for men!
 We borrow the wings to find the way—
 We may hope, and resolve, and aspire, and pray,
But our feet must rise, or we fall again.

Only in dreams is a ladder thrown
 From the weary earth to the sapphire walls;
 But the dreams depart and the vision falls,
And the sleeper wakes on his pillow of stone.

Heaven is not reached at a single bound;
 But we build the ladder by which we rise
 From the lowly earth to the vaulted skies,
 And we mount to its summit round by round.

JOSIAH GILBERT HOLLAND.

HOW TO LIVE.

HE liveth long who liveth well!
 All other life is short and vain;
 He liveth longest who can tell
 Of living most for heavenly gain.

He liveth long who liveth well!
 All else is being flung away;
 He liveth longest who can tell
 Of true things truly done each day.

Waste not thy being; back to Him
 Who freely gave it, freely give;
Else is that being but a dream;
 'T is but to be, and not to live.

Be what thou seemest! live thy creed!
 Hold up to earth the torch divine;

Be what thou prayest to be made;
 Let the great Master's steps be thine.

Fill up each hour with what will last;
 Buy up the moments as they go;
The life above, when this is past,
 Is the ripe fruit of life below.

Sow truth, if thou the truth wouldst reap:
 Who sows the false shall reap the vain;
Erect and sound thy conscience keep;
 From hollow words and deeds refrain.

Sow love, and taste its fruitage pure;
 Sow peace, and reap its harvests bright;
Sow sunbeams on the rock and moor,
 And find a harvest-home of light.

HORATIUS BONAR.

PRESS ON.

PRESS on! there 's no such word as fail;
Press nobly on! the goal is near,—
Ascend the mountain! breast the gale!
Look upward, onward,—never fear!
Why should'st thou faint? Heaven smiles above
Though storm and vapor intervene;
That Sun shines on, whose name is Love,
Serenely o'er life's shadowed scene.

Press on! surmount the rocky steeps,
Climb boldly o'er the torrent's arch;
He fails alone who feebly creeps;
He wins who dares the hero's march.
Be thou a hero! let thy might
Tramp on eternal snows its way,
And through the ebon walls of night
Hew down a passage unto day.

Press on! if once, and twice, thy feet
Slip back and stumble, harder try;
From him who never dreads to meet
Danger and death, they 're sure to fly.
To coward ranks the bullet speeds;
While on their breasts who never quail,
Gleams, guardian of chivalric deeds,
Bright courage, like a coat of mail.

Press on! if fortune play thee false
To-day, to-morrow she 'll be true;
Whom now she sinks, she now exalts,
Taking old gifts and granting new.
The wisdom of the present hour
Makes up for follies past and gone;
To weakness strength succeeds, and power
From frailty springs;—Press on! PRESS ON!

Press on! what though upon the ground
Thy love has been poured out like rain?
That happiness is always found
The sweetest that is born of pain.
Oft 'mid the forest's deepest glooms,
A bird sings from some blighted tree;
And in the dreariest desert, blooms
A never-dying rose for thee.

Therefore, press on! and reach the goal,
And gain the prize, and wear the crown;
Faint not! for to the steadfast soul
Come wealth and honor and renown.
To thine own self be true, and keep
Thy mind from sloth, thy heart from soil;
Press on! and thou shalt surely reap
A heavenly harvest for thy toil.

PARK BENJAMIN.

A TRUE WOMAN.

GIVE ear, fair daughter of love, to the instructions of prudence, and let the precepts of truth sink deep in thy heart: so shall the charms of thy mind add lustre to the elegance of thy form; and thy beauty, like the rose it resembleth, shall retain its sweetness when its bloom is withered. In the spring of thy youth, in the morning of thy days, when the eyes of men gaze on thee with delight, and nature whispereth in thine ear the meaning of their looks; ah! hear with caution their seducing words; guard well thy heart, nor listen to their soft persuasions. Remember that thou art made man's reasonable companion, not the slave of his passion; the end of thy being is not merely to gratify his loose desire, but to assist him in the toils of life, to soothe him with thy tenderness, and recompense his care with soft endearments. Who is she that winneth the heart of man, that subdueth him to love, and reigneth in his breast? Lo! yonder she walketh in maiden sweetness, with innocence in her mind and modesty on her cheek. Her hand seeketh employment, her foot delighteth not in gadding abroad. She is clothed with neatness, she is fed with temperance: humility and meekness are as a crown of glory circling her head. On her tongue dwelleth music, the sweetness of honey floweth from her lips. Decency is in all her words; in her answers are mildness and truth. Submission and obedience are the lessons of her life, and peace and happiness are her reward. Before her steps walketh prudence, and virtue attendeth at her right hand. Her eye speaketh softness and love; but discretion with a sceptre sitteth on her brow. The tongue of the licentious is dumb in her presence; the awe of her virtue keepeth him silent. When scandal is busy, and the fame of her neighbor is tossed from tongue to tongue; if charity and good nature open not her mouth, the finger of silence resteth on her lips. Her breast is the mansion of goodness; and therefore she suspecteth no evil in others. Happy were the man that should make her his wife; happy the child that shall call her mother. She presideth in the house, and there is peace; she commandeth with judgment, and is obeyed. She ariseth in the morning, she considers her affairs, and appointeth to every one their proper business. The care of her family is her whole delight, to that alone she applieth her study; and elegance with frugality is seen in her mansions. The prudence of her management is an honor to her husband, and he heareth her praise with a secret delight. She informeth the minds of her children with wisdom; she fashioneth their manners from the example of her own goodness. The word of her mouth is the law of their youth; the motion of her eye commandeth obedience. She speaketh, and her servants fly; she pointeth, and the thing is done; for the law of love is in their hearts, and her kindness addeth wings to their feet. In prosperity she is not puffed up; in adversity she healeth the wounds of fortune with patience. The troubles of her husband are alleviated by her counsels, and sweetened by her endearments: he putteth his heart in her bosom, and receiveth comfort. Happy is the man that hath made her his wife; happy the child that calleth her mother.

ROBERT DODSLEY.

THE SUPREMACY OF VIRTUE.

VIRTUE may be assailed, but never hurt;
Surprised by unjust force, but not inthralled;
Yea, even that which mischief meant most harm
Shall in the happy trial prove most glory:
But evil on itself shall back recoil,
And mix no more with goodness, when at last,
Gathered like scum, and settled to itself,
It shall be in eternal restless change
Self-fed and self-consumed: if this fall,
The pillared firmament is rottenness,
And earth's base built on stubble.

JOHN MILTON.

INDUSTRY AND GENIUS.

INDUSTRY is a substitute for genius. Where one or more faculties exist in the highest state of development and activity,—as the faculty of music in Mozart, —invention in Fulton,—ideality in Milton,—we call their possessor a *genius*. But a genius is usually understood to be a creature of such rare facility of mind, that he can do anything without labor. According to the popular notion, he learns without study, and knows without learning. He is eloquent without preparation, exact without calculation, and profound without reflection. While ordinary men toil for knowledge by reading, by comparison, and by minute research, a genius is supposed to receive it as the mind receives dreams. His mind is like a vast cathedral, through whose colored windows the sunlight streams, painting the aisles with the varied colors of brilliant pictures. Such minds *may* exist. So far as my observations have ascertained the species, they abound in academies, colleges, and Thespian societies; in village debating clubs; in coteries of young artists, and among young professional aspirants. They are to be known by a reserved air, excessive sensitiveness, and utter indolence; by very long hair, and very open shirt collars; by the reading of much wretched poetry, and the writing of much yet more wretched; by being very conceited, very affected, very disagreeable. and very useless, —beings whom no man wants for friend, pupil, or companion.

HENRY WARD BEECHER

THE LIGHT OF STARS.

HE night is come, but not too soon;
　And sinking silently,
All silently, the little moon
　Drops down behind the sky.

There is no light in earth or heaven,
　But the cold light of stars;
And the first watch of night is given
　To the red planet Mars.

Is it the tender star of love?
　The star of love and dreams?
O no! from that blue tent above,
　A hero's armor gleams.

And earnest thoughts within me rise,
　When I behold afar,
Suspended in the evening skies,
　The shield of that red star.

O star of strength! I see thee stand
　And smile upon my pain;

Thou beckonest with thy mailéd hand,
　And I am strong again.

Within my breast there is no light,
　But the cold light of stars;
I give the first watch of the night
　To the red planet Mars.

The star of the unconquered will,
　He rises in my breast,
Serene, and resolute, and still,
　And calm, and self-possessed.

And thou, too, whosoe'er thou art,
　That readest this brief psalm,
As one by one thy hopes depart,
　Be resolute and calm.

O fear not in a world like this,
　And thou shalt know ere long,
Know how sublime a thing it is
　To suffer and be strong.

HENRY WADSWORTH LONGFELLOW.

A HAPPY LIFE.

OW happy is he born and taught,
　That serveth not another's will;
Whose armor is his honest thought,
　And simple truth his utmost skill!

Whose passions not his masters are,
Whose soul is still prepared for death,
Not tied unto the world with care
Of public fame, or private breath;

Who envies none that chance doth raise,
Or vice; who never understood
How deepest wounds are given by praise;
Nor rules of state, but rules of good;

Who hath his life from rumors freed,
Whose conscience is his strong retreat;
Whose state can neither flatterers feed,
Nor ruin make oppressors great;

Who God doth late and early pray,
More of his grace than gifts to lend;
And entertains the harmless day
With a well-chosen book or friend;

This man is freed from servile bands,
Of hope to rise, or fear to fall;
Lord of himself, though not of lands;
And having nothing, yet hath all.

SIR HENRY WOTTON.

MY MIND TO ME A KINGDOM IS.

MY mind to me a kingdom is,
  Such perfect joy therein I find,
That it excels all other bliss
  That God or nature hath assigned:
Though much I want that most would have,
Yet still my mind forbids to crave.

No princely port, nor wealthy store,
  Nor force to win a victory;
No wily wit to salve a sore,
  No shape to win a loving eye;
To none of these I yield as thrall,
For why, my mind despise them all.

I see that plenty surfeits oft,
  And hasty climbers soonest fall;
I see that such as are aloft,
  Mishap doth threaten most of all;
These get with toil, and keep with fear:
Such cares my mind can never bear.

I press to bear no haughty sway;
  I wish no more than may suffice;
I do no more than well I may,
  Look what I want my mind supplies;
Lo, thus I triumph like a king,
My mind's content with anything.

I laugh not at another's loss,
  Nor grudge not at another's gain;
No worldly waves my mind can toss;
  I brook that is another's bane;
I fear no foe, nor fawn on friend;
I loathe not life, nor dread mine end.

My wealth is health and perfect ease,
  And conscience clear my chief defence;
I never seek by bribes to please,
  Nor by desert to give offence;
Thus do I live, thus will I die;
  Would all do so as well as I!

SIR EDWARD DYER.

SUCCESS IN LIFE.

TAKE earnestly hold of life, as capacitated for and destined to high and noble purpose. Study closely the mind's bent for labor or a profession. Adopt it early and pursue it steadily, never looking back to the turning furrow, but forward to the ground that ever remains to be broken. Means and ways are abundant to every man's success, if will and actions are rightly adapted to them. Our rich men and our great men have carved their paths to fortune, and by this internal principle—a principle that cannot fail to reward him who resolutely pursues it. To sigh or repine over the lack of inheritance is unmanly. Every man should strive to be creator instead of inheritor. He should bequeath instead of borrow. He should be conscious of the power in him, and fight his own battles with his own lance. He should feel that it is better to earn a crust than to inherit coffers of gold. When once this spirit of self-reliance is learned, every man will discover within himself the elements and capacities of wealth. He will be rich, inestimably rich in self-resources, and can lift his head proudly to meet the noblest among men.

HONORABLE EMPLOYMENT.

MY lord, lie not idle:
  The chiefest action for a man of great spirit
  Is never to be out of action. We should think;
  The soul was never put into the body,
Which has so many rare and curious pieces
Of mathematical motion, to stand still.

Virtue is ever sowing of her seeds:
In the trenches for the soldier: in the wakeful study
For the scholar; in the furrows of the sea
For men of our profession: of all which
Arise and spring up honor.

JOHN WEBSTER.

A RHYME OF LIFE.

IF life be as a flame that death doth kill,
  Burn, little candle, lit for me,
With a pure flame, that I may rightly see
To word my song, and utterly
  God's plan fulfill.

If life be as a flower that blooms and dies,
  Forbid the cunning frost that slays
With Judas kiss, and trusting love betrays;

Forever may my song of praise
  Untainted rise.

If life be as a voyage, foul or fair.
  Oh, bid me not my banners furl
For adverse gale, or wave in angry whirl.
Till I have found the gates of pearl.
  And anchored there.

                CHARLES WARREN STODDARD.

INDUSTRY.

THE way to wealth is as plain as the way to market. It depends chiefly on two words, industry and frugality; that is, waste neither time nor money, but make the best use of both. Without industry and frugality, nothing will do, and with them everything. Sloth makes all things difficult, but industry all easy; and he that riseth late must trot all day, and shall scarce overtake his business at night, while laziness travels so slowly that poverty soon overtakes him. Industry need not wish, and he that lives upon hopes will die fasting. There are no gains without pains; then help, hands, for I have no lands; or if I have, they are smartly taxed. He that hath a trade hath an estate, and he that hath a calling hath an office of profit and honor; but then the trade must be worked at, and the calling followed, or neither the estate nor the office will enable us to pay our taxes. If we are industrious, we shall never starve; for, at the working-man's house, hunger looks in, but dares not enter. Nor will the bailiff or the constable enter, for industry pays debts, while despair increaseth them. Employ thy time well, if thou meanest to gain leisure; and since thou art not sure of a minute, throw not away an hour. Leisure is time for doing something useful; this leisure the diligent man will obtain, but the lazy man never; for a life of leisure and a life of laziness are two things.

                BENJAMIN FRANKLIN.

MY WORK.

MASTER! to do great work for thee, my hand
  Is far too weak. Thou givest what may suit
  Some little chips to cut with care minute,
  Or tint, or grave, or polish. Others stand
Before their quarried marble, fair and grand,
  And make a life-work of the great design
Which thou hast traced; or, many-skilled, combine

To build vast temples, gloriously planned,
  Yet take the tiny stones which I have wrought,
  Just one by one, as they were given by thee,
Not knowing what came next in thy wise thought.
Set each stone by thy master-hand of grace,
  Form the mosaic as thou wilt, for me,
And in thy temple-pavement give it place.

                FRANCES RIDLEY HAVERGAL.

THE BETTER LAND.

"The moon doth with delight
Look round her when the heavens are bare;
Waters on a starry night
Are beautiful and fair."

ODE ON IMMORTALITY.

THERE was a time when meadow, grove and stream,
  The earth, and every common sight,
    To me did seem
    Apparelled in celestial light,
The glory and the freshness of a dream.
It is not now as it hath been of yore:—
    Turn whereso'er I may,
    By night or day,
·The things which I have seen I now can see no more.

The rainbow comes and goes,
  And lovely is the rose;
  The moon doth with delight
Look round her when the heavens are bare;
  Waters on a starry night
  Are beautiful and fair;
  The sunshine is a glorious birth,
  But yet I know, where'er I go,
That there hath passed away a glory from the earth.

Now, while the birds thus sing a joyous song,
　　And while the young lambs bound
　　　　As to the tabor's sound,
To me alone there came a thought of grief:
A timely utterance gave that thought relief,
　　And I again am strong:
The cataracts blow their trumpets from the steep;
No more shall grief of mine the season wrong;
I hear the echoes through the mountains throng.
The winds come to me from the fields of sleep,
　　And all the earth is gay;
　　　　Land and sea
　　Give themselves up to jollity,
　　And with the heart of May
　　Doth every beast keep holiday;
　　　　Thou child of joy,
Shout round me, let me hear thy shouts, thou happy
　　　　shepherd-boy!

Ye blessed creatures, I have heard the call
Ye to each other make; I see
The heavens laugh with you in your jubilee;
　　My heart is at your festival,
　　My head hath its coronal,
The fullness of your bliss—I feel, I feel it all.
　　O evil day! if I were sullen
　　While Earth itself is adorning,
　　　　This sweet May morning,
　　And the children are culling,
　　　　On every side,
　　In a thousand valleys far and wide,
　　Fresh flowers; while the sun shines warm,
And the babe leaps up on his mother's arm;
　　I hear, I hear, with joy I hear,
　　—But there 's a tree, of many, one,
A single field which I have looked upon—
Both of them speak of something that is gone:
　　The pansy at my feet
　　Doth the same tale repeat:
Whither is fled the visionary gleam?
Where is it now, the glory and the dream?

Our birth is but a sleep and a forgetting:
The soul that rises with us, our life's star,
　　Hath had elsewhere its setting,
　　　　And cometh from afar:
　　Not in entire forgetfulness,
　　And not in utter nakedness,
But trailing clouds of glory, do we come
　　From God, who is our home:
Heaven lies about us in our infancy!
Shades of the prison-house begin to close
　　Upon the growing boy,
But he beholds the light, and whence it flows,
　　He sees in it his joy;
The youth, who daily farther from the east
　　Must travel, still is Nature's priest,
　　And by the vision splendid
　　Is on his way attended;

At length the man perceives it die away,
And fade into the light of common day.

Earth fills her lap with pleasures of her own;
Yearnings she hath in her own natural kind,
And, even with something of a mother's mind,
　　And no unworthy aim,
　　The homely nurse doth all she can
To make her foster-child,her inmate man,
　　Forget the glories he hath known,
And that imperial palace whence he came.

Behold the child among his new-born blisses,
A six years' darling of a pigmy size!
See where mid work of his own hand he lies,
Fretted by sallies of his mothers' kisses,
With light upon him from his father's eyes!
See, at his feet, some little plan or chart,
Some fragment from his dream of human life,
Shaped by himself with newly learnéd art;
　　A wedding or a festival,
　　A mourning or a funeral;
　　　　And this hath now his heart,
　　And unto this he frames his song:
　　　　Then will he fit his tongue
To dialogues of business, love, or strife!
　　But it will not be long
　　Ere this be thrown aside,
　　And with new joy and pride
The little actor cons another part;
Filling from time to time his " humorous stage,"
With all the persons, down to palsied age,
That Life brings with her in her equipage;
　　As if his whole vocation
　　Were endless imitation.

Thou, whose exterior semblance doth belie
　　　　Thy soul's immensity;
Thou best philosopher, who yet dost keep
Thy heritage, thou eye among the blind,
That, deaf and silent, readest the eternal deep,
Haunted forever by the eternal mind,—
　　Mighty prophet! Seer blest!
　　On whom those truths do rest
Which we are toiling all our lives to find,
In darkness lost, the darkness of the grave:
Thou, over whom thy immortality
Broods like the day, a master o'er a slave,
A presence which is not to be put by;
Thou little child, yet glorious in the might
Of heaven-born freedom, on thy being's height,
Why with such earnest pains dost thou provoke
The years to bring the inevitable yoke,
Thus blindly with thy blessedness at strife?
Full soon thy soul shall have her earthly freight,
And custom lie upon thee with a weight
Heavy as frost, and deep almost as life!

　　O joy! that in our embers
　　Is something that doth live;

That nature yet remembers
What was so fugitive!
The thought of our past years in me doth breed
Perpetual benediction; not indeed
For that which is most worthy to be blest;
Delight and liberty, the simple creed
Of childhood, whether busy or at rest,
With new-fledged hope still fluttering in his breast:—
　　Not for these I raise
　　The song of thanks and praise;
　　But for those obstinate questionings
　　Of sense and outward things,
　　Fallings from us, vanishings;
　　Blank misgivings of a creature
Moving about in worlds not realized,
High instincts before which our mortal nature
Did tremble like a guilty thing surprised:
　　But for those first affections,
　　Those shadowy recollections,
　　Which, be they what they may,
Are yet the fountain-light of all our day,
Are yet a master-light of all our seeing;
　　Uphold us, cherish, and have power to make
Our noisy years seem moments in the being
Of the eternal silence! truths that wake,
　　To perish never;
Which neither listlessness, nor mad endeavor,
　　Nor man, nor boy,
Nor all that is at enmity with joy,
Can utterly abolish or destroy!
　　Hence in a season of calm weather
　　Though inland far we be,
Our souls have sight of that immortal sea
　　Which brought us hither;
　　Can in a moment travel thither,
And see the children sport upon the shore,
　　And hear the mighty waters rolling evermore.

Then sing, ye birds, sing, sing a joyous song!
　　And let the young lambs bound
　　As to the tabor's sound!
We in thought will join your throng,
　　Ye that pipe and ye that play,
　　Ye that through your hearts to-day
　　Feel the gladness of the May!
What though the radiance which was once so bright
Be now forever taken from my sight,
Though nothing can bring back the hour
Of splendor in the grass, of glory in the flower;
　　We will grieve not, rather find
　　Strength in what remains behind;
　　In the primal sympathy
　　Which, having been, must ever be;
　　In the soothing thoughts that spring
　　Out of human suffering;
　　In the faith that looks through death,
In years that bring the philosophic mind.

And O ye fountains, meadows, hills, and groves,
Think not of any severing of our loves!
Yet in my heart of hearts I feel your might;
I only have relinquished one delight
To live beneath your more habitual sway.
I love the brooks which down their channels fret
Even more than when I tripped lightly as they;
The innocent brightness of a new-born day
　　Is lovely yet;
The clouds that gather round the setting sun
Do take a sober coloring from an eye
That hath kept watch o'er man's mortality;
Another race hath been, and other palms are won.
Thanks to the human heart by which we live,
Thanks to its tenderness, its joys, and fears,
To me the meanest flower that blows can give
Thoughts that do often lie too deep for tears.

　　　　　　　　WILLIAM WORDSWORTH.

————◦⟩∘◦◆∘◦⟨◦————

THE DISCOVERER.

HAVE a little kinsman
Whose earthly summers are but three,
And yet a voyager is he
Greater than Drake or Frobisher,
Than all the peers together!
He is a brave discoverer,
And, far beyond the tether
Of them who seek the frozen Pole,
Has sailed where the noiseless surges roll.
　　Aye, he has traveled whither
　　A wingèd pilot steered his bark
　　Through the portals of the dark,
　　Past hoary Mimir's well and tree,
　　Across the unknown sea.

Suddenly in his fair young hour,
　　Came one who bore a flower
And laid it in his dimpled hand
　　With this command:
"Henceforth thou art a rover!
Thou must make a voyage far,
Sail beneath the evening star,
And a wondrous land discover."
　—With his sweet smile innocent
　　Our little kinsman went.

Since that time no word
From the absent has been heard;
　　Who can tell
How he fares, or answer well

What the little one has found
Since he left us, outward-bound!
Would that he might return!
Then should we learn
From the pricking of his chart
How the skyey roadways part.
Hush! does not the baby this way bring,
To lay beside this severed curl,
Some starry offering
Of chrysolite or pearl?

Ah, no! not so!
We may follow on his track,
But he con e ot back.

And yet I dare aver
He is a brave discoverer
Of climes his elders do not know.
He has more learning than appears
On the scroll of twice three thousand years;
More than in the groves is taught
Or from furthest Indies brought;
He knows, perchance, how spirits fare—
What shapes the angels wear,
What is their guise and speech
In those lands beyond our reach—
And his eyes behold
Things that shall never, never be to mortal bearers told.

EDMUND CLARENCE STEDMAN.

THE FUTURE LIFE.

OW shall I know thee in the sphere which keeps
The disembodied spirits of the dead,
When all of thee that time could wither sleeps
And perishes among the dust we tread?

For I shall feel the sting of ceaseless pain
If there I meet thy gentle presence not;
Nor hear the voice I love, nor read again
In thy serenest eyes the tender thought.

Will not thy own meek heart demand me there?
That heart whose fondest throbs to me were given;
My name on earth was ever in thy prayer,
And wilt thou never utter it in heaven?

In meadows fanned by heaven's life-breathing wind,
In the resplendence of that glorious sphere,
And larger movements of the unfettered mind,
Wilt thou forget the love that joined us here?

The love that lived through all the stormy past,
And meekly with my harsher nature bore,

And deeper grew, and tenderer to the last,
Shall it expire with life and be no more?

A happier lot than mine, and larger light,
Await thee there; for thou hast bowed thy will
In cheerful homage to the rule of right,
And lovest all, and renderest good for ill.

For me, the sordid cares in which I dwell
Shrink and consume my heart, as heat the scroll;
And wrath hath left its scar—that fire of hell
Has left its frightful scar upon my soul.

Yet though thou wear'st the glory of the sky,
Wilt thou not keep the same beloved name,
The same fair, thoughtful brow, and gentle eye,
Lovelier in heaven's sweet climate, yet the same?

Shalt thou not teach me, in that calmer home,
The wisdom that I learned so ill in this—
The wisdom which is love—till I become
Thy fit companion in that land of bliss?

WILLIAM CULLEN BRYANT.

THERE IS NO DEATH.

HERE is no death! The stars go down
To rise upon some fairer shore,
And bright in heaven's jeweled crown
They shine forevermore.

There is no death. The dust we tread
Shall change beneath the summer showers
To golden grain or mellow fruit
Or rainbow-tinted flowers.

The granite rocks disorganize
To feed the hungry moss they bear;
The forest leaves drink daily life
From out the viewless air.

There is no death; the leaves may fall,
The flowers may fade and pass away—
They only wait through wintry hours
The coming of the May.

There is no death! An angel form
Walks o'er the earth with silent tread;
He bears our best-loved things away,
And then we call them "dead."

He leaves our hearts all desolate—
He plucks our fairest, sweetest flowers;
Transplanted into bliss, they now
Adorn immortal bowers.

The bird-like voice, whose joyous tones
  Made glad this scene of sin and strife,
Sings now in everlasting song,
  Amid the tree of life.

And where he sees a smile so bright,
  Of hearts too pure for taint and vice,
He bears it to that world of light,
  To dwell in Paradise.

Born into that undying life,
  They leave us but to come again;
With joy we welcome them—the same
  Except in sin and pain.

And ever near us, though unseen,
  The dear immortal spirits tread;
For all the boundless Universe
  Is life—there are no dead.
                    J. L. McCREERY.

"BLESSED ARE THEY THAT MOURN."

H, deem not they are blest alone
  Whose lives a peaceful tenor keep;
The Power who pities man has shown
  A blessing for the eyes that weep.

The light of smiles shall fill again
  The lids that overflow with tears;
And weary hours of woe and pain
  Are promises of happier years.

There is a day of sunny rest
  For every dark and troubled night;
And grief may bide an evening guest,
  But joy shall come with early light.

And thou, who o'er thy friend's low bier,
  Sheddest the bitter drops like rain,
Hope that a brighter, happier sphere
  Will give him to thy arms again.

Nor let the good man's trust depart,
  Though life its common gifts deny,—
Though with a pierced and bleeding heart,
  And spurned of men, he goes to die.

For God hath marked each sorrowing day
  And numbered every secret tear,
And heaven's long age of bliss shall pay
  For all his children suffer here.
                    WILLIAM CULLEN BRYANT.

THE MARINER'S HYMN.

AUNCH thy bark, mariner!
  Christian, God speed thee!
Let loose the rudder-bands—
  Good angels lead thee!
Set thy sails warily,
  Tempests will come;
Steer thy course steadily;
  Christian, steer home!

Look to the weather-bow,
  Breakers are round thee;
Let fall the plummet now,
  Shallows may ground thee.
Reef in the foresail, there!
  Hold the helm fast!
So—let the vessel wear—
  There swept the blast.

"What of the night, watchman?
  What of the night?"
"Cloudy—all quiet—
  No land yet—all 's right."

Be wakeful, be vigilant—
  Danger may be
At an hour when all seemeth
  Securest to thee.

How! gains the leak so fast?
  Clean out the hold—
Hoist up the merchandise,
  Heave out thy gold;
There—let the ingots go—
  Now the ship rights;
Hurrah! the harbor 's near—
  Lo! the red lights!

Slacken not sail yet
  At inlet or island;
Straight for the beacon steer,
  Straight for the highland;
Crowd all thy canvas on,
  Cut through the foam—
Christian, cast anchor now,
  Heaven is thy home!
                    CAROLINE BOWLES SOUTHEY.

ABIDE WITH US: FOR IT IS TOWARD EVENING.

THE tender light is fading where
　　We pause and linger still,
And through the dim and saddened air
　　We feel the evening chill.

Long hast Thou journeyed with us, Lord,
　　Ere we thy face did know;
Oh, still Thy fellowship afford,
　　While dark the shadows grow.

For passed is many a beauteous field
　　Beside our morning road;
And many a fount to us is sealed,
　　That once so freshly flowed.

The splendor of the noontide lies
　　On other paths than ours;
The dews that lave yon fragrant skies
　　Will not revive our flowers.

It is not now as in the glow
　　Of life's impassioned heat,

When to the heart there seemed to flow
　　All that of earth was sweet.

Something has faded—something died,
　　Without us and within;
We more than ever need a guide,
　　Blinded and weak with sin.

The weight is heavy that we bear,
　　Our strength more feeble grows;
Weary with toil, and pain, and care,
　　We long for sweet repose.

Stay with us, gracious Saviour, stay
　　While friends and hopes depart;
Fainting, on Thee we wish to lay
　　The burden of our heart.

Abide with us, dear Lord, remain
　　Our Life, our Truth, our Way,—
So shall our loss be turned to gain—
　　Night dawn to endless day.

HORATIO NELSON POWERS.

SHALL WE MEET AGAIN?

MEN seldom think of the shadow that falls across their own path, hiding forever from their eyes the traces of the loved ones, whose living smiles were the sunlight of their existence. Death is the great antagonist of life, and the cold thought of the tomb is the skeleton of all feasts. We do not want to go through the dark valley, although its passages may lead to Paradise; and, with Charles Lamb, we do not want to lie down in the muddy grave even with kings and princes for our bed-fellows. But the fiat of nature is inexorable. There is no appeal of relief from the great law which dooms us to dust. We flourish and we fade as the leaves of the forest, and the flower that blooms and withers in a day has not a frailer hold upon life than the mightiest monarch that ever shook the earth with his footsteps. Generations of men appear and vanish as the grass, and the countless multitude that throngs the world to-day will to-morrow disappear as the footsteps on the shore. In the beautiful drama of Ion, the instinct of immortality, so eloquently uttered by the death-devoted Greek, finds a deep response in every thoughful soul. When about to yield his young existence as a sacrifice to fate, his beloved Clemanthe asks if they shall not meet again, to which he replies: "I have asked that dreadful question of the hills that look eternal — of the streams that flow forever — of the stars among whose fields of azure my raised spirit hath walked in glory. All were dumb. But while I gaze upon thy face, I feel that there is something in the love that mantles through its beauty that cannot wholly perish. We shall meet again, Clemanthe."

GEORGE D. PRENTICE.

HOME AND HEAVEN.

WITH the same letter, heaven and home begin,
And the words dwell together in the mind;
For they who would a home in heaven win
Must first a heaven in home begin to find.
Be happy here, yet with a humble soul
That looks for perfect happiness in heaven;
For what thou hast is earnest of the whole
Which to the faithful shall at last be given.

As once the patriarch, in a vision blessed,
Saw the swift angels hastening to and fro,
And the lone spot whereon he lay to rest
Became to him the gate of heaven below;
So may to thee, when life itself is done,
Thy home on earth and heaven above be
    one.

JONES VERY.

REST IS NOT HERE.

WHAT 's this vain world to me?
    Rest is not here;
False are the smiles I see,
    The mirth I hear.
Where is youth's joyful glee?
Where all once dear to me?
Gone, as the shadows flee—
    Rest is not here.

Why did the morning shine
    Blithely and fair?
Why did those tints so fine
    Vanish in air?

Does not the vision say,
Faint, lingering heart, away,
Why in this desert stay—
    Dark land of care?

Where souls angelic soar,
    Thither repair;
Let this vain world no more
    Lull and ensnare.
That heaven I love so well
Still in my heart shall dwell;
All things around me tell
    Rest is found there.

LADY CAROLINE NAIRNE.

PEACE.

PEACE, troubled heart! the way 's not long be-
    fore thee,
    Lay down thy burden; say to sorrow, cease;
Be yon soft azure hand serenely o'er thee,
    The blue, bright border to God's sphere of
    peace.

Peace, troubled heart! the hasty word may fret thee,
    The cruel word may coldly probe and pierce;
The Christ who suffered, loves thee, never leaves thee,
    He pours His balm upon the fever fierce.

Peace, troubled heart! though marred thy best be-
    havior,
To thy deep longing, thine aspiring cry,
Listens thy Heavenly Kinsman, thy dear Saviour
    Healeth thy life-hurt, wipeth thy tears dry.

Peace, lonely heart! Be patient. Thou 'lt see, waiting,
    How perfect sympathy and love may meet;
Be patient, praying; all earth's discord grating,
    Will melt at last to love divine, complete.

Peace, troubled heart! O coward, weakly shrinking
    Back from the chalice! Saints and martyrs' meed,
The chrism of suffering. Earthward, poor souls
    sinking,
    Yearn for the heavenly joy, through human need.

Peace, troubled heart! see yon strong ships all sailing
    Through sun and storm, on to the solemn sea;
Through summer calms, through wintry tempest
    quailing,
Thus sailest thou, out to Infinity.

Peace, troubled heart! beyond these bitter breezes,
    Mid Isles of Paradise, in airs of balm,
Where cruel wind or word ne'er wounds or freezes,
    Thou 'lt gain at last the everlasting calm.

Peace, troubled heart! go out beneath the ether,
    Rest in the marvelous sunshine of the sky;
Watch the bees sail and sing in sunny leisure;
    List the waves laughing as they loiter by.

Peace, troubled heart! if minor notes of sadness
    Tremble through Nature's voices, every sigh
Quickens the anthem of her mightier gladness,
    Foretells fruition perfect by and by.

Peace, troubled heart! life's ever-mocking seeming,
    Life's weary dearth, life's aching sense of loss,
Are fitful phantoms of its transient dreaming,
    While Faith stands steadfast gazing on the Cross.

MARY CLEMMER AMES.

THE DEATH OF THE VIRTUOUS.

SWEET is the scene when Virtue dies!
　When sinks a righteous soul to rest,
　How mildly beam the closing eyes,
　How gently heaves the expiring breast!

So fades a summer cloud away,
　So sinks the gale when storms are o'er,
So gently shuts the eye of day,
　So dies a wave along the shore.

Triumphant smiles the victor brow,
　Fanned by some angel's purple wing; —

Where is, O Grave! thy victory now?
　And where, insidious Death, thy sting?

Farewell, conflicting joys and fears,
　Where light and shade alternate dwell!
How bright the unchanging morn appears;—
　Farewell, inconstant world, farewell!

Its duty done,—as sinks the day,
　Light from its load the spirit flies;
While heaven and earth combine to say,
　"Sweet is the scene when Virtue dies!"

ANNA LETITIA BARBAULD.

I SHALL BE SATISFIED.

NOT here! not here! not where the sparkling wa-
　　ters
　Fade into mocking sands as we draw near;
　Where in the wilderness each footstep falters—
　I shall be satisfied—but oh! not here.

Not here! where every dream of bliss deceives us,
　Where the worn spirit never gains its goal;
Where, haunted ever by the thoughts that grieve us,
　Across us floods of bitter memory roll.

There is a land where every pulse is thrilling
　With rapture earth's sojourners may not know,
Where heaven's repose the weary heart is stilling,
　And peacefully life's time-tossed currents flow.

Far out of sight, while yet the flesh enfolds us,
　Lies the fair country where our hearts abide,

And of its bliss is naught more wondrous told us
　Than these few words—" I shall be satisfied."

Satisfied! satisfied! the spirit's yearning
　For sweet companionship with kindred minds—
The silent love that here meets no returning—
　The inspiration which no language finds—

Shall they be satisfied? the soul's vague longing—
　The aching void which nothing earthly fills?
Oh, what desires upon my soul are thronging,
　As I look upward to the heavenly hills!

Thither my weak and weary steps are tending—
　Saviour and Lord! with thy frail child abide!
Guide me towards home, where, all my wanderings
　　ending,
　I then shall see Thee, and "be satisfied."

THE MOUNTAINS OF LIFE.

THERE'S a land far away, 'mid the stars, we are
　　told,
　Where they know not the sorrows of time.—
　Where the pure waters wander through valleys
　　of gold,
　And life is a treasure sublime:—
'Tis the land of our God, 'tis the home of the soul,
　Where the ages of splendor eternally roll;
Where the way-weary traveler reaches his goal,
　On the evergreen Mountains of Life.

Our gaze cannot soar to that beautiful land,
　But our visions have told of its bliss
And our souls by the gale of its gardens are
　　fanned,
　When we faint in the desert of this;

And we sometimes have longed for its holy repose,
When our spirits were torn with temptations and
　　woes,
And we've drank from the tide of the river that flows
　From the evergreen Mountains of Life.

Oh, the stars never tread the blue heavens at night,
　But we think where the ransomed have trod!
And the day never smiles from his palace of light,
　But we feel the bright smile of our God!
We are traveling homeward through changes and
　　gloom,
To a kingdom where pleasures unceasingly bloom,
And our guide is the glory that shines through the
　　tomb
　From the evergreen Mountains of Life.

J. G. CLARK.

IMMORTALITY.

H! listen, man!
 A voice within us speaks that startling word:
 "Man, thou shalt never die!" Celestial voices
 Hymn it unto our souls; according harps,
By angel fingers touched, when the mild stars
Of morning sang together, sound forth still
The song of our great immortality:
Thick clustering orbs, and this our fair domain,
The tall, dark mountains, and the deep-toned seas,
Join in this solemn, universal song.
Oh! listen, ye, our spirits; drink it in
From all the air. 'Tis in the gentle moonlight;

'Tis floating 'mid Day's setting glories; Night,
Wrapped in her sable robe, with silent step
Comes to our bed, and breathes it in our ears:
Night, and the dawn, bright day, and thoughtful eve,
All time, all bounds, the limitless expanse,
As one vast mystic instrument, are touched
By an unseen living Hand, and conscious chords
Quiver with joy in this great jubilee.
The dying hear it; and, as sounds of earth
Grow dull and distant, wake their passing souls
To mingle in this heavenly harmony.

RICHARD HENRY DANA.

THE BETTER WAY.

ND didst thou love the race that loved not thee?
 And didst thou take to heaven a human brow?
 Dost plead with man's voice by the marvelous
 sea,
 Art thou his kinsman now?

O God, O kinsman loved, but not enough!
O man, with eyes majestic after death,
Whose feet have toiled along our pathways rough,
Whose lips drawn human breath!

By that one likeness which is ours and thine,
By that one nature which doth hold us kin,
By that high heaven where, sinless, thou dost shine,
To draw us sinners in, —

By thy last silence in the judgment-hall,
By long foreknowledge of the deadly tree,
By darkness, by the wormwood and the gall,
I pray Thee visit me.

Come, lest this heart should, cold and cast away,
Die ere the guest adored she entertained —
Lest eyes which never saw Thine earthly day,
Should miss Thy heavenly reign.

Come, weary-eyed from seeking in the night
Thy wanderers strayed upon the pathless wold,

Who, wounded, dying, cry to Thee for light,
And cannot find their fold.

And deign, O watcher with the sleepless brow,
Pathetic in its yearning — deign reply;
Is there, O is there aught that such as Thou
Wouldst take from such as I?

Are there no briers across Thy pathway thrust,
Are there no thorns that compass it about?
Nor any stones that Thou wilt deign to trust
My hands to gather out?

O, if Thou wilt, and if such bliss might be,
It were a cure for doubt, regret, delay;
Let my lost pathway go — what aileth me?
There is a better way.

What though unmarked the happy workman toil,
And break, unthanked of man, the stubborn clod?
It is enough, for sacred is the soil,
Dear are the hills of God.

Far better in its place the lowliest bird
Should sing aright to Him the lowliest song,
Than that a seraph strayed should take the word
And sing His glory wrong.

JEAN INGELOW.

THE WAY, THE TRUTH, AND THE LIFE.

THOU great Friend to all the sons of men,
 Who once appeared in humblest guise below,
 Sin to rebuke, to break the captive's chain,
 And call thy brethren forth from want and
 woe,—

We look to thee! thy truth is still the Light
 Which guides the nations, groping on their way,

Stumbling and falling in disastrous night,
 Yet hoping ever for the perfect day.

Yes; thou art still the Life, thou art the Way
 The holiest know; Light, Life, the Way of heaven!
And they who dearest hope and deepest pray.
 Toil by the Light, Life, Way, which thou hast
 given.

THEODORE PARKER.

REST.

LAY me down to sleep,
  With little care
Whether my waking find
  Me here, or there.

A bowing, burdened head
  That only asks to rest,
Unquestioning, upon
  A loving breast.

My good right hand forgets
  Its cunning now;
To march the weary march
  I know not how.

I am not eager, bold,
  Nor strong,—all that is past;
I am ready not to do,
  At last, at last.

My half-day's work is done,
  And this is all my part,—
I give a patient God
  My patient heart;

And grasp his banner still,
  Though all the blue be dim;
These stripes as well as stars
  Lead after him.

MAY WOOLSEY HOWLAND.

ONLY WAITING.

A very old man in an alms-house was asked what he was doing now. He replied, "Only waiting."

ONLY waiting till the shadows
  Are a little longer grown;
Only waiting till the glimmer
  Of the day's last beam is flown;
Till the night of earth is faded
  From the heart once full of day;
Till the dawn of heaven is breaking
  Through the twilight soft and gray.

Only waiting till the reapers
  Have the last sheaf gathered home;
For the summer-time is faded,
  And the autumn winds have come.
Quickly, reapers, gather quickly
  The last ripe hours of my heart,
For the bloom of life is withered,
  And I hasten to depart.

Only waiting till the angels
  Open wide the mystic gate.
At whose feet I long have lingered,
  Weary, poor and desolate.
Even now I hear the footsteps,
  And their voices far away;
If they call me, I am waiting,
  Only waiting to obey.

Only waiting till the shadows
  Are a little longer grown;
Only waiting till the glimmer
  Of the day's last beam is flown;
Then from out the gathered darkness,
  Holy, deathless stars shall rise,
By whose light my soul shall gladly
  Tread its pathway to the skies.

FRANCES LAUGHTON MACE.

LIFE.

LIFE! I know not what thou art,
  But know that thou and I must part;
And when, or how, or where we met,
  I own to me 's a secret yet.
  But this I know: when thou art fled,
Where'er they lay these limbs, this head.
No clod so valueless shall be
As all that then remains of me.
O, whither, whither dost thou fly?
Where bend unseen thy trackless course?
And, in this strange divorce.
Ah, tell where I must seek this compound, I?

To the vast ocean of empyreal flame,
  From whence thy essence came.
Dost thou thy flight pursue, when freed
From matter's base encumbering weed?

Or dost thou, hid from sight,
Wait, like some spell-bound knight,
Through blank, oblivious years the appointed hour
To break thy trance and reassume thy power?
Yet canst thou, without thought or feeling be?
O, say, what art thou, when no more thou 'rt thee?

Life! we've been long together
Through pleasant and through cloudy weather;
  'T is hard to part when friends are dear,—
  Perhaps 't will cost a sigh, a tear;
  Then steal away, give little warning,
    Choose thine own time;
Say not Good Night,—but in some brighter clime
  Bid me Good Morning.

ANNA LETITIA BARBAULD.

TELL ME, YE WINGÉD WINDS.

TELL me, ye wingéd winds,
    That round my pathway roar,
Do ye not know some spot
    Where mortals weep no more?
Some lone and pleasant dell,
    Some valley in the west,
Where, free from toil and pain,
    The weary soul may rest?
The loud wind dwindled to a whisper low,
And sighed for pity as it answered,—"No."

Tell me, thou mighty deep,
    Whose billows round me play,
Know'st thou some favored spot,
    Some island far away,
Where weary man may find
    The bliss for which he sighs,—
Where sorrow never lives,
    And friendship never dies?
The loud waves, rolling in perpetual flow,
Stopped for a while, and sighed to answer,—"No."

And thou, serenest moon,
    That, with such lovely face,
Dost look upon the earth,
    Asleep in night's embrace;
Tell me, in all thy round
    Hast thou not seen some spot
Where miserable man
    May find a happier lot?
Behind a cloud the moon withdrew in woe,
And a voice, sweet but sad, responded,—"No."

Tell me, my secret soul,
    O, tell me, Hope and Faith,
Is there no resting-place
    From sorrow, sin, and death?
Is there no happy spot
    Where mortals may be blest,
Where grief may find a balm,
    And weariness a rest?
Faith, Hope, and Love, best boons to mortals given,
Waved their bright wings, and whispered,—"Yes, in
    heaven!"

CHARLES MACKAY.

THE DYING CHRISTIAN TO HIS SOUL.

VITAL spark of heavenly flame,
    Quit, oh, quit this mortal frame!
Trembling, hoping, lingering, flying;
    Oh the pain, the bliss of dying!
Cease, fond Nature, cease thy strife,
    And let me languish into life!

Hark! they whisper; angels say,
Sister spirit, come away.
What is this absorbs me quite,
Steals my senses, shuts my sight,

Drowns my spirit, draws my breath?
Tell me, my soul! can this be death!

The world recedes; it disappears;
Heaven opens on my eyes; my ears
    With sounds seraphic ring:
Lend, lend your wings! I mount! I fly!
O grave! where is thy victory?
O death! where is thy sting?

ALEXANDER POPE.

DYING HYMN.

EARTH, with its dark and dreadful ills,
    Recedes and fades away;
Lift up your heads, ye heavenly hills;
    Ye gates of death, give way!

My soul is full of whispered song,—
    My blindness is my sight;
The shadows that I feared so long
    Are full of life and light.

The while my pulses fainter beat,
    My faith doth so abound,

I feel grow firm beneath my feet
    The green, immortal ground.

That faith to me a courage gives,
    Low as the grave to go;
I know that my Redeemer lives,—
    That I shall live I know.

The palace walls I almost see
    Where dwells my Lord and King!
O grave, where is thy victory?
    O death, where is thy sting?

ALICE CARY.

HEAVEN.

EYOND these chilling winds and gloomy skies,
  Beyond death s cloudy portal,
There is a land where beauty never dies—
  Where love becomes immortal.

A land whose life is never dimmed by shade,
  Whose fields are ever vernal;
Where nothing beautiful can ever fade,
  But blooms for aye eternal.

We may not know how sweet its balmy air,
  How bright and fair its flowers;
We may not hear the songs that echo there
  Through those enchanted bowers.

The city's shining towers we may not see
  With our dim earthly vision,

For Death, the silent warder, keeps the key
  That opes the gates elysian.

But sometimes, when adown the western sky
  A fiery sunset lingers,
Its golden gates swing inward noiselessly,
  Unlocked by unseen fingers.

And while they stand a moment half ajar,
  Gleams from the inner glory
Stream brightly through the azure vault afar,
  And half reveal the story.

O land unknown! O land of love divine!
  Father, all-wise, eternal,
Oh, guide these wandering, way-worn feet of mine
  Into those pastures vernal!

NANCY PRIEST WAKEFIELD.

HEAVEN OUR HOME.

T cannot be that earth is man's only abiding-place. It cannot be that our life is a bubble, cast up by the ocean of eternity, to float another moment upon its surface, and then sink into nothingness and darkness forever. Else why is it that the high and glorious aspirations which leap like angels from the temples of our hearts, are forever wandering abroad, unsatisfied? Why is it that the rainbow and the cloud come over us with a beauty that is not of earth, and then pass off and leave us to muse on their faded loveliness? Why is it that the stars which hold their festival around the midnight throne are set above the grasp of our limited faculties, and are forever mocking us with their unapproachable glory? Finally, why is it that bright forms of human beauty are presented to the view, and then taken from us, leaving the thousand streams of the affections to flow back in an Alpine torrrent upon our hearts?

We are born for a higher destiny than that of earth. There is a realm where the rainbow never fades; where the stars will be spread out before us like the islands that slumber on the ocean; and where the beautiful beings that here pass before us like visions will stay in our presence forever!

GEORGE D. PRENTICE.

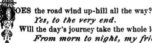

UP-HILL.

OES the road wind up-hill all the way?
  Yes, to the very end.
Will the day's journey take the whole long day?
  From morn to night, my friend.

But is there for the night a resting-place?
  *A roof for when the slow dark hours be-
  gin.*
May not the darkness hide it from my face?
  You cannot miss that inn.

Shall I meet other wayfarers at night?
  Those who have gone before.
Then must I knock, or call when just in sight?
  *They will not keep you standing at that
  door.*

Shall I find comfort, travel-sore and weak?
  Of labor you shall find the sum.
Will there be beds for me and all who seek?
  Yea, beds for all who come.

CHRISTINA G. ROSSETTI.

IN HARBOR.

THINK it is over, over—
  I think it is over at last;
Voices of foeman and lover,
  The sweet and the bitter have passed;
Life, like a tempest of ocean,
  Hath blown its ultimate blast.
There 's but a faint sobbing seaward,
While the calm of the tide deepens leeward,
And behold! like the welcoming quiver
Of heart-pulses throbbed through the river,
  Those lights in the Harbor at last—
  The heavenly Harbor at last.

I feel it is over, over—
  The winds and the water surcease;
How few were the days of the Rover
  That smiled in the beauty of peace!
And distant and dim was the omen
  That hinted redress or release,
From the ravage of life and its riot,

What marvel I yearn for the quiet
  Which bides in this Harbor at last?
For the lights with their welcoming quiver,
That throb through the sacrificed river
  Which girdles the Harbor at last—
  That heavenly Harbor at last.

I know it is over, over—
  I know it is over at last;
Down sail, the sheathed anchor uncover,
  For the stress of the voyage has passed;
Life, like the tempest of ocean,
  Hath outblown its ultimate blast,
There 's but a faint sobbing seaward,
While the calm of the tide deepens leeward,
And behold! like the welcoming quiver,
Of heart-pulses throbbed through the river,
  Those lights in the Harbor at last—
  The heavenly Harbor at last!

PAUL HAMILTON HAYNE.

TWO WORLDS.

TWO worlds there are. To one our eyes we strain,
  Whose magic lens we shall not see again;
  Bright haze of morning veils its glimmering
      shore.
      Ah, truly breathed we there
      Intoxicating air—
  Glad were our hearts in that sweet realm of
      Nevermore.

The lover there drank her delicious breath
Whose love has yielded since to change or death;
  The mother kissed her child, whose days are o'er.
      Alas! too soon have fled
      The irreclaimable dead;
  We see them—visions strange—amid the
      Nevermore.

The merrysome maiden that used there to sing—
The brown, brown hair that once was wont to cling
To temples long clay-cold: to the very core
      They strike our weary hearts,
      As some vexed memory starts
  From that long-faded land—the realm of
      Nevermore.

It is perpetual summer there. But here
Sadly may we remember rivers clear,
  And harebells quivering on the meadow-floor.
      For brighter bells and bluer,
      For tenderer hearts and truer,
  People that happy land—the realm of
      Nevermore.

Upon the frontier of this shadowy land
We pilgrims of eternal sorrow stand:
  What realm lies forward, with its happier store
      Of forests green and deep,
      Of valleys hushed in sleep.
  And lakes more peaceful? 'Tis the land of
      Evermore.

Very far off its marble cities seem —
Very far off — beyond our sensual dream—
  Its woods, unruffled by the wild wind's roar;
      Yet does the turbulent surge
      Howl on its very verge.
  One moment — and we breathe within the
      Evermore.

They whom we loved and lost so long ago
Dwell in those cities, far from mortal woe—
  Haunt those fresh woodlands, whence sweet carol-
      ings soar.
      Eternal peace have they;
      God wipes their tears away;
  They drink that river of life which flows from
      Evermore.

Thither we hasten through these regions dim,
But, lo, the wide wings of the Seraphim
  Shine in the sunset! On that joyous shore
      Our lightened hearts shall know
      The life of long ago:
  The sorrow-burdened past shall fade for
      Evermore.

MORTIMER COLLINS.

WHEN.

IF I were told that I must die to-morrow,
　　That the next sun
Which sinks would bear me past all fear and
　　　sorrow
　　For any one,
All the fight fought, all the short journey through,
　　What should I do?

I do not think that I should shrink or falter,
　　But just go on,
Doing my work, nor change nor seek to alter
　　Aught that is gone;
But rise and move and love and smile and pray
　　For one more day.

And, lying down at night for a last sleeping,
　　Say in that ear
Which hearkens ever: "Lord, within thy keeping
　　How should I fear?
And when to-morrow brings thee nearer still,
　　Do thou thy will."

I might not sleep for awe; but peaceful, tender,
　　My soul would lie
All the night long; and when the morning splendor
　　Flushed o'er the sky,
I think that I could smile — could calmly say,
　　"It is His day."

But if a wondrous hand from the blue yonder
　　Held out a scroll
On which my life was writ, and I with wonder
　　Beheld unroll

To a long century's end its mystic clew,
　　What should I do?

What *could* I do, O blessed Guide and Master,
　　Other than this:
Still to go on as now, not slower, faster,
　　Nor fear to miss
The road, although so very long it be,
　　While led by Thee?

Step after step, feeling thee close beside me,
　　Although unseen,
Thro' thorns, thro' flowers, whether the tempest hide
　　thee
　　Or heavens serene,
Assured thy faithfulness cannot betray,
　　Thy love decay.

I may not know; my God, no hand revealeth
　　Thy counsels wise;
Along the path a deepening shadow stealeth,
　　No voice replies
To all my questioning thought, the time to tell;
　　And it is well.

Let me keep on, abiding and unfearing
　　Thy will always,
Through a long century's ripening fruition
　　Or a short day's;
Thou canst not come too soon; and I can wait
　　If thou come late.

　　　　　SARAH WOOLSEY (Susan Coolidge).

ABIDE WITH ME.

ABIDE with me! fast falls the eventide;
　　The darkness deepens; Lord, with me abide!
　　When other helpers fail, and comforts flee,
　　Help of the helpless, oh, abide with me!

Swift to its close ebbs out life's little day;
Earth's joys grow dim; its glories pass away;
Change and decay in all around I see;
O Thou who changest not, abide with me!

Not a brief glance I beg, a passing word;
But as thou dwell'st with thy disciples, Lord,
Familiar, condescending, patient, free,
Come, not to sojourn, but abide, with me!

Come, not in terrors, as the King of Kings,
But kind and good, with healing in thy wings;
Tears for all woes, a heart for every plea;
Come, Friend of sinners, and thus bide with me!

Thou on my head in early youth didst smile;
And, though rebellious and perverse meanwhile,
Thou hast not left me, oft as I left thee;
On to the close, O Lord, abide with me!

I need thy presence every passing hour;
What but thy grace can foil the tempter's power?
Who like thyself my guide and stay can be?
Through cloud and sunshine, oh, abide with me!

I fear no foe, with thee at hand to bless;
Ills have no weight, and tears no bitterness;
Where is Death's sting? where, Grave, thy victory?
I triumph still, if thou abide with me!

Hold Thou thy cross before my closing eyes!
Shine through the gloom, and point me to the skies!
Heaven's morning breaks, and Earth's vain shadows
　　flee;
In Life and Death, O Lord, abide with me!

　　　　　HENRY FRANCIS LYTE.

"I TOO."

"LET us spread the sail for purple islands,
  Far in undiscovered tropic seas;
Let us track the glimmering arctic highlands,
  Where no breath of men, no leaf of trees
E'er has lived." So speaks the elders, telling
  By the hearth, their list of fancies through,
Heedless of the child whose heart is swelling
  Till he cries at last, "I too! I too!"

And I, too, O my Father! Thou hast made me —
  I have life, and life must have its way;
Why should love and gladness be gainsaid me?
  Why should shadows cloud my little day?
Naked souls weigh in thy balance even —
  Souls of kings are worth no more than mine;
Why are gifts e'er to my brother given,
  While my heart and I together pine?

Meanest things that breathe have, with no asking,
  Fullest joys: the one-day's butterfly
Finds its rose, and, in the sunshine basking,
  Has the whole of life ere it doth die.

Dove, no sorrow on thy heart is preying;
  With thy full contentment thou dost coo;
Yet must man cry for a dove's life, saying,
  "Make me as a dove — I too! I too!"

Nay, for something moves within — a spirit
  Rises in his breast, he feels it stir;
Soul-joys greater than the doves inherit
  Should be his to feel; yet why defer
To a next world's veiled and far to-morrow
  All his longings for a present bliss?
Stones of faith are hard; oh, could he borrow,
  From that world's great stores one taste for this!

Hungry stands he by his empty table,
  Thirsty waits beside his empty well
Nor with all his striving, is he able
  One full joy to catch where hundreds swell
In his neighbor's bosom; see, he sifteth
  Once again his poor life through and through —
Finds but ashes: is it strange he lifteth
  Up his cry, "O Lord! I too! I too!"

CONSTANCE FENIMORE WOOLSON.

NO SORROW THERE.

THIS earthly life has been fitly characterized as a pilgrimage through a vale of tears. In the language of poetry, man himself has been called a pendulum betwixt a smile and a tear. Everything in this world is characterized by imperfection. The best people have many faults. The clearest mind only sees through a glass darkly. The purest heart is not without spot. All the intercourse of society, all the transactions of business, all our estimates of human conduct and motive must be based upon the sad assumption that we cannot wholly trust either ourselves or our fellow-men. Every heart has its grief, every house has its skeleton, every character is marred with weakness and imperfection. And all these aimless conflicts of our minds, and unanswered longings of our hearts, should lead us to rejoice the more in the divine assurance that a time is coming when night shall melt into noon, and the mystery shall be clothed with glory.

DANIEL MARCH.

THIS WORLD IS ALL A FLEETING SHOW

THIS world is all a fleeting show,
  For man's illusion given;
The smiles of joy, the tears of woe,
Deceitful shine. deceitful flow,—
  There 's nothing true but heaven!

And false the light on glory's plume,
  As fading hues of even;
And love, and hope, and beauty's bloom

Are blossoms gathered for the tomb,—
  There 's nothing bright but heaven!

Poor wanderers of a stormy day,
  From wave to wave we 're driven,
And fancy's flash and reason's ray
Serve but to light the troubled way,—
  There 's nothing calm but heaven!

THOMAS MOORE.

THE OTHER WORLD.

T lies around us like a cloud—
A world we do not see;
Yet the sweet closing of an eye
May bring us there to be.

Its gentle breezes fan our cheek;
Amid our worldly cares
Its gentle voices whisper love,
And mingle with our prayers.

weet hearts around us throb and beat,
Sweet helping hands are stirred,
And palpitates the veil between
With breathings almost heard.

The silence—awful, sweet, and calm—
They have no power to break;
For mortal words are not for them
To utter or partake.

So thin, so soft, so sweet they glide,
So near to press they seem,—
They seem to lull us to our rest,
And melt into our dream.

And in the hush of rest they bring
'Tis easy now to see
How lovely and how sweet a pass
The hour of death may be!

To close the eye and close the ear,
Rapt in a trance of bliss,
And gently dream in loving arms
To swoon to that—from this.

Scarce knowing if we wake or sleep,
Scarce asking where we are,
To feel all evil sink away,
All sorrow and all care.

Sweet souls around us! watch us still,
Press nearer to our side,
Into our thoughts, into our prayers,
With gentle helpings glide.

Let death between us be as naught,
A dried and vanished stream;
Your joy be the reality,
Our suffering life the dream.

HARRIET BEECHER STOWE.

A BETTER WORLD.

EYOND the farthest glimmering star
That twinkles in the arch above,
There is a world of truth and love
Which earth's vile passions never mar.

Oh! could I snatch the eagle's plumes
And soar to that bright world above,

Which God's own holy light illumes
With glories of eternal day.

How gladly every lingering tie
That binds me down to earth I 'd sever,
And leave for that blest home on high
This hollow-hearted world forever!

GEORGE D. PRENTICE.

MINISTRY OF ANGELS.

ND is there care in heaven? And is there love
In heavenly spirits to these creatures base,
That may compassion of their evils move?
There is:—else much more wretched were the
case
Of men than beasts: but O, the exceeding grace
Of Highest God! that loves his creatures so,
And all his works with mercy doth embrace,
That blesséd angels he sends to and fro,
To serve to wicked man, to serve his wicked foe!

How oft do they their silver bowers leave,
To come to succour us that succour want!
How oft do they with golden pinions cleave
The flitting skies, like flying pursuivant,
Against fowle feends to ayd us militant!
They for us fight, they watch, and dewly ward,
And their bright squadrons round about us plant;
And all for love, and nothing for reward;
Oh, why should heavenly God to men have such
regard!

EDMUND SPENSER.

TERNITY will be one glorious morning, with the sun ever climbing higher and higher; one blessed spring-time, and yet richer summer—every plant in full flower, but every flower the bud of a lovelier.

"FATHER, TAKE MY HAND."

THE way is dark, my Father! Cloud on cloud
Is gathering thickly o'er my head, and loud
The thunders roar above me. See, I stand
Like one bewildered! Father, take my hand,
  And through the gloom
  Lead safely home
    Thy child!

The day goes fast, my Father! and the night
Is drawing darkly down. My faithless sight
Sees ghostly visions. Fears, a spectral band,
Encompass me. O Father, take my hand,
  And from the night
  Lead up to light
    Thy child!

The way is long, my Father! and my soul
Longs for the rest and quiet of the goal:
While yet I journey through this weary land,
Keep me from wandering. Father, take my hand;
  Quickly and straight
  Lead to heaven's gate
    Thy child!

The path is rough, my Father! Many a thorn
Has pierced me; and my weary feet, all torn
And bleeding, mark the way. Yet thy command
Bids me press forward. Father, take my hand;
  Then, safe and blest,
  Lead up to rest
    Thy child!

The throng is great, my Father! Many a doubt
And fear and danger compass me about;
And foes oppress me sore. I cannot stand
Or go alone. O Father! take my hand,
  And through the throng
  Lead safe along
    Thy child!

The cross is heavy, Father! I have borne
It long, and still do bear it. Let my worn
And fainting spirit rise to that blest land
Where crowns are given. Father, take my hand;
  And reaching down
  Lead to the crown
    Thy child!

HENRY N. COBB.

RIPE GRAIN.

O STILL, white face of perfect peace,
  Untouched by passion, freed from pain,—
He who ordained that work should cease
  Took to Himself the ripened grain.

O noble face! your beauty bears
  The glory that is wrung from pain,—

The high, celestial beauty wears
  Of finished work, of ripened grain.

Of human care you left no trace,
  No lightest trace of grief or pain,
On earth an empty form and face—
  In Heaven stands the ripened grain.

DORA READ GOODALE.

NEARER HOME.

ONE sweetly solemn thought
  Comes to me o'er and o'er:
I'm nearer home to-day
  Than I ever have been before.

Nearer my Father's house,
  Where the many mansions be;
Nearer the great white throne,
  Nearer the crystal sea;

Nearer the bound of life,
  Where we lay our burdens down;
Nearer leaving the cross,
  Nearer gaining the crown!

But lying darkly between,
  Winding down through the night,

Is the silent, unknown stream,
  That leads at last to the light.

Closer and closer my steps
  Come to the dread abysm;
Closer Death to my lips
  Presses the awful chrism.

Oh, if my mortal feet
  Have almost gained the brink—
If it be I am nearer home
  Even to-day than I think,—

Father, perfect my trust,
  Let my spirit feel in death,
That her feet are firmly set
  On the Rock of a Living Faith!

PHŒBE CARY.

THE PILLAR OF THE CLOUD.

EAD, kindly Light, amid the encircling gloom,
     Lead thou me on!
The night is dark, and I am far from home,—
     Lead thou me on!
Keep thou my feet; I do not ask to see
The distant scene,—one step 's enough for me.

I was not ever thus, nor prayed that thou
     Shouldst lead me on:
I loved to choose and see my path, but now
     Lead thou me on!

I loved the garish day, and, spite of fears,
Pride ruled my will: remember not past
     years.

So long thy power hath blessed me, sure it still
     Will lead me on;
O'er moor and fen, o'er crag and torrent, till
     The night is gone;
And with the morn those angel faces smile
Which I have loved long since, and lost awhile.

                              JOHN HENRY NEWMAN.

HEREAFTER.

OVE, when all the years are silent, vanished
     quite and laid to rest,
When you and I are sleeping, folded breathless
     breast to breast,
When no morrow is before us, and the long grass
     tosses o'er us,
And our grave remains forgotten, or by alien footsteps
     pressed —

Still that love of ours will linger, that great love en-
     rich the earth,
Sunshine in the heavenly azure, breezes blowing
     joyous mirth;
Fragrance fanning off from flowers, melody of sum-
     mer showers,
Sparkle of the spicy wood-fires round the happy
     autumn hearth.

That's our love. But you and I, dear—shall we linger
     with it yet,
Mingled in one dew-drop, tangled in one sunbeam's
     golden net —

On the violet's purple bosom, I the sheen, but you the
     blossom,
Stream on sunset winds, and be the haze with which
     some hill is wet?

Or, beloved—if ascending—when we have endowed
     the world
With the best bloom of our being, whither will our
     way be whirled,
Through what vast and starry spaces, toward what
     awful, holy places,
With a white light on our faces, spirit over spirit
     furled?

Only this our yearning answers: whereso'er that way
     defile,
Not a film shall part us through the æons of that
     mighty while,
In the fair eternal weather, even as phantoms still
     together,
Floating, floating, one forever, in the light of God's
     great smile.

                              HARRIET PRESCOTT SPOFFORD.

THE ETERNAL REST.

HEN I bethink me on that speech whyleare
     Of Mutability, and well it way,
Me seemes, that though she all unworthy were
     Of the heav'ns rule, yet, very sooth to say,
     In all things else she bears the greatest sway;
Which makes me loath this state of life so tickle,
And love of things so vaine to cast away;
     Whose flowring pride, so fading and so fickle,
Short Time shall soon cut down with his consuming
     sickle.

Then gin I thinke on that which Nature sayd,
Of that same time when no more change shall be,
But steadfast rest of all things, firmely stayd
Upon the pillours of Eternity,
     That is contrayr to Mutabilitie;
For all that moveth doth in change delight,
     But thenceforth all shall rest eternally
With him that is the God of Sabaoth hight,
O thou great Sabaoth God, Grant me that Sabbath's
     sight!

                              EDMUND SPENSER.

I WOULD NOT LIVE ALWAY.

WOULD not live alway: I ask not to stay
Where storm after storm rises dark o'er the way;
Where, seeking for rest, I but hover around
Like the patriarch's bird, and no resting is found;
Where Hope, when she paints her gay bow in the
   air,
Leaves her brilliance to fade in the night of despair,
And Joy's fleeting angel ne'er sheds a glad ray,
Save the gleam of the plumage that bears him away.

I would not live alway, thus fettered by sin,
Temptation without, and corruption within;
In a moment of strength if I sever the chain,
Scarce the victory's mine ere I'm captive again.
E'en the rapture of pardon is mingled with fears,
And the cup of thanksgiving with penitent tears.
The festival trump calls for jubilant songs,
But my spirit her own *miserere* prolongs.

I would not live alway: no, welcome the tomb;
Immortality's lamp burns there bright 'mid the gloom.
There, too, is the pillow where Christ bowed his
   head—
O, soft be my slumbers on that holy bed!

And then the glad morn soon to follow that night,
When the sunrise of glory shall burst on my sight,
And the full matin-song, as the sleepers arise,
To shout in the morning, shall peal through the skies.

Who, who would live alway, away from his God,
Away from yon heaven, that blissful abode,
Where rivers of pleasure flow o'er the bright plains,
And the noontide of glory eternally reigns;
Where the saints of all ages in harmony meet,
Their Saviour and brethren transported to greet,
While the anthems of rapture unceasingly roll,
And the smile of the Lord is the feast of the soul?

That heavenly music! what is it I hear?
The notes of the harpers ring sweet on my ear.
And see soft unfolding those portals of gold,
The King all arrayed in his beauty behold!
O give me, O give me the wings of a dove!
Let me hasten my flight to those mansions above,
Ay, 'tis now that my soul on swift pinions would soar,
And in ecstacy bid earth adieu evermore.

WILLIAM AUGUSTUS MUHLENBERG.

THE REST OF THE SOUL.

IN that hour which of all the twenty-four is most emblematical of heaven and suggestive of repose, the eventide, in which instinctively Isaac went into the fields to meditate — when the work of the day is done, when the mind has ceased its tension, when the passions are lulled to rest in spite of themselves, by the spell of the quiet starlit sky—it is then, amidst the silence of the lull of all the lower parts of our nature, that the soul comes forth to do its work. Then the peculiar, strange work of the soul, which the intellect cannot do, meditation begins; awe and worship and wonder are in full exercise; and love begins then its purest form of mystic adoration, and pervasive and undefined tenderness, separate from all that is coarse and earthly, swelling as if it would embrace the All in its desire to bless, and lose itself in the sea of the love of God. This is the rest of the soul—the exercise and play of all the nobler powers.

F. W. ROBERTSON.

THE ETERNAL HOME.

THE seas are quiet when the winds give o'er;
So calm are we when passions are no more.
For then we know how vain it was to boast
Of fleeting things, too certain to be lost.
Clouds of affection from our younger eyes
Conceal that emptiness which age descries.

The soul's dark cottage, battered and decayed,
Lets in new light through chinks that time has made:
Stronger by weakness, wiser men become,
As they draw near to their eternal home.
Leaving the old, both worlds at once they view,
That stand upon the threshold of the new.

EDMUND WALLER.

"FOLLOW ME."

THE shadow of the mountain falls athwart the
    lowly plain,
And the shadow of the cloudlet hangs above
    the mountain's head:
    And the highest hearts and lowest wear the
      shadow of some pain.
    And the smile has scarcely flitted ere the
      anguished tear is shed.

For no eyes have there been ever without a weary
    tear,
And those lips cannot be human which have never
    heaved a sigh;
For without the dreary winter there has never been a
    year,
And the tempests hide their terrors in the calmest
    summer sky.

So this dreamy life is passing — and we move amidst
    its maze,
And we grope along together, half in darkness, half
    in light;
And our hearts are often burdened with the mysteries
    of our ways,
Which are never all in shadow, and are never wholly
    bright.

And our dim eyes ask a beacon, and our weary feet a
    guide,
And our hearts of all life's mysteries seek the meaning
    and the key;
And a cross gleams o'er our pathway, on it hangs the
    Crucified,
And He answers all our yearnings by the whisper,
    "Follow Me."

                     ABRAM T. RYAN.

ALL BEFORE.

O HEARTS that never cease to yearn!
    O brimming tears that ne'er are dried!
    The dead, though they depart, return
    As though they had not died!

The living are the only dead;
    The dead live — nevermore to die!
And often when we mourn them fled,
    They never were so nigh!

And though they lie beneath the waves,
    Or sleep within the churchyard dim —
(Ah! through how many different graves
    God's children go to him!) —

Yet every grave gives up its dead
    Ere it is overgrown with grass;
Then why should hopeless tears be shed,
    Or need we cry, "Alas"?

Or why should Memory, veiled with gloom,
    And like a sorrowing mourner craped,
Sit weeping o'er an empty tomb,
    Whose captives have escaped?

'Tis but a mound, and will be mossed
    Whene'er the summer grass appears;
The loved, though wept, are never lost;
    We only lose — our tears!

Nay, Hope may whisper with the dead
    By bending forward where they are;
But Memory, with a backward tread,
    Communes with them afar.

The joys we lose are but forecast,
    And we shall find them all once more;
We look behind us for the Past,
    But lo! 'tis all before!

THE DIVINE ABODE.

YE golden lamps of heaven, farewell,
    With all your feeble light!
Farewell, thou ever-changing moon
    Pale empress of the night!

And thou, refulgent orb of day,
    In brighter flames arrayed;
My soul, that springs beyond thy sphere,
    No more demands thy aid.

Ye stars are but the shining dust
    Of my divine abode;
The pavement of those heavenly courts
    Where I shall see my God.

There all the millions of his saints
    Shall in one song unite;
And each the bliss of all shall view
    With infinite delight.

                  PHILIP DODDRIDGE.

SAFE TO THE LAND.

KNOW not if the dark or bright
    Shall be my lot;
If that wherein my hopes delight,
    Be best or not.

It may be mine to drag for years
    Toil's heavy chain;
Or day or night, my meat be tears,
    On bed of pain.

Dear faces may surround my hearth
    With smile and glee,
Or I may dwell alone, and mirth
    Be strange to me.

My bark is wafted to the strand
    By breath divine,
And on the helm there rests a Hand
    Other than mine.

One who has ever known to sail
    I have on board;
Above the raging of the gale
    I hear my Lord.

He holds me; when the billows smite
    I shall not fall;
If sharp, 'tis short; if long, 'tis light;
    He tempers all.

Safe to the land, safe to the land!
    The end is this;
And then with Him go hand in hand,
    Far into bliss.

HENRY ALFORD.

OVER THE RIVER.

OVER the river they beckon to me—
    Loved ones who've passed to the further side;
The gleam of their snowy robes I see,
    But their voices are lost in the dashing tide.
There 's one with ringlets of sunny gold,
    And eyes the reflection of heaven's own blue;
He crossed in the twilight gray and cold,
    And the pale mist hid him from mortal view;
We saw not the angels who met him there,
    The gates of the city we could not see—
Over the river, over the river,
    My brother stands waiting to welcome me!

Over the river the boatman pale
    Carried another, the household pet;
Her brown curls waved in the gentle gale—
    Darling Minnie! I see her yet.
She crossed on her bosom her dimpled hands,
    And fearlessly entered the phantom bark;
We felt it glide from the silver sands,
    And all our sunshine grew strangely dark;
We know she is safe on the further side,
    Where all the ransomed and angels be—
Over the river, the mystic river,
    My childhood's idol is waiting for me.

For none return from those quiet shores,
    Who cross with the boatman cold and pale;
We hear the dip of the golden oars,
    And catch a gleam of the snowy sail;
And lo! they have passed from our yearning heart,
    They cross the stream and are gone for aye;
We may not sunder the veil apart
    That hides from our vision the gates of day
We only know that their barks no more
    May sail with us o'er life's stormy sea,
Yet, somewhere, I know, on the unseen shore,
    They watch, and beckon, and wait for me.

And I sit and think, when the sunset's gold
    Is flushing river and hill and shore,
I shall one day stand by the water cold
    And list for the sound of the boatman's oar;
I shall watch for a gleam of the flapping sail,
    I shall hear the boat as it gains the strand;
I shall pass from sight with the boatman pale,
    To the better shore of the spirit land.
I shall know the loved who have gone before,
    And joyfully sweet will the meeting be,
When over the river, the peaceful river,
    The Angel of Death shall carry me.

NANCY PRIEST WAKEFIELD.

LOOKING calmly yet humbly for the close of my mortal career, which cannot be far distant, I reverently thank God for the blessings vouchsafed me in the past, and with an awe that is not fear, and a consciousness of demerit that does not exclude hope, await the opening before my steps of the gates of the eternal world.

HORACE GREELEY.

PARTED FRIENDS.

RIEND after friend departs;
  Who hath not lost a friend?
There is no union here of hearts
  That finds not here an end!
Were this frail world our final rest,
Living or dying, none were blest.

Beyond the flight of time—
  Beyond the reign of death—
There surely is some blessed clime
  Where life is not a breath;
Nor life's affections transient fire,
Whose sparks fly upward and expire!

There is a world above
  Where parting is unknown!
A long eternity of love,
  Formed for the good alone;
And faith beholds the dying here
Translated to that glorious sphere!

Thus star by star declines
  Till all are passed away;
As morning high and higher shines
  To pure and perfect day;
Nor sink those stars in empty night,
But hide themselves in heaven's own light.

JAMES MONTGOMERY,

THE ETERNAL.

HE One remains, the many change and pass;
  Heaven's light forever shines, Earth's shadows
    fly;
  Life, like a dome of many-colored glass,
  Stains the white radiance of Eternity,
Until Death tramples it to fragments.—Die,
If thou wouldst be with that which thou dost seek!
Follow where all is fled!—Rome's azure sky,
Flowers, ruins, statues, music—words are weak
The glory they transfuse with fitting truth to speak.

Why linger, why turn back, why shrink, my heart?
Thy hopes are gone before: from all things here
They have departed; thou shouldst now depart!
A light is passed from the revolving year,
And man and woman; and what still is dear
Attracts to crush, repels to make thee wither.
The soft sky smiles,—the low wind whispers near:
'T is Adonais calls! oh, hasten thither,
No more let Life divide what Death can join together.

That Light whose smile kindles the universe,
That beauty in which all things work and move,
That benediction which the eclipsing curse
Of birth can quench not, that sustaining Love
Which through the web of being blindly wove
By man and beast, and earth and air and sea,
Burns bright or dim, as each are mirrors of
The fire for which all thirst, now beams on me,
Consuming the last clouds of cold mortality.

The breath whose might I have invoked in song
Descends on me, my spirit's bark is driven
Far from the shore, far from the trembling throng
Whose sails were never to the tempest given;
The massy earth and sphered skies are riven:
I am borne darkly, fearfully, afar;
While, burning through the inmost veil of heaven,
The soul of Adonais, like a star,
Beacons from the abode where the Eternal are.

PERCY BYSSHE SHELLEY.

BEYOND THE HILLS.

EYOND the hills where suns go down,
  And brightly beckon as they go,
I see the land of fair renown,
  The land which I so soon shall know.

Above the dissonance of time,
  And discord of its angry words,
I hear the everlasting chime,
  The music of unjarring chords.

I bid it welcome; and my haste
  To join it cannot brook delay,

O, song of morning, come at last,
  And ye who sing it come away.

O, song of light, and dawn, and bliss,
  Sound over earth, and fill these skies!
Nor ever, ever, ever cease
  Thy soul-entrancing melodies!

Glad song of this disburdened earth,
  Which holy voices then shall sing;
Praise for creation's second birth,
  And glory to creation's King!

HORATIUS BONAR.

MISCELLANEOUS.

"Silence sleeps on the earth and air,
Never a breath does the sea-breeze blow."

DOWN IN THE HARBOR THE SHIPS LIE MOORED.

DOWN in the harbor the ships lie moored,
   Weary sea-birds with folded wing, —
Anchors sunken and sails secured;
   Yet on the water they rock and swing,
      Rock and swing,
  As though each keel were a living thing.

Silence sleeps on the earth and air,
   Never a breath does the sea-breeze blow,
Yet like living pendulums there,
   Down in the harbor, to and fro,
      To and fro,
Backward and forward the vessels go.

As a child on its mother's breast,
   Cradled in happy slumber, lies,
Yet, half-conscious of joy and rest,
   Varies its breathing, and moves and sighs,
      Moves and sighs,
Yet neither wakes nor opens its eyes.

Or it may be, the vessels long—
   For almost human they seem to me—
For the leaping waves, and the storm-wind strong,
   And the fetterless freedom out at sea,
      Out at sea,
And feel their rest a captivity.

467

So as a soul from a higher sphere,
  Fettered down to this earthly clay,
Strives at the chains that bind it here,
  Tossing and struggling, day by day,
      Day by day,
Longing to break them and flee away,

Strive the ships in their restlessness,
  Whether the tide be high or low;—
And why these tear-drops, I cannot guess,
  As down in the harbor, to and fro,
      To and fro,
Backward and forward the vessels go.

ELIZABETH AKERS ALLEN.

"He took the little ones up on his knee."

THE JOLLY OLD PEDAGOGUE.

'TWAS a jolly old pedagogue, long ago,
  Tall and slender, and sallow, and dry;
His form was bent, and his gait was slow,
His long, thin hair was as white as snow;
  But a wonderful twinkle shone in his eye,
And he sang every night as he went to bed,
" Let us be happy down here below;
The living should live, though the dead be dead,"
  Said the jolly old pedagogue, long ago.

He taught his scholars the rule of three,
  Writing, and reading, and history too;
He took the little ones up on his knee,
For a kind old heart in his breast had he,
  And the wants of the littlest child he knew:
" Learn while you 're young," he often said,
  " There is much to enjoy down here below;
Life for the living, and rest for the dead,"
  Said the jolly old pedagogue, long ago.

With the stupidest boys he was kind and cool,
  Speaking only in gentlest tones;
The rod was hardly known in his school;
Whipping to him was a barbarous rule,
And too hard work for his poor old bones;
Besides, it was painful, he sometimes said,
  "We should make life pleasant down here below,
The living need charity more than the dead,"
  Said the jolly old pedagogue, long ago.

He lived in the house by the hawthorn lane,
  With roses and woodbine over the door;
His rooms were quiet and neat and plain,
But a spirit of comfort there held reign,
  And made him forget he was old and poor.
" I need so little," he often said,
  "And my friends and relatives here below
Won't litigate over me when I am dead,"
  Said the jolly old pedagogue, long ago.

But the pleasantest times that he had, of all,
  Were the sociable hours he used to pass,
With his chair tipped back to a neighbor's wall,
Making an unceremonious call,
  Over a pipe and a friendly glass; —
This was the finest pleasure, he said,
  Of the many he tasted here below;
" Who has no cronies had better be dead,"
  Said the jolly old pedagogue, long ago.

Then the jolly old pedagogue's wrinkled face
  Melted all over in sunshiny smiles; —
He stirred his glass with an old-school grace,
Chuckled, and sipped, and prattled apace,
  Till the house grew merry from cellar to tiles; —
" I'm a pretty old man," he gently said,
  " I've lingered a long while here below;
But my heart is fresh, if my youth is fled ! "
  Said the jolly old pedagogue, long ago.

He smoked his pipe in the balmy air,
  Every night when the sun went down,
While the soft wind played in his silvery hair,
Leaving its tenderest kisses there
  On the jolly old pedagogue's jolly old crown;
And feeling the kisses, he smiled and said,
  'Twas a glorious world down here below;
" Why wait for happiness till we are dead?"
  Said the jolly old pedagogue, long ago."

He sat at his door one midsummer night,
  After the sun had sunk in the west,
And the lingering beams of golden light
Made his kindly old face look warm and bright,
  While the odorous night-wind whispered " Rest! "
Gently, gently he bowed his head, —
  There were angels waiting for him, I know
He was sure of happiness, living or dead,
  This jolly old pedagogue, long ago.

                                    GEORGE ARNOLD.

HERE 'S TO THEM THAT ARE GANE.

ERE 'S to them, to them that are gane;
  Here's to them, to them that are gane;
  Here's to them that were here, the faithful and
    dear,
That will never be here again—no, never.
  But where are they now that are gane?
  Oh, where are the faithful and true?
They 're gane to the light that fears not the night,
An' their day of rejoicing shall end—no, never.

  Here 's to them, to them that were here;
  Here 's to them, to them that were here;
Here 's a tear and a sigh to the bliss that 's gane by,
  But 't was ne'er like what 's coming, to last forever.

  Oh, bright was their morning sun!
  Oh, bright was their morning sun!
Yet, lang ere the gloaming, in clouds it gaed down;
  But the storm and the cloud are now past—forever.

  Fareweel, fareweel ! parting silence is sad ;
  Oh, how sad the last parting tear !
But that silence shall break, where no tear on the
    cheek
Can bedim the bright vision again—no, never.
  Then speed to the wings of old Time,
  That waft us where pilgrims would be;
To the regions of rest, to the shores of the blest,
  Where the full tide of glory shall flow—forever.

                              LADY CAROLINE NAIRNE.

THE TOPER'S APOLOGY.

M often asked by plodding souls
  And men of sober tongue,
What joy I take in draining bowls
  And tippling all night long.

But though these cautious knaves I scorn,
  For once I 'll not disdain
To tell them why I sit till morn
  And fill my glass again.

'Tis by the glow my bumper gives,
Life's picture 's mellow made;
The fading light then brightly lives
And softly sinks the shade.

"In life I 've run all changes through,
Run every pleasure down."

Some happier tint still rises there
With every drop I drain;
And that I think 's a reason fair
To fill my glass again.

My Muse, too, when her wings are dry,
No frolic flights will take,
But round the bowl she 'll dip and fly,
Like swallows round a lake.
Then, if each nymph will have her share,
Before she 'll bless her swain,
Why, that I think 's a reason fair
To fill my glass again.

In life I 've rung all changes through,
Run every pleasure down,
Tried all extremes of folly too,
And lived with half the town;
For me there 's nothing new nor rare,
Till wine deceives my brain;
And that I think 's a reason fair
To fill my glass again.

I find, too, when I stint my glass,
And sit with sober air,
I 'm prosed by some dull reasoning ass
Who treads the path of care;
Or, harder still, am doomed to bear
Some coxcomb's fribbling strain;
And that I 'm sure 's a reason fair
To fill my glass again.

There 's many a lad I knew is dead,
And many a lass grown old,
And as the lesson strikes my head,
My weary heart grows cold;
But wine awhile drives off despair—
Nay, bids a hope remain;
And that I think 's a reason fair
To fill my glass again.

CHARLES MORRIS.

A VISIT FROM ST. NICHOLAS.

WAS the night before Christmas, when all
through the house
Not a creature was stirring, not even a mouse;
The stockings were hung by the chimney with
care,
In hopes that St. Nicholas soon would be there.
The children were nestled all snug in their beds,
While visions of sugar-plums danced through their
heads;
And mamma in her kerchief, and I in my cap,
Had just settled our brains for a long winter's nap,
When out on the lawn there arose such a clatter,
I sprang from the bed to see what was the matter.
Away to the window I flew like a flash,
Tore open the shutters and threw up the sash.
The moon on the breast of the new-fallen snow
Gave the lustre of mid-day to objects below;
When, what to my wondering eyes should appear,
But a miniature sleigh, and eight tiny reindeer,
With a little old driver, so lively and quick,
I knew in a moment it must be St. Nick.
More rapid than eagles his coursers they came,
And he whistled, and shouted, and called them by
name:
"Now, Dasher! now, Dancer! now, Prancer! and
Vixen!
On, Comet! on, Cupid! on, Donder and Blitzen!
To the top of the porch! to the top of the wall!
Now dash away! dash away! dash away all!"
As dry leaves that before the wild hurricane fly,
When they meet with an obstacle, mount to the sky,
So up to the house-top the coursers they flew,
With the sleighful of toys, and St. Nicholas too.
And then, in a twinkling, I heard on the roof
The prancing and pawing of each little hoof.
As I drew in my head, and was turning around,
Down the chimney St. Nicholas came with a
bound.

He was dressed all in fur, from his head to his foot,
And his clothes were all tarnished with ashes and
soot;
A bundle of toys he had flung on his back,
And he looked like a peddler just opening his pack.
His eyes, how they twinkled! his dimples, how
merry!
His cheeks were like roses, his nose like a cherry!
His droll little mouth was drawn up like a bow,
And the beard of his chin was as white as the snow;
The stump of a pipe he held tight in his teeth,
And the smoke it encircled his head like a wreath.
He had a broad face, and a little round belly
That shook, when he laughed, like a bowlful of jelly.

He was chubby and plump—a right jolly old elf—
And I laughed, when I saw him, in spite of myself;
A wink of his eye, and a twist of his head,
Soon gave me to know I had nothing to dread;
He spoke not a word, but went straight to his work,
And filled all the stockings; then turned with a
jerk,
And laying his finger aside of his nose,
And giving a nod, up the chimney he rose.
He sprang to the sleigh, to the team gave a whistle,
And away they all flew, like the down of a thistle,
But I heard him exclaim, ere he drove out of sight,
"Happy Christmas to all, and to all a good-night!"

CLEMENT C. MOORE.

"Soon as the evening shades prevail,
The Moon takes up the wondrous tale;
And nightly, to the listening Earth,
Repeats the story of her birth."

THE SPACIOUS FIRMAMENT ON HIGH.

THE spacious firmament on high,
With all the blue ethereal sky,
And spangled heavens, a shining frame,
Their great Original proclaim.

The unwearied Sun from day to day
Does his Creator's power display;
And publishes, to every land,
The work of an almighty hand.

Soon as the evening shades prevail,
The Moon takes up the wondrous tale;
And nightly, to the listening Earth,
Repeats the story of her birth:
Whilst all the stars that round her burn,
And all the planets, in their turn,
Confirm the tidings as they roll,
And spread the truth from pole to pole.

What though, in solemn silence, all
Move round the dark terrestrial ball:
What though nor real voice nor sound
Amidst their radiant orbs be found:
In reason's ear they all rejoice,
And utter forth a glorious voice,
Forever singing as they shine,
"The hand that made us is divine."

JOSEPH ADDISON.

NEGRO REVIVAL HYMN.

OH, whar shill we go w'en de great day comes,
Wid de blowin' er de trumpits en de bangin' er
de drums?
How many po' sinners 'll be kotched out late
En fine no latch ter de golden gate?

Who's a gwine fer ter stan' stiff-kneed en bol',
En answer to der name at de callin' er de roll?
You better come now ef you comin' —
Ole Satun is loose en a bummin' —
De wheels er distruckshun is a hummin' —
Oh, come 'long, sinners, ef you comin'!

De song er salvashun is a mighty sweet song,
En de Pairidise win' blow fur en blow strong,
En Aberham's bosom, hits saft en hits wide,
En right dar's de place whar de sinners oughter hide!
Oh, you nee'n ter be a stoppin' en a lookin';
Ef you fool wid ole Satun you'll git took in;
You'll hang on de aidge en get shook in,
Ef you keep on a stoppin' en a lookin'.

" De time is right now, en dish yer's de place."

No use fer ter wait twell ter-morrer,
De sun musn't set on yo' sorrer, —
Sin's ez sharp ez a bamboo-brier —
O Lord! fetch de mo'ners up higher!

W'en de nashuns er de earf is a standin' all aroun',
Who's a gwine ter be choosen fer ter w'ar de glory-
crown?

De time is right now; en dish yer's de place —
Let de sun er salvashun shine squar' in yo' face;
Fight de battles er de Lord, fight soon en fight late,
En you'll allers fine a latch ter de golden gate;
No use fer ter wait twel ter-morrer,
De sun musn't set on yo' sorrer, —
Sin's ez sharp ez a bamboo-brier,
Ax de Lord fer ter fetch you up higher!

JOEL CHANDLER HARRIS.

THE OLD SHEPHERD'S DOG.

THE old Shepherd's dog, like his master, was
gray,
His teeth all departed and feeble his tongue;
Yet where'er Corin went he was followed by
Tray;
Thus happy through life did they hobble
along.

If Corin went forth 'mid the tempests and rain,
Tray scorned to be left in the chimney behind.

At length, in the straw Tray made his last bed —
For vain, against Death, is the stoutest endeavor;
To lick Corin's hand he reared up his weak head,
Then fell back, closed his eyes, and, ah! closed
them forever.

"The old Shepherd's dog, like his master, was gray."

When fatigued, on the grass the Shepherd would lie,
For a nap in the sun—'midst his slumbers so sweet,
His faithful companion crawled constantly nigh,
Placed his head on his lap or lay down at his feet.

When winter was heard on the hill and the plain,
And torrents descended, and cold was the wind,

Not long after Tray did the Shepherd remain,
Who oft o'er his grave with true sorrow would
bend;
And, when dying, thus feebly was heard the poor
swain:
"Oh, bury me, neighbors, beside my old friend!"

JOHN WOLCOTT (Peter Pindar).

BOOKS are the true levelers. They give to all who faithfully use them the society,
the spiritual presence, of the greatest and best of our race.

THE BELLS.

HEAR the sledges with the bells,
　　Silver bells!
What a world of merriment their melody fore-
　　tells!
　　How they tinkle, tinkle, tinkle,
　　　In the icy air of night!
　　While the stars that oversprinkle
　　All the heavens seem to twinkle
　　　With a crystalline delight;
　　Keeping time, time, time,
　　　In a sort of Runic rhyme,
To the tintinnabulation that so musically wells
　　From the bells, bells, bells, bells,
　　　Bells, bells, bells,
　From the jingling and the tinkling of the bells.

　Hear the mellow wedding bells-
　　Golden bells!
What a world of happiness their harmony foretells!
　　Through the balmy air of night
　　How they ring out their delight!
　　　From the molten-golden notes,
　　　　And all in tune,
　　　What a liquid ditty floats
　To the turtle-dove that listens, while she gloats
　　　On the moon!
　　Oh, from out the sounding cells,
　What a gush of euphony voluminously wells!
　　　How it swells!
　　　How it dwells
　　On the future! how it tells
　　Of the rapture that impels
　　To the swinging and the ringing
　　Of the bells, bells, bells —
　　Of the bells, bells, bells, bells,
　　　Bells, bells, bells—
　To the rhyming and the chiming of the bells!

　Hear the loud alarum bells—
　　Brazen bells!
What a tale of terror, now, their turbulency tells!
　　In the startled ear of night
　　How they scream out their affright!
　　Too much horrified to speak,
　　They can only shriek, shriek,
　　　Out of tune,
In a clamorous appealing to the mercy of the fire,
In a mad expostulation with the deaf and frantic fire
　　Leaping higher, higher, higher,
　　　With a desperate desire,
　　And a resolute endeavor,
　　Now — now to sit or never,
　By the side of the pale-faced moon.

　Oh, the bells, bells, bells!
　　What a tale their terror tells
　　　Of despair!
　How they clang, and clash, and roar!
　　What a horror they outpour
On the bosom of the palpitating air!
　　Yet the ear, it fully knows,
　　　By the twanging,
　　　And the clanging,
　　How the danger ebbs and flows;
　　Yet the ear distinctly tells,
　　　In the jangling
　　　And the wrangling,
　　How the danger sinks and swells,
By the sinking or the swelling in the anger of the
　bells—
　　　Of the bells —
　　Of the bells, bells, bells, bells,
　　　Bells, bells, bells—
　In the clamor and the clangor of the bells!

　　Hear the tolling of the bells —
　　　Iron bells!
What a world of solemn thought their monody com-
　　pels!
　　In the silence of the night
　　How we shiver with affright,
　At the melancholy menace of their tone!
　　For every sound that floats
　　From the rust within their throats
　　　Is a groan.
　　And the people — ah, the people —
　　They that dwell up in the steeple,
　　　All alone,
　　And who tolling, tolling, tolling,
　　　In that muffled monotone,
　　Feel a glory in so rolling
　　On the human heart a stone—
　　They are neither man nor woman —
　　They are neither brute nor human —
　　　They are Ghouls:
　　And their king it is who tolls;
　　And he rolls, rolls, rolls, rolls,
　　　A pæan from the bells!
　　And his merry bosom swells
　　　With the pæan of the bells!
　　And he dances and he yells;
　　Keeping time, time, time,
　　In a sort of Runic rhyme,
　　　To the pæan of the bells—
　　　　Of the bells;
　　Keeping time, time, time,
　　In a sort of Runic rhyme,

"Humbled beneath His mighty hand,
　Prostrate His providence adore.
'Tis done! — Arise! He bids thee stand,
　　To fall no more.

" Now, traveler in the vale of tears,
　To realms of everlasting light,

And while the moldering ashes sleep
　　Low in the ground,

"The soul, of origin divine,
　God's glorious image, freed from clay,
In heaven's eternal sphere shall shine,
　　　A star of day!

" On thy dear lap these limbs reclined,
Shall gently moulder into thee."

Through Time's dark wilderness of years
　　Pursue thy flight!

"There is a calm for those who weep,
　A rest for weary pilgrims found;

" The sun is but a spark of fire,
　A transient meteor in the sky:
The soul, immortal as its sire,
　　　Shall never die."

JAMES MONTGOMERY.

THE WORLD.

SAW eternity the other night,
Like a great ring of pure and endless light,
　　All calm, as it was bright;
And round beneath it, time, in hours, days,
　　years,
　　　Driven by the spheres
Like a vast shadow moved, in which the world
　And all her train were hurled.

The doting lover, in his quaintest strain,
　　Did there complain:
Near him his lute, his fancy, and his flights,
　　Wit's sour delights;
With gloves and knots, the silly snares of pleasure,
　　Yet his dear treasure
All scattered lay, while he his eyes eyes did pour
　　Upon a flower.

The darksome statesman, hung with weights and
    woe,
Like a thick midnight fog, moved there so slow,
    He did not stay nor go;
Condemning thoughts, like mad eclipses, scowl
    Upon his soul,
And clouds of crying witnesses without
    Pursued him with one shout.
Yet digged the mole, and lest his ways be found,
    Workt under ground,
Where he did clutch his prey; but one did see
    That policy;
Churches and altars fed him; perjuries
    Were gnats and flies;
It rained about him blood and tears; but he
    Drank them as free.

The downright epicure placed heaven in sense,
    And scorned pretence;
While others, slipt into a wide excess,
    Said little less;
The weaker sort, slight, trivial wares enslave,
    Who think them brave,
And poor, despiséd truth sat counting by
    Their victory.

Yet some, who all this while did weep and sing,
And sing and weep, soared up into the ring;
    But most would use no wing.
"O fools," said I, "thus to prefer dark night
    Before true light!
To live in grots and caves, and hate the day
    Because it shows the way,—

"The fearful miser, on a heap of rust."

The fearful miser, on a heap of rust,
Sat pining all his life there; did scarce trust
    His own hands with the dust;
Yet would not place one piece above, but lives
    In fear of thieves.
Thousands there were, as frantic as himself,
    And hugged each one his pelf;

The way which, from this dead and dark abode,
    Leads up to God;
A way where you might tread the sun, and be
    More bright than he!"
But, as I did their madness so discuss,
    One whispered thus,
"This ring the bridegroom did for none provide,
    But for his bride."

HENRY VAUGHAN.

WILLIAM TELL AMONG THE MOUNTAINS.

YE crags and peaks, I'm with you once again!
    I hold to you the hands you first beheld,
    To show they still are free. Methinks I hear
    A spirit in your echoes answer me,
    And bid your tenant welcome to his home
    Again! O sacred forms, now proud ye look!
How high you lift your heads into the sky!
How huge you are! how mighty and how free!

Ye are the things that tower, that shine, whose smile
Makes glad, whose frown is terrible, whose forms,
Robed or unrobed, do all the impress wear
Of awe divine. Ye guards of liberty!
I'm with you once again!—I call to you
With all my voice! I hold my hands to you
To show they still are free. I rush to you,
As though I could embrace you!

Scaling yonder peak,
I saw an eagle wheeling, near its brow,
O'er the abyss. His broad, expanded wings
Lay calm and motionless upon the air,
As if he had floated there, without their aid,
By the sole act of his unlorded will,
That buoyed him proudly up! Instinctively
I bent my bow; yet wheeled he, heeding not
The death that threatened him! I could not shoot!
'T was liberty! I turned my bow aside,
And let him soar away.

In my boat at night, when down the mountain gorge
The wind came roaring—sat in it, and eyed
The thunder breaking from his cloud, and smiled
To see him shake his lightnings o'er my head,
And think I had no master, save his own!

You know the jutting cliff, round which a track
Up hither winds, whose base is but the brow
To such another one, with scanty room
For two to pass abreast? O'ertaken there
By the mountain-blast, I 've laid me flat along

"Ye crags and peaks, I'm with you once again."

Once Switzerland was free! O, with what pride
I used to walk these hills, look up to heaven,
And bless God that it was so! It was free!
From end to end, from cliff to lake, 't was free!
Free as our torrents are, that leap our rocks,
And plough our valleys without asking leave;
Or as our peaks, that wear their caps of snow
In very presence of the regal sun!
How happy was I in it then! I loved
Its very storms! Ay, often have I sat

And while gust followed gust more furiously,
As if 't would sweep me o'er the horrid brink,
And I have thought of other lands, whose storms
Are summer-flaws to those of mine, and just
Have wished me there, — the thought that mine was
    free
Has checked that wish; and I have raised my head,
And cried, in thraldom, to that furious wind,
"Blow on!—This is the land of liberty!"

JAMES SHERIDAN KNOWLES.

THE sword is but a hideous flash in the darkness—right is an eternal ray.

MY HEART 'S IN THE HIGHLANDS.

I.

MY heart 's in the Highlands, my heart is not
  here;
  My heart 's in the Highlands a chasing the
  deer;
    Chasing the wild deer, and following the roe—
My heart 's in the Highlands wherever I go.
Farewell to the Highlands, farewell to the North,
The birthplace of valor, the country of worth;

II.

Farewell to the mountains high covered with
  snow;
Farewell to the straths and green valleys below:
Farewell to the forests and wild-hanging woods;
Farewell to the torrents and loud-pouring floods.
My heart 's in the Highlands, my heart is not
  here,
My heart 's in the Highlands a chasing the deer;

"Farewell to the mountains high covered with snow;
Farewell to the straths and green valleys below."

Wherever I wander, wherever I rove,
The hills of the Highlands forever I love.

Chasing the wild deer, and following the roe—
My heart 's in the Highlands, wherever I go.

ROBERT BURNS.

THE RAVEN.

ONCE upon a midnight dreary,
  While I pondered, weak and weary,
  Over many a quaint and curious volume of for-
    gotten lore,
  While I nodded, nearly napping,
  Suddenly there came a tapping,
  As of some one gently rapping,
    Rapping at my chamber door.
"'Tis some visitor," I muttered, "tapping at my
    chamber door—
    Only this, and nothing more."

Ah, distinctly I remember,
  It was in the bleak December,
And each separate dying ember wrought its ghost
    upon the floor.
  Eagerly I wished the morrow;
  Vainly I had tried to borrow
  From my books surcease of sorrow—
    Sorrow for the lost Lenore—
For the rare and radiant maiden whom the angels
    name Lenore—
    Nameless here for evermore.

And the silken, sad, uncertain
Rustling of each purple curtain
Thrilled me—filled me with fantastic terrors never felt
    before;
So that now, to still the beating
Of my heart, I stood repeating,
" 'Tis some visitor entreating
    Entrance at my chamber door—
Some late visitor entreating entrance at my chamber
    door;
    This it is, and nothing more."

Presently my soul grew stronger;
Hesitating then no longer,
" Sir," said I, " or Madam, truly your forgiveness I
    implore;
But the fact is, I was napping,
And so gently you came rapping,
And so faintly you came tapping,
    Tapping at my chamber door,
That I scarce was sure I heard you," — here I opened
    wide the door:
    Darkness there, and nothing more!

Deep into that darkness peering,
Long I stood there, wondering, fearing,
Doubting, dreaming dreams no mortal ever dared to
    dream before:
But the silence was unbroken,
And the darkness gave no token,
And the only word there spoken
    Was the whispered word, " Lenore!"
This *I* whispered, and an echo murmured back the
    word, " Lenore!"
    Merely this, and nothing more.

Then into the chamber turning,
All my soul within me burning,
Soon I heard again a tapping somewhat louder than
    before.
" Surely," said I, " surely that is
Something at my window lattice;
Let me see, then, what thereat is,
    And this mystery explore—
Let my heart be still a moment, and this mystery ex-
    plore;
    'Tis the wind, and nothing more!"

Open here I flung the shutter,
When, with many a flirt and flutter,
In there stepped a stately Raven of the saintly days of
    yore;
Not the least obeisance made he;
Not an instant stopped or stayed he;
But, with mien of lord or lady,
    Perched above my chamber door—
Perched upon a bust of Pallas just above my chamber
    door—
    Perched, and sat, and nothing more.

31

Then this ebony bird beguiling
My sad fancy into smiling,
By the grave and stern decorum of the countenance it
    wore,
" Though thy crest be shorn and shaven,
Thou," I said, " art sure no craven,
Ghastly, grim and ancient Raven,
    Wandering from the Nightly shore—
Tell me what thy lordly name is on the Night's Plu-
    tonian shore!"
    Quoth the Raven, " Nevermore."

Much I marvelled this ungainly
Fowl to hear discourse so plainly,
Though its answer little meaning, little relevancy
    bore;
For we cannot help agreeing
That no living human being
Ever yet was blessed with seeing
    Bird above his chamber door—
Bird or beast upon the sculptured bust above his
    chamber door—
    With such name as " Nevermore."

But the Raven sitting lonely
On the placid bust, spoke only
That one word, as if his soul in that one word he did
    outpour.
Nothing further then he uttered—
Not a feather then he fluttered—
Till I scarcely more than muttered,
    " Other friends have flown before—
On the morrow he will leave me, as my hopes have
    flown before."
    Then the bird said, " Nevermore."

Startled at the stillness broken
By reply so aptly spoken,
" Doubtless," said I, "what it utters is its only stock
    and store,
Caught from some unhappy master
Whom unmerciful Disaster
Followed fast and followed faster
    Till his songs one burden bore—
Till the dirges of his Hope the melancholy burden
    bore
    Of ' Nevermore'—of ' Nevermore.' "

But the Raven still beguiling
All my sad soul into smiling,
Straight I wheeled a cushioned seat in front of bird,
    and bust, and door;
Then upon the velvet sinking,
I betook myself to linking
Fancy unto fancy, thinking
    What this ominous bird of yore—
What this grim, ungainly, ghastly, gaunt and ominous
    bird of yore
    Meant in croaking, " Nevermore."

This I sat engaged in guessing,
But no syllable expressing
To the fowl whose fiery eyes now burned into my
    bosom's core;
This and more I sat divining,
With my head at ease reclining
On the cushion's velvet lining,
    That the lamplight gloated o'er;
But whose velvet violet lining with the lamplight
    gloating o'er,
She shall press, ah, never more!

Then, methought, the air grew denser,
Perfumed from an unseen censer,
Swung by angels whose faint footfalls tinkled on the
    tufted floor.
"Wretch," I cried, "thy God hath lent thee,
By these angels he hath sent thee,
Respite—respite and nepenthe
From thy memories of Lenore!
Quaff, oh quaff this kind nepenthe, and forget this lost
    Lenore!"
    Quoth the Raven, "Nevermore."

"Prophet," said I, "thing of evil!—
Prophet still, if bird or devil!
Whether tempter sent, or whether tempest tossed thee
    here ashore,
Desolate, yet all undaunted,
On this desert land enchanted—
On this home by Horror haunted—
Tell me truly, I implore—
Is there—*is* there balm in Gilead? tell me—tell me, I
    implore!"
    Quoth the Raven, "Nevermore."

"Prophet," said I, "thing of evil—
Prophet still, if bird or devil!
By that heaven that bends above us—by that God we
    both adore—
Tell this soul with sorrow laden
If, within the distant Aidenn,
It shall clasp a sainted maiden
    Whom the angels name Lenore—
Clasp a rare and radiant maiden whom the angels
    name Lenore."
    Quoth the Raven, "Nevermore."

"Be that word our sign of parting,
Bird or fiend!" I shrieked, upstarting—
"Get thee back into the tempest and the Night's Plu-
    tonian shore!
Leave no black plume as a token
Of that lie thy soul hath spoken!
Leave my loneliness unbroken!—
Quit the bust above my door!
Take thy beak from out my heart, and take thy form
    from off my door!"
    Quoth the Raven, "Nevermore."

And the Raven, never flitting,
Still is sitting, still is sitting
On the pallid bust of Pallas just above my chamber
    door;
And his eyes have all the seeming
Of a demon that is dreaming;
And the lamplight o'er him streaming
Throws his shadow on the floor;
And my soul from out that shadow that lies floating
    on the floor
Shall be lifted—nevermore!

EDGAR ALLAN POE.

THERE IS MIST ON THE MOUNTAIN AND NIGHT ON THE VALE.

THERE is mist on the mountain and night on the
    vale,
    But more dark is the sleep of the sons of the
    Gael.
A stranger commanded—it sunk on the land.
It has frozen each heart, and benumbed every
    hand!

The dirk and the target lie sordid with dust,
The bloodless claymore is but reddened with rust:
On the hill or the glen if a gun should appear,
It is only to war with the heath-cock or deer.

The deeds of our sires if our bards should rehearse
Let a blush or a blow be the meed of their verse!
Be mute every string, and be hushed every tone,
That shall bid us remember the fame that is flown.

But the dark hours of night and of slumber are
    past,
The morn on our mountains is dawning at last;
Glenaladale's peaks are illumed with the rays,
And the streams of Glenfinnan leap bright in the
    blaze.

O high-minded Moray!—the exiled—the dear!
In the blush of the dawning the Standard uprear!
Wide, wide to the winds of the north let it fly,
Like the sun's latest flash when the tempest is nigh!

Ye sons of the strong, when that dawning shall
    break,
Need the harp of the aged remind you to wake?
That dawn never beamed on your forefathers' eye
But it roused each high chieftain to vanquish or die.

O sprung from the Kings who in Islay kept state,
Proud chiefs of Clan-Ranald, Glengarry, and Sleat!
Combine like three streams from one mountain of
    snow,
And resistless in union rush down on the foe!

True son of Sir Evan, undaunted Lochiel,
Place thy targe on thy shoulder and burnish thy
    steel!
Rough Keppoch, give breath to thy bugle's bold
    swell,
Till far Coryarrick resound to the knell!

Stern son of Lord Kenneth, high chief of Kintail,
Let the stag in thy standard bound wild in the gale!
May the race of Clan-Gillian, the fearless and free,
Remember Glenlivet, Harlaw, and Dundee!

Let the clan of gray Fingon, whose offspring has
    given
Such heroes to earth, and such martyrs to heaven,
Unite with the race of renowned Rori More,
To launch the long galley and stretch to the oar!

How Mac-Shimei will joy when their chief shall
    display
The yew-crested bonnet o'er tresses of gray!
How the race of wronged Alpine and murdered
    Glencoe
Shall shout for revenge when they pour on the foe!

Ye sons of brown Dermid, who slew the wild boar,
Resume the pure faith of the great Callum-More!
Mac-Neil of the Islands, and Moy of the Lake,
For honor, for freedom, for vengeance awake!

Awake on your hills, on your islands awake!
Brave sons of the mountain, the frith, and the lake!
'Tis the bugle — but not for the chase is the call;
'Tis the pibroch's shrill summons—but not to the
    hall.

'Tis the summons of heroes for conquest or death.
When the banners are blazing on mountain and
    heath;
They call to the dirk, the claymore, and the targe.
To the march and the muster, the line and the charge.

"Rough Keppoch, give breath to thy bugle's bold swell,
Till far Coryarrick resound to the knell!"

Be the brand of each chieftain like Fin's in his ire!
May the blood through his veins flow like currents of
    fire!
Burst the base foreign yoke as your sires did of yore!
Or die, like your sires, and endure it no more!

SIR WALTER SCOTT.

THE DREAM OF ARGYLE.

EARTHLY arms no more uphold him;
    On his prison's stony floor,
    Waiting death, in his last slumber,
    Lies the doomed MacCallum More.

And he dreams a dream of boyhood;
    Rise again his heathery hills,
Sound again the hound's long baying,
    Cry of moor-fowl, laugh of rills.

Now he stands amidst his clansmen
    In the low, long banquet-hall,

Over grim, ancestral armor
    Sees the ruddy firelight fall.

Once again, with pulses beating,
    Hears the wandering minstrel tell
How Montrose on Inverary
    Thief-like from his mountains fell.

Down the glen, beyond the castle,
    Where the linn's swift waters shine,
Round the youthful heir of Argyle
    Shy feet glide and white arms twine.

"Down the glen, beyond the castle
Where the linn's swift waters shine."

Fairest of the rustic dancers,
  Blue-eyed Effie smiles once more,
Bends to him her snooded tresses,
  Treads with him the grassy floor.

Now he hears the pipes lamenting,
  Harpers for his mother mourn,
Slow, with sable plume and pennon,
  To her cairn of burial borne.

Then anon his dreams are darker,
  Sounds of battle fill his ears,
And the pibroch's mournful wailing
  For his father's fall he hears.

Wild Lochaber's mountain echoes
  Wail in concert for the dead,
And Loch Awe's deep waters murmur
  For the Campbell's glory fled!

Fierce and strong the godless tyrants
  Trample the apostate land,
While her poor and faithful remnant
  Wait for the avenger's hand.

Once again at Inverary,
  Years of weary exile o'er,
Armed to lead his scattered clansmen,
  Stands the bold MacCallum More.

Once again to battle calling
  Sound the war-pipes through the glen,
And the court-yard of Dunstaffnage
  Rings with tread of armèd men.

All is lost! the godless triumph,
  And the faithful ones and true
From the scaffold and the prison
  Covenant with God anew.

On the darkness of his dreaming
  Great and sudden glory shone;
Over bonds and death victorious
  Stands he by the Father's Throne!

From the radiant ranks of martyrs
  Notes of joy and praise he hears,
Songs of his poor land's deliverance
  Sounding from the future years.

Lo, he wakes! but airs celestial
  Bathe him in immortal rest,
And he sees with unsealed vision
  Scotland's cause with victory blest.

Shining hosts attend and guard him
  As he leaves his prison door;
And to death as to a triumph
  Walks the great MacCallum More!

          ELIZABETH H. WHITTIER.

HOW charming is divine philosophy!
  Not harsh and crabbéd, as dull fools
      suppose,
But musical as is Apollo's lute,
And a perpetual feast of nectared sweets.

CHILDHOOD'S PRAYER.

AS now I lay me down to sleep,
May angel guards around me keep,
Through all the silent hours of night,
Their watch and ward till morning light.
Dim evening shades around me creep.
As now I lay me down to sleep.

If I should die before I wake;
If I this night the world forsake,
And leave the friends I hold most dear,
Leave all that I so value here;
And if Thy call my slumbers break—
If I should die before I wake.

"Now I lay me down to sleep."

I pray Thee, Lord, my soul to keep.
The while I wake or while I sleep;
And while I work and while I play,
Give me Thy grace, that, day by day,
Thy love may in my heart grow deep,
I pray Thee, Lord, my soul to keep.

I pray Thee, Lord, my soul to take;
I pray that Thou wouldst for me make
Close at Thy feet a lowly place,
Where I may e'er behold Thy face,
And this I ask for Thy dear sake—
I pray Thee, Lord, my soul to take.

While bending at my mother's knee,
This little prayer she taught to me—
" Now as I lay me down to sleep,
I pray Thee, Lord, my soul to keep;

If I should die before I wake,
I pray Thee, Lord, my soul to take."

NEWTON S. OTIS.

THE LADY'S "YES."

"YES," I answered you last night;
  "No," this morning, sir, I say.
Colors seen by candle-light
  Will not look the same by day.

When the viols played their best,
  Lamps above, and laughs below,
Love me sounded like a jest,
  Fit for yes or fit for no.

Call me false or call me free,
  Vow, whatever light may shine,
No man on your face shall see
  Any grief for change on mine.

Yet the sir so to us both;
  Time to dance is not to woo;

Wooing light makes fickle troth.
  Scorn of me recoils on you.

Learn to win a lady's faith
  Nobly, as the thing is high,
Bravely, as for life and death,
  With a loyal gravity.

Lead her from the festive boards.
  Point her to the starry skies.
Guard her, by your truthful words,
  Pure from courtship's flatteries.

By your truth she shall be true,
  Ever true, as wives of yore;
And her yes, once said to you,
  SHALL be Yes for evermore.

ELIZABETH BARRETT BROWNING.

THE LAST LEAF.

SAW him once before,
As he passed by the door;
And again
The pavement-stones resound
As he totters o'er the ground
With his cane.

" But the old three-cornered hat,
And the breeches, and all that,
Are so queer."

They say that in his prime,
Ere the pruning-knife of time
Cut him down,
Not a better man was found
By the crier on his round
Through the town.

But now he walks the streets,
And he looks at all he meets
Sad and wan,
And he shakes his feeble head,
And it seems as if he said,
"They are gone."

The mossy marbles rest
On the lips that he has pressed
In their bloom;

And the names he loved to hear
Have been carved for many a year
On the tomb.

My grandmamma has said —
Poor old lady! she is dead
Long ago—
That he had a Roman nose,
And his cheek was like a rose
In the snow.

But now his nose is thin,
And it rests upon his chin
Like a staff;
And a crook is in his back,
And a melancholy crack
In his laugh.

I know it is a sin
For me to sit and grin
At him here,
But the old three-cornered hat,
And the breeches, and all that,
Are so queer!

And if I should live to be
The last leaf upon the tree
In the spring,
Let them smile, as I do now,
At the old forsaken bough
Where I cling.

OLIVER WENDELL HOLMES.

THE NOBLE NATURE.

IT is not growing like a tree
In bulk, doth make man better be;
Or standing long an oak, three hundred year,
To fall a log at last, dry, bald and sere:
A lily of a day
Is fairer far in May,
Although it fall and die that night—
It was the plant and flower of Light.
In small proportions we just beauties see;
And in short measures life may perfect be.

BEN JONSON.

OF A CONTENTED MIND.

HEN all is done and said,
  In the end thus shall you find,
He most of all doth bathe in bliss,
  That hath a quiet mind;
And, clear from worldly cares,
  To deem can be content
The sweetest time in all his life.
  In thinking to be spent.

Companion none is like
  Unto the mind alone;
For many have been harmed by speech,
  Through thinking, few or none.
Fear oftentimes restraineth words,
  But makes not thought to cease;
And he speaks best that hath the skill
  When for to hold his peace.

"The sweetest time of all my life
To deem in thinking spent."

The body subject is
  To fickle Fortune's power,
And to a million of mishaps
  Is casual every hour:
And Death in time doth change
  It to a clod of clay;
When as the mind, which is divine,
  Runs never to decay.

Our wealth leaves us at death;
  Our kinsmen at the grave;
But virtues of the mind unto
  The heavens with us we have.
Wherefore, for virtue's sake,
  I can be well content,
The sweetest time of all my life
  To deem in thinking spent.

THOMAS, LORD VAUX.

THE SEA-BIRD'S SONG.

N the deep is the mariner's danger,
  On the deep is the mariner's death;
Who to fear of the tempest a stranger
  Sees the last bubble burst of his breath?
    'Tis the sea-bird, sea-bird, sea-bird,
      Lone looker on despair;
    The sea-bird, sea-bird, sea-bird,
      The only witness there.

Whose wing is the wing that can cover
  With its shadow the foundering wreck?
    'Tis the sea-bird, etc.

My eye in the light of the billow,
  My wing on the wake of the wave,
I shall take to my breast for a pillow
  The shroud of the fair and the brave.
    I'm the sea-bird, etc.

"My eye, when the bark is benighted,
  Sees the lamp of the light-house go out "

Who watches their course who so mildly,
  Careen to the kiss of the breeze?
Who lists to their shrieks who so wildly
  Are clasped in the arms of the seas?
    'Tis the sea-bird, etc.

Who hovers on high o'er the lover,
  And her who has clung to his neck?

My foot on the iceberg has lighted,
  When hoarse the wild winds veer about;
My eye, when the bark is benighted,
  Sees the lamp of the light-house go out.
    I'm the sea-bird, sea-bird, sea-bird,
      Lone looker on despair,
    The sea-bird, sea-bird, sea-bird,
      The only witness there.

            JOHN G. C. BRAINARD.

OR my own private satisfaction, I had rather be master of my own time than wear a diadem.

THE MARINER'S DREAM.

IN slumbers of midnight the sailor boy lay;
　His hammock swung loose at the sport of the
　　wind;
But watch-worn and weary, his cares flew away,
　And visions of happiness danced o'er his mind.

He dreamt of his home, of his dear native bowers,
　And pleasures that waited on life's merry morn;
While memory each scene gaily covered with flowers,
　And restored every rose, but secreted its thorn.

Then Fancy her magical pinions spread wide,
　And bade the young dreamer in ecstasy rise;
Now far, far behind him the green waters glide,
　And the cot of his forefathers blesses his eyes.

The jessamine clambers in flower o'er the thatch,
　And the swallow chirps sweet from her nest in the
　　wall;
All trembling with transport, he raises the latch,
　And the voices of loved ones reply to his call.

A father bends o'er him with looks of delight;
　His cheek is bedewed with a mother's warm tear;
And the lips of the boy in a love-kiss unite
　With the lips of the maid whom his bosom holds
　　dear.

The heart of the sleeper beats high in his breast;
　Joy quickens his pulses,— his hardships seem o'er;
And a murmur of happiness steals through his rest,—
　" O God! thou hast blest me,— I ask for no more."

Ah! whence is that flame which now glares on his eye?
Ah! what is that sound which now bursts on his
　ear?
'Tis the lightning's red gleam, painting hell on the
　sky!
'Tis the crashing of thunders, the groan of the
　sphere!

He springs from his hammock,— he flies to the deck;
　Amazement confronts him with images dire;
Wild winds and mad waves drive the vessel a wreck;
　The masts fly in splinters; the shrouds are on fire.

Like mountains the billows tremendously swell;
　In vain the lost wretch calls on Mercy to save;
Unseen hands of spirits are ringing his knell;
　And the death-angel flaps his broad wing o'er the
　　wave!

O sailor boy, woe to thy dream of delight!
　In darkness dissolves the gay frost-work of bliss.
Where now is the picture that Fancy touched bright,—
　Thy parents' fond pressure, and love's honeyed
　　kiss?

O sailor boy! sailor boy! never again
　Shall home, love or kindred thy wishes repay;
Unblessed and unhonored, down deep in the main,
　Full many a fathom, thy frame shall decay.

No tomb shall e'er plead to remembrance for thee,
　Or redeem form or fame from the merciless surge;
But the white foam of waves shall thy winding-sheet
　　be,
　And winds in the midnight of winter thy dirge!

On a bed of green sea-flowers thy limbs shall be
　laid,—
Around thy white bones the red coral shall grow;
Of thy fair yellow locks threads of amber be made,
　And every part suit to thy mansion below.

Days, months, years, and ages shall circle away,
　And still the vast waters above thee shall roll;
Frail, short-sighted mortals their doom must obey,—
　O sailor boy! sailor boy! peace to thy soul!

　　　　　　　　　　　WILLIAM DIMOND.

————————

RING OUT, WILD BELLS.

RING out, wild bells, to the wild sky,
　The flying cloud, the frosty light;
　The year is dying in the night;
Ring out, wild bells, and let him die.

Ring out the old, ring in the new;
　Ring, happy bells, across the snow;
　The year is going, let him go;
Ring out the false, ring in the true.

Ring out the grief that saps the mind,
　For those that here we see no more;
　Ring out the feud of rich and poor,
Ring in redress to all mankind.

Ring out a slowly dying cause
　And ancient forms of party strife;

Ring in the nobler modes of life,
　With sweeter manners, purer laws.

Ring out false pride in place and blood,
　The civic slander and the spite;
　Ring in the love of truth and right,
Ring in the common love of good.

Ring out old shapes of foul disease,
　Ring out the narrowing lust of gold;
　Ring out the thousand wars of old,
Ring in the thousand years of peace.

Ring in the valiant man and free,
　The larger heart, the kindlier hand;
　Ring out the darkness of the land,
Ring in the Christ that is to be.

　　　　　　　　　　ALFRED TENNYSON.

THE MONEYLESS MAN.

IS there no place on the face of the earth,
Where charity dwelleth, where virtue has birth?
Where bosoms in mercy and kindness will heave,
When the poor and the wretched shall ask and
    receive?
Is there no place at all, where a knock from the poor,
Will bring a kind angel to open the door?
Ah, search the wide world wherever you can,
There is no open door for the Moneyless Man.

Go, look in yon hall where the chandelier's light
Drives off with its splendor the darkness of night,
Where the rich hanging velvet in shadowy fold
Sweeps gracefully down with its trimmings of gold,
And the mirrors of silver take up and renew
In long lighted vistas the wildering view:
Go there! at the banquet, and find if you can,
A welcoming smile for a Moneyless Man.

Go, look in yon church of the cloud-reaching spire,
Which gives to the sun his same look of red fire,
Where the arches and columns are gorgeous within,
And the walls seem as pure as the soul without sin;
Walk down the long aisles, see the rich and the great
In the pomp and the pride of their worldly estate;
Walk down in your patches, and find, if you can
Who opens a pew to a Moneyless Man!

Go, look in the Banks, where Mammon has told
His hundreds and thousands of silver and gold;
Where, safe from the hands of the starving and poor,
Lies pile upon pile of the glittering ore!
Walk up to their counters—ah, there you may stay
Till your limbs grow old, till your hairs grow gray,
And you'll find at the Banks not one of the clan
With money to lend to the Moneyless Man.

Go, look to yon Judge, in his dark flowing gown,
With the scales wherein law weigheth equity down;
Where he frowns on the weak and smiles on the strong,
And punishes right whilst he justifies wrong;
Where juries their lips to the Bible have laid,
To render a verdict they've already made:
Go there, in the court-room, and find, if you can,
Any law for the cause of a Moneyless Man.

Then go to your hovel—no raven has fed
The wife who has suffered too long for her bread;
Kneel down by her pallet, and kiss the death-frost
From the lips of the angel your poverty lost,
Then turn in your agony upward to God,
And bless, while it smites you, the chastening rod,
And you'll find, at the end of your life's little span,
There's a welcome above for a Moneyless Man.

                                HENRY T. STANTON.

O MAY I JOIN THE CHOIR INVISIBLE.

MAY I join the choir invisible
Of those immortal dead who live again
In minds made better by their presence; live
In pulses stirred to generosity,
In deeds of daring rectitude, in scorn
Of miserable aims that end with self,
In thoughts sublime that pierce the night like stars,
And with their mild persistence urge men's minds
To vaster issues.
            So to live is heaven:
To make undying music in the world,
Breathing a beauteous order, that controls
With growing sway the growing life of man.
So we inherit that sweet purity
For which we struggled, failed, and agonized
With widening retrospect that bred despair.
Rebellious flesh that would not be subdued,
A vicious parent shaming still its child.
Poor anxious penitence, is quick dissolved;
Its discords quenched by meeting harmonies,
Die in the large and charitable air.
And all our rarer, better, truer self.
That sobbed religiously in yearning song,

That watched to ease the burden of the world,
Laboriously tracing what must be,
And what may yet be better,—saw within
A worthier image for the sanctuary,
And shaped it forth before the multitude,
Divinely human, raising worship so
To higher reverence more mixed with love,—
That better self shall live till human Time
Shall fold its eyelids, and the human sky
Be gathered like a scroll within the tomb,
Unread for ever.
            This is life to come,
Which martyred men have made more glorious
For us, who strive to follow.
                        May I reach,
That purest heaven,—be to other souls
The cup of strength in some great agony,
Enkindle generous ardor, feed pure love,
Beget the smiles that have no cruelty,
Be the sweet presence of a good diffused,
And in diffusion ever more intense!
So shall I join the choir invisible,
Whose music is the gladness of the world.

        MARIAN EVANS LEWES CROSS (George Eliot).

THE MODERN BELLE.

THE daughter sits in the parlor,
 And rocks in her easy-chair;
She is dressed in silks and satins,
 And jewels are in her hair;
She winks, and giggles, and simpers,
 And simpers, and giggles, and winks;
And though she talks but little,
 It's vastly more than she thinks.

Her father goes clad in russet—
 All brown and seedy at that;
His coat is out at the elbows,
 And he wears a shocking bad hat.
He is hoarding and saving his dollars,
 So carefully, day by day,
While she on her whims and fancies
 Is squandering them all away.

She lies in bed of a morning
 Until the hour of noon,
Then comes down, snapping and snarling
 Because she's called too soon.
Her hair is still in papers,
 Her cheeks still bedaubed with paint—
Remains of last night's blushes
 Before she attempted to faint.

Her feet are so very little,
 Her hands are so very white,
Her jewels so very heavy,
 And her head so very light;
Her color is made of cosmetics—
 Though this she'll never own;
Her body is mostly cotton,
 And her heart is wholly stone.

She falls in love with a fellow
 Who swells with a foreign air;
He marries her for her money,
 She marries him for his hair—

One of the very best matches;
 Both are well mated in life;
She's got a fool for a husband,
 And he's got a fool for a wife.

AUNT TABITHA.

WHATEVER I do and whatever I say,
 Aunt Tabitha tells me that isn't the way,
When she was a girl (forty summers ago),
 Aunt Tabitha tells me they never did so.

Dear aunt! If I only would take her advice—
But I like my own way, and I find it so nice!
And besides I forget half the things I am told;
But they all will come back to me—when I am old.

If a youth passes by, it may happen no doubt,
He may chance to look in as I chance to look out;
She would never endure an impertinent stare,
It is horrid, she says, and I musn't sit there.

A walk in the moonlight has pleasure, I own,
But it isn't quite safe to be walking alone;
So I take a lad's arm—just for safety, you know—
But Aunt Tabitha tells me, *they* didn't do so.

How wicked we are, and how good they were then!
They kept at arm's length those detestable men;
What an era of virtue she lived in!—but stay—
Were the men such rogues in Aunt Tabitha's day?

If the men were so wicked—I'll ask my papa
How he dared to propose to my darling mamma?
Was he like the rest of them? goodness! who knows?
And what shall I say, if a wretch should propose?

I am thinking if aunt knew so little of sin,
What a wonder Aunt Tabitha's aunt must have been!
And her grand-aunt—it scares me—how shockingly
 sad
That we girls of to-day are so frightfully bad!

A martyr will save us, and nothing else can:
Let us perish to rescue some wretched young man!
Though when to the altar a victim I go,
Aunt Tabitha 'll tell me—she never did so.

OLIVER WENDELL HOLMES.

PROVIDENCE.

UST as a mother, with sweet, pious face,
    Yearns toward her little children from her
      seat,
Gives one a kiss, another an embrace,

To this a look, to that a word dispenses,
    And, whether stern or smiling, loves them still;—
So Providence for us, high, infinite,
    Makes our necessities its watchful task,

"Gives one a kiss, another an embrace."

Takes this upon her knees, and on her feet:
And while from actions, look, complaints, pretences,
She learns their feelings, and their various
    will,

Hearkens to all our prayers, helps all our wants,
    And even if it denies what seems our right,
Either denies because 't would have us ask,
    Or seems but to deny, or in denying grants.

RHYMES OF THE MONTHS.

JANUARY.

EATH stormy skies the wintry blast
    Sweeps o'er the hill and down the vale,
While children 'round the farmer's hearth
    Repeat the merry fireside tale.

FEBRUARY.

The forests with their icy plumes
    Are radiant with the rising sun,
Or sparkle like an arméd host
    Before the closing day is done.

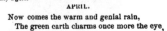
"The earth is set with many a gem."

MARCH.   APRIL.
Now falls the snow, the sleet, the rain,   Now comes the warm and genial rain,
And raging tempests fill the sky —   The green earth charms once more the eye,

"And on the meadow—in the field—
The polished scythe and sickle gleam "

A moment—and the sun peers through   The tender bud, the early flower,
Where clouds with golden edges lie.   Look up to greet the mild blue sky.

MAY.

All nature springs to life once more,
  The earth is set with many a gem;
And while the stars at eve look down,
  The modest flower looks up to them.

JULY.

The sky grows dark, and chains of fire
  Run through the clouds with dazzling sheen;
The thirsty earth drinks up the storm,
  The bow of promise now is seen.

"The north winds howl with dismal wail,
And earth and sky seem cold and drear."

JUNE.

The vine creeps forth, the daisy blooms,
  The very air is filled with song;
The tall grass bends with graceful curve
  When sweeps the summer breeze along.

AUGUST.

Now man and beast alike repair
  To cooling shade and running stream,
And on the meadow—in the field—
  The polished scythe and sickle gleam.

SEPTEMBER.

The golden grain glows in the sun
  Whose rays are scarcely felt at noon:
The maid and swain at eve enjoy
  The harvest and the hunter's moon.

OCTOBER.

The maple leaf is touched with age,
  And fades and shivers in the breeze
Whose mournful whispering now is heard
  Among the naked forest trees.

NOVEMBER.

The mountain-tops are clad with snow,
  The hills and vales look bare and gray;
The moon shines on the gleaming lake,
  And sparkles down the frozen bay.

DECEMBER.

The north winds howl with dismal wail,
  And earth and sky seem cold and drear;
The loud storm swells the grand refrain—
  The anthem of the dying year.

CLARK JILLSON.

A BOOK is a living voice. It is a spirit walking on the face of the earth. It continues to be the living thought of a person separated from us by space and time. Men pass away; monuments crumble into dust—what remains and survives is human thought.

BEAUTIFUL SNOW.

THE snow, the beautiful snow,
Filling the sky and the earth below.
Over the house-tops, over the street,
Over the heads of the people you meet,
    Dancing,
      Flirting,
        Skimming along,
Beautiful snow, it can do nothing wrong.
Flying to kiss a fair lady's cheek;
Clinging to lips in a frolicsome freak.
Beautiful snow, from the heavens above,
Pure as an angel and fickle as love!

O the snow, the beautiful snow!
How the flakes gather and laugh as they go!
Whirling about in its maddening fun,
It plays in its glee with every one.
    Chasing,
      Laughing,
        Hurrying by,
It lights up the face and it sparkles the eye;
And even the dogs, with a bark and a bound,
Snap at the crystals that eddy around.
The town is alive, and its heart in a glow
To welcome the coming of beautiful snow.

How the wild crowd goes swaying along,
Hailing each other with humor and song!
How the gay sledges like meteors flash by,—
Bright for a moment, then lost to the eye.
    Ringing,
      Swinging,
        Dashing they go
Over the crest of the beautiful snow:
Snow so pure when it falls from the sky,
To be trampled in mud by the crowd rushing by;
To be trampled and tracked by the thousands of feet
Till it blends with the horrible filth in the street.

Once I was pure as the snow,— but I fell:
Fell, like the snow-flakes, from heaven— to hell:
Fell, to be tramped as the filth of the street:
Fell, to be scoffed, to be spit on, and beat.
    Pleading,
      Cursing,
        Dreading to die,
Selling my soul to whoever would buy,
Dealing in shame for a morsel of bread,
Hating the living and fearing the dead.
Merciful God! have I fallen so low?
And yet I was once like this beautiful snow!

Once I was fair as the beautiful snow,
With an eye like its crystals, a heart like its glow;
Once I was loved for my innocent grace,—
Flattered and sought for the charm of my face.
    Father,
      Mother,
        Sisters all,
God, and myself I have lost by my fall.
The veriest wretch that goes shivering by
Will take a wide sweep, lest I wander too nigh;
For of all that is on or about me, I know
There is nothing that's pure but the beautiful snow.

How strange it should be that this beautiful snow
Should fall on a sinner with nowhere to go!
How strange it would be, when the night comes again,
If the snow and the ice struck my desperate brain!
    Fainting,
      Freezing,
        Dying alone,
Too wicked for prayer, too weak for my moan
To be heard in the crash of the crazy town,
Gone mad in its joy at the snow's coming down;
To lie and to die in my terrible woe,
With a bed and a shroud of the beautiful snow!

                   JAMES W. WATSON.

EVERY YEAR.

THE spring has less of brightness,
    Every year;
And the snow a ghastlier whiteness,
    Every year;
Nor do summer flowers quicken,
Nor the autumn fruitage thicken,
As they once did, for they sicken,
    Every year.

It is growing darker, colder,
    Every year;
As the heart and soul grow older,
    Every year;

I care not now for dancing,
Or for eyes with passion glancing,
Love is less and less entrancing,
    Every year.

Of the love and sorrows blended,
    Every year;
Of the charms of friendship ended, ·
    Every year;
Of the ties that still might bind me,
Until time to death resign me
My infirmities remind me,
    Every year.

OUR MOTHER TONGUE.

OW gather all our Saxon bards—let harps and
hearts be strung,
To celebrate the triumphs of our own good
Saxon tongue!

"——Far as Orkney's breakers roar."

For stronger far than hosts that march with battle-
flags unfurled,
It goes with freedom, thought, and truth to rouse and
rule the world.
Stout Albion hears its household lays on every surf-
worn shore,
And Scotland hears its echoing far as Orkney's break-
ers roar;
It climbs New England's rocky steeps as victor
mounts a throne;
Niagara knows and greets the voice, still mightier than
its own;
It spreads where winter piles deep snows on bleak
Canadian plains;
And where, on Essequibo's banks, eternal summer
reigns.
It tracks the loud, swift Oregon, through sunset val-
leys rolled,
And soars where California brooks wash down their
sands of gold.
It kindles realms so far apart that while its praise you
sing,
These may be clad with autumn's fruits, and those
with flowers of spring.
It quickens lands whose meteor lights flame in an
Arctic sky,

And lands for which the southern cross hangs orbit
fires on high.
It goes with all that prophets told and righteous kings
desired;
With all that great apostles taught and
glorious Greeks admired;
With Shakespeare's deep and wondrous
verse, and Milton's lofty mind;
With Alfred's laws and Newton's lore, to
cheer and bless mankind.
Mark, as it spreads, how deserts bloom,
and error flees away,
As vanishes the mist of night before the
star of day!
Take heed, then, heirs of Saxon fame—
take heed, nor once disgrace,
With recreant pen nor spoiling sword,
our noble tongue and race!
Go forth, and jointly speed the time, by
good men prayed for long,
When Christian states, grown just and
wise, will scorn revenge and wrong;
When earth's oppressed and savage tribes
shall cease to pine or roam,

"——Lands whose meteor lights flame in an Arctic sky."

All taught to prize these English words—FAITH,
FREEDOM, HEAVEN, and HOME.

J. G. LYONS.

T is well known that he seldom lives frugally who lives by chance. Hope is always
liberal, and they that trust her promises make little scruple of reveling to-day
on the profits of to-morrow.

THE HARP THAT ONCE THROUGH TARA'S HALLS.

HE harp that once through Tara's halls
　The soul of music shed,
Now hangs as mute on Tara's walls
　As if that soul were fled.
So sleeps the pride of former days,
　So glory's thrill is o'er,
And hearts that once beat high for praise
　Now feel that pulse no more!

No more to chiefs and ladies bright
　The harp of Tara swells;
The chord alone that breaks at night
　Its tale of ruin tells.
Thus Freedom now so seldom wakes,
　The only throb she gives
Is when some heart indignant breaks,
　To show that still she lives.

THOMAS MOORE.

THE VAGABONDS.

E are two travelers, Roger and I.
　Roger's my dog:—come here, you scamp!
Jump for the gentlemen,—mind your eye!
　Over the table,—look out for the lamp!—
The rogue is growing a little old;
　Five years we've tramped through wind and
　　weather,
And slept out-doors when nights were cold,
And ate and drank—and starved together.

We've learned what comfort is, I tell you!
　A bed on the floor, a bit of rosin,
A fire to thaw our thumbs (poor fellow!
The paw he holds up there's been frozen),
Plenty of catgut for my fiddle,
　(This out-door business is bad for strings),
Then a few nice buckwheats hot from the griddle,
　And Roger and I set up for kings!

No, thank ye, sir,—I never drink;
　Roger and I are exceedingly moral,—
Are n't we, Roger?—see him wink!—
　Well, something hot, then,—we won't quarrel.
He's thirsty, too,—see him nod his head!
What a pity, sir, that dogs can't talk!
He understands every word that 's said,—
　And he knows good milk from water-and-chalk.

The truth is, sir, now I reflect,
　I've been so sadly given to grog,
I wonder I've not lost the respect
　(Here's to you, sir!) even of my dog.
But he sticks by, through thick and thin;
　And this old coat, with its empty pockets,
And rags that smell of tobacco and gin,
　He 'll follow while he has eyes in his sockets.

There is n't another creature living
　Would do it, and prove, through every disaster,
So fond, so faithful, and so forgiving,
　To such a miserable, thankless master!
No, sir!—see him wag his tail and grin!
　By George! it makes my old eyes water!
That is, there's something in this gin
　That chokes a fellow. But no matter!

We'll have some music, if you're willing,
　And Roger (hem! what a plague a cough is, sir!)
Shall march a little.—Start, you villain!
　Stand straight! 'Bout face! Salute your officer!
Put up that paw! Dress! Take your rifle!
　(Some dogs have arms, you see!) Now hold your
Cap while the gentlemen give a trifle,
　To aid a poor old patriot soldier!

March! Halt! Now show how the rebel shakes,
　When he stands up to hear his sentence.
Now tell us how many drams it takes
　To honor a jolly new acquaintance.
Five yelps,—that's five; he's mighty knowing!
　The night's before us, fill the glasses!—
Quick, sir! I'm ill,—my brain is going!
　Some brandy,—thank you,—there!—it passes!

Why not reform? That's easily said;
　But I've gone through such wretched treatment,
Sometimes forgetting the taste of bread,
　And scarce remembering what meat meant,
That my poor stomach's past reform;
　And there are times when, mad with thinking,
I'd sell out heaven for something warm
　To prop a horrible inward sinking.

Is there a way to forget to think?
　At your age, sir, home, fortune, friends,
A dear girl's love, but I took to drink;
　The same old story; you know how it ends.
If you could have seen these classic features,—
　You need n't laugh, sir, they were not then
Such a burning libel on God's creatures:
　I was one of your handsome men!

If you had seen her, so fair and young,
　Whose head was happy on this breast!
If you could have heard the songs I sung
　When the wine went round, you would n't have
　　guessed
That ever I, sir, should be straying
　From door to door, with fiddle and dog,
Ragged and penniless, and playing
　To you to-night for a glass of grog!

She's married since,—a parson's wife:
  'T was better for her that we should part,—
Better the soberest, prosiest life
  Than a blasted home and a broken heart.
I have seen her? Once: I was weak and spent
  On the dusty road, a carriage stopped:
But little she dreamed, as on she went,
  Who kissed the coin that her fingers dropped!

You've set me talking, sir; I'm sorry:
  It makes me wild to think of the change!
What do you care for a beggar's story?
  Is it amusing? you find it strange?
I had a mother so proud of me!
  'T was well she died before— Do you know
If the happy spirits in heaven can see
  The ruin and wretchedness here below?

Another glass, and strong, to deaden
  This pain; then Roger and I will start.
I wonder, has he such a lumpish, leaden,
  Aching thing, in place of a heart?
He is sad sometimes, and would weep, if he could,
  No doubt, remembering things that were,—
A virtuous kennel, with plenty of food,
  And himself a sober, respectable cur.

I'm better now; that glass was warming.
  You rascal! limber your lazy feet!
We must be fiddling and performing
  For supper and bed, or starve in the street.
Not a very gay life to lead, you think?
  But soon we shall go where lodgings are free,
And the sleepers need neither victuals nor drink;—
  The sooner the better for Roger and me!

JOHN TOWNSEND TROWBRIDGE.

UNIVERSAL PRAYER.

FATHER of all! in every age,
  In every clime adored,
By saint, by savage, and by sage,
  Jehovah, Jove, or Lord!

Thou Great First Cause, least understood,
  Who all my sense confined
To know but this, that thou art good,
  And that myself am blind:

Yet gave me, in this dark estate,
  To see the good from ill:
And binding nature fast in fate,
  Left free the human will.

What conscience dictates to be done,
  Or warns me not to do;
This teach me more than hell to shun,
  That more than heaven pursue.

What blessings thy free bounty gives
  Let me not cast away;
For God is paid when man receives:
  To enjoy is to obey.

Yet not to earth's contracted span
  Thy goodness let me bound,
Or think thee Lord alone of man,
  When thousand worlds are round.

Let not this weak unknowing hand
  Presume thy bolts to throw,

And deal damnation round the land
  On each I judge thy foe.

If I am right, thy grace impart
  Still in the right to stay;
If I am wrong, O teach my heart
  To find that better way.

Save me alike from foolish pride
  Or impious discontent,
At aught thy wisdom has denied,
  Or aught thy goodness lent.

Teach me to feel another's woe,
  To hide the fault I see:
That mercy I to others show,
  That mercy show to me.

Mean though I am, not wholly so,
  Since quickened by thy breath;
O lead me, wheresoe'er I go,
  Through this day's life or death!

This day be bread and peace my lot:
  All else beneath the sun
Thou know'st if best bestowed or not,
  And let thy will be done.

To thee, whose temple is all space,
  Whose altar earth, sea, skies!
One chorus let all being raise!
  All nature's incense rise!

ALEXANDER POPE.

THE talkative listen to no one, for they are ever speaking. And the first evil that attends those who know not to be silent is, that they hear nothing.

THE COLLEGE REGATTA.

HE immortal boy, the coming heir of all,
Springs from his desk to " urge the flying ball,"

Cleaves with his bending oar the glassy waves,
With sinewy arm the dashing current braves.

OLIVER WENDELL HOLMES.

" Now to their mates the wild swans row."

EVENING.

HE sun upon the lake is low,
The wild birds hush their song,
The hills have evening's deepest glow,
Yet Leonard tarries long.

Now all whom varied toil and care
From home and love divide,
In the calm sunset may repair
Each to the loved one's side.

Ah me! my very laurels breathe
The tale in my reluctant ears,
And every boon the hours bequeath
But makes me debtor to the years!
E'en flattery's honeyed words declare
The secret she would fain withhold,
And tells me in "How young you are!"
I 'm growing old!

Thanks for the years!—whose rapid flight
My sombre muse so sadly sings;
Thanks for the gleams of golden light
That tint the darkness of their wings!
The light that beams from out the sky,
Those heavenly mansions to unfold,
Where all are blest, and none may sigh,
"I 'm growing old!"

JOHN GODFREY SAXE.

THE SOLDIER'S DREAM.

OUR bugles sang truce,—for the night-cloud had
lowered,
And the sentinel stars set their watch in the
sky;
And thousands had sunk on the ground overpowered,
The weary to sleep, and the wounded to die.

When reposing that night on my pallet of straw,
By the wolf-scaring fagot that guarded the slain;
At the dead of the night a sweet vision I saw,
And thrice ere the morning I dreamt it again.

Methought from the battle-field's dreadful array,
Far, far I had roamed on a desolate track;
'Twas autumn,—and sunshine arose on the way
To the home of my fathers, that welcomed me back.

I flew to the pleasant fields traversed so oft
In life's morning march, when my bosom was young;
I heard my own mountain goats bleating aloft,
And knew the sweet strain that the corn-reapers
sung.

Then pledged we the wine-cup, and fondly I swore,
From my home and my weeping friends never to
part;
My little ones kissed me a thousand times o'er,
And my wife sobbed aloud in her fullness of heart.

"Stay, stay with us,—rest, thou art weary and worn;"
And fain was their war-broken soldier to stay;—
But sorrow returned with the dawning of morn,
And the voice in my dreaming ear melted away.

THOMAS CAMPBELL.

ABOU BEN ADHEM.

ABOU BEN ADHEM (may his tribe increase!)
Awoke one night from a deep dream of peace,
And saw, within the moonlight in his room,
Making it rich and like a lily in bloom,
An angel writing in a book of gold;
Exceeding peace had made Ben Adhem bold,
And to the presence in the room he said,
"What writest thou?" The vision raised his head,
And with a look made of all sweet accord,
Answered, "The names of those who love the Lord."

"And is mine one?" said Abou. "Nay, not so,"
Replied the angel. Abou spake more low,
But cheerily still; and said, "I pray thee, then,
Write me as one that loves his fellow-men."
The angel wrote, and vanished. The next night
It came again with a great wakening light,
And showed the names whom love of God had
blessed,
And lo! Ben Adhem's name led all the rest.

LEIGH HUNT.

TO MY MOTHER.

WHEN barren doubt like a late-coming snow
Made an unkind December of my spring,
That all the pretty flowers did droop for woe,
And the sweet birds their love no more would
sing;
Then the remembrance of thy gentle faith,
Mother beloved, would steal upon my heart;
Fond feeling saved me from that utter scathe,
And from thy hope I could not live apart.

Now that my mind hath passed from wintry
gloom,
And on the calmed waters once again
Ascendant Faith circles with silver plume,
That casts a charmed shade, not now in pain,
Thou child of Christ, in joy I think of thee,
And mingle prayers for what we both may
be.

ARTHUR HENRY HALLAM.

THE ATHEIST AND THE ACORN.

METHINKS the world is oddly made,
  And every thing 's amiss,
A dull presuming Atheist said,
As stretched he lay beneath a shade,
  And instanced it in this:

My better judgment could have hung
  The pumpkin on the tree,
And left the acorn, lightly strung,
'Mongst things which on the surface sprung,
  And small and feeble be.

"As stretched he lay beneath a shade."

Behold, quoth he, that mighty thing,
  A pumpkin large and round,
Is held but by a little string,
Which upwards cannot make it spring,
  Or bear it from the ground.

While on this oak an acorn small,
  So disproportioned grows;
That who with sense surveys this all,
This universal casual ball,
  Its ill contrivance knows.

No more the caviller could say
  No further faults descry:
For as he upwards gazing lay,
An acorn, loosened from its stay,
  Fell down upon his eye.

The wounded part with tears ran o'er,
  As punished for the sin;
Fool! had that bough a pumpkin bore,
Thy whimsies would have worked no more,
  Nor skull have kept them in.

ANNE, COUNTESS OF WINCHELSEA.

"LOOK on your best friends with the thought that they may one day become your worst enemies," was an ancient maxim of worldly prudence. It is for us to reverse this maxim, and rather say: "Look on your worst enemies with the thought that they may one day become your best friends."

BUENA VISTA.

ROM the Rio Grande's waters to the icy lakes of Maine,
Let all exult! for we have met the enemy again—
Beneath their stern old mountains, we have met them in their pride,
And rolled from Buena Vista back the battle's bloody tide:
Where the enemy came surging, like the Mississippi's flood;
And the reaper, Death, was busy, with his sickle red with blood.

For their hosts are pouring swiftly on, like a river in the spring—
Our flank is turned, and on our left their cannon thundering.

Now brave artillery! Bold dragoons!—Steady, my men, and calm!
Through rain, cold, hail, and thunder; now nerve each gallant arm!
What though their shot falls round us here, still thicker than the hail!

" Lo!—their battery is silenced now; our iron hail still showers:
They falter, halt, retreat!—Hurrah! the glorious day is ours!"

Santa Anna boasted loudly that, before two hours were past,
His lancers through Saltillo should pursue us thick and fast:
On came his solid regiments, line marching after line;
Lo! their great standards in the sun like sheets of silver shine!
With thousands upon thousands, yea, with more than four to one,
A forest of bright bayonets gleam fiercely in the sun!

Upon them with your squadrons, May!—Out leaps the flaming steel!
Before his serried columns how the frightened lancers reel!
They flee amain.—Now to the left, to stay their triumph there,
Or else the day is surely lost in horror and despair:

We 'll stand against them, as the rock stands firm against the gale.
Lo!—their battery is silenced now; our iron hail still showers:
They falter, halt retreat!—Hurrah! the glorious day is ours!

Now charge again, Santa Anna! or the day is surely lost;
For back, like broken waves, along our left your hordes are tossed.
Still louder roar two batteries — his strong reserve moves on;—
More work is there before you, men, ere the good fight is won;
Now for your wives and children stand! steady, my braves, once more!
Now for your lives, your honor, fight! as you never fought before.

Ho! Hardin breasts it bravely!—McKee and Bissell
  there
Stand firm before the storm of balls that fills the aston-
  ished air.
The lancers are upon them, too!—the foe swarms ten
  to one—
Hardin is slain—McKee and Clay the last time see the
  sun;
And many another gallant heart, in that last desperate
  fray,
Grew cold, its last thoughts turning to its loved ones
  far away.

Still sullenly the cannon roared—but died away at last:
And o'er the dead and dying came the evening shad-
  ows fast,
And then above the mountains rose the cold moon's
  silver shield,
And patiently and pityingly looked down upon the
  field;—
And careless of his wounded, and neglectful of his
  dead,
Despairingly and sullen, in the night, Santa Anna
  fled.

ALBERT PIKE.

"And birds most musical at close of day."

EVEN-TIDE.

THE stream is calmest when it nears the tide,
  And flowers are sweetest at the even-tide,
  And birds most musical at close of day,
  And saints divinest when they pass away.

Morning is lovely, but a holier charm
Lies folded close in evening's robe of balm,
And weary man must ever love her best,
For morning calls to toil, but night brings rest.

She comes from heaven, and on her wings doth bear
A holy fragrance, like the breath of prayer;
Footsteps of angels follow in her trace,
To shut the weary eyes of day in peace.

Until the evening we must weep and toil,
Plow life's stern furrows, dig the weedy soil,
Tread with sad feet our rough and thorny way,
And bear the heat and burden of the day.

"There is a calm, a beauty, and a power,
That morning knows not, in the evening hour."

All things are hushed before her, as she throws
O'er earth and sky her mantle of repose;
There is a calm, a beauty, and a power,
That morning knows not, in the evening hour.

Oh! when our sun is setting, may we glide
Like summer evening, down the golden tide;
And leave behind us, as we pass away,
Sweet, starry twilight round our sleeping clay!

MRS. J. M. WINTON.

THE poems which have lingered in the ear of generations have been clear-cut crystals, flashing with varied brightness—ideas set in gold of cunning workmanship.

33

BLINDNESS.

HEN I consider how my light is spent
Ere half my days in this dark world and wide;
And that one talent which is death to hide,
Lodged with me useless, though my soul more
bent
To serve therewith my Maker, and present
My true account, lest He returning chide;
"Doth God exact day labor, light denied?"

I fondly ask; but Patience, to prevent
That murmur, soon replies, "God doth not need
Either man's work or his own gifts; who best
Bear his mild yoke, they serve him best: his state
Is kingly; thousands at his bidding speed,
And post o'er land and ocean without rest;
They also serve who only stand and wait."

JOHN MILTON.

VERTUE.

WEET Day, so cool, so calm, so bright,
The bridal of the earth and skie;
The dew shall weep thy fall to-night;
For thou must die.

Sweet Rose, whose hue, angrie and brave,
Bids the rash gazer wipe his eye;
Thy root is ever in its grave,
And thou must die.

Sweet Spring, full of sweet days and roses,
A box where sweets compacted lie;
My musick shows ye have your closes,
And all must die.

Only a sweet and vertuous soul,
Like seasoned timber, never gives;
But, though the whole world turn to coal,
Then chiefly lives.

GEORGE HERBERT.

THE PLAIDIE.

PON ane stormy Sunday,
Coming adoon the lane,
Were a score of bonnie lassies
And the sweetest, I maintain,
Was Caddie,
That I took unneath my plaidie,
To shield her from the rain.

She said the daisies blushed
For the kiss that I had ta'en;
I wadna hae thought the lassie
Wad sae of a kiss complain;
"Now, laddie!
I winna stay under your plaidie,
If I gang hame in the rain!"

But, on an after Sunday,
When cloud there was not ane,
This self-same winsome lassie
(We chanced to meet in the lane)
Said "Laddie,
Why dinna ye wear your plaidie?
Wha kens but it may rain?"

CHARLES SIBLEY.

THE DAISY.

F all the floures in the mede,
Than love I most these floures white and rede,
Soch that men callen daisies in our town;
To hem I have so great affection,
As I said erst, whan comen is the May,
That in my bedde there daweth me no day
That I nam up and walking in the mede;
To seene this flour ayenst the sunne sprede,
Whan it up riseth early by the morow,
That blissful sight softeneth all my sorow.
So glad am I whan that I have the presence
Of it, to done it all reverence;
And ever I love it, and ever ylike newe,
And ever shall, till that mine herte die;
All swere I not, of this I will not lie.

GEOFFREY CHAUCER.

PLACES OF WORSHIP.

AS star that shines dependent upon star
Is to the sky while we look up in love;
As to the deep fair ships, which though they
move,
Seem fixed, to eyes that watch them from afar;
As to the sandy deserts fountains are

Of roving tired, or desultory war,—
Such to this British Isle her Christian Fanes,
Each linked to each for kindred services;
Her spires, her steeple-towers with glittering
vanes,
Far kenned, her chapels lurking among trees,

"Where a few villagers on bended knees,
Find solace which a busy world disdains."

With palm-groves shaded at wide intervals,
Whose fruit around the sunburnt native falls,

Where a few villagers, on bended knees
Find solace which a busy world disdains.

WILLIAM WORDSWORTH.

THE BEACON-LIGHT.

DARKNESS was deepening o'er the seas,
And still the hulk drove on;
No sail to answer to the breeze,—
Her masts and cordage gone:
Gloomy and drear her course of fear,—
Each looked but for a grave,—
When, full in sight, the beacon-light
Came streaming o'er the wave.

And gayly of the tale they told,
When they were safe on shore;

How hearts had sunk, and hopes grown cold,
Amid the billows' roar;
When not a star had shone from far,
By its pale beam to save,
Then, full in sight, the beacon-light
Came streaming o'er the wave.

Then wildly rose the gladdening shout
Of all that hardy crew;
Boldly they put the helm about,
And through the surf they flew.

Storm was forgot, toil heeded not,
  And loud the cheer they gave,
As, full in sight, the beacon-light
  Came streaming o'er the wave.

When cheering hopes no more illume,
  And comforts all depart;
Then from afar shines Bethlehem's star,
  With cheering light to save;

"When, full in sight, the beacon-light
Came streaming o'er the wave."

Thus, in the night of Nature's gloom,
  When sorrow bows the heart,

And, full in sight, its beacon-light
  Comes streaming o'er the grave.

JULIA PARDOE.

GOD'S-ACRE.

LIKE that ancient Saxon phrase which
  calls
  The burial-ground God's-Acre! It is just;
It consecrates each grave within its walls,
  And breathes a benison o'er the sleeping
    dust.

God's-Acre! Yes, that blessed name imparts
  Comfort to those who in the grave have
    sown
The seed that they had garnered in their
  hearts,
  Their bread of life, alas! no more their
    own.

Into its furrows shall we all be cast,
  In the sure faith that we shall rise again
At the great harvest, when the archangel's
  blast
  Shall winnow, like a fan, the chaff and
    grain.

Then shall the good stand in immortal bloom,
  In the fair gardens of that second birth;
And each bright blossom mingle its perfume
  With that of flowers which never bloomed on
    earth.

With thy rude ploughshare, Death, turn up the sod,
  And spread the furrow for the seed we sow;

This is the field and Acre of our God,
  This is the place where human harvests grow!

HENRY WADSWORTH LONGFELLOW.

DANIEL GRAY.

IF I shall ever win the home in heaven
For whose sweet rest I humbly hope and pray,
In the great company of the forgiven
I shall be sure to find old Daniel Gray.

I knew him well; in truth, few knew him better;
For my young eyes oft read for him the Word,
And saw how meekly from the crystal letter
He drank the life of his beloved Lord.

Old Daniel Gray was not a man who lifted
On ready words his freight of gratitude,
Nor was he called upon among the gifted,
In the prayer-meetings of his neighborhood.

He had a few old-fashioned words and phrases,
Linked in with sacred texts and Sunday rhymes;
And I suppose that in his prayers and graces,
I 've heard them all at least a thousand times.

I see him now—his form, his face, his motions,
His homespun habit, and his silver hair,—
And hear the language of his trite devotions,
Rising behind the straight-backed kitchen chair.

I can remember how the sentence sounded—
"Help us, O Lord, to pray and not to faint!"
And how the "conquering and to conquer" rounded
The loftier aspirations of the saint.

He had some notions that did not improve him:
He never kissed his children—so they say;
And finest scenes and fairest flowers would move him
Less than a horseshoe picked up in the way.

He had a hearty hatred of oppression,
And righteous words for sin of every kind;

Alas, that the transgressor and transgression
Were linked so closely in his honest mind.

He could see naught but vanity in beauty,
And naught but weakness in a fond caress,
And pitied men whose views of Christian duty
Allowed indulgence in such foolishness.

Yet there were love and tenderness within him;
And I am told that when his Charlie died,
Nor nature's need nor gentle words could win him
From his fond vigils at the sleeper's side.

And when they came to bury little Charlie,
They found fresh dew-drops sprinkled in his hair,
And on his breast a rose-bud gathered early,
And guessed, but did not know, who placed it there.

Honest and faithful, constant in his calling,
Strictly attendant on the means of grace,
Instant in prayer, and fearful most of falling,
Old Daniel Gray was always in his place.

A practical old man, and yet a dreamer;
He thought that in some strange, unlooked-for way
His mighty friend in Heaven, the great Redeemer,
Would honor him with wealth some golden day.

This dream he carried in a hopeful spirit,
Until in death his patient eye grew dim,
And his Redeemer called him to inherit
The heaven of wealth long garnered up for him.

So, if I ever win the home in heaven
For whose sweet rest I humbly hope and pray,
In the great company of the forgiven
I shall be sure to find old Daniel Gray.

JOSIAH GILBERT HOLLAND.

"I HOLD STILL."

P**AIN**'S furnace-heat within me quivers,
God's breath upon the flame doth blow,
And all my heart within me shivers
And trembles at the fiery glow;
And yet I whisper—"As God will!"
And in the hottest fire, hold still.

He comes and lays my heart, all heated,
On the hard anvil, minded so
Into His own fair shape to beat it,
With His own hammer, blow on blow;
And yet I whisper—"As God will!"
And at His heaviest blows, hold still.

He takes my softened heart, and beats it—
The sparks fly off at every blow:
He turns it o'er and o'er, and heats it,
And lets it cool, and makes it glow;

And yet I whisper—"As God will!"
And in the mighty hand, hold still.

Why should I murmur? for the sorrow
Thus only longer lived would be;
Its end may come, and will, to-morrow,
When God has done His work in me.
So I say, trusting—"As God will!"
And trusting to the end, hold still.

He kindles for my profit purely
Affliction's glowing, fiery brand,
And all His heaviest blows are surely
Inflicted by a Master's hand;
So I say, praying, "As God will!"
And hope in Him and suffer still.

From the German.

THE BATTLE OF BLENHEIM.

IT was a summer evening;
  Old Kaspar's work was done,
And he before his cottage door
  Was sitting in the sun;
And by him sported on the green
His little grandchild Wilhelmine.

She saw her brother Peterkin
  Roll something large and round,
Which he beside the rivulet,
  In playing there, had found;
He came to ask what he had found,
That was so large and smooth and round.

Old Kaspar took it from the boy,
  Who stood expectant by;
And then the old man shook his head,
  And with a natural sigh,
" 'Tis some poor fellow's skull," said he,
  "Who fell in the great victory.

"I find them in the garden,.
  For there's many here about;
And often, when I go to plough,
  The ploughshare turns them out;
For many thousand men," said he,
  "Were slain in that great victory."

"Now tell us what 't was all about,"
  Young Peterkin he cries;
And little Wilhelmine looks up
  With wonder-waiting eyes;
"Now tell us all about the war,
And what they fought each other for."

"It was the English," Kaspar cried,
  Who put the French to rout;
But what they fought each other for
  I could not well make out;
But everybody said," quoth he,
  "That 't was a famous victory.

"My father lived at Blenheim then,
  Yon little stream hard by;
They burnt his dwelling to the groun
  And he was forced to fly;
So with his wife and child he fled,
  Nor had he where to rest his head.

"With fire and sword the country round
  Was wasted far and wide,
And many a childing mother then,
  And new-born baby died;
But things like that, you know, must be
At every famous victory.

"They say it was a shocking sight
  After the field was won;
For many thousand bodies here
  Lay rotting in the sun;

But things like that, you know, must be
After a famous victory.

"Great praise the Duke of Marlboro' won,
  And our good Prince Eugene."
" Why, 't was a very wicked thing! "
  Said little Wilhelmine.
" Nay — nay — my little girl," quoth he,
" It was a famous victory.

" And everybody praised the Duke,
  Who this great fight did win."
"But what good came of it at last?"
  Quoth little Peterkin.
" Why, that I cannot tell," said he;
But 't was a famous victory."

                    ROBERT SOUTHEY.

JENNY KISSED ME.

JENNY kissed me when we met,
  Jumping from the chair she sat in.
Time, you thief! who love to get
  Sweets into your list, put that in.

" Jenny kissed me when we met,
Jumping from the chair she sat in."

Say I'm weary, say I'm sad;
  Say that health and wealth have missed me;
Say I'm growing old, but add —
  Jenny kissed me!

                    LEIGH HUNT.

A HUNTING WE WILL GO.

HE dusky night rides down the sky,
  And ushers in the morn:
The hounds all join in glorious cry,
  The huntsman winds his horn.
            And a hunting we will go.

The wife around her husband throws
  Her arms to make him stay;
"My dear, it rains, it hails, it blows;
  You cannot hunt to-day."
            Yet a hunting we will go.

Away they fly to 'scape the rout,
  Their steeds they soundly switch;
Some are thrown in, and some thrown out,
  And some thrown in the ditch.
            Yet a hunting we will go.

Sly Reynard now like lightning flies,
  And sweeps across the vale;
And when the hounds too near he spies,
  He drops his bushy tail.
            Then a hunting we will go

Fond Echo seems to like the sport,
  And join the jovial cry;
The woods, the hills, the sound retort,
  And music fills the sky.
            When a hunting we do go

At last his strength to faintness worn,
  Poor Reynard ceases flight;
Then hungry, homeward we return,
  To feast away the night.
            And a drinking we do go.

Ye jovial hunters, in the morn
  Prepare them for the chase;
Rise at the sounding of the horn
  And health with sport embrace.
            When a hunting we do go.
                        HENRY FIELDING.

HOW'S MY BOY?

"O, sailor of the sea! .
  How's my boy—my boy?"
" What's your boy's name, good wife,
  And in what ship sailed he?"

"My boy John—
He that went to sea—
What care I for the ship, sailor?
My boy's my boy to me.

"You come back from sea,
And not know my John?
I might as well have asked some landsman,
Yonder down in the town.
There's not an ass in all the parish
But he knows my John.

" How's my boy — my boy?
And unless you let me know,
I'll swear you are no sailor,
Blue jacket or no,

"Ho, sailor of the sea!
How's my boy—my boy?

Brass buttons or no, sailor,
Anchor and crown or no!
Sure his ship was the ' Jolly Briton '·
" Speak low, woman, speak low! "

" And why should I speak low. sailor.
About my own boy John?
If I was loud as I am proud
I'd sing him over the town!
Why should I speak low, sailor? "
" That good ship went down."

" How's my boy — my boy?
What care I for the ship, sailor?
I was never aboard her.
Be she afloat or be she aground,
Sinking or swimming, I'll be bound

Her owners can afford her!
I say, how's my John?"
" Every man on board went down,
Every man aboard her."

" How's my boy — my boy?
What care I for the men, sailor?
I'm not their mother —
How's my boy — my boy?
Tell me of him and no other!
How's my boy — my boy?"

                                SYDNEY DOBELL.

"And there, 'mid cliffs by lightnings riven,
Gathered her hero-band."

THE HILLS WERE MADE FOR FREEDOM.

WHEN freedom from her home was driven,
    'Mid vine-clad vales of Switzerland,
She sought the glorious Alps of heaven,
And there, 'mid cliffs by lightnings riven,
    Gathered her hero-band.

And still outrings her freedom-song,
    Amid the glaciers sparkling there,

At Sabbath bell, as peasants throng
Their mountain fastnesses along,
    Happy, and free as air.

The hills were made for freedom; they
    Break at a breath the tyrant's rod;
Chains clank in valleys; there the prey
Writhes 'neath Oppression's heel alway:
    Hills bow to none but God!

                    WILLIAM GOLDSMITH BROWN.

THE anguish of that thought that we can never atone to our dead for the stinted
affection we gave them, for the light answers we returned to their plaints or their
pleadings, for the little reverence we showed to that sacred human soul that lived
so close to us, and was the divinest thing God has given us to know.

A CHRISTMAS HYMN.

T was the calm and silent night!
　　Seven hundred years and fifty-three
　　Had Rome been growing up to might,
　　And now was queen of land and sea.
No sound was heard of clashing wars,
　　Peace brooded o'er the hushed domain;
Apollo, Pallas, Jove, and Mars,
　　Held undisturbed their ancient reign
　　　　In the solemn midnight,
　　　　　　Centuries ago.

'Twas in the calm and silent night,
　　The senator of haughty Rome,
Impatient, urged his chariot's flight,
　　From lordly revel rolling home;
Triumphal arches, gleaming, swell
His breast with thoughts of boundless sway;
What recked the Roman what befell
　　A paltry province far away,
　　　　In the solemn midnight,
　　　　　　Centuries ago?

Within that province far away
　　Went plodding home a weary boor:
A streak of light before him lay,
　　Fallen through a half-shut stable door
Across his path. He passed, for naught
Told what was going on within;

How keen the stars, his only thought—
　　The air, how calm, how cold, and thin,
　　　　In the solemn midnight,
　　　　　　Centuries ago!

O strange indifference! low and high
　　Drowsed over common joys and cares;
The earth was still, but knew not why,
　　The world was listening unawares.
How calm a moment may precede
One that shall thrill the world forever!
To that still moment none would heed
　　Man's doom was linked no more to sever,
　　　　In the solemn midnight,
　　　　　　Centuries ago.

It is the calm and silent night!
　　A thousand bells ring out, and throw
Their joyous peals abroad, and smite
　　The darkness — charmed and holy now!
The night that erst no name had worn—
To it a happy name is given;
For in that stable lay, new-born,
　　The peaceful Prince of earth and heaven,
　　　　In the solemn midnight,
　　　　　　Centuries ago.

ALFRED DOMETT.

LOOK ALOFT.

N the tempest of life when the wave and the gale
Are around and above, if thy footing should fail—
If thine eye should grow dim, and thy caution
　　depart—
Look aloft and be firm, and be fearless of heart.

If the friend, who embraced in prosperity's glow,
With a smile for each joy and a tear for each woe,
Should betray thee when sorrows, like clouds, are
　　arrayed,
Look aloft to the friendship which never shall fade.

Should the visions, which hope spreads in light to
　　thine eye,
Like the tints of the rainbow, but brighten to fly,

Then turn, and, through tears of repentant regret,
Look aloft to the sun that is never to set.

Should those who are dearest, the son of thy
　　heart,
The wife of thy bosom, in sorrow depart,
Look aloft from the darkness and dust of the tomb,
To that soil where affection is ever in bloom.

And oh! when death comes, in terror to cast
His fears on the future, his pall on the past,
In that moment of darkness, with hope in thy
　　heart,
And a smile in thine eye, look aloft, and depart.

JONATHAN LAWRENCE, JR.

FAITH.

ETTER trust all, and be deceived,
　　And weep that trust and that deceiving,
Than doubt one heart, that, if believed,
　　Had blessed one's life with true believing.

O, in this mocking world, too fast
　　The doubting fiend o'ertakes our youth!
Better be cheated to the last,
　　Than lose the blessèd hope of truth.

FRANCES ANNE KEMBLE.

COUNSEL TO A FRIEND.

IVE thy thoughts no tongue,
Nor any unproportioned thought his act;
Be thou familiar, but by no means vulgar;
The friends thou hast, and their adoption tried,
Grapple them to thy soul with hooks of steel;
But do not dull thy palm with entertainment
Of each new-hatch'd, unfledged comrade. Beware
Of entrance to a quarrel; but, being in,
Bear 't that the opposer may beware of thee.
Give every man thine ear, but few thy voice;
Take each man's censure but reserve thy judgment.

Costly thy habit as thy purse can buy,
But not expressed in fancy; rich, not gaudy,
For the apparel oft proclaims the man.

*   *   *   *   *   *

Neither a borrower nor a lender be,
For loan oft loses both itself and friend,
And borrowing dulls the edge of husbandry.
This above all—to thine own self be true;
And it must follow, as the night the day,
Thou canst not then be false to any man.

WILLIAM SHAKESPEARE.

BOOKS.

CANNOT think the glorious world of mind,
Embalmed in books, which I can only see
In patches, though I read my moments blind,
Is to be lost to me.

I have a thought that, as we live elsewhere,
So will those dear creations of the brain;

That what I lose unread, I'll find, and there
Take up my joy again.

O then the bliss of blisses, to be freed
From all the wants by which the world is driven;
With liberty and endless time to read
The libraries of Heaven!

ROBERT LEIGHTON.

INDEX OF AUTHORS.

BIOGRAPHIES OF AUTHORS.

ADAM, JEAN.—A Scottish schoolmistress, author of a volume of poems, among which is the famous one of "The Sailor's Wife." Its authorship is erroneously given to William Mickle in many collections. Born in 1710; died in 1765.

ADAMS, CHARLES FOLLEN.—An American humorist, known chiefly from his "Leedle Yawcob Strauss," and poems of a similar character, which have been published in a volume, and enjoyed considerable popularity. Born in Mass. in 1842. At one time a journalist of Detroit, Mich.

ADAMS, JOHN QUINCY.—Sixth President of the United States. Born in Mass., 1767; died in Washington, 1848. He stands eminent among American statesmen as an accomplished scholar, an astute diplomatist, a prolific writer of prose and verse, and a man of inflexible integrity.

ADDISON, JOSEPH.—This immortal essayist, who also ranks high as a poet, was born in Wiltshire, England, May 1st, 1672, and was the son of the Dean of Litchfield. Entering Oxford at the age of fifteen, he early distinguished himself. At twenty-three he published a poem on one of King William's campaigns, which brought him favor and a pension, and he then spent two years abroad. He wrote largely for "The Tattler" (Steele's project), and afterwards for "The Guardian." More famous than either was "The Spectator"—in point of time between the two—and to this he was the leading contributor. The fame these essays won was and is co-extensive with the English language. It was at its height when his "Tragedy of Cato" appeared, in 1713. On this his reputation as a poet principally rests, though he also wrote a few exquisite hymns and some other sacred pieces. In 1717 he was made Secretary of State, but held the office only a short time, retiring on a pension of £1,500 per annum. He died in the midst of busy literary labors, June 17, 1719.

AINSLIE, HEW.—Was born in Scotland in 1792; removed to America in 1822, and died in Kentucky in 1878. The evening of an active business life was spent in literary pursuits.

ALDRICH, JAMES.—A native of Suffolk county, New York. He engaged early in mercantile pursuits, but left them for literature, and was engaged as a writer for various periodicals. Born in 1810; died in 1856.

ALDRICH, THOMAS BAILEY.—An American author, whose writings, both poetry and prose, are endued with the charms of a delicate fancy, playful humor, tender sentiment, and graceful diction. Born in New Hampshire in 1836, he has led an active literary life since his youth; is author of several volumes, and (since 1880) editor of the "Atlantic Monthly."

ALEXANDER, CECIL FRANCES.—The wife of Wm. Alexander, Bishop of Derry, Ireland; author of "Moral Songs," "Hymns for Children," "Poems on Old Testament Subjects," etc. Born near Strathbane, Ireland, about 1830.

ALFORD, HENRY.—Dean of Canterbury, Eng.; a voluminous writer on critical and religious subjects, his chief work being "The Greek New Testament, with Notes." His poems appeared in 1835, and his sacred lyrics in a volume of "Psalms and Hymns," which he edited in 1844. Born in London, 1810; died in 1871.

ALISON, RICHARD.—An English poet, of whom little is known. In 1590 he published "A Description of the Visible Church," and in 1616 "An Houre's Recreation in Musicke, apt for Instruments and Voyces."

ALLEN, ELIZABETH AKERS (FLORENCE PERCY).—Her maiden name was Elizabeth Chase; her first husband was the sculptor Paul Akers. She is widely known as the author of the lines, "Rock me to Sleep, Mother." Born in Maine, in 1812.

ALLINGHAM, WILLIAM.—Began his literary career with a volume of poems in 1850; in 1854 he published "Day and Night Songs," and received a literary pension in 1864. Born at Ballyshannon, Ireland, in 1828.

AMES, MARY CLEMMER.—A versatile and brilliant writer, widely known as the Washington correspondent of the New York "Independent." The author of several novels, and of the memoirs of the Cary sisters. Was born in Utica, N. Y.

ANDERSON, ALEXANDER.—Noted as the first engraver on wood in America. A man of diversified talents and attainments—a poet, musician, illustrator, engraver, naturalist, and physician. Born in New York city, 1775; died in Jersey City, 1870.

ANDREW, JOHN A.—Massachusetts' famous "War Governor," and a distinguished lawyer and orator as well as statesman. Born in Maine in 1818; died at Boston in 1867.

ARNOLD, EDWIN.—An English scholar and poet, born in 1832. Was for a time principal of the Government Sanscrit College at Poonoh, India. After returning to England in 1864, became editor-in-chief of the London "Telegraph." Published in 1879 the remarkable poem entitled "The Light of Asia"; and three years later the "Indian Song of Songs."

ARNOLD, GEORGE.—Was born in New York in 1834 and died in 1865. An edition of his poems was published the year after his death. The most widely known, and perhaps the best, of his pieces is "The Jolly Old Pedagogue."

ARNOLD, MATTHEW.—An English poet and critical essayist, the son of Dr. Thomas Arnold, the historian and head teacher of Rugby. Was born in 1822, and elected to the Chair of Poetry at Oxford in 1857. Is author of several books, and one of the foremost magazine writers of the day.

AUSTEN, SARAH.—Was noted for her elegant translations from the German. Her daughter, Lady Duff Gordon, inherited her talent, gaining by it a similar distinction. Was born in England in 1793; died in 1867.

AYTON, SIR ROBERT.—A favorite in the Court of James VI., and a poet of considerable merit, composing verses of refined elegance in Greek, Latin, French, and English. Born in Scotland in 1570; died in 1638.

BACON, FRANCIS, LORD.—The illustrious philosopher and statesman, whose fame sheds lustre on the reigns of Queen Elizabeth and King James VI. Endowed with every advantage of birth, talent, and education, his career was crowned with the highest honors, and marked by as dire a downfall as is recorded in the history of mankind. The "Novum Organum" was his grandest work, and his volume of miscellaneous "Essays" the most popular. Countless editions of the latter have been sold. Born in 1561; died in 1626.

BAILEY, J. M.—Belongs to the distinctive school of American humorists; earned a national repute by the witty character of his writings in "The Danbury News," and from them derived his familiar title of "Danbury News Man."

(529)

BAILEY, PHILIP JAMES.—Published at the age of twenty-three the poem of "Festus," which secured a swift but transient popularity. The several later works of the author have failed to secure him the fame which his first juvenile production promised. Born in England in 1816.

BAILLIE, JOANNA.—An English poetess who enjoyed great celebrity in her early day, but lived to see her genius eclipsed by later writers. Her chief works were her "Plays on the Passions." Born in Scotland in 1762; died in 1851.

BANCROFT, GEORGE.—An American scholar and author, whose ability as a statesman is forgotten in his renown as a historian. He has fulfilled with great acceptance the duties of Secretary of the Navy, Minister Plenipotentiary to England, American Minister at the Court of Berlin, and Minister Plenipotentiary to the German Empire. His chief work is a comprehensive "History of the United States," begun in 1834 and still (1883) in progress. Born in Mass. in 1800.

BARBAULD, ANNA LETITIA.—An English writer who did much to advance the education of children and the position of her sex. To her belongs the distinction of originating books expressly for young readers. Born in 1743; died in 1825.

BARBOUR, JOHN.—A Scotch poet contemporary with Chaucer. Born about 1320; died 1395.

BARNARD, LADY ANNE.—A Scottish poetess, whose name is preserved by the fine ballad of "Auld Robin Gray." Born in 1750; died in 1825.

BARNES, WILLIAM.—An English clergyman, poet, and philologist. Born in 1810.

BARNFIELD, RICHARD.—An English author who published several poems towards the close of the sixteenth century. Born in 1674.

BARR, MATHIAS.—A Scottish poet, known by the endearing title of "The Children's Poet Laureate." Was born in Edinburgh in 1831.

BARRY, MICHAEL JOSEPH.—An Irish poet who contributed to the Dublin "Nation." His most famous piece "The Place Where Man Should Die," was first published in 1843. Born in 1815.

BATES, CHARLOTTE FISKE.—A teacher in Cambridge, Mass., Born in the city of New York.

BEATTIE, JAMES.—A well-known Scottish poet and metaphysician. "The Minstrel" was his most popular work. Born in 1735; died in 1803.

BEDDOES, THOMAS LOVELL.—A poet and physician, the nephew of Maria Edgeworth. In his nineteenth year he published "The Bride's Tragedy," which excited general admiration as a work of promise. Born in 1803; died in 1849.

BEECHER, HENRY WARD.—A son of the eminent divine, Dr. Lyman Beecher, he is in his turn the most eminent pulpit orator in America. His lectures and sermons afford admirable examples of spontaneous and inspiring eloquence. Since 1847, Mr. Beecher has been the pastor of Plymouth Church, Brooklyn. Born in Connecticut in 1813.

BEERS, ETHEL LYNN.—Was born in New York in 1827, and died in 1879. Her widely-known lyric beginning "All Quiet Along the Potomac" is among the many popular poems of disputed authorship.

BENJAMIN, PARK.—An American poet and journalist. Born in 1809; died in 1864.

BENNETT, HENRY.—An Irish poet, author of "St. Patrick was a Gentleman." Born at Cork about 1785.

BERKELEY, GEORGE.—A celebrated divine and philosopher. Only one poem of his writing has survived, but that contains an element of enduring life. Born in Ireland, in 1684; died in 1753.

BLAINE, JAMES GILLESPIE.—An American statesman of popular gifts and prominent position in the Republican party. Has been a member of both houses of Congress, and Secretary of State under President Garfield. Born in Pennsylvania in 1830.

BLAKE, WILLIAM.—An English artist and poet of great and unique talents. His works were of too eccentric a character to be easily understood, but since his death the genius which created them has received a more just appreciation. He was born in 1757, and after a life of sad struggle with poverty and obscurity died in 1828.

BLOOMFIELD, ROBERT.—An unlettered shoemaker, who performed the wonderful feat of composing a poem of some 1,600 lines while at work over the last, and completing it before a word was written down. The poem, named "The Farmer's Boy," created an immense sensation, 26,000 copies being sold in three years, and several translations appearing. Other works were produced by the author, but none of them equalled the first. Born in England in 1766; died in 1823.

BOKER, GEORGE HENRY.—A dramatic and lyric poet. Was American Minister to Constantinople from 1871 to 1877. Born in Philadelphia in 1823.

BOLINGBROKE, LORD.—An English political writer and speaker, contemporaneous with Pope, Swift, and Addison. He was brilliant, fascinating, ignoble and profligate. Born in 1678; died in 1751.

BONAR, HORATIUS.—A minister of the Free Church of Scotland, whose poetical works consist of "Lyric Consolations" and "Hymns of Faith and Hope." Born at Edinburgh in 1808; died in 1869.

BONNEY, CHARLES C.—An eminent lawyer and jurist of Chicago, distinguished also by successful advocacy of various important reforms in law and government. Born in Hamilton, N. Y. in 1831.

BOURDILLON, FRANCIS W.—While yet an under-graduate at Oxford, he won reputation as a poet by two stanzas, eight lines in all, entitled "Light." Born in 1852.

BOWLES, WILLIAM LISLE.—An English clergyman and voluminous writer. His sonnets have been greatly admired. Born in 1762; died in 1850.

BOWRING, SIR JOHN.—An English statesman and linguist, noted for his attainments in the Sclavonic languages. Born in 1792; died in 1872.

BRAINARD, JOHN G. C.—An American poet and journalist. Born in Connecticut in 1796; died in 1828.

BRETON, NICHOLAS.—An English pastoral poet of the Elizabethan era. Born in 1555; died in 1624.

BRONTE, CHARLOTTE.—The most famous member of a singularly gifted family. Her first published novel, "Jane Eyre," created an immediate and universal sensation by its remarkable power. It was followed by "Shirley," "Villette," and the posthumous story of "The Professor." Born in England in 1816; died in 1855.

BROOKS, PHILLIPS.—A clergyman of the Episcopal Church, distinguished by striking oratorical powers. Born in Boston in 1835.

BROWN, WILLIAM GOLDSMITH.—An American editor, teacher, and poet. Several of his shorter pieces—as "Mother, Home, and Heaven," and "A Hundred Years to Come,"—have enjoyed a wide and lasting popularity. Born in Vermont in 1812.

BROWNE, CHARLES F.—(ARTEMUS WARD.)—A clever and original humorous writer, who won equal favor in England and America by the quaint drollery of his lectures and sketches. Born in Maine in 1834; died in England in 1867.

BROWNE, FRANCIS F.—An editor and literary critic. Conducted the "Lakeside Monthly" magazine (Chicago, 1869 to 1874), and since 1880 editor of the Chicago "Dial." Born in Vermont in 1843.

BROWNE, WILLIAM.—An English author who achieved distinction by poems written before he was twenty, but fell into silence and obscurity after he was thirty. Born in 1590; died in 1645.

BROWNELL, HENRY HOWARD.—An American poet, whose principal book, "Lyrics of a Day," appeared in 1864. He is best known by his stirring poem on "The Bay Fight," and other naval pieces. Born in Conn. in 1820; died in 1872.

BROWNING, ELIZABETH BARRETT.—The greatest female poet of England or of modern times. High as is the standard of the poetry she produced, had she possessed physical powers commensurate with her genius she would undoubtedly have attained a still loftier rank by the force of sustained effort. Many of her poems are among the most popular in our language. She was married to the poet Robert Browning, in 1846. Born in 1807; died in 1861.

BROWNING, ROBERT.—A poet of universal genius, whose fame, on account of the obscurities and eccentricities of his style, has not been equal to his deserts. One of his greatest works, "Paracelsus," was written when he was twenty-three. His repute is slowly increasing, and the title of "the poet of poets" may yet be exchanged for that of the poet of cultivated readers. Born in England in 1812.

BRYANT, WILLIAM CULLEN.—One of America's first and most honored poets. He began writing poetry at the age of ten, and his most celebrated production, "Thanatopsis," was written when he was but eighteen. All his poems, whether early or late, show a rare uniformity of excellence, and a close and fine observation of nature. From 1826 until his death, a term of fifty-two years, Mr. Bryant held with esteem the position of editor of the New York "Evening Post." He was born in Mass. in 1794; died in New York in 1878.

BRYDGES, SIR SAMUEL EGERTON.—An English writer and bibliographer of eccentric character. His shorter poems show imaginative power and some of the high gifts of the poet. Born in 1762; died in 1837.

BUNGAY, GEORGE W.—A newspaper editor and lecturer. Born in New York about 1830.

BURKE, EDMUND.—A statesman, orator and writer of commanding influence and talent; a leader among the great Englishmen of his time. Born in Dublin in 1728; died in 1797.

BURLEIGH, CECIL, LORD.—The renowned statesman who, under Elizabeth, was virtually prime minister of England for a period of forty years. Born in 1520; died in 1598.

BURLEIGH, WILLIAM HENRY.—An eloquent writer and speaker, identified with the anti-slavery cause and temperance reform. He was by nature a poet and enthusiast. Born in Connecticut in 1812; died in 1871.

BURNS, ROBERT.—"The National Poet of Scotland"; was born in 1759, and died in 1796. His simple lyrics sprang from a brain fired with the purest flames of genius, and a heart throbbing with genuine human feeling. A peasant's son, his life was made up of poverty, hardship and sorrow. Its pathos appeals to our charity, and the errors which shadowed it are forgotten in our love. Wherever the poetry of Burns is read, his name will be spoken with tenderness and enthusiasm.

BURROUGHS, JOHN.—An American author, whose writings, chiefly on the scenery and life of nature, are exquisite prose idyls. He looks upon all things with the eye of a poet, and has a rare power of graceful expression. Born in New York in 1837.

BUTLER, SAMUEL.—An English humorist, famed as the author of "Hudibras," a satire on the Puritans, abounding in wit and enjoying a lasting celebrity. Born in 1612; died in 1680.

BYROM, JOHN.—A minor English poet. Born in 1691; died in 1763.

BYRON, GEORGE GORDON NOEL, LORD.—One of the greatest of modern English poets. To genius of a high order he joined an attractive person and many engaging qualities. No poet has been more widely discussed, and none has had his private life subjected to a severer scrutiny. But whatever his failings as a man—and these have been scandalously exaggerated—his position as a poet is of the loftiest. Born in 1788; died in 1824.

CAMPBELL, THOMAS.—An eminent Scottish poet. Published his "Pleasures of Hope" at twenty-one. His lyrics are greatly admired, the choicest being familiar as household words. Born in 1777; died in 1844.

CAREY, HENRY.—An English poet and musician, who composed a number of songs, dramas, and burlesques. Born in 1700; died in his own land in 1743.

CARLETON, WILL.—Author of the popular "Farm Ballads" and "Farm Legends." Born in Michigan in 1845.

CARLYLE, THOMAS.—An English historian and essayist, who produced a greater impression on the thought of his age than any other writer of the nineteenth century. His intellect was mighty in grasp, his character was rugged, his disposition severely critical, and his writings were a mingling of these grand and harsh qualities. His "History of The French Revolution" is graphically denominated the epic of modern times. There is a tremendous stimulus in his works, and an eloquence that is electrifying. Born in Scotland in 1795; died in 1881.

CARY, ALICE.—An American author, whose writings display rare poetic sensibility. Her name, with that of her sister Phœbe, is peculiarly endeared to American readers. Born in Ohio in 1820; died in 1871.

CARY, PHŒBE.—Sister of Alice Cary, and her life-long associate in literary work. Born in Ohio in 1824; died in 1871.

CHATTERTON, THOMAS.—An English poet, whose precocious genius and untimely fate have gained him great notoriety. Born in 1752, and at the age of seventeen committed suicide by poison.

CHAUCER, GEOFFREY.—England's first great poet, called distinctively the "Father of English Poetry." Of good birth, he was connected with royalty by marriage, and held trusted places in the service of Edward III. His principal work was "The Canterbury Tales," said to be written after he was sixty. Born in 1328; died in 1400.

CHESTERFIELD, PHILIP, EARL OF.—Best known as the author of "Chesterfield's Letters," which were written to his son, and never intended for publication. Born in 1694; died in 1773.

CIBBER, COLLEY.—A witty English dramatist and actor. Poet laureate to George II., yet a single poem only of his writing is now remembered. Born in 1671; died in 1757.

CLARE, JOHN.—The Northamptonshire peasant poet. Born in England in 1793; died in 1864.

CLARK, JAMES G.—An American poet and musician. Born in New York in 1830.

CLARKE, WILLIS GAYLORD.—An American poet of prominence in his time, and editor of the old "Knickerbocker Magazine." Born in New York in 1810; died in 1841.

CLEMENS, SAMUEL C. (MARK TWAIN).—An American humorist of quaint and original talent. His books have had an extraordinary sale. Born in Missouri in 1835.

CLOUGH, ARTHUR HUGH.—An English poet, a favorite pupil of Dr. Thomas Arnold; for a time a resident of Cambridge, Mass. His later career scarcely fulfilled his youthful promise. Born in 1819; died in 1861.

COLERIDGE, HARTLEY.—Eldest son of the poet S. T. Coleridge, and the inheritor of much of his father's extraordinary talent. Born in England in 1796; died in 1849.

COLERIDGE, SAMUEL TAYLOR.—One of the towering names in modern English literature. Coleridge was endowed with magnificent genius, but its achievements were sadly limited by a feeble energy and impotent will. His poems, fragmentary at best, are creations of marvelous power. His fame as a conversationalist has never been surpassed. Born in 1772; died in 1834.

COLFAX, SCHUYLER.—Seventeenth Vice-President of the United States, greatly esteemed in public and private life. Born in New York in 1823.

COLLINS, MORTIMER.—Author of several novels and volumes of poetry, and a frequent contributor to "Punch" and other periodicals. Born in England in 1827; died in 1876.

COLLINS, WILLIAM.—An English lyric poet of rare endowments. His brief and sad life ended in insanity. Born in 1720; died in 1756.

COLLYER, ROBERT.—A native of England, of humble birth and scanty education. He came to this country at the age of 27, and worked at his trade of blacksmithing. Soon after he forsook the anvil for the pulpit, and has become one of the most popular preachers in the United States. His literary style is a model of Saxon simplicity. Pastor of a Unitarian church in New York city. Born in 1823.

COLMAN, GEORGE.—Styled "The Younger." An English humorist and dramatist. Several of his plays are still popular on the stage. Born in 1762; died in 1836.

CONSTABLE, HENRY.—An English poet; born about 1560; died in 1600.

COOK, ELIZA.—A favorite English poetess. Received a literary pension in 1864. Born in 1817.

COOKE, JOHN ESTEN.—Brother of Philip Pendleton Cooke, and, like him, a prolific and pleasant writer. Born in Virginia in 1830.

COOKE, PHILIP PENDLETON.—An accomplished man of letters. Born in Virginia in 1816; died in 1850.

COOKE, ROSE TERRY.—Author of many poems and short prose sketches. Born in Conn. in 1827.

COOLBRITH, INA D.—A California poet, whose verses first attracted attention in the "Overland Monthly." A volume of her poems has appeared in print.

CORBETT, MISSES.—Natives of England, the authors of a number of juvenile books which have met with high success.

CORWIN, THOMAS—An American lawyer and statesman, and one of the most popular orators of his time. He was Governor of Ohio, U. S. Senator from the same State, and Minister to Mexico. Born in Kentucky in 1794; died in 1865.

COWPER, WILLIAM.—"The most popular poet of his generation," whose writings modified the tone of English poetry, infecting it with a more earnest and simple spirit. His greatest work was "The Task," but the best known at the present day is the ballad of "John Gilpin." Born in 1731; died in 1800.

CRABBE, GEORGE.—An English poet and divine, who depicted the life of the poor and lowly in verse of simple graphic power. Born in 1754; died in 1832.

CRAIK, DINAH MARIA (MISS MULOCK).—An English novelist, whose voluminous writings are deservedly popular for their healthy moral tone and truthful pictures of every-day life. The best-known of her books is "John Halifax, Gentleman," one of the standard works of English fiction. Born in 1826.

CRAWFORD, JULIA.—An Irish lady, a contributor to the London "New Monthly."

CROSS, MARIAN EVANS LEWES (GEORGE ELIOT).—An English novelist and poetess, standing in the first rank of the authors of fiction in her own or any other language. Her writings were invariably characterized by powerful originality, wide learning, masterly insight and invention, and vigorous and sinewy diction. They procured her fame and wealth, and the world's esteem. Born in 1820; died in 1881.

CUNNINGHAM, ALLAN.—A Scotch poet, novelist, and miscellaneous writer. His most esteemed works were biographical. Born in 1784; died in 1842.

CURTIS, GEORGE WILLIAM—Best known as the editor of "Harper's Weekly," and a champion of civil service reform. The author of a number of charming books of fiction and travel. His writings are marked by exquisite finish, keen penetration, and sound judgment. Also one of the most brilliant orators of his time. Born in Rhode Island in 1824.

CUSHING, CALEB.—An American scholar and jurist of distinguished and varied talents. Occupied a prominent position in public affairs, and produced many literary and political works. Born in Mass. in 1800; died in 1879.

CUTTER, GEORGE W.—The author of a volume of poems published in 1857. Born in Kentucky in 1814; died in 1865.

DANA, RICHARD HENRY.—An American author who acquired repute in the first half of this century. Born in Mass. in 1787; died in 1878.

DANIEL, SAMUEL.—An English poet and historian. Born in 1562; died in 1619.

DARWIN, ERASMUS.—An ingenious English physiologist and poet; author of "The Botanic Garden," and also of several prose works evincing much metaphysical talent. Grandfather of Charles Darwin, the eminent naturalist. Born in 1731; died in 1802.

DAVIS, THOMAS OSBORNE.—An Irish poet and patriot. Born in 1814; died in 1845.

DE QUINCEY, THOMAS.—An English author of wonderful powers, but trammeled in their use by the habits of an opium-eater. He had a masterly command of language, and as an essayist and conversationalist was equally dazzling. Born in 1785; died in 1859.

DE VERE, SIR AUBREY.—An Irish poet and dramatist. Born in 1788; died in 1846.

DICKENS, CHARLES.—One of the first of the great English novelists of the present century. But one or two authors can rival him in the department of fiction, and none equal him in the enthusiasm of his readers. He is cherished by a host of admirers with a feeling of personal love and gratitude, such was the tenderness of his nature and the charm of his transcendent talent. Born in 1812; died in 1870.

DIMOND, WILLIAM.—An English theatrical manager, dramatist and poet; he is now known by his "Mariner's Dream." Born about 1780; died about 1814.

DOANE, GEORGE W.—Bishop of New Jersey. A poet and scholar of refined and cultivated taste. Born in New Jersey in 1799; died in 1859.

DOBELL, SYDNEY.—An English poet. Born in 1824; died in 1874.

DOBSON, AUSTIN.—One of the foremost of the younger English poets of the day, and an accomplished man of letters. Born in 1840.

DODDRIDGE, PHILIP.—A celebrated English hymnist, and author of religious works. His hymns are in use in most Protestant churches. Born in 1702; died in 1751.

DODGE, MARY E.—The accomplished editor of "Harper's Bazar."

DODGE, MARY MAPES.—Widely known as the editor of "St. Nicholas," and a writer of juvenile literature. Born in 1838.

DODSLEY, ROBERT.—An English author and publisher of note. He was the first to give employment to Samuel Johnson. Born in 1703; died in 1764.

DOMETT, ALFRED.—Contributed a number of lyrics to "Blackwood's Magazine," among them his celebrated "Christmas Hymn." Born in England about 1815.

DOUDNEY, SARAH. (Afterwards Mrs. Clark.)—An American, whose title to the authorship of the beautiful and popular poem of "The Water-Mill," claimed by several authors, is not now to be disputed.

DOUGLAS OF FINGLAND.—The author of the original song of "Annie Laurie," which is in two stanzas, and was written prior to 1688. The lady who inspired the poem married a Mr. Ferguson.

DRAKE, JOSEPH RODMAN.—An American poet of precocious genius, remembered chiefly as the author of "The Culprit Fay" and the stirring poem of "The American Flag." Born in New York in 1795; died in 1820.

DRAYTON, MICHAEL.—An English poet, whose name is preserved mainly by his spirited ballad of "Agincourt." Born in 1563; died in 1631.

DRUMMOND, WILLIAM.—An early Scotch poet, the first to write in pure English dialect. Of high repute in his day. Born in 1585; died in 1649.

DRYDEN, JOHN.—An English poet and dramatist, whose writings mark an epoch in the progress of the literature of his country. He excelled in prose as well as poetry. Was poet laureate. Born in 1631; died in 1700.

DUFFERIN, LADY.—A grand-daughter of Richard Brinsley Sheridan, sister of Mrs. Norton, and mother of the Earl of Dufferin, late Governor-General of Canada. Her literary reputation was made by "The Lament of the Irish Emigrant." Born in 1807; died in 1867.

DUFFY, SIR CHARLES GAVAN.—An Irish poet and journalist. Emigrating to Australia, he became Prime Minister of the colony in 1871. Born in 1816.

DUGANNE, AUGUSTINE J. H.—An American poet and novelist. Born in Mass. in 1823.

DURIVAGE, FRANCIS A.—An American poet and magazinist. Born in Mass. in 1814.

DWIGHT, TIMOTHY.—A prominent theologian, and for many years President of Yale College. One of the earliest of American poets. Born in Mass. in 1752; died in 1817.

DYER, JOHN.—A Welsh poet. Born in 1700; died in 1758.

DYER, SIR EDWARD.—A writer of the Elizabethan age. Was employed by the Queen in several foreign embassies. Born in 1540; died in 1607.

EASTMAN, CHARLES GAMAGE.—A journalist and poet. Born in Maine in 1816; died in Vermont in 1861.

ELLIOT, EBENEZER.—The English "Corn-Law Rhymer." Born of the people, he espoused their cause, and with fervid zeal plead in his verses for the relief of their oppressions. Born in 1781; died in 1849.

EMERSON, RALPH WALDO.—An eminent American essayist, poet, and idealist; distinguished for originality and subtlety of thought, for exalted conceptions of conduct, and for a life consistent with his highest teachings. America has produced no writer or scholar of greater influence and renown. His works have had a profound effect in molding earnest minds. Born in Mass. in 1803; died in 1882.

EMMET, ROBERT.—An Irish patriot and revolutionist, whose career excited a romantic interest. Was born in 1780, and executed for treason in 1803.

ENGLISH, THOMAS DUNN.—A physician and poet. Born in Pennsylvania in 1819.

EVERETT, EDWARD.—An American scholar, statesman, and orator, especially famed for eloquence of the most finished character. He filled with credit various important public positions. Born in Mass. in 1794; died in 1865.

FALCONER, WILLIAM.—A Scotchman of humble birth, winning fame by a single remarkable poem, "The Shipwreck." Born in 1732; died in 1769.

FAWCETT, EDGAR.—An American poet, novelist, and dramatist. Born in New York in 1847.

FIELDING, HENRY.—Entitled the "Father of the English Novel." His first fiction was intended as a satire on Richardson's "Pamela," and had a prodigious success. His best novel was "Tom Jones." Born in 1707; died in 1754.

FIELDS, JAMES THOMAS.—An American publisher and author, whose character and writings were equally genial and charming. Born in New Hampshire in 1817; died in 1881.

FINCH, FRANCIS MILES.—A lawyer and judge. Born in Ithaca, N. Y., in 1827. His poetic fame rests chiefly on the fine lyrics of "The Blue and the Gray"—published first in the "Atlantic Monthly," and suggested by the women of Columbus, Miss., decorating alike the graves of Union and Confederate dead—and "Nathan Hale," read at Yale College in 1853. Hale was a captain in the Continental army, who was found by the British within their lines at New York, and, by order of Lord Howe, was executed the next morning, Sept. 22, 1776.

FINLEY, JOHN.—Born in Virginia in 1797; died in 1866.

FLAGG, WILSON.—An ornithologist, and the author of several volume of delightful sketches of nature. A native of Massachusetts.

FLETCHER, GILES.—Born in Kent, England, about 1550; died in 1610.

FORRESTER, ALFRED A. (ALFRED CROWQUILL).—An English artist and humorous writer; the first illustrator of "Punch" and the "Illustrated News," and the author of a number of books combining humorous sketches with pen and pencil. Born in 1805.

FOSTER, STEPHEN COLLINS.—A musician and poet, whose negro songs, original in words and melody, have had a wonderful popularity. Born in Pennsylvania in 1826; died in 1864.

FRANKLIN, BENJAMIN.—An American sage, statesman, and scientist, who is to be named among the great men of the world. A signer of the Declaration of Independence, and one of the framers of the Constitution of the U. S. His writings, on a wide range of subjects, fill ten octavo volumes, and are remarkable for the purity of their literary style as well as for their sagacity and depth of thought. Many of his wise sayings have become proverbs among all English-speaking people. Born in 1706; died in 1790.

FRENEAU, PHILIP.—An able political humorist of the Revolutionary period, and a prolific writer of verse. Born in 1752; died in 1832.

FULLER, MARGARET (COUNTESS D'OSSOLI).—A remarkably gifted woman, noted as a conversationist and writer. She was conspicuous among the company of brilliant personages born in New England at the beginning of the present century. Born in 1810; died by shipwreck in 1850.

GAGE, FRANCES DANA.—An American poetess, and popular public lecturer. Born in Ohio in 1808.

GALLAGHER, WILLIAM D.—A journalist and poet, author of "Miami, and other Poems." Born in Pennsylvania in 1808.

GARFIELD, JAMES ABRAM.—Twentieth President of the United States. A statesman of fine abilities, lofty motives, and manly character, whose assassination while Chief Magistrate of the nation plunged a whole people in mourning. Born in Ohio in 1831; died in 1881.

GARRICK, DAVID.—The most famous actor who has adorned the English stage. He was an accomplished playwright and a writer of considerable verse. Born in 1716; died in 1779.

GAY, JOHN.—A poet, contemporary with Swift and Pope, and best known as the author of " The Beggar's Opera " and the ballad of " Black-Eyed Susan." Born in 1688; died in 1732.

GILBERT, WILLIAM S.—An English dramatist and poet. Associated with Arthur Sullivan in the production of "Pinafore" and other popular burlesque operas. Born in 1836.

GILDER, RICHARD WATSON.—A journalist and poet, associate editor of "Scribner's Magazine" from its foundation, and successor to Dr. Holland as editor of the "Century Magazine." Born in New York in 1844.

GOLDSMITH, OLIVER.—One of the cherished names in English literature. He wrote a vast amount of prose with singular grace and simplicity. He produced less poetry, but it was imbued with an individual charm. "The Vicar of Wakefield" is now his most popular prose work, and his "Deserted Village" has a high place among English classics. Born in Ireland in 1728; died in 1774.

GOODALE, DORA READ.—The younger of two sisters remarkable for precocity. A volume of their poems was published when they were respectively 15 and 12. Born in Mass. in 1866.

GOODALE, ELAINE.—Sister of Dora Read Goodale, and of kindred poetical temperament. Born in Mass in 1863.

GOUGH, JOHN B.—Widely known as a temperance lecturer of rare dramatic power. Born in England in 1817.

GRAY, DAVID.—A Scotch poet of humble birth and early death. Born in 1838; died in 1861.

GRAY, THOMAS.—An English poet and scholar of renown, who produced but little, but that little of a high order of excellence. His "Elegy in a Country Churchyard" is an example of finished poetical composition, which has ensured its author immortal fame. Born in 1716; died in 1771.

GREENE, ALBERT GORTON.—The author of fugitive poems, of which "Old Grimes" is the most famous. Born in Rhode Island in 1802; died in 1868.

GRIFFIN, GERALD.—An Irish poet and novelist. Born in 1803; died in 1840.

GRISWOLD, HATTIE TYNG.—A lady of much poetic talent, author of a volume of verse entitled " Apple Blossoms." Resides in Wisconsin.

HALE, SARAH J.—An American writer, whose long career in literature has been honorable to herself and her sex. For many years editor of " The Lady's Book," and its predecessor, "The Lady's Magazine." Born in New Hampshire in 1795.

HALPINE, CHARLES GRAHAM (MILES O'REILLY).—A well-known poet and journalist; a native of Ireland and an adopted citizen of America. Born in 1829; died in 1868.

HALLAM, ARTHUR HENRY.—Son of the eminent historian, Arthur Hallam, and a youth of great promise. He was the subject of Tennyson's "In Memoriam." Born in London in 1811; died in 1833.

HALLECK, FITZ-GREENE.—Holds an honored place in American literature by his few but excellent writings. His "Marco Bozzaris" is pronounced the best war lyric in the language. Born in Connecticut in 1790; died in 1867.

HALL, EUGENE J.—An American poet, author of several popular volumes of verse. Born in Vermont in 1845.

HALL, NEWMAN.—A prominent English divine and temperance advocate. His "Pilgrim's Songs" have had a wide circulation. Born in 1816.

HANNAFORD, E.—Born in England in 1840. A resident for many years of Cincinnati, Ohio, but now of St. Louis, Mo.

HARRIS, JOEL CHANDLER.—Author of many popular stories and poems of Southern negro character. In 1881 he published a volume entitled "Uncle Remus," which attracted much attention as a study of negro folk-lore.

HARTE, BRET.—An American author, of original and unique talents. In his sketches of pioneer life on the Pacific coast, he struck out a new line in fiction, which he has worked with marked skill and success. Born in New York in 1839.

HAVEN, GILBERT.—A Bishop in the Methodist Church, and a writer of prose and verse. Born in Mass. in 1821; died in 1883.

HAVERGAL, FRANCES R.—An English poetess, whose writings are chiefly of a devotional character. Born in 1837; died in 1879.

HAWTHORNE, NATHANIEL.—The greatest of American novelists. His genius was solitary and melancholy, busying itself with the analysis of the secret motives of human action and character. His literary style was a model of pure, copious, felicitous English. Born in Mass. in 1804; died in 1864.

HAY, JOHN.—An American poet and journalist of conspicuous ability. Author of "Pike County Ballads," "Castilian Days," etc. Born in Indiana in 1839.

HAYNE, PAUL HAMILTON.—An American poet and prose writer. Born in South Carolina in 1831.

HAYNE, ROBERT YOUNG.—An American statesman of fine abilities. Noted for brilliant debate with Webster. Was U. S. Senator and Governor of South Carolina. Born in South Carolina in 1791; died in 1840.

HEBER, REGINALD (BISHOP).—An English scholar and clergyman, whose celebrated missionary hymn "From Greenland's Icy Mountains" is sung throughout the world. He died in the service of missions in India. Born in 1783; died in 1826.

HELPS, ARTHUR.—An able English historian and essayist, the esteemed Secretary of Queen Victoria. Emerson said of him: "There is nothing which Helps might not do." Born in 1818; died in ——.

HEMANS, FELICIA DOROTHEA.—An English poetess, universally admired during her life. Her maiden name was Browne. Born in 1794; died in 1835.

HENRY, PATRICK.—A distinguished American patriot and orator. Born in Virginia in 1736; died in 1799.

HERBERT, GEORGE.—An English clergyman and poet of devout life and saintly character. Born in 1593; died in 1632.

HERRICK, ROBERT.—An English lyric poet of repute during the Commonwealth and Restoration. His songs are replete with sparkling melody. Born in London in 1591; died in 1674.

HEYWOOD, THOMAS.—An actor, dramatic poet, and prose writer, of the times of Elizabeth, James I., and Charles I. Born in 1570; died in 1649.

HIGGINSON, THOMAS WENTWORTH.—A brilliant American writer, who left the ministry to take part in the civil war. Since then has devoted himself to letters. Born in Mass. in 1823.

HOFFMAN, CHARLES FENNO.—An American writer who held a conspicuous place in general literature in the last generation. Born in New York in 1806; died in ——

HOGG, JAMES.—A Scotch poet, known as "The Ettrick Shepherd." Born in 1770; died in 1835.

HOLLAND, JOSIAH GILBERT.—An American journalist, poet, and novelist. Associate editor of the "Springfield Republican" for seventeen years, and editor of "Scribner's Monthly" for the last ten years of his life. His writings have enjoyed a wide popularity, and exerted a wholesome moral influence. Born in Mass. in 1819; died in 1881.

HOLMES, OLIVER WENDELL.—An American author, of many and distinguished powers; he is at once a physician, college professor, poet, and essayist. His contributions to American letters have been varied and valuable. His prose disputes with his poems for popularity. Born in Mass. in 1809.

HOOD, THOMAS.—A favorite English humorist and poet. The most skilled and audacious of punsters. His wit was always conspicuous, yet under it there ran a current of deep pathos. Born in 1798; died in 1845

HOPE, JAMES BARRON.—A native of Virginia, and the author of a volume of poems published in 1857.

HOPKINSON, JOSEPH.—An American poet, whose stirring lyric "Hail Columbia" has become a national anthem. Born in Pennsylvania in 1770; died in 1842.

HOWE, JULIA WARD.—A talented American authoress; the wife of Samuel G. Howe, the philanthropist. Born in New York in 1819.

HOWELLS, WILLIAM DEAN.—A novelist whose writings have won him a distinguished place among American men of letters. For several years he was editor of the "Atlantic Monthly." Born in Ohio in 1837.

HOWITT, MARY.—An English writer of kindred tastes and pursuits with her husband, William Howitt. The lives and labors of the two were so lovingly blended that the history recorded of one must include that of the other at every step. Born in 1804.

HOWITT, WILLIAM.—An Englishman of letters, whose literary fame is inextricably associated with that of his wife, Mary Howitt. He was a prolific author, his writings embracing prose and verse. Born in 1795; died in 1879.

HOWLAND, MAY W.—Born in 1832; died in 1864.

HOYT, RALPH.—A clergyman of the Episcopal Church in New York City, and writer of prose and verse. Born in 1808; died in 1878.

HUGHES, JOHN.—An English poet and essayist. Born in 1677; died in 1720.

HUNT, LEIGH.—A prominent man of letters in his period. The associate of Coleridge, Lamb, Byron, Shelley, and other men of note. His pen was employed with skill in various departments of writing. Born in London in 1784; died in 1859.,

INGELOW, JEAN.—An English poet and novelist, whose writings have had a wide circulation and high favor. Born in 1830.

INGERSOLL, ROBERT G.—An American, of national repute for his oratory. Born in Illinois, in 1832.

IRVING, WASHINGTON.—An American author peculiarly honored and beloved by his countrymen. His gentle and genial nature, together with the beauty of his writings and the early fame he gave to American literature, cause his memory to be fondly cherished. He was a prolific writer and his works were received with universal applause. Born in New York in 1783; died in 1859.

JACKSON, HELEN HUNT.—An American author, whose prose and poetical writings are characterized by ardent imagination and a facile command of language. It is doubtful if as a poetess she has a rival among her countrywomen. Has written chiefly over the signature "H. H." Born in Mass. in 1831.

JEFFERSON, THOMAS.—Third President of the United States, author of the Declaration of Independence, founder of the University of Virginia, and author of the Virginia statute for establishing religious freedom. Born in Virginia in 1743; died in 1826.

JENNER, DR. EDWARD.—An English physician famous as the discoverer of the system of inoculation as a preventive to small-pox. Born in 1749; died in 1823.

JERROLD, DOUGLAS.—An English author distinguished for brilliant wit. Several of his comedies have a permanent popularity. Born in 1803; died in 1857.

JOHNSON, SAMUEL.—A renowned English author and lexicographer. A man of extraordinary power of mind and of eccentric character. He struggled with poverty for many years, and with disease all his life, yet by his literary achievements and his dictatorial disposition he became the intellectual autocrat of his day. Born in 1709; died in 1784.

JONES, AMANDA T.—An American poet and philanthropist; author of a number of magazine pieces, and of a volume of poems published in 1867, and "A Prairie Idyl, and Other Poems," published in 1882. Her poetry is the work of a deeply reflective spirit, and is marked by great sincerity and purity of expression.

JONES, SIR WILLIAM.—A famous English scholar and jurist. Born in 1746; died in 1794.

JONSON, BEN.—One of the greatest of the English dramatists, a contemporary of Shakespeare, and, during their lifetime, a rival. He produced more than fifty dramas and works. Born in 1574; died in 1637.

KEATS, JOHN.—A poet of great promise, whose life was unfortunately brief. His "Endymion" was published when he was twenty-two, and the "Eve of St. Agnes" and minor poems two years later. Had he reached maturity, there is reason for believing he would have added another to the list of great English poets. Born in 1795; died in 1821.

KEBLE, JOHN.—An English clergyman and poet, whose sacred lyrics, the expression of a sanctified life, gained him the reverent regard of men of all denominations. Born in 1792; died in 1866.

KEMBLE, FRANCES ANNE.—Daughter of Charles Kemble, the actor, and niece of Mrs. Siddons. Distinguished in early life for histrionic talent, and, later, as a writer of poems, sketches of travel, and personal reminiscences. Born in London in 1811.

KEY, FRANCIS SCOTT.—An American poet, whose one memorable song, "The Star-Spangled Banner," was composed in 1814, during the bombardment of Fort McHenry, when the author was a prisoner in the hands of the attacking British. Born in Maryland in 1779; died in 1843.

KIMBALL, HARRIET M.—An American poetess, whose devotional lyrics are characterized by a true poetic quality and an artistic finish. Born in New Hampshire in 1834.

KINGSLEY, CHARLES.—An eminent English divine, novelist, and poet. A man of brilliant talents, whose earnest work in the church and in behalf of the English poor give him as honorable a distinction as did his fervent and eloquent writings. The magnetism of a strange and intense nature was felt in all he did and wrote. Born in 1819; died in 1875.

KINNEY, COATES.—An American poet and miscellaneous writer. Born in New York in 1826.

KNOWLES, JAMES SHERIDAN.—An accomplished British dramatist, actor, and theologian. Among his successful plays are "William Tell," "Virginius," "The Hunchback," "The Wife," etc. Born in Ireland in 1794; died in 1862.

KNOX, WILLIAM.—A Scotch poet, whose memory is kept green by the pensive lyric, "Oh, Why Should the Spirit of Mortal be Proud ?" Born in 1789; died in 1825.

LACOSTE, MARIE R.—A teacher, whose only published writing is the touching poem, "Somebody's Darling." Born in Georgia in 1842.

LAIGHTON, ALBERT.—An American poet, a cousin of Mrs. Celia Thaxter. Born in New Hampshire in 1829.

LAMB, CHARLES.—The most popular of English essayists. His writings are marked by a delicate, quaint humor which is peculiarly captivating. His character was expressed by the title, "Gentle Elia." Born in 1775; died in 1834.

LAMB, MARY.—Sister of Charles Lamb, and tenderly associated with his life and literary efforts. Born in 1765; died in 1847.

LANDOR, WALTER SAVAGE.—An English poet and miscellaneous writer, whose style was original, antique, and perfect. His "Imaginary Conversations" form the enduring basis of his fame, yet his poems evince power, and some of them have enjoyed great popularity. Born in 1775; died in 1864.

LANIER, SIDNEY.—An American poet and prose writer, whose life was cut short in the midst of an honored and useful career in literature. Besides many poems of merit and several volumes for the young, he left a substantial treatise upon "The Science of English Verse," and one upon "The Development of the English Novel." Born in Georgia in 1842; died in 1881.

LARCOM, LUCY.—An American writer of note. At one time a factory operative, afterwards a teacher, and finally wholly devoted to literature. Born in Mass. in 1826.

LATHROP, GEORGE PARSONS.—An American journalist and poet. At one time assistant editor of the "Atlantic Monthly," afterwards editor of the "Boston Courier." His wife is a daughter of Nathaniel Hawthorne. Born in the Sandwich Islands in 1851.

LAWRENCE, JONATHAN, JR.—An American poet. Born in New York in 1807; died in 1833.

LEIGHTON, ROBERT.—A Scotch poet of true inspiration. Born in 1822; died in 1869.

LELAND, CHARLES GODFREY.—Author of the "Hans Breitman Ballads," and translator of a number of Heine's pieces from the German. Born in 1824.

LEWES, GEORGE HENRY.—The well-known English philosophical, scientific, and miscellaneous writer, and founder of the "Fortnightly Review." The husband of Marian Evans, the novelist. His chief works are "The Life of Goethe" and "Problems of Life and Mind." Born in 1817; died in 1878.

LINCOLN, ABRAHAM.—Sixteenth President of the United States. A man who rose from the humblest origin. Endowed with strong common sense, tender feeling, great energy and ambition, keen sense of humor, and pure principles. He was one of the most remarkable characters America has produced, and is cherished fondly in the hearts of his countrymen. Was born in Kentucky in 1809; assassinated by J. Wilkes Booth in 1865, shortly after he had entered the second term of his administration.

LINGARD, JOHN.—An English historian of high rank. Born in 1771; died in 1851.

LOGAN, JOHN.—A Scotch divine and poet. Born in 1748; died in 1788.

LONGFELLOW, HENRY WADSWORTH.—The most popular of American poets. His name is not only dear to his countrymen, but is held in high esteem by all English readers. His poems are transparent in thought, tender in sentiment, and perfect in rythm, and are adapted to universal favor. Born in Maine in 1807; died in 1882.

LOVELACE, RICHARD.—An English cavalier poet, who spent his fortune in the service of the king, and, after much suffering, died in extreme poverty. Born in 1618; died in 1648.

LOVER, SAMUEL—A humorous Irish poet and novelist. Was a successful lecturer, giving entertainments made up of songs and stories of Irish life. Born in 1797; died in 1868.

LOWELL, JAMES RUSSELL.—One of the most eminent of American scholars, poets, and writers. His critical essays evince wide reading and fine discrimination, while their style is rich, elegant, and captivating. His humorous poems, chief of which are the "Biglow Papers," are racy and witty to a rare degree, and his more serious poetical writings are distinguished by varied graces. Born in 1819.

LUDLOW, FITZ-HUGH.—An American author of fine natural abilities, who fell an untimely victim to the habit of opium-eating. Born in New York in 1837; died in 1870.

LUNT, GEORGE—An American poet. Born in Mass. in 1807.

LYLY, JOHN.—Called the "Euphuist." A dramatist, whose affected writings set a pernicious example in English literature. Born in 1553; died in 1600.

LYTE, HENRY FRANCIS.—A Scotch poet and divine. The last and finest of his poems was the beautiful hymn, "Abide With Me." Born in 1793; died in 1847.

LYTTON, SIR EDWARD BULWER—A leading English novelist, whose works at one time ranked with those of Thackeray and Dickens, but have since declined in favor. Lord Lytton excelled as a man of letters by dint of ambitious and endless labor, rather than by an inborn creative genius. His three dramas, "Richelieu," "Lady of Lyons," and "Money," have had great success upon the stage. Born in 1805; died in 1873.

LYTTON, ROBERT BULWER (OWEN MEREDITH).—Only son of Lord Lytton. A poet and diplomatist. His most popular work is the poem of "Lucille." Was Viceroy of India from 1876 to 1880. Born in 1831.

MACAULAY, THOMAS BABINGTON, LORD.—An eminent English historian, essayist, and poet, of remarkable eloquence in conversation and writing. His works have had an enormous sale. His "History of England" was read with the eagerness of an exciting novel, and his essays and poems have had a similar popularity. Born in 1800; died in 1859.

MacCARTHY, DENIS FLORENCE.—An Irish poet. Born in 1810; died in 1882.

MACDONALD, GEORGE—A British novelist and poet, whose writings are esteemed for their pure teachings. Born in 1825.

MACE, FRANCES LAUGHTON.—An American writer, contributing to leading periodicals. Her hymn, "Only Waiting," is widely popular. Born in Maine in 1836.

MACKAY, CHARLES.—A Scotch poet and journalist. Author of many spirited and familiar poems. Born in 1812.

MAHONY, FRANCIS (FATHER PROUT).—An Irish poet and priest, witty, scholarly, and mild. His "Reliques" is a most delightful book. Born in 1804; died in 1866.

MANN, HORACE.—A noted American educationist, whose services in behalf of popular education in America merit the nation's gratitude. Born in Mass. in 1796; died in 1859.

MARLOWE, CHRISTOPHER.—An English dramatist, contemporary with Shakespeare, and born in the same year, 1564; died in 1593.

MARSTON, JOHN.—An English dramatist, and friend of Ben Jonson. Born in 1600; died in 1634.

MARTINEAU, HARRIET.—An eminent English author, whose writings range through the departments of history, politics, social economy, and fiction. Her style is clear and lively, securing her works a deserved popularity. Born in 1802; died in 1876.

MARVEL, ANDREW.—Distinguished chiefly as a political writer, but also a writer of verse. Born in 1620; died in 1678.

MASSEY, GERALD.—An English poet, who endured in childhood the hardships and miseries of a factory operative. Born in 1828.

McCREERY, J. L.—An author whose fame rests upon his beautiful poem, "There is no Death." The piece has been widely attributed to Bulwer, but is contained in a volume of McCreery's poems, published in this country, and is undoubtedly his.

McLEAN, KATE SEYMOUR.—A writer of good poetic gifts, but who has published sparingly. A resident of Ontario, Canada.

McMASTER, GUY HUMPHREY.—An American poet. Born in New York in 1829.

MEEK, ALEXANDER BEAUFORT.—An American lawyer, journalist, and poet. Author of the spirited poem on Balaklava. Born in South Carolina in 1814; died in Georgia in 1865.

MERRICK, JAMES.—An English clergyman and poet. Born in 1720; died in 1769.

MILLER, JOAQUIN.—An American poet and novelist. His youth was passed in the rough pioneer life of the Pacific coast. After publishing his first volume of poems, he was lionized in English society. Born in Indiana in 1841.

MILLER, WILLIAM.—A Scotch poet, author of "Willie Winkie;" an artist in wood-turning. Born in 1810; died in 1872.

MILNES, RICHARD MONCKTON (LORD HOUGHTON).—An English statesman and author. Favorably known by his poems and by his amiable personal character. Born in 1809.

MILTON, JOHN.—Next to Shakespeare, the greatest English poet. Author of "Paradise Lost," an epic poem ranking with Homer's "Iliad" and Dante's "Inferno." Some of his minor poems, as notably the "Allegro" and "Penseroso," are masterpieces of thought and diction. In prose, Milton evinced an equal power, his political writings exerting a special influence on his times. His character partook of the stateliness and grandeur of his writings. His later years, including the period of the production of "Paradise Lost" and "Paradise Regained," were passed in total blindness. Born in 1608; died in 1674.

MONTGOMERY, JAMES.—A Scotch poet and journalist, who was twice fined and imprisoned for offensive political writings. His devotional poetry was of a high merit, many pieces being adopted into the hymnology of all Christian denominations. Born in 1771; died in 1854.

MOORE, CLEMENT C.—An American poet and scholar; son of Bishop Moore of the Episcopal Church. His poem, "A Visit from St. Nicholas," is universally familiar. Born in New York in 1799; died in 1863.

MOORE, THOMAS.—A famous Irish poet, the friend of Byron, and a social favorite. His talent was very precocious and prolific. He wrote with remarkable ease, and his songs, set to Irish melodies, were sung by him with much effect. "Lalla Rookh" is his chief work, and was one of the most successful and pecuniarily profitable poems ever published. Born in 1779; died in 1852.

MORE, HANNAH.—An English writer of great distinction in her day. The contemporary of Johnson, Cowper, and Scott, and the friend of Garrick. Her writings were of a distinctively moral character, and did much to elevate the standard of purity in England. Her works comprise dramas, poems, essays, and tales. Born in 1745; died in 1833.

MORRIS, CHARLES.—A British naval captain, who published many songs, none at all equal to his "Toper's Apology." Born in England in 1749; died in 1838.

MORRIS, GEORGE P.—An American poet. Author of "Woodman, Spare that Tree," "My Mother's Bible," etc. Born in Pennsylvania in 1802; died in 1864.

MORRIS, WILLIAM.—An English poet and artist, prominent in the school of the pre-Raphaelites. His "Earthly Paradise" recalls the poet Chaucer, in the simple naturalness of its language and versification. Born in 1834.

MOSS, THOMAS.—An English clergyman, known only by his poem, called "The Beggar." Born in 1740; died in 1808.

MOULTON, LOUISE CHANDLER.—A brilliant American writer and naturalist. Has contributed largely to magazines, and at one time literary criticisms to the New York "Tribune." Born in Connecticut in 1835.

MUHLENBERG, WILLIAM AUGUSTUS.—An American clergyman and poet, grandson of the founder of the German Lutheran Church in this country. Born in Pennsylvania in 1796; died in 1877.

MUNBY, ARTHUR J.—An English poet, author of "Doris" and other charming pieces. His first volume appeared in 1865; his "Dorothy," a long elegiac poem, published in 1882, was less favorably received than his shorter works. Born in 1837.

NAIRNE, LADY.—A Scottish poetess of exquisite tenderness, as evinced by "The Land o' the Leal," and other beautiful poems. Born in 1766; died in 1845.

NEWMAN, JOHN HENRY.—An eminent English scholar and theologian. Prominent in the Tractarian movement in the Church of England. Afterwards made Cardinal in the Roman church. Born in 1801.

NOEL, THOMAS.—An English country gentleman, who published in 1841 a volume of "Rhymes and Roundelays," which included "The Pauper's Drive," the poem by which he is chiefly known.

NORTHRUP, B. G.—An American clergyman and poet. Born in Conn. in 1817.

NORTON, CAROLINE ELIZABETH SARAH.—An English poetess; the grand-daughter of Sheridan; of great personal beauty and brilliant talents. Born in 1808; died in 1877.

O'HARA, THEODORE.—A Kentuckian, author of the famous poem,"Bivouac of the Dead," written on the occasion of the interment, at Frankfort, Ky., of the soldiers of that State who fell at Buena Vista. Born in 1820; died in 1867.

O'REILLY, JOHN BOYLE.—An Irish patriot and poet. Tried for sedition and sent to the penal colony of Australia, he escaped to America, and became editor of "The Pilot," published in Boston. Born in 1844.

OSBORNE, SELLECK —An American journalist and poet, Born in 1783; died in 1826.

OSGOOD, FRANCES S.—An American poetess. Born in Mass. in 1812; died in 1850.

OTIS, NEWTON S.—A resident of Brooklyn, N. Y. Born in 1836.

PAGE, EMILY R.—An American writer, who died at the early age of twenty-two. Her poem of "The Old Canoe" was widely credited to Albert Pike. Born in Vermont in 1838; died in 1860.

PALFREY, SARAH HAMMOND.—An American writer; daughter of the historian, J. G. Palfrey.

PALMER, JOHN WILLIAMSON.—A physician and poet, known principally by his famous piece on "Stonewall Jackson's Way." Born in Baltimore about 1828.

PALMER, WILLIAM PITT.—Author of "The Smack in School," etc. Born in Mass. in 1805.

PARDOE, JULIA.—An English author, whose numerous volumes of travel, fiction, and historical memoirs met with much favor. Born in 1806; died in 1862.

PARKER, THEODORE.—A famous American preacher, poet, and linguist. He is chiefly known as an ardent reformer and an eloquent advocate of simple theism in religion. Born in Mass. in 1810; died in 1860.

PATMORE, COVENTRY.—A favorite English poet. Author of "The Angel in the House." Born in 1823.

PAULDING, JAMES K.—An American statesman and man of letters. A prolific writer of prose and verse. Born in 1778; died in 1860.

PAYNE, JOHN HOWARD.—An American dramatist and actor, chiefly known by the popular and exquisitely touching poem, "Home, Sweet Home." Born in New York in 1792; died in 1852.

PEABODY, S. H.—An eminent teacher and educator, and writer upon scientific subjects. Born in Vermont in 1833.

PEALE, REMBRANDT.—An eminent American painter, and also an author of note. Born in Penn. in 1778; died in 1860.

PENN, WILLIAM.—The founder of Pennsylvania, and an able exponent of the doctrines of the Society of Friends. After establishing his colony in America, he returned to England in 1684, and took an active part in political affairs, enjoying the favor of James II His writings were numerous and much esteemed. Born in 1644; died in 1718.

PERCIVAL, JAMES GATES —An accomplished American scholar and poet, of recluse habits and eccentric character. Born in Conn. in 1795; died in 1856.

PERRY, NORA.—An American poetess; author of the popular piece, "After the Ball." Born in Rhode Island.

PHELPS, EGBERT.—A son of U. S. Senator Phelps, of Vermont. A teacher, officer in the regular army, and afterwards a successful lawyer in Illinois. Born in 1838.

PHELPS, ELIZABETH STUART.—An American prose and poetical writer, whose works are widely read. "The Gates Ajar" established her literary reputation in 1869, and she has since produced a number of popular novels and contributed largely to the leading magazines. Born in Mass. in 1844.

PIATT, DON.—An American journalist and poet. Born in Ohio in 1829.

PIATT, JOHN JAMES.—An American poet and prose writer. Born in Indiana in 1831.

PIATT, SALLIE M. B.—An American poetess, wife of John James Piatt. Born in Kentucky in 1835.

PIERPONT, JOHN.—An American clergyman, prominent in the cause of anti-slavery and of temperance reform. Born in 1785; died in 1866.

PIKE, ALBERT.—For many years a resident of Arkansas, and noted there as a brilliant and eloquent lawyer, as well as poet and journalist. Born in Mass. in 1809.

PITT, WILLIAM.—An English ship-builder, who died at Malta in 1840. His amusing poem of "The Sailor's Consolation" is in many collections credited to Charles Dibdin.

POE, EDGAR ALLAN.—An American poet of rare and unique genius. The best of his writings have been translated into all the European languages. His fame, slight during his lifetime, has increased greatly since his death. Of keen sensibility, delicate organization, irregular habits, and unhappy fate, the incidents of his life have excited the deepest interest, while they have been subjected to conflicting interpretations. Born in 1809; died in 1849.

POLLOK, ROBERT.—An English poet and divine. His principal poem was "The Course of Time." Born in 1799; died in 1827.

POPE, ALEXANDER.—One of the most celebrated of English poets. His verse was moulded with consummate art, and throughout his century was regarded as an expression of the loftiest genius. But it was monotonous in its polished construction, was wanting in the passion which speaks from heart to heart, and has suffered an inevitable decline in favor. Born in 1688; died in 1744.

PORTER, NOAH.—An American scholar and author, eleventh President of Yale College. Born in Conn. in 1811.

POWERS, HORATIO NELSON.—An American clergyman of the Episcopal Church, and an accomplished poet and man of letters. Was an intimate friend of the poet Bryant, and author of an excellent memoir of him. Pastor of a church in Bridgeport, Conn. Born in New York in 1826.

PRENTICE, GEORGE D —An American journalist and poet of great repute in his day. Editor of the Louisville "Journal." Born in Connecticut in 1802; died in 1870.

PROCTER, ADELAIDE ANNE.—An English poetess, the daughter of Bryan Waller Procter (Barry Cornwall). Her poems are tender, serious, and imbued with a delicate fancy. Born in 1825; died in 1864.

PROCTER, BRYAN WALLER (BARRY CORNWALL).—An English poet and barrister-at law. Many of his songs are popular favorites. Born in 1790; died in 1874.

PROCTOR, EDNA DEAN.—An American poetess and miscellaneous writer. Born in New Hampshire.

PUNSHON, WILLIAM MORLEY.—A popular English preacher of the Wesleyan denomination. Born in 1824.

QUARLES, FRANCIS.—A quaint English poet. His "Emblems" are very widely known. Born in 1592; died in 1644.

RALEIGH, SIR WALTER.—A famous English discoverer, sailor, soldier, and courtier. There are forty short poems attributed with tolerable certainty to him, but his prose writings contain the best evidence of his genius. Born in 1552, beheaded by James I. in 1618.

RANDALL, JAMES R.—An American poet and journalist; author of "My Maryland," one of the most stirring lyrics of the American civil war. Born in Maryland in 1839.

READ, THOMAS BUCHANAN.—An American painter and poet, excelling in lyrics, of which one, "Sheridan's Ride," had sufficed to give him national fame. Born in Pennsylvania in 1822; died in 1872.

REALF, RICHARD.—A gifted but unfortunate poet, who emigrated from England to America at the age of twenty, and was associated with John Brown in the political strife in Kansas. Born in 1834; died in 1878.

REDDEN, LAURA C. (HOWARD GLYNDON).—An American poetess. Born in Maryland about 1840.

RICH, HIRAM.—An American poet and magazine contributor. Born in Mass. in 1832.

RICHARDS, WILLIAM C.—A poet of English birth, resident in America since early youth. A clergyman, journalist, and popular lecturer on chemistry. Born in 1817.

ROBERTSON, FREDERICK W.—A distinguished English clergyman, whose sermons and lectures have made him widely known. Born in 1816; died in 1853.

ROBERTSON, WILLIAM.—An eminent Scotch historian, whose works rank with those of Hume and Gibbon. Born in 1721; died in 1793.

ROGERS, SAMUEL.—An English poet and banker, distinguished in the literary and social life of London. His chief poems are "The Pleasures of Memory" and "Italy." Born in 1763; died in 1855.

ROSSETTI, CHRISTINA G.—An English poet, sister of Dante Gabriel Rossetti.

ROSSETTI, DANTE GABRIEL.—An English painter and poet, one of the originators of the Pre-Raphaelite school of painting. Born in 1828; died in 1882.

RUSKIN, JOHN.—The great English art critic and writer. His works have had a profound influence on the age, exciting admiration by their impassioned eloquence and elevating the standard of morals by their lofty teachings. There is nothing in the prose literature of our language equalling in magnificence and splendor some of his descriptions of nature, and nothing more impressive than some of his terse declarations of the duty of men. Born in 1819.

RUSSELL, WILLIAM H.—A distinguished English newspaper correspondent, familiarly known as "Bull Run Russell," from his report of the battle of that name in 1861. Born in Ireland in 1821.

RYAN, ABRAM T. (FATHER RYAN).—A Catholic clergyman of Alabama, who has published a volume of verse, much of it of excellent quality.

RYAN, RICHARD.—A Scotch poet. Born in 1796; died in 1849.

SANGSTER, MARGARET E. M.—An American poet. Born in 1858.

SARGENT, EPES.—An American poet and journalist. Edited a series of school-books—speakers, readers, and spellers, which have been extensively used. Born in 1812; died in 1880.

SAXE, JOHN GODFREY.—One of the most popular of the humorous poets of America. Born in Vermont in 1816.

SCOTT, SIR WALTER.—A Scotch poet and novelist, a man of wonderful, vigorous, and fecund genius, whose works enjoyed an immense popularity in their day, securing him a splendid reward in wealth and fame. His reputation was founded on his poems and crowned by the series of Waverly novels. Born in 1771; died in 1832.

SHAKESPEARE, WILLIAM.—A name which stands above all others in the literature of England or of the world. His works are an inexhaustible treasury of great thoughts delivered with marvelous expression. They comprise thirty-seven plays, the poems of "Venus and Adonis," and "Tarquin and Lucrece," and 134 sonnets. Born in 1564; died in 1616.

SHANLEY, CHARLES DAWSON.—Author of the famous poem, "Civil War," which appeared originally in London "Once a Week." Born in 1830; died in 1876.

SHELLEY, PERCY BYSSHE.—A great English poet, whose genius was underestimated during his lifetime on account of the liberal social and religious views which he proclaimed. His successive writings show a continual development of his powers, but his life was cut short before they were matured. Born in 1792; died in 1822.

SHENSTONE, WILLIAM.—An English pastoral poet and miscellaneous writer. Born in 1714; died in 1763.

SHILLABER, B. P. (MRS. PARTINGTON).—A popular American humorist. By profession a journalist, his humorous sketches and sayings originally appeared in the newspaper press, and afterwards had an immense sale in book form. Born in 1814.

SHIRLEY, JAMES.—A celebrated writer of tragedies, comedies, and poems. Born in England in 1596; died in 1666.

SIDNEY, SIR PHILIP.—A courtly knight adorning Queen Elizabeth's reign. His bright talents were overshadowed by his manly and lovely personal traits. Honored and admired universally, he trod from his cradle to his grave amid incense and flowers. Born in 1554; died in 1586.

SIMMS, WILLIAM GILMORE.—An American poet and novelist, whose writings embrace a list of sixty volumes. Born in South Carolina in 1806; died in 1870.

SMITH, CHARLOTTE.—An English poetess, whose life was full of hardship and sorrow, the result of an unhappy marriage. Born in 1749; died in 1806.

SMITH, HORACE.—A celebrated English wit and writer, associated with his brother James in the production of "The Rejected Addresses." Born in 1779; died in 1849.

SMITH, MAY RILEY.—An American poet and miscellaneous writer. Born in New York in 1842.

SMITH, SEBA.—An American journalist, poet, and prose writer, displaying a rich vein of humor in some of his works. Born in Maine in 1792; died in 1868.

SMITH, SYDNEY.—A political writer, humorist, critic, and preacher, of extraordinary talents. Born in England in 1771; died in 1845.

SMOLLETT, TOBIAS G.—A popular English novelist, the author of a few short poems of much merit. Born in 1721; died in 1771.

SOMERVILLE, WILLIAM.—An English poet. Born in 1677; died in 1742.

SOULE, JOHN B. L.—A clergyman of the Presbyterian denomination; prominently connected with educational interests in Illinois. Author of a volume of poems, published in 1882.

SOUTHEY, CAROLINE A. B.—An English poetess, the second wife of the poet Southey. Born in 1787; died in 1854.

SOUTHEY, ROBERT.—One of the English Lake Poets, associated with Wordsworth and Coleridge, and a poet laureate. He was an able and laborious writer, and his works were voluminous and covered a wide range of topics. Born in 1774; died in 1843.

SPENCER, WILLIAM ROBERT.—An English poet, who wrote chiefly "society verses." Born in 1770; died in 1834.

SPENSER, EDMUND.—One of the foremost of England's poets, his name following next after Chaucer's. His writings helped to make the Elizabethan era illustrious, and the chief of them, "The Fairy Queen," forms one of the treasures of our language. Born in 1553; died in 1599.

SPOFFORD, HARRIET PRESCOTT.—An American poet and prose writer. Has contributed largely to the magazines, and published several volumes. Born in Maine in 1835.

SPRAGUE, CHARLES.—An American, known as "the banker-poet," his long life having been almost entirely devoted to commercial pursuits. Born in Mass. in 1791; died in 1876.

STEDMAN, EDMUND CLARENCE.—One of the foremost members of the "younger school" of American men of letters, of the period when Bryant, Emerson, Longfellow, and Whittier represented the older school. He is distinguished alike as a poet and a critic. His poetry is marked by delicate fancy, purity of conception, and refined and artistic expression; his critical writings, by clear insight, fine judgment, judicial spirit, and warm literary sympathies. Author of a number of volumes in prose and verse, and a frequent contributor to the magazines. Born in Conn. in 1833.

STEPHEN, JAMES.—An English barrister and author. A friend of Wilberforce, and sharer of his religious and anti-slavery principles. Born in 1789; died in 1832.

STILL, JOHN.—An English divine, Bishop of Bath and Wells. Author of one of the earliest comedies in the language, "Gammer Gurton's Needle." Born about 1543; died in 1608.

STODDARD, CHARLES WARREN.—An American journalist and traveler; for many years connected with the press of San Francisco. A small collection of his poems, printed in his youth, attracted the attention of Emerson and others; but he soon ceased to write verse. His prose, however, is peculiarly rich and brilliant.

STODDARD, RICHARD HENRY.—An American poet, critic, and journalist. Most of his life has been spent in New York City, devoted to continuous and arduous literary labors. His first volume was published in 1842, and in 1880 appeared a complete edition of his poems, forming a large volume. Between these periods, a number of his works, in prose and verse, were published. He has contributed largely to the magazines, and held the post of literary critic upon several leading New York journals. Born in Massachusetts in 1825.

STORY, JOSEPH.—A celebrated American judge and law writer; author of "Commentaries on the Conflict of Laws." Born in 1779; died in 1845.

STORY, WILLIAM W.—An American poet and sculptor of a high order of talent. Son of Judge Joseph Story. Born in Mass. in 1819.

STOWE, HARRIET BEECHER.—An American novelist of world-wide popularity. A daughter of Dr. Lyman Beecher, and sister of Henry Ward Beecher. Her story of "Uncle Tom's Cabin" has been translated into more languages and sold more largely than any other novel ever written. Born in Connecticut in 1812.

STREET, ALFRED B.—An American poet. Born in New York in 1811; died in 1881.

SUCKLING, SIR JOHN.—An English poet and courtier, celebrated in the times of Charles I. Born in 1609; died in 1641.

SWAIN, CHARLES.—An English poet and engraver. His songs have had a considerable popularity. Born in 1803; died in 1874.

SWINBURNE, ALGERNON CHARLES.—One of the first English poets of Victoria's reign. Distinguished for a marvelous command of metrical forms. Born in 1837.

SWING, DAVID.—An eminent American clergyman, pastor of a large independent church in Chicago; and popular as lecturer and essayist not less than preacher. Born in 1832.

SYMONDS, JOHN ADDINGTON.—An English writer of native talent and scholarly culture. His "Studies of the Greek Poetry, in Two Series," appeared in 1876, and his great work on "The Italian Renaissance" a few years later.

TANNAHILL, ROBERT.—A Scotch poet. By trade a weaver; he published a volume of lyrics at the age of sixty-three, which attained immediate popularity. Born in 1744; died in 1810.

TAYLOR, BAYARD.—A distinguished American poet, novelist, journalist, and traveler, whose works have obtained deserved popularity. Born in Pennsylvania in 1825; died at Berlin, where he had been appointed American Minister, in 1878.

TAYLOR, BENJAMIN F.—A brilliant American journalist, poet, and prose writer. Author of several successful volumes, in prose and verse. Born in New York in 1822.

TAYLOR, JANE.—An English poetess, who singly and with her sister published several volumes of poems. Her child's song, "Twinkle, Twinkle, Little Star," is chanted in every nursery. Born in 1783; died in 1824.

TAYLOR, TOM.—A prolific English author and dramatist. Has produced over a hundred plays, many of which are popular on the stage. Was at one time editor of the famous "Punch." Born in 1817.

TENNYSON, ALFRED.—One of the greatest English poets of the present century, and the poet laureate since the death of Wordsworth in 1850. His poetry evinces a high order of genius united with a capacity for the most patient labor. In it thought and words are exquisitely adjusted to each other, producing almost the perfection of poetic form. Born in 1809.

THACKERAY, WILLIAM MAKEPEACE.—A great English novelist, the contemporary of Dickens. "Vanity Fair" is commonly accepted as his masterpiece. He was gifted in the use of the pencil as well as the pen, and illustrated some of his own works with designs of much originality and humor. He excelled also as a poet, some of his pieces showing genuine power and feeling. Born in Calcutta in 1811; died in 1863.

THAXTER, CELIA.—An American writer, who has spent many years of her life upon Appledore Island, on the coast of Maine. Her poems and prose writings are remarkable for their reproduction of the color, the odor, the sound and the action of the sea, and of the features of nature with which she was surrounded on her island home. Born in New Hampshire in 1835.

THOMSON, JAMES.—An English poet of distinction, whose writings abound with beautiful descriptive passages which give them permanent fame. His chief poems were those written upon the Seasons, and "The Castle of Indolence." Born in 1700; died in 1748.

THOMPSON, ED. PORTER.—Born in Kentucky in 1834. A contributor to periodical literature of prose and poetry. Author of a "History of the First Kentucky Brigade of Infantry, C. S. Army;" co-author of "The Academic Arithmetic." Now a resident of Arkansas.

THOMPSON, JAMES MAURICE.—A poet and magazinist, resident in Indiana. Widely known through his writings on the subject of archery. Born in 1844.

THOMPSON, JOHN R.—An American poet and journalist of marked talents. Born in Virginia in 1823; died in 1872.

THOREAU, HENRY D.—An American poet, and a naturalist of original and independent mind and solitary habits. He devoted himself to observation and reflection rather than to writing, yet his prose and poetry betray the profound seer and thinker. Born in Mass. in 1817; died in 1862.

TILTON, THEODORE.—An American poet, journalist, and miscellaneous writer, of versatile and brilliant talents. Born in New York in 1835.

TIMROD, HENRY.—An American poet, of considerable gifts. Born in South Carolina in 1829; died in 1867.

TROWBRIDGE, JOHN TOWNSEND.—An American poet and miscellaneous writer. A number of his poems and juvenile stories have attained great popularity. Born in New York in 1827.

TUCKER, ST. GEORGE.—An American jurist, whose fame as a poet rests on the single poem, "Days of My Youth." Born in 1752; died in 1827.

VAUGHAN, HENRY.—A well-known Welsh poet and devotional writer. Born in 1621; died in 1695.

VERY, JONES.—An American poet, whose merits were recognized by Emerson and a few acute critics, but whose poetry has been slow in gaining the public appreciation that it deserves. A volume of his poems was published in 1883. Born in Mass. in 1813; died in 1880.

WAKEFIELD, NANCY PRIEST.—An American poetess. Her poem of "Over the River," which appeared originally in the Springfield (Mass.) "Republican," has been remarkably popular. Born in Mass. in 1837; died in 1870.

WALLER, EDMUND.—An English poet of great popularity in his time, but now nearly forgotten. Born in 1605; died in 1687.

WALLER, JOHN FRANCIS.—An Irish journalist and barrister. Born in 1810.

WALTON, IZAAK.—An English author of contemplative mind and gentle character. His "Complete Angler" holds a place among English classics. Born in 1593; died in 1683.

WASHINGTON, GEORGE.—The first President of the United States. Honored by the title of "The Father of his Country." His abilities as a statesman and a military leader, and his virtues as a man, have gained him a high place among the great men of the Saxon race. Born in Virginia in 1732; died in 1799.

WATTS, ISAAC.—A celebrated English poet and independent minister. The author of the first regular hymn-book used in public worship in England. For many years it superseded any other collection of sacred songs among the Dissenters in England and the Calvinists in America. Watt's hymns numbered about 800. Born in 1674; died in 1748.

WEBSTER, DANIEL.—One of the greatest of American statesmen and orators. A man of immense brain-power, with far-reaching grasp of comprehension, intense energy and feeling, and a power of language adequate to the quick and eloquent expression of all his conceptions. He was the master-spirit in legislative debate during his lifetime. Born in Mass. in 1782; died in 1852.

WEBSTER, JOHN.—A contemporary of Shakespeare, and one of the best of the minor dramatists of the Elizabethan era. Born about 1570; died in 1640.

WEIR, HARRISON WILLIAM.—An English poet, artist, and naturalist, noted for his wood engravings of animals. The successful author of numerous juvenile works written and illustrated by himself. Born in 1824.

WHEELER, ELLA.—An American poetess, a resident of Wisconsin, who has contributed largely to the newspapers, and is the author of one or two volumes of verse.

WHITE, HENRY KIRKE.—An English poet of promise, whose life was prematurely cut short by excessive study. Born in 1785; died in 1806.

WHITE, JOSEPH BLANCO.—An Irish poet and prose writer. His "Night and Death" is regarded as one of the most perfect sonnets in the English language. Born in 1775; died in 1841.

WHITMAN, WALT.—An American poet of eccentric genius. England has been more ready to acknowledge his talent than his own country, but its strange expression, defying the acknowledged laws of poetry, has made it difficult to pronounce upon its order or degree. Born on Long Island in 1819.

WHITNEY, ADELAIDE D. T.—An American poet and novelist, whose writings have enjoyed much popularity. Born in Mass. in 1824.

WHITTIER, ELIZABETH H.—An American poetess, sister of the poet, John G. Whittier, and his companion until her death. Born in Mass. in 1815; died in 1864.

WHITTIER, JOHN GREENLEAF.—A distinguished American poet, whose writings breathe the purest spirituality, patriotism, and humanity. There is no poet of the time who dwells nearer the hearts of the people. His name is beloved and venerated. Born in 1807.

WILDE, LADY (SPERANZA).—An Irish poet, whose writings have generally a political bearing. Mother of Oscar Wilde. Born about 1830.

WILDE, OSCAR.—An Irish poet of very decided talents; his personal affectations have subjected him to much public ridicule, and prevented the recognition due his poetry. Born in Dublin in 1855.

WILDE, RICHARD HENRY.—An Irish poet, resident most of his life in the United States. Was for twenty years a Member of Congress from Georgia. Born in 1789; died in 1847.

WILLIAMS, MARIE B.—An American prose and poetical writer of decided gifts and sincere devotion to literature. Born in Louisiana in 1826.

WILLIS, NATHANIEL PARKER.—A distinguished American journalist and poet. His writings were witty, graceful, and graphic. He allowed a social ambition to hinder the noblest use of talents of no common order. Born in Maine in 1807; died in 1867.

WILLMOTT, AVIS.—An English author, chiefly of devotional pieces. Died in 1863.

WILLSON, FORCEYTHE.—An American poet of marked originality, whose brilliant promise was cut short by his early death. His famous poem of "The Old Sergeant" first appeared as the Carrier's Address of the Louisville "Courier-Journal," in 1863. Born in New York in 1837; died in 1867.

WILSON, JOHN (CHRISTOPHER NORTH).—A Scotch poet and prose writer of splendid abilities. Nature endowed him prodigally with physical and mental gifts. Editor of the famous "Blackwood's Magazine," of Edinburgh. Born in 1788; died in 1854.

WINTER, WILLIAM.—For many years the musical and dramatic critic of the New York "Tribune," and a pleasing and accomplished verse-writer. Born in Mass. in 1836.

WINTHROP, ROBERT C.—An esteemed American statesman and author. Daniel Webster's successor in the U. S. Senate. Born in Mass. in 1809.

WIRT, WILLIAM.—An eloquent American lawyer and writer. Born in Maryland in 1772; died in 1834.

WOLCOTT, JOHN.—An English poet, author of many popular humorous pieces, written chiefly over the signature of "Peter Pindar. Born in 1738; died in 1819.

WOLFE, CHARLES.—An Irish divine and poet. His poem, "The Burial of Sir John Moore," was pronounced by Lord Byron "the most perfect ode in the language." Born in 1791; died in 1823.

WOODWORTH, SAMUEL.—An American poet, remembered by a single vigorous lyric, "The Old Oaken Bucket." Born in Mass. in 1785; died in 1842.

WOOLSEY, SARAH (SUSAN COOLIDGE).—A popular American poet and prose writer. A niece of President Woolsey, of Yale College.

WOOLSON, CONSTANCE FENIMORE.—An American writer, who has gained a considerable celebrity, both by her prose and verse.

WORDSWORTH, WILLIAM.—A great English poet, whose works grew very slowly into favor, but finally have come to be esteemed among the most precious literary legacies bequeathed to the nineteenth century. Wordsworth is pre-eminently the poet of the reflective imagination. Was poet laureate of England, succeeding Southey. Born in 1770; died in 1850.

WOTTON, SIR HENRY.—An English poet and diplomatist. Born in 1568; died in 1639.

YOUNG, EDWARD.—An English poet, most exclusively known by his poem, "Night Thoughts," which had a great popularity in his time. Born in 1684; died in 1765.

Lightning Source UK Ltd.
Milton Keynes UK
UKHW052350031218
333390UK00027B/1113/P